ALF

The Allan Langer Story

Paul Malone

Published by
Random House Australia Pty Ltd
20 Alfred Street, Milsons Point, NSW 2061
http://www.randomhouse.com.au

Sydney New York Toronto
London Auckland Johannesburg
and agencies throughout the world

National Library of Australia
Cataloguing-in-Publication Data

Malone, Paul, 1962–   .
Alf : the Allan Langer story.

ISBN 0 09 183569 0.

   1. Langer, Allan. 2. Rugby League football players –
   Queensland – Biography. 1. Malone, Paul, 1962–   . II.
   Title.

796.338092

Design by Yolande Gray
Typeset by Asset Typesetting Pty Ltd, Sydney
Printed by Griffin Press, Adelaide

10 9 8 7 6 5 4 3 2 1

ACKNOWLEDGEMENTS

Out of the dozens of people who have shaped my life, any list of the people I need to thank starts with my parents, Rita and Harry, sister Desley and brothers Cliff, Kevin and Neville.

I count myself lucky to have grown up in Ipswich and appreciate the help I had through my junior years there.

My wife Janine has been my greatest support since the day she saw me in a Jackie Howe singlet, lugging washing machines around for Waltons. With our children, Courtney, Maddison and Harrison, she has provided a perfect life away from football.

As far as my football goes, I'd like to pay particular tribute to Wayne Bennett. He provided advice on my football and influenced my life.

Also, thank you to all the players I have formed friendships with over the years. When you boil it all down, those friendships are why you play football.

Allan Langer
Brisbane
May 1997

CONTENTS

FOREWORD

It was a typical October night in Manchester. The locals were crammed into their corner pubs warming their bellies with pints of bitter in true Lancashire tradition. The 1990 Kangaroo Tour had just kicked off and the boys were allowed to take advantage of a lull in the schedule to partake of some good old-fashioned bonding.

No sooner had we settled at our first stop when the pub evacuated. Anyone would have thought there was a bomb scare. The locals abandoned their beers and poured out onto the street. We followed them into the chilly night and found the crowd roaring hoarsely. It didn't take long to find out what they were cheering about. It was two blokes, going hell for leather. It was the closest I have seen to the rollicking finale in Clint Eastwood's *Any Which Way You Can*.

The two bodies rolled over the top of a car bonnet, crashed into a garbage can, tumbled onto the bitumen and continued to trade blows down the middle of the road. Not surprisingly, the throng followed. They were having bets and yelling advice— talking through their wallets, of course. All of a sudden the stink stopped. The combatants turned around and a hush enveloped the gathering.

The silence was broken when the two 'pugs' burst into laughter. 'Gotcha!' they cackled. It was none other than Allan Langer and Kevin Walters.

This wasn't the first crowd that trudged back into their watering hole that night. Every pub we visited got caught by the same act.

That was the first time I really got to know the great character we all know and love as Alfie. We both made our debuts in the Winfield Cup in 1988. Alf had made a name for himself by winning the Man of the Match award for Queensland in the decisive State of Origin match the previous year. My first dealings with him came through club football, and then when I was picked for NSW in my first Origin series in 1990. But I didn't really meet him properly until we toured together.

Alf immediately struck me as a genuine bloke.

He has earned every ounce of success he has had in rugby league. In my opinion he has the highest profile in the game. But the most endearing quality about Alf is you could not meet anyone who is more modest. He has never forgotten where he came from and he is immensely loyal to his family, his friends and his beloved Brisbane Broncos.

There are no fiercer competitors in the game than Alfie. And there are no bigger jokers either.

The rivalry between Queensland and NSW was the backdrop to the toughest football I have played. But even in those intense battles, Alf always kept his sense of humour. I will never forget the final Origin match in 1993 when a brawl erupted. This was the brawl made famous by Paul Harragon unleashing on Martin Bella. It was the same blue which saw hooker rivals Steve Walters and Benny Elias go toe-to-toe. All four players were sin-binned. What is not as well known is the way referee Greg McCallum was able to defuse the situation.

While both sides were going for it, a Maroon jumper charged at NSW prop Glenn Lazarus declaring, 'I am going to punch the Christ out of you.' The 'target' recognised the voice. It was Alfie. Big Lazzo couldn't do anything but crack up. And there were plenty of us who joined in the laughter …

The 1994 Kangaroo Tour brought Alf and I closer together. Our competition for the Australian half-back jumper was a constant subject of media attention. It became tiresome. But not more so than on this tour. The speculation reached a height before the First Test, when we were both picked in the starting line-up. We were bracketed together at half-back and the final decision was put off until closer to game day. No-one was prepared to make the call. We both realised how unnecessary this was not only for us, but also the team. Alf roomed with Kevie Walters, directly opposite Dean Pay and myself. We regularly socialised and roamed in and out of the two rooms. Alf and I often shared a joke about the No. 7 scrumbase job, which helped ease a constant burden. I would say that strengthened the bond between us.

In my assessment, Langer is the greatest Bronco. In a team stacked with legendary players, he is the heart and soul of the Broncos' success. Throughout it all, he has remained a wonderful character which has made him extremely popular amongst his peers and the public.

As an opponent, Alfie is the most complete half-back I have played against. It has been an honour to play against him and one of the highlights of my career. If I have any regrets, it is only that I haven't played more games with him. Unfortunately we were always striving for the same position and it was not possible.

The Langer–Stuart debate will probably go on forever. We are two totally different styles of half-back. But we have enjoyed a challenging rivalry. It is a privilege to have my name mentioned in the same breath as his. We have been very competitive over the years and this will continue. However, at the end of the day I am proud to say I can always sit down for a beer with Allan Langer and call him a true friend.

Ricky Stuart
Canberra
June 1997

INTRODUCTION

In my line of work I am often asked the question: 'What is he *really* like?' Being a sportswriter means having a close, if often staged, relationship with the top sportsmen who have their every public action monitored.

Supporters read what the players have to say, witness interviews on television, watch how a player conducts himself on the field and how he relates to other players when games are rolling sweetly—or when the opposition has a blowtorch to their bellies. Over time they can generally pick the lair, the one who folds under pressure, the lazy player, the head case, the champion and the player they wouldn't mind having a chat with over a beer.

But over 10 years, I don't think I have ever been asked what Allan Langer is really like. The reason must be that what you see is what you get. The media can't help but convey his complete lack of artifice, his honesty, his consistency, his uncomplicated wit and his well-defined sense of sportsmanship. In the interview process for this book, I often heard the comments 'a great bloke', 'funny little bloke' and 'hasn't changed'.

Digging a little deeper, there are changes in Allan Langer— changes that are to be expected from someone who aged from 20 to 30 in the 'big fish in a small pond' sports environment of Queensland. Looking at some of the transcripts from my conversations with Langer, his depth and perception are now light years away from the shy, often monosyllabic 20 year old drafted into the 1987 Queensland State of Origin team. And if I have come close to charting those subtle shifts, and the humour and sense of mischief in the man that have come in response to a decade of turbulence in rugby league, then it will be close to a success.

INTRODUCTION

This book would not have been possible without the support of Allan and Janine Langer and Allan's family, particularly Kevin Langer.

One of the easier aspects of compiling Allan's biography was the willingness of people to find time to talk to me when they learned it was being written with his cooperation. In a game driven by commerce more than ever before, their enthusiasm was a tribute to him personally. I was helped particularly by John Ribot, Wayne Bennett, Tom Raudonikis, Ricky Stuart and Bob Fulton—all of whom had focal roles in the Langer career. Allan, Steve Crawley and Shane Edwards thought I was the one for this project and hopefully their opinion hasn't changed.

In addition, my personal thanks to John and Marie Malone, Robert Craddock (for the loan of his computer while he spent the summer off head-butting cricketers), Stephen Gray for the world's slowest—albeit most encouraging—transcription service, Anthony Weate, Cheryl Thurlow, Barry Dick and Kevin Jones. To Gary Smart and Geoff Stead, thanks for the time off work. To the staff at Random House, particularly Roberta Ivers, your patience and enthusiasm was greatly appreciated.

I remember when one of Langer's colleagues became exasperated by a line of questioning about the Broncos—he wondered what it had to do with a book on Alf. My reply remains that what happened to Langer's club over the year *was* his story. That would sit comfortably with Allan, but only when he was sure that the implication was that he belonged to the club, not it to him.

Paul Malone
Brisbane
February 1997

THE DAY ALF LEFT THE BRONCOS

By December, 1995, John Ribot was used to having his mind warp at the latest bomb he was expected to detonate on behalf of Super League.

A boisterous afternoon in Brisbane with the 'Mongrels Club'—a loose collection of Brisbane businessmen and sportsmen—was a welcome break from dealing with uncertain players, administrators and the false alarms about the imminent return of Federal Court judge Justice Burchett. When Allan Langer sidled up to him, Ribot was expecting nothing other than Yuletide cheer and banter from the Broncos captain.

'Ribes, I want to leave the Broncos,' Langer said awkwardly.

For Ribot, in the post of Super League chief executive for seven months, it was a matter of the utmost delicacy. He'd already had a couple of ferocious arguments with Broncos coach Wayne Bennett and chief executive Shane Edwards about the issue of player movement—weaker Super League clubs were agitating for a release of Broncos players to stock their teams. They would have more heated discussions over the next few months.

But this request from Langer, mentioning Super League's fledgling Adelaide franchise as his preference, was dynamite and had the potential to destroy the relations between the Broncos and

Super League. The last thing Ribot needed was a showdown with the Broncos over the defection of their captain. To select an analogy from a more serious war, it was the rugby league equivalent of Douglas MacArthur going to the White House in 1942 and saying he had had enough of the Pacific, but he'd like to give North Africa a shot if it wasn't too much trouble.

After eight seasons Langer was sick of the Broncos. His Brisbane team had been knocked out of the Australian Rugby League finals series with losses on the first two weekends to Canberra and Sydney Bulldogs. Dismayed at Brisbane's inability to build on their 1992 and 1993 titles, the Broncos skipper was annoyed with the airs and graces of some of his teammates and concerned that he was part of the reason for their on-field performances. Even the hectare property of his luxurious colonial home did not provide enough space.

His former Test teammate Peter Jackson had remarked earlier in the season that Langer had become more than a sporting hero in Queensland. 'He's a craze, like yo-yos,' Jackson said. Broncos teammate Kerrod Walters laughs as he recalls a ride in the skylift at the annual Brisbane Exhibition which takes patrons the length of the grounds. 'I could see Alf and Janine walking along sideshow alley, with about 30 kids following them,' he said. There were unfounded rumours about the state of his five-year marriage to Janine, his girlfriend from the days when he was a removalist for a department store and a household name in only a handful of Ipswich houses. Wild speculation about his gambling on horses had also made Brisbane an inhospitable environment, even for this man who was happiest doing what he knew best.

'Ribes was very surprised, but I spoke to him a couple of times over the phone after that,' Langer said. 'I spoke to Janine about it and we were seriously looking at going somewhere else. I was mentally stale playing for the Broncos and starting off in another city like Adelaide was looking good.

'I was disappointed with the way we had gone and I thought I needed a change, a new challenge. I was down on my own performances. The only time I had gone close to leaving was with the Gold Coast (in 1991), and that was mostly about getting more money out of Ribes. I think Ribes didn't want to look like he was doing the wrong thing by the Broncos. He told me I had to speak to the coach about it.'

So determined was Langer to leave the club that he had come to dominate and enrich that he seconded his business partner David Pie to ensure Ribot knew this was no whim or sour reaction to defeat. 'I said to him that Alf felt he needed a change. Ribes said: "If he really wants to go to Adelaide, I'll organise it."' Pie said: 'Later on, Alf rang me and said, "Mate, I'm going".'

'Alf normally handles the media attention and the public very well, but he'd had enough,' Pie said. 'He hated it that every time the media ran something on the Broncos, it was probably about Allan Langer. He could start up fresh where he is not as high profile and live a normal family life. He thought some of the Broncos players weren't up to it and he was being pushed into the corner where he was expected to get them over the line in the big games.'

Ribot made an appointment to lunch with Langer and his wife Janine the following Sunday at their home. But Ribot did not arrive. 'Benny (Wayne Bennett) came over instead and he talked me out of it in an hour or so,' Langer said.

Bennett said: 'He thought for a fleeting moment that he could go away and that would solve the problem. When I got to him, I told him it would never solve the problem. We all think of these crazy things sometimes. He could never leave. His lifestyle is so comfortable in Brisbane, he doesn't have to go anywhere else. He would have been like a fish out of water. He would have hated every minute of it.'

Bennett rejected Langer's argument that he was jaded by playing at one club in an era where few players complete their careers with the outfit at which they started. 'I don't know how he could get tired of the environment. He *is* the environment. You fear for how much you are going to miss him when he isn't here,' Bennett said.

'I didn't think he would leave because this is a tight-knit club. You can't get away from it. The club has done more for them than just use them as football players. It's easy to leave a club when you are dirty on the joint, but not when you are happy about the majority of things that happen at a place and feel a part of it. When you leave, you find the grass is not necessarily greener. The bond, the common thread, that Alf, Kevin Walters, Gene Miles and Wally Lewis have created is there, and we have to build on it for the next generation who are starting to come in.'

Langer realised as Bennett's car pulled away from his house that his coach had hit the pause button on the matter and that, deep down, he had told him what he wanted to hear.

'Ribes did the right thing to get Benny to come, looking back at it. Wayne set me straight that I didn't need to leave. He practically said: "You aren't going anywhere," ' Langer said. 'There wasn't an argument. Mostly, he talked and I listened. The Broncos have looked after me and I owe them a fair bit. That's why I'm here and will stay here for the rest of my career.'

Unless, of course, he becomes expendable, deeper into his thirties like Wally Lewis, like his great friends Gene Miles and Trevor Gillmeister. Like, a year later, his boyhood friend Kerrod Walters, with whom he had played for Ipswich, Brisbane, Queensland and Australia over an 11-year period. 'It does make you think when a player like Gilly goes. We really needed him at the club and I was one bloke who really tried to keep him here,' Langer said.

'The club becomes a big part of your life. I don't love training, but I love being around the boys—bagging and geeing each other up. That's what keeps me playing football, the mates I have. But when your mates leave the club, it makes you think about when your time is coming up. It's why you have to keep playing well, because you are waiting for that phone call at the end of the season to come and see Benny. In the end, you have to keep winning to stay together. I can't come up with an answer, after the success in 1992 and 1993. We had the side to win again every year after that.'

Langer's departure from the Broncos had blown itself out within a fortnight. But through it all, he had learned a few things about himself. That he had become, year by year, a Brisbane Bronco. Almost as much as he was one of the Langers from Sadliers Crossing.

REDSKIN MOUTHGUARDS AND WOODSTOVE FIRES

The name Langer, according to a dictionary of German surnames, means 'tall man'. To be born with such a name provided an appropriate start to life for four boys all short for their ages, uniformly blond and imbued with a sense of fun, adventure and mischief.

The only home Allan Langer knew until the age of 21, when he took a deep breath to earn a living at his hobby, was a weatherboard house with a yard backing onto a horse's paddock in Sadliers Crossing, a suburb of working-class Ipswich. Harry Langer, a carriage builder in the Queensland Railways for 46-and-a-half years, provided shelter, food, clothing, sporting equipment and the annual Christmas holidays to Caloundra for his wife, Rita, and their five children. Rita Langer, one of 15 children herself, worked as a cleaner at the children's primary school, Blair State School, for almost 20 years, on top of her day job as cleaner, cook and referee in the family home.

Equipped with a wood stove and without a telephone (to the exasperation of journalists trying to find Queensland's unlikely star in his first State of Origin series in 1987) the house that was home to the Langers for 33 years in quaintly named Ferrett Street was a model for living comfortably by your means and being grateful for what you had. Even when their youngest son—having risen through the Australian meritocracy by the means most widely respected in a sports-crazed country—offered to move them into a more comfortable dwelling, they declined with thanks. If nothing else, to do so would have meant dismantling the collection built over 33 years of trophies, photographs and mementos of the children's sporting achievements that dominated the walls and shelves, plus the glass-topped dining table enshrining newspaper clippings of their deeds.

The days when the four boys Cliff, Kevin, Neville and Allan, would conduct football and cricket wars in the sloping backyard, either in teams of two or with an expanding guest list, are sadly missed. Watching it all and usually having the good sense to keep a safe distance, was Desley, the eldest child, seven years Allan's senior, and the only daughter.

Now a father himself, Allan is pleased that his football earnings paid for renovations to a number of rooms to the family home, including the kitchen. Which is only fair, considering he and Cliff once almost burned the kitchen down when they threw petrol onto the stove to get the fire roaring on a cold winter's afternoon.

'I still can't believe how they brought up five kids on the money they were getting. We didn't miss out on a lot,' Allan said. 'I'm grateful to football for the money I can give back to my family. I'd do anything to repay my parents for what they did for us. To see their appreciation for the little bit of help I have given them is a fantastic thing.'

'We are happy where we are,' Rita said. 'But I still hate not having them all home. Sometimes, I get so lonely ...'

Harry, a stylish fullback in two first grade teams in the Railways club which won two Ipswich rugby league premierships in 1954 and 1958, married Rita Blaine on December 21, 1958 after a five-year courtship. Rita was the ninth child of Lillian and Jack

Blaine, a railways blacksmith. The family was raised in the Salvation Army, Rita wearing the uniform and playing in the band. 'We were taught the rights and wrongs of life, to do unto others as you would have them do unto you,' she said. 'We taught our children the golden rule, do unto others.'

Their fifth child, born on July 30, 1966, was Allan, allowing Rita and his siblings to launch the soothing nickname 'Bubby' at family gatherings—even 30 years later—whenever his cheek demanded retaliatory action. 'Allan was a shocking eater. Really picky,' Rita said. 'He would never eat his greens and when they stopped making his favourite brand of tomato sauce there was all sorts of trouble.'

Fitting everyone into the house took some doing. Allan would room in one sleep-out, an enclosed verandah, with Neville. This left Cliff with Kevin in the other sleep-out in a double bed. The sleep-out could be both a haven and a place of banishment. When Harry Langer's patience had been rubbed raw by his children's pursuit of a new thrill or adventure, the verdict 'Get on your beds' was the Ferrett Street equivalent of being sent to Coventry.

'Harry was a feared father. Very strict. Every time we were in trouble, he'd take the strap from bed to bed. Allan, being the youngest, would get the strap first and he would be squealing. Waiting would be the worst,' Kevin recalls. There were no doors to the sleep-out and few secrets.

One secret however, stayed that way for twenty-five years. When Harry Langer's change kept disappearing from a jar atop his wardrobe, and he was recently told his suspicions had been right all along. 'The others couldn't reach, so they would put me on their shoulders and hoist me up. We'd go down the shops with the change. Harry used to blame Rita,' Allan said.

But Harry Langer was able to gain a conviction when his newly painted garage door was imperilled by a six-year-old's temper tantrum. 'We were under the house, mixing up this custard powder with water,' Kevin said. 'Allan got upset about something and picked it up and just threw it—all over Harry's garage door. Flies were attracted to it and when Harry came out there were all these flies stuck to it. When he made a few inquiries, the rest of us went: "It was him, it was him".'

Harry Langer could also be protective of his boys, as a neighbour found out when he tired of the shouting, noisy brood hammering sixes over the bordering fence.

Harry and Rita were able to afford their children an all-hours freedom of movement which Allan Langer would not countenance with his own children. 'Growing up in Ipswich, your house was never locked up. We could walk around the streets, play down by the river or run around in the bush … it wasn't a problem. Looking back, we were so lucky,' he said. Some of the boys earned some extra pocket money by collecting and selling manure for fertiliser, Sadliers Crossing being rural in the 1970s to the point where horses and other animals were kept in big yards. 'But Allan wouldn't. He would be the supervisor,' Rita said.

The youngest Langer was also beset by a fear of darkness. 'I think it started from when my brothers used to grab me as I was running up the back steps at night. Mainly Kevin,' he said. 'They would hide under my bed and when I was just about asleep this hand would come up and strangle me or shake me.' His elder brothers would insist on taking him through the dark catwalk under the Dave Trompley Bridge on the way to football at the North Ipswich Sports Reserve. The sibling terrorism worked so effectively that when he travelled away for his club, state and country, he prevented roommates from turning the light off until he was asleep. 'You couldn't believe it. He'd tackle 17 stone props, but was afraid of the dark,' Brisbane Broncos roomie Gene Miles marvelled.

The five Langer children were all christened in the Salvation Army church and attended Sunday school. However, the boys had matters other than religion on their mind, at one stage attending a Lutheran service so they could play for the Lutheran cricket team. 'All we had to do was go to church once and we'd be right,' Kevin Langer said. 'When we went to the Salvation Army once, I remember (the minister) saying: "Everyone, the Langers are back".'

When Allan was eight, the nearby Bremer River flooded its banks, providing the family with stories similar to those sent around at Christmas by all families in south-east Queensland in the summer of 1974. It was a cause for celebration among the children amid all the parental concern. 'The water came up to our third back step. We were ready to evacuate. The house beside us was under,' Allan said. 'But it was great because it meant we didn't have to go to school.'

The Ipswich of the 1970s was a snapshot in Australian country culture for boys. You would play football until your team was out of the premiership race, then you played cricket. Any other pastime was decidedly suspect. The skills for both were forged in the furnace of a backyard competition far more desperately fought than the real, organised thing. It was much more embarrassing to be beaten in defence by your brother than the chubby kid from the Catholic school in the next suburb. The Langer teams were, almost without exception, Allan and Cliff, the youngest and oldest, on one side, with Kevin playing alongside Neville. 'We'd have Test matches, like most families. Our backyard has a slope and you'd always want to run downhill in the first half because sometimes the second half wouldn't end because there would be a fight,' Allan said.

Wayne Bennett, the most influential figure in Allan's career, would come to consider that those hours and hours of learning what worked and what didn't, shaped and enhanced his career.

'The magic he comes up with is partly the product of that environment,' Bennett said. 'These days, he just does things at training that make the other players stand in amazement, and it all started in the backyard. In the 1990s, it's something we don't do enough for our kids, to give them that healthy outdoors upbringing.'

Kevin reminisced: 'Remember those foam pads you used to put inside your shorts? Allan's were the smallest, but he could still use them as shoulder pads. Those Redskin lollies? He'd use them as a mouthguard sometimes. Harry would sometimes come down and referee and we'd put the hose out for the tryline. He'd play sometimes.'

What would Desley do? 'She'd be the tackling bag,' jested Kevin. 'Dad would hold her there and we'd use her for tackling practice. Most of the time she'd stay upstairs and watch television.' Desley played rugby league for Ipswich Norths when she was in her late teens and also touch football. 'She got married early, probably because she wanted to get out of the house,' Allan said.

The scampish brothers developed a comedy routine where they would alarm passers-by, at home and in town, by pretending to pick on Allan. On one occasion, a neighbour ran into the house screaming that Kevin was punching and kicking 'poor little Allan'. 'The big one was when we went into town and Kevin would be throwing me head-first in the garbage bins and lights poles as we walked along,' Allan said. 'I'd bang the bins with my hand or shoulder and just lay there like I had been shot. The boys would drag me around and I'd be screaming for help. People would be coming up to grab them and we'd start laughing.'

Into adulthood, it remained a pet prank of Allan and some of his teammates from the Broncos, as his Kangaroo tour team manager Geoff Carr attests. 'Alf is the master of the dead fall. He would have them petrified in Leeds at night. They have railings on corners to prevent pedestrians walking out into the traffic or cars ploughing into them. Two of the big forwards would pretend to pick on him and throw him around like a rag doll and he would tumble over the railing and lie in a crumpled heap on the side of the road. Buses would come along and he would roll out of trouble in the nick of time. His reflexes were that good, even at that time of night.'

Like so many families in Ipswich, sport became a cheap family outing, as well as a backyard obsession. 'We started our rugby league through our uncle, Snow Hooper, and Harry got involved in the team,' Kevin said. 'Allan was a little fatso. But even then the girls loved him. The girls in my class were always asking about my little brother.' Just four-and-a-half, Allan would play his first season in the second row in the under-sevens, with Neville as halfback. The boys played for Norths, the Railways club their father played for before it changed its name.

'We used to walk to the games, probably five miles to training. In those days, it didn't matter. We would take 20 cents for hot chips, which would feed most of us in those days,' Kevin said. Allan outlines with relish the match day routine for the Langer family. 'It would go all day from under-sevens to under-16s. After your game, you would be sandboy or ballboy and watch your brothers play,' he said. 'You'd have a meat pie and a coke and then go home to play there. Then there might be a (Brisbane premiership) game on television. We put a light up outside so we could play a little longer in the dark before Mum would get us to get ready for bed.'

Pat O'Doherty, who went on to play for the Ipswich Jets and subsequently Wests in the NSWRL premiership, was a teammate that year. 'Allan and I played together until we were 17. We had two years at the Jets together as well,' O'Doherty said. 'From the age of about seven, I'd say everyone knew he was going to be one of the best players around.'

Rodney Clark, the coach of the Ipswich under-sevens and under-eights, echoed O'Doherty's sentiment and soon had to formulate a distinct style for his team after moving Langer to halfback. 'I had to put two boys on either side of him to try to keep up with him, but he still lost them,' Clark said. 'It was hard for the others in the team to know what he was doing. He had everything going for him and he was always a leader. He'd win the game for you.' Clark recalls a big forward connecting with Langer's nose, failing to prompt as much as a wobbling lip.

Harry Langer had long thought Allan was good enough to play for Queensland but did not consider him playing for Australia. 'Allan got the opportunities Kevin never had,' he said with paternal regret.

Harry, like all parents, had to provide transport for his budding footballers. Kevin Langer recalls: 'Dad had a car about the size of a Laser or an Astra or a little smaller, and he used to drive everyone home after training. The record we got in it was 13, the four of us, and the rest of them mates. We'd usually have nine in it.

'We'd have to drop David Herman off at a the top of the hill. There were so many in the car, it couldn't get up the hill.' Norths became a focal point of family life. Rita would work in the canteen and on the social committee. She remembers dealing with unbeatable mounds of soiled jerseys. 'I would tell her she should move her bed down there,' Harry says.

But back to the Langer cars. When Harry upgraded to a EH Holden, he received a scare one day when he was under it, working on the engine. 'Allan was in the driver's seat and let the handbrake off. The car rolled over Harry's legs and crashed into the fence. That was another time where we were off and running,' Kevin said.

One day when Norths took on Booval Swifts in under-eight competition, their opponents included twins Kevin and Kerrod Walters, as well as the more familiar red head of their elder brother

Andrew. 'I think Kevin and I were both on the wing, filling in because they were short in the under-eights,' Kerrod Walters said. 'Alf got the ball and stepped around me and scored. I remember thinking, gee that kid will probably play for Australia one day, even though he was tiny.'

By 1982, Langer had been chosen in an Australian honours side after representing Queensland at the national carnival. 'But even when I was 16, I wouldn't say I was setting the world on fire. There was still the size thing,' he said. The Walters and the Langers had shadowed each other from age group to age group. Steve Walters and Neville Langer played in the Ipswich representative team together for years, teaming in the Queensland under-18 side. Brett Walters, one of three from the family to play the foundation season with the Broncos, had Kevin Langer for company.

'The two sets of brothers played against each other a fair bit in a town that size and made rep teams together,' Allan said.

It would be nice to record that the four youngest Walters boys would venture over the river from Sadliers Crossing, would come over and take on the Langer quartet in their backyard. Nice, but sadly, untrue. 'But the families got to know each other. Harry Langer and our dad were in the schoolboys committee for Ipswich and West Moreton,' Steve Walters said. When the committee meeting was at the Walters house, the Walters boys would be shunted under the house. But Kevin Walters senior had been pestered into erecting a strong light into the backyard for night combat. 'They'd have the meetings every fortnight or so. Our job was to make sure the beer was in the fridge long enough to be cold and then get out of the way under the house,' Kevin junior said. 'Then we'd play footy. Alf was over our place for those games a fair bit if I remember right.'

It wasn't just rugby league at which the Langers excelled. There is a yellowing newspaper photograph on the Langers' dining room table of a cricket clinic. A cherubic Allan, barely able to be glimpsed over the stumps, is beside a skeletal-looking Craig McDermott, the future Australian opening bowler. Allan Langer played cricket for Queensland at under-16 level, batting with invention and a clear eye in the middle order, alongside future first grade players Craig Jesburg, Dean Reynolds, and Gary Hayden, the elder brother and coach of Australian Test opener Matthew Hayden. Having endured the rough and tumble of 12 years of rugby league without serious injury, Allan learned he wasn't indestructible in the national cricket carnival at Adelaide, breaking his right thumb in the third game as he fielded a ball.

Kevin Langer represented Queensland in cricket in the under-15s and under-17s as a batsman, teaming with Biloela's Ian Healy, a pugnacious wicketkeeper-batsman who would captain his state and country. 'He and I top-scored with 48 one year, but NSW beat us,' he said.

When State of Origin caught hold of the Queensland sporting imagination, the Langer boys and their mates would catch the train down to Milton to most matches at Lang Park. 'We used to go down to just about every State of Origin game—all of us, with a few of the Walters boys and some others—and sit in the outer,' Allan said. 'We were there for the first one. The fight with Arthur Beetson was right in front of us. Some games later, the older brothers would be playing in curtain-raisers.'

In 1984, Allan was gutted when his first serious football injury cost him an opportunity to play a curtain-raiser on State of Origin night. Bennett, then director of coaching for the Queensland Rugby League, considers he would have captained the state under-19 team in 1984 had he not broken his right ankle in the final trial match, causing him to miss the rest of the season. It meant Langer would leave his junior days with only one Queensland league selection—in the under-15s. But he had begun his most lasting and important friendship in league, although Bennett would seriously misjudge his potential at least three times before they reached the game's Everest, the premiership in a national competition, eight years later. 'I'd heard of him before I saw him play,' Bennett said. 'He played in my team in a City–Country match, which was unlimited interchange. I put him back on in the second half and he broke his ankle. Wayne Alberts, the guy who tackled him, got his position in a state team which had the Walters twins in it.'

The following year, Bennett declined to include Langer in a QRL youth squad. 'I just hadn't seen enough of him play. The other problem was I thought, he's almost 20 now—if he was going to make it, he probably would have made it by this,' he said. 'To be fair, always in the back of my mind was his size. I just never believed he was going to be big enough.'

Bennett still saw something worth persevering with, even though he misjudged Langer's potential in trying to recruit him for Souths in 1985. 'Benny tried to sign me on for $500,' Langer recounted. 'But he reckoned the best I could do was play C grade that year, so I stayed at Norths. I don't let him forget that. I went back and played first grade for Norths in 1985 and was dropped to reserve grade at one stage by (coach) Jeff Ashe. I wasn't playing well apparently. We stacked our reserve grade for the semi-finals and we still lost the grand final. Then I signed with the Jets.'

Bennett explained: 'I just thought his size was against him— and it was, in those days, in terms of defence. I never held a lot of hope for him. He was only 55 kilograms or thereabouts. There was nothing of him. He was never a good defensive player and he virtually taught himself how to tackle late in his teens when he was playing for the Jets. It was something we worked on at the Broncos as well.'

School was not exactly an overriding priority for Allan Langer. He repeated ninth grade at Ipswich and left school after Grade 10. 'The second year was worse. I didn't apply myself and was only concentrating on sports. I never did my homework,' he said. 'All my mates were leaving school. I wish I had tried harder, but that was me.' Kerrod and Andrew Walters won apprenticeships at the railways. Allan missed out in his examination for an apprenticeship before going on the dole briefly. By the time a vacancy at the railways came up he had begun a job with Waltons department store in Ipswich's city centre. 'My first job was a truckie's offsider. It was pretty hard shifting furniture around when you aren't the biggest 16-year-old around,' Allan said. 'It was $120 a week.

'It used to be great fun on the country run out to Esk, Toogoolawah way to deliver. We would find a couple of nice pubs for lunch. Only problem was the roads were a bit rough out that way. Once I fell out of the cabin of the removalists' van on the way back. I fell down this embankment, maybe five metres, coming into the Ipswich turnoff and wrecked the uniform.'

The first girl Allan brought home was the one he married. Janine Browne was still at Ipswich State School when she started going out with the footballer, three years her senior, who was building a local reputation without being anything like a universal choice as a representative senior player. Allan said: 'I was ahead of her at Blair and she didn't notice me. We wouldn't have spoken at primary school and in high school we just got on. Then she saw me at Waltons one day, with my muscles bulging out of my Jackie Howe singlet, carrying around a washing machine, and that was that.'

Whatever it was, Janine said that even when she was 16 they had reached an understanding.

'It dawned on me straight away that we would get married,' she said. 'I don't know why, we never thought any differently. I

17

always knew I was going to get married and have five kids. Except I stopped at three. I got smart.

'I always called Harry and Rita Mum and Dad, right from the first day I was taken home. I always felt like they were my family. My parents were going through a divorce around that time and they (the Langers) were very supportive. They have been great parents and grandparents. Rita has done such a wonderful job. She will never stop being a mother.'

Allan had other loves, of course, such as riding motorbikes with his cousins Mick Wilson and David Tistle, from which he was forbidden doing by his father. 'Allan still has scars from a muffler burn when he wore shorts on the bike. He wore long pants for a month, so Harry wouldn't notice,' Kevin said.

Eventually, at the age of 17, he settled on a vivid orange, used, XA Falcon. 'I saved $1200 somehow from my first year at Waltons,' Allan said. Kevin Langer said: 'It was this big thing. He had to sit on a pillow to see over the dashboard.' 'Nah, it's a good line, though,' his younger brother disavows. 'I'd have to park a bit away from the house because the muffler was that loud and I used to have to take a four-litre oil drum with me because it used to leak.'

Janine said, 'We lived on a hill and his brakes weren't very good, so I'd have to put house bricks behind the wheels when Allan pulled up.'

Janine's father was trying to shepherd young suitors from their church in to see Janine. 'He thought I was too small and wouldn't make it in rugby league,' Allan said. 'For his youngest daughter to be going out with a rugby league player wasn't the thing he wanted. I was always nice and pleasant when I was there.' Nightspots such as Caesar's Palace and the Roman Lounge, though not as grand in reality as they sound, did solid trade as the Langers, the Walters and other footballing friends went out on the town with their girlfriends.

After the Waltons job ended, for a while Langer drove down to Rocklea, in Brisbane's south, for a job Bennett lined up for him, driving cars on and off the train carriages. 'I'd never seen those push-button windows before. I had my head out the window, when I hit the button and got my head caught in the window. Nearly broke my jaw,' he said. Eventually, Langer got a better paying job with Ipswich City Council as a labourer—female shoppers in the City Mall who snap a heel between the paving stones should know who to send the damages claim to!

'Ipswich wouldn't be the same without me. I built roads, footpaths, you name it,' Allan said. 'I was mainly in the kerb and channel gang. It wasn't too bad. The worst thing was being out in the weather. I pity the poor blokes out in it now. The worst thing was going off to training after the shift.' The sight of Allan Langer standing by the side of the road with a stop-go sign became an essential local landmark and his brothers would make sure he was not short of attention. 'We'd drive past and give him a bit of lip. He'd stand there and have the radio earpiece in to see how the races were going,' Kevin said. As the youngest member of the crew, the responsibilities included boiling the billy for smoko. 'If I didn't have it ready by 9.30am, all the older blokes would blow up at me. The worst thing was when it rained and the wood would get wet,' he said. 'One day, I poured kerosene onto the fire to make it go, except it was petrol.

'The tent almost went up in flames. They had to get the backhoe to tip some dirt on it to put it out.'

It echoed an incident when Allan was 14. He and Cliff were trying to get the fire started on the wood stove at home. 'Rita and Harry were on the way home from the football,' he said. 'Cliff had this ice-cream container full of petrol and threw it on. The stove went up and the flames were all up the walls.

'We splashed water up from the sink and put the fire out, but

19

we had to scrub the walls down in a hurry to try to get all the black smoke marks off. The smell was still there when they got back.'

By age 19, he had graduated to occasional first grade appearances with Norths, although thoughts of earning a decent buck out of football did not enter the equation. 'In those days, you had do to what you were doing. I was happy to get $200 a week from the Council because I was on $120 a week before that. Even at Norths, we were on $40 or $50 a win and going with the flow. I wasn't expecting too much,' Allan said. When he finished the 1985 season with a loss for Norths in the reserve grade final, Langer's horizons were not exactly boundless. But with fateful timing, the Ipswich Rugby League had decided to enter its Winfield State League team into the Brisbane premiership in 1986. The move heralded Allan's first big break.

'YOUR HEART'S AS BIG AS THIS, YOU LITTLE...'

In attitude and distinctly reduced circumstances, North Ipswich Reserve reminded Tom Raudonikis of Lidcombe Oval, the slightly rustic home of Western Suburbs, Sydney's team of proud battlers. The dark, modest, predominantly wooden dressing-rooms used by the Jets for their entry to the Brisbane premiership looked to pre-date those at Lidcombe from which Raudonikis played for Wests through the 1970s.

Those years at Lidcombe had him prepared for the make-do mentality forced on those who embarked on the Ipswich Jets adventure in 1986: the Jets officials and players had the same determination to make do with only a fraction of funds and comforts which other clubs enjoyed.

It was fortuitous for Langer that Raudonikis was his first coach in his approach to the big time—with all due respect to the coaches who went before. Raudonikis' career yielded 20 Tests as a tough, durable halfback who refused to take a backward step to anyone bigger than him in an era that was characterised by violent play and a very liberal interpretation of the high tackle rule. After being narrowly denied the premiership he craved in his brief stint at Newtown, Raudonikis had moved from Sydney to captain-coach Brothers in 1983. Two years later, he was sacked.

Raudonikis had gone in to assist a Brothers player involved in a hotel fight and, the way he tells it, it was seized upon to get him out of the club.

As coach of the Ipswich team playing in the Queensland State League in 1985, Raudonikis was appointed for the premiership entry, carrying with him the local knowledge from coaching Laidley in the Ipswich competition. Reflecting on his impressions of Langer, Raudonikis said: 'I saw a bit of him when Laidley would play Norths. You always noticed the little blond bloke running around. It was hard not to.'

But in the pre-season, Raudonikis came to grips with what raw talent he had at his disposal, including his halfbacks. The officials spent to the limit of their budget, enticing thirteen players from Brisbane clubs, including six from Brothers plus another five from Queensland country to bulk out the Ipswich ranks.

Decisions, decisions. Mark Clarkson, a recruit from Souths in Brisbane, or Allan Langer at halfback, for instance.

When the Jets' team sheet went up on the wall of the dressing-room for the first trial, Clarkson it was. Langer was in reserve grade. Also in reserve grade was lock Pat Shepherdson, a Brothers player Alf had struck up a friendship with in training.

Working on the basis that the Jets would be fitter than most Brisbane sides if nothing else, trainer Steve Nance worked the players hard from September, 1985. 'Nancey reckoned I wasn't in A grade because he found out that Shepo and I had hid under a house when we were doing these five kilometre road run circuits. We did it for weeks. Every time we did it and got away with it, it got funnier,' Langer said. 'We'd always be last in a road run anyway, so we'd wait for everyone to go past and then join them for the last few hundred yards, with a bit of water splashed over us to make it look like we had been running. Tommy wasn't flamboyant as a player himself, and I guess he wanted to see if I was tough enough for him.'

Nance said: 'Mark Clarkson had come down to Ipswich and Tommy might have known more about him than Alf. You have to remember he was only eighteen. Alf was 59 kilograms the first time I weighed him. Tommy always had a lot of time for Alf, but I got the impression he thought he was too carefree in his approach—which he still probably is in some ways. You wouldn't call those days at the Jets amateurish, but we had hardly any money or facilities. At that stage Tommy was selling soft drinks off the back of a truck and it didn't look like he had two bob to scratch together.'

Among Raudonikis' great strengths is his innate resistance to passing himself off as something that he is not, and his ability to find humour in the low times. Happiest in a polo shirt or T-shirt, sometimes splashed with stains of intriguing origins, he finally bowed to pressure from a club official to wear a tie at games— with a shirt which did not fasten at the collar. He recognised a similar attitude to life in Langer, who became the scallywag's apprentice.

'I had the Jets blokes over to my place once and after a while I noticed Alf had disappeared,' Raudonikis said. 'I went inside and there he was, sitting on the floor, over in the corner, reading the scrapbooks my mother kept of my career. A lot of kids didn't see me play. When I came to Queensland, I was on the slippery slide. Until they see it there in black and white, they don't know that this bloke used to be able to play. It showed me that he had that respect. He was cheeky, but never rude or a smart arse. He listened when you said something to him about football. But you want a bit of rogue in them, a bit of laughter. Alf trained hard, but he only did what he had to do, the little ... He quickly showed he could play and take what they threw at him. When I went to Sydney, I was a skinny little bloke too, blond hair as well, and eventually people stopped wondering about me. I didn't know much about Alfie — I was just trying to give some players a chance. He was there before the serious games started and I know I never dropped Alfie from first grade once he made it.'

Langer said there was little by the way of science or reliance on technology with Raudonikis in those days, which was understandable given his lack of access to both. 'I always tried to live up to Tommy's expectations. He wasn't a really tactical coach then. There weren't much by the way of videos. He was a larrikin and a real "get out and give it to them" coach. He was great for comradeship in the team.'

The Jets players quickly learned to expect nothing but the unexpected with Raudonikis. In that pre-season competition, Raudonikis decided his team was playing with too little determination and needed a jolt before a Lang Park game against the better-performed Redcliffe. The coach talked his partner, Terri, into buying a bullock's heart from a butcher for a bout of pre-game motivation. 'Make sure you get one with plenty of blood with it,' were his parting words.

'Tommy told me before the game what he had in mind. He was going to make them take a bite of it before they ran out,' Nance said. 'I said: "You can't make them do that". He said: "Do you think it's overboard?" and I said: "Well, why don't you just get them to touch it?"'

The Jets went out to warm up and when they returned, the dripping bloody heart was on the wall, even if the writing was not. 'There was a six inch nail in this heart nearly as big as a briefcase,' Langer said. 'We had to squeeze it as we ran past. We went out onto the field with blood wiped over the front of our jerseys and our shorts.'

Raudonikis chuckled: 'I shoved it in front of Alfie and said: "Your heart is as big as this, you little …" I think Alfie liked that, in a way. Great generals in wars have to grab the attention of their men. I can go over the top with it.

'With Alfie, his commitment was unconditional. He believed what you wanted him to do and he just went and did it. It didn't matter how silly it was.'

So how did the blood-smeared Jets go?

'They played brilliantly and got beaten by a bloody point. Errol Hunter, who was one of our strike weapons and a goalkicker, was king hit and that would have made a difference,' Nance recalls. Pat Shepherdson recalls a day when Raudonikis' pre-match motivation talk stunned the players. 'He smashed the rub-down table with a baseball bat, with the old Winfield hanging out the side of his mouth, and no-one was able to get a rub before the game,' he said. But when the State League started, the spirit engendered into the Jets had them unbeaten after four matches and joint leaders with Valleys and Wynnum-Manly, stacked with internationals Wally Lewis, Gene Miles and Greg Dowling. One of those matches brought Allan in opposition to his brother Kevin, halfback for Wests.

The *Rugby League Week* edition of April 16, 1986 headed a story 'Lang Park Langers' on Ipswich's 21–12 win. Kevin Langer left the game after 12 minutes with an ankle injury, barely having time to plant a sloppy kiss in a tackle. 'Here's one for you, Bubba,' Kevin mouthed in his ear. Reporter Tony Durkin said the long-awaited battle between the brothers was a 'fizzer'. 'It was the little blond-headed Alan (sic) Langer who stole the show,' Durkin wrote. 'Langer has great maturity and common sense.'

The *Courier-Mail*'s Robert Craddock chose the description 'pint-sized' and noted that the Jets' half had been involved in two spectacular Ipswich tries before scoring the third, match-sealing try himself. Kevin said after the match: 'We let him run the show. It would have been different if I had stayed on. We'll have to wait until next time now, won't we?'

The two Langers played each other twice more. Next time, at Purtell Park, Kevin injured his ankle again. 'I never played in a side that beat him. He is so competitive,' Kevin said. In a 31–12 home win over Norths, there was evidence of the special combination of Allan and former Australian Schoolboys international Gordon Langton, a winger with a dazzling turn of pace from the Cherbourg community. Langton scored twice—one an absolute gum-swallower where Langer kicked on the first tackle from a 22 metre tap kick and the winger sped 70 metres to score. Later in the match, Langer scored over a 50 metre sprint after following through in support of Langton. 'I used to kick for him all the time. He was very quick,' Langer said.

Asked to describe Langton, Langer offers: 'Gordon was very quiet.' At the time, this would have been the equivalent of a pot calling a kettle black, but their lack of verbal communication did not impinge on their silent understanding in attack.

Throughout the 1986 season and the following year, Langer's kick for Langton was a rich source of tries for Ipswich. In 1987, Langton's enthusiasm for training started to wane, but the tactic stuck fast for Langer and became the prototype for his repeated success in the 1990s when he kicked for the Broncos wingers. As a teenager Langer had always been accurate with the high ball, and in those four games for Ipswich he scored five tries. To add to the intoxicating novelty of first grade football, he also pocketed $50 on a bus trip back from Southport, the bounty from a game of pontoon. All-time great winger Ken Irvine wrote in *Rugby League Week* that 'Tommy's tearaway twins tore Gold Coast to shreds' in the 30–14 win.

'While he is only 19, he can only get better with the tough-as-teak Raudonikis in his corner,' Irvine concluded. Langer reflects: 'The Jets was a great club for me to be involved in. Tommy taught the younger blokes a lot and there were a lot of good times. We used to go down the Raceview Tavern all the time. There was the time I wrestled the One Tonner (strapper Darryl Gately) and got him on the ground. Tommy reckoned everyone had to go through the qualification rounds of the wrestling to get a crack at him. Tommy says to this day that I never beat him, but he knows I did.'

Steve Nance confirmed Langer's understated strength. 'Alf was always naturally strong. I took them to a gym one day where they had a chin-up bar and Alf was the only one to get past 20. Tommy put on a carton for the bloke who did the most. And at that stage, Alf had never lifted a weight.'

Raudonikis agrees that Langer got the better of Gately, who, as his nickname would indicate, was built upon generous lines, as well as prop Steve Rohl, but claims the halfback's memory on their own match-up must have been distorted by concussions. 'I won, don't worry about that,' he said. 'I was criticised a lot for getting too close to the players and I still do it, but the players love all that. You don't lose anything, you gain a lot, if they respect you. If they don't respect you, forget about it. Don't coach. Rugby league has become a simple game run by complex individuals, or people who want to be complex. You have to keep up to date with modern trends. But it's a basic game. It's that simple. I can't make every-one happy, but you must get on with people. The Jets trained hard, played hard and made sure we had a good time. Of all the places I have been to, it was closest to Wests in those days,' Raudonikis said.

'I was still living up in Brisbane, about 50 minutes away from Ipswich and I'd pick up some players on the way. I'd have a couple of beers after training and then get one of them to drive. I'd take half-a-dozen stubbies with me for the ride.'

Langer had warmed to Raudonikis at the same time that the

coach began to appreciate his halfback's wry wit and love of a good time. 'Tommy had a lot of influence on Allan in the early days. There was a lot of word around that he was too little,' Shepherdson said. 'He would sort of follow you around, but he would idolise Tommy. He would always be mimicking Tommy and taking the piss out of him. He got confidence from what he did during that first year. He was working pretty hard on the council gang as the billy boy. But occasionally he'd knock off early and we'd go to Bundamba races. He'd snip $20 off me to have a bet.'

Remembering the Langer of the time Raudonikis said: 'He was always stirring the Walters boys. The blokes would go to the discos and come back with cuts all over them. They'd been fighting or wrestling among themselves. But that was okay because they were out together—there was a lot of comradeship.'

But Raudonikis had been through the wringer of Sydney football for so many seasons that he knew the time would come when team spirit and enthusiasm would cease to be enough to win football games. 'We weren't really strong. I thought we went well in 1986, especially with the team we had,' he said. Ipswich lost their unbeaten State League record when they lost 26–14 to Redcliffe at Lang Park. Ipswich scored when Langer laid a chip kick over the top for a Langton try. Later, Langer brought off two try-saving tackles, regardless of his size. 'As small as he was, he used to cover-defend and make tackles on the forwards and the bigger backs,' said Nance, who has been a constant through Langer's senior career, having worked with him at the Broncos and acted as his business manager for more than a year. 'He was starting to put his leg out even then. It didn't raise any eyebrows then. He used it more in the Sydney premiership because they were bigger and stronger. Alf was beginning to do things that were uncanny in attack.'

Harsh reality set in for the Jets in mid-May when Wynnum

assaulted them 36–2 in a State League semi-final. Still, in the first round of the Brisbane premiership, Ipswich were 28–20 victors over premiers Souths—who had lost coach Wayne Bennett, captain Mal Meninga and fullback Gary Belcher in the off-season.

Langer, intensely media-shy as reporters began to consult his fledgling opinions, said after the match that the more serious training was the reason for his improvement. 'Some of the experienced players in the team have made life easier,' he said. The May 21 *Rugby League Week* column of former Kangaroo Bob McCarthy said the QRL should sign up Langer, Langton and Valleys forward Gavin Allen as well as all the State of Origin players to long-term contracts. 'And not to petty contracts either. In my opinion, they are good enough at this stage of their careers to play for Queensland and deserve special consideration,' McCarthy claimed. 'Langer may be a little small, but don't be fooled. He reminds me of a young Steve Mortimer with his little bag of tricks. He is always doing something to probe the line. I don't think I have seen a love affair established so quickly as the one between the Lang Park crowds and Langton, the Ipswich flash. He amazes me with his speed. Add his brilliant swerve, sidestep and change of pace, he can go to the top.'

When the magazine consulted a poll of 50 Brisbane first graders, Langton was rated the best new face with 42 per cent, with Allen on 30 per cent and Langer on six per cent. Langer was rated best halfback in the competition by the same proportion of his peers, with Mark Murray an overwhelming winner with 88 per cent of votes.

In front of a crowd nearing 5000, Wynnum beat Ipswich 34–18 at which Langer and the Walters twins all played together in first grade. Raudonikis played the Walters twins sparingly in 1986, the club saving them for the under-19 grade, but he made an indelible impression on Kevin Walters when he sat the five-eighth on the bench in a game in the second half of the season.

'Tommy said he was going to fire these blokes up by smacking Glenn Haggath across the face,' Nance said. 'He'd seen Glenn, who was captain, about it before. Tommy was ranting and raving about giving it to the other team and how they weren't playing with any ticker. He's said: "Glenny, get up here." And he hit him too hard, more or less punched him. Glenn went to hit him back and we had to pull them apart in the dressing-room. The gee-up had got out of control and I looked over at Kevin and Kerrod and they had their mouths open. Kevin said to Kerrod: "Gee, I hope I never captain this side".'

Langer and dummy-half Kerrod Walters quickly struck up a routine in attack which would elevate their teams in moments when inspiration was short at hand for fully a decade. Langer's gritty style could save the match. 'Alf's always been a bit of an individual player who could take the game by the scruff of the neck,' Kerrod Walters said. 'The reason why he has been such a great player over the years is that he never relied on other players in attack. He would create things for himself, without being what you would call a selfish player.' In response Langer said: 'The marker defence wasn't that great with some Brisbane teams. I'd just about always get the ball out of first receiver and I'd work off Kerrod a lot.'

Raudonikis said publicly in July that Langer, the Walters twins and Langton would be silly to go to Sydney. 'They should consolidate themselves in Brisbane so they can earn more money later,' he said. Langer re-signed with the Jets for $7500 a season— and felt like a millionaire. Langton also stayed with the Jets, but the instant celebrity their combination gave them in the small environment which was Queensland club football had a more intimidating effect on Langton.

With the Jets, he did not repeat the excellence or excitement of his 1986 season and by the mid-1990s was playing for Gatton in the Toowoomba competition. 'I think he had more ability than Alf, taking into account he was a winger,' Raudonikis judged. 'Gordon could do anything. He could have played for Australia. He had speed, a step. It just shows you—the blokes who put in the effort make it and those that don't put the effort in, don't. I'm not saying that because he is an Aborigine. I have seen a lot of white kids go off the rails too. But for Alfie, once he got the taste for it, there was no stopping him. He wanted to go all the way.'

In the second half of the season, the Jets lost four games in succession, winning the consolation of a diplomatic visit from former QRL chairman Ron McAuliffe after a 20–18 loss to Souths at the North Ipswich Reserve. He enthused, 'You may have been beaten today, but your efforts, along with those of your coach, were outstanding in your season. I wouldn't mind betting you win the 1988 Brisbane premiership.' After the 15-round Brisbane premiership season ended, the Jets had won four matches to finish second last. 'All we wanted to do was be competitive and we were. We were starting Ipswich off. We brought Alf along and the Walters twins, although Kevin went to Canberra (for 1987). That year, we almost beat Wynnum when they had half a State of Origin team. We trailed about 30–6 at halftime and they ended up winning 38–36,' Raudonikis said.

In 1987, Ipswich's record was eight wins from 16 premiership games, a considerable improvement on their adventurous, at times riotous, first season. At one stage in the 1987 pre-season, there was concern that the Jets would lose their coach in a swell off the Sunshine Coast. Raudonikis had arranged for the first graders to attend a weekend training camp at Coolum Surf Lifesaving Club, at the princely accommodation rate of $10 a weekend. They brought their own sleeping bags. Nance arrived in the afternoon to find the Jets were training, instead, at the Coolum Hotel.

Recounting the story, Nance said, 'They'd been on the drink for about five hours. Most of them were full. I said to Tommy: "What about the training camp?" and he said: "We'll do it tomorrow." So we all got on the drink.

'The hotel had a raffle and Tommy bought a couple of tickets. Tommy was the only celebrity among us and they got him to draw the raffle. He had kept the two tickets in the palm of his hand—so he won a racing bike. He rode it back to the surf club.'

Few in the Jets camp knew that Raudonikis had recently been diagnosed with testicular cancer. Not the type to court sympathy, he would wage a private fight with all the grit that forwards from Sydney and England would have recognised. 'Tommy told me not to tell anyone that he was on chemotherapy at this stage,' Nance said. His condition was to become apparent. 'When we got to the beach, it wasn't closed, but there was a big sea running and no-one was out,' Nance said.

'For the bet of a carton of beer with one of the lifesavers, Tommy bet he could swim out and back. I was trying to get him out of the challenge without letting anyone know why. He'd had a gutful of booze, he didn't need to do it, but he had been challenged—so that was that. Anyway, the whole beach watched him battle this surf for twenty or twenty-five minutes. He got pounded. He was exhausted and went grey. I had to put him to bed. He slept the rest of the afternoon and all night.' Langer said: 'We didn't have any idea he had cancer. Then it came out in the paper and it didn't seem possible.'

If Langer's career could be sliced like a tree to reveal the rings of development and growth, the two seasons with Raudonikis would be distinct to the eye. The rough-and-tumble Raudonikis delivers just about his supreme compliment.

'If Alfie had played in the 1970s, where the rules were more lenient, he would have handled himself,' he said. 'I belted some halfbacks and Alfie would have belted them, too. If Alfie and that bloke from Norths (Jason Taylor) went back to the 1970s, Alfie would punch him all over the paddock. He is a tough character. He takes the big knocks and gets up. I was always glad I had a little bit to do with him doing well.'

THE BEST MOTIVATION

Late on July 13, 1986, Mark Murray's life changed—and Allan Langer's with it. Murray, at 27 a fixture of the Queensland State of Origin team in the maturing years of the revitalised interstate competition, fell in a playful, happy heap with a Redcliffe teammate onto the floor at a high-spirited Valleys Leagues Club. Fun became concern as Murray noticed his vision was blurred in his left eye. Then a teammate noticed the blood seeping from a cut from a broken beer glass. Operations the next day and a month later left Murray with permanent double vision not unlike a ghosting television picture, his hand-eye coordination greatly reduced.

He soon dropped plans, encouraged by early diagnosis, to resume playing in 1987. Murray had played at halfback alongside Wally Lewis fourteen times at State of Origin, and played six Tests at a time when Peter Sterling and Steve Mortimer made for hothouse conditions for representative halfbacks.

The stocky product of Millmerran, in Queensland's southwest, captained the 1980 Norths first grade premiership team and quickly complemented Lewis and his Maroons forwards with his robust style and no-fuss passing game. In his absence, Queensland needed a halfback who played like Mark Murray, or at least someone new for coach Wayne Bennett (given a second chance after a 3–0 loss to NSW in 1986) to make up for the lost knowledge, combination and composure.

There were also almost weekly stories of some new, richer offer coming from Sydney for Wally Lewis, either alone or in a package deal with fellow international Gene Miles, his clubmate at Wynnum-Manly from 1984. 'There was no shortage of trips to Sydney for talks. Wally and I used to joke about it—let's jump on the plane and have a free lunch in Sydney,' Miles laughed. Those who lived outside Queensland in the 1980s would find it difficult to appreciate just what Lewis meant to the Queensland sporting public.

When Murray's opinion was being courted by the media for who would replace him in the Queensland team, he could not split Langer and Norths halfback Craig Grauf in March. 'I have noticed a change in Langer this year. He doesn't seem to be trying to do as much on his own and he is taking on responsibility for the organisation of his team,' he said at the time.

The search for a new halfback drew a considerable media posse, but the issue was a mere sideshow to the three-ring circus of the Queensland Rugby League and Brisbane Division in deciding whether, and how, a team from the city should be entered into the NSWRL competition. The Brisbane selectors went with Langer for a trial against Northern Rivers at Tweed Heads. I reported for the *Courier-Mail* of Brisbane's 42–2 win that Langer 'confirmed he was the halfback Queensland was looking for in 48 minutes, being the best player on the field in his representative starting debut'.

In truth, there was no queue of contenders out the front of the QRL's offices. If Langer, barely into his second season, was not the answer, it was hard to know where else to look in the wake of Murray's retirement. Langer, playing in the front line in defence to allow Lewis to move to the second line, was involved in the first two tries and scored the third. But the trial is best remembered when Langer, shifting play wide, cut Lewis out with his first touch of the football in senior representative football.

'I only did it once. When a bloke like Wally was there, you give him the ball. I wasn't going to do too much. It would have been my downfall,' Langer remembers.

Based at Canberra, Bennett had taken up a coaching position which allowed him to coach a NSWRL team without assuming the front-man responsibilities. Don Furner, the coach of the undefeated Kangaroos, smiled, shook hands and charmed the media. Bennett tuned in to a telecast of Langer's debut for Brisbane in a Panasonic Cup midweek game against Penrith on April 8. The halfback was replaced at three-quarter time by coach Barry Muir. Brisbane were eliminated 14–2. 'I made sure I watched and I thought he was very ordinary. I saw that defensively he was bloody terrible,' Bennett recalled. 'He never got himself into attack. He never seemed to make anything happen.'

The QRL had scheduled a match between teams Sydney Residents and Queensland Residents at Lang Park on the night the selectors were to name a team to play in the first Origin game, and also a three-match tour of New Zealand. Both the selection trial and the tour were recommended by Bennett as a measure to have the Origin team more match-toughened to meet NSW.

Playing halfback for the Sydney team was Laurie Spina, a slightly built, elusive halfback enjoying a headline-grabbing season with Easts. The smokie in the two-man battle was Kevin Walters, in his first season with Bennett with the Raiders and playing five-eighth, opposite Wally Lewis.

'There was a push on for Alf. I thought, bloody hell. I didn't think Spina was the answer either. I knew Kevin was a very good halfback,' Bennett said. 'To my mind, it was either Kevie Walters or it was Spina.'

Tom Raudonikis did not like what he was hearing: that Lewis was favouring his Wynnum teammate Peter Dawes. He went public with his fears in *Rugby League Week*, the headline reading: 'Raudonikis, Lewis feud—war of words over Langer'. Raudonikis said he had been told by a source that Lewis did not want Langer in the Origin team and that he had heard the Jets halfback would not be selected without Lewis' approval.

'Lewis might be a good player, but he isn't God. If he is going to run the whole show the QRL might as well hand the whole bloody thing over to him—if they already haven't,' he told *Rugby League Week*. 'Maybe Wally is smarter than I give him credit for. Maybe he can see how good he really is and he's afraid Alan (sic) might steal a bit of his limelight.'

Lewis responded at the time by saying Langer was big enough and good enough to do his talking on the field. 'I reckon Tommy has made the whole thing up, just to give him a push,' he said. And with a keen eye for how things seem as well as how they are, Lewis felt compelled to approach Langer about his coach's comments when Wynnum played Ipswich the following Sunday at Lang Park, winning 22–16.

'Langer said he didn't know that Tommy was going to say what he did. Maybe I should let him play his own game a bit more,' Lewis told reporters.

Raudonikis felt he was the only league figure in Queensland game enough to criticise Lewis: 'In four years up here, I haven't seen a bad thing written about him and he has a bad day like everyone else. I stick up for my players.' Ten years later, his stance had softened a little. 'I was critical because it had to be said. It was the truth. Wally was a great player, one of the best five-eighths I have ever seen. He and Bob Fulton were different, but both were great,' Raudonikis said. 'You have to have heroes. Wally Lewis was put on a pedestal, but he was there because he could play.

Queensland needed someone like that. But if Allan Langer hadn't had that chance, who knows what might have happened?'

Raudonikis took his assault on Langer's behalf in still one more direction—the QRL chairman of selectors, Dud Beattie.

'I fronted Dud Beattie, because he was an Ipswich bloke, and said: "If you don't pick this kid, you're kidding. He can play, he is tough and he is big enough",' Raudonikis said.

The idea of Beattie being intimidated into anything is cute—he would have been the last person to be persuaded into picking Langer if he didn't consider him to be the best option. As a player he was a by-word for toughness, most remarkably a 1962 Test against Great Britain in Sydney in which he was sent off in the company of the menacing Lions forward Derek 'Rocky' Turner. Playing in an era where there were no replacements, the pain of a dislocated shoulder convinced Beattie he could not continue, so he baited the fiery Englishman into belting him—so much that they were both sent off.

Bob McCarthy, coaching the NSW team, rated Spina one of the best three players in Sydney Maroons' 20–10 win, with the Roosters half creating a try for lock Bob Lindner early in the second half. Spina also handled twice in a spectacular 75 metre try begun by Walters.

After a match—which was mostly a trial in every sense of the word—the selectors met with Bennett to discuss the teams he would be given. Bennett said he had not canvassed the opinion of Lewis, with whom he had built a sound communication base.

'It had nothing to do with the players,' he said. 'Dud wanted Alf. I wasn't dogmatic about it. I would have been strong, pushing for Kevie, but then I didn't know he was the right one either. Kevie was only a kid,' Bennett said. 'One selector wanted Spina, and as the discussion continued, it was obvious Alf had two votes out of three, so I made it easy. I remember saying: "Look, we have this short tour, I'll try to make it work if you think he is the guy. You've seen more of him than me." I wasn't going to spit the dummy and carry on. In the end, Uncle Dud looked after him. He was an old Norths Ipswich boy and Uncle Dud was in his corner.'

Publicly, Bennett said Langer was going to be the most inexperienced player in the Origin match 'and that's his problem. My only criticism of him now is that he tends to look over his shoulder too much and say: "What am I doing here?" '

The first thing Bennett did when the Queensland residents team gathered to fly to Auckland was to confront Lewis and Miles. 'I grabbed them and said: "Listen, I don't know if you want this guy in the team or not, but he's in. You've got to make him feel comfortable, you've got to make him feel part of it. If you don't, we'll pay the price," ' Bennett said. 'We had two matches in New Zealand to work on it. The tour could not have come at a better time.'

Miles said: 'We didn't really like Bennett when he took over in 1986. It was just a question of us adjusting to him and him appreciating the ways things had always been done in State of Origin. It was a huge surprise to me when Alf made it. I thought they'd go for Spina, for sure.'

Miles had easily shoved Langer aside with a big fend in their first club meeting in 1986. It had seemed like a grown-up teaching his enthusiastic nephew a lesson in the backyard. First impressions are strong. So the double act of Queensland league went to work to make the 20-year-old, who had played in a beaten Ipswich reserve grade grand final side less than two years before, feel right at home. With his usual good humour, Langer quipped: 'Yeah, they kept calling me the gimp from Ipswich and told me to get down the back of the bus.'

Those unacquainted with the workings of football teams, the checks and balances system which keeps egos and morale on an even keel with the right blend of personalities, might wonder how all this was making him feel welcome. Miles recalls: 'He'd just lobbed from Ipswich with his brown port (suitcase). He always brings it up when we're out, even now with comments like: "You wouldn't talk to me ten years ago, you big-headed bastard."'

Miles agreed that there was a pecking order with Queensland teams which would carry through to the first two years of the Brisbane Broncos. 'Quite a few of us had played together for Queensland for a few years and gone away on the 1986 Kangaroo tour. It was only natural he would have felt a bit intimidated. You are always a bit intimidated the first time you go into a State of Origin camp.'

Raudonikis said Langer had confidence in his ability to compete even at this juncture, although it did not help matters much when Lindner said after the Lang Park trial that Langer did not do 'much at all' in the trial and the selectors should have gone with Spina. Mark Murray chided Lindner publicly, affirming that he thought Langer to be a better all-round player. 'Lindner will be his teammate next week and that's not the type of encouragement a kid needs from a senior member of the side,' he said.

It was nothing compared to what Bennett said to Lindner when the Queensland team convened, with team management confronting the potential unpleasantness by rooming Lindner with the rookie halfback. 'I was bloody seething. I told Bob that his job was to play football and keep his bloody nose out of it,' Bennett said.

When Queensland toured New Zealand, a group of American tourists asked Langer and Redcliffe's James Sandy if they were part of a schoolboy team. Sandy, a utility back built on Langer's dimensions, provided comfortable company for Langer among the star studded team. Like Langer, Sandy was not out of place at this level, having scored the match-winning try for Castleford in that year's Challenge Cup final before more than 85,000 spectators at Wembley against Hull Kingston Rovers. But 9500 at Auckland's Carlaw Park was the biggest stage of the career of Sandy's mate to that point as Queensland edged home 18–14 over a New Zealand President's XIII.

Langer, running off a trademark one-hand pass from Miles, scored the winning try 11 minutes from fulltime, beating off fatigue and equally tired pursuers as he ascended the quaintly sloped corner at the ground. It seemed the screws were loosened, with the Origin battles ahead. 'At least I didn't fail,' he remembers.

The second match of the tour, in the sulphurous air of Rotorua, brought Sandy four tries in a 72–6 embarrassment of Bay of Plenty, best summed up by hooker Greg Conescu's try on the right wing and his duffed conversion attempt from in front, taking his career record with the boots to one from two. Bennett, keen to pair Lewis and Langer for every minute of the tour, was frustrated when Langer withdrew on the morning of the match with a stomach upset. He said: 'On that tour of New Zealand, his sense of humour started to come out. We started to work out what sort of bloke we had.'

When the Sydney-based players arrived in Brisbane to prepare for the first game on June 3, Langer was firmly in the spotlight at Bennett's first team meeting. Paul Vautin said: 'I was watching his face as Bennett was talking about where he was going to play Langer in defence. Alf was looking down at the ground and he was obviously uncomfortable about what was being said about him. I thought if that was me, I'd want to get up and say, "Hang on a minute." So I got up and said: "Hang on, he's Queenslander, he'll do the job." Bennett accepted it. He did some great things in that game and it carried on from there.' Bennett adds: 'I remember I looked at Alf and said: "Well, how do you feel about it?" and he said: "I won't let you down." It was never discussed again.'

Langer said the first Origin match preparation was the most stressful of his career. 'The hardest thing to cop was that the coach and half the team didn't want me there, didn't think I could do it. I was surprised I was there, where I was coming from. I appreciated Fatty Vautin standing up for me. But I knew if I didn't perform in that game, I was out. The best motivation was to shut the critics up. When I got to the State of Origin camp, one of them came up with the nickname, the Alien Lifeform from Ipswich. I think Badge (Gary Belcher) and Fatty gave it to me. You don't have a choice,' Langer explained.

A comparison to a furry puppet from the American sitcom of the year, 'Alf', and a jibe suggesting that the only hometown he had ever known was even more unworldly than he thought … Just as well the coach asked them to go easy on him.

'After a day or two of being called a niff-nuff in the State of Origin camp, he gave as good as he got. He was one of the boys,' Vautin said. Langer said the first night he was in camp, Lewis, an accomplished mimic, rang him in his room. 'It was one of those prank calls where he takes off a journo and interviews me. I just sat there, answering the questions, even though they got sillier, wrapping me as a great player,' Langer said.

He played his first State of Origin match as 'Alan' Langer. It was not until the preparation for the third game that the Queensland management found out through a third party that an 'l' had been lost in transit and told the press. Not wanting to look like a big-noter, Langer said nothing until asked. Part of the press contingent, Peter Frilingos, from Sydney's *Daily Mirror*, summed up the prevailing atmosphere of disbelief over Langer's ability to compete.

'Queensland half Alan (sic) Langer will probably run onto Lang Park on Tuesday night wearing a blue suit, cape and a big "S",' Frilingos wrote. 'The tiny No. 7 must be Queensland's secret weapon or at least the best halfback to escape the Sydney clubs in a dog's age. The Queensland selectors have a tradition to commit to weird and wonderful choices, but if Langer is a better halfback than Easts' Laurie Spina then Peter Sterling's Test spot is in extreme peril,' he said. 'The Queensland selectors' decision to omit this Rooster from the starting line-up will prove to be a decisive step to oblivion. It's desperation time up north. Another 3–0 loss will see long queues featuring maroon-clad types waiting their chance to plunge from the Gateway Bridge.'

Queensland league fans pored over every mundane skerrick of information about State of Origin for weeks ahead. They took it more seriously than the Queensland players, who operated on a policy of fun first, football second until a day or two before the game.

'You couldn't have told the general public what the State of Origin team got up to in those days. They wouldn't have been able to sell tickets,' Miles said. 'When I went into my first Origin camp (in 1982), I couldn't believe a team could drink that much over five nights. You'd be sick of it after a couple of days. In the old days, we used to go for a walk at 6am and half the time you'd just be coming back into the foyer. So you'd go for a walk with the team in the gear you went out in the night before.'

Casual fans who had absorbed none of the pre-match publicity were astonished by the tiny Langer. He was so small his jersey number almost tucked into his shorts. Regardless of his stature, Langer stood his ground. In that first game, big NSW forwards snapped him around like a wet towel. His education in the backyard had taught him when to fight a tackle and when to hit the ground and cover up.

'Ron Willey (NSW coach) would have said, "Right, let's sort out this little prick." And he took everything they threw at him,' said John Ribot. The rising star Langer said: 'The pace of the game was something I wasn't used to. I was glad halftime came. In that first year, I was just wanting to do my best and hopefully they would accept me. I was never confident of staying there. The thing I remember best was trapping ET in goal after a kick. The crowd just got behind me. It gave me a great lot of confidence.'

Another moment which won hearts was his failed footrace with Michael O'Connor as O'Connor scored one of the great solo Origin tries. A football thoroughbred, O'Connor scored NSW's first try from his own half after breaking the line and kicking ahead. Langer was never going to reel in the metre or two advantage O'Connor had. But he kept chasing until the dual international had stooped to gather and roll over the tryline in a fluid motion. The effort—the pride—involved was what galvanised public support behind Queensland Origin teams.

As families grouped around televisions, mothers wanted to make him a cup of tea at the end and give him a chocolate biscuit. Fathers wanted to buy him a beer. Some of the daughters...well, let's just say he had a lot of fans!

Every schoolboy around a television could feel for him as he tackled forwards more than 30 kilograms heavier than him, acting out their Boys' Own adventures. But there would be no heroic last chapter from the rookie.

Queensland had recovered from a 16–6 deficit with tries by wingers Dale Shearer and Tony Currie, the second a masterly piece of field vision from Lewis who had spotted a blindside hole. But with the scores locked at 16–all entering the last minute, Langer could do no more than watch as a pass from NSW centre Mark McGaw was deflected backwards by a desperate Currie, leaving McGaw and Peter Jackson to drive towards the ball, rolling innocently towards the dead-ball line. In a pile of arms and legs, referee Mick Stone came up with the correct decision, fair try, NSW win 20–16. A television camera recorded Bennett in the stands. He looked disbelievingly and grimaced: 'Oh, no.'

Langer felt like he had won the lottery and lost the ticket.

As the players sat and stared at nothing, talking in anguished bursts or not at all, Bennett waited for the media. The Brisbane and Sydney press contingent, their attitudes to his team's performance no doubt shaped by the last minute and not the previous 79, did not show.

'Bloody typical. They only want to talk to the winners,' said Bennett, unaware that on the night in which he suffered a fourth loss in succession the scribes had been called out on strike by their union. In the week that followed, Bennett told team management he would not be seeking a third term if they lost. His state coaching career was at match point down.

For the second game in Sydney, the selectors moved Currie to the reserves, changing positions with specialist fullback Colin Scott, a former international, in the last line. The only other change was lock Bob Lindner, back from injury and forcing out Gary Smith, of Brothers, from his first and only Origin team. 'I've always had an intuition, I suppose, when I know things are right and when things are wrong,' Bennett said. 'I knew we had lost four straight, but I wasn't at panic stations because I knew we were on the right track … It was just a matter of holding our nerve and hoping we got a little bit of luck.

'And if you don't, you know you won't have the job next year, but at least you'd have known you did the best you could—no regrets. I never had any doubts about Alf since that first game in State of Origin. He belonged.'

Langer said: 'I didn't have the confidence that Wayne had at the time, that I would make it. I was only one bad performance away from the sack.' The attitude had been drummed into him by Raudonikis. 'If you have a bad one in the second game or they lose, you're out. Don't forget that,' he told Langer.

In camp in Sydney, Langer took a call from world champion boxer Jeff Fenech. Once he was reasonably sure the caller was not Lewis in another room, they spoke freely.

'It came out of the blue. He said he really admired my game at Lang Park. It was a really nice gesture from a New South Wales bloke,' Langer said.

The second Origin game on June 16 was lashed by rain which reduced the pace advantage the Blues enjoyed and inspired such noted mud-runners in the Queensland pack as Trevor Gillmeister, Greg Dowling and Greg Conescu. It did not deter a 42,048 crowd from attending, a notable stamp of approval on the eight-year-old concept from Sydneysiders.

Five successive penalties from Mackay referee Barry Gomersall assisted Queensland to withstand a NSW surge begun by a try to second-rower Steve Folkes after Shearer had fumbled the ball on a kick return. Shearer, as he so often did throughout his never-a-dull-moment career, repaid his debt to the team when, shortly before half time, he moved into dummy-half behind Langer and burrowed over. Scott's conversion, from a handy position, hit the crossbar and Queensland again rued the absence of Mal Meninga, who was out with the first of four fractures to his left forearm.

The Maroons took an 8–6 lead when Miles, pressing home the advantage of a searching run by centre partner Peter Jackson on the previous tackle, found an unstoppable Dowling on his outside. In the last 10 minutes, Lewis and Miles worked the numbers to the left, where winger Colin Scott skidded over for the last score of the game, a 12–6 win.

At fulltime, the series still alive and a number of careers in the visitors' dressing-room saved, a euphoric Lewis slung an arm around Langer and puckered up for the photographers. Langer squirmed, grinned and waited for the photographers to finish.

'I don't know what that kiss was about. Maybe he was just elated with the win,' is as deep as Langer wants to go. Going on to analyse the game he added: 'I was happy with my game, especially winning, which made it easier for all of us. I might have been out if we hadn't have won in Sydney.' Reflecting on the incident Raudonikis said: 'I don't know Wally that well, but you have to give him credit. With that kiss, he was saying he was wrong about Allan. Everybody can make mistakes.'

Former Australian halfback and grand final referee Keith Holman sought Langer out. 'Well done, son. You have what it takes,' Holman said warmly. The *Daily Mirror*'s Tony Adams reported Langer as saying to him: 'It was nice of him to say that. Who is he again?' In the same newspaper, Wayne Pearce's column was headed 'Prince Allan'. 'It has taken Allan Langer only two matches to prove himself the heir to King Wally's throne,' Pearce said. 'Langer is the man to lead Queensland league in the 1980s. For a 20-year-old kid who has played all his football in the country, the game is at his feet.'

Bennett, his face and clothes smudged with mud from embraces, mined the deep well of resentment in the soul of born-and-bred Queensland league players. 'No matter who we are against or what we do, they say we can't play. It's been the same for cricket, whatever. But someone has to start realising soon we have a good football team here,' he told reporters. Sterling had the consolation of taking the man-of-the-match award and would go on to play halfback against New Zealand, where, after one of the most complacent preparations by Australian players in modern history, they would be embarrassed 13–7 at Lang Park.

But for Langer, having persuaded his coach, teammates, the media and fans that he could cut the mustard in the big time, there was a new and potentially devastating problem.

Before the third game, on June 26, Allan's elder brother, Kevin, answered a charge in the Brisbane District Court on alleged fraud and stealing offences during November and December 1986 from the bank that employed him. The next day, he was sentenced to six months jail.

'I was a bad punter at the time,' Kevin Langer said nine years later. 'I was about to get married. We were saving for a deposit and I didn't want to tell Donna I had lost it. I remember when I was sentenced, Allan was in tears. We are a very close family. When they came to visit me, we would sit there, with the glass between us. It straightened me out.'

Allan said: 'He had the gambling bug, which a lot of people do. Working in the bank, there was that temptation. He is the character of the family. To see him taken away was ...' Rita still shudders when she remembers the emotions of the time. In camp for the series decider, Bennett watched his young halfback closely for signs of frayed nerves or emotions. 'We talked about it once or twice. Alf handled it really well. He's got that attitude to life which allows him to put things behind him. He wasn't embarrassed—he just felt for Kevin and his Mum and Dad,' Bennett said.

On July 7, eight days before the third game at Lang Park, Langer told the Brisbane *Telegraph*: 'I want to play my guts out for Kevin. It's hard to accept and I try not to think about it all that much. I try to concentrate on my football. But everyone makes mistakes. I won't be deserting him. I am very proud of Kevin and what he has achieved. I look up to him as an older brother.' At that stage shy and uncertain of what reporters would do, it was the lengthiest media interview Langer had given and at its source was a desire to lift his brother's spirits at the lowest point of his life. Kevin Langer and a viewing audience of more than two million Australians saw the Maroons halfback provide a fitting dedication to his brother as Queensland won one of the most remarkable

Origin matches of all, 10–8.

Allan came within one metre of scoring the first try from his second touch. In an elaborate Queensland team play which started with Miles beating NSW five-eighth Cliff Lyons and prop Phil Daley, Langer evaded Garry Jack, the world's best fullback, and was collected by winger Brian Johnston. Langer handled twice again in Queensland's well-drilled penalty tap move for Lindner to score after eight minutes.

When NSW hit back through a Pearce chargedown of a Lewis clearing kick, Queensland slapped another card on the table two minutes later when Shearer, roaming to the right side of the field from his left wing, called for a grubber by Dowling and swooped for an 8–6 lead. Twice in the first half, Langer stole the ball from Ettingshausen, once on the NSW 10 metre line and then near halfway.

The Blues levelled at 8–all through a penalty Lewis conceded when he saw how slowly his teammates were retreating. Change kicker Shearer put the Maroons ahead just before half-time when Gomersall ruled O'Connor had been fractionally in front when Lyons laid a chip kick over from his 30 metre line.

The second half, although scoreless, was a monument to the game. Both teams, played to a standstill by the pace of the game and their indomitable wills, had the chance to win on at least three separate occasions. After a Langer grubber had forced an error on the NSW quarter, an unmarked Scott, both hands to his head in self-admonition, was unable to bring in an awkward, if catchable, pass from Miles. Miles was held up over the line after Lewis had chanced a tap kick.

The Queensland captain then launched himself off the ground in a masterpiece of a covering tackle on the dangerous O'Connor, anticipating a sidestep in much the same way a clay target shooter aims along the trajectory of the flight. Queensland fullback Gary

Belcher saved tries with tackles on Johnston and Lyons, before the Maroons forced three line drop-outs in the last eight minutes.

Lewis, the scoreboard proclaiming 'King Wally', lifted his little halfback off the ground in the jubilation greeting Queensland's 10–8 win. At the microphone for the official presentations, he paid special mention of Langer and Bennett—'the best coach in the world'—before inviting the crowd to cast their eyes out on 'fourteen of the bravest footballers ever to play on Lang Park'. As testimony to his team mate and Man of the Match, Lewis said of Langer, 'He is only ten stone—and nine stone 13 pounds is in heart.'

Channel Nine commentator Darryl Eastlake told Langer: 'You're the King. Where do you go from here?' Looking at Eastlake as if he was hallucinating, Langer lurched into classic Alf-speak: 'Hopefully keep the good efforts up and keep playing State of Origin football, mate.' He became more serious. 'I just want to thank my brother Kevin. I did all this for him tonight.'

In the dressing-room, he told reporters, 'I want you to put in that everything I did tonight was for Kevin. When he wakes up in the morning, I want him to read the paper and know that. I'm going to see him (in Boggo Road) on Saturday and I can't wait.'

Kevin Langer was just about to obey the lock-up time orders when he heard his brother's words at the official presentation. 'We were allowed to stay up. It helped me inside because they loved Allan,' Kevin said. He added, 'Just as we were going to bed, I heard Allan say in an interview that he dedicated his match to me. It choked me up. I thought it was great. The Ipswich battlers-thing came out in him. He went for it when he had the chance.'

Langer and Vautin, covering the front and back ends of Origin history respectively, regard the 1987 series as the best they have played in. In the days that followed, Langer was accorded a civic reception in his home town.

The *Queensland Times* reported: 'Youngsters were trampled by screaming fans as local rugby league hero Alan [sic] Langer hurled footballs into a crowd in Ipswich last night. The crowd of hundreds turned out to cheer Langer in a street parade organised by his employer, the Ipswich City Council. Langer was driven through the Ipswich city centre on an old fire engine.' Now an old hand at public speaking, Langer said he was embarrassed by all the fuss. 'Thanks for the turnout,' he added.

After the third State of Origin match, Raudonikis said: 'Wait until the kid grows up. I played my best football later in my twenties and he has skills I only dreamed of. He'll go all the way. Some of those who had to be convinced weren't only members of the public, believe me.'

Langer ventured out of Australia for the first time to play for Queensland in the ARL's experimental exhibition Origin match, at a speedway venue in Long Beach, California. NSW won the match at Veterans' Stadium 30–18, with Sterling pocketing his second best player award of the season. But the match—a novelty piece in ARL history as the League has yet to venture back in anywhere near the same numbers—became almost as well known as a body-building contest.

Paul Vautin recounts: 'At the hotel where we were staying, we were invited into the bar for a few drinks. They have a professional body-building circuit and the body-builders are getting pumped up and oiling themselves down. We're going: "What about these blokes? They have to be kidding." Alf's going: "Yeah, I can do better than them." Unbeknownst to him, some of us entered him in the circuit. When he was announced, he didn't want to go up, but he eventually got up on the stage. He started getting into it, doing one-arm push-ups and the crowd was going berserk. The pros were filthy, saying, "Who is that guy?" He ended up running third and won $50, which he threw on a red or a black.'

Back in Sydney, Laurie Spina was coming to terms that his Origin career was probably over before it began. Looking back Spina is as philosophical as a North Queensland cane farmer's son should be. 'Allan has gone on to become a great player, even though I thought I had the form on the board that year. I don't argue with it,' Spina said in 1990.

Soon Langer would be joining Sterling and Spina in week-by-week combat without following the path out of Queensland to Sydney that was beaten by so many dozens of players over the previous 20 or 25 years. In April, 1987, the Brisbane Division and the Queensland Rugby League approved the entry of a team from Brisbane into the NSWRL premiership, to be funded by Brisbane businessmen Barry Maranta, Paul Morgan, Gary Balkin and Steve Williams.

This ended almost nine months of the QRL and Brisbane Division committees debating all the way down the line. It was one of the difficult gestation periods in Australian sporting history, with Brisbane clubs and country divisions fighting the move, either out of self-interest or a misguided belief in tradition.

A big club crowd in Brisbane at the time was 2000 punters, with the rank-and-file supporters providing company only for the big representative matches at Lang Park. All this saved Langer from a move to Sydney to make a decent dollar. The poignancy of this, against the financial difficulties of Kevin Langer, is impossible to miss.

'Alf being Alf, I really don't think he could have lived in Sydney. He just wouldn't have done it,' Bennett said. Langer says: 'Illawarra were chasing me at one stage even though I was signed for the Jets for 1988. Bob Millward (Steelers chief executive) came up and watched me, but he didn't want me because I was too small.

I could have been at Illawarra, but it wasn't to be.'

Once Bennett had accepted the Broncos coaching role, joining newly-appointed chief executive John Ribot, Langer was sure to follow. Bennett had denied reports throughout the Queensland tour of New Zealand that he was interested in coaching the team to be known as the Broncos. Ultimately, the desire to return home and put together his own NSWRL club outweighed his anguish at leaving the Raiders after one season.

'We had plenty of contenders in mind, but when we spoke to Jack Gibson, we had one name on the list. Jack said Wayne was the one we had to get,' Paul Morgan said. 'My choice for number two was John Lang. Langy had been successful with Easts and he was the sort of bloke we were after. Gary (Balkin) would have wanted Bob McCarthy.' With laughter erupting from his barrel chest, he added: 'But we weren't not going to get Wayne.'

Bennett played against Morgan in the Toowoomba competition in the 1960s, remembering him as one of the most competitive players and most driven trainers he had encountered. He knew he could keep saying no, but also that Morgan would keep coming at him. Allan Langer's life would irrevocably change course, taking him away from his home town.

And for the central figures in Alf's big year, life also marched on. Kevin Langer was home for a more emotional family Christmas than normal in 1987, resuming his career the following season with Wests, a club at which many observers felt he stayed too long. 'We didn't win much, but we had a great time. It's hard when you are in a losing side,' Kevin said. He won the 1988 Rothmans Medal, taking the *Courier-Mail* best and fairest award as well, to put next to his 1985 award of the same.

Leaving Wests in 1990, Kevin captain-coached Beaudesert to two Gold Coast-Group eighteen premierships in three years and guided Ipswich to a second grand final loss before the Jets, unable to muster the finances to compete, declined sadly. He had a NSWRL premiership trial with Wests in the pre-season of 1991, but his chance at the top level of club football in Australia just did not come.

'I went all right in the first game against Newcastle. The coach, John Bailey, was pretty pleased. There was another trial against Penrith which I played with a broken bone in my foot. Maybe I shouldn't have,' he said. 'People ask me if I'm jealous of Allan's success. Well, you know those Alfie dolls that came out? He was suffering bad headaches for a while. So the pins worked! But at least I'm able to say I won a Rothmans Medal in Brisbane, which he never did. Allan might come across as a bit stuck-up to some of the public, but it's just shyness. I love being in the limelight, but he'd prefer to sit back. But once you get to know him, he's a rat too. Loves practical jokes.

'Allan's success was good because it opened doors for me. You'd love to have it yourself, but good luck to him.' One of the opened doors was a transfer to the London Broncos. Returning to Queensland, Kevin coached Runaway Bay in the 1997 Gold Coast premiership.

Cliff and Neville Langer would play the 1996 season for Norths in Ipswich, turning out in both first and reserve grade.

Tommy Raudonikis would recover from cancer and take Ipswich to the grand final in 1988 without Langer and Kerrod Walters. 'We lost to Valleys by four points and should have won it,' said Raudonikis, who would move to Wests in the ARL premiership in 1995. 'In Sydney they think it's a shit competition. But it's still producing good footballers. Paul Green and Adrian Lam got their starts in Brisbane.

In late 1996 there was a reunion of Jets players. Raudonikis brought his friend John Singleton, the successful advertising executive, who championed his cause to the point of helping him get the job with ARL club Wests. 'Singo couldn't believe that none of these blokes were playing anymore and here was Alfie out with them and picking up the bill for $400 at the Chinese restaurant,' Raudonikis said.

'Alf loves it. He takes control now, too. He is the boss now. He remembers the people on the way up. One night he got us back to City Rowers where there was this mechanical bull. I was half shot and there was no way I was getting on it. Alf told me: "You're sweet. I've got the controls. I'll put it on a slow speed and you'll win the prize". So he conned me into it and put it on full bore— and sent me flying off it! I couldn't get him on it.'

The paths of Kevin Langer and Tom Raudonikis crossed when they were involved in a Queensland Residents representative team and team bonding was carried out in the typically enthusiastic Raudonikis style. Allan Langer would have loved to have been with them.

But destiny was calling.

EVERYBODY'S LITTLE MATE

The most stressful day of Allan Langer's first two seasons with the Brisbane Broncos wasn't when he proved correct the ten or 12 years of predictions that he would play for Australia. It wasn't when the Broncos management and the Ipswich Jets club had a summer-long donnybrook about whether Brisbane would pay $30,000 or not for his services—a laughably small sum for such a dispute when it is considered in retrospect.

It wasn't when he broke his ankle in a State of Origin match, forcing him to surrender the Test jersey he had worn so proudly. It wasn't even on either of those two dark occasions when the Broncos fell one win short of making the NSWRL's finals series when not doing so was widely seen as a failure and a criminal waste of talent.

The most stressful day of Allan's life came early in 1988 when Langer had to break the news to his parents that he was moving out of Sadliers Crossing. 'It was one of the hardest decisions I had to make, to leave home,' he said. 'I didn't tell Dad until the morning I was going to Brisbane that I was moving out because it was a long way to travel each day. I was sitting at the breakfast table, trying to work up the courage to tell them. Being the baby of the family it was hard for them.'

Coming from a familiar and comfortable environment in 1986, Langer was now a celebrity in the small arena of Queensland sport, dealing with people who would have unknowingly sheeted dust or sprayed puddles over him as they drove past him on the Ipswich road gang.

'It was something he had to adjust to. He came out of a recluse-type environment at Sadliers Crossing and when things got a bit tight in the early days, or a bit rough, he'd get the rattler (train) to Ipswich and get away. He didn't have a car at that stage,' said John Ribot. 'I'd have to send someone to find him at Sadliers Crossing because his parents didn't have the phone on. It was his insulation from the rest of the world.'

Langer and his girlfriend, Janine, moved into a flat in Red Hill, a few blocks from the club which would become central to his future affluence and success.

'When I went to the Broncos, I didn't think I had made it, even though I had played State of Origin,' he recalls. 'I still had to justify my position in first grade. I knew they were trying to buy Des Hasler and I really had to struggle to keep my spot early in that first year.'

Ribot, appointed general manager of the Brisbane team to enter the NSWRL premiership as one of three new clubs, wasn't as convinced about Langer's longevity in Sydney's uncompromising competition as coach Wayne Bennett. In the time between his first and second Origin matches of 1987, Ribot declared Langer 'a priority player', but admitted they were negotiating with other Sydney halfbacks, including the tireless Hasler, a Manly inter-national. Ribot remembers: 'I'd be fibbing if I said there weren't some doubts about how Alf would handle the week-to-week grind. We realised how good he was, but in those days he was small and a bit frail.

'To tell you the truth, Des Hasler was our first choice and we couldn't get him. It wasn't a case of "Hey, this bloke is a super-star".' Bennett has a different recollection: 'He was always our first-choice halfback. Ribes is bullshitting himself there.'

Ribot had engaged in a poker-game style negotiation with the Ipswich Jets over their $30,000 demand for Langer's release from the last year of the 21-year-old's Jets contract. It went most of the summer, the Brisbane press wrestling with the prospect that Langer would be the only Origin player in Australia not playing in the expanded 16-team competition. 'I don't think the Broncos were ever going to drop off. The Jets got $20,000 in the end and I got $10,000 of that. It was part of the deal,' he remembers.

Ribot clinched the compromise deal less than two weeks before the Broncos were to play their first pre-season match against grand finalists Canberra at Lang Park, the ground adopted as their home ground after a lengthy wrangle over hiring terms which set the stage for more bitter and vengeful confrontations. Jets official Gary Parcell, a former Test prop, was prepared to concede on a reduced fee for Kerrod Walters, but stood firm on Langer, forcing the issue to arbitration with the Queensland Rugby League.

'They probably got more than they thought by playing such a straight bat, although I was pleased with the deal we got,' Ribot said. 'The thing that both I knew and they knew was that Alf had other offers. When Illawarra dropped off, we were the only ones who were in the race.' The Broncos also had to pay another $15,000 to the Jets because Langer was a State of Origin player. 'It was more a publicity stunt to keep the papers happy and it gave the Ipswich people some credibility,' Ribot said.

The dispute also added fuel to the fire of conviction among the local clubs that the Broncos management was only happy when they got their own way. The 'whingeing Broncos' tag was born. A case in point was Ipswich coach Tom Raudonikis' February, 1988 column in *Rugby League Week*, in which he claimed Brisbane would not make the final five, despite their massed stars. 'One thing against them is their management team. I reckon a lot of people would see some of their antics as that of the big bully,' Raudonikis said. 'The case of Allan Langer is typical. Ipswich put a $30,000 transfer fee on him, the Broncos whinged and got it reduced on appeal and then whinged some more. Naturally they paid the money because they know he is worth more like $50,000. The Broncos should be trying to foster the relationship with the Brisbane clubs, not crush them.'

Langer said he was paid $10,000 a year for 1988 and 1989, despite his Origin record. 'He upgraded me for 1989 when I went all right—up to $30,000,' Langer said, dissolving into laughter. When he learned Lewis and Miles had been signed for $125,000 a season, he filed the information away for future reference.

But there were other benefits being a Bronco. Being a member of the club gained instant credibility when Wally Lewis signed on June 10, 1987, Gene Miles the following day, and internationals Greg Dowling, Greg Conescu, Colin Scott and Bryan Niebling in the hectic weeks that followed. Only three Sydney players were brought north: Chris Johns and Billy Noke, both regular first graders with St George without being permanent, and Easts under-21s lock, Terry Matterson.

Leaving the billy, shovel and stop-go sign behind, Langer was groomed by Broncos director Gary Balkin in the hotel trade and put to work at the St Paul's Terrace establishment, Bonapartes. Briefly, that is.

'You'd go down there to the public bar on Saturdays and he'd have the same old fellas there every week,' Langer's friend David Pie said. 'He'd have them all entertained. He knew all their names and he was forever putting shit on them. They loved it. But he wasn't big on getting there at 9:30 every morning and smelling the stale grog from the night before. He didn't last there long.'

Only a little reserved around the senior players, Langer felt quickly at home at the Broncos, which operated out of the newly bought bottom floor of the Wests Old Boys club at Red Hill. It was christened the Cockroach Inn, and was a step down from the temporary riverside offices of Paul Morgan, one of the four directors of the NSWRL's first private enterprise club. Ensconced at Red Hill were Ribot, Pie (as merchandising officer), public relations manager Kev Keliher, marketing manager Richard Winten and Ribot's secretary, Robyn Maranta.

Boxes were piled in walkways and it was OK to swing a cat in the offices, provided it wasn't a particularly big cat.

'The cockies used to fly. They looked like bats,' said Pie, who played Australian football in Brisbane and Victoria both before and after his employment there. 'But from the start, it was a professional organisation. You knew they were in it for the long haul. Alf was always good fun in those early days because he wasn't usually working. He used to hate being at home by himself. He'd be there at 7:30 in the morning because Janine had gone to work. I'm sure she thought he used to work there. He became my little offsider—he'd come everywhere with me, which means he would just get in my way. Ribes would tell me to stop encouraging him to come to the club.' The Broncos organised a small car for Langer through sponsor Ron McConnell. 'He was over the moon with it. He thought it was the greatest thing of all time,' Pie said.

Ribot, Bennett and their four bosses made the management of the club up as they went along. Conventional ways of operating a football club were thrown to the wind.

'I've got to tell you, it wasn't a compatible board. There were personalities there—and they weren't going out for a drink with each other,' Ribot said. 'In their own ways, they all had different strengths. Take this the right way: their greatest strength, in some ways, was that they didn't trust each other. There was a lot of emotion involved, but they were analytical at the same time. Gary (Balkin) had a great feel for the marketplace. He would come in sometimes, full of gloom and doom saying: "The coach ... people are saying he has no personality and we've lost the feel for the community and we've got to change the coach, that's what people are saying." But, in the same breath, Gary was very supportive of Wayne. Initially, Wayne had to earn that from Gary.'

Taking their cue from American sports, as the Broncos would continue to do, the public address at the club's first trial match on February 20 sounded cracking whips and neighing. Smart alec remarks were made towards the Canberra players by the ground announcer and the operator of the scoreboard. Dancing girls prowled the sidelines and a band stationed behind the goalposts blew a brass raspberry at Canberra's Gary Belcher as he lined up a kick.

The next day, NSWRL chairman Ken Arthurson, who had previously been at his diplomatic best in predicting that Brisbane would make the finals at their first attempt, said the 'bad sportsmanship and juvenile behaviour' may be fine for basketball, but could drive traditional fans away.

After a media saturated pre-season, an inauspicious crowd of 9744 created an echo chamber effect on the grounds, but Langer excelled in a 22–16 win in which Brisbane immediately established their trend to concede leads by falling eight points behind in the first half.

A 20 metre solo try by the Broncos halfback was bookended by scores from Matterson and Dowling in an 11-minute flurry in the second half. The Broncos went on to make the club an instant success in the attacking football which Bennett and the directors had deduced was essential for the club's financial future, given the absence of the poker machine money which fuelled Sydney clubs.

Accounting for a New Zealand President's 13 team in the second trial, Brisbane approached the premiership debut they had ringed on the calendar for months—premiers Manly at Lang Park. Two days before the game, there was an interesting perspective in Brothers coach Ross Strudwick's column in the *Daily Sun* as he predicted a big win over the Sea Eagles.

'Langer does not exploit his exceptional skills when Wally is outside him,' said Strudwick, who was Lewis' first senior coach with Valleys. 'When Wally is there, Langer obviously thinks he's there to give Wally the ball and that dulls Allan's potential. I think Wally should be playing wider of the ruck. As it is, Langer appears to be cramped up and restricted.'

But Langer remembers: 'Wally didn't try to tell me to back off at all. He encouraged me to play my game. As soon as we got used to playing alongside each other, I thought we played well.' Lewis, who had been force-fed for years the opinion he would not be able to aim up in Sydney, unfurled one of his finest afternoons before a disappointing crowd of 17,451. It was as if after all the hype, the Brisbane public was sitting back, arms folded, daring them: 'Show us what you have.' And what a show they missed. The premiers were ambushed—44–10!

Lewis was irresistible, scoring two tries, one over 25 metres, which defeated six Manly defenders, and giving the last pass for two others. Matterson marked his 21st birthday and his second game in first grade with 24 points, a club record which still stands.

Langer had been off the field when Brisbane scored their first try—a bomb brought down by second-rower Brett Le Man—because he had been collared by Manly prop Phil Daley, and this re-ignited the debate over his stature and whether he could handle the week-to-week buffeting. 'When I came back on, I tried to pack in at lock, which was funny because I hadn't played in the forwards since the under-sevens! So I could understand why people were concerned,' he reflects. Bennett said: 'I was worried once. He is smart and when he gets tackled, he has good body protection. He gets low to the ground when he thinks he is in trouble.'

The atmosphere in the Broncos' dressing-room couldn't have been headier. It was as if they had shared Armstrong's first step on the moon. But among the laughter and smiles of exultation there was Bennett, aloof and trying to practice his personal belief that success should not send spirits soaring too high or defeat casting them too low.

He was right. It was too good to be true—but what an afternoon. For anyone who remembered the interstate thrashings back in the days when State of Origin had everything to do with Charles Darwin, it carried a surreal quality.

It wasn't just the north that was getting carried away with the new boys from Queensland who would go on to win their first six premiership games. Just one win was enough to spark the reaction from Sydney that the NSWRL had created a monster. No less an authority than Parramatta's premiership-winning coach John Monie opined that the Broncos could 'almost take a stranglehold' as the only team in Queensland. The *Daily Telegraph* wondered if the Broncos would win the grand final in their first year. Manly coach Bob Fulton was more circumspect when discussing the prospects for the winners. 'It's a hard school and you shouldn't get carried away. If a team is able to put pressure on Wally Lewis, it will be a different story,' he said with foresight.

Their second match was more down-to-earth, a 20–18 escape against the physical Penrith. Flamboyant winger Joe Kilroy—so popular with the Lang Park faithful that he would soon take his own cheer squad to Sydney to dance his praise—scored a late, length-of-the-field match-winner. 'Alf is fascinating,' Bennett remarked afterwards. 'In that try, he stood two defenders up, stood and unloaded to Joey.'

At halftime the game had looked only a matter of how and when with the Broncos leading 16–2. But when they returned at fulltime, Bennett was doing one of his Easter Island impressions and warning them that their lack of discipline would prove costly.

It was all so new and exciting and the adrenalin was rushing. Morgan was talking about chartering helicopters to take the players to Campbelltown for round three against Wests to prevent the players getting tired. Miles didn't play and travelled to the ground in a white stretch limousine with Morgan, Barry Maranta, Gary Balkin and Steve Williams. 'At Campbelltown we couldn't believe it,' he said. 'I swear some of them had never seen a limousine. We won that game easily and when we got back they had been throwing cans and rocks at it as if we were the toffs from Brisbane heading out to fibro town. Wherever we went in Sydney, we copped it, particularly in Balmain. The obvious reason was they thought we were the Queensland State of Origin team.'

The presence of Wally Lewis particularly engendered that depth of feeling. The Broncos skipper had been abused as the visitors wended their way from the dressing-rooms and spectators hooted at every action during the 38–4 win over Wests. It may seem contradictory but, at the end, about 300 fans and five police lined up as he signed autographs. Three kids were shooed away by the boys in blue after they had comically bopped Lewis—deep in scrawling concentration—repeatedly on the head with plastic soft drinks bottles. Twice, more menacing attention was escorted away from the huddle—and still he kept signing.

Six weeks later, a punch was thrown at Lewis as he walked off the ground at Cronulla, with trainers hurrying him away to the rooms. Langer said: 'A lot of league fans hated him because he is such a great player and has had such a lot of success.'

Making the most of their winning streaks, Brisbane prevailed

24–18 over Parramatta in an authentic big-match atmosphere with a Lewis try that stemmed from a miscued Langer grubber kick.

For the next game at Newcastle, Langer's now-legendary aversion to flights was established. During the Sydney–Newcastle flight aboard a twenty-seater that was buffeted by winds and rain, a petrified Langer, white knuckles gripping the armrest, dared not look at anything but the floor, as teammates hammed it up with each lurch and drop. Bennett, another nervous passenger, was another who did not laugh. He, Langer and Scott commandeered a hire car for the return to Sydney airport after the 24–10 win over the Knights before a 30,220 crowd.

'He has become better over the years—he had to—but he's still a terrible flier,' Bennett says with a chuckle. 'It's one time when his teammates can just give it to him. If he is nervous, he just sits there and hopes and says nothing. When he is on the long haul flights, you see him up the back of the plane talking to some bloke from Queensland he doesn't know or one of the stewardesses.' Langer agrees: 'The small planes are the worst. I just get scared. It's part of the job these days, but I still hate it, even the bigger jets.' Psychologically, it stems from his helplessness in the air. Langer likes to be in familiar surroundings, with people and situations he knows. 'He's just one of those guys who has a comfort zone and doesn't try to be anything else,' Bennett offers.

An off-hand comment by Ribot that Langer could become the first league player to become a millionaire—hey, at the rate he was paying Langer, the misplaced choir boy would need to play for about 70 years to turn seven figures—was the stuff of newspaper headlines.

Fan mail for Langer at the Broncos office began to assume Lewis-like quantities. Keliher explained: 'Kids see themselves as Alf being the little guy taking on the adults and winning. When they swarm around him for autographs he talks to them in kidspeak.'

Power Brewing were sending Broncos to hotels in Brisbane and Queensland country, even though there was no product. 'They couldn't use Alf on the television advertisements because he wasn't old enough, but he was the epitome of their product,' he said. 'Here was a working class product and a little battler on the field trying to match it with the big guys and winning.'

Alf would go to these appearances and he slowly found his feet despite his shyness among strangers. He is not a confrontationalist—he has different ways of dealing with situations. He is very particular who he picks as his friends. It might seem that he's friendly with everyone but his greatest strength is to just shut people out. He will be social and respectful though. But the best way for him is to say nothing and work people out, see what they are like.'

Langer was encouraged, briefly, like other players, to attend a Toastmasters course. 'He didn't go to many, but that was fine because we quickly worked out that Alf was Alf and you wouldn't want to change him,' Ribot said. 'That natural side of him is what makes him so good with people. There are no airs and graces with Alf, even after nine or ten years at the top.'

The endorsements and the win bonuses of $1500 Man of the Match awards meant Langer was in need of urgent financial advice. His friend from the Jets, Steve Nance, was recruited by Bennett into the Broncos training staff, and volunteered when he could see Langer in danger of being picked off by advisers more protective of their own interests. 'When I first started to look after his financial affairs, I was really worried about him on the punt. He'd started to earn decent amounts of money and he was going to the races midweek, and on Saturday if the Broncos weren't playing,' Nance said.

'I got him off the punt completely for a couple of months there in 1988. But it was more than the punt. We went to Expo one day when Janine was away. He was trying to find his pass in the glovebox and there was this Dally M award cheque for $500 in his glovebox along with another for $500 Man of the Match award. They'd been there a couple of months because he hadn't got around to banking them. I took him to my accountant and he got a couple of angles on his tax. I got him some corporate deals, nothing near as big as he was going to get. He bought into a video store, but it would be later on before he had the money to do well with real estate. He got a lot of help from a lot of people because he is the sort of bloke you like to help.'

Langer's lack of schooling is compensated by his sixth-sense, his antennae which detect when he is being taken advantage of.

'His common sense is good and his work with numbers is good, probably because of the punt. When he lends someone money, he remembers to the cent how much it was: "Pay me back next week". It was his upbringing,' Nance elaborates. 'He can be sitting there reading the paper and if he doesn't understand a particular word, he'd say: "What's this bloke mean?" When he was at school, he wasn't interested in reading.'

The football education of Langer and the Broncos deepened when Balmain destroyed their unbeaten record in round seven with a 26–18 win at Lang Park. In the following week, Tigers coach Warren Ryan aired his reservations about the legality of Langer's tackling style in a Sydney newspaper column. Langer would sling opponents over his outstretched leg.

Bennett was incensed. 'Sydney used to be happy just to throw dirt at Wally. Now they want to tarnish the image of a kid whose attitude and skill epitomises everything that is healthy about rugby league.' But it was the sort of issue the Broncos got off on: the 'us against them' mantra used to motivate and maintain the rage of players.

When radio commentator Ray Hadley accused Lewis of manhandling referee Greg McCallum in the round six win over Newcastle, Bennett stormed: 'It's us against the media. Anything adverse is coming from the media.' Ribot admits the 'us against them' card was played often, both publicly and behind the scenes, and it presented him and Bennett with a delicate balancing act. 'Them' could be anybody the Broncos wanted to turn their minds to in scorn—the referees, the NSWRL, the Sydney media, the Brisbane media, the Sydney spectators, the QRL. That was the beauty of it. Ribot explained: 'We were careful not to use it as an excuse for performance though… it could have had a detrimental effect on us because the players' mindset could be: "The ref's going to give it to us today". We made sure our performance was always at an elite level, so when some of the judiciary decisions came back I didn't have to go back to the players and say "we've been done again"—they knew they'd been done.'

'If you have some individuals in the club who thought another influence was taking control, either refereeing decisions or the (NSWRL) administration, they can use it as an excuse.' Bennett, for instance, was never fined for criticising a referee in all the nine years before Super League, picking his words off carefully after some of the more contentious losses. The loss to Balmain supported the developing theory that the Broncos were vulnerable to a physical team, making life difficult for them as they tried to punch the ball out from their defensive end.

Lewis, his kicking distance in general play impaired by injury in that season, was unable to force opponent possession far enough away from Brisbane's danger zone. Miles had a hefty, but erratic boot and Langer was strictly a purveyor of chips or grubbers in those days. Bennett argued the condemnation of his forwards, but by round 11 he took the measure of introducing a reluctant Miles to the second row to provide some running and size to a pack of willing forwards, if all too similar in size and style.

The Broncos had lost two of the intervening three matches, the first a 38–8 thrashing at Cronulla which showed telltale signs of a team gradually running low on the raw enthusiasm which had buoyed their earlier performances. The Sharks rattled up an 18–0 lead in the first eight minutes, the stunned visitors standing behind their own tryline. And the then Gold Coast-Tweed, all seething injustice at the advantages enjoyed by the big-heads up the Pacific Highway, created a 25–22 upset made all the more shocking by a sledgehammer tackle by Ron Gibbs which injured Lewis' shoulder so badly he was in doubt for the first State of Origin match. After a week of will-he won't-he medical bulletins, Lewis' unbroken run of 20 Origin games was over.

At the time, it was as plausible as Jerry Seinfeld not starring in the show or John Gielgud subbing himself out of *Hamlet* at the last minute and handing the skull to the most promising of the local amateur dramatics society. Effervescent Peter Jackson, with considerable claims to the tag of ham actor himself, thought he could play five-eighth for Queensland. So did Bennett, his mentor in Souths' Brisbane premiership-winning team three years earlier. But to most, the equation was simple: Lewis out meant a NSW victory. His shadow was so large it obscured the worth of the 15 he left behind.

Instead, Bennett and stand-in captain Paul Vautin served a potent cocktail of emotion. If one game can be pin pointed as the hour when Langer made the transition from an exciting young player to a genuine box-office smash, it was when Queensland harassed NSW to a 26–18 win at the new Sydney Football Stadium. It wasn't promising when NSW centre Michael O'Connor scored the first try. But when controversial Mackay referee Barry Gomersall allowed a Queensland scrum win against the feed, Sterling came up with a clean one-on-one miss on Langer, who cruised over for a stunning reply four minutes later.

With Jackson expertly kicking for position behind a dominant pack, Langer taunted the Blues six minutes from halftime. He chanced another chip 35 metres out and this time he toed the loose ball away from the path of Blues winger Brian Johnston and gathered for a 14–6 lead. Before the change of ends, he provoked a groan from the three-quarters full stadium with a copyright, try-saving tackle on NSW prop Steve Roach, despite a 38 kilogram disparity in body weight. The man of the match award could only go to one man when Langer put the match away in the second half by producing a try for Queensland fullback Gary Belcher. All but three of 64 media representatives at the game voted him into the Winfield award: an unprecedented landslide.

'When you consider the best 26 players in the world were out there, Langer is arguably the best player in the world,' said Lewis, his personal disappointments forgotten in his euphoria about the team's performance. 'It was unbelievable. Their forwards had no fire, they didn't hurt us at all,' Vautin said.

Langer faced the media with ingenuous modesty about his own performance. 'The kicks were just spur of the moment decisions and some work. It was one of my best matches, but the front-rowers made it for the backs. I think they were over-confident,' he shrugged.

The presses whirring in Sydney and Brisbane did his talking for him. 'Langer puts Sterling out of business,' trumpeted The Courier-Mail's back page headline in reference to Test selection matters, a little prematurely as it turned out. The Daily Sun returned serve: 'Brilliant Langer the best by far!' And then: 'Yes, there is life after King Wally,' declared the Sydney Morning Herald's back page. 'Alf: He's worth $120,000,' the Daily Mirror estimated in the sports section.

The Herald's John MacDonald said Langer had staked a case for selection in Australia's team for the 100th Ashes Test against

Great Britain, to be played between the second and third Origin games. 'Even Peter Sterling's greatness may not be enough to deny Langer a Test jersey,' he worried. The *Daily Mirror*'s Peter Frilingos claimed: 'Queensland's mini genius Allan Langer is the world's most valuable player. Langer is only 21 and on the threshold of a career that will see him become one of the game's greatest stars.'

In the days that followed, as Langer's corporate appearance fee climbed to $1000 and an estimated throng of more than 2000 crammed into the Toowoomba shopping centre he was attending, Raudonikis called for Langer's Test debut. 'He cleaned up NSW and anyone who can do what he did to the mighty Blues is ready for the Poms, that's for sure. Great player that he is, Peter Sterling's time has come,' Raudonikis said. 'Sterlo has been cleaned up by him the last three times they have met. He was whipped in Sydney.'

With the win and the return of Lewis, the bookmakers who had considered Queensland 5–2 underdogs before the Sydney Football Stadium game made them 1–2 favourites for the second at Lang Park. Only his teammates knew Langer had started on a secret course of antibiotics two days before the match. In a match best remembered for the beer-can throwing demonstration by the crowd, Queensland prevailed 16–6 to clinch the series.

Continuing the best season of his career, Canberra and Queensland prop Sam Backo scooped the awards pool scoring an unstoppable match-turning try. But Langer was comparatively uninvolved, losing ground to Sterling, although he did score the last try off a reverse pass from the rejuvenated dummy-half Conescu. A joyous Lewis returned to the field, raced to Langer and carried him, the pair resembling a ventriloquist and his dummy. 'I think if you asked him, that would be Alf's most embarrassing moment,' Ribot recalls. 'While Alf is a little guy, he doesn't like being treated like a little guy. Wally wouldn't have meant it like that, but I know at the time Alf thought he was being disrespectful of his ability. He didn't want any concessions.'

Interestingly, Bennett reckons he has never heard Langer make reference to his own height in any way. 'I've never had the impression he has a hang-up about what people were saying. Maybe he was thinking to himself, I'll show you, but he is pretty secure in himself.'

On the night of the second game of the series, Langer missed the post-match celebrations in favour of a doctor's examination. Initial diagnosis was glandular fever, which created another media furore about what it would mean to his club's faltering season. He spent two days in hospital with what was found to be tonsilitis. Back for the 13th round of the premiership, the Broncos remained tied for second place with Penrith, behind Canterbury, in a tightly-bunched field of finals-chasing teams with an unconvincing 26–22 win over St George before their biggest home crowd yet: 19,954. The match saw a too-smart-by-half scam in which the Broncos players stayed on the field at halftime corralled within a 30 metre Power's banner. Dancing girls displayed placards bearing a letter apiece, spelling not only Power, but the word Brewing which the Trust had banned the club from displaying at the ground.

Chairman Barry Maranta was required to apologise to the NSWRL and the Lang Park Trust. The Broncos' signing of Power Brewing as major sponsor for $1 million a season, an unprecedented deal, put them on a collision course with the Castlemaine Perkins contracts which the QRL and the Lang Park Trust had to defend. The Broncos had their own corporate loyalties to serve. Bernard Power had written a personal cheque for $250,000, an advance on his company's sponsorship, when funds for setting up the club were needed.

The *Daily Mirror* claimed that Brisbane could be ejected from the premiership because of the disobedience, a story from which Arthurson distanced himself. 'I often said Arko was a politician par excellence, a smoother politician than Bob Hawke,' Morgan says. 'Quayle carried the axe and did the board's bidding. When you see the composition of the board, there were some people on the board who had ridden high for a long time and were doing it tough on the footy field. I think they thought we had a hidden agenda, which we didn't.'

The manufactured second-rower Miles wrenched a muscle in his neck so severely in a twisting scrum in Brisbane's horrendous 16–4 loss to South Sydney that he missed the next, heavier, loss to Canterbury into the bargain. 'That Souths game,' Langer remembered with a wince. 'It was a game we had to win and it was one which taught us a lot about playing in Sydney. The crowd was small, it was a Friday night and we were all talking about what we were going to do over the weekend. We weren't tough enough mentally that first year and we were found out.'

The new boys had won three of their past nine games. It was becoming a long season. Langer skippered Brisbane for the first time in the 25–10 loss to Canterbury at Lang Park, running on the sixth tackle to create a try for Le Man, giving Brisbane a 10–9 lead early in the second half.

Despite an eye-catching starting performance from former Ipswich hooker Kerrod Walters, Canterbury's physical superiority and a Brisbane error count of 21 says much about that first season. Yet this team of contrasts and contradictions would still find the mettle to win their next two matches against Manly and Penrith, the latter game becoming a byword at Red Hill for toughness and victory against the odds. Lewis and Conescu missed the Penrith collision, resting injuries suffered in the third Test against Great Britain.

A third injury from Australia's disinterested loss to the Lions gave Langer the next advance in his career. Sterling had badly injured a shoulder and was unavailable for the July 20 Test against Papua New Guinea at Wagga Wagga. Langer was selected ahead of Kangaroos Hasler and Greg Alexander, of Penrith. Wally Lewis was the man who broke the news to him over the telephone.

A disbelieving Langer said: 'I wasn't that sure he wasn't gee-ing me up at first.' His mentor Raudonikis was on the line soon after. 'I wanted to be the first to tell him his football life had just started. I knew it would happen, from the first time I laid eyes on him. He always had the ability and as I got to know him I was sure he had the desire. I was sure he'd keep his feet planted on the top of the ladder. He worked too hard to let it slip. Some people think he hasn't done his apprenticeship and has reached the top too soon. I must say he got there quicker than I thought. A lot of people expected him to crumble under the pressure in Sydney, but he showed them. He showed them ability and, most of all, guts.'

Wagga Wagga's Eric Weissel Oval, crammed with 11,685 on a Wednesday afternoon, saw Australia's 70–8 margin break the world record for a Test match against PNG, who treated players like Lewis and Mal Meninga with the reverence normally reserved for royalty. 'The PNG halfback wanted to swap jerseys but there was no way I was giving away my first one,' said Langer, who scored two tries and led Arthur Summons to call his linking between the forwards and backs 'exceptional'. 'I hope to be able to show that jersey to my kids one day. I felt sorry for PNG. They were good blokes and never stopped trying'.

Next was the Bicentennial match against a Rest of the World team coached by New Zealander Graham Lowe, a representative fixture to extend a season already containing three Origin games and four Tests. Manly coach Bob Fulton, who would follow Don Furner into the Australian coaching position in 1989, wondered in his newspaper column what his Sea Eagles half,

Hasler, had done to lose out to Langer. 'The match is make or break time for Langer. He will take the field under intense pressure. It is a game which will shape his immediate future in representative football,' Fulton claimed. As it panned out, Australia's 22–10 win at the Sydney Football Stadium was remembered for little other than Meninga's fourth—and mercifully last—fracture of his left forearm.

The smoke had cleared to illuminate the run down to the semi-finals and Brisbane arrived at the last round, away against Balmain, with four possible scenarios stemming from the result. They could make the sudden-death semi-final, making it the best debut season of any team since 1909; be forced to qualify through a midweek play-off for fifth even if they won; get a second chance in a play-off if they lost; or be eliminated altogether.

The biggest and most experienced forward, prop Dowling, was ruled out for the fifth week in succession with a shoulder ailment. And it was the forwards where Balmain, all surging muscle and know-how, dictated terms even after Langer's most astonishing try, two minutes from halftime when his team was gasping for air and inspiration, down 12–2 at Leichhardt Oval. The Broncos' half sliced through a gap and, seeing Tigers fullback Garry Jack advancing across-field, angled a grubber kick in behind him, leaving the Test custodian without a play.

But Balmain, also playing for their finals lives, scored twice in the last seven minutes. With Roach, Sironen, Pearce and Ben Elias making their presence felt, they deserved their win. And Bennett declined the chance to offer excuses. 'I accept our limitations out there today,' Bennett told the media huddle, remarking that his plans for 1989 had started five minutes after fulltime. 'I am more than satisfied with the year as a whole. I don't think we will be guilty next year of the same performances and losses we had. I said from day one this would be the hardest year. I have no doubt about it.' Bennett has been right about a lot of aspects about his Broncos over the years but that comment at Leichhardt was not one of them.

Langer, who had played in 21 of the 22 premiership games to dismiss the suggestions that he was not physically up to the NSWRL, won the inaugural Broncos best and fairest award before going to Auckland for the World Cup final against New Zealand. His growing certainty in representative teams was noticed by Australian team manager Peter Moore. 'The first time I met Allan, he was with some of the other Australian players at the bar at our hotel in Auckland,' Moore said. 'I came over after the team because Canterbury had won the grand final, so it was a big couple of days. When I got to Auckland, I walked up to Alf and introduced myself. He looked me in the eye and said: "I saw you on TV. You carried on like a goose." ' The footnote to the exchange came after Langer captained Brisbane to their first premiership. He received a fax from Moore: "Dear Goose. Congratulations on winning the grand final!" '

Australia won 25–12 against a New Zealand team that was so steamed up, they evaporated. Langer's two tries propelled him to the man of the match award. Soon after, Langer was invited in his guise as the Australian game's hottest newcomer to play for a Rest of the World team against Great Britain at Headingley, Leeds.

Rugby League Week's Dave Hatfield reported: 'Langer still has a lot to do to persuade the English rugby league public he will be the successor to Peter Sterling. It proved a bit of an anti-climax all round.' Great Britain coach Malcolm Reilly offered: 'He doesn't seem as effective if Wally Lewis isn't there.' Always self-deprecating, Langer told the English press: 'I didn't do a great deal and I was a little disappointed.'

• • •

The Broncos entered their second season with Currie being joined by two more Queensland Origin players, Jackson and Backo. Looking back at the era, Morgan admits: 'After going close in 1988, I expected us to win the competition in 1989 and 1990 and thought we should have won it in 1991.' But Brisbane looked unstoppable as final five contenders, winning nine of their first 10 games, including a 22–18 win at Manly despite playing the last 55 minutes with 12 men. Miles—now permanently in the second row—and Dowling were mighty leaders when Lewis was sent off on a charge later dismissed by the NSWRL judiciary.

The one defeat as the Broncos sailed along in the premiership lead came when a measure of reality arrived in the unmistakable form of Balmain. Ryan, who had added to his mystique by taking the Tigers to the grand final in 1988, had told the Brisbane media that his injury problems were so bad that Brisbane would play 'the limping, the blind and the weak'.

After form in the early weeks of the premiership which encouraged Sydney speculation that his Test spot was in jeopardy, Langer won maximum points in three successive games in the Broncos' best and fairest in the wins over Wests, Newcastle and Parramatta. When Brisbane played a Panasonic Cup match Parramatta at Townsville's Sports Reserve, an alarmed Ribot sent security guards as police onto the field to save Langer from hundreds of enthusiastic fans after fulltime. 'I wanted to stay on the field, but the crush was so bad I couldn't move,' Langer said. 'The security guards couldn't stop them. I'm glad they listened to the public address announcer when he asked them to give me a path off.' Explaining the phenomenon Ribot said: 'In the country, there were some crazy scenes over the years. They weren't used to seeing the top players except on television.'

The Broncos would win the Panasonic Cup, a maiden trophy which lent assurance in the minds of most at Red Hill that the right formula was close at hand, in a 22–20 thriller over Illawarra in the final. After being booed by the Steelers faithful on the club's biggest occasion to date, the team made a pointed gesture when they returned to Broncos Leagues Club for a celebration function, captured and aired by Channel Seven. 'Wally was on the microphone and said the (NSW) fans could kiss their ... and they all turned around and pointed to their backsides,' said reporter Pat Welsh. 'Including the coach. When we put it to air, it angered Wayne somewhat, you could say, but I maintain we were justified.'

The season rolled on for the six Broncos chosen in the Queensland team making light of five-time premiership winner Jack Gibson's first term as NSW coach, blasting open the biggest margin in State of Origin, a 36–6 annihilation at Lang Park. Bella was named Man of the Match and Langer was not far behind in the voting, playing with striking confidence and vision. He started the scoring when he took a quick tap penalty 40 metres and, drifting across field, picked out winger Alan McIndoe with a 15 metre cut-out ball. After 28 minutes, it was 18–0, with Langer being first to a well-weighted grubber kick ahead of NSW fullback Garry Jack. 'That may have been the best Queensland team I played with. We had Mal Meninga back and Geno was in the second row and it was Kerrod's first year,' Langer said.

Brisbane suffered their second loss of the season, 20–10 to St George on a Kogarah mudheap.

After 19 minutes of the second Origin match in Sydney there was no way Langer could have known that would be his last match for the Broncos for eleven weeks, and that the season would slip through Brisbane's fingers again. Langer slipped on the soft centre of the field as he attempted a tackle, his senses locating the sensation he had felt once before. He had broken his left ankle, four years after breaking his right. Helped off by trainers with a face more of surprise than pain or anguish, there was massed cheering, the first adverse personal crowd treatment for him in Sydney. Coming in the face of a pre-game appeal for sportsmanship over the public address system, it illustrated just how seriously Sydneysiders were taking the Origin after two successive series losses, followed by a record losing margin. Stretched out on a table as doctor Keith Woodhead confirmed what he already knew, Langer was not long without company when injured teammates joined him as though on a conveyer belt.

After 29 minutes, Meninga came off, his right eye closing by the second with a fractured socket, courtesy of a punch from NSW firebrand Peter Kelly. It would be the subject of a citing and two-week suspension. Vautin did not return for the second half because of a dislocated left elbow which would also sideline him from the third game. With 20 minutes to go, winger Michael Hancock succumbed to a shoulder injury, leaving Beetson without any more reserves.

For 15 minutes, Bob Lindner played with a broken bone in his leg, leaving the Maroons one short only when he was unable to stand up and accepted a stretcher ride to the dressing-room. Langer's replacement, Newcastle's Michael Hagan, gave the last pass for Queensland's final two tries. The second came after Gillmeister had smashed the ball from the grasp of NSW lock Brad Clyde. Hagan found Lewis and the sliding NSW players underestimated the Queensland skipper's acceleration. Lewis kept going, the retreating defence more concerned about his supports (because a 40 metre solo try was not exactly in his job description), and he skidded through Jack's tackle.

Lewis celebrated the 16–6 lead with a war dance, and with 13 minutes left NSW were within four points. The Maroons kept turning up in defence to take the series with a 16–12 win which remains the most remarkable in Origin history. Nothing is even in the same neighbourhood.

When Queensland won the dead third game in Sydney with Hagan comfortable at half, a record twelve Queenslanders made the 20-man team to tour New Zealand. Seven Broncos were lost for the three week duration of the tour, plus Langer and Miles, who had broken his thumb. They lost all three matches to fall to equal fourth place. The humour of Broncos management was not lightened when after the third Test in Auckland, Lewis and Jackson bungee-jumped off the roof of the grandstand. Not the sort of gravitas they were after.

Langer whiled away the time as easily as he could, taking Janine away for a weekend to Morgan's Gold Coast holiday house. 'In retrospect, it's funny seeing how out of place he could be. He had nothing to say,' Morgan said. 'Little Alfie sat there and just looked out to sea, as if he was thinking: "What am I doing here?" '

Power Brewing made use of Langer's open diary, particularly in an often-recalled company conference at the Southport Yacht Club. Bernard Power, chairman of the company, was unable to attend the silver service dinner which began in restrained fashion. Still, not to worry. 'All of a sudden, there is a tap on a glass,' John Crane said, setting the scene. 'Alf says: "Can I have your attention please? In the absence of Bernie Power, it's been decided I will take the role as chair for tonight. We are in a beautiful place tonight and I want to make sure the standards are kept high and I would like to make the first toast." With that, he takes his shirt off, grabs the jug in front of him and starts to scull. Some of it has gone down his throat, some of it is running down his chest. Even the waiters were laughing. It broke the ice and set up a relaxing evening. He has the uncanny ability to make people feel at ease. He was quite happy and when we got back to the motel he had a few games with fire hoses and things. We used Alf's ability at Power's to make people feel at ease.'

When Brisbane regathered their Test players for the game

against Balmain, there were no excuses. A 24–8 win by the Tigers followed the familiar themes set in their previous three meetings. It was their seventh loss in eight matches and left them in equal sixth. To add to the creeping despair, Greg Dowling, enjoying a much better and fitter season now he was unavailable for Queensland selection, was sent off on a charge of deliberately kneeing Balmain halfback Gary Freeman. Freeman was pictured in the *Daily Mirror* on the following afternoon with a wide, smashed and bloody smile, resembling a piano which had been taken to with a wrecking ball.

If it did not hurt Dowling's chances at the judiciary, it certainly would not have helped. Guilty. Eight weeks. Ribot looks back: 'There was certainly unfairness given to us in judiciary hearings. I still can't believe someone who has never been sent off in his career of something like 400 games of football can get eight weeks in his first appearance.'

Running into a soft section of the draw, Brisbane won their last four matches, including a 16–8 win over Parramatta at Lang Park which attracted 33,245 spectators, the NSWRL's biggest home and away crowd in seven years. The total attendance for the season was up 12 per cent on the home game crowds in the first season.

When Langer and Miles returned from injury, Walters and Dowling were missing. It was that sort of season. When Langer made a cautious return as a reserve in the round 22 match against North Sydney, the 30–0 win was only good for a tie for fifth against Cronulla. This would not have normally been a problem, except Australia was crippled by the long-running pilots' strike at the time. To ensure the match would take place the Broncos suggested that the play-off at Parramatta Stadium be played at Tweed Heads. Once the laughter died down at the NSWRL's Phillip Street headquarters, Ribot reluctantly chartered a private aircraft to

Sydney at a cost of $27,000. Bennett opted to leave Langer on the bench again and start with French against Cronulla, who were belted 42–10 by Brisbane ten weeks earlier. One of Bennett's favourite sayings in such end-of-season decisions is: 'I'll dance with the ones who brought us.'

The Sharks were a different team this time, with skipper Gavin Miller and five-eighth Michael Speechley in destructive form. Langer drummed his heels on the bench as the 2–5 favourites struggled to keep the margin as close as six points at halftime. Bennett sent Langer out for the second half and within ten minutes he had levelled the game at 14–all with his signature chip-and-chase play, extended to a 50 metre team try run-in by Lewis.

But the Sharks scored four converted tries without reply, running the Broncos' defence utterly ragged. 'Our inability to win any of the three matches during the tour of New Zealand when we had half a team away was the biggest factor for us being out now,' Bennett said. 'I'd like to keep this team together for a full season. Then I'd tell you how good the Broncos could be.'

Gene Miles watched as Bennett went up to Ron Massey—a shrewd judge and Jack Gibson's right-hand man during Parramatta's premiership years. 'Mass, what do I have to do to get this side performing?' Bennett asked. Miles remembers: 'Mass said that for a start we were all too fat. He was probably right. I was playing at 112 kilograms. I haven't been 112 kilograms since.'

That was point one. Point two was that Bennett had told confidants he would resign as Queensland State of Origin coach. Point three, he had a rough idea about and it would be a bombshell unparalleled in Queensland sport.

Harry and Rita on their wedding day. *Photo: Langer family*

The Langer children on holidays at Caloundra, (*from left, top*) Kevin, Desley and Cliff and (*bottom*) Allan and Neville. *Photo: Langer family*

Scrum down — the footballing Langer brothers (*from left*) Allan, Neville, Kevin and Cliff. *Photo: Langer family*

The harder they fall ...
A bare-footed Allan
Langer gives a bigger
Ipswich junior oppo-
nent a taste of what is
to come. *Photo: Langer
family*

A ten-year-old Allan
Langer probes away for
Norths in an Ipswich
junior game.
Photo: Langer family

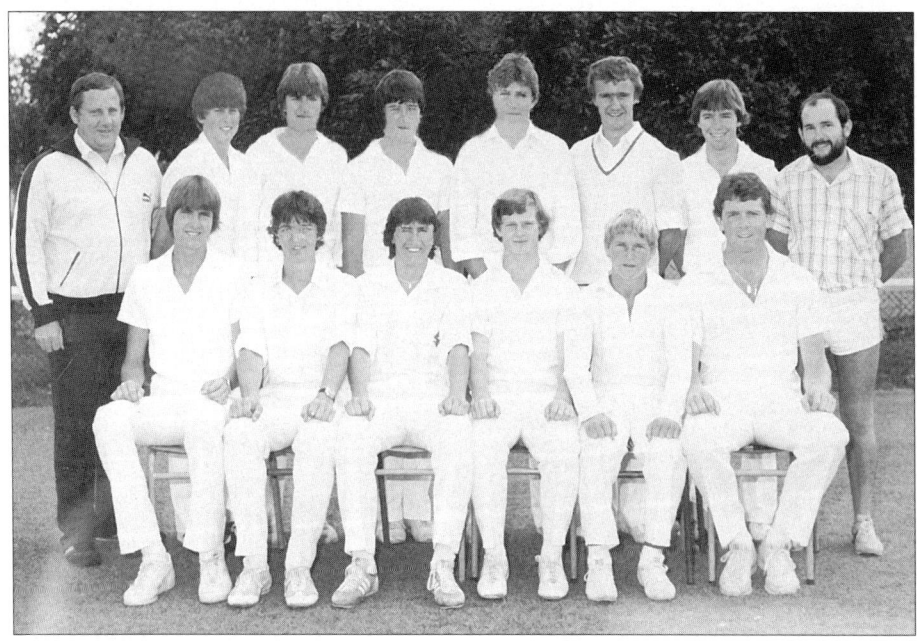

Allan makes the Brisbane West team for the 1982 Queensland Secondary School Cricket Association Carnival. He is sitting at right in the front row, next to Ipswich's future Australian opening bowler Craig McDermott.
Photo: Langer family

Allan Langer, 11, takes strike in a school cricket game. *Photo: Langer family*

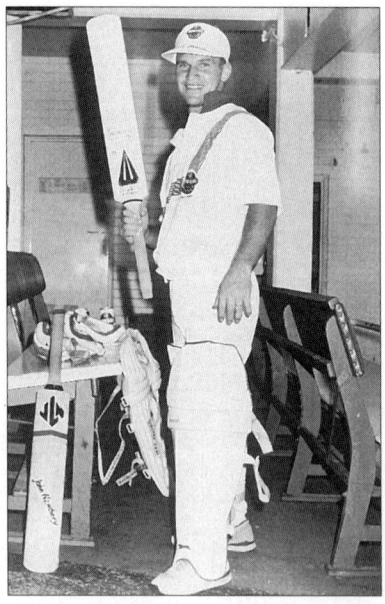

Preparing for a charity cricket innings in 1990. *Photo: Derek Moore*

The under 16s team from Norths which won the Ipswich competition. Allan is in the front row. His father, Harry, a team manager, is in the second row.
Photo: Langer family

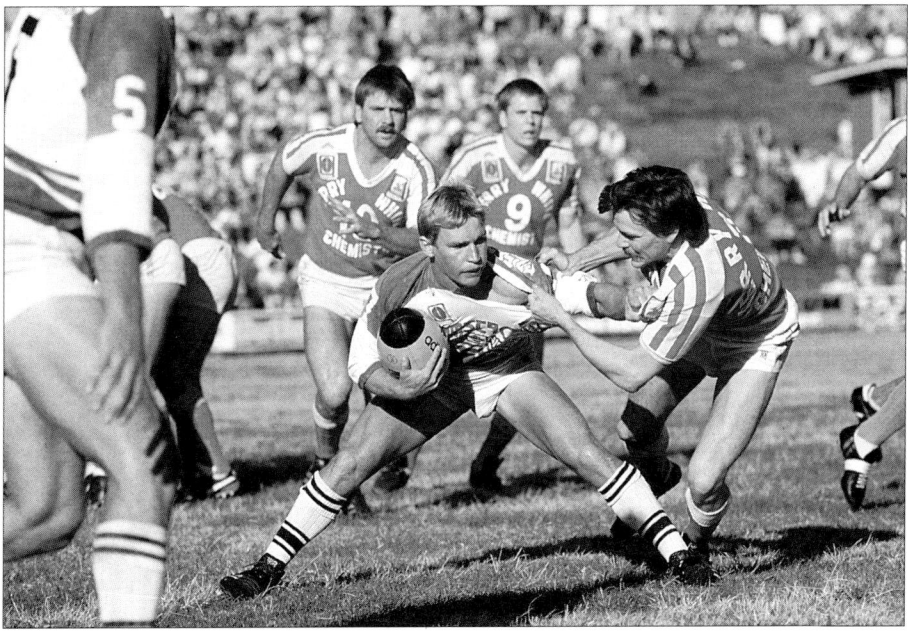

Redcliffe's Trevor Benson slings Allan Langer to the ground in a Brisbane premiership match at Dolphin Oval in 1986. *Photo:* Rugby League Week

On the road gang — Allan Langer with his shovel in late 1986. *Photo: Langer family*

Striking a classic half-back's pose in a club match at North Ipswich Reserve in 1987. *Photo: Rugby League Week*

The first of many meetings. Allan Langer talks to Penrith halfback Greg Alexander after Combined Brisbane's 1987 Cup loss to the Panthers. *Photo:* Rugby League Week

Allan Langer wipes away a tear after receiving the Man of the Match award
in his debut State of Origin. He dedicated the award to his brother Kevin
who was in Boggo Road jail at the time. *Photo: News Limited*

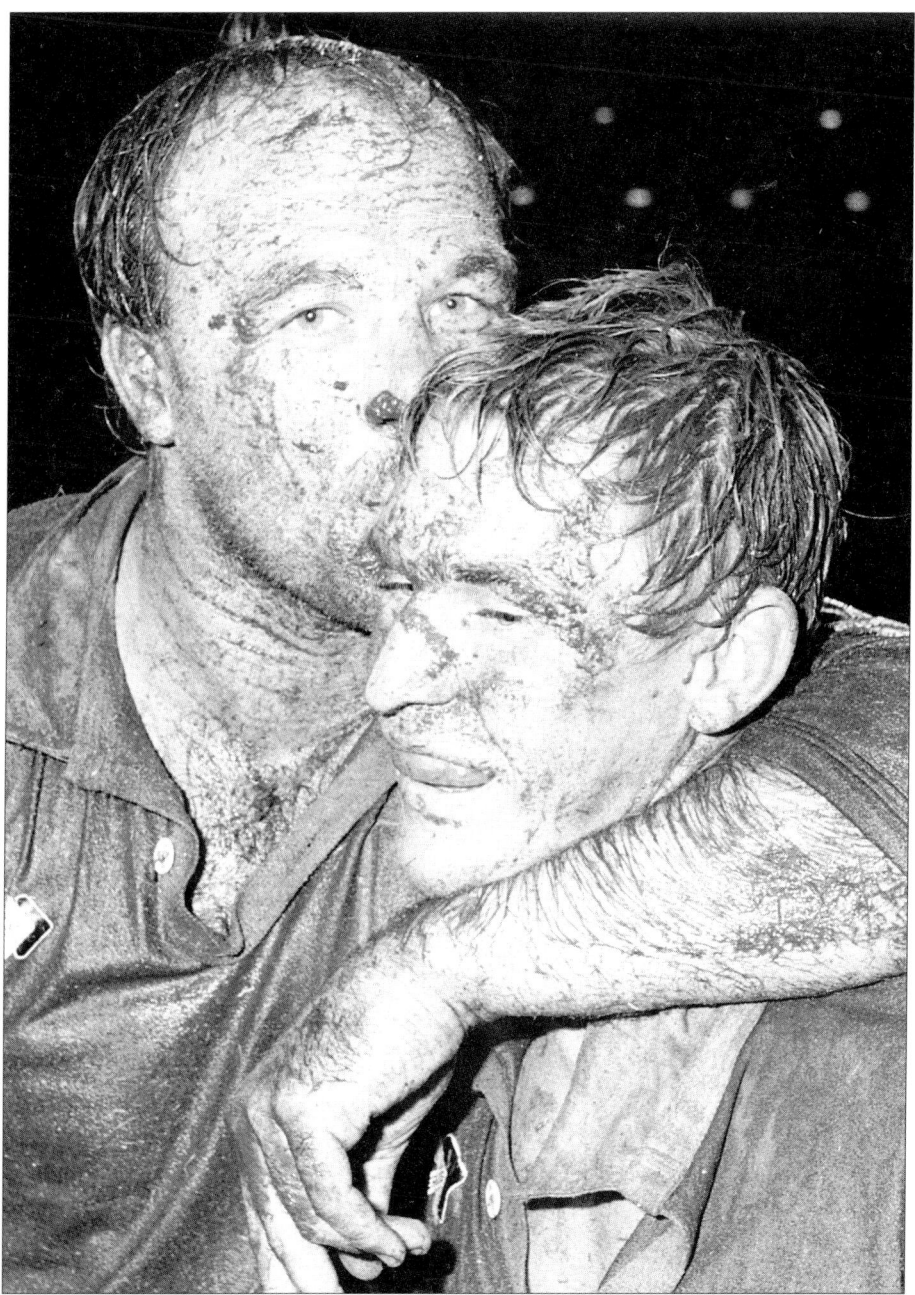

The kiss. Wally Lewis welcomes Allan Langer into the big league after winning their second game in the 1987 State of Origin at the SCG. *Photo: Fairfax Photo Library*

Ipswich Jets coach Tom Raudonikis welcomes Allan Langer back to the club during his 1987 State of Origin breakthrough series. *Photo: Langer family*

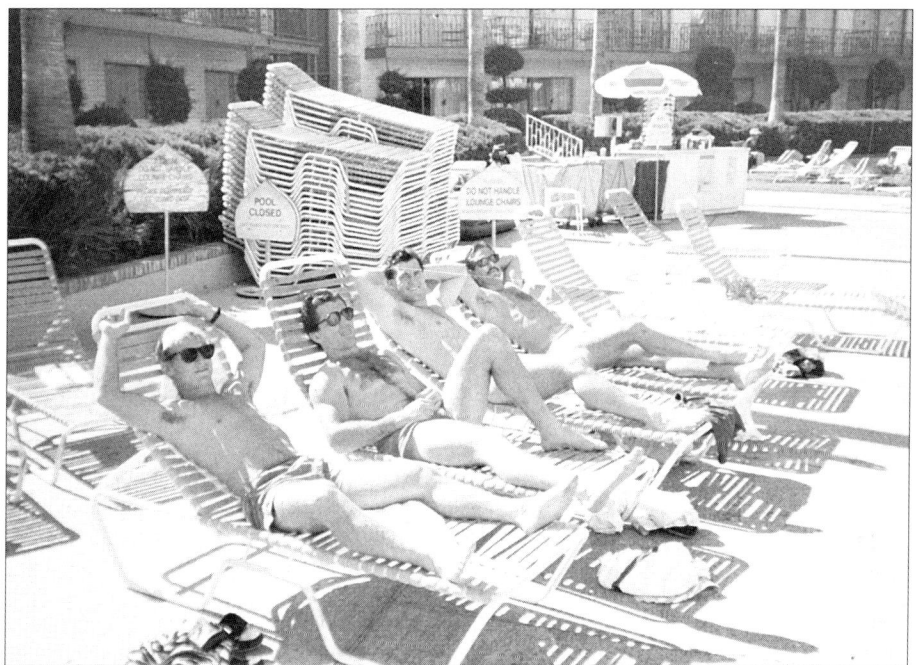

Allan Langer leans back in the Californian sun with some of his Queensland team-mates on the 1987 trip to play NSW in an exhibition game. *Photo: Langer family*

Away from it all — Allan and Janine Langer on a cruise ship departing New Orleans in 1993. *Photo: Langer family*

In the days before he got his own T-shirt ... Allan Langer in 1988. *Photo: Brisbane Broncos*

Well, somebody at Castlemaine Perkins thought it was the definition of sartorial elegance: Allan has a beer with Brewster in a promotional shot. *Photo: Brisbane Broncos*

It's not every player who gets his name on a speedway car. Broncos team-mate Greg Dowling signals his approval to the man at the wheel. *Photo: Langer family*

Plenty to prove: getting the feel of the NSWRL premiership in a 1988 game at Lang Park. *Photo: Brisbane Broncos*

Wests halfback Kevin Langer breaks from the scrumbase with future ARL grand final referee David Manson for company in a Brisbane premiership match at Lang Park. *Photo:* Rugby League Week

Allan congratulates his brother Kevin on his win in the 1988 Brisbane Rothmans Medal poll. Former Australian halfback Barry Muir, Allan's first senior representative coach, joins them. *Photo: Brisbane Broncos*

Allan Langer with his own 1992 Rothmans Medal. *Photo: News Limited*

Allan Langer, in his second game as captain of Australia, strains to beat the defence of the French President's XIII at Paris during the 1990 Kangaroo tour. Kangaroo teammate David Gillespie supports. *Photo: News Limited*

There is a God — Ricky Stuart breaks clear in the dying moments of the second Test against Great Britain in Manchester, 1990. *Photo: News Limited*

Allan Langer grapples with New Zealand fullback Frano Botica in the second Test of the 1991 series at the Sydney Football Stadium. Australia won 44-0 to square the series. *Photo: News Limited*

Allan Langer, with a cut nose the price of success, celebrates the 1991 Test series win over New Zealand in the Lang Park dressing-room with team-mates Steve Walters (*left*) and David Gillespie. *Photo: News Limited*

BIGGER THAN THE CLUB

John Ribot sat in the restaurant at Sydney's Camperdown Travelodge, absent-mindedly drinking a cup of coffee as he focused on the harsh glare of failure. It was the morning after the night before. Brisbane had been freshly eliminated from the 1989 premiership. In the bus outside, a team of well-lubricated footballers were about to begin the 12 hour trip back to Brisbane.

Talking to himself as much as his fellow diners, Ribot uttered: 'All I know is that this can't go on.'

The plane strike which was crippling the country? The restaurant? The coffee? No more late nights?

The others around the table knew he was talking about the inability of the Broncos to make the finals in their first two years. But if they were given 20 guesses at what would happen in response, they still would have come up empty. At the end of an extensive interview process with established and younger players, Wayne Bennett was further convinced of what he had already decided—Wally Lewis could no longer be his captain.

Bennett's ethos as a coach, as far as it is possible to capture in one sentence, is that every individual's self-interest and feelings are secondary to the welfare of the club.

A dinner at the Parkroyal Hotel was attended by most senior

players. Lewis didn't attend because of prior commitments, but it was one meeting he may have, in retrospect, wished he'd made it to. 'There was also a meeting in the boardroom. I didn't have much to say. Plenty of blokes did, Wally included. But I never knew it would get to the stage it did,' Langer said. Ribot's response to the common perception of the Broncos as a one-man band was: 'That was the thing that was holding them back. Everything centred around Wally and the analysis was always of Wally.'

Langer could not decide if the players had spoken to Bennett out of their dissatisfaction with Lewis' manner or out of plain jealousy. 'But I think it was a bit of both,' he said. 'The one-man team thing didn't worry me. He was a great player and that was why he had the media attention. We just didn't put it together on the field. A lot of us were still learning.'

In the first two years of the Broncos, there was a distinct caste order among players. While it is not unusual for senior players to form their own clique at a club, Lewis fraternised most readily with his contemporaries from Wynnum, Gene Miles and Greg Dowling.

Having decided to do something about it, Bennett carried his decision through, telling Lewis impassively on September 22 that he would not be captain in 1991. By that time, Miles reveals, Bennett had already offered him the captaincy at the Parkroyal dinner.

'I fully agreed with the decision of taking the captaincy off him, although I never thought I was in line for it, or that it was ever going to happen,' Miles said. 'I told Wayne that I needed a few weeks to think about it and he said he had some time.' Lewis later numbered off Bennett's reasons, as best his memory was amid the shock of it all, to his biographer Adrian McGregor: that he had been away too much during the representative season; he did not talk to the younger players; he didn't mix well; he didn't arrive

early enough at training to engender unity; he was not approach-
able as a club leader; and that some players were unhappy with his
leadership.

Bennett has never spoken publicly of his reasons for taking
the captaincy off Lewis, a stance which did nothing to staunch
the flow of wild and damaging rumours in the months that
followed. He and Ribot did not speak their minds out of deference
to Lewis. They also knew it was an argument they would never win
with the Queensland public acting as judge.

The episode set in train, faster than before, the unpopularity
of the Broncos. It alienated sections of the Queensland public,
building upon a solid bloc of supporters loyal to Brisbane club
football who thought the Broncos a little too arrogant for their own
good. Lewis angrily rejected Ribot's offer to portray the change of
captaincy as his resignation from the post, and went on holidays in
California with his family with the agreement that it would be
embargoed from the media until his return.

While Lewis was away, Sydney's *Sunday Telegraph* broke the
story. To the ever-present question—why?—Ribot responded that
the Broncos wanted a full-time captain and Lewis' captaincy duties
for Queensland and Australia meant he couldn't devote the desired
time and energy to the Broncos, their lower grade players and
sponsors.

That response was so pat that no-one swallowed it, and gave
rise to the inevitable behind-the-scenes rumours which made the
divide between player and club management wider still. Ribot says
now: 'When we signed him to a three-year contract, we were
planning even then for life after Wally. We appreciate that he got
us up there from day one but it was Wally and the Broncos and we
had to change it to the Broncos. Father Time marches on and the
amount of money he was commanding and the amount of time he
was in the park meant we had to make a conscious decision for the

best interests of the club. Wally to this day is the best player I have ever seen. But we were building something and when Wally left we needed someone who could give the place a feeling. A bloke like Alfie, who is a great character and a great player, was the whole package when he took over the captaincy whereas Wally became bigger than our whole organisation. Alfie gave the place a heartbeat.'

Ribot readily concedes that Lewis was shaped by his environment. For years, his football ability was his passport to do whatever he liked and he largely responded to a committee of one. Ross Strudwick, his first senior coach at Valleys, Ron McAuliffe, Ken Arthurson, Arthur Beetson, Don Furner, the Queensland media mostly accepted his excesses, tacitly encouraging them.

Wally was capable of charm and tact. His private efforts in support of charity or his willingness to brighten the lives of sick children showed great humanity. But he was also guilty of self-aggrandisement and impatience with those he did not respect.

Ribot reflected: 'The media was a bit to blame with Wally. He was this megastar and we lost track of the club. Wally just took everything over—it was the roadshow he took along with him. In some ways, because he was so big, the players were sitting back and were in awe of what Wally was. As time goes on, I think Wally has mellowed now and he appreciates where we were coming from, what we could achieve.'

But in the white-hot emotion of the time, Bennett and Ribot came in for public denouncement from Lewis supporters: from Test coach Bob Fulton and Queensland deputy Paul Vautin down to talkback radio callers. They were also targeted for the worst form of personal intimidation from anonymous callers. 'There were threats. I don't want to go into it too deeply,' Ribot said. Miles asked the ARL for permission to retire from representative football in recognition of services rendered. This prevented the pro-Lewis forces from at least accusing Bennett and Ribot of double standards, as well as everything else. In the mid-1980s, Lewis-and-Miles were almost a single identity in Queensland league. Manly courted both in a package deal. But they were rarely, if ever, billed as Miles-and-Lewis.

When Miles accepted the captaincy, Lewis took it as an act of disloyalty. They went from the closest of mates one week to walking past each other, one studying the sky and the other the ground, the next day. 'I honestly believed it would ease the pain of the King by me taking it. Oh jeez, was I wrong. In hindsight, it was probably the worst decision I ever made in terms of our friendship,' Miles said. 'He looked at it as if I had stabbed him in the back. I wouldn't do that to anybody. He just couldn't accept the fact that I was taking over.' On the tender subject Langer said: 'I wasn't worried who was captain. But it became a problem when Wally and Gene weren't talking.'

Bennett said he did not involve Langer in his considerations on how to find some harmony in the team when the two biggest names were not talking to each other. 'He was only young. I wouldn't put that type of pressure on him,' he said. 'I also knew Alf and that if he thought I was doing the right thing by the team, he'd be fine with it. Gene was his great mate and I knew he'd be supportive of him as captain.' Miles remembers: 'Alf would just gee everyone up, the same as always. When the team was eating together, he'd be down one end of a table with me. Wally would be at another table. Alf would go: "Aw, Geno, you can't say that about Wally"—and I hadn't said a thing about him. It was Alf's way of trying to lighten the situation.'

Ribot explained: 'It was a great period for Alf to sit back and analyse how things were done. He might not be eloquent in his speech and all those things, but he reads situations well. He is street smart. People underestimate that with him.' Bennett maintained the silent treatment he adopted for most aspects of the Lewis affair in later crises. When Trevor Gillmeister was released in 1993, he said nothing and let Gillmeister's bitterness burn itself out through the media. Just as when Kerrod Walters and Willie Carne were released in 1996.

'Alf learned from Wayne that sometimes it's best to say nothing,' Ribot remarked. 'One of Wayne's sayings is that if you have nothing to say, don't say anything.'

To make matters worse for the Broncos, the team did not immediately justify the captaincy decision on the field. When Brisbane salvaged just seven points from the first seven games, the pressure became intolerable for Miles.

'After the seventh game, I went to Benny and said: "What the hell have I got myself in for?" The public wanted Bennett and me out and the King reinstated,' Miles said. 'Wayne said that we had to stick it out because we could do the job together.'

The 1990 season was the first that the senior players left behind the habits of Brisbane club football, and started training with weights, following the example set by clubs such as Canberra and Canterbury. There were some transitional problems. 'We had some weights at Wynnum, but you didn't see them used too much,' said prop Greg Dowling. Kelvin Giles, a British athletics coach who had left the Australian Institute of Sport program was head-hunted by Bennett from Canberra as head trainer.

With a zealot's glint in his eye and a military quotation for every occasion, Giles set the club on its head in the 1990 pre-season, barking out taunts and insults. The players responded by calling him 'Mad Dog'. The weight gain started tongues wagging that the improvement did not all come down to hard work in the gym. 'There were rumours that players were on steroids at

Canberra, but we had never done weights seriously until he got here,' Langer said. 'That's why we never put on beef. If there were steroids, I didn't see them being used. I'd be extremely surprised if they were.'

It wasn't just the predictable channels through which the club was being attacked, as Kevin Walters found out, Bennett preferred Walters as five-eighth with Lewis shifted out to lock for the start of the 1990 premiership. By that stage, Walters was amassing form of such consistency and brilliance that he would be voted the Dally M players' player and be a runaway winner of the Broncos Best and Fairest award. Still, it wasn't enough to satisfy one 11 year-old, who approached him at a clinic in Gladstone in June. 'Gee, Mr Walters, you're not a very good player are you? Wally should be five-eighth,' the urchin said.

Walters reflects: 'It was probably my best season, 1990. I had to keep performing. I probably was Wayne's Pet, like people kept saying about me. Wayne wanted me at the club and that's a coach's prerogative, isn't it?'

Lewis became an alternative leader within the club, a rallying figure for the dissatisfaction of the aftermath of the 1989 finals exit. The suggestion is that Bennett was proactive, getting Lewis out before the Broncos board could act. In truth, there was never any real likelihood of Lewis being appointed captain-coach in place of a sacked Bennett, not that those rumours did anything to engender harmony.

Had the Queensland captain played a full season, the Broncos could have halted his slide. By the end of the season, he had started in five matches and been a reserve four times. A reserve! At the age of 30 he was susceptible to injuries, as with the majority of players. Lewis played the first three games at lock, tore a hamstring at Leichhardt, missed two games and tried to make a comeback as a reserve against Newcastle. Lewis' comeback from the hamstring injury had become largely a matter of pride. He knew there had been private suggestions around the Broncos that he was putting himself in cotton wool for the State of Origin series. Lewis told author Adrian McGregor: 'They made out I was wasting time, sulking about the captaincy. I thought: "Bugger them, I'll show them I can do it their way."'

Brisbane looked a better team with him on the field for all eight minutes before a low pass—it just had to be thrown by Miles—forced Lewis to scoop the ball low, tearing his hamstring. 'Great pass,' he said. Tony Currie snapped his Achilles tendon, forcing him out for the season, and Lewis was out of the first Origin game. The 14–12 loss to Norths left Brisbane with seven points in seven rounds, in ninth position.

Langer entered the Origin series with Hagan as his five-eighth colleague. Hagan was a positive, calm influence when he played halfback in the third game of the 1989 series. 'Everyone has been saying Langer's game has been down this year because he hasn't been scoring three tries a week,' said NSW coach Jack Gibson. 'He's their most ambitious and best player. I reckon he has been working the joint down this year.'

Playing without his normal spark despite a full off-season of training since his broken leg, Langer marked Ricky Stuart. It was the first of their on-field meetings and the two career paths would bump and ricochet off each other in the years to come. 'I have to put up with the criticism I get,' the Queenslander said before the match. 'I'm not really happy with my form, but I'm getting more confident every week.'

Gibson, a five-time premiership winner coming off the biggest Origin series ever in the winter of a magnificent career, infuriated the Maroons by declaring the fabled Queensland team spirit to be a 'load of crap'. Vautin, deputising as Queensland captain, responded: 'Gibson hasn't been part of our set-up, so what does he know? Probably 90 per cent of our wins can be attributed to the spirit we have.'

Canberra hooker Steve Walters, playing his first game in the absence of his injured younger brother Kerrod, was relieved to room with Langer. 'They didn't train as hard as I thought they'd train. You'd think the further you go, the harder you'd train,' he said.

NSW prevailed 8–0 in one of the least eventful Origin matches ever played, leading Queensland coach Beetson to declare that the return of Lewis and the injured Backo were prerequisites for the second game, which the ARL had taken to Melbourne's Olympic Park.

Lewis missed Brisbane's 20–8 win over Cronulla which featured a 75m, 16-pass try which made the Harlem Globetrotters seem obsessed with ball security in comparison. It was the second of what would become an 11-match winning streak. Lewis broke ranks when Vautin was dropped, along with Wally Fullerton Smith, another member of the mid-1980s Queensland champions. 'No, I don't think it's fair. I feel very disappointed for him,' he said.

Recollections of the first big ARL representative match in Melbourne start and end with the 'stolen ball' penalty issued against Langer in NSW's 12–6 win which ended their three-year sequence of Origin series losses. With the score tied at 6-all with seven minutes left, Langer emerged from a two-man tackle of Blues forward Glenn Lazarus with the ball, looking up to see that the shrill blast of referee Greg McCallum's whistle was against him.

Several Queenslanders thought they had heard McCallum call 'play on'. McCallum said he had called 'held' once and 'let him go' three times before penalising Langer. Rod Wishart goaled for the Blues, who sealed the result when Brad Mackay scored an intercept try.

Langer's upper-body strength and low centre of gravity made him a renowned ball 'thief', a skill which would be banned internationally after the 1990 season. It was the first, but not the last occasion in which a Langer attribute was cut from the rulebook. 'It was a disappointing night. I thought Lazo was still going forward. I didn't hear McCallum say anything,' Langer recalled. 'I haven't seen too many more angry dressing-rooms than that. The blokes were just so frustrated at losing the series on that note. I still think the rule is best if it's legal for one-on-one tackles. Players started to milk the penalties. It became a real eyesore.'

But on that night, the unflappable Langer was close to tears as he faced the press. Lewis, who played out a colossal 80 minutes on adrenalin despite playing exactly eight minutes in the previous two months, said: 'It was one of the bummest decisions of all time. It was a very appropriate penalty, right in front of the posts.' Beetson stormed: 'We expected some trouble. I didn't want McCallum. I wanted (Bill) Harrigan and I know Gibson did. So who wanted McCallum?'

The darkest conspiracy theories Queenslanders harboured about their treatment from NSW officials fermented into a potent brew. As far as the Sydneysiders could see sour grapes were the main ingredient. Gibson said: 'For everything Queensland reckon went wrong for them, I can find two which hurt us.' Lewis was subsequently fined $5000 for abusing a touch judge in the match, although the QRL paid his fine. Back in Broncos colours, he was used as a replacement five-eighth for the second time during the season, Brisbane scoring two tries in his first five minutes on the field as they thrashed Gold Coast 30–14.

Seagulls coach Bob McCarthy credited Lewis for lifting the Broncos and Bennett said he had supplied the necessary enthusiasm. 'He is our ace in the pack,' said Bennett. Among his other comments, he included the use of the word 'juggle', which made some commentators wonder if the coach was pondering the formation with which he finished the match—Lewis at five-eighth, Kevin Walters in the centre and Miles at lock.

Queensland won the third Origin game 14–10, gaining eight of the 15 places in the Australian team to meet France in Parkes a fortnight later, and NSW players choked on the statistic that a 2–1 win was good for only seven of the 15 positions. 'What a farce,' was the *Daily Mirror*'s back page headline.

On the last day of the financial year, Lewis broke his left forearm in Brisbane's 18–14 squeak against St George. A couple of hours earlier, Peter Jackson, unwanted for first grade, had said in a radio interview that the lines of communication between him and Bennett were down. But the Broncos hit the top of the table anyway before a Lang Park sell-out of 32,124 as Brisbane beat Canberra 22–20 in a classic, breakneck contest which would draw misty-eyed nostalgia among Queensland league fans for years to come. As fatigue set in during a second half which Brisbane began 10 points behind, Hauff was released by Langer down the Hale Street side. Canberra and Australian fullback Gary Belcher converged in cover, diving at Hauff, all legs, and coming up with ... nothing but a boot. 'When he was at his best, he could only be tackled one leg at a time,' Langer marvelled. Even more remarkable was a 24–22 win at Parramatta from a position of a 14-point deficit with 22 minutes left. Even Bennett was a disbeliever that day.

When a sellout crowd of 32,168 became inevitable two days before the match against Balmain, Ribot went public with the Broncos board's desire to relocate to the QEII Stadium, a 62,000 capacity stadium which had been monstrously underused as a spectator facility since the 1982 Commonwealth Games. 'We are rapidly outgrowing Lang Park. Balmain is our third sell-out in the past 12 months,' Ribot said. Two years later, Brisbane would play their last match at Lang Park, the NSWRL reasoning that the Broncos had the right to play home games where they wanted. QRL managing director Ross Livermore publicly opposed the NSWRL's stance, maintaining the Broncos had an obligation to play at Lang Park.

Balmain, the physical team who were the last of the clubs Brisbane had not beaten in three seasons of trying, surrendered their perfect 5–0 record to the Broncos in a 30–16 loss which sealed a final five berth for Brisbane. 'A lot of people labelled us a soft pack over those years,' Miles recalled. 'Balmain used to really give it to us (verbally). Not that some of us said much back when we got on top that day.'

With Miles in the grandstand nursing a knee injury which would hamper his finals preparation, acting captain Greg Dowling enjoyed one of his finest days for Brisbane, as younger men like Andrew Gee and Gavin Allen buffeted the Tigers in defence. Behind such authority, Langer flourished, creating three of Brisbane's six tries in what became a watershed moment in establishing self-belief. It was their 11th win in succession. 'They are a 100 per cent better team than they were 12 months ago,' Balmain captain Wayne Pearce said.

For three weeks, the Broncos management had been refusing to comment to reporters on rumours that two or three Brisbane players had returned a positive drug test to marijuana. This could not be proved, Ribot and media manager Kev Keliher said, because of the NSWRL's policy of maintaining confidentiality with drug tests. But the story was splashed on the front page of Sydney's *Daily Mirror*, 24 hours after Brisbane's greatest moment as a club.

The Broncos management was incensed by what they regarded as an attempt to destabilise their finals campaign. Whatever the effect of the publicity, Brisbane lost their next two games, away against Manly and Penrith, results which ultimately gave Canberra the minor premiership on a points for-and-against basis. Manly coach Graham Lowe used a pre-match tactic also much loved by Phil Gould, in which he made sure the Broncos were praised to the heavens in the Brisbane media in the days leading up to their clashes. 'The Broncos are a world-class team, one of the two best in the world with Wigan. I can't separate them,' said Lowe, who knew the advantages of appealing to the complacency instincts of Queenslanders from a coaching stint in Queensland.

Lewis, meanwhile, was recuperating from the broken forearm which would eventually lead to the controversial non-selection for the Kangaroo tour on the medical opinion, opposed by Lewis' specialist, of ARL doctor Nathan Gibbs. To add insult to injury, Broncos insiders were intimating it would be his last year with the club. From mid-July, the Brisbane press were reporting that Lewis, in the last year of his three-year contract with the Broncos, was privately resigned to not being with the Broncos in 1991. Gold Coast Seagulls quickly took up the position as the club most keen to pay Lewis top dollar.

It is likely the decision not to present Lewis with anything other than a token offer was made much earlier. Much of the money Lewis was paid in 1990—one-tenth of the club's salary cap—had already been distributed to five first graders re-signed to upgraded deals for 1991 and beyond.

For weeks, Ribot and Bennett successfully kept the issue on a low flame, trying to hold the storm from breaking before the end of the season. They cited the new draft system as a complicating factor in assessing a final offer. Then Ribot applied to have Lewis declared outside the salary cap. The NSWRL's refusal surprised no-one. It was the greatest display of trying to play time out since the English cricketer Geoff Boycott retired. But Lewis was desperate to prove his fitness for the Kangaroo tour and the media began cranking out speculation stories of how, or if, Bennett would use him in the finals.

Brisbane were pistol-whipped by Penrith in their first finals game, the score of 26–16 being artificially narrowed by three late Broncos tries. Brisbane endeavoured to take the game to Penrith's forwards, having been bustled by the Panthers in their previous meeting three weeks earlier.

At the last training session before their sudden-death final against Manly, Lewis asked Bennett to play him off the bench and was turned down on the basis that he had been to three training sessions in twelve weeks. Asked how Lewis had received the verdict, Ribot responded memorably: 'Not real well, I think.' As it turned out, the issue ground on for seven more days because Brisbane wore down Manly to 12–4 for their first finals win. Kevin Walters rebounded from a ghastly defensive miss against opposite number Brad Izzard against Penrith to play his way onto his Kangaroo tour. All in all, Bennett has never been as excited by a win, before or since.

'That's fair comment,' he remembered. 'There was always a lot of pressure on us and the thing the media would have then come at us with was "You choke in the finals" or "You can't live without the King". Queensland, at that time, hadn't won a Sheffield Shield, so we would have started reading that Queenslanders can't win the big ones. You know it's not true, but you hear it and someone gets the doubt in their mind. It just makes the job harder. We had a lot of players busted up that day and James Donnelly stood up for us. The twins were outstanding that day.'

Brisbane's *Sunday Mail* reported that it was a formality that Lewis would sign with Gold Coast after a meeting with Ribot in the next week.

As Lewis ran short of patience over the contract impasse, a decision came on September 13—three days before the preliminary final against Canberra—out of a concern that the team was being distracted by the output of reporters ping-ponging between Lewis and Ribot for updates. Lewis' mood on the morning of the meeting was understandably not lightened by a colourful comment from a frustrated Giles. 'Everyone else has these emotional problems about it. I don't. To me, he is a human organism, not Wally Lewis,' Giles said.

Lewis emerged with an offer that was one-third of his 1990 money plus the normal match bonuses. It was an offer he could not accept, although he told Adrian McGregor that he had half a mind to, just to see Ribot's reaction. He later rejected an offer to retire. Six years later Ribot said: 'From a salary cap point of view, to give Wally what he was worth to Gold Coast was going to impact on the club. We made a conscious decision not to let anyone become bigger than the club. The hardest thing to argue against was emotion. People would say: "He played 30-odd Origin games and won ten of those single-handedly." We had to evaluate on 1990 performances, not the 1980s. The board said to me: "Can we utilise Wally?" and I said we could, provided we didn't expect him to put in 40 hours a week.

'They went to him and said that they thought his best football was behind him and offered him a sum to retire gracefully and get involved with the corporate side of things. The amount was huge then. I could understand where Wally was coming from. It's hard for a champion to adjust and he had a lot of frustration with injuries. He saw it as a smack in the face and responded accordingly. I don't think people should ever fear adversity. It was a time which was not much fun, but it was a great learning period for Wayne, Alf and myself. Gene can sit back and say it was the worst year of his life, but if he analyses it, he got a lot out of it.'

Bennett said: 'We didn't want to lose him. But name me the

four or five first graders we should let go to keep within the salary cap.'

In 1993, Lewis would tell his biographer: 'People say Bennett was jealous, that I was detracting from him, that he couldn't handle big names. But he got rid of me, not Ribes, not the board. Why? I don't know. He's the only bloke who would know. I changed so many different attitudes to go along with his plans, changed my opinions on how the game should be played. After I did, I got the flick.'

Langer looks back on the release of Lewis as a black mark on his club's reputation. 'I think it was disappointing the way the Broncos handled it,' he said. 'He deserved better for what he did for the Broncos and what he had done. I think it was a bad thing for Queensland rugby league the way they went about it, dropping him from the club.' When asked if he thought the Broncos wanted Lewis out of the club, Langer replied: 'That's the way it looked.'

Miles said the timing of Lewis' departure manifested itself in Canberra's 32–4 win in the preliminary final which terminated Brisbane's dreams of a premiership in their third season. 'It certainly didn't help anyway. We got what we deserved,' he said. That day, the Broncos trooped out of the Sydney Football Stadium to the mischievous refrain of the Last Post from a busker with a bugle. It was hard to find much by the way of alibis about a 28-point defeat in the second biggest game of the season.

Raiders captain Mal Meninga, saved two first half tries, with an intercept and a wrestling tackle which held Mark Hohn up over the line when Brisbane had held a four-on-two overlap. Jackson, with a nice line in gallows humour, complained at halftime to Bennett that Meninga, steaming past to Canberra's second try with an abrupt fend, had failed to stop when Jackson called 'touched'.

After a healthy chorus of 'We want Wally', Lewis ran on for the last 16 minutes with his forearm heavily padded. He declared the run proved his recovery for the Kangaroo tour. Arthurson called it inconclusive and said he would have to satisfy ARL doctor Nathan Gibbs in a special medical two days later. Dr Gibbs said Lewis' arm would not be fully healed for at least six weeks and ruled him unfit. Lewis' Brisbane specialist, Dr Peter Myers, felt the arm was ready for the tour, with the protection of the arm guard.

Lewis, his emotions raw, deployed the words 'set up' and 'conspiracy'. He said an anonymous source had told him a senior Sydney official had assured him Lewis would not tour because it would mean Reg Gasnier's record of 36 Tests for Australia (which Meninga would eventually surpass) would be broken.

Lewis would go on to have a stunning farewell in the 1991 Origin series, the last time a full-strength Queensland team would win a series by the end of the 1996 season. In his absence, many learned he was an even more influential player than previously thought.

He entered the coaching ranks with Gold Coast, first as captain-coach in 1992 and coach in 1993. In 1993, he accepted a long-standing offer to coach the Queensland team. The Seagulls won six games in 1992, including a farewell win for Lewis as a player against premiers Penrith, and just one in his second year, which was marred by personality clashes with chief executive Greg Bandiera and League club executive Vic Folitarik.

Lewis worked in radio on the Gold Coast and then with Channel Seven in Brisbane, reading sports bulletins and reporting on a variety of sports. 'He has changed a lot, for the better,' said his Channel Seven colleague Pat Welsh. 'I never had much trouble with him. Some people just don't get along with him. He has been a great manipulator of the media. I have seen him with those displays of arrogance even he will admit to now. But he is a great worker, becoming a sports reporter on a broad spectrum of sports.

His attitude to people, his gruff manner on the phone, has changed a lot.'

In the intervening years, there had been a mending of the bridge between Lewis and the Broncos, even Lewis and Bennett. Lewis accepted an invitation to open the extensions to the Broncos Leagues Club with Miles and Langer, the only other club captains to that point. When Lewis enters all-in post-match media conferences, their exchanges are cordial, even friendly, as if Lewis' knowledge of the game is a welcome addition to the cut-and-thrust of the questions posed by those who have never played.

Six years after he left the Broncos, the denouement was complete when Bennett made a special presentation to Lewis at the annual Broncos ball on October 2, 1996. 'We have matured a lot and I would like to publicly thank Wally for his contribution from 1988 to 1990,' Bennett said. 'He was an absolute priority for us. His signature meant we were just about assured of success from day one. He brought to the club an attacking style of play on which the club was founded.'

In reply, Lewis said he had a meeting with Bennett two months earlier. 'A lot of those troubles came through ignorance of my own and arrogance alongside it,' Lewis said. 'The only time I felt true dislike for the club was when I was playing for the Gold Coast against them at Lang Park. Every one of those guys at the club in the first year was the basis for what I believe was the greatest rugby league club.'

Langer said he was glad the club and the foundation captain had 'healed their old wounds'. 'Maybe it was a bit late,' he said.

ENGLAND'S UNPLEASANT PASTURES

For Allan Langer, it was nearly the tour that wasn't. The Kangaroo tour of 1990, his first, was the natural extension of a representative career in which he had taken over the Test halfback spot in the light of Peter Sterling's retirement from the international arena. Except he came so close to watching the tour at home on television. 'I wanted to drop him coming into the 1990 finals,' Brisbane coach Wayne Bennett revealed.

'It was the worst he ever played. We won 11 games straight at one stage, but Alf was way, way down. Even when we went into the finals series that year, my mind was telling me he was out of form and he had to be put into reserve grade. My heart was saying: "Don't drop him because this guy is a long-term investment player" and to do it would have absolutely destroyed him. The selectors wouldn't have taken him on the Kangaroo tour. So I weighed up whether we were best off taking a short-term loss in 1990, our first semi-finals series.'

To put the decision in its proper context, a premiership or a grand final appearance would have helped much of the criticism over the treatment of Wally Lewis, and Bennett felt the most likely way to achieve that success was with Langer on the bench. The alternative halfbacks were Kevin Walters and Gary French, who deputised competently and often constructively for Langer, especially in 1989 when the Test half was recovering from a broken ankle.

French was not Allan Langer. But, as Bennett saw it, neither was the man himself, the way he was playing. 'I think he lacked a bit of confidence in his ankle. He wasn't playing with any zip. He was missing tackles, not running with the footy,' Bennett said.

'Alf can get extremely negative when something goes against him—it's only ever happened once or twice and never really with me, on both occasions it was with Ribes. He does absolutely the worst dummy spit I've probably ever seen. He would be bitter on me for not making the Kangaroo tour. We'd never have the same rapport that I need because he'll always harbour that in the back of his mind. The fallacy with these QRL and ARL selectors is that they pick guys who are out of form and when the players come back to their clubs and the coach says: "Look, you're playing terrible football for us", they say: "What do you mean? I've been playing State of Origin, Test football",' Bennett explained. 'So I went with him, he went on the tour and he came back the next year and was great for us.'

When Langer learned of Bennett's agonising he concluded the coach had read him accurately again. 'It could have been a problem. It would have been disappointing to miss out on the tour and I would have lacked a lot of confidence where I stood,' Langer said. 'But as far as me being a dummy spitter is concerned, he should refer to himself. He mustn't have seen himself. When we beat him in tennis or indoor soccer, he just hates it. He is one bloke who is up with me in that regard.'

As events transpired, Bennett came to believe nothing would have seen the 1990 premiership go to the Broncos. The season was to be a rites of passage exercise which set the compass coordinates for success and see six players from the club—Langer, the Walters twins, Dale Shearer, Michael Hancock and Chris Johns—make the Kangaroo tour. Langer and Kerrod Walters left for Manchester, the base for the 17th Kangaroos, as the incumbent Test halfback and hooker, but only after a domestic season of intense pressure from their NSW opposites Ricky Stuart and Ben Elias. Coming into the third State of Origin game, Queensland had lost the series, with Elias taking the Man of the Match award for the first game in Sydney and Stuart honoured from the second in Melbourne.

Three former Australian halfbacks were polled for their opinion in who should play for Australia against France by Brisbane's *Sunday Mail*: Peter Sterling, Steve Mortimer and Mark Murray. Sterling plumped for Stuart because Langer had 'not been in the best of form yet', adding, 'every rule change in the past few years has made field position and kicking an important part of league. Stuart's kicking game is such a big plus.'

Mortimer and Murray both suggested Langer be named to the position he relinquished in 1989 due to his broken leg. 'I'm a big believer that a player gets into the Australian team on merit and once he is there someone has to play a lot better than him to get him out. Also Langer can create things in attack which Stuart can't and I think he is more involved in the play,' Mortimer said.

Langer was chosen for the June 27 Test on the back of a 14–10 Queensland win in which he created the match-winning try for replacement forward Steve Jackson with 10 minutes remaining. 'I was thinking a lot of negative thoughts ... things like, maybe I can't play any more. Wayne sat me down and got me thinking more positively,' Langer remembers. 'He saw I was getting down on myself about my form.'

NSW coach Jack Gibson criticised the selections of Queensland front-rowers Kerrod Walters and Sam Backo ahead of Ben Elias and Ian Roberts. Langer had held the Test halfback spots for wins over France and New Zealand during the domestic season. He was criticised for his lack of running in Australia's 34–2 win in Parkes, a night which became a byword among those in attendance for miserably cold weather. Langer and Walters retained their spots for the August 18 match against New Zealand in Wellington.

The question mark resting over the judgement of the national selectors remained when the tale emerged that former Manly, Easts and NSW fullback Marty Gurr, two years in retirement, had been urged by a NSW member of the national panel: 'Keep punching, son. We've got an eye on you. Keep playing well.'

The Broncos ball-handlers enjoyed one of their most penetrative afternoons in green-and-gold on an Athletic Park mudslide, Walters creating the game-breaking try for clubmate Michael Hancock. Australia won 24–6 despite a 14–3 penalty count in favour of New Zealand from Englishman Robin Whitfield. This prompted Fulton to ask reporters if they thought he would be subject to the NSWRL's fines for commenting on referees who came from outside the territorial boundaries of Australia. The tour was both enticing and repulsive to Langer. He had an idea from his 1988 visit to Leeds that the emerging chill of October and November in the north of England was not his idea of a good time. 'You wake up in the morning and it' cold and foggy outside. It's really hard to get used to compared to the sunny mornings in Brisbane,' he said. 'The idea of an hour or two around your pool looks very good after a while. As far as the football goes, I just didn't like the greasy surfaces and the rain.'

Allan had married Janine Browne barely eight months earlier, on January 27, 1990 at Albert Street Uniting Church, Brisbane. Kevin Langer was chosen as best man, Janine playing under a no-tears edict. 'I was told if there were any tears he wouldn't marry me. It was extremely hot—I don't know how we didn't pass out at the altar. But it was a fairytale wedding,' Janine said. Except, perhaps, for an unscripted arrival from the Fire Brigade. The big red trucks had, coincidentally, been called to the same church, a week or two earlier, for the wedding of Dale and Delyse Shearer. 'Kevin's speech was hilarious. He told them we met at the skating rink, eating an ice block,' Janine said.

The timing for 11 weeks in Europe did nothing to raise his enthusiasm for the tour. Langer's friend Steve Nance, on the training staff at the Broncos remembers: 'He thought about not going, but in the end he wanted to play for Australia and that kind of overrode everything. Before the team was picked, he spoke about missing home too much, but you kind of knew he wasn't going to knock it back. Once he was over there, he'd get on the phone and ask how the golf was going, who got the money, who did what at the barbecue or out on the town,' Nance said. 'Sometimes, you'd wonder if he was going to start crying on you.'

Langer, assured of support from Queensland's selectors, could be sure of selection in the 28-man touring team to be selected on the night of the grand final. Incredibly, Stuart thought he could not, even when he finished second to Cliff Lyons in the Dally M awards on September 11, five days before Canberra's 32–4 preliminary final win over Brisbane.

'I was talking to Don Furner the night of the Dally Ms and he made it known I needed to have a very good game in the grand final to get picked,' Stuart said. 'Don is a family friend and I knew where he was coming from. He was telling me as a mate. Straight away it put a lot of pressure on me to perform in the grand final.'

Furner, the foundation coach of the Raiders who had become an ARL selector, knew his man. The word in Stuart's ear would inspire and motivate, not intimidate. Stuart's grand final opponent, Greg Alexander, had dominated the major semi-final, won in extra time by Penrith. Two weeks later, Stuart won the Clive Churchill Medal in Canberra's 18–14 verdict over the Panthers, having a hand in Canberra's first two tries. He was one of five Raiders named in the 28-man Kangaroo touring team on grand final night.

Furner remembers seeing Stuart in a first grade Canberra union match early in his career. 'An old hard-head hit him with a stiff arm. Ricky hauled himself up, looked him straight in the eye and said: "That's why you have never gone very far in the game." But Ricky's greatest ability was to read the game and make the right decisions.'

Stuart had grown up in Canberra in a rugby league family. His father, Les, had played for Canberra Workers and then played and coached at Captain's Flat, Braidwood and Lakes United in Newcastle. His uncle Garry Marmont captain-coached future Raiders premiership player Chris O'Sullivan at Captain's Flat, a rural hamlet an hour's drive from the national capital. 'All my uncles played rugby league. So football was in the blood. Garry played halfback for Monaro for many years and could have gone to Sydney to play,' Stuart said. 'I got my kicking game from him and he has a similar style of play to me, but I don't tell him that. I used to be the ballboy when my dad coached Garry. I love being close to the action.'

He was never short of a word, a scam or an eye for the main chance, even then. 'I would always hang around the captains when they were doing the toss, so I could ask for the 20 cent piece. I'd go and get some lollies or whatever at halftime,' he said. Stuart toured Argentina with the 1987 Wallabies as a mid-tour replacement, having been overlooked in favour of Nick Farr-Jones and Brian Smith. When he returned, Balmain coach Warren Ryan approached him in Sydney at a union trial and tendered an offer the following night at a pub. He stopped short of signing because he had promised Furner, years earlier, that the Raiders would know before he signed with another league club. The Raiders stumped up enough money to keep him at home.

He would never know if he could have exerted pressure on the halves combination of Nick Farr-Jones and Michael Lynagh, which held firm to Australia's 1991 World Cup triumph. 'That doesn't worry me. I would have always gone to rugby league. It was only a matter of when,' he said. 'I had played SG Ball, the under-16s. I came from a league family. I enjoyed rugby union, but when people asked me what I wanted to do when I finished school, the answer was always that I wanted to play footy.'

After an educational season playing mostly five-eighth, Stuart turned out in 26 first grade games in Canberra's first premiership year. And as he grew in certainty, Stuart brought his renowned long-kicking game, as effective as any in the modern era, a commendable left foot under pressure, a clearing pass half the width of the field to a precise target, the ability to get the simple play done expertly, the reverse flick pass, and the talking that never stopped.

Early in the 1990 tour, Langer and Stuart eyed each other off a trifle warily. Both had a deep well of self-belief matched with a desire to be the best in their position. Both also had that most blokey of desires to be accepted by their teammates, to be one of the boys—especially on a Kangaroo tour.

The team hotel, especially early on, appeared to be run by someone trying out scripts for a television sitcom. Room-mates Michael Hancock and Cliff Lyons spent more than £500 on telephone calls in the first week, until they realised with a mixture of astonishment and fury how much it cost to make calls through the hotel switchboard.

Langer was quicker to learn that long distance phone calls should be made from the box in the foyer. 'I'm not a real big traveller and to go away for two and a half months was going to be hard. I'd spend an hour on the phone a day back to Janine and other people back home,' he said.

Fulton, too, after five Test wins to begin his international coaching reign was a little anxious about the early days of the tour, his first Ashes series. The 1982 and 1986 teams had left the legacy of undefeated Kangaroo tours. The first coach to lose the Ashes, since 1973, would have some serious explaining to do.

He was less than sure the ARL had done the right thing by basing the Kangaroos in Manchester, rather than Leeds, where the previous three groups of tourists had been. 'It wasn't a rugby league town. We had trouble with training venues. We trained on one park which we called Leaf Park and another we called Dogshit Park,' Fulton said. 'Coaching representative sides is a lot different to coaching club teams. There are tracks you have to go down and things you have to do. As a coach, you have to treat the players fairly. If they are happy, you have a good time socially.'

In the years since Fulton captained the 1978 Kangaroos to a series win in Britain and a 2–0 loss in France (the last time an Australian team lost a Test series) he had become less driven to achieve in football, while maintaining a pride which would not let him cut corners in preparing his team. A champion five-eighth and centre chosen by *Rugby League Week* as one of four 'Immortals' among Australian players, Fulton had won a premiership with Manly, in 1987, and been beaten in two grand finals with Easts and Manly, without dislodging the opinion of many that he should have done better with the talent at his command. A director of a chemicals company among other sound investments, Fulton did not need to coach for a living when he returned to Manly in 1992 after a three-year absence when Graham Lowe resigned for health reasons. When he returned to football, he had become adept at time management, juggling football and business, and sought to gather the best possible staff, bigger than ever before for an Australian team, when he took over the Test team in 1989.

Fulton was twenty years older than some of the players alongside whom he drank and laughed at a punishing pace when the schedule of games allowed. 'It's part and parcel of representative football when you are together for a shorter period of time, you have to make sure there is a good balance between preparing them properly and having a good time on the run through,' Fulton said. 'There have been coaches who neglected the latter and paid the price. I do it for the challenge. I like the involvement of working with the best players in Australia. The pressure to keep winning, keep the record intact, is something we all accept.'

Along with his clothes, football gear and essentials from home, Stuart brought with him on the plane to Manchester a sternum injury which would worsen with impacts in his first two matches in Kangaroo colours. Langer, as incumbent, was chosen for the tour opener, a 34–4 cuffing of St Helens. Three weeks without a match had a positive effect, his willingness to run with the football, the gauge of his form, having been restored. He and Laurie Daley, his Test five-eighth partner in Wellington, combined to spread to the right for the first try of the tour, scored by captain Mal Meninga in the third minute. Later in the first half, he reefed the ball from a Saints forward near the home team's tryline and the Kangaroos scored.

Second-rowers Paul Sironen—who set up two tries in quick succession—and John Cartwright muscled the mid-table Saints out of the way to a 22–0 halftime lead and shared the various best player honours.

The British press reacted with alarm the next morning, helped by Fulton's comments that the team would only get better. The *Daily Telegraph*'s John Whalley wrote that the team had more than lived up to pre-tour predictions that it might be a better team than the unbeaten tourists of 1986. 'Allan Langer was a superb orchestrator at halfback,' Whalley wrote. Still, former Kangaroo centre Chris Mortimer, who had seen the 1986 halfback combination of Wally Lewis and Peter Sterling operate from close quarters, felt the Daley–Langer pairing suffered in comparison. 'I think Bozo will go with Daley and Stuart in the Tests,' said Mortimer, who was playing English club football.

Stuart, playing three days later against Wakefield Trinity, marked his first league game for his country by being sent off two minutes from the end of a 36–18 win which is dusted off and re-told lovingly every time an Australian team has returned.

The match is partly remembered for the send-offs of Stuart (on a charge of fighting) and forwards Mark Carroll (fighting) and David Gillespie (abuse). The Kangaroos were baited from the terraces with abuse, words such as 'pigs' and 'thugs', with a scattered chorus of 'Go home, you bums' thrown in for good measure.

Stuart's dismissal, which the bemused halfback said was the result of a swinging arm tackle which connected with the ball, was the first of his career. He and Gillespie were cleared by a special judiciary. Carroll and Wakefield's John Thompson were fined £40 for fighting.

To top off the match drama was Fulton's post-match dissection of the performance of veteran referee Kevin Allott and his 24–7 penalty count against the Australians. Fulton's nature is not to suffer penalty counts such as those at St Helens and Wakefield indefinitely. He saw Allott at halftime. 'I asked if we could get a couple of penalties in the second half—to practise our tap moves,' he said later.

Fulton's critique to reporters was that Allott's performance was like something out of Fawlty Towers, suggesting the referee would be better off, given his length of service, in front of a fire

110

with a cup of cocoa. Despite Stuart's quick-witted 78 minutes at Wakefield, Langer effectively placed his Test spot under lock and key in Australia's match against English double-winners Wigan. The unofficial fourth Test finished 34–6. Great Britain captain Ellery Hanley, an explosive runner who had never quite ignited against the Australians, went out like a candle after an enterprising start. Fulton praised Langer's performance to set Daley and the rest of the back line alight. 'Alf reacted well to the subtle pressure of me having Ricky on the bench,' he added.

The team encountered further adverse comparisons with their predecessors on tour when they recovered from a 10-point deficit to win 22–10 at Leeds. Great Britain's effervescent team manager Maurice Lindsay said Leeds had given the Test side heart and showed 'the Aussies aren't Supermen'. Still, a spectator was overheard in the Headingley souvenir shop before the match: 'No, I'm not going to get another T-shirt. I've still got the Kangaroo-Busters one (from 1986). My wife uses it to do the dusting.'

The Kangaroos ventured south for the first Test at Wembley Stadium to London, where it was the best of times and the worst of times to be an Australian. A British teen girls magazine poll had revealed *Neighbours* star Jason Donovan to be the 'most famous person in the world', with Margaret Thatcher second, George Bush third and Kylie Minogue a most deserving fourth. Australian television soap operas exerted such a fascination that the Rugby Football League, eager to make a dint, any dint, in the consciousness of the national capital, arranged for Donovan to appear at a photo opportunity with the Kangaroos at Wembley Stadium.

One photographer muttered darkly that he did not 'want this turning into a rugby thing'. Another urged Mal Meninga to balance a ball on Donovan's head. Paul Sironen shook his head and walked away when asked to put his arm around Donovan. Langer, standing at the front, worked on the basis that if he kept smiling he would not be asked to do anything. Had they cared, the Kangaroos would have noticed the next morning that the country's two most popular newspapers had declined to run any pictures and one did not mention the Test at all in its London edition.

Of greater importance was the withdrawal of Daley the next morning, two days before the Test, with a broken bone in his hand, suffered in an all-in brawl at Leeds. With the form of Cliff Lyons and Kevin Walters being less than authoritative, Fulton played Stuart at five-eighth with Langer at halfback.

'I stuck with Alf for two reasons—his form was as good as Ricky's in the lead-up games and he was the incumbent Test halfback,' Fulton later recalled. 'I thought it was the fair way to go. It was basically a new era and I had to find the right combination. It didn't work. And Alf, in my opinion, played okay in that first Test.' Kerrod Walters and Bella retained their Test places, Fulton ignoring a clamour in some sections of the Sydney media for Glenn Lazarus and especially Elias to be in the front row.

Great Britain coach Malcolm Reilly worked to overcome any inferiority complexes his players held towards the world champions, claiming the Kangaroos could be bustled into error if they played with discipline. 'They are so confident. Our aim is to shut them up,' he said.

It was the first Ashes Test at Wembley since 1973 and most of the Australians had never played in front of a crowd as big as 52,274. The bracing effect of a first visit to Wembley, where Australian sports fans had seen so many Challenge and FA Cup finals on television over the years, was underestimated by the Australians. The Rugby Football League maximised the advantage by having the teams enter at a leisurely pace, down the famous race, over the dog track and to a position in front of the Royal Box, while the stirring 'Land of Hope and Glory' boomed over the public address.

Television cameras showed the Australians to be pale for reasons other than the autumnal chill. As the camera panned across during the national anthem, Kerrod Walters' eyes batted furiously and Langer looked as if he had eaten something that had disagreed with him.

The first half was a lull, finishing 2–all after Alain Sablayrolles—combining the usual French refereeing cocktail of flamboyant gestures and nothing more than a rudimentary command of English—found cause to deliver 17 penalties.

Ah, yes, Sablayrolles. But more of him later. In the meantime Hanley beat Sironen three minutes after the break to send young winger Paul Eastwood over for a try which brought the crowd into the contest more vigorously. But Meninga scored soon after, a rumble down the Twin Towers sideline which relieved the estimated 4000 Australian supporters in the stadium of the thought that their side would be in danger at 6–all.

Great Britain regained momentum with a try from a bomb in which fullback Gary Belcher may or may not have been taken out of the contest by chasers, depending mostly on your nationality. Five-eighth Garry Schofield, like Hanley, creating trouble with a short kicking game in positions where most Australian players would opt for safer tactics, snapped a field goal for a 13–6 lead with 20 minutes left. Then, McGaw scored a remarkable try over 45 metres, Meninga's conversion from touch reducing the margin to one point before Schofield, chipping and regathering, ignited the Wembley faithful by creating a second try for Eastwood.

As the Kangaroos trooped off, their sequence of 37 wins on British soil broken and one loss from an unimaginable fate, their anger over Sablayrolles, responsible for a 17–7 penalty count to the home team, boiled over behind closed doors.

As the touring Australian press moved in on eggshells, there was a shrill laugh from Fulton to greet them. It was so bad, it was funny. 'We had the ball for 39 tackles in the second half,' said Fulton.'I said to the players if you get 13 drunks out of any pub and give them the ball for 79 minutes, they are going to beat the best team in the world. It was a bad example, but it got the point across. When we were getting penalised for offside, Sablayrolles was even doing the old two-step. We'll win the series if we are given a square deal.'

But ARL chairman Ken Arthurson later added: 'You can't get away from the point that the better team won.'

Fulton's comments caused a sensation in a media coverage understandably more interested in examining the depth of British Bulldog spirit, a supposed lack of flair in the Australian team and the issue of whether Hanley was the best player in the world. Half-back Andy Gregory enthused: 'The Australians have spent so much time at the top they just don't believe in giving credit to anyone. It's time they realised they are not the be-all and end-all. We won't be satisfied until we get our hands on the Ashes.'

Langer was unfavourably compared to Sterling in two national newspapers. Sterling was something of an icon from his two tours and impact on English club league with Hull. The verdict was as inevitable as it was correct—Langer was still learning how to best act as a playmaker at the top level. Alex Murphy, the talismanic Great Britain halfback of the 1960s, considered Fulton would have been best off making Penrith's Greg Alexander half instead of Langer or Stuart for the second Test in Manchester two weeks later.

'I think Langer is a tough kid with a ton of guts, but he just lacks that yard of pace to be a real Test halfback,' Murphy said. 'This team is nowhere near as good as the 1986 team. I bet they wish they had Wally Lewis.'

Langer said a number of the team had been awed by the Wembley experience. 'A few of the players were relieved because people would stop talking about another undefeated tour, which I couldn't work out. Losing shook us all up, me included,' he said.

Six years later, Fulton maintains his team was attacked by Sablayrolles, who had been spotted by the Australians with the friendly arm of a RFL administrator around him as he walked out for the second half. 'Sab-lay-rolles,' says Fulton, as if pronouncing an inedible vegetable. 'He couldn't referee at all. Maurice Lindsay got him from somewhere in France and no-one has seen him before or since. He did a job on us, a good job, and it made it hard for us to play the football we wanted to play.'

When the Kangaroo team for the vital Sunday match against Castleford was announced, it was manager Keith Barnes who faced the media at the team hotel, Fulton having departed for training. In announcing that Stuart, Elias, Lazarus, Dale Shearer and Brad Mackay would play in positions held by Langer, Kerrod Walters, Bella, Michael Hancock and John Cartwright at Wembley, Barnes alluded to a sea-change in selections which was not missed by the omitted Queenslanders. 'This team is more able to adapt to an attacking style. Bob was disappointed with the one-out running. It's not the way they have been coached. It boils down to a lack of support play,' Barnes said.

Earlier, Fulton explained to the five that they were not out of the running for the second Test team and their rivals had deserved a chance to advance their claims among the Test players. Langer was made captain of the team to play Halifax two days later. It was the first time he had captained Australia. Despite the accolade, the selections had the aura of consolation about it for him. 'Bob told me during the week he was happy with my form, but you do have to wonder what good it will do me to play well against Halifax.'

In the 28–8 win over Castleford, Stuart engineered the first try for Ettingshausen with a double-around and it was a knife through Langer's competitive heart when he chipped and regathered to lay on Australia's last try. The Queenslander was given the last five minutes against Castleford and felt his Test position slip away in slow motion as the Kangaroos laboured to a 36–18 win over Halifax.

Langer was sent to the sin-bin in the 75th minute for kicking an opponent, a charge teammates said was one of mistaken identity. After leading 32–4 at halftime, the second half had taken an eternity. 'It was the most amazing match I had ever played in. We had it given to us with the penalties again (15–5). Kevie Walters was penalised for not playing the ball fast enough. Of course, then I found out what could go on in France,' Langer recalled.

The next morning Langer and Walters resigned to disappointment. But hoping against all logic for the best, they heard the second Test team announced to the players.

Kerrod Walters, who thought it a 'bit strange' that so many changes to the team to play Castleford were made, reveals with a chuckle that he knew he wasn't going to play at Old Trafford. 'I walked into a lift at the hotel to go down to get the Test team and Benny Elias' parents were in there and I thought "shit, what's going on here? The writing is on the wall". I never thought my position in the Test team was in danger. I thought both Alf and I did okay. Later on, Laurie Daley tells me the story about how he was talking to Benny's parents somewhere before we went away and they told him they would be over (in England) when they heard the news that Benny was the Test hooker. They had obviously heard the news.'

Fulton said Elias' parents could not have known for sure. 'You don't suddenly jump on a plane, do you? How would they have known what the side would be? There was plenty of speculation that Benny and the others would be in the team. But I don't tell the players beforehand. It was made clear to the players that I was the person selecting the sides. The blokes who weren't in the team were all told before the selection announcement, except Martin Bella. He had borrowed my car to see his wife and kids, who were staying in Halifax. He was told when he came back. Glenn Lazarus came in and was one of the players of the tour.'

Four Queensland Test players, along with Cartwright of Penrith, were omitted, although Hancock was not considered because of an ankle injury. The team announcement created a backlash in Brisbane that Fulton was against Queensland players. It was a familiar refrain, a distant chord of the tumultuous 1985 season in which Terry Fearnley was coach, and not one with which Langer was, or is, comfortable.

'I think he was more comfortable with Ricky and Cliff Lyons playing together in the halves,' Langer said. 'I was obviously shattered, but at the same time you don't want to look like a dummy spitter. I was told the reason was that Fulton had to improve the kicking game. The worst part of it was that my parents and Janine were coming over that week before the second Test. All the way to England, and I wasn't in the Test side.'

Fulton's six changes, including the unavailable centre McGaw, who had been outed for the rest of the tour with a severe knee injury sustained against Castleford, did not sit well with his repeated assertions that Sablayrolles' refereeing was the main factor in the Wembley loss. 'It was backs-to-the-wall for the second game and I thought there were changes that had to be made,' he recalls.

'But the fact is that some players look for excuses when they don't make a side. You only have to look at the number of Queenslanders picked in the side and the number of times Alf played in those teams, and you can see that I don't have anything against Queenslanders. I'm comfortable with anyone if they can play. If there was a push in Sydney, it didn't come from good judges, who realise that both Ricky and Alf are exceptional players.'

Fulton confirms that he believes the ultimate criterion of selection is the win-loss column in Tests. 'I certainly do think that. I'm not saying that if we hadn't have gone with the same side again Australia wouldn't have won. The selections weren't made willy-nilly. They were made through hours of video. Combination did come into it. Certain players are more comfortable with others,' he said. 'We had to win the second Test in one of the great Tests and in the wash-up those changes proved to the right decision. Alf, in my opinion, handled it superbly. He never gave less than his best for the rest of the tour.'

Back in Brisbane Wayne Bennett was acting as a long-distance counsellor for the deposed hooker and halfback. 'Alf didn't shrug it off real well. He handled it well publicly, but he rang me a lot. Probably once a week,' Bennett said. 'The calls were initially about why he was dropped and being homesick and that he was just trying to keep his spirits up. I really felt like I was doing Fulton's job, trying to keep their spirits up. They were telling me that he had shafted them. I knew Langer needed support, but you don't bullshit him. He doesn't want to hear that stuff. He's very realistic,' Bennett said.

'You try to put some balance back into their lives. They have no-one they can go to over there. So you act as a filter. It's the making of the administration over there, but you know if they can't handle it properly it is going to get worse and worse. You don't want to see Australia fail, so you do it.'

It wasn't until later that Fulton learned of the amount of contact Bennett was having with Brisbane players. He didn't know what to make of it. 'When Bennett was coaching Queensland, I had some Manly players who used to ring me about certain things. They weren't ringing up blueing about anything, they just wanted a bit of a chat and talked about training—all sorts of things,' Fulton said. 'It's a relationship club coaches and their players have at any time of the day. So I might have been doing his job for him in the 1980s for Queensland. I didn't undermine any representative coach. 'Alf proved to me he was comfortable with the reasons I gave him. I got on famously with him. I have nothing against Alf ringing Wayne Bennett, but it depends on what he is saying to them.'

The five Broncos players not in the Test team began spending more time in the company of the four Penrith players with indelible consequences. In the week before Old Trafford, it was generally agreed late one night that a tattoo declaring 'Roo 90' on the rear end was what was needed.

'Janine was arriving the next day and I wasn't game to get it done,' Langer said. 'I snuck out as they were ready to go out to get the tattoo. They were that sore the next day. People kept smacking them.' Kevin Walters went back to the same tattoo shop in Manchester in 1994 to get a comma and '94' added to his derriere. 'It wasn't that good, it probably ruined it,' he said.

Langer and the Walters twins, playing in their specialist positions together for the first time on tour, took some satisfaction from the 34–4 win at Hull in the last week of the tour. 'It was one of the plusses later in the tour. At least we kept trying,' he said. Like almost every player on the tour, Langer came away from the tour with a special regard for Johnny Lewis, the quietly spoken boxing trainer who took Jeff Fenech and Kostya Tszyu to world titles.

'Johnny was as homesick as Alf and the twins and they helped each other through it,' Bennett said.

Preparing his team for the second Test, Fulton had spotted

on the video that Hanley was more dangerous running from his left to right and back-rowers Sironen and Mackay assumed special responsibility to close down the runs which had given the Kangaroos so much trouble at Wembley. He had alerted Meninga to look for Hanley smearing the ball with grease from his legs at the kick-off. When Sablayrolles was prompted to replace the ball for the start of the Test it was a minor victory for the tourists.

For Ricky Stuart, the second Test at Old Trafford would allow him to learn what it would be like to lose the Ashes for his country and save them, all in the space of 13 minutes.

Australia's first half drove Fulton to the brink of despair. There was brilliant attack as Stuart's passing game cleared matters for the deep back line, but all they had to show was a 4–2 lead through a Shearer try in which he capitalised on indecisive cover defence from Schofield with explosive acceleration.

Worse, Great Britain brought the near-capacity crowd of 46,615 behind them when second-rower Paul Dixon, running off Schofield, bounced up, stopped but not held, by Meninga and Gary Belcher, to score a try. Australia replied with one of the great tries in Ashes history, a 14-pass extravaganza covering 50 metres in which Shearer and Belcher ran into dead-ends and flung the ball behind them in ad-lib fashion. Cornered on the right wing, Ettingshausen aimed a cross kick and Lyons made a difficult bounce look easy through anticipation.

So with ten minutes to go, the Kangaroos led 10–6, until Stuart, enjoying a clever game, didn't see Great Britain centre Paul Loughlin. Loitering with intent out of Sablayrolles' offside radar, Loughlin intercepted a clearing pass near halfway. Daley, chasing back, at least forced the conversion attempt from winger Paul Eastwood to be placed about 15 metres from the left upright, rather than in front. Ten–all, kick to come.

Stuart, the scene of pandemonium swimming before his eyes, was in no mood to look on the bright side. 'When I walked into the in-goal area, I felt like a prick. I might have cost Australia the Ashes. It was like a death in the family,' he remembers. 'Mal walked past me and said: "Seven minute drill." That lifted me a bit and made me think we had to go again here.'

The comment from Meninga was a reminder of one of the training drills Tim Sheens ran at Canberra. 'You have seven on seven, playing for seven minutes. What that does is show you how much time there is in seven minutes. It teaches you not to panic,' Stuart said. As Eastwood approached the ball, Stuart, Meninga and other Australians cursed him beneath their breath. This was for the Ashes. The left-footed Hull kicker sliced it to the loudest groan ever heard by the banks of relieved and jubilant Australian supporters.

Doing their maths on their way back to the re-start, the Kangaroos worked out they would retain the Ashes with a draw and a win in the third Test at Leeds. But a draw at Old Trafford would leave themselves and Fulton's selections open to a storm of criticism from back home.

A field goal attempt called by Stuart was not heeded by team-mates and the Australians were buried deep within their own 20 metre zone three minutes into injury time. A draw it was. But then Stuart, ball in his outstretched right hand and eyes peeled for the most tiny of holes, sold the defence a dummy. Hanley gave chase, only to give up, to Stuart's surprise. The Australian halfback ran on and on, beyond halfway, eyeing the support of Meninga and Ettingshausen, still too far away to use, while maintaining his speed. Reilly was to lament that if Offiah had not been forced off early in the second half with a leg injury, the fleet-footed winger would have run down Stuart.

Over the British 20 metre line, Stuart knew he was going to be collared. Inside, he saw Meninga bursting clear, shouldering aside two defences. The pass hit the mark, the Test was won, the series was alive.

Television cameras captured two Kangaroos, Mark Carroll and Kerrod Walters, in suit and tie, open-mouthed as they marvelled at the sporting drama which had been played in front of them. No hard feelings from Walters—he wanted to see Australia win. Out of shot, Langer watched with the same emotions. 'Now I know there is a God,' Stuart told reporters later.

Time has barely reduced the shudder Stuart feels when he thinks about how close he came to life-long notoriety. 'It would still be burning in my guts had we lost. It was an amazing experience,' he said. 'All I was trying to do was position the bloke who got the pass and I could see Mal screaming for the ball. Everyone was absolutely buggered, it was that sort of game. It was a case of mind over matter.'

What happened on the tour after that was an academic footnote to a moment in which two players had composed and performed, under unspeakable tension, one of the sweetest notes ever heard in Australian league. Australia duly retained the Ashes 14–0 in the third Test at Leeds' Elland Road. Stuart created the first try for Ettingshausen with a floating pass which revisited, for everyone but the halfback, the horror of the Loughlin intercept. Elias scored the second-half try which sealed the retention of the Ashes.

Stuart reflects: 'The first half of the tour was a learning experience. When I got the first Test start when Laurie was injured, I tried to make every post a winner from five-eighth. We didn't play well. It was hard for Alfie to be dropped. It wasn't his fault we lost the first Test.'

In the final days before the third Test, Fulton told me Langer would still 'go down in ten years' time as one of the great halfbacks we have had, in the same breath as Peter Sterling and Steve

Mortimer'. The comment was a genuine accolade. Fulton is a master at keeping players sweet, but this was no calculated attempt to massage an ego. But there is a mutual liking. Fulton admires Langer's skills as a player and his mixture of respect, cheek and love of a good time.

Over the next four or five years, the Test halfback issue would fill more newspaper space and radio airtime than any other in the game. It can be seen now as a time of some innocence in light of the bitterness and jealousies which were to afflict the game in 1995 and 1996.

Langer was less than pleased when Stuart withdrew on the day before the last club match against in-form Widnes. He felt that Stuart was regarding him as expendable to injury. It prevented him from taking a weekend break with his wife. Teammates knew, but it is not Langer's style to confront over such a matter. Stuart said: 'I ripped my stomach muscles in that run (for the Meninga try) and I needed the time off before the third Test. I got man of the match for the third Test. It turned out to be a very successful tour for me.'

It was also the sort of tour manager Keith Barnes probably enjoyed most when the team returned to Australia on December 9. Most serious was an incident at an indoor cricket centre outside Manchester on November 11, the day after the second Test. One Australian player was fortunate not to be sent home. Sketchy details made newspapers in England and Australia, but it was well defused by Fulton and Barnes, with the assistance of the cricket centre's management.

In his published tour diary, *Kangaroo Confidential*, Belcher recorded on November 12 that Fulton had asked the players 'in pretty strong terms to cut down on our drinking'. He noted four days later that Barnes had called a team meeting to discuss the breakage of windows on the players' floor and that hotel management had 'virtually threatened not to let us stay here for the next week unless it is all fixed up'. Some of his teammates did not react well to Belcher's forthright comments that touring players tended to drink too much, and it tended to detract from performances both in matches and at training. Belcher and roommate Bob Lindner, the player of the tour, were among the lighter drinkers on the tour. Unlike some teammates who remained at the hotel to play cards or generally while away time, they enjoyed sightseeing in cities like London and Paris.

Never a great sightseer or sampler of different cultures, Langer does not share the sentiments of Belcher and others in hindsight. 'It was a very enjoyable tour, you could say,' Langer said.

The Broncos players were not duly thrilled with a report in Sydney's *Daily Mirror* earlier in the tour which claimed two Broncos had fought each other in the hotel's foyer bar. Rumours vary on this—some players swore that it was simply one of the mock fights between Langer and Kevin Walters in which the blows sound and look real, only for the victim to regain his feet laughing.

But there was a heat-of-the-moment clash between Langer and Johns as the tour dragged on in France. 'Johnsy and I had a blue in France. It all started through me flicking Kevin's cauliflower ear,' Langer said. Kerrod Walters said television commentator Warren Boland had to intervene between Langer and Johns. 'Alf and Johnsy had started off joking and it got serious. Alf had come back to our room with blood everywhere and then Johnsy followed him in. Then I had to try to break it up,' he said.

It was the sort of incident which often happens late on rugby league tours and resulted in a late night knock on the door of team doctor Nathan Gibbs. 'Nathan did a good job considering … Kevie had him in a headlock at one stage as he was stitching my ear,' Langer said. 'Kevie wouldn't let him put more than three stitches in my ear because he gave Kevin three stitches the night before. I wasn't allowed to have four.'

Langer's flat vowels would never send a television executive rushing with an offer, but Boland seconded him for a Test in France as expert commentator for the ABC. 'It was an absolutely freezing day and I had two jumpers, a pair of gloves and a blanket. Alf arrived to call the game in the open air in a tracksuit top and singlet,' Boland said. 'He wasn't saying much towards the end of the first half and I turned to see him looking blue. I was about to put a third jumper on, but reluctantly gave it to him.'

One night in France, Langer forgot his fear of heights and began to scale a drainpipe as his mates killed themselves laughing. 'I had my Jackie Howe singlet on and must have got 12 or 15 feet up it when someone looked down from a window and tossed a bucket of water down on me,' he said. 'The water was freezing and I was just drenched.' Kevin Walters said Langer forgot to add that he had threatened to jump.

'He was shouting "Get out of the way, I'm going to jump," as if he was going to end it all. The French people were yelling back at him, "Don't jump." In the end he just climbed down. Then we went for a swim in the fountain,' Kevin Walters said.

Former St George forward John Fifita was out that night with the Kangaroos and piled a few of them into his small sedan. Langer solved the squeeze problem and was riding on the bonnet, stretched out and holding on for dear life. 'Johnny Fifita was racing through the narrow streets. It was freezing outside and my face was sort of pressed up against the windscreen,' Langer described. Kevin Walters adds: 'Alf was looking in at us screaming at us to stop. He was pretty shaken up at the end of it.'

In Carcassonne, the team management secured tickets for American actor Kevin Costner and his entourage. Costner was filming *Robin Hood, Prince of Thieves* around the walled city and its environs. Langer, a casual film watcher rather than a buff, wondered who the bloke in the dressing-room standing next to Mal

Meninga was. On a more serious note, Kevin Walters and Cartwright were temporarily blinded when a Perpignan shop-keeper sprayed mace in their eyes.

The tour was the last but one in the full Kangaroo tour format and Langer, for one of many, was sorry to see the passing of that tradition. 'Yeah, it was all training and playing and drinking. But we had a lot of fun,' Langer said.

RIBES NEEDS A BIGGER CAKE

John Ribot thought Allan Langer was bluffing. Almost certainly bluffing that he was going to leave the Broncos—but still he could not be sure. If 1991 was the worst season the Broncos have experienced on a win–loss basis, it was also the year when Langer rewrote the textbook on how to negotiate a rugby league playing contract.

The Broncos, once again backed as premiership favourites due to their 1990 blooding in the finals series, launched their season with the panache of an aristocrat knowing he was about to come into possession of the family fortune. A memorable newspaper photograph pictured Bennett kneeling to receive a knighthood from comedian Gerry Connolly, dressed as Queen Elizabeth II. They had traded a King for a Queen. Try as one might, it was difficult to imagine a man in a dress gaining admission to a Souths function during Bennett's time at Davies Park. It was somehow analogous to a more assured and relaxed outlook for the Broncos with the storm over Lewis' departure at least calmed, if not completely dissipated.

Unusually for Langer, he told close friends in early 1991 that he really wanted to regain the Australian Test position taken over by Ricky Stuart on the Kangaroo tour. Slapping his cards on the table, Langer won the Man of the Match award in all four games as Brisbane won the pre-season Lotto Challenge.

Brisbane beat North Sydney 24–10 in the first round match at Bundaberg's Salter Oval. Newcastle were next, overcome 28–13 at Tamworth's Scully Park, despite skipper Gene Miles' dismissal on a punching charge. Against Illawarra at Dubbo, the Broncos fell behind 12–2 before Miles (found guilty by the NSWRL judiciary but not suspended in view of a spotless record) and Dale Shearer worked some second half magic after previous personal mistakes. Twice Langer stole the ball from Steelers opponents to provide possession for Broncos tries. 'Once (referee) Bill Harrigan was looking the other way when Alf put the ball down for a try,' Bennett said.

When Langer was announced Man of the Match as they walked off the field 16–14 winners, his teammates chanted 'Wally, Wally', a cheeky reference to Wally Lewis' domination of such awards in the early years of State of Origin. 'How embarrassing,' he said. 'They reckon it's in my contract. I have to get it.'

Penrith coach Phil Gould, defending an unbeaten 6–0 record against Brisbane, said before the March 9 final at Broken Hill that Langer received preferential treatment from referees in his ball-stealing exploits. 'Other players get penalised. It depends on the referee's interpretation,' he said.

The trip to Broken Hill for the Lotto Challenge final against Penrith remains a fond memory for anyone who joined one of the NSWRL's most enjoyable and relaxing frontier missions. The far western mining town provided a green oasis of a field amid the red dirt and slag heaps. Miles was unable to play because of injury, leaving Langer to hoist the second trophy won by a Broncos first grade team and Bennett to confirm that the Kangaroo halfback was being looked at, along with Kevin Walters, as Brisbane's next club captain.

It was another hair-raising ride for the coach, as they were behind 16–2 in the shadows of halftime, heading towards a fifth straight loss to Penrith and another round of condemnation revolving around the 'soft Broncos' theory. Second-rower Trevor Gillmeister, secured by the Broncos in the NSWRL player draft which would be ruled invalid by the Federal Court later in the season, made his statement on that score in a first half set-to with Penrith's Mark Geyer which saw both sent to the sin-bin.

Bennett was not backward in advancing a few theories of his own: 'The most important thing about us and Penrith is that we never felt we couldn't compete. If you believed everything you read and hear about the Broncos, we should have been bombed out of Broken Hill at 16–2.' The Brisbane coach was thrilled with Langer's pre-season after being disappointed in his 1990 season. 'Penrith closed him down and last season he would have put his cue in the rack. Today, he kept pressing, opened them up and ended up in his own league,' Bennett said.

The match against Manly was the first premiership encounter to be played under an unlimited interchange rule and Bennett was one coach to adapt well to the scope offered by the rotation of an eight-man forward pack. The crowd at Lang Park and elsewhere did not react kindly to the turnover of players. When the rule was discontinued after five rounds, there were those at Red Hill who thought it was because Bennett had worked it to the advantage of his team too successfully.

Stuart hardly did his bit to play down his first battle against Langer in 1991. When he was talked into posing for a photograph on the cover of *Rugby League Week*, dressed in military fatigues, he held a high-tech firearm to accompany the headline 'Alfie in his sights.' He later added, 'I'm not real sure about it and I don't think I'd do it again.'

129

Canberra lowered their colours 26–12 at Lang Park on a steamy, sapping afternoon. Two contentious try decisions went against the Raiders. The halfback match-up was a no decision. The match was played on April 1. Langer's April Fools' Day joke on Ribot was to tell reporters that he had been unable to agree with the management on terms for a new contract for 1992. The joke would last seven weeks and prove to be Ribot's most difficult contract signing in his eight years at Red Hill.

Into the bargain, Allan and Janine Langer were expecting their first child. The looming birth drew such media attention in Brisbane—would he be able to play or would the baby be born on game day?—that an exasperated Bennett eventually told reporters: 'Look, he's not the first man to become a father.'

When their daughter was born and named Courtney, team-mates ribbed Allan about calling her after a West Indian fast bowler. Similarly, when Maddison was born two years later, he was accused of stealing the name from Steve Renouf's brand of headgear.

Even though Wally Lewis' departure had loosened up the Broncos' salary cap of $1.5 million to some extent, most of the money saved on the transaction had already been promised to other players. As players compared notes from their trip to the chief executive's office, a routine emerged. 'I'd say fellas, I'd love to give you more, but there is only so much to the cake and I can't give you a bigger slice if I'm going to be fair to the others,' Ribot said.

The Bennett–Ribot partnership was an identikit fit of individual strengths. Bennett was the stoic, even-tempered disciplinarian and developed a fatherly relationship with many of his younger players. Ribot was more comfortable with sidling up to a player over a beer if there was tension or an issue to be addressed. 'Wayne doesn't drink or smoke, but he gets kind of intoxicated on the atmosphere, not that he'd be out with us at a nightclub,' Langer said. 'He likes being with the boys.' Ribot said: 'I picked my moments to go and get on the drink with them and have a good time or sort some problems out in the confession box. But there had to be a cut-off point.'

More often than not, Bennett played good cop to Ribot's bad cop. 'That comes with the job description. The buck stopped with me,' Ribot said. 'Wayne and I were very aware we must control and manage that properly because if it was used the right way it could be a real positive.'

Director Paul Morgan said: 'Ribot had to keep himself that little bit above the players. That demarcation has to be necessary because Ribes increasingly had to be a businessman as well as a chief executive. We had a luxury because Ribot filled the role as football manager and chief executive. The Broncos were turning $3 million or $4 million in the late 1980s and were turning $11 million by the mid 1990s.'

It was Ribot's job to retain Langer, their most recognised and popular player now, within a strict budget. There were epic meetings in which Ribot talked and talked and Langer sat and looked at him. 'Alf didn't probably realise what a strength it was, but he'd sit there and say nothing,' Ribot said. 'Then you'd hear the rumours he was going to play for the Gold Coast and that put more pressure on me. Especially when he kept playing blinders.' Bennett adds: 'I remember him getting the shits real bad with Ribes and I knew I had to stay out of his road. Alf's not going to argue with you, he's just going to do a job on you his way. Alf would just sit there and get filthier and filthier. He knew what his market price was and he wasn't going to let Ribes get him cheaply again. He'd tell me a little bit and I knew Ribes had his hands full.'

Gold Coast Seagulls made Langer a priority, offering him the chance to become the first Australian player to be on an admitted wage of more than $200,000. The deal was $700,000 over three years, plus the captaincy, when Wally Lewis retired. Easts and Canterbury were also interested in Langer.

Ribot felt Langer's manager Richard Winten was encouraging Langer to leave the Broncos. Winten had left his position as marketing manager of the Broncos after the 1988 season to start his own business with relations between the two men extremely strained. Ribot preferred managers, in general, who would make themselves scarce around contract time. He had also clashed heatedly with Steve Nance when Nance represented Langer in 1988.

Asked if he thought Langer was on the verge of joining another club, Ribot recalls: 'That indication certainly came from Richard. He was flogging Alf around the clubs and if the money had have been poles apart, we might have struggled. Luckily, we were able to get to Alf and say to him: "We don't want you to go. This is what the club is all about, people like you. Can we be fair about this?" The stalemate was more frustrating for me than him.'

On May 21, Langer confirmed two NSW clubs had made him offers and to accept one would make it worthwhile to move south. Eventually, Ribot seconded Bennett to broker a peace. 'He was asking for a lot of money for that time, we both compromised because we couldn't pay him that. Say the figure he wanted was 100, I brought him back to 90 or 95,' Ribot remembers.

'As a last resort, we could pull Wayne in and start dealing with the players. They felt a bit easier talking to Wayne. They saw me as the hard-nosed bloke. We knew we had to get him to put an extra dimension on Allan Langer the person off the field. If he was going to stay, he would have to do more endorsement work. Easts, for instance, could write him a cheque for the full amount.'

On May 23, the Broncos called a press conference at which

Langer announced he was staying for two more years. Bennett said: 'He just screwed Ribes right down, the best job on Ribes anyone ever did. I thought there was a time when we would be shopping for a new halfback. Over the years since, I occasionally say to Alf: "Gee, it would have been a great move for you to go to the Gold Coast. They'd win one game all year—mate, you really missed an opportunity there." '

Even at the time, Langer endorsed TDK tapes, The Plains Video (briefly owning one franchise at Jindalee), an Arnotts snack food, Broncos Cheese Rings, and football equipment. When Power Brewing were legally able to use him in television commercials the following year, he would endorse beer as well.

When he thinks about the period when he left the club dangling for weeks, Langer's rapscallion grin breaks: 'I wasn't going to leave unless they offered me a really ordinary deal. I knew Ribes got me for the first couple of years and I kept hanging off. We're still great mates, me and Ribes, but I'm glad I got him the second time around.'

With Miles nursing injured ribs, Langer was acting captain in a round seven match at Campbelltown. Wests beat the 12-man Brisbane team, deprived of Kerrod Walters, who had been sent off on a punching charge. The score was 17–16 despite a masterful personal performance by Langer. Walters was sent off by referee Greg McCallum, and subsequently suspended for two matches. This suspension included the first Origin encounter which stoked the fires of indignation at Red Hill to the point where the club prepared a report to the NSWRL on McCallum's handling of their matches since 1988. The referee would go on to control Brisbane's two NSWRL grand final wins.

Lewis had needed minor knee surgery in early April and

played only once on his return before the first Origin match. Test fullback Gary Belcher withdrew with knee damage, giving Bronco Paul Hauff—juggling his football with his career in the police service—a debut at Lang Park one day before his 21st birthday. The 197 centimetre Hauff stooped to conquer, saving three tries with cool defence, but it was Lewis who grabbed the headlines with a Man of the Match performance rekindling his chances to play for Australia again. Running off Langer, Lewis conjured Queensland's only try in a 6–4 win when he put the NSW defence in a number of minds and sent Mal Meninga rumbling over the top of Alexander.

On the club front, Brisbane suffered successive losses at home to Easts and Balmain to leave them languishing in 11th position. The season had slipped away before the crucial nature of the mid-season games had struck them.

Channel Ten ran a viewer phone-in poll on whether Bennett should coach the Broncos. 'Off with his head', the public said decisively. Bennett responded by saying, 'I notice that when we win, it is because everyone does their job and when we lose it's my fault. There are no major problems and it's a matter of persevering. If the board doesn't think I'm doing the job, they can make a decision.'

Langer and the Walters twins encouraged Bennett to keep with the job. Kerrod Walters said: 'I know there was a time when he was going to chuck it in. The three of us got hold of Benny at different times and let him know he had our 100 per cent support. I spoke to Trish (Bennett) and she said Wayne was really despondent.'

With Kerrod Walters' elder brother, Steve, holding down the Queensland hooker spot in victory, the two Origin teams went at it again in Sydney in one of the most sensational and bad-tempered encounters. Lewis, sensing when his team needed a lift when they fell behind 8–6 at halftime, confronted NSW enforcer Mark Geyer. The pair pushed, growled at and threatened each other and referee David Manson physically separated them in a 30 metre tango of bravado on the way to the tunnel. Geyer had been involved in two all-in brawls in the first half and 11 minutes after the change of ends he caught Hauff's jaw with a forearm and the Queenslanders picked the nearest Blue jersey for a square-up.

While Langer and Lewis worked play to the left to send Dale Shearer slicing through for a 12–8 lead, Stuart would have a crucial say four minutes from fulltime when he spun a long pass for centre Mark McGaw to crash through three defenders. From near touch, Blues centre Michael O'Connor scraped the conversion in by the left upright for a 14–12 win.

The nerveless finish by the Blues was swamped by the uproar from the Queensland dressing-room in defeat. Coach Graham Lowe, a New Zealander head-hunted by the QRL to replace the revered Arthur Beetson, called Geyer a 'lunatic'. The ARL cited Geyer for five weeks, ruling him out of the decider at Lang Park, won 14–12 by Queensland.

The lead-up for the Maroons had been atrocious. Lowe, hospitalised before and during the series because of a blood clot in his leg, addressed his team over the telephone from his bed in a Sydney hospital, before flying north to coach with the assistance of a cane. Then Lewis discovered late in the campaign that his young daughter was profoundly deaf, making his performance in what would be his last match for Queensland all the more remarkable, given his emotion.

The Maroons were told of Lewis' decision to retire from Origin football shortly before the kick-off. The Queensland Rugby League timed an announcement over the public address system to coincide with Queensland nosing ahead 14–12 by a Dale Shearer try and a conversion from near touch by Meninga.

The ARL must have hardly believed that the Origin series had developed into such a money-tree, commanding as if by right three of the top five places in the annual television ratings in Sydney and Brisbane throughout the 1990s. And aside from Lewis, Langer was as much a part of the success as any figure. When Channel Nine produced an advertisement playing on the one-time derisory cockroach and canetoad nicknames, the canetoad which devoured cockroaches was named 'Alfie'.

It is interesting to look at critiques of Langer's Origin performances in this series. Many judges felt he was too conservative, not risking the darts and kicking variations which were his stock-in-trade for the Broncos. In time, he would be accused of relying too much on himself to breach the NSW defence.

Had a pundit forecast in Queensland that in 1991 Langer had just played in his last Origin series win at the age of 24, there would have been much merriment in the Maroons camp.

When the Australian team was announced for the July 3 series opener against New Zealand at Melbourne's Olympic Park—the first Australian Test played outside NSW and Queensland—there were seven Maroons in the starting 13, an appropriate outcome from a knife-edge series. Hauff made his first, and, as it turned out, only Test appearance. Langer and Lewis were selected in the halves, but the ARL Board, as expected, retained Meninga as Test captain on a 6–2 vote.

Steve Walters' selection, ahead of NSW rival Ben Elias, meant the family from East Ipswich had become the first in Australian league history to provide three brothers for Test representation.

Canberra revealed Stuart had been playing for a month with pain-killing injections to deaden a torn abdominal muscle. In later years, Raiders coach Tim Sheens sailed into the breach in support of his playmaker, saying Stuart's incumbency coming into 1991 did not count as much as Langer's in subsequent years. 'I was disappointed why I wasn't given the right to play a game as the incumbent,' Stuart admitted five years later. 'I realise I was playing with a bad groin, but all they had to do was pick me, rule me out in a fitness test and I'd have been happy. I thought they were weak pricks. I was at my father's house and I heard the team over the radio. I thought: "Thanks for letting me know." It's always been the disappointing factor. I have never played a Test in Australia and that's incredibly disappointing.'

Langer thought his tenancy as Test halfback would last exactly 80 minutes after a listless Australian team were beaten 24–8 by a fiercely committed New Zealand. It was the third time in succession New Zealand had won the first trans-Tasman Test played after a successful Kangaroo tour.

'It was a disappointing game. We always seemed to lose the first game in most series when I was there,' Langer recalls. 'In those games, we took the other side too lightly. I thought I was lucky to hold my spot. I don't think I had the best of games. Luckily, we played a lot better in the last two.'

From the grandstand, Peter Sterling rated Langer's defence as outstanding and the half finished third in the Australian tackle count behind Walters and Ian Roberts. Lewis was not so fortunate, his 33-Test career at an end after New Zealand had inflicted the biggest Test defeat on Australia since 1971. Five others joined him through the out door for the second Test in Sydney. His replacement Peter Jackson—now with North Sydney—and Langer would reprise their halves combination from Queensland's 1988 triumph in Sydney when Lewis had been injured.

Langer's Man of the Match award in Australia's 44–0 romp was precisely the steadying hand his international career needed. His performance, described by coach Bob Fulton as 'simply sensational', came despite a broken and lacerated nose—a souvenir of a high tackle and knee early in the second half. 'The Kiwis were perplexed by his probing and nimble footwork,' assessed reporter David Middleton.

Langer engineered three of Australia's eight tries, the first for a back-in-favour Geyer. Canberra pair Laurie Daley and Brad Clyde also sparkled behind a new-look Australian engine room.

New Zealand were mugged 40–12 in the third game at Lang Park, which was the stage for Meninga's eclipse of Mick Cronin's world record of 201 points in Tests. His 16-point haul won him most of the awards going, but forwards Geyer and Martin Bella, and Langer were all outstanding.

In retrospect, the 1991 series can be seen as Langer's most potent and certain in Tests. The performances of the Australian pack in the second and third Tests were timely for him and gave him a springboard, for following seasons.

While Langer had scaled the heights internationally, the sky had fallen in on his club's ambitions. Allan and centre Chris Johns had missed three premiership matches, and winger Willie Carne two, due to the ARL's insistence on standing down players from club matches on the weekend before Tests. Brisbane lost two of those three to Illawarra and St George by the time Langer had backed up in body but not entirely in spirit after the second Test. They suffered a 26–0 embarrassment by Manly into the bargain.

Even with the salve of two premierships to distance the day of disaster, a mention of the St George loss at Lang Park in round 17 will still put a crinkle in the brow of those involved. The defeat was cut from the same cloth as the one by Canterbury during the Origin series, when six Broncos had been prevented from playing. They were ahead in the last minute, but beaten by a try from fullback

Mick Potter, the result of ball-handling which had utter desperation as its genesis.

'Every time that happens a little bit of you dies,' said Ribot after a 28–26 result which left Brisbane's chances of making the finals in the realms of the mathematical. Langer recalls: 'It was very frustrating sitting there on that day. You didn't have any control over things. I just think we had a lot of bad luck in 1991. There were a couple of games we could have won and didn't, like the St George try. The thing about playing for the Broncos, even then, was that there was always pressure to win.'

Eight times in 1991 the margin in Broncos games was fewer than ten points and Brisbane won only twice. The players drove their coach to the brink of despair. They beat grand finalists Canberra, at Bruce Stadium when both teams were missing their Test players, and Penrith, effectively 'out-Penrithing' the Panthers in late June with a 20–10 win at Lang Park.

Brisbane won all of their last five games, which only compounded their sense of loss, their victims including runners-up Canberra and semi-finalists North Sydney (caned 44–6) and Wests. They finished one win out of the final five.

Prior to the win over Norths, the Broncos directors reappointed Bennett. Some of the Brisbane media came to the press conference in the expectation that the coach would be announcing his resignation. But Bennett's handshake agreement was extended to the end of 1995 and Morgan, to assume the club chairmanship in 1992, was quick to offer the man he called 'the Supercoach' a lifetime term.

'He just looked at me for a second and said he didn't want it. He said he didn't know if he could put up with us that long,' Morgan said. Ribot said: 'To set Wayne up as the long term coach was the right decision and one of the great decisions they made. That's not to say there wasn't a lot of soul-searching involved because they were getting a lot of feedback from outside. It ran on the back of the Wally decision, so it wasn't popular. The other thing is if you look around at world sport, there aren't too many examples where people go and back the sports-person and come up trumps. I'm a great believer in the sports-person getting a better deal, but you've got to have someone running the business.

'We got the two decisions right and you wouldn't get two harder decisions to make.' It is hypothetical, but irresistible, to wonder how long Bennett would have been given without providing a premiership. 'If we had had a bad year in 1992—and by bad, I mean ninth or 10th—I think we would have had to make adjustments, whether in playing, coaching staff, or management. Those decisions would have had to be looked at,' Ribot said.

When Ribot and Bennett looked to the future, it was Miles who became surplus to requirements. He had missed four of the last six matches through injury. Hauff and prop Andrew Gee were re-signed during a period when Miles found Ribot an elusive target when it came to naming a price. In contrast to the Langer negotiations, this time it was Ribot employing the delaying tactics. Miles said he was offered a reduced sign-on, with incentives for playing more matches.

'It was so disappointing because after 1990 we were expected to go on with the job. Players just weren't putting in, week in— week out,' Miles concludes from the perspective of retirement. 'I got undone at the Broncos because I was injured a fair bit that year (playing 16 of 22 games) and had two knee operations.

'That was probably the most disappointing thing—after all the bullshit we had been through together in 1990 and 1991, and then to be told your services were no longer required unless you play this amount of games,' he said. Miles remains convinced that

Morgan and head trainer Kelvin Giles had 'put their heads together'.

'Porky was always into me about being injured. The other directors were great. They understood if you play a contact sport, you get injured,' Miles said. 'Whether Wayne took the advice of Kelvin Giles, I don't know. Kelvin was asking me if I really wanted to play (in 1992) and if I could really perform. I had no doubts on both counts. I applaud him for what he did in the early days, but by the end he was unreasonable in a lot of ways with me. I remember sitting there with Ribes and saying I wanted to win the premiership for the guy sitting in the other room, who was Benny. I went to Wayne and he said there wasn't a great deal he could do, which I found very hard to believe because if he wanted to keep a player, he would have kept him. I probably didn't put my case forward enough, certainly not with Ribes. I didn't say Benny and I had to put up with all the crap that came from the King's axing and now they basically wanted to do the same to me.'

As luck would have it, Wigan chief executive Maurice Lindsay, who had professed a wish to bring Miles to England in the past provided he played a full season, was in Australia at the time that the negotiations had stalled. 'Maurice caught me at a time when I was filthy at the Broncos about how could they do that to me. It's a disappointment that I couldn't play for the Broncos in 1992 because the ARL had a law then that players had to be back from England by February 1,' Miles said. Wigan, coached by Australian John Monie, won the Championship-Challenge Cup double in Miles' only season at Central Park.

When he retired to Brisbane to work harder than he had done in his life in his own dry cleaning business, he had some regrets— his biggest was that he had played four years for the Broncos and missed out on the cream of achievements the club would reap. 'If I had my time over again, I would have gone to Sydney after the

1982 or 1983 Kangaroo tour,' Miles said. 'It would have made me a better player. That's where Alf and some of the younger blokes were lucky in the whole timing of the Broncos.'

Miles, Dowling and Shearer left the club. Dowling started in nine first grade games in his last season, but could feel satisfied with his contribution to the club. Shearer joined Gold Coast before moving on to South Queensland and Sydney City.

The youngsters, Langer and the Walters twins, had come down from the treehouse and assumed permanent residence to become the senior Broncos, along with Gillmeister who had been a deserved winner of the club's best and fairest in his first season. Bennett believes the Broncos would have won their first premiership in 1991 had they made the finals.

'The State of Origin and Tests hurt us, as they did in 1989 when we lost five in a row because we had six guys on the tour of New Zealand,' Bennett said. 'We played above ourselves and threw it away against Canterbury. Over the years, we tried a lot of things to get them through the rep season. They come back to the club physically and mentally exhausted. The competition is so darn hard, if you are down 15 per cent, you are going to lose. We usually start the season well and finish it well. Why? Because we have no distractions, we play one game a week and can focus on one game as a team.'

In no mood for individual honours, Langer finished second in the Rothmans Medal count behind Canterbury utility back Ewan McGrady. Kerrod Walters, keen student of the game that he is, spotted an anomaly in the voting. 'Alf actually should have won the Rothmans that year. I reckon 1991 was Alf's best season, even though 1992 was when he got all the accolades,' he said. 'In the second Test, he won all the Man of the Match awards and it was one of those years when the Tests were counted in the Rothmans polling because the Test players couldn't play for their clubs. The referee (Holdsworth) didn't give him a point. And he was beaten by a point. So Alf should have won two Rothmans.'

Having fought with such resilience to win back the Test jersey and play in a successful series, Langer gave it away for the two-Test tour to Papua New Guinea in October, submitting himself to a nose operation. 'They cut under his nose and pulled it back to clean his sinuses. They put an artificial bone graft into his nose,' Janine Langer said. 'When he came out of the theatre, he looked as if he had been beaten up. He had no eyes, he was so swollen. When they sent him home, he was so sick he couldn't breathe because of the packing in the sinuses.' Langer, in his hard-to-impress manner, offers confirmation in his own way. 'I'd never advise anyone to get a nose operation. It worked, but the pain wasn't the best,' he said.

A BOY'S OWN YEAR

For most of the summer leading into the 1992 season, Wayne Bennett had his mind made up that Kevin Walters was going to be his third club captain. Four matches before the 1991 finals, Bennett had chosen Kevin Walters as Broncos skipper in place of the injured Gene Miles ahead of Langer. 'It was neither temporary nor permanent. I was very pleased with the job he did when we won in Canberra when Alf was away with the Australian team,' he said.

Tom Raudonikis remembers playing with Bennett in a touch football side contesting the 1990 Masters Games in Brisbane and discussing Langer as a potential captain. 'I was walking back to the car with Wayne and we were just talking football. He got to talking about Alfie and I said: "Wayne, you make him captain." He said: "Oh, mate," and not much else,' Raudonikis said.

If on-field communication was central to the captaincy role, then Walters was the man. He calls many of the plays when he plays alongside Langer, even though the Broncos have had one of the least structured offences of Australian teams. Aside from that, he was much more verbally assertive on the field. On the other hand, Langer as captain would assist the marketing operation of the Broncos, as he had a higher profile. Langer says that he was not fussed either way. 'Wayne pulled Kevin and myself aside after the end of the 1991 season and said he hadn't made his mind up,' he said. 'If he had have gone with Kevin, it wouldn't have been a problem for me. It wouldn't have worried me.'

Bennett sought the opinion of players, including Gene Miles. 'Allan was the logical choice to me, when Wayne was saying he was leaning to Kevin Walters,' Miles said. 'I said: "Allan is your man. He has the respect of the players and communicates with everyone." I can honestly say you can count his enemies on one hand. The only way he can upset someone is in a fun sort of Alf way. How would he have an enemy in the world? He wouldn't hurt or abuse anyone. He is the underdog, comes from Ipswich, he's three-foot-six and manages to do all these fantastic things on the field, so the public is on his side. Why wouldn't he have been a good captain?'

In late January, Bennett decided on Langer, Walters accepting the verdict with the public good humour, as well as with private mock indignation among his teammates.

'I just thought, in the end, I could potentially get more out of Alf by making him captain,' said Bennett, who had been saying privately since 1988 that Langer would retire as one of the game's all-time greats. 'I didn't think he was starting to mark time, it wasn't that. He had been a bit patchy in the previous two years even by his high standards, but it was more that I thought the responsibility would bring more out of his football.'

Over the years, Langer had become a more wily customer on the field, with a functional verbal component to his game. He had a firmer grasp of what worked on the field and had become more keen-eyed in reading trends, getting the ball to where the opposition least needed it to be.

'I can have more in-depth talks with him and he's got a

great grip on things,' Bennett said in 1996. 'On tactics, I just say to him: "Mate, will this work or am I wasting my time?" and he'll tell me whether it is the way to go. You hardly ever see him being flippant during training these days. He'll go into team meetings and be leading the team in stupidity, but the moment the meeting starts, he's locked in. Normally, his concentration span is about one second, but when it's business and I can cover things in 15–20 minutes he will be precise and not miss a point.'

'I don't make any speeches,' Langer says of his captaincy. 'I just do a bit of light-hearted stirring, but I also try to make sure they are geed up to play. If we have conceded a soft try, I might say a few words, but nothing too deep.' Kevin Walters said: 'If things aren't going right and everyone gets a little panicky, and a few adjectives are being thrown around, he's the one to tell us where to go.'

Miles said: 'As he got more confidence over the years, he would bag the opposition a little—like yelling out for the rest of us not to run at such and such a player. You'd know the player he was referring to was a little ordinary and the idea was to run at him as much as possible.'

'One day early in a game against the Broncos, Alf was geeing Steve Walters up,' Canberra's Ricky Stuart tells. 'He was saying: "Gee, you're looking fit, Boxhead (Walters). You're going to kill someone today. Hey, fellas, we'd better keep away from Boxhead today".'

With Canberra's Glenn Lazarus aboard the Broncos after a bitter departure, Langer and his team needed a brisk pre-season. Lazarus took time to settle into Brisbane, but his initial intensity about the pressure he felt from being the mantle of the 'last piece in the puzzle' subsided.

In the Tooheys Challenge, Brisbane edged out a 28–16 win over a weakened Raiders team at Lang Park. Afterwards, Laurie Daley said he expected Brisbane to make the top three. They overcame Gold Coast 14–10 at Wagga Wagga and next beat Wests 16–10 in Wellington in a manner which left Magpies skipper Joe Thomas to declare the Broncos had developed an aggressive edge which had been lacking. Exhibit A was Trevor Gillmeister's punch to the head of Bob Lindner, his rival for a Queensland State of Origin position. 'I don't know why he did it. I was just standing there,' said a non-plussed Lindner.

Brisbane lost the Challenge final 4–2 to Illawarra at Dubbo. Bennett said: 'We haven't had a better preparation in any of our five seasons.'

In late March with the premiership under way, Brisbane edged out Gold Coast 24–18 in Wally Lewis' last appearance at Lang Park. A late Langer solo try was the difference in a second half which continued Gold Coast's tradition of envy-stoked defiance. Brisbane got to within 10 metres of Gold Coast's line with two penalties within three tackles and Langer spurned the two points, even though the Seagulls were two points ahead. Four tackles later, Langer penetrated by stepping off his right foot, then his left, to score under the posts.

When Brisbane played Canberra at Bruce Stadium and won 24–16, the Raiders were without internationals Daley, Ricky Stuart, Gary Belcher and Gary Coyne—and they lost Brad Clyde with a knee injury in the first half. It was to be a trend in a season of rebuilding after a salary cap dispute with the NSWRL. 'If we had Allan Langer and Kevin Walters taken out of our side, we'd have troubles too,' Bennett sympathised with his former club. But from Brisbane's viewpoint, one of their major opponents was out of the way. Another would soon bite the dust.

After winning three in a row to add to the string of five wins which finished the 1991 season, Brisbane were outgunned 24–10 by premiers Penrith at Lang Park. Greg Alexander outpointed Langer, carrying on his general play kicking excellence which had turned the second half of the grand final against Canberra. In a *Rugby League Week* column, Sherlock—the nom-de-plume adopted by a veteran sportswriter went to work. He said the singles championships for halfbacks had just come to hand: 'G Alexander (Penrith) d A Langer (Brisbane) 6–0, 6–0, 6–0.'

Brisbane rebounded, however, to overcome Newcastle 12–8 at Marathon in a game Bennett rated as among the best ten he had watched after Langer put Brisbane ahead 12–2 midway through with a deceptive right foot step. The season was becoming something special.

But NSW's 14–6 win in the first State of Origin match in Sydney was the first and biggest blemish on Langer's and his six clubmates' season in the Queensland team. The series was the second and last time New Zealander Graham Lowe guided the Maroons, and Lowe had a particular regard for Langer's individual skills.

'Alf does a great Graham Lowe (impression),' said Paul Vautin, who did not have the same rapport with Lowe. 'Before the game, he would go through every player, 1–17. He'd get to Alf and he'd usually say: "Alf—you're like Felix. You've got the bag of tricks. About the 20-minute mark, you open it up and pull a couple out. Then with 20 to go, you open them up, and you pull them all out, Alf." Now, you go to Alf, "How are the bag of tricks?" He'd go: "Yeah, mate, yeah." '

Ribot interviewed the Brisbane State of Origin players to question them on their drinking after their match. Ribot said he was alarmed by reports that some players had still been out at 5am, with a game against Illawarra only four days away. 'Wayne has always said to us: "Have a drink, but don't come back full the next

148

day." ' Langer said. 'You do get carried away a bit, especially after a win. As senior players, we should watch what we do.'

But when Illawarra duly won 10–8 at Lang Park, it deepened the muted accusations of unprofessionalism at Red Hill. The complacency of the Broncos players had manifested itself not only in tired representative season performances, but in the ever-present slow starts. This trend, which allows opponents six or 12 points start before the team reluctantly kicks into more resolute effort or in massive leads which evaporate in second halves, has been a theme over Brisbane's seven years. Some of their greatest wins have been despite themselves—a case of talent and fright winning out over contentment. Sometimes the increased effort does not rein in the opponents.

'That's the nature of the beast with Alf and those guys,' Bennett said. 'Their biggest problem is keeping concentration. When they've got a game sewn up, they are challenging themselves, because they are very competitive by nature. It's a case of: "We are the Broncos. Someone will do something to get us home." When they get behind, you sometimes think they do it deliberately to give themselves a gee-up. They get some interest in the last 30 minutes and away they go. They come back physically and mentally exhausted from State of Origin. They are there in spirit, but they are not there in body.'

Yet in that 1992 season, Brisbane beat South Sydney 26–18 without six Origin players—Hancock, Johns, Kevin Walters, Langer, Lazarus and Allen. Willie Carne and Andrew Gee were injured and Alan Cann was suspended. And the Broncos won the sort of loose, free-scoring game they often lose in the middle of a season, in a heart-stopping 20–18 win over St George at the Adelaide Oval, which cost them fullback Paul Hauff for the rest of the season with a shoulder injury. That win came four days after a draining Origin match at Lang Park, and exemplified the greater steel and motivation in the Brisbane team after the disappointments in the previous three years.

Langer's status as the heir to the Lewis mantle was exemplified by a radio station's distribution of cardboard masks of his face to be held up as a sign of mass solidarity. Previously, the masks bore Lewis' features.

That second Origin game, which was condemned for its defensive bent, was one of Queensland's stoutest efforts, especially from the seventh to the 17th minutes in the first half when they played with 11 men. Referee Bill Harrigan sin-binned Martin Bella and Peter Jackson. Langer himself sailed close to the wind in the second half when he unleashed a short, sharp retort to the awarding of a NSW penalty. Queensland won 5–4 on a Langer field goal, snapped from 17 metres with all of 66 seconds left. 'Usually they go along the ground when I practice field goals, so I'll take that one,' he said. The field goal was another brushstroke to the public's picture of a one-size-fits-all sporting hero.

In the view of Langer's predecessor in the Maroon No. 7 jersey, Mark Murray, that moment of solo inspiration was one of many that captured the essential difference between the games of Langer and Stuart.

'There is no doubt who is the better individual footballer, although I'm sure the Canberra and NSW players would love to play with Stuart because of what he adds to the team,' Murray said. 'Stuart is the sort of halfback who pushes his team around the field and wins the game in 80 minutes. Langer can take a game over in five minutes because he is a machine-gun player in attack. He can hit you with a try and then in the next possession make a bust and there's 12 points. With Ricky, you know 95 per cent of the time if he is going to pass or kick. He organises better for his teammates.

Alf doesn't know what he is going to do, often, until he has the ball in his hands. His coach doesn't know, so the defence certainly has to wing it when he has the ball. You have to be ready for anything.'

The deciding game was a dead-end of frustration in a freeway season. Early, prop Martin Bella was left in a one-on-one contest with Stuart which he could not be expected to win defensively.

After two Meninga goals to level accounts, Daley created a try with a grubber, backing up on the inside to find Andrew Ettinghausen for a score which was slickly worked and impossible to defend against. A barging try by John Cartwright through tired, frustrated defence left the result 16–4 and the series to NSW.

Despite NSW's series win, Langer retained his Test position against the visiting Great Britain team—Stuart had missed key early season club games and the first Origin match with a knee injury.

For Greg Alexander, another of Langer's rivals, representative football had become so low on his list of priorities that it just didn't matter: on June 21, his younger brother Ben had lost his life driving away from a function at Penrith Leagues Club. Alexander and Mark Geyer, a close family friend, were particularly distraught and would eventually flee for a Greek Islands holiday to deal with their grief. For Penrith, football and their premiership defence lost meaning. But the football industry ground on without them.

Before the first Test, Australian coach Bob Fulton's gift for making every advantage for his team manifested itself in his capture of a leaked document, a tip sheet prepared for Great Britain coach Malcolm Reilly by a former Australian Test player. It detailed the strengths and especially the weaknesses of the Australian players, which were occasionally expressed in insulting terms. Fulton gave the sheet to Meninga to read to the Australians before the game.

Langer began uncertainly. A clearing kick speared off like one of his mis-hit five irons to Martin Offiah's left wing, providing the quicksilver Lions winger with space to embarrass the exposed Australian defence. Offiah beat his opposite number, Rod Wishart, and proved too mobile for Meninga, only to be deprived of a try by a stunning cover defensive tackle by fullback Ettingshausen.

There were the usual confrontations which would normally interest the ARL judiciary had the contest been at domestic level. A defiant Lazarus had to be physically dragged to the blood-bin with a cut brow, the souvenir of a British forearm. And Peter Jackson was floored by a high tackle by halfback Andy Gregory which New Zealand referee Dennis Hale considered a sin-bin offence. Briton Ian Lucas was sent to hospital with concussion after being felled by rookie Australian prop Paul Harragon and his career would never again reach the same heights.

Despite their five-day preparation, the Australians produced a stunning 75 metre try scored by Meninga after both he and Jackson had handled three times. A 22–6 win, never quite comfortably achieved, was theirs.

Rugby League Week's David Page regarded Langer's game as 'his probing best—the big British forwards had no answer to his explosive stepping, jinking and dummying'. The Queenslander made breaks of 50 metres and 30 metres, without being able to position his supports for tries. Langer said after the game: 'I was determined to play well after losing the spot on the Kangaroo tour. I lost my hunger, but I have it back now. I want to keep my place for the entire series.'

Instead, the Broncos halfback was bracing himself a week later for the sack as the Australian camp came to grips with Great Britain's 33–10 win at Melbourne's Princes Park. Australia had reigned the Ashes since 1973 and an Australian defeat was an oddity. But a 23-point humiliation. The biggest losing margin ever conceded to Great Britain?

So many things went wrong that the proceedings carried a strange fascination. When else in his career has Laurie Daley lost the ball twice in his own 20m zone in one game? Players in green and gold skidded over on the slippery, dewy surface when trying to change direction under pressure or remain upright with the grace of a novice ice-skater.

'I can remember Bozo blowing up about the tags [boot studs]. At halftime, there was ET trying on Rod Wishart's ankle boots. Bozo said: "Get those things off," ' Langer said. 'Jacko got the hook at halftime and he was full by fulltime, he was that disappointed.'

Former Brisbane Wests prop Andy Platt won Man of the Match honours to emphasise his standing in world league and Gary Schofield again tormented Australia with his short kicking game.

Fulton said: 'You can look at all the excuses in the world. The fact is we were beaten by the better side on the night.' He added: 'The last place I wanted to go for a Test was Melbourne. I'm confident we can win the third Test.'

Langer's fears for his position, however, were unfounded as Peter Jackson was the only casualty for the decider at Lang Park a week later. Wishart and Mackay were forced out with injury. Fittler and Carne came in, with Laurie Daley moved to five-eighth. Australia prevailed 16–10 to retain the Ashes, buoyed by two Meninga tries as he broke Reg Gasnier's record of 36 Tests for Australia.

A knee injury to Schofield sidelined him for the last 10 minutes, but he was gracious enough to concede Australia had been a better side. But Great Britain half Shaun Edwards, who came off the field in tears, was in no such mood for equanimity. 'If we had the space Langer and Daley had, we would have created more chances than they did,' Edwards said.

• • •

During the club period, Bennett sat Langer on the sidelines for the 20–4 win over Parramatta, playing Kevin Walters at half-back. Easts' competition lead melted in the winter sun at Lang Park. The 46–22 scoreline prompted Roosters coach Mark Murray to compare his team to the fabled Dutch boy trying to subdue a leaky dyke with one digit. 'They have been working hard to get together a champion side and they are very close,' Murray said.

Langer's growing difficulty with referees, particularly Graham Annesley, became a more urgent matter for Bennett when the skipper was sin-binned by Annesley for dissent when the premiership favourites lost 25–16 to Wests at Campbelltown. It was one of those aimless, niggly team performances which blighted every Brisbane season, even the season that had for weeks borne an 'at last' feel to it. *Rugby League Week*'s Sherlock sarcastically noted: 'Gee, I was thrilled for Allan Langer. The bloke played all those years alongside Wally "The King" Lewis and I was honestly starting to worry about whether some of the magic had worn off. Then there he was when a penalty was given against the Broncos and he is in there arguing his little head off, abusing the referee and got 10 minutes in the sin-bin for his trouble. Fabulous and sentimental stuff.'

But a four-point win at Cronulla added to the feeling of destiny which can sometimes accompany a sporting campaign. It featured a fluke try in which Langer, following his own chip kick, miscued a toe-ahead with the upper part of his instep. The ball spun back from its landing point one metre from the dead ball-line like a well-struck pitching wedge, and Kevin Walters pounced on it.

Moments like that and the Lang Park field goal had made

Langer's public recognition even more pronounced, especially with all Langer's advertising campaigns in Queensland. There was a television commercial for Allgas: soaped-up under the shower Langer corrected the voice-over man: 'That's Alfgas'.

When Tip-Top bread combined the authentic maternal feel of Rita Langer advising a green-and-gold clad Allan that he could go out to play if he had finished his sandwich, their sales increased 500 per cent initially. With an abashed look to camera it was his finest acting moment. 'Up to the moment it went to air, Rita was saying: "It took 144 takes, but it worked out well in the end,"' Kevin Langer said. 'The first time we saw it on TV, they had voiced over Rita's voice. We killed ourselves laughing. They reckoned it was too nasal, but the voice they got was just as bad anyway. She was cut but she still gets the free bread now.'

Tony Currie, his eye on the main chance as ever, suggested to Langer the idea of an Alf doll. The response was: 'Whatever you reckon, mate.' The blond, skinny doll was only a minor success. The craftsmen did their best, although the only similarity was the colour of the hair!

Allan said of the increasing attention: 'Wherever you go in Queensland you get noticed. It's good in a way, but it takes a lot of getting used to, getting stared at like that. I just try to go with the flow. It's good for me in terms of getting endorsements, but I don't go out of my way to promote myself.'

As the Broncos moved to within two matches of the semi-finals with six points clear of second-placed St George and consecutive wins over Canberra, Penrith and Manly, the jury remained out on their premiership chances. Lowe, the Manly coach, said after their 22–10 loss at Lang Park that some teams would be happy enough to meet Brisbane in the finals. And Phil Gould said after Penrith that while he would not put his money on a Broncos premiership, the refereeing style of Bill Harrigan would suit the flamboyant Broncos.

Bennett looks back at the 12–6 win at Penrith as the night he thought his team would win their first premiership. Winger Carne scored from a copybook backline play executed in the first 10 minutes and the Broncos matched Penrith, blow for blow, for the rest of the match until aggressive second-rower Alan Cann smashed over in the last minute.

Langer says: 'In 1992, we were the best side and I never thought we weren't going to win it. We were playing so well as a team late in the season, winning in Wollongong and Penrith, which were games a lot of people expected to find us out. Penrith didn't make the semi-finals, Canberra missed out and so did Manly. There were a bunch of teams who hadn't been in the semi-finals before, so our experience (in the 1990 finals and numerous representative games) was better than anyone else there. The enthusiasm and the comradeship was incredible. We really put in for each other that year.'

Ribot remembers murmuring to Bennett, in fear of mocking their chances, that the team was looking good. 'We were healthy. We didn't get many injuries towards the end of the season and it was back in the days when Gould and (Warren) Ryan would come out and imply the Broncos were soft in the underbelly, just arm-wrestle them and you'll get them in the end,' Ribot said. 'We were pretty well bullet-proof by the time we made the semi-finals.'

Langer counted down towards the finals series with concerns raised again over his trip tackle. Wests coach Warren Ryan re-activated his claim, first made in 1988, that Langer's tackling style of throwing runners over his leg was illegal. He added that winger Michael Hancock kicked out dangerously when he was tackled and that second-rower Alan Cann was sailing close to the wind with the height of his defence. Writing for the *Sydney Morning*

Herald, Ryan said: 'I suppose it is fundamental we try to find fault with a side that has done everything we ask of them. The thrust of my comments was that it was surprising certain things had not been cleared out of the repertoire of Langer, Hancock and Cann.'

With Brisbane getting the first week of the finals off because of their minor premiership win, Langer, Ribot, Lazarus and the Walters twins were able to fully enjoy their night out at the Rothmans Medal awards in Sydney. Until, that is, the polling got to the point where Langer could win the game's premier individual prize. After a nerve-racking wait, NSW premier John Fahey announced Langer as the winner, two points ahead of Manly's John Jones and Newcastle's Robbie McCormack. Rattling a speech off the top of his head, Langer, with a mischievous grin, declared a truce with the referees. 'I like referees now,' he said, adding later the award would not mean as much if Brisbane did not proceed to win the grand final. Ribot recalls: 'Alf was scared. Having to get up there and speak in front of everyone would have over-ridden the importance and the joy of winning it. That's just the sort of guy he was. When the speeches were over, he'd go back and relax with his teammates.'

Eleven days later, having declared the 26-year-old playmaker could only improve as a player, Bennett took the Broncos back to Sydney for the major semi-final against Illawarra. The Steelers started more effectively, scoring first through a converted try by Wishart, but by halftime Brisbane were in front with tries by Kevin Walters and Langer, the latter the result of a clever offload by Terry Matterson. Langer scored his second try midway through the second half and played out the 80 minutes with considerable aplomb—given their week off—to record a 22–12 win to book with little noticeable emotion a place in their first grand final. 'We didn't panic when we got behind, which shows how much we have improved,' Langer said later.

• • •

Bennett and trainer Kelvin Giles now set in motion the schedules that would bring the Broncos up to the grand final, in mind and body, despite one match in a month. 'It would now be a tragedy if after five years we let it all go with a substandard performance,' Bennett said cautiously.

The grand final berth was the cue for a sequence of events which embroidered the first time adventure and made it unique. No other club in the code has gathered, or weathered, such a circus around the biggest game of the season. To begin with, a record borrowing more than a little from a Monkees tune, called 'Hey, Hey, We're The Broncos' was released under the name The Ipswich Connection. Kerrod Walters and his manager, Barry Collins, hatched the idea, drafting in Kevin Walters and Langer. 'I was surprised we talked Alf into it,' Kerrod said. 'We released it for a bit of fun and to get a bit of exposure, mainly for my and Kevin's benefit because Alf had plenty of exposure by then.'

In grand final week, it was at number one in the Queensland charts and number 28 nationally, making Victorians and West Australians scratch their heads about the identity of this breakthrough band. It sold 7000 copies. 'I'm sure people who have them get them out occasionally for a bit of enjoyment. You can just see them—"what did I buy this for?"' Kerrod laughed. Shane Edwards, the Broncos marketing manager, said: 'The timing was just right, more so than the singing or the record. They recorded it and we made the grand final. The following year, they were going to do another one and we advised Alf to move onto his next opportunity. But it was a great initiative.'

Brisbane's Olympic 1500 metre swim champion Kieren Perkins sent a letter of encouragement to the team, which was read out on the day of the game. A farmer on the Darling Downs left rows of his fields without seed so that by September the words 'Broncos to Win' could be seen by air passengers flying over. Almost as remarkable was the Thursday afternoon when about 3000 fans clogged the Red Hill training ground as the red-hot favourites trained to rock music blasted out by the club's radio sponsor.

Through it all, the players and Bennett kept their nerve. For Bennett, the premiership would be the greatest validation—of his coaching methods, his ability to get the best out of a perennially strong team, and even his personality. 'It's just my nature and a mechanism I have so you don't get hurt along the way. I've been in this game a long time and seen a lot of guys get hurt along the way,' he explained. 'I have never gone out and sold myself to the media or the fans. It has never been about a publicity campaign for Wayne Bennett. Over the years, I have compromised and I can see other people's points of view as well.'

Bennett says he did not consider after being to hell and back over three years, what would happen if they did not win the grand final. 'We were just thinking about winning. I tried to take that pressure off them. I would have tried to make sure they were relaxed and focused,' he said. 'To tell you the truth, I was as loose as a goose all week, which in retrospect wasn't a bad performance.'

St George had edged out Illawarra 3–2 in the preliminary final and seasoned observers glimpsed the signs of a team that had popped its cork as captain Michael Beattie and teammates threw themselves into on-field celebrations. 'They have only one player in the backs who worries me at all—Alf Langer,' said Beattie.

Saints' chief executive Geoff Carr confirmed three years later that a feeling of achievement had inflicted the mood at Kogarah in grand final week. 'The Broncos were everyone's pick. They'd sorted everything out,' Carr said. 'Every week we got through the finals, it meant a real heart-stopper. We just beat Newcastle, just beat Illawarra. By the time we got to the grand final the Broncos were really hungry and I think our blokes were a little "Gee, isn't it great we got here?" It was a case of us over-achieving that year and the Broncos finally doing what they had been threatening to do.'

The Broncos players noticed Bennett's hands were shaking as he wrapped up his pre-match address. 'Wayne gets really nervous before a game. His teeth start chattering if it's even a bit cold,' Langer said.

St George started more assertively, Kerrod Walters having to scramble Saints winger Ricky Walford into touch two metres short with the first serious attacking raid of the game. But Langer, running on the sixth tackle, beat Saints second-rower David Barnhill with a left-foot step and doubled around Gavin Allen, accepting the arms-high offload which bounced fortuitously off the head of fullback Michael Potter. 'He's the new king of rugby league,' enthused Paul Vautin on Channel Nine's telecast.

Six-nil after 10 minutes, but St George coach Brian Smith's instructions to have his bigger, more mobile forwards run at the Broncos halves paid dividends when Scott Gourley beat Langer near halfway. Support queued up to supply Walford, who skidded over in the corner.

A 6–4 lead was taken uncertainly into halftime and it took 10 minutes for the Broncos to bury themselves into the St George 20 metre zone. Johns and Carne completed a breakneck chase of a Langer kick weighted into the in-goal and Potter, skirting to the sideline, was crunched into touch just in the field of play. On the third tackle, Langer ghosted out of dummy-half to his right, using —as many felt—referee Greg McCallum as a shepherd. He twisted past Saints hooker Wayne Collins, and, grabbed by prop Tony Priddle, kept his right elbow off the ground long enough to avoid the double-movement. Under high pressure, it was the instinctive play acquired through hour after hour in the backyard and training paddock. 'The great players make it look easy,' Peter Sterling commented.

Four minutes later, the grand final was won. Running again on the sixth, the Broncos back row ran in waves of support—Matterson, Gillmeister, Cann. The chunky Cann, turning the cover defence inside-out with the ease of a father teasing his toddler son under the Hills hoist, got rid of Walford, Potter and five-eighth Peter Coyne. Cann smiles are even rarer than those from Bennett, but he spiked the ball into the turf with joy. It was 18–4 and the last 25 minutes had become a lap of honour.

From there, Renouf's 90 metre runaway try after the halves had spun play to the right, was appropriate tribute to Brisbane's willingness to chance their ability in circumstances when many teams lock the ball under the arm and play towards the sixth tackle. Cann scored again, with even greater ease and cheek.

At fulltime, and 28–8 victors, Langer fought off teammates trying to chair him in, the traditional manner for the benefit of photographers on the swarm. 'He wouldn't allow himself to be in the spotlight without his teammates getting the same attention after a big match like that,' Ribot said. Bennett, a smile of satisfaction aboard, moved around his players. Unlike some recent on-field title celebrations, there was not a wet eye to be seen. It's not the Broncos way. As Renouf had raced away for his second half try, Bennett was puzzled at the arm-waving of assistant coach Steve Calder beside him. 'Steve said he was ceremonially throwing the monkey off my back,' he said.

The tee-totalling coach spurned the flowing champagne and an attempt to force-feed him a can of the sponsor's product, promising he would mark the occasion later with 'happy chocolate'. 'This is the ultimate for me and I'm pleased most for my family and everyone who has stuck up for me when I was getting back. The critics will have to shut up for a while,' he said. The victory speech of the captain, an automatic choice as the Clive Churchill Medal, atop a red-carpeted podium was classic Alf-speak.

'First of all, I'd like to thank St George for a great game,' Langer started. 'They put a lot of pressure on us, but it was also … thanks, St George. But also you have to look on the other side of the board, our blokes played great all year, they were under pressure coming down to Sydney. But also I'd like to thank all the supporters who travelled down from Brisbane (cheers) to support us today (more cheers). And also, to all the supporters in Queensland, waiting for us to come back home tonight. But also, Wayne Bennett has put five years of hard work into us and it comes down to 80 minutes of football today. So thanks very much.'

A hat of comically unspeakable taste was bestowed on Langer. It was made entirely of Power's cans, looking a cross between a toilet roll cover and a tea-cosy. 'The Power's hat came from a man in Mt Isa: a big guy with a beard, Mal Brosnan, who is a relative of Wayne's,' Edwards said. 'Porky (Morgan) got it and you could say it went missing at Porky's house for 12 months before it was resurrected for the 1993 grand final. Mal got it again and I think he still has it.'

In a Broncos room crammed with media and well-oiled sponsors wearing uniform maroon caps, Queensland premier Wayne Goss sought out Langer. 'I think it's going to have to be Sir Alf,' Goss told reporters. 'We cancelled knighthoods three years back, but we will have to bring them back.' Langer remembers being struck by the realisation as day became night of how much the Broncos meant to Queensland. 'I never realised we had that much support. That premiership changed a lot, all our blokes were getting recognised when they walked down the street,' he said.

With the Winfield Cup strapped into a seat next to Renouf on flight AN4002 at 7pm, the plane was filled with players, officials, relatives and sponsors. Down the back of the plane, unobtrusive as always, were Harry and Rita Langer, keeping watch over the latest addition to the 200-plus trophies displayed in their home—the Churchill Medal.

They knew the best was yet to come. But the scope of it, few could predict. At Ansett's arrival lounge at Brisbane, they started arriving for the 4.45pm flight from Sydney, evidently faithful that Alfie and the boys could do anything that day—even do a lap of honour, change and make it to the aiport in five minutes. Televison host Bert Newton was mildly surprised that so many maroon clad people would turn out to welcome him!

By 8.15pm, it was a sea of people. But that was nothing compared to the reception at King George Square, which was nothing again when it was stacked up against what happened around a stage erected on Gilbert Park, Red Hill. Langer, Kevin Walters and Renouf body-surfed across the crowd, estimated at around 3000, hands gliding them more than two metres off the ground.

The Broncos Leagues Club had a 24-hour licence. Forty kegs and 1800 cartons of beer were consumed in that time. People would spend the night under trees and on the field, being part of history in their own way. Inside the clubhouse, the night extended into slapstick as the Walters twins turned on a cake fight, team-mates grabbing and firing at each other. Hairdressers Janine Langer and Sharon Gee obliged the wish of the players to have a mass crewcut, shaving their jersey numbers to the scalp. Reserve John Plath had a red mohawk, with matching marker pen autographs of teammates. And Wayne Bennett compromised by allowing a C, for coach, to be shaved into the back of his head.

• • •

In the days after the grand final, eight Broncos were named in a 22-man team for a three-match tour to England, which would culminate in the World Cup final at Wembley—Langer, Johns, Carne, Hancock, Renouf, the Walters twins and Lazarus. Then there was a civic reception and street parade for the players, Lord Mayor Jim Soorley presenting Langer with the key to the city.

During this time, Ribot tried to rush together plans for a World Club Championship match against English champions Wigan. As well as being potentially lucrative, it had come to take the mantle of an extended grand final celebration, allowing wives or girlfriends a holiday at the club's expense. Canberra and Penrith, premiers in 1989 and 1991, treated the match with little seriousness, with players taking the field so underprepared it was a miracle the games were not one-way traffic in the direction of their British opponents two months into their winter season. The game at Wigan's Central Park raised the question of whether a mutiny of players had to be put down by Bennett and Ribot.

'What made me burr up about that was when I rang Ken Arthurson and I asked him whether we could play Wigan the week after the World Cup final, he said he'd have to ring Bob and ask whether he would allow it to happen,' Ribot said. 'I said: "The coach?" He said Bob (Fulton) didn't want his team interfered with. I remember (Australian team manager) Geoff Carr was involved then and even he was embarrassed by some of the things he was saying to me. A coach was running the game. Unbelievable.'

Fulton takes up his version of the dispute played out over the telephone lines between Leeds and Brisbane. 'The Brisbane players over there, leading into the final, didn't want to play in the World Club Challenge. The players were coming to me en masse. There was Johnsy, again, as a spokesperson, and they were putting all sorts of pressure on and asking my advice,' Fulton said. 'I spoke to Wayne Bennett on a number of occasions, trying to pacify the

scene. We are trying to prepare for the World Cup final and we
have this on our plate. My stance on it was that whatever the club
wants, you basically have to do. They have to heed some of your
requests, too. They had confidence in me sorting it out and it was.
Maybe it would be seen that I was doing Wayne Bennett's job. It
stopped what would have been a major problem for the Broncos.'

Bennett has a different version: 'The players were overseas
and we found out the reason the game was off was because Bozo
didn't want his players being distracted before the World Cup
final. I rang Bozo and he said he didn't want wives distracting the
players with the game coming up. I said that I understood he didn't
want us having anything to do with them before the final. I said I
would give him a guarantee that there would be no wives there
until the Saturday night. He said he had no problems with the game
going ahead provided that happened. We duly arrived in England
and the ARL were carrying on like a mob of gooses. They didn't
want to let them go that Saturday night with us and they took some
daily allowances off them because they weren't there on the
Sunday and Monday. Bob Lindner wasn't there, but he got paid all
his allowance. Lazo was concerned about being away from home
for another week. Also, he was in the inner sanctum with Bozo.
Lazo would have said to Bozo he didn't want to play. Players are
like that. If one player says he didn't want to do something, the
other players in the group will say they don't want to do it either.
When you get them one-out, they give an opinion.'

Langer, who injured his sternum in the World Cup final,
admits there was some resistance to the game among the Broncos,
but felt a one-in, all-in decision was always going to clarify the
issue. 'I wasn't over-keen to play. It had been a long year. But if
the blokes back in Brisbane wanted to come over, have a good time
and play Wigan, I wasn't going to say I wasn't playing,' he said.

Fulton's caution after Australia's scare on the 1990 Kangaroo tour was well justified. Australia only prevailed 10–6 at Wembley when Kevin Walters, coming on as replacement five-eighth, directed an out-ball to Renouf, who had changed the line of his run to the outside of opposite number John Devereux. Renouf brushed through the tackle and skidded over the greasy surface virtually untouched.

'Kevie actually called it a couple of plays earlier, but I didn't want to do it. He went looking for me again and it worked,' Renouf said. 'We had already done it quite a lot for the Broncos, but I guess it was good because the Poms weren't familiar with it. You know, I feel bad about it because I got all the wraps and Kevie was hardly mentioned. His pass did it.'

The Broncos internationals travelled north to the Lancashire countryside to prepare for the game against Wigan. But only after re-topping their fluid levels when the rest of the team arrived from Brisbane with a thirst. 'When we went up north, we were training up in the cold and I could see some of them weren't interested,' Bennett said. 'We had a meeting on the Thursday and I said: '"Look, we have a problem, some of you blokes don't want to play this game. We have to turn this around. I know Trevor Gillmeister and Alfie Langer will have a go regardless. If the rest of you don't want to play, let's get it out in the open and we can all play tiddlywinks and get beaten by 40 points." I left them to it. Lazo was adamant he didn't want to be there. The rest said they would play. Lazo played anyway. We got the job done. If Alf had a broken leg he wouldn't tell you. He had a busted sternum. We needled him up and he went out there. He didn't play great, but he was there for morale.'

Smoke from fireworks left an eerie blanket over the stands at Central Park, but soon gave way to explosions at ground level as prop Andrew Gee let rip at opposite number Andy Platt, sparking an all-in brawl. But the match would become a triumph for some of the less-heralded Broncos. Teenage fullback Julian O'Neill showed the Brits his ability as a runner with the first try. A number of players, Langer included, had backed O'Neill at odds of 16–1 to do just that and a windfall of almost $1000 helped to defray the costs involved with living next door to the Leeds Casino for three weeks. And lock Terry Matterson gapped the Wigan defence on halfway, and three supporters on the inside gave Kerrod Walters a clear run to the posts. Two second half tries by Hancock gave Brisbane a 22–8 win, fully 33 days after their grand final win.

'They put us under immense pressure, the sort of pressure we normally put on other teams. They were quite simply the better team,' said Wigan's Australian coach John Monie.

The victory, added to the home-and-away season and the finals, meant 21 wins from 25 games, the most successful in the club's history. The four losses for the year has been matched once, by Manly (four in 1996), and bettered twice (Manly's three in 1973 and Easts' three in 1975) in the past 25 years. 'It was a real credit to the team that we were able to back up when there were so many reasons to not give it everything,' said Langer, who had been taken out of the game after 45 minutes, with his team ahead 16–2.

Kevin Walters looks back at the year with nostalgia: 'I don't think the Broncos will ever get back to the level we had that year. We were hungry, but we still knew that we were better than the rest. We delivered that year.'

ST GEORGE CAN'T PLAY

Wayne Bennett had studied the phenomenon of premiership teams not being able to muster the necessary hunger when defending their prize. He was acutely aware of the early signs. But despite the conscientiousness of Bennett and others, season 1993 was the year when the Broncos became less soap opera and more comic book. As a series of cliff-hanger endings left observers wondering time and again: 'How are they going to get out of this one?'

Bennett held his tongue after Brisbane were eliminated 18–10 by South Sydney at Lang Park in the first round of the pre-season Challenge, but behind the scenes, Langer was told that he had to lose at least four kilograms. 'I feel sluggish. Maybe I ate too much in the off-season, but I'm not going to go silly after one loss,' he said.

When they lost their second game to Canterbury in Auckland, Bennett thundered to the press that a number of his stars had one more match in which to avoid the axe. The next day, the senior players turned the tables. Bennett remembers: 'It was just stupid of me. Our blokes are tremendously proud. They didn't need that publicly. Alfie and Johnsy said that I wasn't good to be around any more. I just couldn't relax with them.'

Bennett's anguish was typical of the pressure felt throughout the club to excel in their title defense in a first season at ANZ Stadium. The crowd of 51,517 to turn up to see Parramatta win the first ANZ game was the biggest ever to attend a league game in Queensland and the biggest in Australia for 13 years.

The success was disparaged, along the lines of 'What do you expect when you give away 20,000 tickets?'. 'My answer to that is we had to condition the people to not going to Lang Park to see us,' Morgan said.

The following week, 46,001 was the official figure for Brisbane's 12–10 defeat of Canberra, giving the Broncos more through the gate in two games than some clubs like South Sydney and Balmain managed in 11 home games all season. But the result, giving them two wins from four games, was more welcome than the support. 'It means we will have a week without the pressure of questions about what is wrong with us,' Langer said.

Brisbane ended St George's six-match unbeaten start to the season with a 20–14 win at Kogarah in which Langer, scoring one try and sparking the other two, owned the second half. St George prop Tony Priddle spent the night in hospital with concussion after being collected high by Langer and Kerrod Walters, both men having their feet off the ground as they leapt to contend with his size. NSWRL general manager John Quayle deemed the Langer tackle did not merit a citing. A suspension would have ruled him out of the State of Origin series opener. Walters was not so lucky, being called before the judiciary and outed for four weeks. The Walters suspension was the catalyst for a 20-page report in which the Broncos recommended changes to the judiciary process of the League. Ribot claimed in the submission to the NSWRL Quayle harboured a 'serious misapprehension' as to his role, and branded the citing system 'amateurish'.

Representative games were costly for Brisbane. Steve Renouf broke his ankle in NSW's 14–10 State of Origin win at Lang Park and Andrew Gee played 50 minutes with what he discovered later to be a broken jaw. 'I hate seeing what is happening to these players. It's like the Battle of the Somme at this club—and it's being done by external forces,' said Kelvin Giles, who as an Englishman found the annual demolition derby between the states beyond understanding.

NSW halfback Ricky Stuart's Man of the Match award, his second in as many games, was siezed upon by his admirers in the Sydney media to push his claims for that winter's Test series against New Zealand. Indeed Bennett sensed what he felt was a building Sydney media push in support of Stuart's return to the Test team. When Brisbane came from 22–8 down against Illawarra with 18 minutes remaining with two tries by John Plath and another by Terry Matterson, Bennett tried to claw back some ground for his captain with the senior Sydney media men in attendance for the match of the day.

'There is a certain television commentary team which doesn't miss too many chances to push the Ricky barrow,' the coach said. 'He wasn't the Man of the Match in the State of Origin match. But Alf, my God, he carried the ball today. He was probing and pulling defenders to him all day.'

Commentator Peter Sterling, a calculating playmaker like Stuart opted for the Queenslander when the *Daily Telegraph Mirror* published a poll of former halfbacks after the second Test. In contrast, Tom Raudonikis said he leaned towards Stuart on form. Up until then the worst result for his Ipswich protégé was for Raudonikis to say he was sitting on the fence.

When the notebooks or television cameras came at him, Langer would knot his brow and produce the pro forma answers that he rotated in and out of circulation when Stuart rivalry was in

Bradley Clyde is flattened by Allan Langer in the second State of Origin game in 1992. Queensland won 5 – 4. *Photo: News Limited*

The boot that did it — Allan Langer with daughter Courtney on the day after his match-winning field goal in the 1992 State of Origin match at Lang Park. *Photo: News Limited*

Courtney doesn't look too sure about new addition Maddison as Dad shows his girls to the media. *Photo: News Limited*

Brisbane captain Allan Langer scores and team-mate Kerrod Walters jumps for joy during the 1992 grand final. *Photo: Fairfax Photo Library*

Hail the new King Alfie. Allan on a lap of honour after the 1992 grand final win. *Photo: Fairfax Photo Library*

The best thing since sliced bread. Rita Langer congratulates her premiership-winning son after the 1992 grand final. *Photo: News Limited*

Great Britain captain Ellery Hanley watches and waits as Allan Langer comes his way in the 1992 World Cup final. *Photo: News Limited*

'Now this is what you do about the budget ... ' Allan Langer speaks with Queensland Premier Wayne Goss, a strong Broncos fan, in the ANZ Stadium dressing-room after a 1993 game. Trainer Steve Nance also has his say. *Photo: Brisbane Broncos*

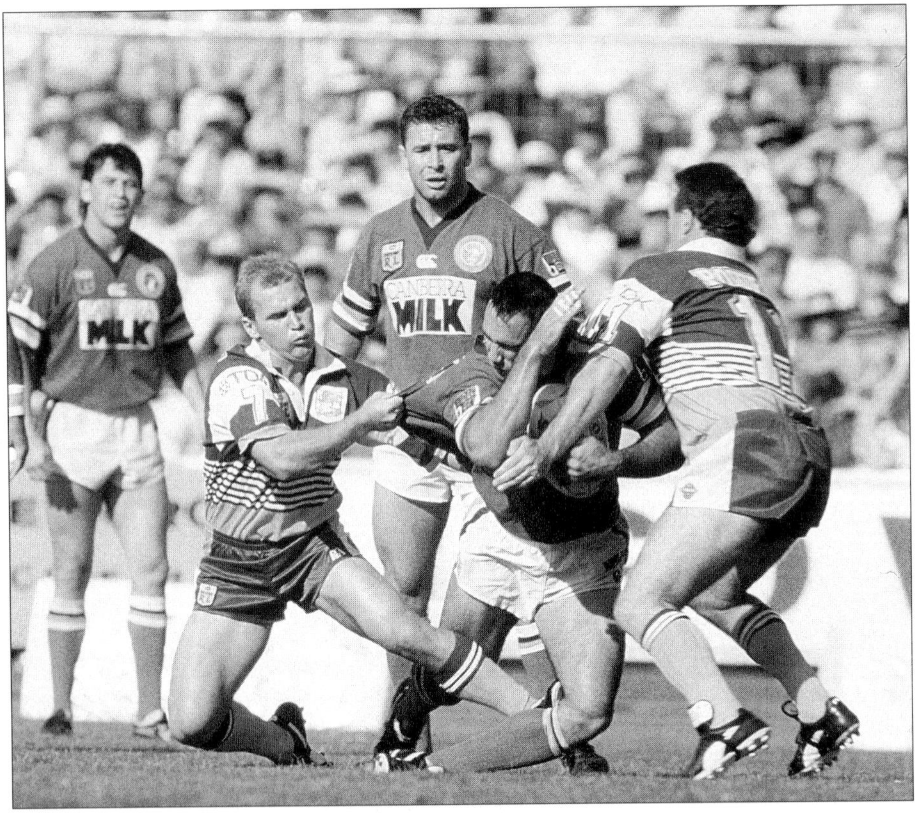

Get your leg out of there! Allan Langer moves into a two-man tackle on Canberra champion Laurie Daley in the classic 1993 match which was won by Brisbane. The game stirred premature talk of a NSWRL grand final without a Sydney team. *Photo: Brisbane Broncos*

The Powers beercan hat. Allan after winning the 1993 grand final. *Photo: Fairfax Photo Library*

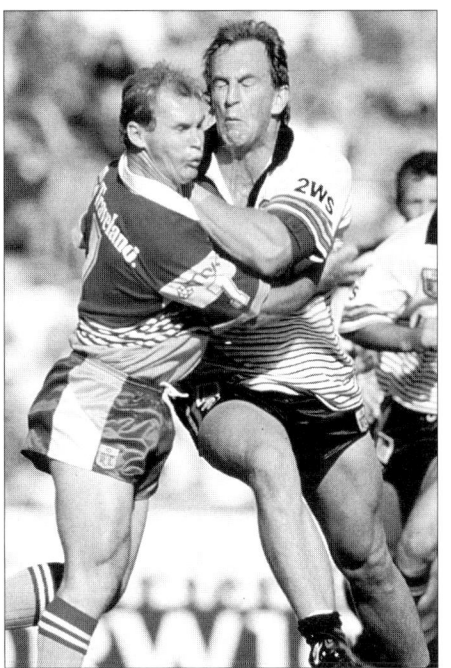

Penrith second rower John Cartwright, a 1990 Kangaroo tour teammate of Allan Langer's, is a handful in defence in this ANZ Stadium match in 1994. *Photo: Brisbane Broncos*

Diamonds are trumps. Allan Langer offloads in the love-it-or-hate-it night jersey in a 1994 club game. *Photo: Brisbane Broncos*

Allan torments the Auckland defence in the last game of the 1995 season at Lang Park which dashed the hopes of the Warriors to make the ARL finals. *Photo: Brisbane Broncos*

A few hours after he signed a Super League contract at Lachlan Murdoch's house, Allan Langer had his mind on football in Brisbane's 26-0 win over South Queensland in the first derby match at ANZ Stadium in 1995. *Photo: Brisbane Broncos*

In action against the North Queensland cowboys at Stockland Stadium, April, 1997. *Photo:* Super League Magazine/Jay Town

upswing. 'There is a bit of pressure on me ... I have to do it on the field and concentrate on my own game ... I don't have anything against him,' he would intone.

Attracting much the same questions 1200 kilometres to the south-west of Brisbane, Stuart was for once struggling to button his lip under his frustration. 'For the past two years, I've been injured every time I played against him and on my form I probably didn't deserve the job,' Stuart said. 'What I can't believe are the calls to overlook form this year and stick with Langer. It's annoying that since the first Origin game, every time you turn around somebody is saying how well the other guy is playing.'

Langer retained the Test position despite NSW's 2–1 series win, which will be examined later, and the *Sun-Herald*, polling all premiership coaches, published a list of their top dozen players. Langer was No. 1, followed by Daley, Clyde, Lazarus and Stuart.

In the premiership, the Broncos were locked into one of their phases where the game did not begin until they fell far enough behind that perhaps they had better start playing. Wests scored three tries in the first 20 minutes—bang, bang, bang—before Brisbane creaked into action. 'Even at 16–0, I thought: I hope Wests aren't getting too cocky for their own sakes. The fat lady hasn't sung yet,' said Bennett after a 36–16 win before 40,733 at ANZ.

The following day, Canberra and Australian captain Mal Meninga was cited and suspended from the same first Test against New Zealand on a charge of attacking the head of Manly centre John Devereux. The ARL then appointed Laurie Daley as stand-in captain, the first from NSW to do so in a Test since Max Krilich 10 years earlier. Daley had two State of Origin series wins, Langer one premiership, having yet to captain his state. While making it clear he had no problems with playing in a side skippered by

Daley, who was three years his junior, Langer said he hoped to be considered to captain his country one day.

'Alf has been around long enough to know that in the political games in league, jobs can be done on you if you don't go into bat for yourself,' commented Bennett, impressed at the assertiveness.

On balance, the ARL looked at blooding Daley as a long-term option. As he could play centre as well as five-eighth—and was indeed picked by Fulton in the centres for the first Test to accommodate the in-form Kevin Walters at pivot—Daley was a more certain selection, year after year, than Langer. He had three positions open in the starting team, Langer one.

As it eventuated, Langer believes he was fortunate to even make the tour as the spectre of his tackling style raised its head. The incident which made the issue snowball over the following months was not even the trip-tackle: it was alleged to be where Langer uses a leg to sling to ground bigger opponents. In Brisbane's 26–22 verdict over Easts, Langer had been wrong-footed by a sidestep from Roosters fullback Rod Silva, shooting his left leg out in what he claimed later was a reflex action. Silva, a man unmarked beside him, fell heavily and with five minutes left the Broncos held on to remain in fifth place.

'This was a good old fashioned trip—the sort of desperate and potentially dangerous act which earns an automatic send-off,' wrote Steve Ricketts in the *Sunday Mail*. Referee Stephen Clark elected to penalise Langer rather than take sterner action and there was disagreement between Langer and Silva over whether Clark had remarked on the field if the trip had been deliberate or not. Langer said: 'I was lucky in that Silva tackle that I had been picked for the tour of New Zealand. It was one time I think I was lucky. Maybe I should have been cited. The judiciary has been very inconsistent. When they kept going on about it, it was hard to take. I knew I had to make some changes because so many people were on the bandwagon, but it was hard to do. It was the way I learned to tackle.'

Pragmatic is rarely a word associated with Daley, an instinctive player and leader, but after his 25 metre field goal, two minutes from time to give Australia a barely deserved 16–all draw, there was no other word. The skipper said he ran the tactic past Langer as Australia ground ahead earlier in the set of six tackles, gaining Langer's agreement. Bedevilled by poor ball security which did not allow Langer and Kevin Walters to shine, Australia was again attacked successfully by short kicking, this time by the redoubtable Gary Freeman.

Under intense media pressure, NSWRL general manager John Quayle consented for Renouf—in New Zealand as a stand-by for Meninga—to be released to play for Brisbane against Manly a day after the second Test in Palmerston North. Fulton had been in an invidious position. The Broncos had insinuated that if Renouf had remained on tour the national coach's influence would have resulted in a weakened opposition for his club team. In 1989, Brisbane had been unsuccessful in trying to gain Peter Jackson's availability for club duty under similar circumstances.

So Fulton enormously enjoyed Manly's 24–8 win at Brookvale, having caught the first flight out of 'Palmy' the morning after Australia's 16–8 win in the second Test.

Daley had a bottle thrown at him, hitting his leg, as the Australians and New Zealand ran off the field through spectators milling on the sidelines. 'I personally feared we would be king hit and I know other players felt the same,' Glenn Lazarus said. Four footballs were stolen by the crowd during the course of the game, leaving the players to stand in the cold and rain for almost three minutes until a fifth could be found in the sheds. 'The cold was amazing. We would have walked off if it hadn't meant losing the game,' Langer said.

In the third Test at Lang Park only four days later, and the third in ten days, Australia again had difficulty with a well-organised, typically determined Kiwi team, before prevailing 16–4.

While the Test players had been in New Zealand, there had been Brisbane newspaper reports on Ribot's headache in retaining the internationals, plus Julian O'Neill and Trevor Gillmeister, under Brisbane's salary cap of $1.6 million. Brisbane's ability to retain all their internationals had become a source of wonder, even though the NSWRL auditors had not found them guilty of offences. But by 1993, Ribot was coming under more intense pressure to make some sort of tacit acknowledgment that they could not group larger and larger numbers of internationals.

The *Daily Telegraph Mirror*'s Ray Chesterton poked fun at Ribot's attempts over three years to assure all that players were happier to live in Brisbane and play with their teammates for less than they could get in NSW. Especially if they could pick up some employment or endorsement money, both legitimate under the salary cap rules.

'Ribot's grasp of fiscal policy seems superb enough to warrant a chance to wipe out Australia's balance of payments deficit,' Chesterton wrote on June 23. If Ribot was in charge of negotiating the release of the Middle East hostages, they would have been home years ago, feet up, having a cup of coffee.

'Brisbane have 10 internationals. Throw in (four State of Origin players). Tone down the amounts and average the internationals at $110,000—I can hear Alfie Langer and Lazarus laughing—and the Origin players at $80,000 and it still explodes the salary cap. The Broncos salary cap must be the only thing that expands in the sun.'

Regardless, Ribot said a senior official of the QRL-backed South Queensland Crushers had complained to NSWRL officials that Brisbane had 'rorted the salary' at a meeting in late June. 'It's a cheap shot and a distraction,' he said.

The richer, more successful clubs had been able to attract sponsors keen to throw individual endorsements and employment offers at players, which would not count towards the salary cap, which was increased to a maximum $1.8 million per club in 1994. Langer, for instance, had been employed with Gene Miles in the complaints department at major Broncos sponsor, Power Brewing. It was employment which would not have been forthcoming had they not known their way around a football field, but it is also worth remembering that at the time league was a semi-professional sport in Australia. Langer resigned in 1992, claiming the time at work was affecting his football —at that stage he was limiting promotional appearances, despite a loss of income. 'We thought it was perfect for Alf and Geno to do the job,' said John Crane, then Powers' marketing manager. 'They'd struggle out, have a chat, present a six-pack or whatever and then write a one-page report. There was a lot of innuendo that it was only something to help the Broncos with the salary cap. While they had allowances made for them for training, which was their No. 1 priority, I can tell you they reported in with Power's every day. Although sometimes you would get a call where you could hear golf balls being hit in the background.'

Quayle said on July 23: 'What the players earn above their football payments is their own business. To me that sort of comment is a cheap shot at clubs like Canberra and Brisbane.' On the other side of the debate, Quayle said Canberra and Brisbane could not expect rebates towards the salary cap for representative players they produced.

Looking towards the future, Ribot and Bennett regarded Renouf—sounded out by Easts and the Crushers for when he came off contract in 1995—and O'Neill as essential retentions for the future. However, Gillmeister and Mark Hohn, both 29, were expendable, unless they accepted less money than they had asked for in unfinished negotiations. Young forwards like Kerrod Walters, Andrew Gee, Peter Ryan and Alan Cann had been re-signed earlier in the season.

On July 9, Bennett broke the news to the two hard-working forwards. He tells the story that he walked up and down the training field three times before entering the dressing-room to tell Gillmeister he would have to accept what the Broncos were to offer him if he wanted to stay. Then he brought the team together and told them of the decision. It caused a furore among the players. An across-the-board pay cut was raised as an option by a senior player, but dismissed by Gillmeister.

It was one of the very few times when the Brisbane players were so incensed by a management decision that it was leaked to the media, in this case the *Courier-Mail*. 'I can't fathom it—I was ready to kill someone yesterday. They talk about club loyalty. I'll have to leave. I don't know if this means I will be in the team, but I can't give them a chance to drop me,' Gillmeister said.

The unrest of the players, exemplified in their well-meaning, but immaterial support, showed in a 38–34 home win over Cronulla after being outscored 8–24 in the second half. The result left them one win behind joint premiership leaders Canterbury and St George with six rounds before the finals.

Ribot remembers: 'It was reported in various places that our offer to Gilly was a bit of a joke. But it was a bloody good offer. We offered him a six-figure contract. 'I think he'd set his mind on a fixed figure. If he didn't get it, he was going. That was one of his strengths, that he was so focused. When we went into a game—

bang—he was unbending. How did we win? We were called salary cap cheats and had to release valued players. Mark Hohn was a similar case. He had signed a one-year contract and he was thinking about retiring. I said I couldn't guarantee anything beyond that. I really like Gilly as a bloke and I think that may have wavered over the years because of that. That's one of the hard parts of the job.'

One particularly agitated forward offered to Gillmeister, without a smile, to 'sort out' Ribot if he okayed it. That was the depth of feeling the nuggetty second-rower stirred among his teammates.

While Gillmeister left the club for a richer deal at Penrith, Hohn stayed on with the Broncos in 1994 before agreeing to play for South Queensland Crushers—the benefits of which were staying in Brisbane with a salary upgrade. He became the oldest Australian forward on debut against France in 1994. Twelve months later, Gillmeister relieved him of that distinction when he played for the ARL players-only team against New Zealand at Lang Park.

A week after the Cronulla scare, Brisbane produced their most authoritative game of the season, a 38–18 home thrashing of Canterbury featuring four tries by Steve Renouf. Bennett reviewed: 'Steve is up there with the really great centres to have played the game when he is on.' Three weeks later, Renouf had his jaw badly broken in two places, in a domestic disturbance in his home town of Murgon. 'When I got off the phone, I just thought how unfair it is to Steve and the club. We don't hold much hope of him being back this year,' Ribot told reporters.

Canberra had underlined their premiership claims with a convincing 20–4 win over the Broncos on a sub-zero Friday night in the national capital which left frost down the outside 10 metres leading into either sideline. New Zealand forwards John Lomax and Quentin Pongia tore into the Brisbane pack, reviving an old theme. But the Raiders would suffer their own devastating loss, with Stuart dislocating and fracturing his ankle late in a 68–0 humiliation of Parramatta, just two weeks before the semi-finals.

Bennett would paper over the cracks left by Renouf's loss, trying and discarding Plath as a manufactured centre before settling on Carne for the finals. By contrast, Canberra were annihilated by the loss of Stuart. He accepted the Rothmans Medal solemnly on crutches. The sight of him lurching away, deep in thought, down Driver Avenue after his team's exit from the finals at the Sydney Football Stadium was poignant.

On the morning of Brisbane's match on August 21 at Penrith, a shell of the 1991 premiership team which had still been good enough to embarrass St George the previous week, Panthers coach Phil Gould raised the stakes in the Langer tripping issue in his Sydney newspaper column.

'I'll be quite frank—I think Langer trips people,' Gould claimed. 'He might not mean to. He might genuinely believe that his tackling style is all right and so might his club. But they are all wrong. Just because Langer gets his hands to a player first sometimes does not mean when he uses his legs immediately afterwards it can be excused for being a trip.'

Langer reacted impassively when the newspaper was handed to him at breakfast and went out to score once with a hand in four of Brisbane's other six tries in a 34–14 win that was studded with Chris Johns' first hat-trick of tries for the club. Referee Graham Annesley was not influenced by Gould's comments, ruling play on when Langer brought second-rower Phil Adamson's head-of-steam run to an abrupt halt in the first half. It enticed a furious reaction from the home crowd.

'What he said disappointed me and fired me up. It's an obvious campaign to put pressure on the Broncos and myself in the run-up to the semi-finals. Some people must be keen to see us upset so another team wins the premiership,' Langer said after the game.

The pertinent law, as it stood in 1993, was that a tackler could introduce a leg into the tackle once he had made contact with either hand. Langer's style, except in aberrations like the Silva incident, complied with those rules, even if the results for the attacking player could be dangerous. There was, of course, no law which prohibited injury caused to an opponent in a manner which did not contravene the rules. The defect in Langer's tackling style was, and occasionally still is, that he has trouble tackling to his right. He tries to time the introduction of a leg to a tackle when he is side on, or in extreme cases, almost facing his own tryline in trying to wrench the ball-runner over.

The next week, newspapers rounded up former and current players to pass verdict on whether Langer's tackling style was dangerous. They included Cronulla back-rower David Boughton, who had dislocated his elbow and missed five weeks in 1992 when he fell in a Langer tackle. Langer remembers: 'For a couple of weeks, I wrote this campaign off as old news, because the first time it was raised was by Warren Ryan when he was coach of Balmain (in 1988). I was dirty at the other coaches because it was a ploy to put me off my game. They really pushed ahead in trying to do something against the Broncos. You know, maybe it was one of the things that held us together in the semi-finals, just another setback we had to overcome.'

Langer was disappointed, but not surprised, when his Queensland and Australian teammate Martin Bella was one player to attest to the danger of the tackle. 'Munster just loves to jump on the bandwagon, whatever it is. It's disappointing when your fellow players do that to you in public. Why don't they say it to your face?' he said.

However, Bennett says Langer hates confrontation and actively avoids it. 'In a lot of ways, I'm too soft,' Langer agreed. 'Too soft to say no, too soft to be upfront with people who have said things I don't like. They get away with a lot more than I should let them.' Asked why, he said: 'I have plenty of common sense and road sense, but I don't think I'm the smartest bloke going around.'

Depending on the results of the last round, Brisbane and St George could both finish in positions one to five. Canterbury, on 33 points, held a one-point lead over three teams—Brisbane, Canterbury and St George—with Manly on 30.

No other team could make the final five, but it was one of league's modern dictums that it was nigh impossible to win the premiership from fourth or fifth place, requiring four sudden-death wins in as many weeks. It had been done once since the system's introduction in 1973, by Canberra's emerging 1989 team.

The lights were turned off on Brisbane's top three ambitions, both literally and figuratively. 'We kicked off late because the stadium lights went out. St George got away from us and had trouble with some of their bigger forwards,' Langer recalls. 'What made it even more frustrating was the slowing tactics they used. Blokes hurt, blokes taking their time to play the ball, they slowed the game right down, which was obviously what they wanted.' Bennett went further after St George's professional 16–10 win. 'It's not in the spirit of the game,' he said.

Langer remembers the mood: 'It was disappointing, but it wasn't like we were humiliated. We were in the clubhouse after the game and this bookmaker reckoned we couldn't win the premiership from fifth. He gave us 4–1 and I was geeing Johnsy up for it. I wanted 5–1, so I missed the price. But Johnsy had $5000 on it.

We had to do it the hard way with the pressure on us and a few injuries. We were confident in each other that we could get there. It was just that Johnsy was more confident.'

On Sunday morning, Bennett's inability to put the match out of his mind led him to ring all 17 players, something he could not remember doing before. 'I just asked them to come to training on the Monday with a great attitude. Regardless of where we had finished we could get the job done. I turned myself around and that helped the players turn themselves around.' And it was emerging that Renouf would be back for the preliminary final if his teammates could get him there. At training, Bennett pulled aside his forwards—including Gillmeister, who was playing with a shoulder injury he was keeping secret, mindful his next loss with Brisbane would be his last. His message—for them to play as a unit rather than individuals—would not get a place in his hall-of-fame motivational speeches, but Kerrod Walters remembered it struck a note which rang throughout the finals series.

Brisbane punished Manly 36–10 in a knock-out semi-final, the Sea Eagles starting without the injured Geoff Toovey and losing their other creative force, Cliff Lyons, after 15 minutes with rib cartilage damage. The Broncos struck with a ruthless half hour, leading 20–0. After Kerrod Walters scored early, O'Neill crossed when Langer took a quick penalty tap option, the six-point dividend looking more a formality than a 3–1 bet. The only discordant note was when Lazarus (ankle) and lock Terry Matterson (dislocated shoulder) were ferried down the Sydney Football Stadium tunnel in the NSWRL's new medi-cabs, which whisked injured players off the field. Matterson's dislocated shoulder gave him such pain that he was given a morphine injection and spent the night in a Sydney hospital.

In retrospect, Brisbane were lucky to next play Canberra when they were so vulnerable. Brisbane next eliminated Canberra

30–12 in the minor semi-final despite Lazarus lasting only six minutes before his ankle gave way, forcing him out for two weeks. In his absence, Hohn's finest moments as a Bronco would occur over the next two weeks, as he and Andrew Gee took the match up to the opposition.

Bennett's right-hand man, Kelvin Giles, became the filter for the influx of home remedies and offers from get-rich-quick merchants that flood in whenever a Broncos player suffers a high profile injury.

'We were given some some special calcium tablets for Steve's jaw, but that was one of the saner ones,' Giles said. 'One letter suggested chants and incantations. Another letter suggested I had to get the players sleeping with their beds north-south to avoid injuries. Over the years, there were dead animals and lots of tablets, which we packed off to the drugs agency for analysis.'

Kevin Walters enticed Lazarus to use an electric impulse machine, which he claimed helped him be available for Canberra's 1989 grand final. 'Anything to do with Alf or Kevie, you have to wonder if there is a gee-up involved,' Giles said. 'Glenn wasn't sure if he was going to spend two hours hooked up to some machine and have everyone laugh at him the next day.'

In the preliminary final against Canterbury Renouf scored a try his first touch of the football. After everything that had happen-ed, not an eyebrow was raised. The amazing had become common-place. But Canterbury led 16–10 at halftime, given impetus by a mix-up between fullback O'Neill and Kerrod Walters in which neither claimed a bomb.

Walters repaid the debt to his team in gold, making two breaks from dummy-half in the second half for the tries by Langer and second-rower Alan Cann to salvage the operation and claim a 23–16 victory. Langer's try came after Walters spotted the Bulldogs marker defence unprepared for him to put the pedal to the metal. From the side, his captain moved into his peripheral vision with the precision of a NASA satellite.

For 25 minutes, the teams were locked at 16-all. Brisbane did not carry the ball into Canterbury's 30 metre zone for the first 27 minutes of the second half, emphasising just how close they had come to elimination. When they did, it was through Hohn's reflex catch of an ill-advised chip kick from fullback Scott Wilson. It gave Langer the field position to snap the third field goal of his career for a 17–16 lead, with 12 minutes left. The fatigue and stretched nerves of the Broncos could be no better exemplified than this. The Broncos players regarded field goals as an act verging on cowardice. It took them five seasons to land their first.

Incredibly, Langer knocked on from the kick-off. He leaned on the ball for support. His luck was in. Canterbury's English centre Gary Connolly took so long to steady for a field goal that Kerrod Walters was able to charge it down. Five minutes from time, Cann reprised his grand final try of 51 weeks earlier with two right-foot steps beyond Connolly and Darren Senter, throwing in a sidestep off his left for variety to wrong-foot the scrambling defence. It meant a grand final replay against St George, four weeks after their bitterly fought ANZ Stadium encounter.

Langer remembers being mentally drained by the week-by-week pressure in the finals series. In grand final week, he needed daily treatment on a shoulder injury—that physiotherapy franchise at Red Hill in September, 1993 would have earned enough to retire on. 'All week, you would think about the expectations that we were certain to make the grand final and win it. People in Queensland just took it for granted,' he said. Ribot seized on a comment from Brian Smith in an interview with ABC Radio that St George had wanted to beat Brisbane, not Canterbury, in the grand final.

'I'm certainly glad we're getting a shot at them because they're not good at handing out accolades,' Smith had said. 'If they hadn't got there, they would have told the world: "We didn't get there, so you haven't beaten the best." ' Ribot accused Smith of being 'childish'. 'I can't see how he can justify those comments. I'd like to think, if there is a rivalry with St George, it was a healthy one. The Brisbane–Sydney thing appears to be becoming bitter,' Ribot said.

This was akin to the Sex Pistols complaining about the decay in modern etiquette. It only added to the mix of emotions in one of the most rancorous grand final weeks in Australian league history.

Asked at the grand final breakfast why he thought St George would win the grand final, Smith replied that he had a better team and that he was a better coach. It was obvious he meant his team were better than in 1992 and he had improved as a coach in 12 months. The Broncos players chose to believe he meant 'better than the Broncos'. But the mind games were not all one way. Smith claimed early in grand final week that Bennett had said Brisbane would win more easily than in 1992. Bennett said Smith had twisted his words around in a bid to motivate his players. 'You know me well enough to know it's something I wouldn't say,' he told Brisbane reporters.

Smith distributed to his players copies of Lazarus' column from the *Sunday Mail*. The day after the final round loss at ANZ Stadium, Lazarus had said he did not rate Saints a premiership threat. Two weeks later, Lazarus had changed his opinion, warning that if St George beat Canterbury in the major semi-final, they would be 'virtually unbeatable'. In grand final week, he conceded favouritism to Saints.

Still, Saints supporters in Queensland sent streams of faxes of Lazarus' most contentious column to date to their club's Kogarah offices. Lazarus had, by now, been cleared to play in the grand final. 'The players are highly motivated by what Lazarus has been saying about them, to say the least,' Carr told the media. Bennett does not begrudge Lazarus his right to call a spade a spade when others, Langer included, would rather chew off their own arm than give the opponents any more motivation. 'Sometimes you wish he wouldn't. But he is a prop. What more can they do to him that hasn't already been done to him?' Bennett said.

The dogged enthusiasm of the Saints fans landlocked into enemy territory by family history or employment was nothing compared to what was going on in southern Sydney suburbs. 'The district went mad,' Carr said. 'The boys were better prepared to be celebrities than they were in 1992. I remember Mark Coyne saying every time he came home, the tape on his answering machine was full up from messages from media and well-wishers. They were more steely, more focused. We had a very good chance to upset the Broncos because they had had a very hard campaign.'

At the final training session, which was the lightest presided over by Giles in three seasons, Bennett remarked mysteriously to reporters that he hadn't played all his cards. 'I've still got the joker,' he added.

What he did not have in mind was Langer almost knocking himself out at Doomben races that afternoon. Rushing to watch Pregong, one of the horses he owned in syndicate with Matterson and Gillmeister, he was felled by a bookmaker's stand—moving in the other direction, he reckoned—and suffered a small cut above his right eye. He sat down to avoid fainting, took a glass of water and found out Pregong ran fourth. It was going to be a tough weekend.

'I wasn't feeling 100 per cent anyway with the flu and a sore throat, but you soon forget about it in a grand final,' Langer remembered.

• • •

American pop star Tina Turner, the figurehead of the NSWRL's long-running and successful advertising campaign, walked out to mime the anthemic 'Simply The Best' in the pre-game entertainment. As she walked past the opened Broncos dressing-room door Turner said, 'I'm rooting for you.' Folklore has it that a Broncos team staffer replied: 'Come in here after the game.'

After a long delay, St George suffered a horrific start to the grand final. 'Our guys knew by the way they had played the Broncos in the past that they were capable of beating them and the way was to keep running at their little guys, like Alf and Kevin,' Carr said. 'We had Scott Gourley, David Barnhill and Jason Stevens, just to name three, in that regard. Jason was determined to have a big game against Lazarus. All our players expected Lazo not to go the distance. Instead, after 60 seconds, Jason comes off with a thumb that was nearly severed from his hand. Of all the things that can go wrong … Lazo, on the other hand, didn't have to come off and played a typical Lazo game.'

Stevens was gone with blood streaming down his arm from a gash, and a double dislocation of his right thumb, and Smith was a prop short for 79 minutes. On top of that, centre Mark Coyne, one of St George's most talented backs, injured his knee after 10 minutes and spent more time off the field than on. At times, Saints would seem to operate without a back line at all.

Bennett had done his homework on St George's tactics of sending big forwards running at Langer and Kevin Walters. 'For one thing, Wayne tried to put us on either side of the field in defence as much as possible,' Langer said.

The opening 20 minutes of the game were so flat, so strewn with error, that Tina Turner must have wondered what on earth she had lent her name to. Saints forwards Barnhill and Priddle were particularly errant with their passes, a Priddle fumble giving Brisbane possession near halfway for their first try. Kevin Walters beat Barnhill and Priddle, and running free to the last line, drew to send the unopposed Johns over to score with all the excitement of a man with a $20,000 dividend hinging on the result.

The Broncos five-eighth reveals he was on a part of the action. 'Johnsy had let me in for $500 and when we got to the grand final, I gave him the chance to take the whole bet for himself,' Kevin Walters said. 'He said he'd see when we ran out on the field. We've run and it was one of those feelings you get before a game—you know the team is going to play well. Just before the kick-off, Johnsy grabbed me: "You're in." He's looked at it the other way. He was that sure we were going to win.'

Matterson, experiencing no residual soreness from his previously dislocated shoulder, made it 10–0 on the half-hour mark when Kevin Walters put the tryline defence in two minds. Then St George went to work with improved ball security and the kicking game of Noel Goldthorpe, pocketing three penalty goals by winger Ian Herron. Saints forced two line drop-outs midway through the second half, the latter a heart-stopping moment for the Broncos as winger Carne just barely recovered to force out a bomb which had taken a drunken bounce.

But the deciding passage of the grand final began when Goldthorpe had some 30 metres knocked off a clearing kick by a partial chargedown from Kerrod Walters. Brisbane methodically played their set of six and Langer weighted a grubber kick well enough to reap a drop-out. Hit-ups by Hohn and Kerrod Walters gave Langer the width to work the numbers to his right and Gee, feet planted in a tackle, gave Carne sufficient space to beat the cover defence to the corner.

A 14–6 lead with 12 minutes remaining was enough. With relief and satisfaction rather than the raw excitement which typified their success 12 months earlier, the Queenslanders greeted a fulltime siren as a release from purgatory. That it would soon install them in another is the price to be paid by winners. It never stops.

But at least the Broncos would get the chance to teach Tina Turner their team song. Langer procured a kiss at the presentation, and Kevin Walters would swing an arm around her. 'She went up to the best looking bloke,' the match-winning pivot claimed later. After a stressful week and what Coyne considered to be their worst first 40 minutes of the season, and on the day that mattered most, Smith was gracious. 'They might have moved into the great category,' he said of the winners.

Quayle prevented Gillmeister from joining Langer on the podium to accept the trophies as the Broncos players wanted. The ARL's advertising script for next year's campaign called for Langer and Lazarus, mirroring the long and the short of the figures on the Winfield Cup, to stand, grin and raise the trophy.

After the game, Langer and Matterson made pointed references to Smith not having won a premiership. Renouf said: 'See, Wayne doesn't have to open his mouth like Brian Smith does … he doesn't have to blab it out.' Smith was perplexed by what he was supposed to have said to have angered the Brisbane players. In time he would find out. '(What I said at) the grand final breakfast wasn't a reference to Bennett or anyone else,' Smith told *Inside Sport* magazine the following April. 'It was just that I thought I'd improved. If I haven't, it's time for me to get out. I was really disappointed with some remarks that were attributed to a couple of their players. You know, I think sometimes there is a bit of a lack of leadership in their place. I don't know who is in charge but all I'll say is that I'd be very disappointed if anyone in my club behaved like that after winning a grand final.'

Smith's comments on leadership were partly a reaction to the one incident that brought public criticism down on Allan Langer's head more than any other. It occurred when the Brisbane players, high on emotion and success and with the first furlong of the Melbourne Cup drinking distance in front of them, made a triumphant appearance back at the Broncos Leagues Club. In a voice either too well oiled or not oiled enough, Langer sang flatly in a tune of his own making: 'St George can't play ... St George can't play'. Urging the crowd to join, they followed uncertainly. That night, they would have followed Langer up to Mt Coot-tha if he thought it was a good idea. Earlier, Kevin Walters had asked a bigger crowd at King George Square: 'Have St George scored yet?'

Sectioned off from the fans, Langer, Johns and Kevin Walters made frequent phone calls through the night and well into the morning to Carr's mobile. 'They were saying, "How is the loser's drink tasting?" and "Carry, have you scored yet?" They were yelling and screaming. I was in the boardroom until 6 am getting these calls, so at least we all had our sense of humour,' Carr said.

The next morning, Channel Seven ran footage of Langer's sing-along and newspapers the next day detailed a subdued reaction from the Saints camp, with Carr being quoted as saying he could not be bothered getting into it. Carr recalls: 'I know there was a lot of confusion in our camp when the "St George can't play" thing happened. No-one was dirty on Alfie because everyone knew that whatever happened would have been in jest, knowing Alfie. He is one of those blokes who can say and do anything. He's just a bloke having fun.' But whatever the forgiving reaction of Saints players and Carr, the mud stuck.

Readers of *Inside Sport* in 1994 voted Langer their least favourite sportsman in Australia, prompting Lazarus to comment that the poll must have been conducted exclusively in the St George district. Langer reflects: 'It's one thing I do regret because it looked like bad sportsmanship. I wish to this day I hadn't done it. It was a spur of the moment thing. We had a few drinks and we were trying to get the crowd buzzing.'

Bennett thought the airing of Langer's song and another report by ABC Television showing players in a clear state of disrepair after at least 15 hours on the drink represented an invasion of the players' privacy.

Seven reporter Pat Welsh said it was his decision to put the footage of the song to air. 'I don't know we can be held to blame for that. It happened in a public place in front of thousands of people,' Welsh said. 'Knowing Alf so well, the St George players would be thin-skinned if they took offence. There aren't many people in league who don't like Langer, as cheeky as he is. Had another couple of Broncos players said it who don't have the same outlook on life that Langer does, then maybe you would think twice because it may be maliciously meant. You have to remember there was a lot of pressure taken off them by winning a grand final they were expected to win. Benny took it all very hard and went into siege mentality—protect the players at all costs.'

Through it all, Bennett refused to make public what his joker had been for the 1993 grand final—until June 17, 1995. In his column in the *Weekend Australian*, Bennett detailed how he had run into an acquaintance at Sydney airport, when the team had gone down for the 1993 grand final breakfast.

An eyebrow had crooked characteristically as he listened to how this man had come into possession of St George's game plan and tip sheet for the 1992 grand final. But the game plan, when it arrived by fax that afternoon, did not excite Bennett as anything that the Saints had not demonstrated by their play already. But the tip sheet, a common end-of-week practice to pinpoint the strengths, weaknesses and foibles of opposition players, was another matter entirely.

Back in Brisbane later in the week, Bennett arranged a half-hour with Bob Bax, a member of his match committee and coach of Norths' most successful era in the Brisbane premiership. Where the Kevin Walters entry read: 'Good hands, quick off the mark, not strong defensively on the left side', Bennett and Bax cackled as they added: 'Along with Langer and his brother Kerrod, known as the Ipswich connection. Kevin is the weakness ... he's over-rated and the other two run around trying to make him look good'. For another they added: 'not tough', and to another, 'thug'. To a third, they added 'lair', a charge to which the player concerned pleaded guilty at the end of the team meeting when the lure was released.

Bennett tells the story: 'Terry Matterson had a bung shoulder, Glenn Lazarus missed two games with an ankle injury, Steve Renouf had played one match back from a broken jaw and Alf was exhausted after Canterbury. We needed something special. My biggest dilemma was when to use this. I knew if we went too early, they'd be angry, but it would be gone by Sunday. So I held it back until the morning of the game and said everyone should sit down and listen to what Brian had to say about them, but more importantly about their teammates.' The Broncos players could not believe their ears. But the key is they wanted to believe.

The Brisbane players were told how Bennett had tinkered with the tip sheet early in 1994. 'We didn't know until then. It did get the boys going a bit, the way Brian Smith was supposed to have bagged some of them. It was a great ploy,' Langer said. Early in 1995, Bennett received a telephone call from a merry Chris Johns. 'Brian Smith has just found out. He's trying to find the mole at St George. He's ripping the place apart,' Johns laughed.

Carr was sitting in a hotel room in Adelaide, awaiting a club game the next day, when he read Bennett's confession, 21 months after the fact. 'Benny had an outstanding team and for them to finish out of the top three, well he must have felt like giving them a jolt to keep that motivation,' Carr said. 'Obviously, there are no rules about that sort of thing. If you can get your team up no matter what, it's the end result that really counts. We couldn't work out why they were so dirty on us. Obviously it came back to Benny's motivational stuff. That's football.'

And without Bennett's mischievous subterfuge, it is likely the 'Saints can't play' incident would not have taken place.

Leaving the 1993 season, it seemed only a matter of time before the players went on the same route in the year to come: the series of comic book escapes during the season until they won the grand final, the silly hat, the lap of honour, the jolly plane trip home, the rapturous welcome at the airport, the even more rapturous function at King George Square, the barely controlled return to Red Hill.

Or so Queensland, and many in NSW, thought.

OPERATION ALF

In Allan Langer's first six years as a State of Origin player, Lang Park was nothing less than a fortress. Over eight successive games, Queensland repelled the NSW invasion from the deciding game of 1987 through to Langer's field goal triumph in 1992. But then the stronghold was stormed and captured by Phil Gould with a hefty arsenal at his command. In the five visits to play against Queensland teams from 1993–96, NSW lost only one game—a dead third rubber in 1993, the Blues having already tied up the series with wins at Lang Park and the Sydney Football Stadium.

In the five series after Wally Lewis' retirement as a player, Queensland won the best-of-three contest once, when Super League players were overlooked in 1995 and Paul Vautin, a television star-cum-hobby coach, struck the right emotional chord in Origin's all-time long-shot team. It left a regrettable tinge of failure on the Origin career of Allan Langer, and the dominance of NSW would eventually cost Langer his four-year unbroken reign as Australian halfback.

Gould, a thoughtful, observant coach who measures his words and instructions with precision, had watched NSW win one series between 1987 and 1991. He had listened to Jack Gibson—a winning coach in 1990 after sustaining the heaviest series defeat the previous year—dismiss Queensland's professed Origin spirit as a myth. He considered some more. When his Penrith team won his second premiership as coach in 1991, Gould's time had come.

'I had never played representative football, but from the outside, it seemed to me that Queensland were winning over the years for some reason other than football,' Gould said in 1993. 'There is so little time for game planning effectively for these games and there are so many players who could win the games, but that wasn't coming out to the same extent [in NSW teams]. I decided winning was important to them as Queenslanders. In NSW, we don't walk around saying we are New South Welshmen. We were St George players, Canberra players or Brisbane players. As a team last year, I wanted us to sit down and decide what playing for NSW meant to them. The players seemed to be inhibited in showing how much it did mean to play for NSW. They played it down in front of the other players. They decided they were proud to play for NSW—so the ingredients were there. It just had to be brought out.'

Gould would lose plenty of dust-ups with the NSWRL officialdom and selectors over the years, having little of the clout that Bob Fulton wielded at national level. But he would get his choice as captain and main manager.

The first was Laurie Daley, the gregarious and universally popular 22-year-old who played in the Canberra side captained by Lewis' successor as Queensland leader, Mal Meninga. One player who would never have his position in doubt, Daley made a point of enjoying life whatever hand fate dealt him, culminating in his memorable fumble of the Winfield Cup onto a Canberra street during a parade after the 1989 grand final. Thinking ahead, Gould saw Daley's permanence and personality as assets.

Daley had been blooded in the 1989 State of Origin series under Gibson. Bloodied more like it—in the biggest landslide series Origin has seen. But over the next three years, he, Brad Clyde, Ricky Stuart, Glenn Lazarus and Brad Fittler were among the under-25 talent introduced.

As his right-hand man off the field, Gould wanted Geoff Carr, chief executive of St George. For a start, he was a night owl like Gould, who watched video tapes deep into the night and shared his liking for a contemplative beer.

Under chairman Don Furner, the NSW selectors came to the crucial though belated conclusion that changes had to be made constructively, and with a long-term view. Gould used 21 players in 1992. He would have used fewer had he been given the players he wanted. But John Peard had worked with 27 players in three matches under a two-reserve system in 1988. A year later, 29 players had been handed a blue jersey when Gibson operated with 17-man teams.

Daley attributes the Blue Reign in some part to this continuity, which reached its apogee when Gould convinced the NSW selectors to name 17 players for all three matches in 1996, even though a player like Jim Dymock was in need of knee surgery, according to his club doctor at Parramatta. 'NSW have stuck to the same nucleus for a few years. But Gus finds new ways of making the right point you need to be thinking going into a game,' Daley said. When the team convened at the Holiday Inn at Coogee Beach for the first game of the 1992 series, Gould was intent on combining the social excess woven into the fabric of the representative team format with the steady professionalism of the club scene.

'Gus and I talked about it and he was concerned that the party side of it could be overdone,' Carr said. 'The best idea he had initially was to get them into camp on the Monday and send them home at lunchtime Thursday after all the fun and bonding. They'd get things sorted out at home and come back on the Saturday morning, ready to focus on the game. The Queensland guys were so close and had such a good time together, they were prepared to go onto the field and do whatever it took to get the result. They had this myth that they couldn't get beaten because they had the Queensland spirit, whereas NSW's situation seemed to be fairly bland. Steve Mortimer managed one year (in 1985) to get that emotion among the players, but other than that ...'

The internal catchcry of the 'new' Blues became: ' "They can't be enjoying themselves any more than us". We viewed it that they weren't going to out-spirit us or out-enthuse us. It was going to come down to football. If we could get them to enjoy each other's company and to enjoy winning, we could get them to have the same respect for each other, the same as Queensland,' Carr said.

Gould felt Daley might have been intimidated by being captain in the same match as Meninga, who had been his Canberra skipper for most of his first grade career. 'Gus is a 24-hour coach and even during those bonding sessions when you're out having a beer and at nightclubs, Gus would go over to Laurie and say: "Now, Laurie, I want you to (do this or do that)," or "Laurie, they're relying on you," ' Carr said.

In that 1992 series, the Blues developed their 'golf' game, a pub crawl which became such a part of the folklore that it was never attempted again. Daley and Stuart devised an 18-hole lay-out in and around the city and the eastern suburbs. Craig Salvatori's gold sports jacket became the leader's jacket, as in the yellow shirt in cycling's Tour de France. A leaders board was fixed atop a pole, as in golf tournaments, and taken from hotel to hotel.

At each stop, Tim Brasher, a non-beer drinker, would decree the par for the hole—a par three meaning three seven-ounce beers (or another size if he felt so inclined) had to be downed in whatever time he set for each hotel stop. When Brasher called time, the players had two minutes to finish. Four beers would be a birdie for a par three, two a bogey.

Salvatori set a punishing pace in the first three holes, one count had him six under par after one hole, only to suffer the fate of many early leaders in golf tournaments. The ultra-competitive Chris Johns and David Gillespie were declared joint winners, Johns going the distance despite a moment of dismay in which he charged out through some swinging doors to the footpath, and the next hole, only to find both doors were bolted shut.

Queensland, meanwhile, were making their own adjustments. Graham Lowe returned as coach on the back of his 1991 success, but a blood disorder prevented him from giving the position his 100 per cent attention. Vautin believes Queensland 'lost the plot' in the two years under Lowe, reasoning that a New Zealander, such as Lowe, could not tap into the spirit which put steel into the spine of the Maroons in the 1980s. It is fair to say that in the 1990s the unquestioning belief of Queensland teams in the powers of the maroon jersey was not of the fever pitch instilled by the likes of Lewis, Arthur Beetson and Vautin in the state's golden Origin era.

Champion Canberra and Queensland hooker Steve Walters freely admits: 'Spirit helps, but you win those games on ability. It used to frustrate me that they (the 1980s Queensland teams) did so well. I struggled a little because I came from a really professional environment in Canberra. If we had a big game in Canberra or a semi-final, we'd be taking it low-key and resting up. For State of Origin, it would be the exact opposite. I tried not to get into the really late nights. They were always so successful with it. The hate for NSW was something that took a bit of getting used to. I'd be playing against Brad Clyde, Laurie Daley, Ricky Stuart and Brett

Mullins, blokes I'd spent 10 years of my life with, some of them. I'd be out on the drink in camp with someone who I met the day before and was telling me how much he hated these blokes.

'I'd look at them and think to myself: "I spent 40 hours with that bloke last week". That's why premierships mean the most to a lot of players because you are with those blokes day after day, year after year. But I was stoked to play for Queensland and I'd give my best. But the spirit … you'd read about it in the paper, like it was a competition—we're bigger mates than you are. I think they get carried away with that sort of stuff.'

After time, a distinct belief grew within the ranks of the QRL that Queensland were losing because it meant more for the Broncos players involved to be Broncos than to be Queensland Origin players. A loss of 'the faith', as a QRL executive remarked once, as if the Broncos were Sunday morning Christians. 'You want to win every game you play. It's as simple as that,' Langer said. But as comfortable as Langer was in the Queensland camp, he was even more sure of himself in the week-to-week environment off the field at the Broncos, as well as his own playing role and the strengths and weaknesses of the clubmates around him. 'It's a fair point,' Langer responds. 'You become comfortable with players you know.'

While refusing to apportion any blame to any of the three coaches—Lowe, Lewis and Vautin—it stands to reason that Langer and the rest of the Broncos would have preferred Bennett, who exiled himself from the Queensland team after 1988 to concentrate on his club and had not been invited back by the QRL. When Bennett accepted for 1995, he quit in the wake of the Super League raids when it became clear rebel players would not be selected by the ARL.

Langer denies the Queensland players felt as if they were playing in the shadow of the retired Lewis. 'There might have been some in the first year he was retired. Then it wore off. It's an interesting stat that we (Super League players from Queensland) still haven't won a series without him, but I don't think it's the real reason,' he said. Steve Walters said: 'Kevin (Walters) in particular would have found it tough. I'd have hated to play five-eighth for Queensland on the heels of Wally Lewis, who won some of those games by himself. I remember in 1993, Kevin was voted players' player for the second game and they sacked him for the third.'

When Queensland dropped Kevin Walters to the bench for the third, dead rubber, Australian coach Bob Fulton felt compelled to speak out on his behalf and encourage him that he was still in the international picture. 'After watching Kevin's performances in the first two games, the decision has left many people shaking their heads in disbelief,' Fulton said.

Kevin Walters, though possessing a unique understanding with Langer, did not convince the Queensland selectors that he was an Origin five-eighth. He reflects: 'State of Origin was the disappointing thing in my career, no doubt about that. We blew a couple and we didn't get a lot of luck in some of them.'

Approaching the first series without Lewis in 1992, Peter Jackson had scored a bullseye with his description of what Lewis meant to the younger Queensland team. 'Looking across at Wally before a game was like being a lost kid crying at the supermarket and then seeing your mum's face. But we're fortunate to have Mal Meninga,' he said.

Like Steve Walters, Meninga openly agreed that he did not like playing against Daley, Stuart, Clyde and the other Canberra players. Langer, similarly, does not and never has played with hate in his mind. Competitiveness, yes, and absolute desire to succeed, but not hate.

• • •

So the high octane resentment that fuelled Queensland through the 1980s was not sending the pistons racing in the hearts of the key players in the Queensland teams of the 1990s. But to distill the practical reason for Queensland's demise requires a return to the nuts and bolts of football, eliminating the mind games on the players which were the absence of Lewis and the team spirit.

Gould's selectors were able to give him such continuity that from the teams of 1992, Daley, Brasher, Fittler, Lazarus, Andrew Ettingshausen, Paul Harragon and Rod Wishart would still be involved in 1996. Stuart and Brad Clyde would probably have been involved were they not injured and they were constant influences when they were fit.

Gould was able to nurture and maintain a dominating forward pack in an era where Queensland seemed to stop producing big forwards, certainly of the quality of Lazarus. Harragon, Clyde, Ian Roberts, David Gillespie and Dean Pay would, over the years, provide that size, bulk, mobility and skill that their Queensland counterparts, however willing and industrious, could not match. It is worth noting that between 1990 and 1996, the two series of the seven which Queensland won were 1991 (in which Lazarus, hampered by a painful sternum injury, played only one game, and that as a reserve) and 1995 (when no Super League players were selected).

'Things go in a cycle and it was NSW's turn to really dominate after Queensland had all those strong sides in the 1980s,' Stuart said. Langer maintains: 'They had the edge in the forwards. We had a hard-working pack who did their best but we just weren't good enough to make our own luck. We were under too much pressure and you have to give NSW credit for that.'

Steve Walters offered: 'The only reason Alf didn't have the impact in those years was because NSW dominated in the forwards. Queensland won in the 1980s because their forwards were so much better and they had Wally, of course. The problem with the Origin games was you didn't have the combination of a good club side in attack, but because the best players were there, the defence was fantastic. It makes it twice as hard to make a break. I'd rather watch a club game between two top sides because everyone is more confident and knows exactly what their role is.'

Stuart said that Gould's concentration on controlling Langer as an attacking threat was remarkably thorough. 'He used to be at us all the time that you can't assume what Alf is going to do. If you think he is going to kick, he'll pass. If you think he'll pass, it'll be a dummy,' Stuart said. 'By the time we got to play, the players were all determined that no matter what happened, Alfie was going to finish on the ground. He'd still be one of their best players, but our defence just about always stopped him—and that's because we were so good, individually, in defence.'

The shrewd Stuart revealed he has a particular routine when he matches up against Langer, more so than other halfbacks. 'I always try to keep eye contact with Alf, so he knows where I am when we are in defence. We name-drop him of course, without over-playing him,' he said. 'I try to keep in the back of my mind where he is at any given moment when they have the ball.'

Over the four series involving Super League players under Gould's reign, Queensland would total 115 points at an average of 9.5 points per game. NSW averaged 14.6 points (indeed they won with 14 points on four occasions).

Only twice in 12 games did a team score more than 20 points—by Queensland in a dead rubber in 1993 and NSW, in the 27–12 win in Brisbane in the deciding game of 1994, which set the Gould era in an historic perspective by being the first time a state had managed a hat-trick of series wins.

Looking on as a spectator, Bennett chided Gould publicly (albeit subtely), for imposing a rigorous, percentage game on a team studded with brilliant attackers, and praised the bloody-minded success which the tactics achieved. 'A lot of us might prefer to see a more open State of Origin, but he has been so successful with his methods,' Bennett said.

While the frustration was apparent in the Queensland players, there was equal frustration among the coaches. Made Maroons coach in 1993 to public acclamation, Lewis was re-appointed after a 24–12 win in the dead third game. It would have been unfair of the QRL board not to do so. 'I thought we were unlucky in a couple of those games he coached,' Langer evaluates. 'It's hard to know how a coach goes when he has a team for a week three times. He was the king of Origin football and he really wanted to be involved.'

Steve Walters said: 'Wally came in a tough spot. The coach doesn't have a great deal to do with it compared to what happens in club football. You have no combination, so you can't have a great deal of strategy. There wasn't enough chance to judge them properly.'

Suffice to say, in the NSW camp, they were not looking to swap. 'I'm not being derogatory of Queensland's coaches, but Gus probably out-coached a few of them,' Carr said.

Gould had played a motivational card before the series-deciding second game in 1993, when he addressed why some wins were more special and memorable than others. 'I said they were usually the wins where the team is filled with your mates, where the game is close, the opposition tough to beat, the match alive late in proceedings and some adversity involved,' he said the next week. 'You can have all the money, cars and houses. You can't get away from the passion of playing the game and wanting to win for each other.'

That match encapsulated the era—Queensland's 16–12 loss coming as they butchered two clear try-scoring chances in the first half and had a fair try taken away by a refereeing mistake. Meninga passed to a marked, and eventually crunched, winger Adrian Brunker when his size could conceivably have propelled him across. Then Shearer, the leading try-scorer in Origin history, astonishingly lost the ball over the tryline attempting to plant the ball in a tumbling motion.

After the game, the Maroons would centre their disappointment on referee Eddie Ward's refusal to award a try to winger Willie Carne after he had climbed to bring down a Langer bomb— a planned move which has served the Broncos well over the years. Television replays proved Carne had been onside in his chase.

In the second half, which started with Queensland 6–0 ahead, Daley scored early, evading prop Mark Hohn and carrying Kevin Walters and Bob Lindner over the line. Three minutes later, NSW were in front with a try which confirmed the sense of impending doom every Queenslander had at the Sydney Football Stadium. A Stuart clearing kick was touched in flight as Queensland replacement forward Billy Moore attempted a chargedown. Fittler, leading the kick chase, turned to see the ball arrowing towards him and, played onside, he positioned Mackay.

But more surreal moments were to come. Five minutes from time, Kevin Walters fought his way over to get Queensland as close as four points behind. In the last minute, Meninga steamed down from the right wing from his own 20 metre area. Forty metres he ran, eyeing the chase across in cover from Daley, his eyes bulging with exertion from the pace of what had been a breakneck contest even by Origin standards. Coming to Brasher in the last line and Daley bearing down to his left, Meninga made the snap decision to slow and try to position the support trailing him. It was Hohn, doing magnificently even to be there, but he was the wrong man in the right place at the right time. The pass crashed to ground. The siren sounded and the series was lost.

How many times in his career had Meninga—he holds the record for the most records in the game—reacted instinctively in a big play and made it count? Now, he had twice misread the play in a four-point game.

The third match featured one of the wildest Origin brawls. Props Bella and Paul Harragon came up swinging from a 24th minute scrum. Steve Walters and his bitter hooking rival Ben Elias went blow for blow. Langer made a beeline for Stuart, the first and only time their rivalry had led to flying fists. The Queenslander was dragged out of it by Lazarus, the clubmate who would complete eight full seasons at the top level, in the toughest position of all, without throwing a punch.

Trailing 12–8 midway through the second half, Queensland turned the corner with a 24–12 win which allowed the retiring Bob Lindner to complete a farewell victory lap of honour. Lindner scored off a Langer pass over the top of Stuart and NSW fullback Tim Brasher before a Carne try settled the issue, and with it, Langer's retention of the Test position to meet New Zealand in a three-Test series.

As a study of helpless acceptance, it is instructional to sit through a replay of extended highlights from the 1994 series with Langer and see how close Queensland came. In the first game in Sydney, Queensland scored through fullback O'Neill after Langer had chanced a quick tap of a penalty with no conference with captain Meninga. 'I like to keep the game going. I have taken the wrong option a few times and should stop and think more often. You have to score off the set of six or it is a waste of an opportunity—and you don't get many in State of Origin,' Langer said.

But with 15 minutes to go, NSW had established a 12–4 lead, with back-rower Brad Mackay scoring a try off Daley, Ben Elias pumping his fist theatrically in the air with Mackay still 15 metres from the tryline. 'When we were watching the tape of the match later, we really enjoyed watching how they were rubbing it in during the game,' Langer chuckled, even though he knew how this movie would conclude in the last reel. 'We used to give it to Johnsy and Lazo when they would come back to the Broncos after a NSW loss. But as time went on, I'd feel a bit sorry for them. They were outnumbered. Of course, Queensland didn't win as often as they used to. That might have had something to do with it.'

Absent-minded in his bearing, he passed no comment when Willie Carne scored with five minutes remaining, but certainly covered everything that followed next. If you are from Queensland, you probably know it by heart anyway. Langer and Kevin Walters spread to the left to Queensland's back line, Carne releasing Renouf with a one-hand pass over the top. To Renouf's right they came in waves—winger Michael Hancock, replacement Darren Smith and Langer, for his second touch of the movement, following down the middle of the field. 'I didn't know where the defence was, but when Brad Mackay got to me I was able to get it to Mal,' Langer said.

Meninga grasped the ball and then replacement Mark Coyne, all under the stress of knowing that one handling mistake or misread option would mean defeat. Coyne, twisting and swivelling in a tackle, kept his right elbow off the ground and grazed the tryline with a lunge of utter desperation. He hit the ground as an able State of Origin player and rose from it with the unalterable fame which comes from deeds on a big sporting stage.

Langer laps up the scenes of celebration. 'You just see the elation on the faces—and you hear people reckon State of Origin didn't mean as much to us as the other Queensland blokes (from the 1980s),' he said. 'It was just natural ability. Coynie did a great job to get over from where he was. Maybe sometimes we could have played a bit more like that, but then you see later in the series how we killed ourselves with mistakes.'

The second game brought 87,161, an Australian record league crowd, to the Melbourne Cricket Ground and a Cheshire cat smile to the face of Quayle, who had heard for months that a half-filled MCG was no place to take the game's show-case contest. But with the Blues suffocating Queensland 14–0 to level the series, the vast crowd was all too often silent, either underwhelmed by the spectacle or failing to comprehend it. 'It was great to play in front of a crowd like that, but we were never in it and it was a shame it wasn't a flash game,' Langer said.

In the first half, referee Graham Annesley ruled play on when Queensland prop Andrew Gee, standing at marker on his tryline, was held back by Dean Pay momentarily, preventing Gee from tackling Lazarus, unstoppable from close range. It looked as if Gee was going at his clubmate and Stuart can be seen rushing in from the side of the frame to remonstrate with Gee. 'Sticky (Stuart) knows how to get up the noses of the other team when he wants to,' Langer said.

There was a graphic moment of defence in the second which captured the essence of the Gould Blues. O'Neill was barely 2 metres from a try, when he was converged upon by four NSW defenders. Blues centre Paul McGregor then tied the game up with a try off a reverse pass from Stuart, drifting across the face of the Queensland defence. 'It was a set play and Ricky had room and time. One of our forwards didn't trail across and there was the gap. If you relax, that's where good players like Sticky can create something,' Langer assessed.

The third game was at Lang Park, and was Meninga's farewell to Queensland before taking his second Kangaroo touring team away (after a third Canberra premiership). 'It is a game you don't like to remember,' said Langer. 'I see a few highlights or lowlights occasionally and just get out of the room. Until then, we had always played well at Lang Park. We lost Jason Smith early in that tackle by Ian Roberts and Gorden Tallis with an elbow injury in the second half, as well as Willie Carne getting knocked out by Brad Clyde.'

Three NSW tries in their 27–12 win in Brisbane came off unforced errors by Broncos backs Langer, Renouf and Kevin Walters. Firstly, Langer, pressing his luck on the sixth tackle 40 metres from his line, was stopped by the second defender he tried to beat and offloaded to the second kicker. The only problem was Elias, evaded the first time, had followed back to intercept and the hooker's quick hands gave Clyde a clear passage to the line. Then Daley, time and again the man most likely to make a decisive break in this Origin era of dominating defence, made it 12–0 with a breathtaking try, featuring three steps off his left foot to beat opponents, Langer being one of them. 'You have to stay on his inside, but it's easier said than done,' he remarked. The second unforced error came when the Blues led 18–0 and Brett Mullins came up with a misdirected pass from Renouf. It is a footnote that Queensland recovered to possess a shot at 19–12 down with 25 minutes to go—and especially forgotten is a Renouf try in which Kevin Walters split the NSW ruck off a reverse pass by Langer. But ultimately, the last mistake occurred when the Maroons five-eighth speared a pass above the outstretched hands of Meninga and Fittler swept in for an intercept try. 'He reckoned Mal didn't jump high enough for it,' Langer said.

Of course there was no 1995 series, not for Langer anyway. But it was a measure of his popularity with his Origin teammates and his ability to skirt controversy and recrimination that even though Super League players were persona non grata, as far as the ARL's representative scene was concerned, Langer was invited into the loyalist team's camp on one of the nights he missed so much that year. Channel Seven reporter Pat Welsh remembers walking into Brisbane's Treasury Casino late one night to find Langer and Queensland captain Trevor Gillmeister holding court at one of the blackjack tables.

'It was one of the funniest nights at the casino I've ever seen,' Welsh said. 'The hierarchy might have been at war but Allan was so well respected by the team that he was invited the night they went to the casino. It was just about mateship. The players transcended all the drama that was going on. I walked in there to see Gilly and Langer sitting side by side by the blackjack tables, with plenty of amber fluid aboard. There was cheering and high-fiving and punting up. The scenes were like something out of a Monte Carlo casino, the crowd that was standing around watching them winning. Gilly won something in the order of $18,000 and Alf won something like $13,000. They say he becomes Captain Invisible on the drink and he was Captain Invisible that night, sitting there, thinking no-one would recognise him.'

Langer laughed: 'They wouldn't let me cash my chips because I didn't have any ID. I got (Broncos team mate) Ben Walker to cash them for me. When I left, the sun was coming up, so it was time to go home.'

When it had become apparent weeks before that the Super League rebel players would not be in the Origin teams in 1995, experts looked at the holes left by the likes of Langer, the Walters brothers, Renouf, Hancock and the rest and concluded the Maroons had no chance.

Vautin had his senior coaching career limited to one season with the Brisbane team that won the Queensland State League, and happily accepted the coaching post when Bennett resigned. He looked at the glass as though it was half full, rather than half empty. There was a sprinkling of Origin regulars and nine players who had not played at that exalted level. 'I knew that with all those players, Queensland had lost three series in a row. I thought we could make the players realise what it meant to play for Queensland when we were all playing together and winning,' he said.

Although they were sent out 9–1 on favourites in the first game, NSW lost 2–0, 20–12 and 24–16. Lightning had struck twice in the same spot and then it struck a third time. Sydney City halfback Adrian Lam, drafted into the Queensland team despite his acceptance of Test honours for Papua New Guinea, left the series as one of the best five halfbacks in the game.

'That 1995 series was one of the best efforts I have ever seen from a team,' Langer marvels. 'They were never ever going to win, almost everyone said, and they scrambled in defence, saving so many tries, just having a go for each other. I was hoping they would win, but I didn't think they could. To win 3–0 was unbelievable.'

When the Federal Court decision in February, 1996 ruled Super League illegal pending an appeal, the ARL brought the rebel players back into the fold for the Origin series. Vautin recalls it was apparent in the first few days of the camp, that even the Queensland State of Origin team, a bastion of old style values of team spirit, had become a victim of the Super League war.

'In 1995, we had extenuating circumstances. It was something very special that team had,' Vautin reflects. 'Talking to the players who played again in 1996, they were saying the feeling wasn't the same. I said: "It doesn't matter. You won't get the same feeling you got last year, that was something special. We weren't supposed to win and we did. This team can do exactly the same."

'A few of them—Mark Coyne, Tony Hearn—felt intimidated by the Broncos being in the side. Tony Hearn came to me after the first game and said "a few of us are a bit intimidated". I couldn't understand it. I said to them: "There is no reason to feel that way. They are terrific blokes and they want to win like you do. Use their abilities." It was really hard for me. I knew there were a couple of problems, which I couldn't put my finger on. I tried to get it to gel, but I couldn't work out how to do it. They were a bit stand-offish from each other. We separated most of them in rooms. But I wouldn't say they were cliqueish.'

Langer's friend Gene Miles set the scene in another context. 'Alf said to me that it would be hard going into the camp because there were a lot of new faces. He didn't have Kevin or Kerrod Walters. Never for one moment would he have thought he couldn't win that game,' Miles said. 'He didn't agree with a lot of the selections, which was understandable. He had quite a few question marks over a number of players in the side. I don't want to mention the players, for his sake, but the side that he would pick and the side he was playing with were two different sides.'

To that, Vautin replies: 'Most of the teams you play in there are blokes there you wouldn't necessarily pick yourself. But you get on with it and sometimes you find your opinion changes.'

The dynamic worked the other way with NSW. Rebels such as Daley, Lazarus and Ettingshausen had watched their Origin teammates of years' standing lose the unlosable Origin series. 'They were just rapt to be back together. They wanted to win together again and the politics weren't important to them,' Gould said.

The choice of Jason Smith, who had excelled at five-eighth in

1995, was another matter. Smith had played a bare handful of matches in that position and would pick up Fittler and Daley, as the two more elusive NSW backs alternated positions. Kevin Walters missed selection, even on the bench.

Langer was sick in the dressing-room before his searching return to Origin football, but it does not signify in itself that he was especially anxious about the significance of the result. 'I get sick before every game,' he says. 'I can get sick before the game, at halftime and after the game, but mostly before. It doesn't do me any good. I get headaches sometimes during games. I can't eat a lot on match days. Then I feel all empty later. By the end of a game, I'm starving. Sometimes I don't feel like going to games.'

The wonder of it is that he can be churning so badly internally and usually appear so composed and quick-witted on the exterior. But Langer was especially uncertain before this opening match of the 1996 series, with the pervading atmosphere in the camp. He was hopeful, rather than confident.

Though skilful with the ball, Smith had played little football coming into the game because of a knee injury and as NSW's 14–6 win unfurled it was apparent the combination between the halves was bordering on non-existent. Twice Smith knocked on from Langer passes which fell short of the target without being exactly uncatchable.

In a series to be dominated by tries from kicks as both teams struggled to make incisions in attack through more fluent means, both NSW tries came from kicks by captain Fittler. The Blues forwards reasserted supremacy—it was often narrow but invariably discernible over these five series—and dummy-half Geoff Toovey made valuable ground.

Early in the second half, Langer scored from a quick tap. Referee David Manson ignored Toovey's complaints, justified according to video replays, that the Queensland half had slammed the ball down short of the line. The home team were within six points.

When Langer plied his craft in the sixth tackle, the Blues either closed them down—Wishart and Daley reading and covering grubber kicks—or looked on as a lack of understanding between the Queenslanders became evident time and again. Vautin described the Queenslanders as 'pansies'.

Langer was made captain for the second game in Sydney when Gillmeister was dropped. 'I'm pleased to captain Queensland, but not at the expense of Gilly,' he said. Steve Walters returned from a shoulder injury in the place of the improved Wayne Bartrim but he dismissed the notion from some commentators that he could be a one-man antidote. 'I came in for the second game with one game in six months. I was pleased Kevin (Walters) was brought back on the bench and I'm sure Alf was as well,' Steve said.

The Brisbane defeat had triggered even greater second-guessing and third-guessing within the Queensland camp—what did that bloke mean when he said that? What was he really thinking? What was he being told by his mates in the ARL/Super League faction outside the camp?

Vautin was learning, as many do, that coaching is no sequence of brilliantly perceived strategies and motivational points executed by players with their wits about them. His legion of admirers from his television appearances see a brash larrikin brimming with self-confidence. Friends insist there is a sensitive side to his personality which reacts best to acceptance and goodwill. But the point is that Vautin is not the bullet-proof persona seen on the small screen. At a time, one-down, two to play, when he craved approbation, he found the forces at play in rugby league in a wider context too hard to suppress.

Vautin said Steve Walters was the only rebel to offer feedback on his coaching, during or after the series. 'He came up to me after the third game and said he was really impressed with what I had done—he didn't have to, it was nice of him to say that. I'd like to think he was genuine. I'm sure he was,' he reflects.

'The Broncos players handled the reintroduction (of Super League players) to Origin football better than ours did. They played to their potential, whereas ours didn't. I can't offer any excuses. I don't know what they said when they got back to the Broncos, what they thought of me, what they thought of the whole thing. I do know Wayne Bennett was ringing them all every day ... anyway. I wish he had have rung me and asked how it was going. I'm thinking: "What is he saying to them? Is he telling them to play their own game?" I still don't know. I must be off with Wayne. The other thing that happened (before the second game) was that a Sydney newspaper said I didn't want Langer in the side, I wanted Lam as halfback. It was absolute, total fabrication.'

However, Danny Weidler from the *Sun-Herald*, stood by his report of June 9 which said that sources in the Queensland and NSW camps told him there was an internal push within the Queensland camp for Lam to start at halfback. Weidler also stated Lam was Vautin's personal preference ahead of Langer for the second game.

Vautin said: 'Weidler is Adrian Lam's man. I said to Adrian a couple of things along the line of: "Last year is last year, this is this year and you have to bide your time. When I can use you, I will use you. I can't use you as halfback". Out of all that, Adrian Lam has said to this journalist, "Oh, I think Fatty wants to use me as halfback". Next thing this is in the press and I'm going back to Alf and saying: "This is bullshit". He said: "Don't worry about it". But I know it didn't affect his on-field performances.'

Weidler said Lam had backed the newspaper report completely a week later after the furore erupted. 'It took courage for Adrian to come out and say that and I appreciate what he did,' he said.

Also before the second game, rumours spread in Brisbane of a comment Vautin was supposed to have made after an interview in a radio commentary box, to the effect that he would be happy if the selectors gave him the 1995 team of ARL loyalists in total for the second game.

'That was ridiculous. I didn't say anything like that. But some other people might have been saying that and telling people all sorts of things,' Vautin said. Langer responded: 'I didn't have to ask him. He came straight up to me and told me the rumours were wrong. I had to take his word for it. I didn't have a problem with him.'

Undoubtedly there were those in the Queensland Rugby League, and certainly at least one member of the Queensland team management, who would have been thrilled if there had been no Super League players.

'To be honest, if I played in 1995 and won the series, it would burn me if I didn't get the chance to play against the best NSW team, with Daley and Lazarus and the rest, which isn't to argue (the merits of) ARL or Super League,' Steve Walters said. 'They did exceptionally well in 1995. If they'd picked the team from 1995, I wouldn't have whinged about it. I would have been curious to see how they went, myself.' Langer said: 'I can agree with that. I wouldn't have complained. But I was glad to play for Queensland again. Not playing in that series was disappointing for the Super League players. There was pressure on us in 1996.'

But in Sydney, as he awaited the result of the Federal Court appeal brought by Super League, John Ribot bristled at criticism of Langer. 'The stories I was hearing that he wasn't having a dig was an absolute insult. You can't say that about that sort of player—Alfie would play you for your last two cents,' Ribot said.

Queensland started promisingly at the Sydney Football Stadium, Brasher just beating Wendell Sailor—one of the few individual successes in his team in Brisbane—to a Langer chip. Steve Walters was curiously sin-binned by Manson for packing into a scrum over-vigorously, but Queensland scored the first try when Wishart was caught slightly out of position by a Langer bomb. Renouf pounced on the loose ball for a 6–2 lead. Then there was the introduction of Kevin Walters to five-eighth, with O'Neill switching to fullback.

Vautin said: 'They were all saying Alf goes no good unless Kevin Walters is beside him. The selectors picked him (Walters) and I put him on after 20 minutes and nothing happened.' Kevin Walters often played for Queensland as if he were all too aware that he was on his last chance, none more so than in this game. Trying too hard to make something happen under the pressure exerted by the NSW defence late in the first half, his fluffed chip was swiped almost off his boot by Daley and taken half the length of the field.

Manson then awarded a highly contentious penalty to NSW for a late tackle on Ettingshausen by O'Neill. Fittler gambled for six instead of two and the Blues were able to stretch Queensland to breaking point to the right wing, where Wishart made it count with a strong finish. Three minutes into the second half, Toovey penetrated from dummy-half and sent Mullins across. Then Andrew Johns, the cultured Newcastle halfback packing in at hooker as an expedient, launched a magnificent bomb fully 30 metres across the field. It landed squarely on the chest of the unmarked Mullins for a 16–6 lead. In contrast, luck or a high degree of skill under pressure eluded Queensland as an O'Neill chip bounced off the shoulder of the leaping Sailor. With 25 minutes remaining, Langer lost the ball on a reverse pass from Steve Walters.

215

Langer probed too much, as he readily admits: 'When we got a chance, we tried too hard. I certainly did. I was too worried about other players, rather than worrying about myself.' His attack, increasingly of a solo nature in this series, carried the telltale signs of a playmaker lacking in confidence in the players around him. 'I never thought I'd say it, but Allan Langer has probably run the ball too much tonight,' Channel Nine commentator Peter Sterling said.

Kevin Walters was left out of the 17 for the third game in Brisbane altogether. He was cheered up, in the perverse way of footballers, only by the fact that his clubmates were not overdoing the sympathy for him, with Langer nicknaming him 'Chipsy'.

The countdown for the match was dominated by speculation about whether Super League players would or would not accept selection by the ARL for a Test series against the Super League-aligned New Zealand. The NZRL had said it would refuse to sanction the series and ban Kiwi players who turned out for an ARL-conducted All Golds side. Among the Australian rebels, it was understood in the days leading into the third Origin match that they would decline Test jerseys if selected. Their response on the subject was that they would make their minds up if named.

Any chance of Langer figuring in the ARL's team was lost when Johns beat him near halfway and rounded fullback Willie Carne, prone from an untimely slip, before flicking an audacious reverse pass to Ettingshausen. A typical example of Queensland's lack of spontaneity occurred when Smith, restored to the back row, smuggled Langer through a hole and Billy Moore grassed a straightforward pass with a try beckoning.

Fittler's boot took the score to 15–2 with a bomb which Mullins, running from deep, soared highest of a pack of players to claim, and a 35 metre field goal, taken as insurance which proved uncanny in its perception. But Queensland scored two tries in the last eight minutes, through two members of the class of '95—Mark Coyne and Matt Sing.

With 30 seconds left and the Brisbane crowd bracing in their support, Langer was put off a grubber kick momentarily by a chase from dummy-half and by the time he rolled it under the posts, Coyne, first to the ball, had run 2 metres in front of the kicker to be ruled offside. No try.

The series went to NSW 3–0 and a fresh batch of if-onlys to Queensland and their fans. Operation Alf had been accomplished by Gould one more time. The following year, Gould resigned as NSW coach.

Looking back at the experience, Vautin agrees that rugby league as a whole has never been less enjoyable. 'I used to love playing every game. You'd be laughing during a game and cracking jokes. I don't see that any more,' he said. 'Players are cranky. They are getting plenty. They should be happy. Money is the root of all evil—you don't get a bigger cliché than that—but it has caused all sorts of problems. I can honestly say I would have played for nothing. Wally would probably be the same because we were brought up that way.'

Vautin brings the 1995 success in as evidence when asked if the Queensland bonding sessions had become passé and other buttons needed to be pushed to motivate the team. 'Everything was the same in camp. Why change something when it worked so well with Queensland sides for so long? It was the best three weeks of the year,' he said. 'This professionalism might be inhibiting. Players are humans too. They want to relax when they aren't training. They did train—even when they were feeling a bit seedy they trained 100 per cent. If you want to have a camp where they are in bed at 8 pm and only drinking water, I think you'd get beaten by 50. It's been traditional and it works. No-one puts a gun to the head of the players and says you have to go out on the drink.'

Asked about his working relationship with his captain, Vautin said: 'Alf was our playmaker and we got on really well in camp. We were in each other's room, punting all the time. Football-wise, obviously he plays his own game for the Broncos, does whatever he likes. For Queensland, I had that little bit of structure, I wanted him to do certain things—I don't know if it took him away from his game plan. I can't argue with how he played. He tried as hard as he could. Unfortunately, we are used to seeing him make the breaks, have those little kicks go back into his arms. He was among our top three players each game.'

Vautin said he thought Langer was a 'deserving' winner of the Wally Lewis Medal presented by the QRL. Five years after Lewis' retirement, the irony in Langer receiving the award named after the heart and soul of Queensland's greatest interstate era was unable to be missed. It was to be the only recognition he received. The next morning, Chris Johns, as rebel players' representative, collected the signatures of nine Super Leaguers on prepared letters advising the ARL that they would not play against a New Zealand team not sanctioned by the NZRL. Daley, Lazarus, Ettingshausen, Mullins, Renouf, Steve Walters, Sailor and David Furner were selected and declined their places. Langer, alone, signed in vain, missing out to the Johns-Toovey ball-handling combination.

Langer does not argue that he should have been selected on Origin form, even though he was leader of three of the major best player awards in the ARL premiership in 1996—and would go on to win every available individual honour except the Rothmans Medal. 'I just didn't deserve to be picked ahead of them, as disappointing as it was,' he said. Bennett said: 'One thing about Alf is there is no ego or falseness. He is totally honest about himself. He wants to do his best for the team and the coach and he absolutely hates letting you down. I thought he had a magnificent game in the second, but not enough were going with him. He tried plenty of things but he didn't have the greatest series and he accepts that.'

BEATEN BY TWELVE POMS

By late 1994, Ricky Stuart, shadowing Allan Langer as Test halfback for four full seasons, was growing heartily sick of gritting his teeth and saying what was expected of him. Langer had played 11 of the 13 Tests between the Kangaroo tours of 1990 and 1994, missing action only when he withdrew from a short tour of Papua New Guinea in 1991 to undergo nose surgery. Stuart had also gone for end-of-season repairs after playing with a damaged groin.

Langer won the 1992 Rothmans Medal, the game's premier individual award and Stuart had followed suit the following year.

In almost four years, Stuart had not improved on the five Tests he had played in Europe—and he doubted he ever would. Even as far back as the 1992 World Cup tour, Stuart had indicated he might not tour with the Kangaroos in 1994.

Team manager Geoff Carr said, 'I remember having a beer with Ricky in Leeds and it burred with him a bit that he missed out. He was umming and ahhing about whether he would go over in 1994.' Later in the tour, Stuart said his concerns to the coach, Bob Fulton. 'It was obvious we had one game to go and Alf was going to be the halfback. Sticky said: "Do I have to fight this incumbent thing all my life?"' Fulton said.

'I said: "If the roles were reversed, you wouldn't mind the rules being the same." He said: "Fair enough". Even though there is a selection panel, the players know that nine times out of ten I get my own way. Anyone who watches rugby league in Australia and has half a brain can usually pick 13 or 14 out of 17. Then there are decisions where you can go either way. It can be a bit of a problem for the selectors and the coach, when journalists can get on the phone and get someone to blow up. It's an easy back page. But Sticky handled it superbly over that period.'

Stuart said his failure to dislodge Langer in 1992 had particularly 'burned' because he had won the NSW player of the series. 'There were two different sets of rules. A lot of people said the halfback should be the bloke in the winning State of Origin series,' he said. 'Fulton might have rung me a couple of times to see how I was going and letting me know I wasn't forgotten. He probably did the same to other players. I didn't know what more I had to do and that was when I really questioned the ability of the selectors. They were all about 55 or 60 and had been out of playing or coaching for a while, with the exception of Don Furner. I'm a believer that the Test team should be picked by the coach, the captain and the senior manager.' Stuart thought the three Queensland selectors fought the corner of the Maroons players more sternly than their NSW counterparts. 'I give the Queensland selectors a wrap for that,' he said.

When NSW won the third and deciding Origin game, a highly placed NSWRL official told Stuart that he had it on good authority that Stuart would be the Test halfback for the only home Test of the season against France.

But 12 hours later, it was announced Langer had been retained on a split vote, leading Fulton to take the remarkable step of publicly declaring that Stuart, in his opinion, deserved the spot on form. Stuart publicly wondered what he had to do to be picked again. Fulton's response could only be interpreted as a shrewd move to keep Stuart 'sweet', a reassurance that he would be a valued member of the Australian team on the Kangaroo tour that followed.

'I don't know who told Ricky what,' Fulton explains. 'I also said at that press conference, it didn't automatically mean Alf shouldn't be in the side. To be honest with you, it was one of the times I said to the selectors: "I'll leave it to you guys" and I'm glad I did. I had a bet each way. I wanted them both in England. I knew Ricky would have been terribly disappointed. It was one occasion when form maybe should have overridden incumbency.'

NSW coach Phil Gould had no doubt. Commentating on a Friday night telecast involving Canberra, Gould said that Stuart was the best player of all time. In his newspaper column, Gould said he was not critical of Langer's selection. 'He is individually a great player. I just fail to understand the logic,' Gould said. 'In a comparison of their various skills, Stuart outpoints Langer—sometimes marginally—in all of the vital areas. The only edge Langer might have is that he runs the ball more as an individual, but that is not necessary in this team.'

When the Kangaroos left for England, there is no doubt Fulton intended to play Stuart at halfback in the first Test, for reasons of team-playing style and the probable presence of dummy-half Steve Walters, five-eighth Laurie Daley, centre Mal Meninga, back-rower Brad Clyde and fullback Brett Mullins—all clubmates from Canberra's 1994 grand final triumph.

Langer suspected he was fighting from behind and was determined to apply as much pressure as he could in the three weeks before the selection of the first Test. 'In 1990, I didn't like the conditions and I hated being away from home. In Australia, we don't play on many wet grounds and I didn't have to knuckle down to the slog of playing on heavy fields,' he remembers. 'But I think

I had become mentally tougher and kind of kept going better when things aren't going my way. I sat down before I left Brisbane and tried to work out why I have never really fired in England.'

Before the tour opener, a 52–8 win over a Cumbrian selection in which neither played, Fulton told Stuart and Langer that he considered them to be 'about even' on form displayed over the Australian season. But that changed when Langer scored three tries and was involved in four others in Australia's 48–6 caning of Leeds before a 18,581 crowd which made Headingley more of an echo chamber with every Australian score. Langer showcased his running game, his ace card in his battle against Stuart, in his second try, in which he barrelled through the tackles of internationals Richard Eyres and Alan Tait, and his third, a 45 metre effort, in which he pinned his ears back before wrong-footing Tait with a dummy. 'It's a long time since I have scored three tries in a game—since the under-sevens probably,' he said.

Fronting the press, Fulton said: 'Alf hasn't made it difficult for me at all. It will be selected on form and Ricky will get his chance against Wigan.' Stuart, however, had to take pain-killing injections to play because of rib cartilage damage in his first appearance in the 30–20 win at Wigan's Central Park. His physical discomfort was evident when he missed Wigan's tearaway winger Jason Robinson in a one-on-one tackle on Australia's tryline. But he was involved in three Australian tries.

Wigan forward Barrie McDermott was cited for a hideous forearm to the jaw of Paul Sironen and appeared before a judiciary panel of three Englishmen—Carr having been precluded from duty because he was a team manager, RFL chief executive Maurice Lindsay explained. McDermott's subsequent suspension did not prevent his availability for the first Test.

If McDermott's suspension tacitly declared open-season for the Ashes series and the violent acts that followed, it also preserved international league's right to dance to a different tune from Australian club football. Fulton and Carr gave the players the opportunity to let off some steam by hiring a rural pub for the day. As a rule, the players did not punish themselves as hard as they had four years earlier.

'In 1990, we might have gone out four times a week and that wasn't the case on the second tour,' Daley said. 'There were older players on the 1990 tour used to the way things used to be and we know we can't afford to go to training the next morning after a big drink and just go through the motions. Not if you want to stay in the Test team.' Langer added: 'The 1994 tour wasn't as much fun. The players were more professional and we had players who don't drink.'

Fulton split time between the halfbacks against Castleford, starting with Langer, who handed the baton to Stuart at halftime of a fog-bound 38–12 win. Now on their third tour together, the two playmakers were more relaxed about the scrutiny, more confident about what the other was thinking. 'At 4 am on the morning of the Castleford game, Alf was in my room, eating turkey sandwiches,' Stuart said. 'We were in opposite rooms. You opened the door and there he was. The pressure doesn't come between us. Some of the boys who weren't playing woke everyone up when they came in. We were standing there drinking water and they were drinking XXXX.'

The team was more focused in running up a 22–4 halftime lead. Langer sent Rod Wishart—at this stage the No. 4 winger on tour—over with Australia's first possession and scored himself from a chargedown of a kick by former Newcastle player Tony Kemp. Stuart, though, flourished with a magnificent pass to first-time tourist Jason Smith and a perfectly weighted kick for Wishart's second try.

Kangaroo hooker Steve Walters remembers: 'It wasn't just

Ricky and Alf who were getting the shits. It became very boring after a while. It never stopped. I got on well with both of them. I thought it was a toss of the coin job, even though I was obviously more comfortable with playing with Ricky, being from Canberra. Bozo had to be careful that people didn't think he was playing favourites, so he was trying to give them both as much chance as possible. He was in a no-win situation and I think he did a pretty fair job.'

Fulton's next step in keeping harmony was to start Langer at hooker, in the absence of injured Steve Walters, against Halifax. Stuart would swap positions with him for the second half. 'The trainer will have to bring a stool out for the scrums,' said Glenn Lazarus, as a bemused Langer posed for press photographs draped off the shoulders of Lazarus and Paul Harragon with his feet ten centimetres off the ground.

Langer said: 'I didn't even play hooker in schoolboy matches. I'll play there if I'm required. The only other time I had packed into the scrum was when Phil Daley knocked me out (in Brisbane's first premiership game against Manly in 1988) and I packed in at lock for some reason.' Two years later, he reflected: 'In one way, I didn't want to play hooker, but in the other, it was good to be in the team, even if it was on the bench.'

Bennett was stunned to hear of the selection of Langer as rake when he arrived in England with a party of holiday-makers from the Broncos management. 'What disappointed me most about Fulton's handling of the tour was when he made Alf play hooker. That was an absolute insult,' Bennett said, giving public vent to his spleen for the first time. 'Alf copped it—he's that type of guy. Regardless of whether Bob Fulton wants to recognise it or not, Allan Langer is one of the greatest players to have ever played the game.'

Fulton replies: 'I certainly don't think it was an insult. He ended up playing three Tests he wouldn't otherwise have played in. I'm sure he's happy about that. It's no more an insult than the Australian and Manly coach playing his club captain and halfback as dummy-half for Australia at the 1995 World Cup. Geoff Toovey didn't have any problems with it. The decision was made for what was best for the team at the time concerned, same as in 1994.'

Players being players, Stuart and Langer turned their discomfort into a double comedy act when facing the media after the Kangaroos' laboured 26–12 win over Halifax. Langer took great pains to strap his ears and put on shin-pads before the game. Asked about a shiner, Stuart quipped that it came from Langer punching him at halftime because of two lost scrums against the feed when the Raiders man was at half. Langer shot back: 'That was the fault of the second-rowers. Why did you kick to the sidelines so much for in the first half anyway?'

Fulton said he was pleased with the outcome of the experiment, so much so that it remained in force for the four Tests to follow. But he was in the minority. 'If I never play there again, it wouldn't worry me,' Langer said.

Bozo was fully into vaudeville mode when speaking about referee John Holdsworth's 9–6 penalty count in favour of Australia, petty crime compared to the exhibition of referee Kevin Allott against Wakefield Trinity four years earlier. In one of Fulton's most famous diatribes against referees, he accused Allott, who had issued penalties 26–7 against the tourists and sent off Stuart, David Gillespie and Mark Carroll, of being like 'something out of Fawlty Towers' and advised him to spend cold winter nights in front of the fire with a mug of hot cocoa. Reminded of his review of Allott's short-comings, Fulton cracked: 'He (Holdsworth) should be drinking 44 gallons of the stuff.'

The penalty count was 9–6, albeit with two sin-bin calls against Brett Mullins (dissent) and Brad Fittler (holding back a kicker). It was hardly, for instance, the 18–1 count conjured by Frenchman Georges Jameau against the Fulton-captained Kangaroos of 1978 in their 14–3 loss in the second and final Test of the series. But the performance of Holdsworth, hampered by a hamstring injury and slowing the pace of the game down to his level, forced the Kangaroo coach to scour his memory to recall where he had last encountered the man in black. Kangaroo Paul Sironen located an 'atrocity' from the French leg of the 1990 tour.

'That's it,' Fulton said, with a wince of someone who had remembered by accident something he had tried for years to suppress. 'Diabolical. It was possibly the worst refereeing display we have encountered in two tours. He was getting around like he had a wooden leg. He is not physically capable of refereeing at this level. He is as old as me.'

Fulton would nominate his team the Tuesday before the first Test. Informed members of the Australian press contingent had been writing for at least a week that Langer was certain to be selected at halfback for Wembley. Langer would not be truly confident until the number was in the frame. Fulton named a squad of 17, with Langer and Stuart bracketed at half, intensifying the uncertainty, rather than defusing the situation. The coach said he appreciated he would be accused of copping out, but he was intent on making Great Britain coach Ellery Hanley wait as long as possible to know the Australian composition. 'I know who will start. You take every advantage you can,' Fulton said.

The next day, you only had to watch the pair train at Headingley to know who had been told by Fulton. Langer was full of spirits and involvement, and Stuart was on the periphery, sitting out most of the session, deep in thought. They had been summoned to Fulton's room together, and Langer had withheld his reaction, just as Stuart bit down hard on his disappointment. 'Deep down I was elated, but it was hard with Ricky there. We were good mates, but it makes it hard for me to be happy,' Langer said.

Two years later, Fulton considered that first Test selection: 'If Alf Langer hadn't have been in that first Test team, there would have been hell to pay. I could easily have picked Ricky, but his form didn't warrant it through injury.'

When the Kangaroos arrived in London on the Thursday, there was further upheaval for Langer and his Broncos teammates, Test new cap Wendell Sailor, centre Steve Renouf, injured winger Michael Hancock and the overlooked pair, Glenn Lazarus and Kevin Walters. In London for the launch of the ARL's World Sevens, ARL chairman Ken Arthurson revealed that Broncos chief executive John Ribot had confirmed he had been speaking to organisers of a breakaway Super League competition. An angered Arthurson said Brisbane could have contravened their conditions of entry and could be expelled by the ARL board from the 1995 premiership.

British bookmakers had Australia entering the first Test as 5–1 on favourites to win their country's 11th successive Ashes series. Australia always started these series with a well-tuned superiority complex. That's what happens with a series-winning streak of more than 20 years. One player remembers Fulton at the team meeting on the day before the Wembley match making some light-hearted comments on the ability of a couple of British players, and wonders whether that contributed to an overall lack of endeavour.

On a man-to-man basis, it was hard to see Daryl Powell containing Daley, Alan Hunte shutting down World Cup winner Renouf or prop Karl Harrison withstanding Ian Roberts or Paul Harragon. And could Jonathan Davies, the slight Welshman who had not figured in Malcolm Reilly's Test plans, live with Brett

Mullins, the flashy, long-striding Canberra fullback? What many Australians had not absorbed from Davies' stay with Canterbury was how fast, brave and instinctive he was. They knew four minutes from the end of the first half though, when Davies, dummying between Fittler and Renouf, accelerated clear and took advantage of Mullins' charity in showing him too much sideline.

It was exactly the filip Great Britain needed before the surging crowd of 57,034 after a moment of foolishness by skipper Shaun Edwards who lurched high and wrong-footed to bring down Brad Clyde. Referee Graham Annesley sent Edwards off, to a chorus of disapproval that might be explained by the fact that the whistle was in the possession of an Australian.

'In a lot of ways, Edwards did me a favour by doing such a job of it. I didn't really have any choice. It made it an easier decision to make,' Annesley remembers. 'I was refereeing the first Test against Great Britain since the idea of having referees from a neutral country. I didn't get any feedback after the game from the English management or the media. Jonathan Davies said to me a few minutes later that it was a stupid thing to do, meaning Edwards' actions, not my decision.'

Enterprising St Helens halfback Bobbie Goulding, rated more highly by Langer than Edwards, was quickly subbed on. Not only did Australia lose a probable try, with Clyde having unmarked supports on either side, they lost Clyde for the entire second half after the champion Canberra back-rower collapsed in the tunnel and was taken to hospital for a brain scan. In a game of 'if onlys', Langer would have cause to dwell on the loss of Clyde. There was a chronic lack of awareness, support and endeavour, Langer spending a busy if unfulfilled afternoon. It was as if his attacking game was operating on a different frequency to that picked up by the antenna of his teammates. A progressively more cluttered game, due to the shrinking 10 metres allowed by Annesley, also contributed to the ability of the home team to spoil in defence.

Former Great Britain halfback Alex Murphy remarked from the sidelines during the first half of Channel Nine's telecast: 'Allan Langer is having one hell of a time. He is looking for runners and there are none about.'

As 12-man teams often do, the British found hidden strengths because they had no choice in the matter. None more so than Davies who was faultless against Australia's moderate kicking game, and who guessed right when faced with a two-on-one defence dilemma as the home team defended a 6–0 lead with half an hour remaining. As Brad Fittler bore down on him with Langer in support, Davies left Fittler in the split second in which the Kangaroo lock passed, collecting Langer before his first stride in possession had been completed. However, Davies left the field six minutes later to a rapturous ovation—his proper due on the biggest stage for a rugby league career sandwiched by two stints for the Welsh rugby union team—but with a shoulder injury which would keep him from playing in the second and third Tests.

A subsequent video study of the remainder of the second half made for blood-curdling viewing as the world champions unwittingly devised new and interesting ways to fall to an eventual 8–4 loss. Four minutes after being denied by Davies, Langer forced a line drop-out with a grubber. From that possession, Fittler was almost in reach of the tryline, but played safe, flipping a pass to a call. The ball evaded a desperate stretch by Andrew Ettingshausen, who paddled the ball beyond Meninga to a British player minding his own business after missing Fittler. Later, Sironen dropped the ball when in the clear, coming to stand-in fullback Gary Connolly.

The sight of Daley limping off, with Stuart sent on to play

five-eighth, heightened the chilling feeling that the nightmare of Wembley in 1990 was revisiting the Kangaroos.

When a Renouf try off a backline sweep brought Australia to within two points, David Furner, making his Test debut off the bench, could not tie the game with an angled conversion attempt under intolerable pressure. Langer tried to force another line drop-out in the 75th minute, the ball rolling dead as his face contorted with annoyance.

Fulton praised the British for producing the best defensive performance he had seen. 'You could ask whether there was complacency, but we probably dropped down a cog or two when they had a player sent off. We were a lot better prepared than we were in 1990. No excuses,' said Fulton. 'We made any number of half-breaks, but their last-ditch defence was sensational. They dropped the ball three times in 42 sets of six and I have never heard statistics like that, even though they did play it one out, except when they moved it laterally and Davies scored.'

Thousands of Australians—many of them having spent their life savings on supporters' tours—drifted out of the famous stadium with the mind-altered bearings of a cinema patron just emerging from the dark of a particularly violent or futuristic film. Beaten. By the Poms at Wembley again. By twelve Poms!

On a London night which didn't know if it wanted to rain or not, I ran into Bennett at the foyer of the Wembley Hilton. Pleased to learn that Langer had been voted players' player by his peers, Bennett was sure there was no reason for his club captain to feel the selection axe again and felt energised by the excellence of the British defence.

But Langer said: 'I ran into Wayne later and I knew I was gone. I told him that. I was hearing things by the time we got back to the function.' He remained determined to enjoy himself and the stayers were treated to the comical sight of a set table—the remaining china and glassware rocking from side to side—walking by itself across the floor with Langer hunched beneath the drink-stained tablecloth.

Cocky in defeat, the northerners were irresistible when cast in the role of winners against the Australians. As the unmistakably marked Kangaroo team bus sped up the M1 motorway to Leeds, a car drew alongside it long enough for a passenger to wind down the window and ... 'Yeah, he mooned us,' Fulton chuckled later. 'They were past us before we had a chance to do anything about it. You can't blame them for enjoying their win, I guess.'

In the week between the first Test and the naming of the second Test team to play at Manchester's Old Trafford, Fulton would disclose only that two un-named players were in doubt.

It was the fourth time in five series that Australia had been unable to win the opening match against Great Britain or New Zealand. Steve Walters tried to explain this trend: 'Whether Australia is playing at home or away, a lot of players are coming off a big high for the first Test of a series. If we were at home, it was off the back of a State of Origin series. In 1994, Canberra had won the grand final four weeks before the first Test and while it sounds like a lot of time, it isn't. We cruised through the lead-up games and then they hit us with a loss. The first Test sharpened us up. We didn't lose the first Test because Alf was there and we didn't win the second Test because Ricky was there. Alf was unfortunate. We were so lethargic and so slow to get into positions in the first Test, that was something Bozo wanted, urgency, before the second Test. The team was in a better frame of mind. There was no way we weren't going to win.'

Fulton himself considers the same question: 'I think at home, the three State of Origin games are so tough, it drains the players most mentally and physically. The Kiwis and Great Britain have improved heaps. In 1990, we had a lot of blokes together who hadn't played much with each other. In 1994, we just played poorly. But early in both those tours, we won games by big scores. Even against Wigan, which the players really concentrated on. When that happens, even though they are told, they think: "Yeah, but we won by 30 or 50." You drop a bit in defence and ball control and the other team gets a sniff. The losses in the first games (of each series) shook the players into action and when you look at it we never lost a series.'

With Fulton assuring all players that the second Test team had not been decided, Stuart took his chance in the rarefied atmosphere of an 80–2 humiliation of Sheffield, having a hand in seven of the 14 tries. Rod Wishart laid siege to Sailor's Test place with a Kangaroo tour record 12 goals. From the team which made Sheffield look like so many cardboard cut-outs, Stuart, Wishart, Dean Pay and Glenn Lazarus would make the starting team for Old Trafford and go on to justify their coach's confidence.

Langer went to the next match in Cardiff convinced he would not start in the second Test, but his combination with Kevin Walters created two of the first three tries in a 46–4 win over Wales.

The Melbourne Cup provided a pleasant diversion on the return to Leeds, which required the touring party to scramble out of bed at 4.30am to watch the race live on television. Langer, inevitably, organised the sweeps—two of £20, one of £10. When Langer drew out Major Decision, an outsider, in the race won by Jeune, Fulton muttered that it should have been his.

Just prior to announcing the second Test team to the players, Fulton again called the two halfbacks to his top-floor room. There was no bracketing this time. Langer, Sailor, Harragon and Sironen were out and the four who played against Sheffield were in. Langer knew only too well the consequences of Wembley, but it didn't make the sense of loss any less painful. Stuart said: 'We walked out in silence. There was not much to be said. I actually said in the room it would probably be easier on both of us in such circumstances if we didn't get on.'

Fulton told Langer that the overriding reason for his demotion had been the need to improve Australia's kicking game. He remembers: 'It was that in a combination of things. The Canberra blend thing was in the pot pourri of selection considerations.'

Carr said teammates who arrived for the team meeting had initially thought Langer had kept his place. 'He was cracking jokes. He handled it well, which is what we wanted from the players. Before the first Test, we said to the players: "Don't spit the dummy, keep working and you might make the next Test",' he said.

Langer said the experience of playing the next three Tests off the bench was probably a waste of time. 'It was a hard decision for him, but he might have been better off having Kevin on the bench instead. I just went along with it.'

Stuart, for his part, ended a 48-month wait for a Test start. 'There was a time when I thought I'd never get back. But it wasn't as though I had a halfback in front of me who couldn't play and that helped me to deal with the frustration,' he said.

It is difficult to see how Fulton could decide that Stuart's form had been better than Langer's. But, on balance, Fulton had influenced the Australian selectors at times to choose Langer in the past and it remains unfair to accuse the coach of disloyalty or fickleness. Fulton's regard for Langer's abilities is best illustrated by the statistic that he started in 15 Tests for Australia, plus the 1992 World Cup final, during Fulton's tenure, compared to Stuart's seven Tests at halfback.

Paul Vautin, on tour with his television duties, said he was surprised Fulton dropped him. 'But I can see why he did and it seemed to work. He wanted Ricky alongside Laurie. I think Alf is a minuscule percentage better player. He has more range and

The Langer children at Lone Pine Sanctuary. *(From left)* Kevin, Cliff, Desley, Allan and Neville.
Photo: Langer family

Preparing for future Man-of-the-Match presentations Allan Langer accepts the award as best player in the under sevens from Norths president Ken Molloy.
Photo: Langer family

Allan and Janine Langer on their wedding day, January 27, 1990. *Photo: Langer family*

The five of us — Allan and Janine Langer on the back deck with their children (*from left*) Maddison, Courtney and Harrison. *Photo: Anthony Weate*

With skipper Wally Lewis and Peter Jackson looking on, Allan Langer sizes up the NSW defence in the decisive game of the 1991 State of Origin series at Lang Park, won 14-12 by the Maroons. *Photo: Brisbane Broncos*

Still the champs — Mark Geyer and Allan Langer after Australia's smashing 40–12 win in the deciding game of the 1991 Test series against New Zealand.
Photo: Brisbane Broncos

Winners at Wembley — the 1992 Australian World Cup team after the final against Great Britain.
Photo: News Limited

Allan Langer, Tina Turner and the Winfield Cup after the Broncos won the 1993 premiership. *Photo: News Limited*

Time running out on his Test incumbency, Allan looks for support in Australia's first loss to Great Britain at Wembley in 1994. *Photo: News Limited*

Langer had his hands full with the size and strength of Manly's Test forward Ian Roberts in the knockout semi-final at the Sydney Football Stadium in 1994. *Photo: News Limited*

Allan Langer puts his foot to the floor to evade Cronulla's international centre Andrew Ettingshausen. *Photo: Brisbane Broncos*

Do as I do. The Broncos skipper surveys his troops. *Photo: Brisbane Broncos*

Allan Langer in his Queensland Super League jersey. *Photo:* Super League Magazine/*Jay Town*

runs more. They are both fantastic players.'

Bennett, who left for Australia soon after the first Test, began fulfilling his 1990 tour role as unofficial morale officer for touring Broncos players. 'To Allan Langer's great credit, he saved the situation by the way he handled it. I think the rest of them handled it poorly,' Bennett said. 'The whole tour would have been a disaster, the ARL would be embarrassed. I'm not critical of Stuart or anyone else making the teams. They are all selection decisions. The point I'm making is that Alf and Laurie Daley were never going to work together in a tough situation. They're not communicators. Bob was better off saying: "Look, this is what we need in the team. Sorry Alf." If I had Laurie, Kevin and Alf, I'd put Laurie in the centres. It's a complement thing. They won the World Cup in 1992 when Fulton whacked on Kevin at five-eighth. It's a case of coach's prerogative. He went with Cliff Lyons in 1990 because he knew what Lyons did for him at Manly. I'd do the same [as national coach]. There is no nice way to sack someone, but the bottom line is you try to avoid it. You try to get it right the first time, so you don't have to sack someone.'

Langer's mates in Brisbane were getting regular phone calls. 'He wanted to be home. He doesn't normally talk that much about the football. Deep down, he didn't really think Fulton gave him a fair go. He thought that at the time,' David Pie said. Langer confirms this: 'I was dirty. But I'm not a bloke to go out and argue with anyone. I just cop it on the chin. I've had some good times with Bozo.'

The Stuart decision was almost unanimously greeted as necessary in the Sydney media. 'You need a heart of stone not to share Allan Langer's pain,' sympathised Ray Chesterton in the *Telegraph Mirror*. 'Langer has been kicked out because he cannot consistently kick out himself. To lose your Test place because of poor form is one thing. To lose your place when you have been playing well, no matter how justified the decision, is an examination of character. Stuart is very, very close to being the best rugby league halfback I have ever seen. He makes chances for other players. Langer makes and takes chances for himself. The need for Stuart to be halfback is paramount.' Later in the tour, Chesterton wrote: 'Langer has been one of the characters of the tour and a man of enormous character to accept the loss of the Test halfback role in the interests of the team.'

There remains a suspicion in Brisbane that the Canberra connection had acted in Stuart's interests, with Meninga and Daley in one of Fulton's ears and fitness trainer Shaun McRae in the other. Fulton said: 'Mal was consulted on selections. When I was captain in 1978, Frank Stanton consulted me. Wally Lewis was the same with me in 1989. I have to say that when it came to the halfback position, Mal didn't want to voice an opinion and I respected him more for staying out of that one. Sure, I spoke to Bomber [McRae] about certain things. He had an opinion in that area. The homework I did was backed up by Geoff [Carr]. The way we won the second Test justified the selections.'

Carr said Langer was unfortunate that the style of play Stuart possessed suited the rest of the team. 'The theory Shaun McRae picked up from his English contacts like Phil Larder was that Alf, as good a player as he is, is an English-style halfback and Great Britain had more trouble defending against Ricky,' Carr said. On the question of consultation, Daley told the *Daily Telegraph*: 'Sure, Bozo did ask and I gave my opinion, just as part of a general conversation. There were other players who were asked as well. I'd prefer Ricky. But I'd accept whatever decision was made. Alf is a very good halfback as well.' And Clyde said prior to the first Test: 'I honestly believe Ricky is the most skilful player in the game.'

Langer holds no bitterness towards the Canberra and NSW players who made their preference for Stuart's style known. 'The

Canberra players were all good blokes. It probably would have been the same in reverse, if the Broncos players were there in force,' he remembered. 'I have never really been comfortable in the Australian team. I liked going into camp, the blokes were great, but even there the Queensland camp always seemed more relaxed. Wayne said to us early in 1994 that the further we went in the semi-finals, the more of us would make the Kangaroo team and we paid the penalty there. The way things turn out, if Brad Clyde stays on the field, we win the first Test and I stay in the team. And they certainly played better with Goulding there.'

But in the heat of his disappointment, Langer grew more introspective as he absorbed his sacking. Becoming more home-sick, he welcomed the arrival of his wife and daughter in Leeds. 'Janine arrived after the first Test, just as she did in 1990, and again I was out of the Test team,' he remembers. Janine said Langer was not as shattered as he had been in 1990. 'It's a long time for the players to be away from their families and I thought Allan needed us over there at some stage around the middle of the tour,' Janine said.

Publicly, he set the coordinates for the rest of his career in his column in the *Courier-Mail*. The immediacy of his reaction is valuable because time would see him introduce new justifications to the sequences of events in his usual desire to remain on good terms with everyone. 'The Broncos have to be the one big priority next year. After I finished training with the Test team, I just sat in my room thinking to myself about what happened because it was too early to ring home. It is clear to me that winning another premiership with the Broncos is the most important goal of all. I have had a lot of rewards from the Broncos over the years and it's time to really pay them back on the field. It is great to play for Australia, but at this stage of my career it is more a bonus than anything. There is nothing much I can do about it. I was happy that

I did my best on the day. I haven't been told whether I will be used at halfback or hooker. Gee, I hope Steve Walters lasts 80 minutes.'

Langer was required all of two minutes at hooker for a sin-binned Walters as Australia flourished to the country's fourth biggest win in the 110th Test against the old enemy, a 38–8 win. Stuart, showing the ball around like a street vendor, allowed Daley to stand a little wider at five-eighth and snapped the point of attack around at will, luxuriating in his options. Australia scored three tries in eight minutes to take an 18–4 lead, the first a Meninga intercept of a Goulding pass, which the Kangaroo skipper took 80 metres to the other end before finding Ettingshausen for a thrilling finish.

Clyde scored the second after new British fullback Graham Steadman had failed to commit himself to a midfield bomb by Stuart and the Canberra halfback would later find his clubmate, Mullins, for a morale-sapping third try. Clyde's fine tour was all the more remarkable because he delivered under enormous physical menace, with Harrison and McDermott both collecting him high in the first 50 minutes. Annesley sent Walters to the sin-bin in McDermott's company after the Kangaroo hooker had sailed in to Clyde's assistance and punched the Wigan firebrand, who had been on the field for all of one minute. The bad feeling between the teams seeped over into two all-in brawls—the first after only two minutes when Pay went for Golding. Appropriately it was the eve of Guy Fawkes night.

The second half became a seething medley of resentment from the sell-out crowd, as Australia reasserted their hold on the Ashes. Annesley, looking back, said: 'The crowd at Old Trafford was a lot more heated than the one at Wembley and it wasn't just the result. Someone threw a lolly from the crowd which ricocheted off a touch judge and hit me in the face. It could have taken an eye out.'

Fulton and Meninga did well to keep the minds of the players attached to the task: Arthurson was returning to Sydney for a meeting with News Limited chairman Ken Cowley over the multinational corporation's plans for an elite competition, the buzz phrase for which was Super League. Back in Australia, the ARL offered contracts to all but two of the 20 teams to contest the expanded 1995 premiership. John Ribot said publicly that the absence of such an offer to Brisbane and Canberra meant those teams had to fear for their positions. 'We are being hanged before appearing before a jury,' Ribot said. But that would come soon enough.

On November 14, Arthurson held a stormy meeting of the twenty clubs, in which all indicated they would sign a five-year loyalty agreement. In Leeds, players fed off scraps of information from home and the touring press. 'Whatever the Broncos do, I'm with them. I'm sure they will look after the players and do what is in the best interests of the club,' Langer said at the time. There was even speculation that the Broncos would pack their entire team off to the London Broncos (which they owned at that stage) if they were expelled from the ARL.

Captain Mal Meninga, one win from becoming the first Kangaroo captain to win two series, had to deal with the publicity of a paternity case in a Leeds court concerning a 10-year-old girl. He met the girl for the first time in the week before the third Test and agreed to start paying child maintenance. For an intensely private individual it was especially unnerving—here was under the circumstances, a long trip to Gateshead for a meaning-less match against a Great Britain under-23 team, was not going to fire the imagination of the players unwanted for Test starts. On the bus going north from Leeds, Langer nudged Stuart awake. 'Geez, Stick. I'm feeling a bit crook. You'll have to play,' he groaned.

With eyelids barely apart, Stuart responded: 'Sorry, Alf. I've already told them I'm too crook to play.'

Amid this sort of mayhem, Australia attempted to win an Ashes-deciding Test, which they accomplished 23–4 after more than an hour of struggle, and sometimes fretful uncertainty. Daley gave them some breathing space with a first half try of quite freakish quality, a chip kick which he gathered on the full while executing a big right-foot sidestep of Connolly. But if ever the result of a big match could be assigned to the efforts of one man, it was the third Test and Steve Walters' grinding, buffeting performance from dummy-half. Walters put Australia ahead 11–2 midway through the first with a 40 metre bust through the middle of the British ruck. Stuart and Daley cleared wide to the left on the next tackle and Wishart scored unopposed. Then, with 10 minutes remaining, Walters dragged four British defenders, at various stages of a 10 metre charge, twisting and spinning to score in a crumpled heap of humanity. Langer was on the field when the fulltime siren sounded, but not long enough to strip off a tracksuit top to ward off the chill in the on-field celebrations. 'I had to keep myself fit for France,' he joked.

Fulton claimed the 1994 tourists should have been regarded as 'probably the best side to leave Australia, given the quality of the opposition'. He found few in agreement, although Langer does consider the 1994 team to be more skilful than the predecessors of four years earlier.

After the official function back at the Holiday Inn, Leeds, Kevin Langer caught up with his youngest brother, having travelled north from where he was playing for the London Broncos. 'I was grabbing Allan and wrestling with him at one stage and big Ian Roberts grabbed me by the collar. Allan said: "Nah, he's my brother". He kept apologising and I'm saying, "Ah, don't worry about it". They shut the bar about four different times that night,' he remembers. Langer and Kevin Walters ruined their tour double-breasted suits by wrestling good-naturedly amid the dirt and spilt beer on the floor of the Wig and Pen Bar. Later Ricky Stuart and Dean Pay were in their room re-enacting the stunning try in which Stuart flicked a reverse pass to Pay for Australia's last, celebratory try—with empty cans of the sponsor's product.

The Langer brothers crashed in the room Allan shared with Kevin Walters, who was to arrive later. If the Broncos pivot did not get to bed at all prior to a 6.30am flight to Paris, he would not have been the only one. In retrospect, the performance of team management in keeping the 28 players together may have been the single greatest performance of the tour.

Langer was selected at hooker for a tour match at Perpignan against a Catalan selection, earning the rare distinction of making the ultra-professional Stuart stop playing briefly in a 60–16 win because he was laughing so hard.

'We were killing them. Alf is carrying on like it's a grand final, sprinting up out of the line and making a couple of tackles and saying: "Come on,"' Stuart recalled. Late in the second half, just as Stuart scored for his first try of the tour, Fulton replaced him, moving Langer to halfback. Langer signalled the substitution, bending his elbow in exaggerated fashion and stretching his thumb just to make sure Stuart knew the way to the sideline.

Australia would go on to demolish France 74–0 in Mal Meninga's final Test, running in thirteen tries.

By 1996, after two years outside the Test arena because of his allegiance to Super League, Langer's summation of his Test career is typically honest. 'I don't think I have played my best football for Australia, not to the same extent as with Queensland and especially the Broncos. It's one thing I'm unhappy about with my career,' he said. 'I have had a couple of good games for Australia—especially that World Cup in 1988—but I have never had a top series. When we went to England, I really wanted to stand out and it was very disappointing. I'm sure Bozo had a lot of influence in the selections and I had a lot of chances to really cement a spot with all the matches I played in Australia. He gave me the chance and I didn't really grab it with both hands. I got on really well with him, I think. He went out with the boys, but he didn't overdo it. He is the king of the gee-ups as well.' To that, Fulton retorts: 'They'd be calling for the developed print between him and me.'

The chance to play for Australia came again in 1997, when Super League excluded ARL-signed players, leaving players of the quality of Brad Fittler, Tim Brasher and Geoff Toovey to glimpse the view from the outside, looking in. In the early weeks of Super League, Stuart had severe troubles with a torn hamstring muscle and Langer played his twentieth Test against New Zealand on Anzac Day at the Sydney Football Stadium. Langer made that team despite playing in yet another beaten Queensland team, this time the Tri-Series. Containing eleven Broncos and coached by Bennett, it went out 2–5 favourites and came back with a 38–10 defeat.

Depending on which insider you spoke to, Langer would have missed or made Test selection depending on the fitness of NSW's in-form Greg Alexander, who played a part in six tries against Queensland before departing for foot surgery. Reunited in the halves, Langer and Daley featured—either together or separately —in five of Australia's six tries in a 34–22 win over New Zealand. Twice, Langer's grubber-and-chase plays destroyed the Kiwi defence, the second occasion provided the match-sealing try for lock Darren Smith, one of 11 new Test caps.

'It was a relief more than anything. I have lost a few Test

matches in my time and to play in a winning side—and one which played so well—was very pleasing,' Langer said. 'Had we lost that game first-up, there would have been a lot of people on the bandwagon bagging us as not being as good as the ARL Test team. Laurie and I spoke before the game about how there were no reasons why we shouldn't be able to play well together. We decided to play our own games.'

Stuart returned to fitness, his eyes on reviving the fortunes of Canberra in the Super League and maybe playing halfback in Australia's four Tests in October and November, 1997.

As Fulton once said, it continues. Even though the Super League split seemed to make it probable that he would never coach Stuart or Langer again in Test level, Fulton could not be coaxed into a definitive choice on which half was better. 'It's too hard. Players can be rated in decades. Alf and Ricky can be rated as players of the 1990s, along with obviously Hasler, Toovey and now Andrew Johns,' he said.

Stuart made an easier call: 'He is the hardest halfback to play against and I have played against Mortimer and Sterling. If I had to play against one of them this week, it wouldn't be Alfie because he has so many tricks.'

THE EVOLUTION OF FRUSTRATION

When the Australian Rugby League outlawed Allan Langer's trip tackle for the 1994 season, it was another brick in the Super League wall. And the season itself, which included the suspension of five players, was the mortar. Broncos chairman Paul Morgan pinpoints 1994 as the year when suspicion in the club administration became a conviction that the ARL was going to disadvantage Brisbane at strategic junctures.

In the furore that followed the ARL's decision to rewrite the rule pertaining to the use of a leg in defence, the words 'vendetta' and 'witch hunt' had been taken out of storage in the pre-season by chief executive John Ribot. ARL chief executive John Quayle, long stylised by the Broncos as the man in the black hat, told Langer of the impending rule change when the Brisbane captain represented his state at a function in Melbourne to promote the upcoming State of Origin match there. ARL referees director Michael Stone had been instructed to compile a dossier on tackles by Langer and other players deemed to be dangerous. In future, the leg could be introduced to the tackle only when both hands had been applied to the attacker, not one as in the original rule. It meant Langer would have to be more upright as he went in to tackle bigger players.

'It's extraordinary. I'm not the coach, but I wouldn't advise Alf to modify his defence because of a witch hunt,' Ribot said. 'It shows how good he is. They didn't change the rules to stop Ray Price, or any of the others over the years who have used the Cumberland Throw-style tackle.' Arthurson said: 'It's absolute rubbish to suggest this was a plot hatched up by NSW to curb Langer. I personally see nothing wrong with Langer's style. I have always had tremendous admiration for him.' Langer complained he had been utilising a leg in defence for a long time, but said he would try to modify it. 'The whole thing has become a big pain in the rear end,' he said.

This was the second time a Langer skill had been largely responsible for a change to the game's rulebook. It resulted in the oft-quoted comparison in Queensland to the supremacy of Walter Lindrum which gave rise to alterations to the rules of billiards. As the season panned out, the worst treatment dished out to Langer would be the odd penalty after a heart-stopping delay. 'It just developed from tackling bigger blokes. It was an easier way to bring a bigger player down,' Langer reflected two years later. 'It was hard to get out of my game, although I do it less than I used to.'

Still, the affair amounted to another event leading the Broncos to mutter darkly to each other about the ARL. 'The year of 1994, when they just bloody bludgeoned us out of the competition with suspensions, was when we knew. The thing about Arthurson and Quayle was we knew they were going to give it to us in the end.' Paul Morgan said. 'The thing that stands out in my mind was this repeated threat we'd get (from the ARL) that we'd be kicked out of the competition if we didn't do what they said. It may have been a throwaway threat, but we had to take it seriously. We'd just signed a 20-year lease at the stadium and signed players like Alf on five-year contracts. Every so often, we went down to Sydney and had long lunches with Arko, all the brotherhood of man bullshit, and we'd all leave as good mates. Then the next thing would happen.'

Ribot had tried to court Arthurson and Canterbury chief executive Peter Moore—a key numbers man on the NSWRL and ARL boards—over this period. But after the 1993 grand final, the chief executive of the dual premiers was voted off the NSWRL premiership policy committee, chaired by Moore. 'I was told I was just too outspoken,' Ribot said. 'I was asking too many questions that were close to the bone.'

Bennett said: 'Maybe they said we would be kicked out of the competition so many times that some people got to thinking that we wouldn't be part of the competition. I have never had a love affair with Sydney because I think they have always had two rules—one for them and one for everyone else. The league always operated in a network and we weren't in that network. I know they think they are right as much as I think they are wrong.'

In 1994 the Broncos had picked up News Limited as a major sponsor on a $2 million a year deal which was the result of a remark from Paul Morgan to Rupert Murdoch at a cocktail party that his company should put something back into the Brisbane community. In August 1995, Pacific Sports Entertainment, which had Morgan as chairman and News Limited as 33 per cent majority shareholder, bought out the remaining Broncos directors —Ribot, Bennett, Barry Maranta, Gary Balkin and Steve Williams.

In November, 1993, the ARL had introduced to the 1995 premiership a team that was endorsed and, despite official denials at the time, part-owned by the QRL—the South Queensland Crushers.

The Broncos had lobbied relentlessly against the addition of a second team from Brisbane. When the bombshell dropped,

Arthurson and Quayle had included three others—one each from Auckland, Townsville and Perth—to create a 20-team competition.

'It has been proved that two teams in south-east Queensland didn't work,' Morgan said. 'It was obvious all they were trying to do was root the Broncos.'

The Crushers, who agreed to the placement of voluntary administrators in August, 1996, claim their debts ran to $4 million due to the effects of the Super League war. Morgan conceded Quayle's valid point that the Broncos were operating out of self-interest. 'Yes, but we believed there had to be an elite competition. I don't care if there were 20 teams, but the reality is there were not enough players for 20 teams,' he said.

There were myriad disputes between the Broncos and the ARL/QRL/Crushers axis in 1994. Through May and June, there were proposed changes to the ARL's salary cap rules which led Ribot to declare the Broncos to be on 'death row'. 'If this goes ahead, four internationals would have to leave our club against their wishes,' he said.

When Andrew Gee (broken jaw), Steve Renouf (ankle) and Willie Carne (concussion) came back from State of Origin duty beaten up and unavailable for club action in 1993 and 1994, there were dark mutterings from Ribot about clubs in future refusing to release players for representative games. The next part of the dance was usually for the media to take a quick two-step to the phone to get a rebuke from Arthurson or Quayle and then bounce it off the Broncos.

In a function at ANZ Stadium on the night of the World Club Championship match which Wigan deservedly won 20–14, Quayle overheard a heated comment made by Morgan and dared him to repeat it 'in front of my chairman'. Morgan obliged and the cold war dropped a few more degrees in temperature. It was also the night the ambitious Broncos directors discussed with English

Rugby League chief executive Maurice Lindsay the subject of taking over the struggling London Crusaders club. The mood of conviviality smoothed the relationship between the Broncos, Lindsay and News, which, as a 40 per cent owner of British Sky Broadcasting, figured highly in Lindsay's plans to raise the profile of the game in England. The match between the champions of the two hemispheres drew 54,426. Between 1993 and 1995, Brisbane would draw five of the top seven biggest home-and-away crowds in the NSWRL competition's history, figures which only added to the conviction of the Broncos directors that their way was the best way.

But over the season, Brisbane's 'us against them' mentality seemed to spiral out of control after a mournful start in which they had taken one point from their first six, drawing fortuitously with Parramatta, being ambushed by Gold Coast and paying dearly for the 'St George Can't Play' mishap by losing to Saints at ANZ Stadium.

'As time has gone on, I have become pretty sure who the "us" is. It's the "them" I have trouble working out. The problem with "them" is they keep coming week after week,' Bennett said.

Get one of the Broncos administrators off in a quiet corner for a moment and he might agree the antipathy towards the ARL became self-defeating. Then in the next breath, he will recount, as defence, an instance such as the time Langer and Kerrod Walters were cited for a dangerous tackle on Canberra's David Furner in a bleak round 12 match at Bruce Stadium (which could be viewed with hindsight as a premature passing of the championship from Brisbane to Canberra). The 29–10 verdict left the premiers wallowing in ninth place, three points out of the top five. Langer was booed onto the field, booed off, cited, exonerated and abused by two drunks on the way out of the NSW Leagues Club after the hearing. The trip to the judiciary would be Langer's first, and to date only, visit to a place he had heard much about, none of it good.

Earlier in 1994, centre Steve Renouf was suspended for two matches on a dangerous tackle charge, prop Gavin Allen was outed for eight games on a charge of using a forearm to the head, and Alan Cann missed four games for a high tackle. Gavin Allen's sentence particularly incensed the club though it was hard to see why. Before the season ended, Peter Ryan was suspended for three weeks on a contested charge of biting. Walters had been to the judiciary twice before in 1991 and 1993 and given a two-week suspension both times on punching and high tackle charges. When he was suspended for two weeks—Langer being found not guilty—the Broncos hooker could maintain his anger no longer. 'There is so much prejudice against the Broncos. All you want is a fair go, but the majority of players who go to the judiciary seem to be guilty until proven innocent,' Walters said. Quayle, in response, said he would have been surprised had the Broncos not whinged about the verdict. 'They didn't call today to say thanks for letting Langer off,' he said.

Walters was eventually fined $5000 by the ARL for bringing the game into disrepute and three years on he says he did not regret speaking his mind. 'I just felt they had decided they were going to get one of us. If they had gotten the both of us, there would have been an uproar. Had it been Alf, there would have been an uproar, but by getting me there wasn't,' Walters said. 'I'd been there three times and dudded three times. I'd just had enough.'

Langer does admit that he may have come in for special consideration, because of his standing in the game, when Walters was suspended for two weeks. 'I have seen tackles a lot worse than that not even make it to the judiciary. It wasn't very dangerous and I have to feel for Kerrod in that instance,' he said. 'I felt as though Kerrod was a scapegoat because they might not have wanted to suspend me.' Asked to consider the 'us and them' phenomenon, Langer said: 'In some cases, we were victimised and in others we have gone over the top. In this case, they were trying to upset our team.'

Langer and the other Broncos in the Australian side against France were booed by a near-capacity crowd at Parramatta when the team was read out by a public address announcer. 'It's disappointing to get that sort of reaction when you're playing for your country,' Langer said after Australia's 56–0 win. 'They even cheered when I got tackled.' In his column in Sydney's *Sunday Telegraph* in early July, commentator Ray Hadley claimed Brisbane's 'us-against-them paranoia is nothing more than a giant smokescreen to hide the club's miserable performances so far this season'.

The mistrust the Broncos held towards anyone associated with Phillip Street affected Langer's dealings with referees, notably Graham Annesley and Greg McCallum. Langer was required to apologise to Annesley for comments made at a scrumbase during Queensland's 14–0 Origin loss at the Melbourne Cricket Ground. And he was sin-binned for dissent by McCallum in a crucial stage of the round 15 loss to Newcastle, the first time their colours had been lowered by the Knights. It left Brisbane still in ninth position and the premiers were seemingly headed for oblivion.

The sin-binning was the last straw for Bennett, who had tolerated Langer's crankiness with referees for more than a season. 'Wayne told me it was the most disappointed he had ever been in me,' Langer remembers. 'He talked and I agreed with everything he said.'

The images of the scallywag with the beer-can hat and the cheeky smile, and the angelic featherweight lopping down big NSW forwards in 1987 were becoming a little tattered. Langer addressed the source of his frustration and has rarely been punished for dissent in the past two years. 'I have tried hard to overcome the problem. You can't change the referee's mind and you can't pass the buck when you're responsible for letting your team down,' he said. Annesley reflects: 'In general terms, over that period there was a number of Broncos players feeling some frustration on the field. Allan was one of those. It becomes a self-fulfilling prophecy when teams worry about things like that. They feel the referees are against them and the penalty counts won't go their way. They get frustrated when a decision goes against them and make a mistake which means another penalty.'

Bennett was also frustrated by the loss of Carne, with an ankle injury (which was alleviated by the improvement of the explosive teenage winger Wendell Sailor); Lazarus, troubled by a knee injury; and Kerrod Walters, who missed several weeks with viral meningitis. Nevertheless, Brisbane won six of their last seven matches to qualify for a knockout semi-final against Manly. It had not been without a bombshell decision to play Lazarus in reserve grade, and then upon the reserve bench on his elevation, as Bennett tried to promote more urgency and enthusiasm.

'I realised I had two options. I could go through the motions and stop caring, and I'm not the sort of bloke who gives in too easily, or I could work my butt off and get back in the side. But yeah, I was angry,' Lazarus said later in the season.

In retrospect, it can be seen that the historic 1993 premiership won from fifth place had fanned the fires of self-confidence of a talented team beyond healthy and realistic heights. 'After that second premiership, every player in the club seemed to be known when we were out and about. That takes a bit of getting used to and there's not much doubt that a few of the blokes got carried away,' Langer recalled.

A hard-nosed 17–0 win at North Sydney Oval two rounds

before the semi-finals sealed a berth in the play-offs, and the purposeful way in which Brisbane subdued the physical style of the Bears augured well for the finals. 'Lazo wasn't the only one who needed to get his head straight. You had to be Blind Freddy not to see what was happening to all of us,' Langer said at the time. 'I don't think it was cockiness ... well, yeah, it probably was. It was all about realising that we still have to show up and play near our best to win.'

In Brisbane's reassuring 16–4 win over Manly in the first weekend of the finals, Langer, as he so often did, inspired through his defence rather than verbal motivation. His hefty tackle on Manly's Test prop Ian Roberts forced him to hit the deck drew gasps from a Sydney crowd which had come to bury the Broncos, not praise them. The same player crashed to ground later in a tackle which McCallum judged to be an illegal trip tackle, the third such penalty Langer had conceded in 1994. Renouf was released at the scrumbase for an 80 metre runaway try and the first score of the game, moving like a Derby winner among solid midweek racehorses. Brisbane back-rower Peter Ryan scored the match-turning try in a furious contest, after Chris Johns' chase of a beautifully weighted Langer kick had trapped Manly fullback Matthew Ridge for a line drop-out.

But 10 minutes from fulltime, Renouf, who had set a club record of 23 first grade tries for the season, collected Manly winger Jack Elsegood in the back with his knees as he slid into a tackle. Manly was granted a complaint which led to the classy centre becoming the seventh Bronco to appear before the judiciary in one season. Langer had been the only one to escape suspension and the total weeks on the sidelines amounted to 19—far more than any other club. Ribot went on the attack.

He said he had heard rumours in Sydney from a reliable source that it had been decided that Renouf would be suspended out of grand final contention. This provocative move, which amounted to a virtual dare to the NSWRL to suspend Renouf, created a sensation. Sullivan said at the outset of the hearing that Ribot's comments would not intimidate the judiciary, and asked the Broncos chief executive if he wished that the panel dismiss themselves. Ribot replied that he was replying to rumours.

Renouf was found not guilty.

Still, Brisbane's 15–14 loss in the minor semi-final to North Sydney—a team they had overwhelmed three weeks earlier—ended their bid to become the second club in the limited tackle era to win a hat-trick of premierships. Like a bad film on SBS, little made sense: the language of defeat after so much victory was a foreign tongue and there were no explanatory subtitles to be seen. Norths scored two tries in the first 11 minutes and two in reply by Sailor kept the premiers as close as six points behind at the change of ends. A converted try by Kevin Walters, from a Ryan offload, squared accounts at 14–all, although Cann (broken ankle) and Lazarus (groin) were in the stands as the teams arm-wrestled up and down the park relentlessly.

Then the gifted right foot of Norths halfback Jason Taylor, calm in the eye of a storm, landed a 35 metre field goal with six minutes left. Twice in the last two minutes, Brisbane worked methodically into position for field goal attempts. The Broncos traditionally spurn field goal attempts as an act verging on football cowardice, but Kevin Walters steadied and got a good shot away, swinging wide to the left. With 50 seconds left, Langer, harassed by a chase out of the marker position which was the hallmark of Norths' effort, wobbled off an attempt which did not rise half the height of the crossbar. He turned and hurled his mouthguard away in fury. The sight of the skipper's mouthguard in the Sydney Football Stadium dust was an appropriate image to end the season. And, on the way out, he was serenaded by Sydney fans chanting 'Brisbane can't play, Brisbane can't play'.

Bennett looked beyond the previous 80 minutes to where Brisbane had effectively lost their premiership—the losses to Gold Coast, Illawarra and Penrith. If a team does the sudden-death dance often enough they will die a sporting death. 'Last year, we beat Canterbury in the preliminary final when Alf kicked a field goal. We shouldn't have been in the position of needing a field goal,' he said later. 'They went out trying their hearts out, as premiers should. You can't win the premiership every year.'

Looking back soon after his resignation as Broncos chairman in November 1996, Morgan said: 'Winning the premiership in 1993 was probably, in a lot of ways, the worst thing that could have happened to us. In a lot of ways, we shouldn't have won it. A lot of decisions would have been made then if we hadn't won it. When the players put so much into winning it under all that pressure, the intensity was bound to drop off in 1994. To me, I believe Benny realises his loyalty to the players probably went a little bit too far.'

Bennett reflects: 'If you win back-to-back premierships, it's hard not to reward them. What do you do, not win a premiership to have a better team down the track? It's unsolvable. They probably did enough to stay there. Sport is about hunger and wanting to achieve things. One of the fallacies about life is it is hard to climb the mountain—that's easy enough—but the tough part is staying at the top of the bloody thing. They had to learn again how to handle that. All the things they want … they want success, they want premierships, they want representative jerseys and get everything out of the game. The commitment they had before is not as important to them. The game is not as important to them. They have to re-learn why it is important. If they don't you have to make other decisions and you have to give them the benefit of the doubt initially. Alf's great credit is he has been our best player year after year. No matter what has happened, he aims up.'

The dual premierships had bestowed on the Broncos players celebrity and endorsement opportunities not available to other clubs. There was a lengthy list of products endorsed either by the clubs or by individuals and half the team had private car deals. Taking their cue from the successful 'Men of League' calendar, Walters and his manager Barry Collins arranged to produce a beefcake calendar of Broncos players. On the photo shoot, Walters sat back in a bubble bath, looked at the rubber duck floating majestically on the suds and wondered how he had let himself be talked into water this hot.

'Give us a sexy smile,' urged the male photographer.

'You're kidding. How do you do that?' was the best rejoinder Walters could come up with at the time.

Had the photographer said the same thing to George Piggins or Noel Kelly, two of Walters' predecessors as Test hooker, he might have had a little difficulty relocating his light meter for a while.

Two days after the exit from the finals, it was only Bennett's intervention that saw Ribot deviate from his intended path of releasing Julian O'Neill from the last two years of his contract with the Broncos under disciplinary clauses. Senior players, including Langer and Johns, also urged Ribot to give O'Neill one last chance. 'The great thing about this organisation is they do care about each other. The players were most distraught when they read the papers,' Bennett said.

O'Neill was 21 as he entered the 1995 season, a genuinely likeable rogue who had been causing merriment and also concern with his preference for a good time. As far back as the 1993 pre-season, he arrived from an all-night toga party at Queensland University to board a bus at Red Hill bound for a trial match. Bennett angrily sent him home. But on August 15, 1994, O'Neill had been charged with cheating at blackjack at Jupiter's Casino. The team had flown back from a forgettable loss to Penrith— which placed their finals chances in severe question—he had been punting with Langer and other teammates on a long night out.

On April 20, 1995, the fullback was found not guilty in the Southport Magistrates Court and George Wilkie, SM, was scathing of the prosecution case. O'Neill received $3000 in compensation. But four months later, O'Neill pleaded guilty to a charge of behaving in an offensive manner. And the Broncos management, protective of the image of the club conveyed to the corporate clients who were their financial life blood, cringed every time. O'Neill walked up the courthouse steps before television cameras.

'Benny was adamant the only club where Julian had a chance was the Broncs,' Morgan remembers. 'That was where John and he disagreed. John said he [O'Neill] was having such an effect on the club and he had broken the rules so many times ... if every player did that the place would be a shambles. Benny's softer side said he would make a go at trying to turn him around. It didn't quite work. Benny might have learned some lessons from that as well.'

Bennett is regarded fondly by many acquaintances as a sort of footballing Mother Teresa. If talent dictates, he takes every opportunity he can to recruit players from the wrong side of the tracks, or just youngsters who would otherwise struggle to make something of themselves.

From his country upbringing near Warwick in south-western Queensland Bennett took as his credo a line from his uncle, Eddie Brosnan, a hard-as-nails Test prop from the 1930s: 'Show 'em nothing, take 'em nowhere'. By the time he came into contact with

Langer in 1987, Bennett had decided coaching football clubs was not just about making players better footballers, but, more importantly, making footballers better men. He was part-coach, part-social worker.

'It's a very fair comment. I don't think it's a bad thing,' Morgan said. 'That's why Benny's use-by date hasn't come up. I reckon Benny has corrected and pulled so much from the day-to-day slog of football coaching. It's been a good thing for the club. You see so many coaches who are so intense that not only do they become pissed off and stale, the players do as well. Benny said on a number of occasions that the aim for a coach has to be to leave your club in better shape than he found it. Allowing them a bit of free rope translates on the footy field. They are coached to show flair.'

Langer concurs: 'He has done a lot for the players, on and off the field. I have never had a better coach or a close friend like him. He isn't a football coach alone. He has enough personal commitments of his own, at home. But he is always ready to help the players in their personal lives. Wives or girlfriends of the players ring him up when something is wrong, if they are having problems with their relationship.'

If players over the years have taken advantage of his willingness to cut them some slack in their discipline, Bennett's treatment of players has also been a major factor in the compilation of so many readymade players who came to the Broncos from southern clubs over 10 years—Chris Johns, Tony Currie, Peter Jackson, Sam Backo, Trevor Gillmeister, Glenn Lazarus, Darren Smith, Gorden Tallis and Anthony Mundine. They want to come for reasons other than having representative players assembled around them, the greater likelihood of titles and private honours, and the money they can make through endorsements in Brisbane. 'It's because players are treated like men. There is no politics in our place and that's the best thing I can say about our club,' Bennett said.

In fact, a case can be made that the bigger league operations in Australia, the Broncos included, do so much for their players that the players are sustained in a state of arrested development, saving them from taking total responsibility for their own lives.

In September, 1995, O'Neill and Willie Carne were banned from the Brisbane Treasury and Jupiter's Casinos. When O'Neill arrived in England later that week, for a short season with the London Broncos, eager to put some distance between himself and Brisbane, a judge in the north of England recognised O'Neill on television as a motorist in a 1993 drink drive charge which only came to trial by the time he had left for Australia. A furious London Broncos chairman Barry Maranta terminated O'Neill's contract with his club and on November 10, 1995, O'Neill was released by the Brisbane Broncos for other Super League-aligned clubs to bid. During his second season for the Perth Reds, he was sacked for disciplinary reasons.

As early as 1994, Kelvin Giles had been publicly warning that Bennett needed to introduce new blood to the dual premiers to prevent the team becoming stale, increasingly injury-prone as the collective core began to move towards the barrier of 30 years and running shorter in ambition. But Bennett favoured drip-feeding new talent such as Sailor, Brad Thorn, Darren Lockyer, confident that the premiership winners had the right stuff, provided their desire and preparation was better. However, when the Super League war began in April, 1995, Bennett no longer had a choice. The players joined en masse because Ribot, as the head of the rebel movement, banked on the Broncos players being one-in, all-in.

Rugby league players were being paid beyond their already considerable wildest dreams. Some had their wages trebled. Renouf was to move his young family to a ten hectare farm to

Brisbane's west. Carne soon shifted to a lavish riverside house. Andrew Gee bought an acreage property. Sailor took possession of a sleek black BMW and a two-storey house in a blue ribbon suburb. And O'Neill would be able to upgrade his sports car a couple of times before the 1995 season was out.

The 1995 and 1996 seasons for the Broncos were so similar as to be interchangeable. In the pre-season and deep into the premiership season, the players vowed to apply themselves in a bid to re-create the sense of unity and passion of 1992. In 1995, they won nine out of their first 10 premiership games. The following year, they forfeited their first round match due to the boycott by Super League players, then won their next eight.

From that juncture in 1995, Brisbane won two of the next five games, coming up with the theory that the players were involved in *too few* games during the split rounds. The ARL had disregarded Super League players from State of Origin or Test matches.

A loss of 34–18 to Illawarra, prompting the first protest evacuation of the ANZ Stadium stands before full time, jolted the players badly, as they were out-scored 32–6 in the second half. But three weeks later, they were not hurting enough to prevent Cronulla rattling up a 26-point lead early in the second half before prevailing 36–22. To make matters worse, Langer broke a bone in his right hand on the jaw of his Sharks opposite number, Paul Green, and would miss the next five matches. At least it gave him time to rest an ankle injury which had unravelled a dynamite first half of the season.

In 1995, the Broncos had won their last six matches before the finals, with some big wins over down table teams serving to inflate the worth of their performances.

In 1996, the streak was eight and included creditable wins

over Cronulla—a last minute escape in which Langer ran on the sixth tackle and Renouf scored—and another finals team in Wests.

In both years, Brisbane would enter the finals series with key personnel missing, but with the apparent advantage of playing their first finals match at Suncorp Stadium.

From here, we split the two seasons to examine how the Broncos of 1995 became the Broncos of 1997.

On August 21, 1995, two weeks before the start of the semi-finals, Kevin Walters and Chris Johns took their geeing-up of Peter Ryan a step too far in a Monday club outing to the Paddington Tavern. Ryan responded with a brief but effective barrage and before peace was restored, police were called but no arrests were made. When the media ran the story the Broncos management discredited it. They and the players saw it as a crossing of the shifting line between what is in the public interest and the 'boys will be boys' protection afforded in less competitive and complicated times for the media. As Langer said: 'It wasn't just that day at the Paddo Tavern. Other footballers get away with things that we can't. Julian O'Neill wouldn't have got that much bad publicity if he hadn't been a Bronco. The Paddo Tavern day was the sort of thing the Brisbane Bears or the rugby union team can do and not get reported because they don't have the same spotlight.'

The 1995 semi-final against Canberra, the first to be played outside Sydney, was a lip-smacking spread, with 19 internationals at Suncorp Stadium. Langer had been troubled in the week preceding the showdown with a quadricep muscle strain and the ankle ailment, but his claustrophobia kept him out of the $130,000 hyperbaric chamber brought to the club by Giles for just such a crisis. In two minutes, the Broncos had a dream start, Renouf collecting a Langer bomb and offloading in a two-man tackle for his captain to score. In two minutes, he had also broken a self-imposed ban on kicking. Late in a first half which was so pretty it belonged on a Milan catwalk, the muscle in his right leg was starting to report its displeasure. Langer went out after the break out of necessity. He regretted it when he was unable to accelerate in pursuit of Brad Clyde and the Canberra lock cruised away to a dazzling solo try for a 13–6 lead. Taking to the bench with ice-packs, he soon had lock Terry Matterson for company who was playing his last season with Brisbane, and the loss of two seasoned ball-handlers and kickers left their team badly disorganised.

Bennett considered later that although Brisbane had finished behind on the scoreboard 14–8, they were not defeated—even though they would be drinking at the 'last chance' saloon when they played Canterbury eight days later. Canterbury, treading the same four-week, sudden-death path to the premiership travelled by Brisbane in 1993 and Canberra in 1989, were a team on a mission, despite the defection of four players from Super League ranks earlier in the season.

The Bulldogs led 14–4 at halftime through two tries by centre Matt Ryan from short kicks, although Brisbane were able to absorb their constant harassment well enough to reply in the 56th minute, when former Canterbury player Darren Smith swept onto a Kevin Walters kick which took a fortuitous hop. Brisbane would have closed to within two points with 14 minutes remaining had referee David Manson ruled a try to Carne rather than disallow it on the advice of touch judge Col White that Cann had knocked on earlier in the movement. Instead, two minutes later Canterbury were leading 22–10 and another 10 months of effort had come up empty. Bennett charitably replaced Langer immediately.

Langer said he had a clear view of Cann's pick-up and that it tallied with Manson's on-the-spot gesture of tapping his foot, to indicate play on. 'I wanted to give the referee a mouthful. David Manson said it came off his feet and the bloody linesman...' he said in the deflated atmosphere of the dressing-room. 'He hasn't been our favourite referee. We have a long time to think about it. All over summer. It's been a disruptive year all round, what with Super League and us not playing rep football and getting a few injuries at the wrong time.'

Picking his words off carefully, Bennett claimed Manson had abrogated his responsibility in making the touch judge's opinion law when the referee had unobstructed vision. 'I even said to the players today—and this is something I hardly ever say—that in any line-ball decisions, he will find it easier to go against us. Next morning, he isn't in the headlines so much,' said Bennett, who added Canterbury had been the better team. 'This time, he took the try off us, when to give us the try was the hard decision.' Canterbury forwards Dean Pay and Jason Hetherington said Manson had been correct from what they saw and Manson said White was in a better position.

During the finals series, Bennett had been sounded out by Canberra chief executive Kevin Neil about whether he wanted to return to the Raiders as coach for 1997. He came close to accepting and declined, but the offer began a painful assessment of what had gone wrong and what the future would bring.

At the 1995 presentation night, at which Langer landed his fourth club best-and-fairest in nine years, Kelvin Giles marched to the podium to deliver his warnings one more time—one last time as it turned out. 'There is a greatness out there to be had—and we haven't grabbed it,' Giles said. Warming to his theme, he said some Broncos players were grossly overpaid, considering the amount of time they put into training in comparison to, returning to his true sporting love, scrimp-and-save Olympic athletes. 'I will continue to seek out the ultimate performance with those who are willing to fight to the death to protect their God-given right to be excellent—

excellence despite the inconvenience, excellence no matter how long and hard the road may be,' said Giles, lead balloons on steep descent throughout the auditorium. 'Gentlemen, on that matter I leave you with your consciences.'

Asked by the *Courier-Mail*'s Wayne Smith a few days later what he thought of Giles' outburst, Langer said: 'I don't agree with any of it. Olympic swimmers and athletes don't have their rivals belting and bashing them when they compete.' In the same article, Lazarus voiced what many had been wondering about Bennett's closeness to the players and length of tenure.

'A lot of the players didn't respect him as much as in the past, but I'm sure that will change,' Lazarus said. 'Wayne is the first to admit he didn't coach the side as well this year as he has done. Still, he can't coach mental toughness into the players. If they don't want to get out of the comfort zone, then the team is going to suffer.' Lazarus said a number of players did not have their minds on the job. 'Their social lives took precedence and football came about No. 4 or No. 5 on their list of priorities,' he said.

Langer was not sorry to see Giles leave the club later that month, having refused an offer of a scaled-down consultancy when Bennett recalled Steve Nance from North Queensland Cowboys to head up the training department. Giles was soon on board with South Queensland Crushers. None of the players would be asked to leave, as was their understood right under their Super League contracts. It was inevitable that Langer—who leans to under-statement as much as Giles strives to voice the most exact and colourful idea he harbours for a given topic—would become disenchanted with the Englishman. 'I think he was starting to get stale with some of the players. It was time to move on. Maybe he was a bit light on some of the players in the last year, myself included,' Langer said. Bennett agrees: 'We haven't always been as committed as Kelvin—and I include myself here.'

• • •

Again the players had a series of meetings with Bennett pledging their restored enthusiasm to train as part of the full-time professionalism ushered in by Super League. They no doubt meant it too. 'We have had meetings and meetings. As Fatty Vautin says, Wayne has more meetings than the Australian Jockey Club,' Langer said. 'What we needed was doers, not talkers.' In short, when the boys of 1992–1993 went to the well, the water was not as plentiful as it had been.

Langer had enjoyed one of his best seasons in 1996, during which he passed the footballing landmark age of 30 and produced the same sustained quality of his 1988 and 1992 campaigns. Individual awards fell at his feet—the Dally M Award for best player, the *Rugby League Week* player of the year, the award presented by radio 2UE and his fourth successive Broncos best and fairest award by a record margin.

His abilities as a playmaker dwarfed what he could do when he first came to the Broncos. Even though Kevin Walters still ran the back line, to all intents and purposes his captain had become uncanny at taking the attack to the point of least resistance. His long kicking game—so often used to batter him over the head in comparisons to Stuart—had improved from 1994 onwards through uncharacteristic repetition work at training, as he practised weighting his kicks into a target area from different distances. His short kicking game developed new subtleties as he tried to keep a step ahead of the coaches studying his habits late in the tackle count. He popularised a grubber kick across his body to the opposite direction to which he was running. Two or three such tries in 1996 were downright comical in the way opponents were left stranded.

Yet, when it really mattered, the Broncos were again unable to redress the statistic that they had not won a finals match since their 1993 verdict of Manly. By the end of their 'straight-sets' exit at the hands of Norths and Cronulla, it meant five successive losses in the rarefied atmosphere of September football.

Again, there were contributing factors through injury— Lazarus (groin) and Smith (broken cheekbone) did not play in either game and prop Andrew Gee (broken thumb) was absent from the 21–16 loss to Norths at Suncorp Stadium, in which both teams had the double chance in event of defeat.

Running so short of forwards that Johns started at lock in his swansong finals series, Brisbane played on the solo attacking skills of Langer and fullback Robbie Ross. Ross was a Super League transient who wanted to play for the Broncos so badly that it looked like at one stage he would have to be carried bodily onto a plane to the fledgling franchise Hunter Mariners to fulfil his allocation by the rebel organisation for 1997. Young centre Tonie Carroll was a similar agent of change.

Norths led 12–0 after 25 minutes, playing the percentages and rallying behind Taylor's kicking game. When Kevin Walters punished a momentary disorganisation in the Bears defence to send Langer over untouched soon after, Norths dealt with the best blows the home team would muster. Five-eighth Michael Buettner took the margin out to 19–6 again, 10 minutes into the second half.

In the infuriating manner of the Broncos, they next put together two tries in seven minutes to be within three points. Ross scored, the result of subtleties by his halves, and Langer exposed the lateral movement of props Gary Larson and Steve Trindall for his second try, which ignited the faithful. Still, unforced errors flowed from Brisbane and Taylor pumped a late penalty goal over for a 21–16 win. As the clock wound down, two Langer grubbers failed to make the mark—one ricocheted off the shins of a Norths player to safety and the other occurred when a pass might have been a better option.

As the siren sounded, Langer steadied for a bomb and in an spectacular scramble, Kevin Walters briefly had the ball over the Norths tryline, only to have it slapped clear.

Gee's brave decision to play in the elimination final against Cronulla with a pain-killing injection gave Brisbane one of their injured threesome back. Lazarus made a pragmatic decision to wait, on the chance that his teammates would win without him and he could play a week later against Manly, the eventual premiers. Cronulla's team bus broke down on the way to the Sydney Football Stadium, forcing players to walk 25 minutes to the ground—but later it would be the Broncos who required breakdown service. Brisbane's 22–16 loss was emblematic of the era which would end a few days later as Bennett trawled through the ashes of the season.

They trailed 12–0 after 15 minutes and fought back to finish with three tries apiece Bennett's decision to rely on Carne as goal-kicker caught up with them. The most unexpected thing about the day was when Langer landed himself in a toe-to-toe fight with Les Davidson, one of the hardest forwards in the game. Davidson dragged Langer out of the play and the Broncos skipper swung a punch, saw how much he was fighting out of his weight division, covered up and waited for referee Kelvin Jeffes to sound the bell at the end of the round. At the end of such a richly studded season, Langer's personal performance against the Sharks did not do him justice.

To be fair to the Broncos, over three years they produced some of the most entertaining, genuinely uplifting football in the country—which was, after all, supposed to be part of the whole deal back in 1988—and came up with nothing except intense disappointment and popular condemnation.

The production against Cronulla by Langer and some of the

senior Broncos provided a sobering reminder that winning in sport does not come down to which athlete or team wants it more—regardless of what the amateur psychologists among us say. 'If anything, Alf tried to over-achieve in the finals,' Morgan says. 'He was doing it almost by himself in various matches, against various teams, through the season. I don't think he had total confidence in all his teammates. That's why he thought he had to (do more).' Janine Langer says: 'I say to him, you can't win it on your own.'

Paul Morgan saw 1995 as a year shrouded with the anxiety and distortion of the Super League fallout, then '1996—that wasn't the case. In the end, we weren't good enough,' he said. 'There were a few holes in the team created by guys who had been there a bit too long.' The charismatic chairman's season review in the hour after the loss set the public agenda for the personnel changes which Bennett came to realise were imperative to the future of the club.

'Some of them are past their use-by date,' Morgan told reporters. 'I was embarrassed for the players, embarrassed for the people of Brisbane who have supported the team so magnificently for so many years and embarrassed for the shareholders.'

The Broncos players were predictably less than thrilled by this, but the ever-game Morgan—resembling a Christian saving the Romans the trouble and throwing himself to the lions—fronted at an advanced stage of the wake two afternoons later. Deep down, the players agreed with me,' Morgan said.

It was important to Langer when his five-eighth and mate from Ipswich dropped plans to ask for a release to join his elder brother Steve at North Queensland. For a hundred reasons, Kevin Walters is a big factor why Langer feels so much at home at Red Hill. One is their annual $100 bet over which of them will score the most number of tries in a season. Almost every try by one or the other leads to a wisecrack that makes the internal pressure of a match more bearable. 'I've lost the bet the last four years and I haven't settled,' Kevin Walters said. 'But that's okay. Alf once had $200 bets with Lazo and me that he could keep off the punt longer than we could keep off the cigarettes. I blew the bet one night when I had a few beers after a game and he sprung me. I settled and he got straight to Lazo to call that bet off. Then he backed something at the races at 5–1 and it won.'

Again, the annual Broncos ball was the setting for the telling of home truths. Retiring fullback Paul Hauff, presented with a memento, said he was getting out of the game because he did not have the enthusiasm for the hard work any more and suggested those in first grade above him were guilty of the same lack of application. 'Hauffy is very outspoken, doesn't hold back,' Langer said. 'But if the cap fits, wear it.'

When Super League won a stunning victory before the full Federal Court to become a legal entity for 1997, Wayne Bennett took his cue. Kerrod Walters and Hancock—both foundation players—and Cann and Carne were told they could not be guaranteed first grade positions in future and would be granted a release if they wanted to join other Super League clubs. Walters, a close friend of Bennett's, was alternately livid and philosophical over the next week, pondering the meaning of loyalty. He joined Adelaide Rams, and Cann, who lost the second half of the season to a knee injury, also moved to the Super League frontier city. Carne turned to rugby union with ambitions of becoming the first dual rugby league international with a league–union sequence. Hancock decided to stay and fight. He and Langer would be the only Broncos first graders to play in the opening premiership match of the first season and the 10th season.

Asked to review the period 1994–96, Bennett began: 'I tried

everything possible. What is important is we were better in 1995 than in 1994. We were better in 1996 again. We had to go through a phase of rebuilding the hunger again to get them in a position to challenge for a premiership. If you look through the history of the game in the past decade, you will see a club take three or four years or longer to rebuild after winning a premiership. Canberra didn't come back from 1990 and win it until 1994. Manly didn't win between 1987 and 1996. I don't know why that trend is.'

Bennett is sensitive to questions which imply a conclusion of failure on the three years. 'Look, the bottom line is, over nine years, we have won more games than any other club,' he says. 'We might be doing a few things wrong, but we have done a lot right. We had to start from nothing and remain competitive all the way through. Winning in 1993 gave some of these players an extra couple of years on their contracts. We didn't win in 1994, 1995 and 1996 and a few of them got lost in the system in that time. If they don't go well in 1997, a few more will be looking at the cold reality of life. If we do win, they might be finished as players, but still get another year or two on their contracts. Everything revolves around success.'

Langer sympathised with Bennett and believes he waited as long as he could to get tough. 'We can't keep making the semis and then not going all the way. A few changes had to be made and Benny has the hard task of making it. He thinks it's time to use those young players,' he said. 'You hear people say Benny isn't as strict as he needs to be with the players. But when it comes to the hard decisions, some of the players he has dropped over the years have been close friends—Peter Jackson, Kerrod Walters. It will be interesting to see how long he coaches. I think he'll be Broncos coach when I stop playing in two or three years. He has wondered if he was the problem in the last few years, how competitive he is—but he can't go out on the field. He'd find it hard to leave on the same basis that I'd find it hard to leave.'

The departure of Walters, in particular, continued the process where established players make way for younger men with more to prove, in this case John Driscoll. 'It's a process of giving someone else the opportunity, an opportunity they themselves received when they were younger,' Bennett said. 'It's a process where if this club is to remain competitive, it has to be ongoing. There are some who will be able to finish their careers here and there will be some that won't. I don't see it ever changing.'

Eventually coming to accept Bennett's right to hire and fire, Kerrod Walters laments the changing face of the game. 'In the early days, the Broncos were 70 per cent a club and 30 per cent a business. Now I think it's the other way around,' Walters said. 'It's become too business oriented and I think that's detrimental.'

But Bennett's nostrils flare like the club's logo mascot when such a proposition is put to him. 'It doesn't create a problem in the team, but individually the players become too commercial. The players have an obligation to get the job done in football. It's about performance,' he said. 'But individual players get consumed by the nature of the business and become more business oriented. They chased a buck. To Alf's credit again, he has never let business influence him about how he approached the game. Kerrod would love to be getting $300,000 a year and still have sport as a sport. If he wants it to be a sport, go back to West End (Ipswich) and get $5 a game.'

Despite his club's frustrations, Langer's standing in the game seemed to be as high as it had ever been. In the tenth year of the ARL's annual yearbook, editor David Middleton named Langer as one of the five best Australian players of the period covering 1987–96 he was in the company of Lazarus, Clyde, Steve Walters and Mal Meninga. The criterion was the number of times a player figured in the annual list of the best five players of a year. In a tribute to Langer's consistency, he was the only man to make the annual lists four times—1988, 1991, 1992 and 1996.

Asked where Langer fits in the pantheon of great Australian halfbacks, Tom Raudonikis replied: 'Among them all, Alfie is in the top category. I would always take him if I was Test coach, even though Ricky Stuart is a great halfback, too. I think Alf won the battle there, but to be honest, I am pro-Alfie. I'll always push his barrow. In the (1996) semi-finals, the Broncos were dreadful. We (Wests) would have beaten them. But he tried his ass off and almost won it himself. He can still pull things out of thin air that other people can't do. All those tries from kicks, it's not luck. I just know I have seen him get the Broncos out of the shit so many times. He will leave an awful gap there when he retires.'

Despite publicly criticising Langer for his stance in support of Super League, Raudonikis said Langer had handled the disputes better than the vast majority. 'A bloke like Laurie Daley went off and Alfie was smart enough not to say anything outlandish. People don't give him enough credit for being smart,' he said. 'It's the way he is and I hope he doesn't change. If Alfie ever changes himself, that's when he goes backwards.'

Paul Vautin wondered if the corporate aspect of the Broncos was creating barriers to the team's greatness, which had seemed assured in 1992 and 1993. 'They don't seem to play with the same enthusiasm, the same grit,' Vautin said. 'They need a new Trevor Gillmeister in their side. Gilly was there the two years they won it. He is such a great clubman that I was surprised when he let them go. I can understand he was going towards the end of his career, but he was going well enough. They missed him. I think the Broncos have turned into a one-man team. Sure, there were other players every now and again who put in, tried hard and were brilliant on their day. But Alf is doing it every week. I think he has been the best player in the game for the past five or six years.'

SAY HELLO TO UNCLE RUPERT FOR ME — THE SUPER LEAGUE WAR

In the first week of April, 1995, the Australian Rugby League were moving mountains. Having seconded representative coaches Bob Fulton and Phil Gould to head their player retention against the Super League menace, they had rattled up 214 signatures by the fourth day of their response to the news of March 31: that the six-month promise of a rival competition had been delivered. They would finish with more than 500 signatures. For both the ARL and Superleague camps time was short and headaches were arriving with every second call. As the week lurched from sensation to sensation more and more money was thrown at fewer players.

But if you speak to the right people at Brisbane, Canberra and the ARL, given the perspective that time lends, it emerges just how close Super League came to being a hideously expensive, one-week wonder. Indeed, the week when it was most vulnerable, Super League stayed intact because of two major developments. Firstly, the ARL had misread the allegiance of the Broncos players to the revolution which the club's management had spoken about darkly for years. The second factor was the announcement Super League would make on Thursday, April 6 of their monopoly on international matches with Great Britain and New Zealand from 1996 onwards.

Allan Langer believes a telephone call two or more from the ARL's bunker over the frenetic first weekend would probably have drawn defections from Broncos players he regards as being greedy, if temporarily. 'They took for granted that our blokes had signed with Super League. But there were only three of us who had signed by the Sunday,' Langer said.

A significant weakening of the Broncos' private enterprise club which was the cradle of the Super League movement would have torn at the fabric of the breakaway competition as a whole. 'The Broncos could have been our Achilles heel,' John Ribot, installed as chief executive of Super League, admitted candidly later in 1996.

Broncos hooker Kerrod Walters said there were 'a few disgruntled players' as the mutterings of Friday had not materialised into offers by Sunday. 'I think a lot of the players felt as if they were a bit left out in the cold. They were a bit dirty,' he said. 'We didn't know for sure there was an offer in it for us.'

Fulton remembers the method by which the ARL bunker had tried to make order out of chaos. 'It was advertised fairly well on the front page of the *Telegraph* who they signed up,' he said. 'We had a meeting to map out what we wanted to do. We had a plan, which was what Super League didn't have. They just threw a gun over the whole shop. We decided to attack the players who were the dominant figures at the club. What we had to do straight away was look at the players who weren't as high profile. We knew ET (Andrew Ettingshausen) was getting three times as much as Pearl (Steve Renouf) and that set the cat among the pigeons. It wasn't any sort of plan to say: "Oh, the Broncos are gone". We just found out too late, as it turned out.'

The ARL's on-the-run decision to consign the Broncos to the lost column was understandable. Reasoning the whingeing Broncos would have their players signed up before the whole enterprise was partially exposed on the evening of March 31, they turned their attention to more achievable recruiting targets. As it happened, through February and March 1995, key Broncos players had known *something* was going on and many were ready for the revolution so often spoken about. But like most of the league community in Australia they could not picture what News Limited had in mind and exactly what the role of the rebel clubs would be.

'We didn't know too much about it. Ribes was trying to dangle the carrot without letting us know what was on,' Langer said. 'He was away a lot and nobody could say what it was about.' And Ribot, thinking back said: 'Alf played an important role for me. A lot of times he wouldn't totally understand where I was coming from, just because of his conservative nature. I would have started sowing the seed with Alf late in 1994, but he wouldn't have realised it. I knew I could confide in him and we could share each other's confidence. I couldn't say this is the game plan—bang, away we go. Chris Johns was another person I really confided in. They're the only ones who knew more than anyone else, but I wouldn't say they knew exactly what was going on. I was always confident about the players.'

The colours of the Broncos had finally been nailed to the mast in November, 1994. At a stormy meeting of ARL chief executives, Ribot, as Brisbane chief executive, admitted in a conversation to John Quayle with chairman Ken Arthurson present that he had been speaking to organisers of a rival, elite competition. Over four months it had been reported that News Limited (major sponsors of the Broncos and joint partner in the embryonic Foxtel pay television services) had ambitions to be involved in an elite Super League of ten or 12 teams, and it did not require much imagination to work out which organisation for whom Ribot was acting as Trojan horse.

'The Broncos directors, as a group, were unconsciously

discussing where the game should be going in the early 1990s—1991, 1992,' Ribot said. 'I remember Barry Maranta said to me one day: "Did you think our battles are finishing with the QRL? The real battle of this is with the ARL." Which was just so true.'

On May 26, 1994, Ribot, Morgan and Broncos marketing manager Shane Edwards had gone to News Limited's Sydney headquarters with an outline of an elite competition. As a Test and grand final winger, Ribot had played to bigger crowds, but never for bigger stakes. In the audience for Ribot's address were News Limited executive chairman Ken Cowley, British Sky Broadcasting boss Sam Chisholm—rated by British magazine *Total Sport* in 1996 as the most powerful man in British sport—and London-based Ian Frykberg, a former Nine Network executive. The old winger, however, didn't drop the ball. He was to run with it, work with assigned News executives, and see what the reaction of other clubs and the ARL was.

What becomes evident in the Super League story is how it could not have happened without the Canberra Raiders and to a lesser extent Canterbury, the one traditional Sydney power recruited by News. In August 1994, rumours circulated, and were denied of course, that Canterbury had 'gone' to News Limited. As chief executive Peter Moore was an ARL and NSWRL director it seemed as likely as Ronald Reagan attending a Politburo meeting at the height of the cold war.

Super League sources insist Moore did not know about the agreement until later in the piece and that Canterbury League Club president Gary McIntyre had been a vital contact for News. But while Brisbane was the cradle of Super League and Canterbury provided a powerful godfather influence, there would have been no-one to rock it had it not have been for the Canberra Raiders. The key support came from Raiders officials Kevin Neil and Les McIntyre, coach Tim Sheens and Raiders stars Ricky

Stuart, Laurie Daley and Brad Clyde. The ground for revolution in Canberra was as fertile as it was in Brisbane. Even more so in a sense, because the Raiders were convinced they were within weeks of being picked apart by Sydney clubs under the benign eye of the ARL.

And just as the Broncos felt badly done by the ARL over a period of time, Canberra were similarly ready for a change in the ways in which rugby league was run. 'As soon as we won the 1989 grand final, the next year there was a salary cap. They tried to fix us well and good,' Stuart said. 'When we won in 1990, they found a way to split us up. Other clubs were over the salary cap, Wests and Parramatta, but you didn't see anything of that.'

Broncos chairman Paul Morgan remembered: 'I was surprised at the depth of angst towards the ARL from someone like Les McIntyre, who has never forgiven Ken Arthurson for what happened over the salary cap. The newer teams were a lot more commercial in their outlook and forward-thinking. It was logic that a national competition could not be run by four blokes from Sydney. But during 1994, I still thought Super League was a pipedream. A good idea which wouldn't go much further. I didn't think the will was there to do it, that there was as much support for Super League as there was.'

Shane Edwards, who became Broncos chief executive when Ribot joined Super League, assesses: 'Kevin Neil was very import-ant to Ribes when he was kind of isolated among the clubs. He gave Ribes someone to run off and there were a lot of similar atti-tudes between the two clubs.' Clearly, common fear between the two biggest 'out of town' clubs was the League's professed desire for salary cap reform, tied in with the introduction for 1995 of four new teams. Ribot remembers the mood of early 1995: 'I was saying: "We're all in the electric chair, we're all in death row. It's just a timing thing of when they are going to turn the switch". The (rebel) clubs each had their own reasons for frustration with the way things were being run and the players weren't being listened to by the League. Enough was enough. It was what you might call the evolution of frustration.'

At Canberra, Neil let his major players, Laurie Daley, Ricky Stuart and Brad Clyde, know as much as he felt he could tell them through late 1994 and into 1995. 'They knew as much as any of the players at the other clubs, I'd say,' he said.

After weeks of uncertainty, Arthurson called a meeting of all 20 clubs on February 6 to hear details of the News proposal from executive David Smith and a short address from Cowley. The clubs who would emerge as the eight rebels—Brisbane, Canberra, Canterbury, Cronulla, Auckland, Penrith, North Queensland and Western Reds—voted in the unanimous 20–0 rebuttal of the News proposal, because they were afraid that raising their hands could have led to their immediate expulsion and the syphoning of their players to other clubs while court cases ensued.

'We kept finding out about how these little deals had been done quietly, like at that February meeting when it emerged Kerry Packer had got the pay television rights for only $1 million,' Ribot said. On March 23, 1995, Ribot delivered his blueprint, once more with feeling—the audience now including News Corporation International executive chairman Rupert Murdoch—on the fourth floor of the company's offices in Holt Street, Surry Hills. Super League folklore holds Murdoch's farewell to be: 'I like the idea. Good luck.'

Ribot said: 'That is when the momentum went to another level—overdrive. The thing about the pay television rights being sold, no-one knew that. Kerry Packer is a great businessman because he doesn't pay the going rate for rights. He has been paying that for the rugby league coverage for so long.'

Wayne Bennett believes the key issue with the Broncos, the

one which resonated through the playing ranks at any rate, was the refusal of Quayle to initially register the contract of Wendell Sailor. Sailor toured with the Kangaroos in 1994 as a player valued at $10,000 a season. Quayle questioned the valuation of his and 10 other valuations by Ribot. After legal action against the ARL, Sailor was eventually registered at a compromise amount, but it still meant John Driscoll, a fresh-faced young hooker, could not play in first grade without jeopardising premiership points won, in the event of the Broncos losing the court case.

In early 1995, rumours were swapped in the rebel network that the ARL was going to scrap the salary cap for the 1996 season and the recruiting efforts of inner-circle clubs such as Manly and Easts—to be marketed as Sydney City—did nothing to quell that suspicion. The suspicion among clubs such as Brisbane and Canberra was that certain clubs had been given the nod that the salary cap rules would be changed or scrapped altogether.

Ribot said: 'You had things like Kevin Neil having Easts trying to knock off Ricky Stuart, Laurie Daley and Bradley Clyde from him and offering dead-set Super League money. We were saying: "Hang on, we can't control our own destiny". We realised at the Broncos that unless something changed, our club was going to die too. The way things were going, two clubs in Sydney were going to run the rugby league world. It was going to be run by the ARL's inner sanctum.'

When the Canberra defection became known, Ken Arthurson said the Raiders should 'get down on their knees every time someone from the ARL walks past' in reference to their 1990 financial crisis. Les McIntyre said the extent of the ARL's financial assistance was to act as a guarantor on a $400,000 loan. In the 1996 biography *Good as Gould*, written by Ray Chesterton, Phil Gould said Stuart contacted him soon after his appointment as coach of Easts in August, 1994, saying that he wanted to play for the Roosters. Indeed Stuart revealed in November 1994 he had a handshake agreement with Neil that he could get out of the last two years of his contract with Canberra if a Super League began. 'My deal with the Raiders would be finished and I would negotiate another deal,' he said. Stuart reflected: 'I went to Kevin in 1994 and said to him: "This is what I can get". He said: "Who is it?" and I said it was no club (making an offer), it was just what I thought I could get in Sydney. Kevin said: "This will be fixed," and it was basically what made Kevin go really hard for it.'

Gould said Stuart had attended a Roosters home match in early March, 1995, reaffirming his desire to leave the Raiders as part of a desire to be coached by Gould full-time. Stuart told Gould his escape was possible because Super League was coming. He cannot recall, but does not dispute, Gould's claim that the Raiders star told him Ribot would be chief executive of Super League.

'When I went to the Sydney Football Stadium I got a phone call from James Packer, inviting me to come to Sydney and talk to him and (Roosters president) Nick Politis. I said I was happy to listen to what they had to say,' Stuart said. 'James Packer couldn't make the game, so when I arrived there after halftime, I spoke to Nick Politis. He got a phone call and asked me to go around to James' unit at Bondi the next day. Gould said in his book that I approached them and I was bored. That's where me and Gould fell out.'

Stuart, at this time, was probably the highest paid player in Australia at a little more than $200,000. 'By going to Easts, I could have got four times what I was on at the Raiders. No-one is going to knock that back. Brad Clyde was in the same boat,' he said. 'Brad would have been the first to sign with Easts if Super League hadn't have happened when it did. Why it happened so quickly was because Brad was on the verge of signing with Easts.'

Clyde reveals that the Roosters offered $800,000 a season—not as a base contract, but endorsements and other extras added—at their final meeting. 'Easts were putting the squeeze on me for an answer. Easts offered me $800,000 a year and I would have wanted to sign for at least three seasons, so it was just enormous money,' Clyde said. 'There was every likelihood I would be living in Bondi. I didn't want to leave Canberra and neither did my wife, Toni. I was looking for a way to stay.'

Clyde said he and his manager, George Mimis, let Neil know on Thursday, March 30 that the Raiders had to decide what they were going to offer the champion lock. When Neil came back with an offer of $300,000 a season, more than any other player had ever been paid in Australian league, he was told the Raiders were not even close. 'I was fairly well satisfied after that meeting with Kevin that Bradley was going to the Roosters,' Mimis said.

'Kevin indicated he'd like to keep Bradley in Canberra and the News organisation might be prepared to assist the Raiders in keeping him. At that stage, we were to give Easts a decision by Friday.' Neil had remembered advice from Cowley to call him if there was a major problem at the Raiders. 'That's where the idea to sign players came from, from our need to keep Bradley. That's what Ken Cowley told me later,' Neil said. 'If Brad hadn't have been signed that weekend, we would have lost him to Easts. Ricky had had a very good offer. I don't know Laurie would have ever gone.'

While the turmoil about the future of Canberra's irreplaceable back-rower was progressing, News had received the opinion of their legal team, headed by solicitor John Atanaskovic, that the ARL's five-year loyalty agreement constituted an unfair monopoly. And so on Thursday, March 30, News Limited launched a Federal Court challenge against the ARL, citing Trade Practices Act breaches in the five-year loyalty agreements entered into with the

20 clubs, naming six clubs—Canberra, Brisbane, Canterbury, Cronulla, Newcastle and the Western Reds—as co-respondents.

At that stage, the Newcastle Knights had been thought to be ripe for defection, although there was concern from Ribot that the directors in favour of Super League would buckle under anticipated public reaction in Newcastle in favour of the ARL. The Knights were literally driven to Phillip Street, with Test prop Paul Harragon at the wheel of a mini-bus.

On the night of March 30, with the media diverted by the Federal Court challenge, Canterbury players had been directed, with coach Chris Anderson as the messenger, to the offices of solicitors Atanaskovic Hartnell.

Earlier that morning, Anderson, Cronulla's John Lang and Canberra's Tim Sheens had been the first coaches to sign on the dotted line. Sheens had had serious second thoughts earlier in the week.

The order of approach to players was to be: Canterbury, Thursday night; Brisbane, Friday morning in Brisbane; Cronulla, Friday night in Perth; and Canberra, Friday night in Townsville. The strategy was that a domino effect would be created and the rest of the clubs and players would consider, when the signings became public that the success of the News venture was a fait accompli. At this stage, News Limited envisaged offering the contracts of the players back to the ARL on Monday, in return for News' terms for a pick-and-choose 10-team elite league to be run by News, with the ARL to still control all other levels of the game.

'I went to Canterbury first because it was the heart of them, the heart of Sydney. I suppose I was punting a bit,' Ribot said. 'We acted on the word of the lawyers that they believed there was every likelihood we would be allowed to start. We did look at where the teams were going to be geographically. It helped that Cronulla and Canberra were playing away.'

• • •

Meanwhile, up in Brisbane, the Broncos were entering the picture. 'Benny was talking to me about what was going on and he said I could probably expect a phone call from Ribes,' Langer said. Langer got the call and met Ribot at Lachlan Murdoch's Hamilton residence on the Friday morning of the home match against South Queensland. Then 23, the younger Murdoch was general manager of Queensland Newspapers and had been to Broncos social functions. He had been brought into the Super League framework, acting as a player negotiator in a move which, to many players, provided the stamp of authenticy.

'A lot of what they said was probably over my head,' Langer said of his briefing. 'I was told not to say anything, signed and left. I wished them good luck. I said something to Janine and Benny knew, of course. The main reason I signed was I thought the club was going there. I knew Ribes was involved, I was sure Wayne was going to be involved. In the end, I thought it was a winner and I knew I could get Ribes again. He had a lot bigger cake and I could get more of it.'

The contract, for $500,000 a year, plus $100,000 up front, was to play for three years from 1997 in a competition to be called Star League. There was a standard 60-day confidentiality clause, which, with so many rugby league people coming into the know, was the height of optimism. Ribot said: 'Alf basically trusted me. I said: "You'll be paid the highest amount of anyone". We did the whole thing in 30 minutes. That shows how the guy has matured. I'd still be talking to him now if he was back in Ferrett Street.'

Channel Seven news in Sydney at 6 pm reported that Super League had started signing players and radio reports quickly ran with the news. 'I know where it (the leak) came from, not that it matters much now,' Ribot said. 'It got out early on us. Had we have got the weekend, or even an extra day, it would helped us enormously.'

The extent of the security surrounding the exercises extended to assumed names for travelling. The aliases 'Mr Lachlan' and 'Mr Bresac' (Ribot de Bresac is Ribot's full surname) were used early. But the strength in the News strike was also an inherent weakness. There were too few negotiators on the ground because of an understandable necessity to let as few as possible know the full picture of what News had in mind. For instance, player managers were not brought into the process. Gould felt that was a major error, because the nature of their job is to trade one side off against the other. In retrospect, it was a huge mistake that only players from Super League-friendly clubs were approached. But again, the reason was the need for secrecy. The Super League negotiating team had also seriously underestimated the ability of the ARL to mount retaliatory strikes.

But in Brisbane, most of the crowd of 49,607 to attend the first—of only two, as it panned out—Brisbane derbies at ANZ Stadium had no idea that news of the player raids had broken. As he prowled the sidelines during the first half, Broncos chairman Paul Morgan denied the rumour that Ribot had resigned as chief executive of the Broncos. When the media entered the Broncos dressing-room, Brisbane's 32–0 win a mere footnote to the main event. Langer, Bennett and Renouf denied they had signed with Super League, as several reporters had been told. Like the ARL, most reporters took it for granted that all the Broncos had signed and assumed they were operating under the frequent in-house rule of a football club: 'Deny everything'.

Joining the Broncos in dispatches were Canberra's internationals, Cronulla's Andrew Ettingshausen, Canterbury's Terry Lamb, Simon Gillies, Dean Pay and coaches Anderson, John Monie and John Lang. Ribot could not be found at ANZ Stadium.

The Broncos management concocted a personal alibi, as if to scold reporters for even thinking they were being lied to.

In fact, Ribot was back in Sydney at the Super League 'war room'. Lachlan Murdoch and Smith had travelled by private jet to Townsville to speak to Canberra players awaiting their Saturday night match against the Cowboys. Canberra had flown their players to Townsville on Friday morning, along with several of the key advisers to senior players on the premise of a relaxing weekend in the tropical city. Neil and Smith had rung Mimis and cordially suggested it would be in his best interests to take the next flight to Townsville to meet them at the Townsville Breakwater Casino.

With Raiders coach Tim Sheens as the tour guide, senior Canberra players, then other members of the team filed into room 1601 to listen to Murdoch and Smith outline the plans for Super League. By the time the briefcases were closed, 18 Raiders had signed.

'We didn't know Super League would be talking to us until we got up there. There was speculation something was on, but we didn't know what was going on,' Clyde said. 'I listened and thought: "You little beauty. It gives me a chance to stay in Canberra". As it turned out, the offer from Easts (before the boom in salaries triggered by Super League) was in excess of what I got by signing with Super League later on. But I'm glad I'm still here.'

Clyde, eventually the beneficiary of a Super League contract over seven years totalling $4.3 million, looks back at the contest for his signature with a rueful shake of the head. 'I was getting phone calls from the Packers and phone calls from the Murdochs and I was stuck in the middle trying to stay onside with both of them,' he said. Mimis had the job of ringing James Packer on Saturday to confirm the newspaper reports of Clyde's move to Super League.

On Saturday morning, Bennett awoke to see his name among a list of players and coaches in all the metropolitan newspapers. League reporters had a telephone call early on Friday night from a lobbyist, drafted in by News Limited for the early days of the exercise. His reaction was typically sharp. He thought his team and himself were being used as negotiating cards by News Limited to improve their negotiating stance with the pool of unsigned players.

'Wayne stopped them from meeting me as planned on the Saturday morning,' Ribot said. 'He told the players to keep away [from ANZ Stadium, where Ribot was waiting with Lachlan Murdoch]. That was a real kick in the teeth. I spoke to Wayne over the weekend and he was really upset at how it came out. His confidence was abused—and not abused by me. It leaked from within and it shouldn't have.'

Willie Carne, who became friends with Lachlan Murdoch during his tenure of a little over 12 months in Brisbane, was the only player to materialise at ANZ Stadium and sign. Once again, Ribot and the senior News Limited executives had to make a judgment on the run: 'We let it go a few more days, hoping they (the ARL) wouldn't get to us. Wayne wasn't a loose end that worried me.' Ribot knew he would be made aware of any rush by the ARL to sign Brisbane players, but it was still a gamble to rely on the residual mistrust the Broncos players held towards Phillip Street and their desire to remain together. 'I knew I'd hear about it, but I was worried about how quickly I could react if the ARL went crazy,' he said.

Letting on nothing of the turmoil behind the scenes, the Broncos management held a noon press conference. Morgan announced that Ribot had resigned as club chief executive in a 30-second telephone call without saying where he would be working. It stretched the imagination, especially as the Broncos directors and staff had been talking of the need for a breakaway competition for so long. 'The directors didn't know what was going on,' Morgan maintained 18 months later. 'The answer is it was kept very close to Ribot's and my chest, for the sake of everyone else. What Barry Maranta said in court [and was slammed by Justice Burchett, in his first judgment document] was a fact—he didn't have much idea what was going on and neither did Steve Williams.'

The ARL enacted their own packages for players, funded by television rights holders Optus Vision and Channel Nine, on that April Fool's Day. Moore resigned his directorship. Then, while flying back from Townsville on Sunday, April 2, Neil rang Cowley at a short stopover at Brisbane airport to suggest it would be best for the senior Raiders players to confirm they had signed with Super League. On Sunday night, Daley, Stuart, Clyde and Brett Mullins confirmed on Channel Seven that they had signed with News Limited.

When Langer heard, he asked Ribot for permission to confirm to the *Courier-Mail*, the newspaper with which he was a columnist, that he had too. 'I didn't want to keep lying. I don't like lying,' said Langer, saying also that he hoped he had not forfeited a chance to captain Queensland's State of Origin team for the first time.

On Monday, April 3, while players at a morning session were told Ribot wanted to meet them at his home, Renouf and Carne admitted they had signed with Super League. Bennett went for a slow, extended walk down the centre of the field with a distressed Brad Thorn, a promising New Zealand-born forward who wanted to play State of Origin more than anything else in football. Later, Bennett told players: 'You've got to work out what you are going to do yourself'.

But the coach also urged them to stick together. Ribot spoke to the players collectively and then negotiated individually. 'No managers were involved. That's how it was done at the Broncos,'

Kerrod Walters said. 'It didn't worry me. But I don't think it sat too well with some of the other players.'

Ribot recalls that some players were harder to sell to than others. The offers to Kerrod Walters and Darren Smith were not what they had been led to expect by media reports of News Limited's spending spree. Both players left Ribot's house thoughtful and uncommitted. Every other regular first-grader signed, bringing the total to 18. The cake was bigger, but still not big enough for everyone. 'That's the only thing I felt was probably handled badly. We didn't know if we were getting a fair price or not,' Walters said.

On Tuesday, April 4, 18 Broncos players were announced as having signed with News Limited by Johns, who was presented as players representative because of his grasp of the issues and his relative comfort with media interrogation. His captain was pleased to do as little talking as possible. The 'one-in, all-in' ethos at Red Hill had struck again—and would do so under greater pressure to come.

On the same Tuesday afternoon in Canberra, a press conference was being held to announce that 20 Raiders players had signed with Super League. It became a matter of when Canberra and Brisbane, plus a core of rebel club managements and an ever-changing list of ARL clubs being courted by News Limited, moved lock, stock and barrel to Super League, and whether the Federal Court would block their plans.

The day before, Ricky Stuart had caused a stir at Super League when he arrived at Phillip Street with his manager John Fordham. Stuart had been in the Hunter Valley with Fordham for promotions when he took two mobile phone calls from Bob Fulton. 'I get on well with Bozo and I got on well with Gould then. I said no the first time and the second time I said I would go in. But it was only to pay them the respect of talking to them because of my involvement with them,' Stuart said. 'We called in that afternoon to meet them at Phillip Street. I could understand the players from other clubs and even the Canberra boys, because I had been in Sydney since the Sunday we flew back from Townsville. But at no stage was I going to renege on my agreement.'

Stuart rang Cowley the next day, to tell them he was meeting again with the ARL negotiators in Canberra on Wednesday and nothing would happen until he spoke to him again. On April 5, Fulton, Quayle, Gould, James Packer and solicitor James McLoughlin flew to Canberra aboard a Packer-owned Lear Jet, with Fordham also on board.

The offer was precisely $1 million a year—$500,000 a year more than Stuart's Super League contract. It was intimated that Stuart would be well placed to also get the ARL Test captaincy, although Fordham and Fulton said no specific guarantee was made. 'They told me they were going up to sign half the Brisbane blokes as well, but they were bullshitting there. They were trying to get me to sign so they could say to the Brisbane boys that they already had me,' Stuart said. 'If I was going to sign for money, I would have signed with the ARL. People accused me of not being loyal to the ARL. I was loyal because I stayed with the Canberra Raiders. After the meeting with the ARL I said: "You know, if I decide to go back to the ARL, I'd want to confront the team and let them know of my reasons." I wasn't interested in going back. At Canberra, we had all made a pact to join Super League together. I had no reasons to want to go back. It was all very attractive.' Fulton said: 'I don't think we said we were going up to sign them (the Broncos players). We weren't going to say anything that would come back to us later. We might have said we thought we could get them.'

Stuart emerged from a two-hour meeting to tell reporters he would announce a decision within 24 hours. 'I spoke to Ken

Cowley the next day and he told me the Rugby Football League (British) board had signed up to play Tests against Super League. It was the icing on the cake. A big part of the ARL's bargaining power was that if you go to Super League you will never play rep football again,' he said. Neil said Stuart was told by a member of the ARL's negotiating team that all Raiders players would be welcomed back, except Daley. This, Neil believes, was a contributing factor to Daley's heart-on-sleeve comments against the ARL later in the dispute.

From Canberra, the Packer Lear jet deviated to Brisbane for a secret meeting with eight Broncos players arranged by Fulton under a veil of secrecy. 'We got a call from two players on the Sunday. Then I rang a couple and arranged a meeting,' Fulton remembers. 'Brisbane were neglected by Super League financially. From what players of comparable ability were being paid by Super League, the Brisbane blokes were totally underpaid.'

Bennett's column in the *Weekend Australian* later in April claimed: 'Fulton told Lazarus that if he wanted to get out of it, that he had a solicitor sitting next to him and they could challenge the contract because it had been signed under duress. Lazo said: "To be honest, I wasn't under too much duress. I left the room with the biggest cheque of my life and felt like dancing on tables." Bennett added later: 'What strikes you about it is they were most interested in signing NSW players so the NSW State of Origin team and the Test team would be strong. Who would be in the Queensland team was an afterthought.'

It was noteworthy that Langer and Johns did not receive a call from the ARL.

Ribot said: 'That's Alf. He made a decision and stuck with it. I don't think it would have mattered if they offered him $10 million. They knew they wouldn't get Alf.' Fulton confirmed: 'Yes, basically. That's the type of person he is. Alf was never a possibility as far as we were concerned. He was always one of the highest paid in Super League.'

The uncommitted Kerrod Walters and seven Super League signees—Carne, Lazarus, Wendell Sailor, Steve Renouf, Kevin Walters, Michael Hancock and Julian O'Neill—arrived for the next secret meeting with the ARL to find newspaper reporters, photographers and television crews waiting for them outside the meeting place, the Qantas Club at Brisbane Airport.

'We spoke to them as a group. James Packer had a say, John Quayle and I had a say,' Fulton recalls. 'They wanted to see what we had to offer—let's not beat around the bush. Contrary to what has been said in Brisbane, they were ready to come. The indications we got over the phone was, yes we'll go (to the ARL). The facts we put to them were about representative football. They had been told by Super League that the ARL was gone. When we spoke to them individually about money, they could see there was a fair bit more on offer with the ARL.

'If the English Rugby League thing didn't come off, I reckon the whole lot of them (the eight Broncos) would have been with the ARL and so would Sticky (Stuart)—without a shadow of a doubt. The whole Super League plan would have fallen flat on its face on the Thursday. They would say something different. But that's my opinion after listening to and watching them. There was no way they would have stayed with an organisation which hadn't done anything. The rep football was a big thing. It would have been a catalyst, which put the ARL out of the equation (to encourage them to defect back to the ARL). Some of them were upgraded, from what I understand. But it wasn't in line with what they should have got, for both ARL and Super League. What Lazarus was on was ludicrous, if they didn't upgrade him.'

On the way out of the Qantas Club and down to their parked cars, Lazarus and Kevin Walters were collared by the media. They both said they had attended merely to get the ARL's side of the story. Walters sounded rock solid with Super League, a thoughtful Lazarus less so, on the surface. Sailor, trapped at the wheel of his sports car by a television cameraman and two reporters, said: 'I'm a Bronco. One in, all in.' Carne and O'Neill sprinted down the length of the arrivals hall. Renouf, on crutches because of his injured knee, escaped being asked for comment when he was let out through a side door by a sympathetic airline employee, leaving one reporter to argue with his boss that the Test centre was in fact quicker on crutches as he is off them. Kerrod Walters looks back and claims that he, for one, was never going to leave. 'I hated the ARL, I wasn't going to go back to them after the duddings I had at the judiciary. I went for curiosity and to hear both sides,' he said.

That afternoon, all eight players returned for a second training session at Red Hill, the atmosphere strained. 'The most disappointing thing of the whole Super League war was when most of the players had signed and then those players went and spoke to the ARL,' Langer said. 'I was shitty with them and didn't speak to them at training that afternoon. No-one bent their arm to sign the Super League contract and they were just chasing more money with the ARL. They were trying to do the right thing by themselves, I can understand that, but I found it greedy they were doing it. They turned their back on a lot of money to turn down the ARL, so at least you have to give them credit they made the right decision in the end. But the ARL might have swayed a few blokes if they got in earlier.'

Ribot arranged a telephone hook-up at short notice involving the players who had gone to the airport for Thursday, April 8, at the Morrison Hotel. 'The biggest thing about someone like Glenn Lazarus is you've just got to tell him all the facts and once he absorbs it and makes his decision he is fine,' Ribot said. 'If you aren't totally open with him then he can get a bit bloody nasty, which he is entitled to be. But he's been great.'

Required to sweeten Stuart's Super League contract by $100,000 as part of the retention process, Ribot voluntarily increased the payments to top-earners Langer, Clyde and Daley and other dress-circle players, including Renouf. The top four were now officially on $600,000 a season. When some of the Broncos learned what some lesser players had received from Super League later in the first week of April, there was some anguish.

'Maybe they had been got on the cheap, maybe they hadn't. But no-one forced them to sign with Super League,' Langer said.

Super League would end up with enough players of differing quality to put together a ten-team competition for 1996, although a couple of clubs thought the more realistic number was eight to assure a good standard. The ARL selected no Super League players in the state or national teams in 1995, their spokesman maintaining a public stance that the best players were considered with an eye to the ARL's future. In March, 1996 Quayle would concede the obvious in a television interview. The representative neglect served to convince the rebels that they had done the right thing in leaving the ARL.

Super League players were now mixing in corporate circles even the Broncos players weren't used to. Ribot remembers Langer's sign-off line to Lachlan Murdoch after a dinner in mid-1996. 'Lachlan's a fairly big player on the world scene and Alf's said to him: "Say hello to Uncle Rupert for me." Lachlan had a laugh about it,' Ribot said. 'Allan wasn't being disrespectful and it was the larrikin coming out in him. When I'd run into him, he'd ask if the cheque was in the mail or ask how business was going and if he could give us a hand.'

But on February 23, 1996 the optimism and commitment of rebel players and officials would receive its greatest challenge. Justice James Burchett returned with his orders in the Federal Court case in which the ARL had tried to have Super League ruled illegal.

He granted all 29 orders sought by the ARL.

It was, in Arthurson's words, a 100–nil rout to the ARL and celebrations continued to the small hours at Phillip Street. The severity of the orders was not even in the worst-case scenario imagined by the rebel clubs. Chris Johns, a players' representative, likened it to a 'return to slavery'.

It was two weeks before the start of the ARL's second season with a 20-team league. Super League were ready to execute the program for a competition comprising the eight rebel clubs and two new franchises at Adelaide and Newcastle. The rebel players vowed to stay out, as injunctions on the players were granted, overturned on appeal and then reinstated. Like players from all eight rebel clubs, the Broncos voted not to play in the first round ARL premiership match against Auckland at ANZ Stadium. In all, only four of the 10 matches, all involving ARL teams, were played that weekend.

On March 17, the rebel players were heartened by the lifting of eight orders, effectively allowing the players to choose their own destinies as long as News Limited or its affiliates were not involved in funding a competition. A delegation of players headed by Johns, Daley, Gillies and Matthew Ridge and coaches Bennett and Monie worked with solicitor Geoff Applegate and English Rugby League chief executive Maurice Lindsay on a player-conducted competition to be known as 'Global League'.

Bennett came back from Global League meetings with a briefing for the Broncos players, as Super League sources revealed to select reporters that the rebel players would refuse to play for their clubs. Edwards said his top 91 players were all contracted to Super League and joked that Bennett and director Steve Williams, a former Queensland and North Sydney five-eighth, might have to make a comeback. Neil, Edwards and Cronulla chief executive Shane Richardson said it would be foolhardy and in the event of injury, possibly litigious to field 16- and 17-year-old players—for that was all they had left—in first grade against trained men.

An emotional Bennett was not ready for his encounter with the Broncos players when he returned to Brisbane. 'I got the boys together before Wayne came in,' Langer said. 'I knew Kevin (Walters) could keep a straight face and he got up at the meeting and said: "Wayne, we have had a team meeting by ourselves and we really think we have to stick together and play football. We're playing in the ARL premiership on the weekend". All the blokes had their heads down because they were about to start laughing. Benny's jaw dropped. He didn't know what to say next and then we went: "Ah, gotcha!"'

But on March 25, the full bench of the Federal Court ruled that rebel players could only be paid by News Limited if the players competed in the ARL premiership. The players' delegation expelled much nervous energy in a draining couple of days in which a list of 15 points was put forward. The most contentious were a call for the ARL to admit News franchises Adelaide and Hunter into a 22-team competition; that rebel players would not play in the winter's State of Origin series; and that Foxtel be allowed to broadcast 'certain games'.

The ARL, being in the legal position to dictate terms, not receive them, declined all the acts of bravado. They could like it or lump it. An emotional Daley said the ARL had treated the players like 'dogs' and said he would not play in the ARL premierships— they were remarks he would come to regret. While Daley and Johns wore their hearts flapping on their sleeves, the comments of

Langer were more ambiguous about the extent of their continuing support for the rebel cause. 'I have never been someone to get involved in controversy and I didn't want to say too much about it. I try not to get on the wrong side of people. But it wasn't as if I was wavering and I think the people who mattered knew that,' Langer said.

But that week the Broncos players had to make a deadly serious decision about whether they were going to play in the second round, starting on March 29, or sit out the season without pay. Edwards said publicly that the club would respect their decision, but hoped they would play, as a refusal would have serious consequences on the Broncos as a business. At the time it was too difficult to tell if this wasn't part of an intricate dance choreographed by Super League. Five players—Langer, Lazarus, the Walters twins and Hancock—spoke at a meeting of players about going back. Johns would have been a sixth, but was in Sydney.

'I don't think there was ever going to be a split on that. But if we (the five) wanted to sit things out, I think the younger blokes would have sat out too,' Langer said. '[But] we spent a lot of time on the phone to each other and there were more in favour of going back. So we did.'

Playing with greater concentration than many Super League clubs, particularly Canberra, the Broncos finished equal fifth in 1996.

On October 4, the full bench of the Federal Court ended months of helplessness and worry among rebel ranks. Justices Lockhart, Von Doussa and Sackville overturned the key orders imposed on Super League, freeing the rebels to start their own competition in March, 1997. An ARL application to seek leave to appeal to the High

Court was denied. When the league world reeled for the second time in seven months, Paul Morgan was at a city restaurant, determined to enjoy his birthday regardless of the whims of the trio of wigs in Sydney.

'It was a vindication. I personally didn't think we would go from 0–100 to 100–0,' Morgan reflected. 'I was semi-confident Super League would get up on business principles alone. It was more relief than a feeling of anything else.' The next month, Morgan would resign as chairman of Pacific Sports Entertainment, effectively severing his official ties with the Broncos, while remaining a consultant to News Limited. Five months short of the 10th anniversary of the advent of corporate ownership of rugby league, Morgan pondered if it had truly been worth the trouble. 'I'd probably not do it again if I knew,' he admitted.

Asked to consider the same question, Ribot said: 'If you had told me what would have happened over three years, I would have thought: "Gee, do I want to do this?" At a meeting with News Ltd, I remember being told: "Kerry Packer is going to go ballistic," so I went into it with my eyes open. But last year (1996) I got sick of it all.'

The Broncos players? They gathered secretly to hear the verdict at Bennett's house, to prevent the media from capturing the measure of the disappointment had Super League been put on hold until the year 2000, as the Justice Burchett orders had it. The mood was one of relief, rather than the pandemonium at Sydney's Marriott Hotel, where Richardson and Neil were throwing themselves around in excitement, embracing colleagues. But as the television at Bennett's house blared the results borne by subdued Channel Nine employees, a loud ring cut through the atmosphere. Langer rushed to the phone and picked it up. 'Yes, Rupert!' he fired.

ON THE PUNT

Everyone loves a rags to riches story. Australians cherish the Don Bradman story, Merseysiders the phenomenon that was The Beatles, and Americans the rise of Abraham Lincoln to the presidency. Allan Langer has shown he can handle a bat in celebrity cricket matches and can lay claim to the most oddball No. 1 hit in the history of Queensland's musical charts—and his rise from road gang worker to national icon is the stuff of dreams. But what close friends of Allan Langer are concerned about is that this might not unravel into a rags to riches to rags story.

Why?

The punt.

Under a barrage of well-meaning advice and words of caution Langer has moments of introspection and knows that his love for the adrenalin rush and the good times associated with gambling will have to be curtailed. From $120 a week as a removalist to around $600,000 a season from Super League, the amount of cash at his disposal carries a surreal quality.

'Everyone tells me I should give it up and I think it is a disease,' he said quietly. 'It's hard to get out of your system. I have tried many times. I have given it away for months at a time. It gets back to you when the horses you like are winning when you aren't on them. I have too many bets. That's the main problem. I have to learn to control it and not try to back every winner on the day. I enjoy it, but I'm not always going to have the income to punt like this for too many more years. I have to rein it in and that's something I have to start working on. I have been to friends of Wayne's and I have had friends of mine try to talk to me. I've never been to Gamblers Anonymous or anything like that. I couldn't bring myself to go there.' In a quiet moment, he can become scared that he may look with regret back at the money he has wasted: 'The scariest thing is that I want to live comfortably and be sure there is plenty of money for the family. Janine's not too rapt about the situation.

'I do it just because it's such a great day out. I win some days and lose others. I just enjoy the winning side of it. I get a big buzz out of it.'

With close friends like Broncos coach Wayne Bennett, there is an additional, unspoken concern, stemming from the six-months jail term of Langer's elder brother, Kevin, which had resulted from his need to repay gambling debts. 'Kevin Langer is like Alfie. He's a good fella, he's an honest guy too. It was just a situation Kevin got into with the gambling,' Bennett said. 'That's my great fear for Alf—that down the track somewhere the income is not there and he's still going to be doing this. But I have never seen so many people want to help someone. Good people, giving him advice on how to punt smarter. He listens, but he doesn't act on it. It's a great disappointment and there are very few things I have ever been disappointed about in Allan Langer. He's bullet-proof because he has the income and he doesn't listen to them right now. I'm not going to give up on him but he's the one who can make it happen.'

Janine Langer remains patient, but watchful of her husband's hobby. 'I wouldn't say he is a compulsive gambler. I'd say he was still in control of it,' she said. He would never put his family in any serious situation or pain. I really think it's an illness to be treated. They become so withdrawn and secretive from everyone else, whether it's a shame thing or whatever it is. It's one thing I'm aware of with Allan, if he becomes quiet or is talking outside on the phone, then I get concerned. If he can't make a bet in front of me, which is what I want him to do, then that worries me.'

Kevin Langer has rebuilt his life with his wife Donna and two children. He lapses occasionally out of the light-hearted framework of his relationship with his youngest brother to make his feelings known: 'It's dangerous how gambling can get away from you. I say to Allan: "Make sure you can afford it".'

'He still punts within his means. I think he will be right. I don't punt much these days. Donna is totally against it. But it's in your blood and you love it.'

Through 1993 and 1994 rumours spread in Brisbane and the Australian rugby league community and had him owing leading Brisbane bookmaker Brian Ogilvie $500,000. Others had him being in debt for anything up to $1.5 million to various bookmakers and casinos. A common conversation starter among the public was that the Broncos had to bail him out for his gambling debts, or at least advance him a year's wages to make up for the spree.

Undoubtedly, the rumours were fed by Langer's appearances on television, a medium with which he is rarely comfortable. A stock line when accepting a Man of the Match cheque, or just winning a game carrying with it a $1300 win bonus, was to crack that he would make something a favourite with it or how handy it was after his latest race meeting disaster. It saved him revealing too much about himself, his team or his game.

John Ribot said he dismissed the rumours because Langer never sought an advance from him. Ribot's successor, Shane Edwards, says the same. 'I'd be the first bloke to know if it was right because he would have needed to say: "I need a bit of a hand here",' Ribot said. 'It was the honesty and the scallywag in the bloke. He'd go on television and accept a Man of the Match award and say: "I need this because I went bad on the punt." Because of his profile, everyone would see him if he had $500 each-way on something at the track. Now that's relative to his income—he can afford it. I remember saying to him once: "Your way of seeing the funny side of things will come back to haunt you." He created the monster himself and didn't realise how people made mountains out of molehills.'

Harry Langer, a keen punter in much smaller denominations than his sons Kevin and Allan, has deeply pondered his part in all this. 'I wondered if it was something about how I was a punter, whether I could have said or done something different to get them to stop betting,' he said. Even when he was briefly on unemployment benefits, the lure of an afternoon visit to a midweek meeting at nearby Bundamba racecourse was irresistible for his youngest son. 'I'd save up and go to the races. I'd take about $20 and have, say, four $5 bets,' Allan said. 'If I won, I'd have $10. I remember having $5 on a thing called Swap Style, which paid 28–1. I felt like I owned the place,' he said.

Bennett said: 'He's always been a punter. I can appreciate that. He can't limit himself to the $5 bets now. He's got to have a $500 bet or whatever and he keeps going with it. It controls him—he can't control it. That's where he has his problem.' And his friend Pat Welsh, a Brisbane television sports reporter, shudders when he watches Langer on the warpath at the track or in the TAB. 'By no stretch of the imagination is he a good punter. He is convinced that if there are 24 races in three states, there are 24 winners for him to find,' Welsh said. 'He may go out there with one or two good tips. They may win, but he leaves losing because he has had 15 or more bets. And is filthy because he can't back 15 winners. They said about Michael Jordan, who lost even $500,000 on the golf course one year, what does it matter out of earnings of $60 million. Langer is close to seven figures in income, with his outside earnings.'

One area where Bennett encourages the gambler's instinct in Langer is with his predilection for tap penalties in goal-kicking range. Damn the two, we'll get four. Put more on, you win more is the sentiment.

'The difference is that on the footy field, that is something he controls,' the coach argued. 'We've had a lot of good results with it because his instincts are good on the field. He'll sense when the other team is tired or vulnerable. He never overplays it … well, maybe once or twice. The punting issue is different—someone else is riding the horses, someone else is training them. He doesn't control it. When he is having a losing streak, it affects his attitude. Betting is an emotional thing. I was in his room on the day before a game and he had the mobile and the phone in the room, going together, making bets. For a week, we had the boys going that I had tumbled into a $500 bet on Alf's winner in the last race.'

In 1990, Bennett and Broncos general manager John Ribot applied a game day punting ban on players after a loss to St George. 'I remember going into the warm-ups and could hear the bloody races on the radio,' Ribot said. 'Alfie lost a bit of money on a horse and there were other players and other people involved. It just wasn't the professional way to prepare. It was Wayne's call. Alf was certainly a better player on a Saturday when he didn't punt on the races. I wouldn't say that unless he agreed with it.'

Sometimes the situation would go over the top. Bennett remembers: 'I saw Kelvin (Giles) out on the field with a headset, which I had never seen before. I thought it was strange, but didn't worry any more about it. We led 10–0 early and then fell in a heap. We fought back and got beaten. I make a few inquiries after the game and Kelvin tells me: "Alf and Geno wanted the race results". Someone got them the result of the Golden Slipper and the race was run when we were 10–0. The horse they were on lost. So I banned them. He doesn't bet on game days.'

Langer being Langer, the restraint manifested itself in humour. Broncos teammate Trevor Gillmeister remembers a Saturday afternoon game at the Sydney Football Stadium, where spectators can swivel their heads quickly to see a replay on the big video screen at the western end, only to find out the result of the sixth at Caulfield instead. 'We had this game under control in the second half and I remember the forwards were packed down for a scrum, waiting for Alf to feed it,' Gillmeister said. 'We're wondering what is keeping him and I stick my head up out of the second row to see Alf looking at the screen and he says: "Bugger it, Gilly. I told you that thing would win". I said: "You are an idiot". I don't know if Benny ever heard about it.'

Langer, Gillmeister and Terry Matterson were involved in syndicates that owned racehorses. Bronson's Beat and Pregong won at Brisbane tracks, both landing plunges and being costly on different days. But way before his six-figure contract days, Langer was an owner. As far back as 1986, he leased a gallant steed called Ernest, in partnership with Kevin and Andrew Walters and Kevin Walters' future father-in-law Buddy Facer. It won three out of 12 starts, including Bundamba and a particularly memorable success at Gatton. Kevin Walters, an apprentice carpenter at the time, cannot forget a particularly unsuccessful mission with Ernest to the Caloundra track.

'I had my life savings on it, $300 or $400, and around the turn, the jockey dropped the whip,' he said. 'I'm nearly crying, Alf's going right off and then I wanted to fight the jockey. On the way home, I was picked up for speeding. So it was a great day.'

The irony in all this is that Langer is extremely wary around horses. Shane Edwards said when Langer had to appear for a promotional shoot with Buck, the horse that does a circuit of ANZ Stadium when Brisbane score a try, he appeared to be both holding the bridle and running at the same time.

Looking at his lifestyle as a whole, his love for the races, the golf course and the night out in Brisbane was part of his persona, part of what made him one of the boys. Occasionally, when the planets are aligned his way, he can land the trifecta on the same day. Like the morning at a Gold Coast resort course, the afternoon at Border Park racecourse, followed by an evening in a public bar, staggering through a pool tournament at the Palm Beach Hotel. Later in the night, his mates had realised he had been gone a while. He had walked onto the main road, leaving his golf bag and clubs in the hotel, hailed a cab and told the cabbie to take him back to Brisbane. He rang up the next day to see if his mates had saved his clubs.

On Australia's 1993 tour of New Zealand, team manager Geoff Carr was asked by a New Zealand racing magazine if he had a player who would be their guest tipster, a role which carried with it a $500 free punting account for the meeting in question. 'If he wins, he keeps the money. If he doesn't, it's not his money. So I said: "Do I ever have a player for you …",' Carr said. 'I had a bit of trouble pinning Alf down and it came down to waking him up one morning to show him the form guide and get a tip. He looks at me with his head cocked on the side. He spent about two seconds looking at it and came up with a 4–1 chance. He went back to bed and I never thought any more of it until I got a phone call a few days later: "Where should I leave Mr Langer his $2500?" I've gone down and suggested to Alf he should put the money in the team fund. He said: "No, mate. I put a lot of time and effort into that".'

Beyond the joking, Langer's fearlessness on the punt is symptomatic of the explosion in wages in the 1990s, particularly from April 1995 onwards. The Super League contracts and the ARL's resourceful fightback plan in reponse to it was the stuff of fantasy as players tried to work out what to do with their massive rise in disposable income.

But Langer's problems with the rumour mill did not rest with gambling. As much as the Brisbane he settled in during the late 1980s prided itself as a maturing city and dynamic new base of business and development, there was still in essence traces of its less assertive days. The Commonwealth Games in 1982, the World Expo in 1988 and Queensland's golden era in the two rugby codes all helped to engender a robust, outward confidence. 'International' is a term of reference, justification even, used for a city truly comfortable in where it stands in the world.

Few born-and-bred Sydneysiders, on the other hand, see any such need for self-justification. To them Sydney *is* the world. Periodically, Brisbane commercial television stations run documentaries, rounding up the same familiar politicians and business figures, out of a perceived need to re-establish that the city is a major player nationally. And despite expanding beyond the one million population, Brisbane retains the small town love of gossip. Every civic leader or television personality is subjected to keen scrutiny of his or her private life. So, during 1993 and 1994, Allan Langer was not the first Brisbane sporting identity to hear of the sensational exploits he was supposed to have enjoyed. Nor will he be the last.

'I was supposed to be living in a council house because I had done all my money on the punt and the Broncos were having to give all my wages to the bookie or the casino. And Janine was living with the kids in a refuge. Every second person I ran into had heard a rumour about us,' Langer said. 'The casino owns the house or a bookie does, I'm bashing Janine and she's in hospital. People say they get these stories from people on good authority.'

Janine Langer retells with relish a story where Terry Matterson arrived at a lunch with a few other Broncos players. 'Before he sat down, Terry looked at the people at his table and said: "And in case you are going to ask me—no, Alf isn't bashing his missus",' she laughed. Langer said: 'It has probably brought me and Janine closer together. At least the girls weren't at school yet. The worst thing was that my family and her family were being asked about it and getting upset.' Indeed Rita Langer said that for a while she stopped going shopping in the city because the questions from casual acquaintances were perplexing her so much.

Allan said: 'Close friends, or reasonably close friends, [or so] you thought, were starting to question if things were true. I was filthy on them. It's died down now. The only ones you hear about now are the punt.'

Ribot remembers reacting with a laugh to the rumours of violence by his player who threw one out-in-the-open punch in his first nine years at the Broncos—and broke a bone in his right hand on the jaw of his Cronulla opposite number Paul Green. 'The things about him beating Janine—well if anyone is going to beat anyone, Janine would beat Alf for coming home late,' Ribot said. 'He might say to a few of us: "Well, if she gives me any cheek, I'll give her a clip under the ear". But it was in total innocence. He has paid the penalty for his like of joking around, but he's probably learned from that.'

Janine Langer consulted Wayne Bennett about the best way to quieten the rumours. Eventually, they decided, at the recommendation of Edwards, to take it to a women's magazine. It was exactly what some friends in the media had told them not to do, as it could perpetuate the rumours, even expand the range. But the couple felt helpless, doing nothing week after week.

So on April 15, 1995, a double-page spread appeared in *New Idea*, headlined 'Battling the rumours—Broncos captain Alfie Langer finally denounces the gossip and stories that torment him'. The colour photographs of the Langer family at their new, sprawling Queenslander home on one hectare in Brisbane's western outskirts were most notable for a rare action photograph of the husband in the kitchen, doing to a tomato what he does to the game plans of opposition coaches for a living. 'We just felt we had to do something, our families were so upset,' Janine Langer said 18 months later. Harry Langer said: 'We knew it wasn't true, but you didn't like the innuendo. It was jealousy.'

The Langers welcomed daughters Courtney in 1991 and Maddison in 1993. In 1996, their son Harrison was born, 'Harry' for short, in honour of his paternal grandfather.

In many ways, the Queenslander home has the space of the Ferrett Street of Allan's youth. There are horses, geese and other farm animals. A playhouse for the girls. There is a dam which has played host to two of the most embarrassing moments of Alf's life. As much as he stays home when he wants to get away from football, true solitude for Langer is to straddle his ride-on lawn mower. But even in that chore he can be relied upon to make the humdrum flare into incident. 'Allan keeps driving them into the dam. He has sunk two mowers,' Janine said. 'He was wearing thongs one day and the thong got stuck on the pedal to put it in reverse. So he reversed into the dam. It didn't occur to him to turn it off. The police happened to be patrolling our area at the time. Allan was very embarrassed because this policeman had to jump the fence to help him pull the mower out of the dam. No common sense at all.'

Janine Langer is probably too honest and forthright to be

universally popular among the Broncos or league communities. Secure enough in herself not to court complete approval, she has often said to people what her husband thinks but prefers not to say to avoid confrontation. 'I say to people about Allan: "What you see is what you get." He has one of the most consistent personalities you will find. He doesn't try to impress people. I don't try to change him. I've had to make a lot of allowances for him but he's not moody and doesn't get himself into stressful situations. We like a bit of peace. When he gets home he has talked himself out about football and I'm selective about when I talk to him about it. I don't know if any professional player needs his family giving him any conversation about football.

'He likes the end of the season. He came home from the last end of the season drink and said: "This is our family time." He came home, drunk, and said: "I am lucky to have you". I have to play the role of two parents sometimes throughout the year. But football has given us a lot.

'He is very protective of me, as far as the media goes. He hates reading about himself or seeing himself being interviewed on television. He's likely to switch the channel. I have to say "Hang on, I wouldn't mind looking at this".'

Langer's friend, David Pie, said: 'Alf doesn't live the life of someone who gets $700,000 or $800,000 a year. He loves barbecues, having a game of golf every few days and a few beers and a punt.' Until the big contract of 1995, Langer drove around in a Telstar. After that, when he served a suspension for using all his licence points for speeding offences, he took possession of a top-of-the-line Holden. None of those smart European cars.

At the end of football seasons, the Langers have a same-time, next-year rendezvous with the Pies, the Nances, Andrew and Sharon Gee, and Peter and Jane Ryan. And, of course, Christmas at Caloundra. Just as the Sadliers Crossing Langers always did.

Janine said: 'We prefer to go to something simple for a family holiday, although the best holiday we ever had was the two of us on a cruise on the Caribbean. At Caloundra, after a few days with the kids, Allan likes to be a few hours away from Brisbane so he can have a game of golf.' Langer plays to a handicap of 18. That is to say, he can play to 10 occasionally and to 25 too often for his liking. With an agricultural swing, which looks as if he has experienced a stroke on the downswing, it's a marvel he can play at all.

Until 1995, the major dilemma nagging the Langers was what he would do when he lost football. 'I used to really lie there at night wondering what I would do,' he said. 'I've been lucky that I've never had a really bad investment. I've had good advice. But I realised I needed to start something business-wise before I stopped playing football.'

After years of investing heavily in the Queensland real estate market, Langer and Pie—a fellow knockabout he met when Pie was a merchandising officer for the Broncos in 1988—decided at a backyard barbecue that polo shirts were the way to go. It says a lot about Langer that his new business strategy automatically included one of his closest friends. No interviewing process. Just: 'Hey, Piesie, why don't you run it?' Then Kevin Langer came on board when Allan Langer Clothing operated out of a small office rather than Pie's mobile telephone. And in May 1995, Langer and Pie went after the Super League contract to produce T-shirts, polo shirts and caps for 500 players and officials. They sealed the deal before a proposal from two Canberra players, who were thinking the same way, could hit the table.

'Alf made the comment to Ribes at the meeting in Sydney: "This is what I want to do for the rest of my life." He doesn't say things like that every day,' Pie said. 'He feels comfortable sitting down with customers and answering their questions. He picks things up about the industry very quickly. He rings two or three times a day to see how the different orders are, or to set meetings up. I can't believe how hard-working he is to tell you the truth.'

The Super League contract was an entrée to sales to Broncos sponsors such as Ansett and Traveland and unaligned organisations such as Surf Lifesaving Queensland. But the very same contract was used to support a theory that was gathering steam that Super League would play host to the comfort zone of the 'old mates act' about which rebel administrators have been so scathing of the ARL for so many years. 'Yes, I hear what you are saying,' said former Broncos chairman Paul Morgan. 'But if Alf and Piesy don't deliver on quality they would lose the contract.' Pie elaborates: 'One of the ideologies of Super League was if one of the players came up with a viable business proposition, they would get the support.'

Janine Langer launched her own line of children's clothing, under the label Tin Can Kids. 'I love being a mother, but I needed some stimulation outside the home,' she said. 'I don't mind being known through my husband because I love him very much and I am very proud of him. I meet people who are amazed that I don't have a full-time nanny because Allan makes a lot of money. We made our own fabric by getting all the kids in the neighbourhood, including Courtney and Maddison, to draw a picture of themselves, or Mum and Dad, or another person. Then we put the pictures on the fabric.'

In early 1996, Langer held a meeting with Broncos chairman Paul Morgan about his business future. After it, Pacific Sports Management, the company of which Morgan was then chairman, had taken a small share holding. 'It's a rare talent Alf has got and he is starting to use it. I remember him signing autographs for 45 minutes after full time in that game at Broken Hill, in that heat.

The next day, he was talking to the managing director of Ansett in exactly the same manner. Most footballers are seen as dumb. There is no doubt he isn't a dummy. Alf surprised me with his tenacity in terms of getting in doors and making sure you made appointments for him. They could make a good go of it if they want.'

But not such a success was a Sydney company's range of Langer Australia toiletries. It didn't get the distribution needed. The public would accept Alf flogging cars, hot water systems, bread, cereal and muesli bars but offering free tips on what shampoo and toiletries to use stretched the bounds of credibility. 'Blokes were putting shit on him left, right and centre. I'd say these shampoo bottles are only half full. Is that because you have half a head of hair?' Pie said. 'But the greatest thing to me is that when he retires, he won't be going into a $60,000 a year job at the Broncos, where they ring him if they need him. He needs something that keeps him busy. Some of the blokes wouldn't mind a job like that when they retire from playing, where they have to get up by 11 to go to lunch. He does need a challenge.'

Langer's contract with Super League takes him through to the end of 1998, by which time he will be 32. It may be his last contract, he says, despite a well-known quip at the time he signed with News Limited that his contract had a four-year option clause, working his way.

'From my point of view, Allan Langer is going to be irreplaceable,' Bennett said. 'He has done so much for us as a player, his performances make him one of the all-time best players. They come along once in a lifetime possibly. Our task is to find the next one in Queensland. But you've got to be lucky to get any more than one every 20 years or so. I wouldn't be game to talk to him about the end of his career yet. The one thing I know about him is that if he isn't performing then he won't continue to play. It's one thing about him, he is such a competitor. He'd hate the idea he could let his team down. Losing is really personal with him and the day he feels he can't be at the top is the day he will get out. He's honest enough to realise that before anyone else does.'

Langer said he could never see himself coaching a major team. 'I haven't got that much hair to lose. I have seen what Benny goes through. No thanks,' he said.

How far divorced Allan Langer's life is from what it might have been was shown in sharp relief as he drove along the Logan Motorway early in 1996. Passing a steamroller and a gang of workmen with shovels, he turned to his passengers.

'You know, if I'd have stayed with the council, I'd have probably been driving one of them rollers by now,' he said, as if a major chance in life had passed him by.

FAVOURITES

Over ten seasons with the Broncos, 19 Tests and 24 State of Origin matches, Allan Langer has teamed up with almost every rugby league player of quality in Australia. In his own words, here are the players he rates as the best in individual positions.

Fullback

Paul Hauff at his prime. *Garry Jack* and *Gary Belcher* were great fullbacks, but in 1990 and 1991, Hauffy would make you feel so safe with him back there. I have never played with a fullback you had so much confidence in when the ball was kicked to him. The way he brought the ball back was unbelievable. I remember a try he scored against Canberra in which he beat Laurie Daley and Badge (Belcher). His cover defence against NSW was as much a reason as any why we won that series. A few injuries went against him and he never recovered. In 1991, he was dropped from the Australian side after one game and that didn't help his confidence. Then he had trouble with injuries and he was never the same again.

Winger

Willie Carne, at his prime, for similar reasons to Hauffy. When he first came to the club, he was the most competitive player I have ever seen in the games we'd have at training. He'd hate to lose. He was so aggressive in a game. A few injuries and the head knocks he took didn't help him. The way he ran—stepping off his left foot—made him a little vulnerable.

Of the others, *Mick Hancock* used to take so much heat off his teammates. He has a short fuse on the field and he can be cranky off the field, but he is the sort of bloke who would do anything for you. He has a kind heart. *Andrew Ettingshausen* has been great for Australia on the wing. Wing was his position, instead of centre. His defence is just outstanding.

Centre

Gene Miles: Mal Meninga played a lot longer than Geno and his record speaks for itself. I just felt that Geno would lift his team more than any other centre. I remember a game at Penrith in 1988. It was very physical and he was doing more than any other player on the field. When a team was in trouble, Gene was one bloke you would want in the centres because he would do more to help the forwards. He was aggressive and had those skills—that one-arm pass—that no-one else had. He is a good mate of mine, but I wouldn't rate him that high if he couldn't back it up.

Mal Meninga was a great big match player for Australia. He'd turn up when a series was on the line. He did it a few times. *Steve Renouf* became a very exciting player and his defence improved a lot with Wayne's help.

Five-eighth

Wally Lewis: Definitely. His knowledge and the scope of his game was fantastic. He read the game so well he knew when to turn up and when he could sit back a bit. In Origin games when I first came in, he helped my game a lot.

Laurie Daley is a big game player and he really showed his wares in State of Origin over the years. We didn't ever really click on the field, probably because we were used to playing with other styles of teammates. I was more used to playing with *Kevin Walters*. We had played together since under-18 and we formed a combination over a period of time. We could read each other's games. Kevin could easily have played more rep football than he did. The Queensland selectors kept putting him in the team and then dropping him after a loss.

Lock

Brad Clyde: His workrate is just unbelievable. The other team kicks downfield and Clydie is back early in the count to hit it up. You feel sorry for him, the number of injuries he has had. The game needs players like him on the field. He has copped a lot of punishment. *Brad Fittler* has a lot of strings to his bow. He is very level-headed on the field now. He hasn't changed as a bloke since he went on the 1990 Kangaroo tour and kept annoying the team manager Keith Barnes by setting off his rockets down the hotel floor or out the windows.

Second-rower

Trevor Gillmeister: It's not me picking one of my mates again. He is a player blokes love playing on the same team as. His defence was inspirational and he was one bloke you know would give 100 per cent against. One of the toughest blokes I have seen.

Prop

Glenn Lazarus: You start and finish with his record. He is one of those go-forward players and his quick play-the-balls gave the Broncos and NSW a lot of momentum. For a man of his size, his mobility is great. He plays with so much discipline. He doesn't get niggled much because the other players know he won't retaliate and give away a penalty.

With his teammates, he was easier to get along with over the last couple of years. He isn't the most liked player around—he has a temper—but he has given the Broncos a lot. We missed him in 1996 when he was injured for the finals.

Greg Dowling: At the Broncos I only played two or three seasons with him. He had a great year for us in our second year. Like Gene Miles, he was a bloke who started playing in Sydney late in his career and might wish the Broncos had have gone in earlier. *Sam Backo* had a couple of sensational State of Origin series for Queensland. *Martin Bella* wasn't my favourite team-mate, but he was great for Queensland over the years on the field. He'd give his best every game and he was certainly a proud Queenslander. *Paul Harragon*, the same. He seems to play a lot better for NSW than he does for Newcastle. I remember Chris Johns telling us that Harragon got up at a team meeting before a State of Origin game and told them he was going to do this and that—and he had a big game.

Hooker

Steve Walters: I didn't play my best football with him. I played better with *Kerrod Walters*. We were at the Jets for a couple of years and then the Broncos for another seven or eight. I only played a couple of games a year with Steve. He's a bit bigger than Kerrod or Benny Elias and his strength out of dummy-half was a great help to us.

Ben Elias, love or hate him, he was a great hooker. In Origin, everyone wanted to bash him. The Walters boys weren't that keen on him, same as he of them. But he gave a lot to their team.

Halfbacks

Ricky Stuart: In his kicking game and passing game, he is just about the best at both of them at the same time. Talking too, he would get his team going and make sure their minds were on the job. He allowed Canberra to play the way they did and was the player they missed most when he wasn't there. We get on great now. The rivalry was beaten up through the media, and it made it hard for us for a while. We were playing in the same positions and desperately wanted the same spot for Australia. Can be a funny bloke and a pest late at night, with his gee-ups. Loves pinching for some reason.

Peter Sterling: His kicking game was always precise and the way he would set up play when he played under Jack Gibson changed the game a bit. I never had any awe of him when I first played against him, but I soon saw why he was rated that highly. I lifted my game because I played against him. His consistency, from what I saw, was something else.

Des Hasler: He was quick and tough, very hard to play against. He wasn't the organising player like the other two. The players he played against knew how good he was. Off the field, you wouldn't meet more of a gentleman in rugby league. His nickname, as almost everyone knows, is 'Sorry'. You can't say enough about him.

Greg Alexander: He had a couple of sensational years at Penrith. His running game alone and his fitness was exceptional. He won a couple of semi-finals for Penrith almost by himself. Before we went away on the Kangaroo tour in 1990, we had a scuffle or two on the field and never got on. But on the tour, the

Broncos blokes got on best with the Penrith blokes. We had a great time.

Geoff Toovey: His best football will probably be in front of him. There are four very good players ahead of him. Toovey has come ahead in leaps and bounds in the past two years. His defence is unbelievable for a man his size.

STATISTICS

ALLAN JEFFREY LANGER

Born: July 30, 1966, Ipswich.

Clubs represented in first grade: Norths (Ipswich) 1985,
Ipswich Jets 1986–87, Brisbane Broncos (1988–).

BRONCOS CAREER (1988-)

Premiership games, including finals

Year	Starts	Repl	Tries	Goals	FG	Points
1988	21	—	8	—	—	32
1989	11	2	5	—	—	20
1990	24	—	6	—	—	24
1991	17	—	3	3	—	18
1992	22	—	12	—	1	49
1993	24	—	11	—	1	45
1994	24	—	11	2	1	49
1995	19	—	12	1	—	50
1996	22	—	11	2	1	49
TOTALS	**184**	**2**	**79**	**8**	**4**	**336**

NB: Langer has not played reserve grade and has only once worn a number other than seven—in 1992, when he backed up from an Ashes Test, wearing jersey No. 42, in Brisbane's 28–22 win over North Sydney at Lang Park.

BRONCOS RECORD

Year	W-D-L	Finished	Premiers	Club best and fairest
1988	14-0-8	Seventh	Canterbury	Allan Langer
1989	14-0-9	Sixth	Canberra	Greg Dowling
1990	17-1-7	Third	Canberra	Kevin Walters
1991	13-0-9	Seventh	Penrith	Trevor Gillmeister
1992	20-0-4	Premiers	Brisbane	Kerrod Walters
1993	20-0-6	Premiers	Brisbane	Allan Langer
1994	14-1-9	Fourth	Canberra	Allan Langer
1995	17-0-7	Fifth (tie)	Canterbury	Allan Langer
1996	17-0-6	Fifth (tie)	Manly	Allan Langer

Total win-draw-loss record: 146-2-65 (win percentage 68.5)

NB: Forfeit to Auckland in first round, 1996 is not included as win or loss.

FINALS RECORD

1990 L Penrith 16–26, at SFS.

W Manly 12–4, at SFS.

L Canberra 4–32, at SFS, preliminary final.

1992 W Illawarra 22–12, at SFS.

W St George 28–8, at SFS, grand final.

1993 W Manly 36–10, at SFS.

W Canberra 30–12, at SFS.

W Canterbury 23–16, at SFS, preliminary final.

W St George 14–6, at SFS, grand final.

1994 W Manly 16–4, at SFS.

L Norths 14–15, at SFS

1995 L Canberra 8–14, at Suncorp Stadium, Brisbane.

L Canterbury 10–24, at SFS.

1996 L Norths 16–21, at Suncorp Stadium.

L Cronulla 16–22, at SFS.

Won 8, Lost 7.

WORLD CLUB CHAMPIONSHIP

1992   W Wigan 22–8, at Central Park.

1994   L Wigan 14–20, at ANZ Stadium.

NSWRL/ARL CHALLENGE

1988   Lost in first round v Penrith 10–24, at Parramatta Stadium.

1989   Won final v Illawarra, 22–20, at Parramatta Stadium. In earlier rounds, d Canberra 18–13, at Parkes, d Parramatta 42-6, at Townsville, d Souths 24–4, at Bathurst.

1990   Lost in first round v Penrith, 10–18, at Toowoomba.

1991   Won final v Penrith 20–16, at Broken Hill. In earlier rounds, d Norths 24–10, at Bundaberg, d Newcastle 28–13 at Tamworth, d Illawarra 16–14, at Orange.

1992   Lost in final v Illawarra, 2–4, at Apex Oval, Dubbo. In earlier rounds, d Canberra, 28–16, at Lang Park, d Gold Coast 14–10, at Wagga Wagga, d Wests 16–10, at Wellington, NZ.

1993   Lost in first round v Souths, 10–18, at Lang Park.

1994   Lost in final v Souths 26–27, at Lavington Sports Reserve, Albury. In earlier rounds, d Canterbury 16–14, at ANZ Stadium, d Norths 26–22, at Parkes, d Illawarra 14–0, at Alice Springs.

1995   Won final v Cronulla 30–14, at Lavington Sports Reserve, Albury. In earlier rounds, d Sydney City 12–0, at Coolum, d Illawarra 26–4, at Coffs Harbour, d Newcastle 28–8, at Bega, d Norths 36–6, at Cobar.

LANGER IN STATE OF ORIGIN

Year	Games	T	G	FG	Pts	Qld W-L
1987	4	—	—	—	—	2-2
1988	3	4	—	—	16	3-0
1989	2	1	—	—	4	2-0*
1990	3	—	—	—	—	1-2
1991	3	—	—	—	—	2-1
1992	3	1	—	1	5	1-2
1993	3	—	—	—	—	1-2
1994	3	—	—	—	—	1-2
1996	3	1	—	—	4	0-3
Totals	**27**	**7**	**—**	**1**	**29**	**13-14**

* denotes Langer was injured for third game of 1989, won by Queensland. The record covering the period 1987–96 was 17–14, including Queensland 3–0 series win in 1995, when no Super League players were selected.

NB: Totals include the 1987 exhibition game in California.

LANGER IN TEST MATCHES

1988 v Papua New Guinea, Eric Weissel Oval, Wagga Wagga, W 70–8 (Langer 2 tries).

1990 v France, Pioneer Oval, Parkes, W 34–2.

      v New Zealand, Athletic Park, Wellington, W 24–6 (Langer 1 try).

      v Great Britain, Wembley Stadium, London, L 12–19.

1991 v New Zealand, Olympic Park, Melbourne, L 8–24.

      v New Zealand, Sydney Football Stadium, W 44–0 (Langer m-o-m).

      v New Zealand, Lang Park, Brisbane, W 40–12.

1992 v Great Britain, Sydney Football Stadium, W 22–6.

      v Great Britain, Princes Park, Melbourne, L 33–10.

      v Great Britain, Lang Park, Brisbane, W 16–10.

v Papua New Guinea, Townsville Sports Reserve,
W 36–14.

1993 v New Zealand, Mt Smart Stadium, Auckland, D 14–14.

v New Zealand, Palmerston North Showground, W 16–8.

v New Zealand, Lang Park, Brisbane, W 16–4.

1994 v France, Parramatta Stadium, W 58–0.

v Great Britain, Wembley Stadium, London, L 4–8.

v Great Britain, Old Trafford, Manchester (as reserve,
repl. G Florimo), W 38–8.

v Great Britain, Elland Road, Leeds (as reserve,
repl. S Walters), W 23–4.

v France, Stade de la Mediterranée, Bezier
(as reserve, repl R Stuart), W 74–0.

Totals for Tests: 19 Tests (16 as halfback, 3 as reserve), 3 tries,
12 points.

LANGER IN OTHER MATCHES FOR AUSTRALIA

1988 v Rest of the World, Sydney Football Stadium. W 22–10.

v New Zealand, World Cup final, Auckland. W 27–12
(Langer 2 tries, m-o-m).

1990 played in 10 other games on Kangaroo tour, including
one as reserve. Scored four tries, 16 points. Captained
Australia in five games, v Halifax (won 36–18), Halifax
(won 34–4), French President's XIII (at Paris, won
46–18), France B (at Lyon, won 78–6) and Languedoc
Rousillon (at Carcassone, won 38–9).

1992 v Sheffield, Don Valley Stadium, W 52–22
(Langer 2 tries as captain).

v Cumbria, Derwent Park, Workington, W 44–0.

v Great Britain, World Cup final, Wembley Stadium,
London, W 10–6.

1994   played in eight other games on Kangaroo tour, including two as reserve. Scored five tries, 20 points. Captained Australia in three games, v Castleford (won 38–12), Warrington (won 24–0) and Great Britain under-21s (at Gateshead, won 54–10).

Totals in all games for Australia: 42 games (including nine as captain), 16 tries, 64 points.

AT THE SCRUMBASE
(A look at who played Test halfback for Australia and when, 1988–96)

Year	Player	Opponents	Games
1988	Peter Sterling	Great Britain	3
1988	Allan Langer	PNG	1 (A)
1989	Greg Alexander	New Zealand	1 (B)
1989	Des Hasler	New Zealand	2
1990	Allan Langer	France, NZ, GB	3
1990	Ricky Stuart	GB, France	4
1991	Allan Langer	New Zealand	3
1991	Geoff Toovey	PNG	2 (C)
1992	Allan Langer	GB, PNG	4
1993	Allan Langer	New Zealand	3
1994	Allan Langer	France, GB	2
1994	Ricky Stuart	GB, France	3
1995	Geoff Toovey	New Zealand	3 (D)
1996	Geoff Toovey	Fiji, PNG	2

NB: Stuart played five-eighth with Langer half at Wembley, 1990. Langer played halfback in World Cup finals of 1988 and 1992, Toovey in three games of 1995 World Cup and Andrew Johns one game in 1995 World Cup.

Legend:

A: Sterling unavailable through shoulder injury.

B: Langer unavailable through broken ankle.

C: Langer unavailable through nose surgery.

D: Super League players not considered for selection by ARL.

INDIVIDUAL HONOURS

1988 *Rugby League Yearbook*, Player of the Year, with G Miller,
    W Lewis, B Elias, G Jack.

1988 Broncos Best and Fairest.

1991 Lotto Challenge Player of the Series.

1991 *Rugby League Yearbook*, Player of the Year,
    with G Alexander, M Meninga, E McGrady, S Walters

1992 Rothmans Medal, for ARL Best and Fairest.

1992 Clive Churchill Medallist, for Best in Grand Final.

1992 *Rugby League Yearbook*, Player of the Year,
    with G Lazarus, S Renouf, S Walters, G Freeman.

1993 Broncos Best and Fairest.

1994 Broncos Best and Fairest.

1995 Broncos Best and Fairest.

1996 Wally Lewis Medal, for Best Queensland Player
    in State of Origin series.

1996 Dally M Award, for Best Player, as voted by
    Daily Telegraph Mirror newspaper.

1996 *Rugby League Week* Player of the Year.

1996 Broncos Best and Fairest.

1996 *Rugby League Yearbook*, Player of the Year,
    with G Toovey, T Brasher, L Daley, D Gartner.

Statistics as at February, 1997
Source: *Rugby League Yearbook*, edited by David Middleton.

INDEX

CW01511839

THE DEEPENING STREAM

Persephone Book N° 141
Published by Persephone Books Ltd 2021

First published in 1930 by Harcourt Brace

Endpapers taken from a design for chiffon voile showing
2 colour schemes: a 1914–23 pencil and watercolour on
tracing paper by Margaret Macdonald Mackintosh.

Typeset in ITC Baskerville by
KSPM, Wolverhampton

Printed and bound in Germany by
GGP Media GmbH, Poessneck

978 191 0263 310

Persephone Books Ltd
8 Edgar Buildings
Bath BA1 2EE
01225 425050

www.persephonebooks.co.uk

Dorothy Canfield published fiction under the name Dorothy
Canfield and non-fiction under the name Dorothy Canfield Fisher.
Nowadays she is almost always referred to as Dorothy Canfield
Fisher and this is the name Persephone has chosen to use.

THE DEEPENING STREAM

by

DOROTHY CANFIELD FISHER

with a new preface by

SADIE STEIN

PERSEPHONE BOOKS
BATH

PREFACE

✟✟✟

By the time Dorothy Canfield Fisher wrote *The Deepening Stream*, she was already a well-known author of works for both adults and children. (In 1921 her novel *The Brimming Cup* was surpassed in sales only by Sinclair Lewis's more cynical portrait of small-town Americana, *Main Street.*) She had translated Maria Montessori's works and popularised her theories in the United States. She was also known as a committed reformer whose causes included adult literacy, women's rights, prison reform, aid for disabled children, and racial equality. Some years later, Eleanor Roosevelt would call her one of the ten most influential women in the United States.

In *The Deepening Stream*, she tells a story that is drawn largely from her own extraordinary life. Like her heroine, Matey, she was the daughter of midwestern intellectuals (she was named for Dorothea Brooke). Like Matey's family, hers was led to Europe by her father's academic career. Like Matey, Canfield Fisher – she wrote variously under her maiden and married names for tax reasons – had two children, and was a committed idealist who followed her husband to Europe when war was declared. The obvious difference between them is that Matey is presented as an everywoman – a contemporary review described her as 'one of those genuine, honourable and rather commonplace characters, in whose depiction Dorothy Canfield Fisher has always excelled'.

Perhaps unsurprisingly, given her involvement in Montessori schooling, Canfield Fisher also takes a deep interest in the emotional lives of children. Like many Americans, I first came to her work via her 1916 children's novel *Understood Betsy*, which only as an adult do I appreciate as a non-didactic argument for the Montessori values of independence, education, and responsibility. Although *The Deepening Stream* is not a 'Montessori novel' as such, it demonstrates the author's unusual sensitivity to children's particular concerns. In the book's early section, we see Matey and her two older siblings at the mercy of their parents' unhappy marriage. Although widely admired by outsiders for their sophistication, the Gilberts' home life is a minefield of insecurity, petty power struggles and acts of casual cruelty. The children cope, each in their own way. Matey grows tough: 'The vivid little girl whose small person had been shaken by rapture and panic in the ups and downs of games, the adolescent who had trembled at the sunset and at the injustice of poverty, was growing into a dry young woman, every day adding another thickness to the soundproof walls around her.' It's only a series of happy accidents – the love of a dog and of music; a sabbatical year boarding with a French family, the Vinets – that leave Matey receptive to love.

The great love that forms the second part of *The Deepening Stream* comes in the modest form of her distant cousin Adrian, a Quaker deeply rooted in the gentle rhythms of his small town, Rustdorf. Their marriage provides Matey with the stability and purpose lacking in her more worldly youth, and it allows Dorothy Canfield Fisher to treat her favourite grown-up themes – equality in marriage, a frank appreciation for sex, the importance of family, and of course the raising of children – with characteristic assurance and delicacy. If this were the novel in total – the story of a woman overcoming a difficult childhood and learning to love – it would be enough, a quiet and nuanced portrait of coming-of-age in the early twentieth century.

In the third section, however, the novel assumes a new scale altogether. Moved by the plight of their French friends the Vinets, already embroiled in the horrors of the Great War, Matey and Adrian shock their acquaintances by moving their family to Paris, where – like Canfield Fisher's actual husband – Adrian volunteers as an ambulance driver. What follows is an unsparing, sometimes shocking, very personal account of the war and of the limits – and necessity – of human generosity. Even as conventional black-and-white morality recedes and the death toll mounts, Canfield Fisher shows us clearly that what redemption there is to be found will only be found in the small acts of kindness, the accidents of fate, the humble individual.

It is a mystery to me why the *The Deepening Stream* is not listed alongside *Testament of Youth*, *A Farewell to Arms*, and *Parade's End* as a definitive World War I novel. Certainly, as any war novel must, it conveys the arbitrary horror of the conflict itself – but to this, it adds a sense of the cost to every aspect of home front life. Without ever taking the reader into the trenches, Dorothy Canfield Fisher makes us feel how war grinds you down, until one's receptivity to tragedy is necessarily blunted – a sort of adaptability that no one should have to learn, but which, thankfully, we can. The buffetings of an unhappy childhood may not seem to call forth the same resources as the Great War, its material deprivations and lost homes, literal maimings and losses. Yet, as the author shows us, human resiliency is a blessed, sometimes shocking constant. As Matey's father-in-law tells her after the family returns, changed forever, to a physically unaltered Rustdorf: '"why do we talk melodramatically, as if war were in an outside compartment different from life? All that can be found in war – appeal to the beast in us – to the man – isn't it in every day of life, if lived with imagination?"'

Recently, a venerable Vermont children's book award named after Dorothy Canfield Fisher decided to change its title on the grounds that her attitudes did not live up to our contemporary standards. The specifics don't hold up to close scrutiny – but the change was justified in part, the librarians said, because hers is no longer a recognisable name. While readers around the world would beg to differ – I still have that copy of *Understood Betsy!* – in the eyes of some modern arbiters, perhaps she seems too earnest and maybe too essentially optimistic for modern tastes. Her sheer productivity may count against her, too; to those minds that cannot separate art from struggle, there may be something distastefully wholesome about such a prodigious output. And then, too, hers are ultimately domestic stories – unashamedly focused on women, children, families at a moment when few middle-class women moved as she did, outside the domestic sphere. Perhaps critics have dismissed her as too much a domestic writer to be a great war novelist; maybe the early chapters, of girlhood, strike them as too slight. But, as is clear to the close reader, it's her brilliance at the one task that so well suits her to the other.

However, it would be a mistake to confuse earnestness with lack of sophistication. *The Deepening Stream* is strikingly modern: domestic hurts are addressed with complete seriousness; the pain of the war, meanwhile, is rendered intimate. The focus remains tight, unsparing, humane. Indeed, the prose feels so ageless that the occasional bit of dated language or generalisation – the sort of insensitivity her critics might point to – strikes the reader as jarring.

As one might expect of such an ambitious novel – or trilogy, really – *The Deepening Stream* falters at times. There are odd shifts in tone. Adrian can seem more saint than man. For me, Matey's very normality is an occasional stumbling block. Matey is presented as a regular person – a person of culture, conviction and compassion, certainly, but her will to action and her superhuman determination are never quite justified. Canfield Fisher's relief work earned her citations from Madame Chiang Kai-shek and the government of Denmark; while in France she organised a Braille press for veterans blinded by mustard gas and she established the Bidart Home for Refugee Children. Her energy was everywhere conspicuous. Matey, by comparison, is loath to engage with the cynical cogs of Big Government, and her continued unwillingness becomes hard to understand. Of course, Matey is a character.

But when the truest, most persuasive accounts are so obviously drawn from the author's lived experience, the abrupt lack of synergy is frustrating and a bit confusing. I wonder if Canfield Fisher thought she, herself, was simply too improbable, too energetic, too successful.

There were moments, while reading *The Deepening Stream*, when I would underline a passage about Matey's early memories and think, 'this is a wonderful evocation of childhood'. Later, when she marries, I was similarly struck by the deft and humane way Canfield Fisher conveyed the complexity of happy marriage, and found her description of new parenthood so completely apt that I stopped to read it aloud to my husband and our baby son: 'Matey had not laughed so much – or scolded so much – or cared so intensely about anything – or been so tired – or felt herself so flooded with vitality – not since she had been a little girl, playing.' By the time I read her taut description of the ravages of the Somme, I realised I had come to respect Dorothy Canfield Fisher as what she is – a great American writer – and *The Deepening Stream* as a neglected treasure of the last century.

Sadie Stein
New York City, 2020

THE DEEPENING STREAM

PUBLISHER'S NOTE

✾✾✾

The Deepening Stream is a novel in four parts, each one starting afresh with Chapter One.

PART ONE: Matey's girlhood.

PART TWO (page 139 onwards): her marriage.

PART THREE (page 299 onwards): her life in France during the War.

PART FOUR (page 517 onwards): the first few months of post-war life.

PART ONE

CHAPTER ONE

When people talked about things they could remember Matey always wondered which kind of remembering they meant – the kind that was just a sort of knowing how something in the past had happened or the other kind when suddenly everything seemed to be happening all over again. Why did time fade out some memories so that they didn't seem any more real than a story in a book? And why were others, whether you liked it or not, a living part of you at any moment when they come into your head? These were among the many questions for which Matey never found an answer.

Perhaps it was the ring of Aunt Connie's old voice, usually so dim, which had hooked the first of these living memories into Matey's four-year-old mind. Yet that was always the end of the memory. With the last echo of Aunt Connie's word all the rest vanished . . . the pale dreaming sky, the wide bare river, the leafless spring trees towering over the moist sweet-smelling earth of the flower beds.

When some chance reminder made the contact which clicked this picture up before her eyes she was again the very little girl who, holding confidently to a cold, soft old hand, scuffed her feet unrebuked on the gravel path as she walked slowly beside Aunt Connie's billowing black, camphor-scented skirts. With the remembered smell of camphor came instantly the old knock at her heart . . . how *could* the tulips be there, finished, shapely, when the last time she had looked there had been nothing but a few skimpy, rolled-up leaves?

There they were, as much themselves, though so new, as Matey was herself. Steady on their strong stems they stood, seeming at Matey's 'Oh!' to look off into the distance as though (she thought) they were trying not to show how proud they were of the surprise they had given her. What struck the small Matey was not so much that they were beautiful as that they were there at all so quickly! How ever had they done it? Dirt and stones and manure-stained straw lying at their feet. That was all they had to make themselves out of!

Matey's astonishment was too big to keep inside her. But she could not get it out without saying something, and she didn't know any words that fitted. The hand which held her little fingers always gave her what she wanted. She jerked imperiously at it, tipping her head back to peer up into the bitter withered face above her. It was looking at her now with tenderness. But Matey was only four years old. She took the tenderness for granted.

'Oh, Aunt Connie!' she cried, her mind full of her own feelings. And then because she could think of no word which fitted the tulips she could only cry again, longingly, 'Oh, Aunt *Connie!*'

Aunt Connie had known at once a word to say. She cried out, 'Incredible!' She said it queerly, not in her usual quiet voice, but almost roughly. It sounded to Matey hardly like a word at all but like the sudden noise a feeling makes inside you before you can think of a word when you get knocked off your sled on a hill or see the Christmas tree for the first time.

It was so strange for old cross silent Aunt Connie to have a sudden loud feeling that Matey was startled. She did not dare to look up again but made herself small, bending her head to look fixedly at the tulips. They seemed in the instant she had glanced away from them to have turned their faces toward her.

Matey knew from the sound part of what Aunt Connie's word meant. It meant that something you hadn't thought possible was really so.

But what was it that Aunt Connie hadn't thought possible?

For an instant, every time this memory came, just before they all winked out into the dark, it seemed to Matey that the tulips looked wise and conscious as though they knew.

This was the instant which did not die like things forgotten, nor like most remembered things, shrink and dwindle into something so much less than itself that it could be put into little words. No matter how long an interval passed between the infrequent times when Matey was reminded of it the memory always sprang freshly into life, as big as all outdoors, just as it had been . . . the sky as lofty, the Hudson as broad, the tall old leafless trees life-size; yet all that bigness less than the bright flowers which stood looking with a wise intentness at the little girl; while Aunt Connie's voice, like a gust of wind, shook the trees as it shook Matey's heart, and carried its cry out across the wide bare river. It never stirred a petal of the tulips.

CHAPTER TWO

✿✿✿

The children had honestly thought, at least Priscilla and
Francis had, that they were quite sure of the path up Izcohébie
Hill to the lookout rock. Matey had thought nothing about it.
She was nearly six – two long years of life had passed since she
had stood with Aunt Connie, looking at the tulips beside the
Hudson so far from her now – but she was still in the age which
takes no responsibility about finding the right path.

Also they had honestly meant to keep their promise to
Dominiqua about not leaving the right path for an instant.
Leave it? Priscilla had laughed and asked Dominiqua how far
off the path she supposed anybody *could* take Matey's short legs
through that prickly *genêt*?

Matey needed no commands from her big sister to make
her hold the exact middle of the winding trail as she trotted
after her elders. The tall broom on each side bristled furiously with what Matey called when she was talking English
'stickers', and when she was talking French *'piques'*, though
Francis told her that wasn't right in either language. She
turned her head from one side to the other to look at the
prickly stiff green bushes. Like rough sprangling-branched

little trees they were, millions of them, every one separate. How different *genêt* looked when you saw it through the window of Dominiqua's house in Biriatou, the smooth carpet of its yellow blossoms laid like seamless silk, fitted to every roll and shoulder of the hills. You wanted to lean out from the window and stroke your hand over a mile or two of that soft gold.

Of course, after these weeks of staying with Dominiqua, she knew what broom was. She had known all the time that the shining gold which she saw out of the windows was nothing but *genêt,* with skinchy little blossoms not so very big any of them, not such an awful lot of them to any one bush. She couldn't say that it was a surprise to see that the soft gold velvetiness was made of something just the opposite, prickly and rough and dark; but it did make many thoughts for her – dim six-year-old thoughts that were mostly feelings.

'Here we are,' said Priscilla from on ahead.

Matey was glad to know they were there. Her legs were tired and her stomach was empty. She could see Priscilla against the sky already running up on the lookout rock, the wind blowing her fair hair and fluttering her short skirts.

She saw Francis scrambling up the rock. And now Matey herself was at the foot of the boulder. The others shouted down patronising directions where to put her feet. *She* knew where to put her feet! 'I want my *goûter,*' she said rather crossly, as soon as she was up beside him. They wanted their *goûter* too. Priscilla was already getting it out from the paper bag.

For a time they gnawed and chewed and swallowed hard, in silent blissful gluttony, seeing distinctly the big brown crusts and nibbled-at lumps of chocolate, and dimly the distant blue sheet of the ocean to their left and the heaped-up Spanish Pyrenees to their right. Yet, even while she was still revelling in the mightiness of her jaw-muscles setting hard on their bones as they triumphantly brought her teeth together through the hardest crust, Matey was noticing that, there! the *genêt* blossoms had all melted together into one shining sheet of gold again.

But the outlines of what she saw begun now to blur, as everything awake in her let go in the first loosening of drowsiness. Francis and Priscilla were talking about the view like grown-ups. 'That little scriggle of dirt-colour must be the road from Hendaye to San Sebastian. When Father and Mother came up here they said they could see clear to Bayonne.' But their voices were to Matey's deliciously dulled ears like the hollow murmur of an echo.

She could not rouse herself even when they gave her such a rare and priceless chance to show off, by wondering if this was the place where the witches were supposed to gather at night. Matey could have told them. Being too young to do lessons, she spent her mornings hanging around the kitchen and back terrace, where she heard more witchcraft and black magic stories than Priscilla and Francis dreamed of. She could have pointed out – Dominiqua's aunt had pointed it out to her dozens of times – the very valley up which, as soon as the dark began to fall, the demons flew in from the sea on their leathery wings to join the witches on Izcohébie, leaning down to snatch the souls of any innocents whose mother left them out after dark. But it was bright daylight now; witches and demons couldn't do anything as long as the sun was up.

‡‡‡

'You mustn't go to sleep there, Matey,' said Priscilla responsibly, her eye catching the limpness of her little sister's arms and legs. 'You'd roll off. And anyhow we must be starting back.'

'I wasn't going to sleep,' said Matey, nettled, sitting up and stretching.

And then they were lost!

Of course it couldn't have happened like that. They must have been following paths through the *genêt* for ever so long – several hours perhaps – before Matey knew they were lost, for when she did, the sun was quite down. But her memory included none of what happened in the late afternoon. Probably she had trotted along, still in a golden half-sleep, still blandly unquestioning the wisdom of those who led her, the green walls on each side of the path sliding by, sliding by.

But she was awake – quite – when Priscilla and Francis stopped and stood still. It was awful that in spite of the terrified look of Francis's back, the path was so narrow they couldn't huddle together, but had to stand in single file. All Matey could do was to wiggle past Francis till she was between him and Priscilla and had caught her sister's hand.

'What'll we do?' said Francis, his voice trembling. Now that Matey was around in front of him she could see that his face looked even more frightened than his back.

Priscilla did not answer. For one horrible never-forgotten instant Matey thought Priscilla was going to be scared, as scared as she was, as Francis was, crazy scared. It was not just being lost, like getting lost in the woods at home, bad as that would be. It was being out alone at night on Izcohébie Hill.

Matey looked up into the greyness over her head. The wind was rising and making long, awful rustlings as it swept towards the top of the slope. A stray gust fumbled coldly at her hair.

Terror flung itself at the door of the little girl's heart, rattling and shaking the latch. Her lips were parted to let out a shriek, when Priscilla spoke. She said in her ordinary Priscilla voice, 'It won't hurt us any, even if we have to stay out till morning. It's warm, at night.' Oh, rock-like twelve-year-old courage! Oh, great-hearted big sister! The panic clattering at the door of Matey's heart reeled back a step.

But was Priscilla only pretending not to be scared? Matey longed frightfully to be sure that Priscilla was not, deep inside, afraid of . . . of . . . what Matey did not dare even to think of in words, lest the rapidly darkening sky turn into . . . into . . . she longed so terribly to know whether Priscilla was really afraid that she dared not ask.

She took another way to find out. She dropped Priscilla's hand, put her arms tightly around Priscilla's waist, and pressed her little body as hard as she could against her sister's. No, Priscilla did not feel afraid.

'Oh, ouch! *aie!* Matey!' she said. 'You're squeezing the wind out of me. Let me go, for goodness' sakes!' No, Priscilla did not sound afraid. Her voice sounded beautifully natural and cross.

The panic terror at the threshold of Matey's little heart shrank farther back. The whooshing of the wind died down from being a shriek to a great humming sound, and that was partly in Matey's ears as her blood unfroze and begun to trickle along its usual channels. She looked up adoringly at the older sister as she went on, 'We must have made a wrong turn and got into a sheep path. But we'd never find the right one now. If we tried we'd probably just get farther and farther away. We'd better stay right here till they come to look for us. Dominiqua'll be sure to raise the roof when we don't come in. You know how scared she is of anything happening to us while Father and Mother are away. I bet she gets the whole village out.'

Because of the humming in Matey's ears she did not hear a word of this. But she heard the sound of it perfectly. The sound meant that they were safe as long as Priscilla could talk in that sort of voice.

The relief made Matey feel faint. Her legs gave way under her and she sat down, dragging Priscilla with her.

'That's a good idea,' said Priscilla. 'We've got a long wait, perhaps. Sit down, Francis, and rest your legs.'

Francis sat down as close to his sisters as the crowding prickles would let him. Crouched there, on the ground, their heads were quite below the surface of the broom. Above them, Matey could hear the wind loudly blowing the blackness up the hill. It did not touch her now. Night had quite fallen so that she could see nothing at all, not Francis as he lay up against her, not Priscilla, although her arms were still around her. But, though she could not be seen, all of Priscilla was there, solid and warm and breathing, stronger than the mortal wickedness roaring over their heads.

'Oughtn't we holler a little to let them know where we are?' said Francis. His voice was still trembling. Matey moved a little to one side, not to take more than her share of Priscilla.

‘Oh, they wouldn't have got out so far from the village as this, so soon,' said Priscilla, reaching around behind her waist and undoing Matey's hands. 'You'd better let go of me and curl up your legs so you'll be more comfortable, Matey. You'll probably drop right off in a nap. You were half-asleep up on the rock.' She pushed the child down till her head rested on what small lap was made by Priscilla's short cotton skirt. It was enough for Matey. She let Priscilla do whatever she would with those warm sisterly hands. But as to going to sleep . . . with that panic creeping closer! She saw him plain . . . the lean demon sprawled face down on his dark cloud spreading out his arms as he swept overhead, stretching out his stringy arms to clutch at the hair of any helpless child out under the night sky. . . .

Dominiqua's voice sounded in her ears. . . . 'They can smell innocence, the fiends can, as flies smell meat, and flock to it – children after baptism and before they have lived long enough to commit any deadly sins – that's the age – '

That was Matey's age. . . .

The black wind stooped lower, fumbled with long stringy arms in the broom. By this time the air above them must be filled with evil spirits, lying out along the wind, drawing the ragged clouds around them, their devil's eyes gleaming through.

Matey's start of horror woke her up . . . she had almost dozed off, even the part of her she had left on guard to remember what it was that kept her safe . . . for an instant she did not know what that was. Quick! Quick! before she died with terror . . . what had it been that had made her safe? There *had* been something, hadn't there?

✿✿✿

Her hand, clawing out in the dark, clutched something, something knobby and hard and warm . . . Priscilla's knee. Oh, yes, it was all right, Priscilla was there. The blood ebbed languidly back into her sickened body. She laid her head down again on Priscilla's lap. My! but she was tired!

Was Francis all right? She felt in the dark for him. Yes, there he was, on the other side of Priscilla's other knee. He felt warm and limp and sound asleep. Oh, dear big sister!

'Don't nestle around so, Matey,' said Priscilla's voice through the darkness. 'Do get yourself in a comfortable position and *stay* there!'

What could the powers of hell and the demons of all evil do against a Priscilla? Nothing. Nothing.

To that refrain and to the now very distant murmur of the night wind, Matey fell soundly asleep, this time with all of herself, just as she did in her bed, at night. She left nothing on guard. Priscilla was on guard.

So sound asleep was she that when she woke she was inexplicably in bed, back at Biriatou in her nightgown, the sun shining on Dominiqua's sleek hair and kind face as she stood beside the bed, holding her black-eyed baby over one shoulder.

When she saw Matey's eyes open, she stooped to kiss her, saying, 'I'll run get your chocolate, it's all ready on the fire.'

Matey lifted a face of stupefied wonder from her pillow. There through the window stretched the old smooth miles and miles of golden blossoms. On the edge of his bed sat Francis, bright and glowing, just as usual. Priscilla looked around from the table where she was writing, a smile in her eyes. 'Well, Matey,' she said, 'you're a seven sleeper all right. It's ten o'clock.'

No, the rescue was no part of the memory for Matey, although she heard from others a great many times all about it. How, sure enough, Dominiqua had raised the roof and got the village out with lanterns, and how she, Matey, had slept through it all, even when Dominiqua's husband picked her up and carried her – even when Dominiqua undressed her and put on her nightgown.

'Just like a sack of meal you were,' said Francis, laughing.

She could remember none of that. But it took her an hour or two that morning, after she opened her eyes, to subside into her usual rate of living. Her mind went right on recording sharply the commonplace impressions of an ordinary day, as vividly as it had recorded the roar of the black wind over the *genêt*. Part of the memory of being lost was the anxious look on Priscilla's face when she said, 'Now, kids, look here. Don't let's tell Mother and Father about getting lost. Dominiqua would get blamed like everything. *You* know Father would. . . . Will you keep still? Promise.'

Sure they would. Matey had less than no wish to talk or think about that night. And it would be meaner than dirt to get Dominiqua into trouble over something that was no fault of hers. If Father came back from the trip to Italy as cross as he'd been when he started, he'd be sure to make an extra fuss over anything that would help show that it had been silly to go . . . and all Mother's fault for wanting to. Matey's experience of life as a whole was limited. Her experience of her parents, however, was quite sufficient to let her foresee this result. Over her bowl of chocolate she nodded seriously. Francis said with emphasis, 'Gracious, no! Absolutely not a word!'

The two elders applied themselves to their lessons. Matey got herself dressed and loitered sleepily down the stairs to get another *tartine* of bread and jam. Dominiqua evidently had her usual visitors. Matey could identify each staccato voice. Probably, she thought, they were saying how wonderful American children are, not to cry and get excited when they are lost, but to stay calm and . . . What they were really saying as she went into the kitchen plucked her sleepiness roughly away. 'Why, Mai Iturbe's boy, not eleven yet, went last week, a day's journey, and the path not half so well marked. And did he lose his way like these babyish foreign . . . ' Seeing Matey come in, they stopped hastily and smiled down at the little foreigner with a kind-hearted unadmiring pity.

Matey was only six, but she had lived long enough with herself to scringe, even before she felt it, at the pang which she knew was aching itself into her mind. She knew this pang. It hurt. She snatched up hastily one of her usual weapons against it. As she watched Dominiqua spreading jam on her slice of bread, she tried to think with all her might that Dominiqua was nothing but an ignorant cook, and that nobody cared whether she looked down on you or not. But alas, as usual Matey did care.

She moved away. But even leaning on the low stone wall which ran around the far side of the garden terrace, she could still catch echoes of their lack of admiration. She chewed loudly to drown out their voices. She swallowed hard, trying to swallow down the heaviest of her discomfort with her bread and jam. By and by, she listened cautiously again to the tick-tick-ticking of the talk.

'. . . every seventh year,' said Dominiqua's voice, once more getting it all wrong about Father's sabbatical. She was saying again that all Americans worked hard for six years and fooled around the seventh – getting paid for it into the bargain. Well, let her. It never did any good to tell her it was only college professors who were allowed to do that – and this year wasn't even a 'sabbatical', just a leave of absence without salary – and Father had worked like a dog writing textbooks to pay for it.

Now they began to talk about something else. Matey couldn't make it out at first. About somebody who had been very brave, although so young, who had gallantly played the part of a real little man, had comforted and quieted his fright-ened sisters – and then hadn't bragged about it afterwards. In fact it had been hard work to get him to say a word about himself, as it always was. Matey made it out now, all right.

An angry impulse sent her running toward the kitchen to tell them what Francis had really . . . but halfway across the garden she stopped short. She stood still. Something was again the matter inside her. She bit hard through her *tartine* of bread and jam, and chewed thoughtfully. To tell on Francis . . . ? Wouldn't that be – well, wouldn't it be sort of like what Francis had done, the other way around? Yes, it would.

With a sigh she turned back and went again to lean on the wall. It was strange, but that inner heaviness and misery was gone. Oh, goody! For the first time since it had begun she felt quite light and comfortable inside, and fell happily to watching an ant fetch and carry to a tiny anthill between the cracks of the stones.

Presently Francis came running out to play ball. 'I've got my verb learned,' he called defensively to his small sister, tossing his *pelota* up on the sloping roof of the cow-barn and catching it as it rolled down and off.

Matey was only six, but she knew that the women watching him from the kitchen were thinking how graceful the little boy was, and how beautiful his sunny hair looked, tossing about in the wind. It *did* look nice. Priscilla looked out of a window and saw him leaping in the sunshine, a small smile on his face. At once she drew in her head and came running out on the back terrace. 'See here, Francis,' she said seriously, speaking in English so that the people in the kitchen wouldn't understand, 'you really *mustn't* tell Father and Mother.'

Francis turned his clear blue eyes on her, pausing as he leaned his supple spine backward to launch his ball. 'Why, *I'm* not going to tell them,' he said in a surprised voice.

He threw the ball and ran nimbly to catch it.

Priscilla walked up close to him. 'Francis,' she said in a threatening voice, 'if you ever *do* – I'll tell Father and Mother about the time you . . . ' She said the last words so low in Francis's ear that Matey could not hear them. She heard very distinctly, however, Francis's quick answer. 'Why, of course I won't tell them. Didn't I say I wouldn't? What in the world makes you *think* I would?'

Would Priscilla say what in the world made her think he would? Matey's heart shrank together. But of course Priscilla wouldn't. Couldn't. From under her dropped lids Matey could see that Francis went on briskly throwing and catching the ball, and that Priscilla stood a moment longer looking at him. Then she turned around and went back into the house.

What had Matey encountered on Izcohébie Hill which had driven that long memory so deeply into her mind? Into her mind alone. For when a few years later she had grown up enough so that she could speak of it, she was astounded to find that Priscilla had forgotten their being lost.

'Were we?' she said vaguely.

She thought of talking it over with Francis, but on second thought decided not to. He *had* told – the next time he had needed something to divert Father's attention. And Priscilla hadn't told on him. Matey had known she wouldn't – and so had Francis – even while she was threatening him.

This was a night-time memory, one of those that never come to you at all in daylight, but when you get about so far asleep, start to unroll themselves in the dark. All at once Matey would not be flat on her bed, but trotting unquestioningly along the winding path behind Francis and Priscilla, turning her head from one side to the other to look at the tall green bushes, thinking busy little thoughts about how different it looked when you were down in the midst of it . . . all those millions of separate little trees, rough, dark, the blossoms so scattered and few. . . .

CHAPTER THREE

✸✸✸

Somewhere between that first memory at four and the next one at six, Matey had stopped being a baby and had begun to be a person. The process continued during the following seven years of school life at Logan Bluffs.

Not that there was any traceable connection between growth and her school life. The public school building where year after year she spent six of her waking hours was only a block away from her house, and yet when she walked through its doors she might as well have walked off into another planet. It was as far away as that. It was farther away than that. On another planet she would have gone on being herself. It was a little as though she stopped breathing when she went into her schoolroom and began again as she passed out. She was not Matey there, and to the real Matey waiting outside, she took back in return for those six hours nothing but the queerest collection of scraps – not even of ideas, only of impressions.

Years afterward, when she thought of her schooldays, what came to her mind, after a picture of her own battered desk in this or that classroom, and the blackboards and dingy books, and the frowsy hair of a little boy who sat ahead of her in the fifth grade, was a photographic reproduction of gold glittering in the front tooth of one teacher, or elegant white ruching sewed in the high-boned collar of another, of wisps of hair straggling down at the back over the cords of a thin neck from a badly adjusted back comb, of the tightness of stout woollen stuff strained over a corseted waist; of the beauty (never equalled by any later jewellery) of a cameo pin on blue velvet; of the grotesque, self-willed stylishness of huge stiffened sleeves. These bits of various teachers stayed with her. The rational explanation of subtraction – all the rational explanations so carefully expounded – vanished forever as soon as she had recited on them.

And yet it would not be fair to say that Matey learned nothing at school. She learned how to hide and dim and dull her natural wonder about the huge whole of which she saw so minute a corner. She learned how not to try to understand what is hard to understand, but only to learn how to use it. And the capacity to shut parts of life off from other parts, to live in pieces, this was a branch of learning not listed in the school syllabus, but thoroughly acquired in those classrooms. Matey learned it well.

Once outside the school *donjon*, life ran free and full. Full and free ran the current of play into which the children plunged. They lived for play. There were interruptions of course, and not only classroom hours. Precious time had to be wasted on a few light household tasks assigned to them, or, worst of all, before the piano. Such intervals were endured with the forced resignation which wilts to passivity travellers waiting for a train at a junction.

✸✸✸

What was this 'play'? What did the children find to do in all those hours after four o'clock till bedtime, not to speak of blessed Saturdays? Why, what do human beings find to do all day long when they are in love? Or how do they get through the hours when they have stepped off from the deadliness of everyday life into the enchantment of a religious conversion?

Matey and her comrades were mystics of play. They were in love with games.

They had more games to play than there was time for, because like the gods on Olympus they wearied not of familiar joys. When they had run through all the ones they knew, they started over again, with as sharp-toothed an appetite as though they had just begun. But they seldom needed to start over.

There were great games that needed a dozen or twenty children, loud dramas like 'Run, sheep, run!' or prisoner's base, and 'Red rover, come over!' In these each child, shrieking and running with all his might, felt his single personal excitement magnified by the screams and agitations of his fellows beyond anything he could have achieved alone. In others the excitement ran deep and silent, as in mumble-de-peg, and jackstones and marbles, played by a silent group squatting or kneeling on the earth. There were in-between games, like duck-on-a-rock, in which moments of hovering suspense alternated rhythmically with explosions into communal screeching and racing about.

For rainy days when play must be carried on under cover, in barns or attics, there were eerie games of ghost-like silence, variations on blind man's buff. 'Still-pond-no-more-moving-I-give-you-three-steps!' screamed out the blindfolded 'it', all in one many-syllabled word. At the end of the formula, the other players, fleeing for their lives, halted in their tracks. A barn full of children scattered about, and not a sound. As far as the senses of the blindfolded player could tell him, the world was as empty as before Creation. Into this silence the 'it' ventured out, feeling his way with his feet, groping with his hands. Sometimes he stopped, listening intently, within a few feet of a wild-eyed child pressing his hands over his mouth. Sometimes, taking a chance, he sprang forward at random, flinging his arms out wide and bringing them together on whatever he found – vacancy, or a fellow being.

There were moments when Matey was 'it' when, almost strangled by the obscuring handkerchief, she knew the bewildered thought, 'Oh, if you could only *see* . . . ' but of course, she knew well enough, if you were not blindfolded there would be no game.

When you were not 'it' but one of the statue-children, you never could remember in the least how the lonely 'it' felt – roaming blindly in vacancy. You had no room left in you for anything but the frightfulness of your present situation, only three paltry steps between you and this incalculable Destiny with hooded eyes. Those endless seconds when it stands within reach of you, when you have used up the last of your poor three steps and by the rules of the game must stand defenceless to take what comes! And that sudden shrinking together in noiseless terror when the hooded hunter springs straight at you!

✹✹✹

Once in the early days when Francis was not too grown up to play with the kids, he thought of an ingenious variation on the game. While the blindfold was being tied over the eyes of Skid Lathrop, who was 'it', Francis in rapid dumb-show explained his plan. He touched his chest, he waved a hand to include the whole group standing about him on the barn floor, he pointed to a broad beam about shoulder high across the end wall. Yes, yes, they all nodded understanding. They had caught the idea. In the moment of running allowed while the 'it' was calling out the formula, they all dashed to the beam and swarmed up on it.

That game was one of the things Matey did not remember, but lived over again whenever she thought of it. Francis's strategy was successful. The 'it' did not dream that the other players were not as usual about him. Perched on the beam, clinging like swallows to the rough boards of the wall back of them, the silent children, in perfect safety for once, looked down on their blindfolded comrade, going through a grotesque panto-mime of befooled activity on the empty barn floor – creeping forward, his head bent to listen intently, stopping short, dash-ing suddenly to one side with outstretched arms, calling out, 'I hear you,' in the old ruse to trick a child into some audible movement. All this with emptiness about him.

Francis's face was half-hidden by one hand as he stifled his laughter. His blue eyes sparkled. Most of the other children were following his example. The antics of the deluded blind-folded Skid were too ridiculous. Absurd and self-deceived, he careered about, snatching at nothing, listening fatuously to vacancy. 'Now I've got you!' he cried, foolishly, dashing ahead and closing his arms on nothing. Francis doubled forward in a paroxysm of silent delight.

Matey sprang down from the beam on the loose floor boards with an audible thud.

'I hear you!' shouted Skid, darting towards the sound. Matey had not yet taken the three steps to which she was entitled by the rules of the game. Nor did she now. She stood still, her eyes on Francis, her head flung up, while Skid's hands ran over her, looking for some identifying mark. There were few. Starched percale playdress – all little girls wore those. Cotton stockings and stout buttoned shoes – any child on the block. Long hair braided in two pigtails. Might be any eight-year-old out of half a dozen. How about hands? Calloused palms, rough hands that seldom wore gloves and had often clung to tree branches and thrown baseballs. Like anybody's hands. But here was something different – long, long fingers and knuckle joints that melted as you took hold of them. 'It's Matey Gilbert!' he proclaimed instantly, snatching off his bandage.

'Well, Matey, you're a great one!' cried Francis, scrambling down with the others. He came up to his little sister, out of patience with her. 'You spoiled all the fun! We weren't doing anything against the rules! What'd you do *that* for?'

Matey did not answer because she did not know why she had done it, except that it would have made her sick not to. She looked stubborn and closed her lips tightly. Francis said, 'Must be you're stuck on Skid.' For a moment the other children hung about listening to this family quarrel, and then with their unerring instinct when play was concerned, knew that for the time being the virtue had gone out of

Still-pond-no-more-moving. 'Come on, everybody, let's play Cops and Robbers . . . last fellow to Warren's maple tree'll be the cop.' They were off, Matey scampering as madly as the rest.

In Priscilla's day, only six years before, little girls had stayed indoors and played with dolls, or sat passively on the porch rocking like the grown-ups, and listening to their talk, but by the time Matey was old enough to run, public opinion had advanced with such a rush that only old ladies thought it tomboyish for the more active of the little girls to play with the boys up to adolescence – and there were extremely few old ladies in that young town. So it happened that Priscilla's mind became coloured by the accumulation, vast beyond reckoning, of impressions made on it by sharing her parents' life, while in Matey's little girlhood they tinged only the few hours spent away from school and from games. For from her sixth to her twelfth year this life of play made up the vital part of Matey's existence. Her small body – and her mind – became strengthened, hardened and toughened by it to a vigorous, insensitive vitality like that of a little savage. She acquired a profound respect for the principle of fair play and for stoical endurance. Most of the other Matey qualities, good and bad, stuff of sorrow or joy, lay weakly curled up in embryo, giving Matey twinges of feeling which she neither recognised nor welcomed. There was very little time left over from play for the exploration of personal emotions. Every child in good health played as hard as he could till he was ready to drop. And then he went to bed. At eight o'clock, 'recall' was sounded from every back porch. Not always from the Gilberts', Matey's mother having more on her mind than most of the housekeeping mothers on the block. But when the other children scattered to their tepees, Matey knew playtime was over. Breathing rather fast, she came scampering in from the dusk, her eyes glowing like those of a romping kitten, her hair tousled, often sparkling with dew, nothing inside her head but pictures of the game just finished.

After the sweet freshness of the outdoor air, the lighted living room felt thick and stagnant with people's breaths. Often enough it was still heavier with a hot something she was beginning to recognise. It was usually Priscilla's taut expression that told Matey things had not been going smoothly. Sometimes she could guess from the tone in which she was spoken to where the trouble was. 'Have you learned your geography lesson?' or 'Don't forget to brush your teeth.' These were neutral remarks, but they were coloured by the prevailing tone and gave her an accurate account of how everybody stood. If it was Father who asked about the geography lesson and if he asked it in a certain harsh voice, Matey knew he had not come out on top. If it was Mother who spoke about brushing teeth with a certain resentful heat in her tone, Matey guessed that she had once more been made to seem of less importance than Father. If by chance Matey had been there all the evening like Priscilla, she too sometimes tried timidly and awkwardly as Priscilla did to smooth things over, and felt as Priscilla looked, taut and strained by bedtime. But when she had been out to play she saw her family as through the wrong end of the telescope. Long before she could have unfocused and refocused her attention on any particular emotional crisis, the impetuous fatigue of a young playing animal would have dulled her eyes. She could have fallen asleep on the floor like a kitten. Still, although she brought in from play enough of its air to protect her somewhat, it was safest of all to find, as she often did, some sort of social goings-on, a card party, a rehearsal of a scene from one of Professor Marlin's plays, or even callers sitting around. For then she was sure of getting comfortably to bed, skimming safely along on the smooth surface of company manners. Once in her own room she dropped quickly off to sleep without any of the wakeful period of tossing and sore-heartedness over echoes of tones and looks which generally followed a quiet evening at home with the family. After a bout of hide-and-seek, it was all she could do to keep her eyes open long enough to take off her clothes and get into her nightgown.

Fainter even than her contact with her own family was her sense of the reality of the rest of the community. Somewhere in the back of her mind was registered a sort of composite picture of the other children's fathers and mothers and the houses they lived in. It furnished a perspective through which she saw life.

Nearly everybody – banker, carpenter, plumber, professor, grocer, butcher, doctor, storekeeper – lived in badly-built comfortable two-storey wooden houses, painted grey or brown. These homes were all supplied with a pleasant front yard of lawn-mowered grass, and a back yard of scythe-cut (if at all) weeds, occupied by a clothes line, a barn, a chicken-house, and a small vegetable garden – well kept if the family in that house were of foreign extraction, ill kept if they were of pioneer American stock, still expecting shortly to move on again. There were practically no fences dividing these lots from each other as in the older towns of Ohio and Wisconsin. Each square block made by intersecting streets was like one large roughly cared-for flat field, with houses, barns, and young cottonwood trees scattered about on it.

Over this territory, like a pack of young dogs the playing children scampered wildly with nothing to stop them. Certainly there was nothing in the minds of the elders to stop them. Nobody could have conceived of any reason for limiting their devotion to play, except possible harm to property. What else should children do? What *was* there for them to do? No one on the porch so much as turned his head when 'it' screeched his wild warning cry through the twilight:

> Bushel o' wheat!
> Bushel o' rye!
> All that ain't ready
> Holler out 'I'!

No one paid more attention than a distant nod of recognition when the porch itself was invaded by a panting hunted child darting up on tiptoe to hide behind a grown-up's chair.

After supper, 'Can-I-go-out-to-play?' rose in every dining room. It was a mere formula. It meant, 'I am going out to play unless I am stopped,' and it was followed – in spite of occasional grasping but usually futile grown-up efforts to get some chores done by the children – by a running dive out of the kitchen or dining room door into enchantment.

There were always children around, who met like meeting drops of water. To the yelling and shouting of the game which they instantly started, flocked all the other children as soon as they were freed – freed from sitting respectably at table to eat, from helping wash dishes or mind the baby, or from a spelling lesson to make up. Encountering in the twilight a group of children madly scattering, a newcomer needed but to shout, 'Who's it?' and 'Where's the goal?' and he was ready to turn and to race as madly as the others, his heart contracting in the terrible joyful anguish of the pursued, although the moment before he might have been sadly emptying out the garbage pail.

A foreigner would have thought them completely abandoned by their elders. But he would have been mistaken. Any child at any moment could be fished out of the sea of play. Their apparently lawless freedom was governed by one ordinance. No child under any condition was to 'go off the block' without permission. A call from any porch could reach the children wherever they were. 'Your *mother's* calling you!' had a certain fixed speech-tune to which it was always sung, preordained by tradition.

Moreover, the children were always either audible or visible to the mothers, who, as they worked inside their homes or sat on the porches sewing, watched over the playing children with as unforgetting a reflex faithfulness as that of the sentries of a grazing herd jerking their heads up after every three bites to make sure that all is well. It is true that nobody even glanced out of a window so long as the shrill chorus of screams was audible, near or far. But if a silence fell, the inmates of the houses, no matter how absorbed in their own affairs, soon looked to see what was happening. If there was no visible explanation of the silence in the shape of a mumble-de-peg or jackstone group, mothers stepped out. One called to another, who passed it down the line, 'What are the children up to?' Almost always a reassuring bulletin was passed back, such as 'They're in Schaumberger's barn playing still pond.' By the unspoken tradition Mrs Schaumberger then became special guardian. She knew exactly how much noise and how frequent bursts of it were natural to that game, and if there were not enough, felt herself called upon to go out unobtrusively on an errand to the barn. That a silent child meant a child in mischief was an aphorism of all those parents.

It was the other way around for the grown-ups. With the exception of a very few academic and professional families, the grown-ups on any block were silent enough. Life for them was work, as life for the children was play. When they stopped work at traditional resting-times it was as though they stopped living. They sat indoors in upholstered 'stationary rockers', their eyes fixed on the newspapers held up in front of them, or they sat outdoors in wooden or wicker rockers on the front porch, their eyes fixed on nothing at all. Either way, silence was a by-product of the hour.

Sometimes they recognised their dullness and felt depressed, but for the most part they thought they were too tired to do more than sit in a peaceable quiet in their own houses, rocking and letting the drained-out pool of energy fill slowly up so that they could go back to work the next day. The disagreeable sensation of stagnation was averted from the men by the occasional attentions needed by pipe or cigar, from the women by crocheting or darning.

These sagging grown-ups did not purposefully thus create vacancy about them in their leisure hours. What was there for them to do which would be interesting enough for people of their age to pay for the exertion of doing it? The block was divided into children who played for their lives, and adults who worked for their livings. Such elders cast a reflection into the lives of the children. Not only of their own, but of all the hard-playing throng streaming around them like a school of swift small fish, flashing about barnacle-covered barges. The children could not help seeing that the grown-ups were not having half 'such a good time' in their off hours as they. Half? There was no comparison. Day is not merely twice as bright as night: it is something different. The children saw this and knew that the grown-ups saw it too. Their own instincts told the children that it was a great pity to grow up and stop playing and go to work. Since the grown-ups thought so too, there could be no doubt about it.

Once a man left behind him at the end of business hours the grim interest in exacting work, he saw nothing for it but to give himself up to resignation. But resignation could not shut his eyes to the vitality of the child who darted quivering out of the twilight to hide behind his chair. At the sight of it, his own middle-aged flesh felt lead-heavy on his bones.

Envying the children their passionate enjoyment, they sat heavily in their rockers, their cigar-tips red in the twilight, the kindly bored wistful fathers on the block, carpenter, plumber, butcher, storekeeper, grocer, too conscientious, too tired, too responsible to look for passionate enjoyment in whisky and women, the only grown-up sources of it of which they had ever heard. They envied the playing children, and out of the love for them which was perhaps the deepest joy in their own lives, they pitied them, because every day was taking them farther away from the best and happiest passage in human life.

CHAPTER FOUR

❦❦❦

It couldn't last – such Arcadia! Day followed day and a thousand gossamer threads of familiarity and custom drew Matey closer to her family circle.

It was a perfectly lovely home, and she was a mighty lucky little girl to have such a fascinating father, such a wonderfully young-for-her-age mother . . . such wonderful parents both of them! . . . and such a perfectly wonderfully interesting family life! Matey heard this so many times from enthusiastic student guests that she came to know by the expression of their eyes and lips when she was about to hear it again. 'Such perfect manners!' 'And you can *speak* French!' Matey and Priscilla took speaking French as much for granted as having clothes to wear, but it greatly impressed the untravelled inland young people of Logan Bluffs. 'What a liberal education for our boys and girls just off the farms, to listen to such brilliant conversation!'

In a way it was an education for Matey too. Without asking any questions, merely by listening when she couldn't dodge, she learned the answer to many a problem which had always puzzled her.

One rainy evening when she hadn't been able to drum up a single playmate in any of the usual rendezvous she came disconsolately home and found Professor Marlin sitting with Mother by the living room lamp. Nothing extraordinary in that. They were always endlessly discussing plans for some sort of a show they were getting up. Matey sat down on the sofa, resigned to wait the required civilised interval before escaping to her room. Father was leaning back in his armchair and talking. That was a little unusual – not that he was talking – but talking to Mother and Professor Marlin. Matey remembered one visit when he hadn't lifted his eyes from his book, and another when he had got up and said, 'If you charming people will excuse me, I'll run over to Chandler's and try to do a little serious work on my department.' But she never remembered seeing him join in the conversation as if he were enjoying it.

'Ever been in Italy in August, Marlin?' Father was asking.

Professor Marlin said apologetically that he hadn't – in August or any other time.

'Well, take my advice and don't. We did once, and believe me or not, I'd gladly have changed places with any of the seven thousand nine hundred and sixty-seven representations of St Lawrence in his martyrdom I looked at during the three hundred and forty-three actual measured miles of gallery floor we walked over that excruciating fortnight . . . Oh, I knew it was a foolish venture, but not how foolish – imagination failed! We were quite comfortable in a little *trou* on the Basque coast, but Jessica had promised a friend . . . a *very dear friend* . . . Mathewson of the art department out at

Millerton . . . you knew I spent some miserable years there, didn't you . . . trying to inject a little appreciation of the Grand Siècle into the solid Nordic ivory headpieces of Nils and Olav and Olga. Well, Mathewson was a fellow sufferer, weary of casting Giotto into the feed-trough, and we joined forces . . . especially Jessica . . . *you* know how ardently she throws herself into any novelty! And the upshot was that she solemnly promised to make a pilgrimage to the Holy Land of the Quattrocento as soon as she could. So there was no help for it.'

Professor Marlin remarked that even with the heat it must have been a remarkable experience.

'Oh, quite,' Father went on, 'but not exactly what Mathewson had led us to expect. *Il faut souffrir pour être belle* – or to appreciate painting. But the dear man had omitted to warn us how much suffering was necessary – not to speak of the number of fleas one collects per kilometre or the mosquitoes on the Grand Canal or the aroma of Italian open plumbing. And to cap the climax, when we got back didn't we find that the "jewel" to whom Jessica had entrusted the children had taken her cares so lightly that she'd let them get lost and wander all night halfway to Spain.'

'Why, Morris Gilbert, of all the preposterous misleading exaggerations!' broke in Mother hotly.

But protests against Father were like throwing stones into a stream. They made a splash but had no other effect. He flowed on, 'Oh, I admit they came to no visible harm. But think what might have happened . . . for that matter we found out about it quite by accident . . . Heaven knows what catastrophes we never discovered . . . however, perhaps it was all worthwhile.

We acquired endless culture. Just by chance I came across our old volume of Vasari this evening . . . it brought back so vividly those evenings at the pension when Jessica used to read it aloud. I thought I'd repeat the experiment tonight . . . It will remind us of our old interests – of our old friend Mathewson.'

'You'd a good deal better save your voice for your public lectures, Morris,' Mother broke in briskly. 'At the last one some people at the back went out while you were speaking. I don't think you can fill a large hall the way you used to – or maybe they get tired hearing you quote so much French.'

Matey saw her Father's eyebrows twitch. His eyes started roaming around the room. Her stomach contracted just as if 'it' were reaching out a hand. The eyes rested on her.

'Little daughter,' he said with a smile, 'in the way of real education, there's of course no comparison between our talk and your textbooks, but the silly world still clings to its examination shibboleths, and your natural flair for geography is hardly robust enough to see you through without occasional study. . . . '

Matey waited for no second hint.

Another thing you learned from living with your family was not to blush and wriggle when you were being talked about. Matey got lots of practice, for as the youngest child she was naturally the central figure of some of the best-remembered family reminiscences. She got tired of hearing them over and over again, but it was always sort of interesting to watch Father fixing them as he went along and trying all his little tricks and manners to make them go off better.

✿✿✿

'The last time we paid a visit to Rustdorf . . . ' he would begin. Then he would give a little start and go on in a different tone, as if a new idea had just struck him – though he always did this part the same way – start and all, 'But, I forget, you don't know Rustdorf. Don't feel apologetic. The joke's not on you. The other way, I assure you! How can I make you see it? Rip Van Winkle might have been its first mayor. If he came back today, he'd be re-elected – unanimously. To speak grandiloquently, it is the ancestral seat of my family and my wife's. To speak realistically – the most torpid pool of stagnant humanity to be found on this continent. Also, it used to be the home of my Aunt Constance. She's difficult to do justice to – unless' – here he would wrinkle up his forehead and look quizzically around the circle – 'unless you've known someone of the sort in your own families. My Aunt Connie was one of those amiable people who had it in for the world because it hadn't given her what she wanted. All her brothers had been allowed to follow the light as God gave them to see it – doctor, lawyer, merchant, chief – whatever took their fancy; but when she made up her mind that she wanted to be a woman doctor, her family met in convocation and fell into fits, and told her to get herself a husband and some babies. Well, what would you expect? She was born too soon. Let me see, when was she born? Matey was born in '83, and Aunt Connie was as old as the hills then – she must have seen the light before 1810. How could she expect any family in a mouldy Hudson Valley town of that period to allow a daughter to be so unwomanly as to study medicine? Knowing the lady, I judge that she put up a pretty stiff fight; but it did her no good. She was never allowed a penny to carry out her wild ideas, and when she finally survived her elders and inherited the family strong box, such as it was, she was too old to begin. So, as I said, she got back at Fate by hating the human race in general and her relatives in particular. And yet when one summer little Matey was sent back to Rustdorf – we had measles or something of the sort in the house – didn't the old Gorgon appear to be quite softened – actually to take a shine to her, or so we fondly imagined.'

Here Father would make a long pause, smile broadly and say, 'I shouldn't go on, really, and exhibit the skeletons in our family closet, but it was such an absurd fiasco – our one attempt at legacy-hunting. Well, the fact is that a year or so later, my wife's strong maternal instinct decreed that we should pay at least a short visit to the old homestead, so that if there *should* turn out to be anything left to bequeath ...'

Somewhere along here, Mother would rustle in her chair till people looked at her. Then she would purse her lips and slump down her shoulder, as if to say, 'It wasn't a bit like that, but what can *I* do?' And Father would arch his eyebrows, and twist his moustache in a way that made it clear that of course his way was right, but if Mother felt ashamed of the truth he wouldn't be mean enough to insist . . . and go on, 'Well, suppose we just say that for some reason or other we did go to Rustdorf, and that our reception was less cordial than we had hoped for. To warm things up a bit, it occured to Jessica that a little showing off of the infant prodigy was in order. So one evening at table she said, "Matey, are you learning to spell at school?" Matey said, yes, she was; but when her mother asked her to spell cat, she shook her head and stopped her mouth with mashed potato.

'"Why, Matey, darling," said her mother, "you must know how to spell *cat*."

'"No, honest," said Matey, looking as brightly intelligent as a horseblock.

'I was making signs to her in dumb-show that I'd spell it to her with my lips, but she paid no sort of attention to me. Jessica was frantic, and Aunt Connie was looking around and around at all of us with those gimlet eyes of hers.

'"Why, child," said Jessica, "I thought you were reading little stories with lots of words in them."

'"Oh, yes," says Matey, as cool as you please, "I know how to spell it at school, c-a-t. But I didn't know for sure that it spelled itself that way at home."'

At this there was always a shout from the audience. It seemed to Matey that the story itself didn't amount to much compared to all the introduction it needed, but she always joined cravenly in the laughter. So did her mother. For somehow the way Father told it made it as necessary for Mother to laugh as for Matey. Priscilla only looked with a shadowed face from her father to her mother. The laughter always rose to a howl when Father, twisting the end of his moustache between his fingers, with a judicious reflective air, brought out, 'Need I add that Matey was *not* remembered in Aunt Connie's will?'

Somehow it must be funnier than she could understand, for Mother liked to tell it too. Only when she did, Matey noticed, she said it was Father who suggested the visit and the spelling show-off.

But what Matey found out for herself about behaving was as nothing compared to what Priscilla taught her. Priscilla was the realest person in her life. She not only loved and depended on her sister, but they were room-mates, so that just in the matter of time spent together Matey saw much more of her than of Father or Mother or Francis, who were all, as Matey was, absorbed in their own interests, meeting for the most part only at meals.

All during the early part of her life, when Matey didn't know what to do, she consulted her older sister; not in words, for things obvious enough to be put into words are seldom very puzzling, but by noticing what Priscilla did. After a time, as Francis grew up into a tall handsome boy in high school, people began to talk to her about that perfectly charming big brother of hers, and Matey looked at Priscilla to see how to answer. Her sister went right on using the same replies that Matey had always heard her use when people said those older things about their perfectly lovely home and so on. She smiled brightly back at them with her company face, murmuring in her company voice one of the company formulas, 'Oh, you're very kind,' or 'How nice of you to say so.' So Matey followed suit. Closely watching her almost grown-up big sister, the little Matey learned other transition formulas, which varied only in accordance with whether it was Mother's or Father's evening in the spotlight. 'There are some good seats left right near the folding door. Professor Marlin is going to pick the final cast for *The Winter's Tale* tonight. Mother's trying for Hermione. Isn't it exciting?' or 'Let me find you a chair up near where Father is going to read?'

After one of these 'informal unpretentious open house evenings', Matey and Priscilla were always too tired to do more than undress and get into their respective beds without so much as saying goodnight. To the last minute Professor and Mrs Gilbert, and later Francis, stood brilliantly at attention, looking their most vital, shaking hands with their guests. Along with them, the two parlours, even the dining room across the hall, in spite of its after-refreshment frowsiness, kept up the enamelled brightness suitable for the occasion, to the very moment when the front door closed on the last guests.

It was astonishing – used though Matey was to it – how instantly haggard and ill-natured the very chairs and curtains looked after this effort. The sofa pillows, especially, looked as she felt, as everybody acted, crushed into shapelessness by the pressure of others on them, all their professional soft pluminess packed into hardness and lumps. Francis, leaping up the stairs in long bounds, was always on the top landing before the last guests were off the front porch, and inside his room with the door shut before the family stirred and breathed. Sometimes he was called peremptorily back to do his share in the 'picking-up' which Mother insisted on. But often nobody had the energy to shout up after him, and then remember whether he had come or not, and shout again till he appeared. Priscilla often said, 'Never mind, I can easily stay up a little longer. I'm not a bit sleepy.'

Matey revelled in the admiration with which the Gilbert guests repaid the Gilbert hospitality, but she certainly did not enjoy the picking-up. Nor the breakfasts of the morning after. She early learned that company manners are not to be had for nothing. Yes, she and Priscilla dreaded those breakfasts. At least Matey did. Priscilla never said whether she did or not.

Matey had indeed, during those Logan Bluffs years of intimate sharing of every smallest detail of physical life, very little idea and not a great deal of curiosity as to what was going on in Priscilla's mind. Her moods were those of an adolescent, while Matey was still in the Stone Age of childhood. Priscilla was often silent and preoccupied. Matey adjusted herself to this inattention as naturally as she did to the queerness of grown-ups, or to the vagaries of the weather. She had a guess that these silences were not happy ones, and she even made a half-conscious connection between these moods of Priscilla's and her habit of looking anxiously from her father to her mother and nervously trying to smooth things over. But Matey was still a little girl and when her sister was silent and moody, she generally thought no more than that Priscilla wasn't so much fun as she used to be.

When Matey had 'homework' to prepare for school, the two girls often sat of an evening studying their different lessons at their tables on opposite sides of their bedroom. Sometimes Matey would feel that Priscilla had stopped looking at her high school textbook and was looking at something invisible to Matey. The stillness between them that had been quiet and studious became tight and strained. Matey too stopped looking at what was on the page of her book, although she still stared hard at it. When, as often, Priscilla's head slowly drooped lower and lower till her face was hidden in her arms on the table, her little sister dared not seem to notice, much less ask for an explanation.

It did not seem strange to her that, though she and Priscilla loved each other dearly and lived as closely as two sisters could, there were all sorts of things they did not talk over, or even mention, or even recognise by a look. That habit of family life had been set too long ago for Matey to imagine anything different. This did not at all mean that the Gilberts were a silent family. Quite the opposite. Their admirers said their home was one of the few in which real conversation was carried on. In the light of this repeated saying and of the home talk with which she was familiar, Matey defined conversation to herself as talk intended to cover up what you were thinking about. If it gave you a chance to show off, so much the better. Not knowing any other, she accepted this definition matter-of-factly, and quite approved of it, being very well aware that it would be no fun for anybody if what you were thinking about showed through the talk too clearly.

Thus, when Priscilla's eyes were opening for their first long look at life, as far as she could guess at it, she was to the rest of the family a child living with grown people. In her own room she was a grown person living with a child. She was never alone, and she lived in a perfectly lovely home and in the midst of a Christian community of at least twelve thousand souls; but Matey's big sister might as well have been solitary on a desert island at the moments when she could no longer endure what seemed to lie there before that first long look ahead into life, when shutting her eyes she laid her young head down on her arms, drawing a long defeated sigh that echoed forebodingly in her little sister's heart.

It was not that no attempts were made to help her. On the

contrary, her parents, noting how pale and thin she was in her senior year at high school, did all that parents possibly could do. They took her to the doctor.

He conscientiously gave her an examination, although he said to begin with he was sure an examination would bring to light nothing but what he knew already, that the only trouble with Priscilla was that she had been growing too fast. Oddly, nothing else was brought to light by his examination. He prescribed cod liver oil and a tonic that had iron in it.

But in spite of oil and iron, Priscilla did not gain either in weight or spirits. She continued to be very 'nervous', often looked tragic, occasionally burst into tears. It was all quite according to the most traditional pattern of troubled adolescence.

The family reaction to the situation also followed traditional lines. Priscilla's father tried to raise her spirits by a play of wit about her 'soul-symptoms' and 'growing pains', but with little success. Priscilla received his sallies in an ungrateful silence. 'Their feet and hands may grow to full size in adolescence before the rest of them,' he often remarked with irritation, 'but, by George! their sense of humour remains embryonic.'

Mother did not joke with Priscilla about her unsteady nerves. She never joked anyhow, and in this case she had another theory as to what would help her daughter. 'If you would only throw yourself into something worthwhile!' she used to say earnestly. At that time, 'something worthwhile' clearly meant the University Dramatic Club. Between them, she and Professor Marlin had fairly swept the faculty circle (not Professor Gilbert, of course) into their enthusiasm for dramatics as an alleviation to the dumb inexpressiveness of American civic life. Rehearsals were then going on, gathering momentum every week, for an outdoor performance of *A Midsummer Night's Dream,* the first of its kind, the beginning of Professor Marlin's famous career, it afterward turned out.

Mother was absorbed by the enterprise, not only by her own rôle of Helena, but by the endless labour over costumes, scenery, rehearsals, quarrels, changes of parts, which fill the last weeks before a dramatic performance. As the date of the play drew nearer, Matey noticed that instead of needing to wait the usual moment until Mother could get her mind on what you were saying, you now spoke two or three times before you could get her attention.

'Same old cycle,' grinned Francis behind her back. He was trying, with some success, to form himself on his father's conversational line. 'I can remember her back in Millerton, just as dead to the world when she and Mathewson were getting up an exhibition of Copley prints.'

But for all that Mrs Gilbert was a careful mother, and often enough she looked anxiously at Priscilla's downcast young face. One morning at breakfast, 'See here, Prissy darling,' she said urgently, as she said most things, 'you're the colour of a tallow candle and you haven't eaten one mouthful of your oatmeal. Do try to eat regularly, that's a good child! You're growing so fast. I'm sure that what you need is something to take you out of yourself – an absorbing interest. I *wish* you'd go in for dramatics! There's a rôle vacant now. That Nelson girl has flunked out two studies and has to leave college. She was going to play Hippolyta. Why couldn't you take her part? It's not long to learn.'

Priscilla shook her head and murmured that she didn't feel like acting.

'How can you know unless you try?' Mother's tone was changing from tenderness to eagerness. 'It's going to be such a success! The rehearsals are going better and better. Mrs Conrad's brother is visiting her, and he said last night that he was really astonished to find so successful a communal effort toward dramatics going on west of the Mississippi. He thought it a revelation of what might be done in other towns. He promised to write an article about it in his paper. And he's a *New York dramatic critic!*'

Matey hardly heard what she said. A premonition made her start bolting her oatmeal at top speed. Father said nothing, ate his orange with attention, but as he sat stirring the sugar into his coffee, something about his eyes, fixed reflectively on his wife's happy animated face, made Matey decide that she didn't want any more oatmeal and would better get her finger-exercises off her mind.

But the piano was only in the next room, and as Matey sat before it, she could see from the corners of her eyes the rest of the family around the breakfast table in Saturday morning leisure.

'Aren't you about through with rehearsals?' asked Father finally, sipping his coffee delicately.

Matey knew from the look of him, from the tone of his careless voice, that Mother was in danger. But Mother never did, apparently, until it was too late. She answered him now, honestly, earnestly, literally, 'Oh, *no!* We're determined to give our very best to it!'

'You haven't an illusion, have you, that rehearsals from now to Doomsday would make the acting anything but amateur?' remarked Father, smiling and looking down into his coffee cup.

Mother knew now something was in the air. Her pleased enthusiasm turned to resentment. 'At least there's a difference between good amateur acting and poor!' she answered hastily and hotly.

'Oh, dear!' Matey scringed on her piano stool. There was the opening Father was looking for. She hoped he wouldn't see it. But of course he did, he always did. And never witheld his hand.

'*Is* there, really?' he enquired delightedly, edging his tone with a false brightness of surprise, driving his neat thrust deep home by a pleased ironic movement of his lips, very familiar to his family.

Matey saw Mother flush darkly, saw the look of helpless anger blaze up in her eyes, heard her begin clumsily, 'I notice there's no question of "amateur" when *you* are the one who wants to . . . '

She stopped abruptly and looked across the table. 'Well, Prissy, how about it?' she said with forced brightness. 'Can I tell Professor Marlin you'll try for Hippolyta?'

Priscilla said nothing, but she stopped looking at her mother and father and began to finger her napkin. From her down-dropped eyes the ever-ready tears began to flow.

Mother put out her hand with an affectionate gesture of anxiety. 'Prissy dear, do *tell* Mother what the matter is?' Matey heard ever so faint a tincture of impatience in the energy of the voice. So did Priscilla apparently, for she pushed her chair away from the table and ran upstairs.

Matey saw Francis grin as, reaching across the table for Priscilla's oatmeal, he began to whiten it with sugar. She heard her father explode irritably to her mother as he folded his napkin, 'What's the use of asking her what the matter is, Jessica? *She* hasn't any idea!' He took a drink of water, and gave the quick turn to each end of his moustache with which he expressed exasperation. 'It's a phase that all families with children have to live through, I suppose. But I'm free to admit that it'll be a glad day when she outgrows it. She's about as enjoyable an element of domestic life as a wet sponge lying around wherever you want to sit down.'

He added, 'Of course she'll be all right as soon as she outgrows it . . . when she begins to have her share of beaux, probably.'

Mrs Gilbert said earnestly, 'I *wish* she'd try dramatics, I know it would occupy her mind.'

Matey's fingers had not, during this talk in the next room, stopped their regularly timed treading up and down the keys. But somewhere inside her was a click. Ever since Priscilla had begun to act queer, a mechanism in Matey had been registering how other people took it. That impression was now complete. A time clock was set, ready to sound its warning bell six years from now, when Matey would be Priscilla's age, or whenever she began to feel queer, if she ever did. 'No matter how queer you feel, you must not show it. Not to anybody, c,d,e,f,g – g,f,e,d,c,' went Matey's fingers, arching their necks like proud little horses, conscientiously pawing at the keys as hard as they could without making the wrist stiff.

'Matey, do you know, you sound as though you might have a nice touch on the piano,' said Mother, passing through the room with her hat on, looking stylish and filling the air with purposefulness. She went on to her rehearsal, leaving her words behind her. For two or three days Matey had been looking for something to lighten a persistent heaviness caused by Teacher's praise of Lena Weingartner's beautiful handwriting. Would this do? She examined it in her mind as she slid down from her stool. But she knew beforehand that it wouldn't do. Not that there was anything the matter with it. Except that Lena hadn't heard it. Although in moments of madness Matey herself sometimes told the Lenas about such things, she was always set upon and shamed so fiercely by another part of herself, that she was worse off than in the beginning. She never could manage it neatly as Francis did. She had plenty of troubles of her own, Matey had, without taking Priscilla's on.

She ran into the yard, taking care not to go to her room, because she knew Priscilla was there, perhaps still crying, and sitting down in the swing, began to push her feet vigorously against the earth. She swung forward and back, faster and faster, till, just as she had hoped, she had pushed the idea of Priscilla off and away, and was thinking of nothing but the flight up and down, with the fascinating sickness at the pit of her stomach on the downward swoop. It is not only table manners and English which are learned with no effort by unconscious imitation of one's elders.

Sure enough, as Father had predicted, Priscilla did get over it all right, thus proving how sensible they had all been not to get excited. Her way out seemed to be tennis rather than beaux. At least tennis was the only suggestion the doctor made that did any good. For after her graduation from high school, Professor and Mrs Gilbert, anxious to neglect no possibility of improving their daughter's health, took her once more to the doctor. It was much against her will.

'*I* don't want to see the *doctor!*' she told her father when he spoke of it. She said this in a high uncertain voice as if the idea were not the most reasonable one in the world.

'Well, my dear child,' said Professor Gilbert, in the tone of imitation patience which goes with that phrase, 'if you can suggest anybody else who you think is more likely to help you back into a normal state of nerves . . . ?'

His daughter looked at him. Finally, 'No, there isn't anybody,' she said in a flat voice which her father thought self-consciously tragic.

'Well . . .' He tried to go on being patient. No, it was too much! 'I don't believe a doctor or anything else would do any good in your present mood,' he rapped out dryly, and left the room.

Mrs Gilbert drew her daughter close. 'Prissy, darling,' she said, 'you mustn't take this time of your life so hard. It has nothing to do with your mind or soul – no more than tooth-ache. It's only the changes that are taking place in your body as you grow to be a woman. Your nerves haven't got used to them yet. That's all. If you keep your physical health good, all these ups and downs that you think are emotional will soon pass off. Now do remember this and take it more calmly!'

She had been determined at all costs to be kind, but in spite of herself impatience pushed its way into the intonation of the last sentence. She had not intended this, but perhaps it was just as well to give the child a glimpse of what a nuisance she was making of herself.

Priscilla looked fixedly at her mother during this speech and at the end of it replied, at once, with no expression in either voice or face, 'All right, let's go to the doctor.'

The doctor this time suggested that plenty of outdoor exercise might be a good thing for Priscilla's lack of appetite and sleeplessness. Tennis was a new game then, just beginning to be talked about in the Middle West. Some of the younger professors at the university had achieved a court on the campus that spring, and during the summer it was open to the resident faculty families. Priscilla threw herself into the game. Her devotion to tennis became as desperate as her face. She played all day long, every day, with anyone who would stand on the other side of the net, doubles or singles, and when no one else was to be had, stood in the torrid Middle Western sun, beating the ball against the wooden fence at the back of the court and returning it furiously on the volley.

And still she did not sleep very well; she was nearly always reading in bed when Matey dropped off in the evening, and several times when Matey woke up in the middle of the night, she found Priscilla's lamp lighted and her sister propped up against the pillows, a book open before her. Once, when Matey woke up, there was no lamp lighted in the room, but the moon was shining enough to show Matey something that startled her very much. Priscilla was kneeling by her bed, her hands clasped, and crying. Matey was a little shocked as well as startled. They went to church once in a while; indeed some of them went nearly every Sunday, in order to have somebody in the Gilbert pew because of Logan Bluffs' disapproval of non-churchgoers. But who ever heard of getting up in the middle of the night to pray? It made her feel very uncomfortable to hear Priscilla sobbing. She wondered if Priscilla did this other nights, when she slept through and didn't hear her. It was, because Matey was only half-awake, like a bad dream.

Indeed the next morning, seeing Priscilla now burned by the sun to saddle colour, muscular and active, beating the tennis ball heartily up against the back fence, Matey thought it certainly must have been a dream.

It was at any rate a dream she never had again. Shortly after that, September came, school absorbed much of Matey's time, Priscilla entered the freshman class at college, and threw herself into university life as into tennis. Every one said she was much improved. She had been a sober, responsible child with eyes that looked rather too deeply at people to be quite pleasant. And she had shown few of the social gifts so marked in her father and mother and brother. But, as often happens to growing girls, a marked change in her character seemed to begin as she emerged from adolescence. Little by little during all of her freshman year she grew more animated, talkative, like other girls. Her parents were relieved by the gradual emergence into a normal condition of a child who had caused them some anxiety. She no longer looked anxiously from one to the other, because she was seldom with them. Somebody was always calling her up on the telephone to go somewhere, or she remembered that she had something to look up in the University Library, or a date to keep with someone. In her sophomore year she was elected vice-president of her class. Her health seemed quite normal. By her eighteenth birthday she had at last become a fitting adjunct (with the exception of a rather restless manner) for her perfectly lovely home.

CHAPTER FIVE

✤✤✤

When Matey was thirteen, Father's sabbatical year came along, and it was spent in France of course, for the sake of his studies. In planning for it, the family had wondered what they could possibly do in Paris with Matey, who was still very much of a child, while Priscilla at nineteen was quite, and Francis at seventeen was almost, grown up. But the problem solved itself. Matey was provided for and her family left free for all the occupations they had feared she would interrupt. For Priscilla it was almost like a 'coming out', as those wander-years in foreign pensions and hotels often were for Anglo-Saxon young ladies before there were so many of them abroad. She was, it is true, 'taking courses' at the Sorbonne; but they were the open lecture courses, given by the fluent professors, popular with lady listeners, courses where you went when you pleased and took notes or read novels – just as you liked, and nobody knew or could tell on you.

Thanks to this free enlightened lack of supervision, Priscilla managed to pursue her studies without seriously interfering with social activities. Several young American students were dangling around her, getting up excursions to 'do' the cathedrals, museums, and cafés. A good deal of what was then called 'serious attention' was paid to her. Everybody thought she would be engaged by spring. One of the young men was sure she would be. Matey heard her parents talking about this prospect quite with approval. But Priscilla did not become engaged. She liked her young suitor very much. But – when it came to the point – no, she didn't want to be married, she didn't want to be loved, she didn't want to be talked to about momentous matters. She went through a manoeuvre which she was to repeat many times. She laughed him off, she laughed off her parents.

When discussion of serious feelings of any kind was imminent – at the first look which threatened it, Priscilla began competently to create the mood in which only small and cheerful feelings can be spoken of. Her eyes set the note. Like her talk, they were sparrow-quick, bird-bright, always warily on the lookout, always hopping briskly just out of reach.

Only Matey, still Priscilla's room-mate, ever saw a different expression in them. Sometimes, half-wakened from her first sleep by the entrance of Priscilla, in from same gay evening, Matey lay in bed, watching through half-closed eyes the sister who did not dream she was being observed. What stuck into the little girl's heart was Priscilla's expression as she sat before the mirror, brushing her long fair hair. The young face before the mirror gazed deeply at the young face in the glass as it never looked into any other human eyes, and the reflected face looked darkly back.

Matey felt the impulse to say something kind and loving – but what could she say that would do any good?

To everyone else Priscilla was a finished and successful young lady. Her father was proud of her and liked to show her off, not only to the Americans whom he knew, but to the French families who had grown up around the friends of his student days. Yes, it was considered on the whole a successful year for Priscilla even if she did act childish about her first suitor.

It did not seem to be a good year for Francis. He was in a boys' *lycée*, supposed to be doing the regular school work, and he certainly spent most of his waking time there, the hours of school attendance being cruelly long. But as far as anyone could see, he learned little beyond a quite astonishingly idiomatic command of spoken French, which he already knew familiarly. He wrote it abominably, so badly that his father, who naturally took correctness in French very hard, was outraged. And his monthly *carnet de notes* brought marks from his teachers in all his subjects, which made Professor Gilbert ask his son, angrily, 'Don't you ever look at your lessons? What do you *do* with yourself from eight in the morning to six at night?' Francis always faintly smiled at such questions and preserved a silence which his father considered insubordinate. Matey, pursuing her unconsidered youngest-child way, often heard things not intended for her. Once that winter she heard her father say to her mother, 'Just when one child gets through the detestable age, another falls neck-deep into it!'

As to Father and Mother – Father's main occupation seemed to be going to the Bibliothèque Nationale, doing, Matey supposed, the something-or-other which professors do in their sabbatical years. He was enjoying it greatly, whatever it was. He always seemed twice himself during a sabbatical year in France.

Mother – Mother was just the opposite. She hardly seemed like Mother when they were in Paris. She had, with her immense energy and determination, learned to speak French with correctness, but she had not so good an accent as the rest of them. It was unbelievable, the difference that made. Matey could not understand why it seemed to add so enormously to Father's advantage over Mother. Such a little thing – how you pronounced your r's! Why should anybody care – let alone permit it to darken the whole sky?

Mother wanted very much to make a visit to Germany and Austria that year – or to Scandinavia – or to Greece. But this time she couldn't have her way. Father's manuscripts, or whatever, were too exacting to allow him to get away for more than short trips. Matey's heart was heavy for Mother, and at first she wished they could please her by going out of France for a time. But once that winter they all took a flying trip for a few days up to Holland to see the Rembrandts and the Vermeers. After that Matey was quite willing to have them all stay in France. Father's state of mind over the figure he cut, stumbling and making gauche mistakes in a language he wasn't sure of . . . it was *terrible!* Matey didn't know how they lived through it. How small they made themselves – all but Mother, who hid a smile – whenever Father tried to put a question to a policeman or a tram conductor. And as for the awful day when a gentleman in The Hague stopped them and asked something in Dutch, too fast for Father to guess at a word . . . even as it was happening, even as Father, red and furious, rejoined his family, obviously wishing they had all been dead rather than there, Matey recognised it as stuff of one of the things she couldn't bear to remember. She began to cram it down into the black hole in her mind where she tried to hide such memories. When they crossed the frontier back into France and Father could begin speaking his beautiful French again, she drew a long breath as though she had escaped from a danger.

But such experiences, indeed any intimate contacts with her family, were rare that winter. One of Father's old student friends, now a professor in a *lycée*, had married a music teacher who in spite of the arrival of four children had always gone on adding to her husband's small income by giving piano lessons. As soon as the Gilberts were settled in Paris, Matey began to take music lessons from her. Then, as it was impossible for her to practise on the piano in the old stuffy salon of the small hotel where the Gilberts lived, an arrangement was made for her to practise on the extra piano in the Vinet apartment, the battered, old (but always scrupulously tuned) piano that stood in the bleak 'children's room'. The small sum which this brought in was very welcome to the Vinets, who were hard put to it to pay for the luxury of four children on the salary of a professor in a *lycée*.

The Vinet children, at least the three older ones, Henri, Mimi, and Ziza, were usually in the children's room doing their lessons when Matey went in to practise, and were obliged to stay there, the apartment being anything but spacious. Matey, although not a shy child, was at first rather abashed by their serious pale faces as they bent their dark heads over their books and wrote carefully in their blue-lined copybooks. But

✠✠✠

Mimi and Henri were near her age, and Ziza not very much younger. All four were natural children in different ways, and it was not long before they were on comfortable friendly terms.

The Vinets were being educated at home, and very soon Matey was sharing the attention of the teacher who came to give them lessons, while Professor Gilbert was sharing the expense of paying him. This arrangement pleased the Vinets, and it certainly gave the Gilberts a priceless freedom from having to take care of Matey.

Matey thus became for this year and a half almost a Vinet instead of a Gilbert. The first result was that she worked more than in all the rest of her life put together. Not that they 'worked' as Matey was used to seeing people work around at home. This was still in the days when every province was a never-failing reservoir of fabulously cheap domestic service. Poor though the Vinets were, poorer in many ways than the carpenters and plumbers with whose children Matey had played in Logan Bluffs, poor to the point of never having expensive cuts of meat and of wearing large patches on their coarse strong underwear, they were true bourgeois of their period, and never lifted a finger to do housework. A dull obstinate little Breton woman in her slightly grotesque, not very clean, and picturesque costume, marketed, carried coal up and ashes down the stairs, cooked, scrubbed the red-tiled floors of the kitchen and dining room, made the beds, and swept the floor of the living room. No matter how tired she might look, none of the family ever dreamed of helping her. Indeed, Matey had the impression that most of the time they did not see her. Twice a week her old aunt, grimly carved in weather-beaten oak, came in to do the heavier cleaning. A lean underfed floor-polisher came once a fortnight to skate breathlessly back and forth over the polished wooden floors on a waxed flannel-covered brush tied to his foot. And every Wednesday an old sewing-woman, who was paid two francs and her lunch, mended and darned and patched in a corner of the children's room. The Vinet life was of incessant effort, but almost wholly disembodied. No part of any Vinet body was active save his fingers in handling pen or piano keys. One of the many things which astonished Matey in this new life was to find that not one person in the Vinet family had ever washed or wiped a single dish. But for all that, the children led, and Matey led with them, a life of taut, driving activity, compared to which Matey's existence till then seemed like a sprawling, dawdling vacation. There was, it seemed, vastly more than she realised to be accomplished before children grew up. No time was to be lost.

Before them, Matey seemed to gather, once they were grown up, there lay not only work and earning their living, but new vivid interests and pleasures that children knew nothing of, compared to which hide-and-seek was as silly as playing with a baby's rattle or rubber dog. These pleasures and interests – music, reading, the theatre, study, conversation, art, friends, thinking – could not be enjoyed or even approached by people who had not been rigorously fitted for them. But they seemed to be within the reach of even hard-working, impecunious teachers like the Vinets. They were open not to money, only to those who held the right keys. With all haste and effort, one's childhood was scarcely long enough to learn how to handle the keys which opened the doors to the world.

✲✲✲

None of this was explicitly stated, indeed never stated at all. But the air was full of it. Casual conversation at the lunch table between Monsieur and Madame Vinet was a daily humbling reminder of how much there was for children to learn. Sometimes they talked soberly of the weather or the children's lessons or remedies for colds in the head. But often Matey could scarcely follow: they spoke with ardour, with delight, of things she had never heard if – of having the evening before seen Mounet-Sully play King Oedipus; of a discussion at dinner with a guest over a new theory that the classical tradition had continued into Gothic architecture; they disagreed to the point of squabbling over the reading which had been given of some Sonata or other at a concert, or fell into fits of laughter over the ridiculous noises made by the amateur orchestra in which M Vinet played the flute, when confronted by the unexpected intervals of a new composer called Debussy.

They might have been talking Hebrew for all the under-standing Matey had of their words, but she perfectly recognised the expression in their eyes and voices. It was one quite familiar to her, an eager living expression which, she had thought, belonged only to childhood and hide-and-seek.

Henri was the bridge between the grown-ups and the children at the lunch table. He was far enough along to ask questions about what went on in his parents' world. Their answers to him, some of which were almost intelligible to Matey, were like outstretched hands of strong climbers to those below them on the path, as if they called, 'Come along up where the view is better.'

Nothing expressed more clearly to Matey this desire to

have children grow up than the difficult abstract subjects given them for their compositions. 'Discuss the valuable and dangerous results of good humour in everyday life.' She told old M LaPlante volubly that she couldn't possibly write on such a subject. Never in her life had she ever thought about such things. He dismissed the protest drily. 'Why not begin now?' he asked her. 'You have had other people around you, always, who have either been good-humoured or not. You have presumably been sometimes good-humoured and sometimes not. *Think* about it. You have as much material as anyone.'

For the first time Matey turned her eye inward. Her capacity to think stretched its stiffened joints and emerged from its long seclusion. She gazed up at the ceiling and began to ponder certain things she had always seen.

When her composition was handed in, 'There!' said M LaPlante. 'You see you could do it as well as anybody. Why not?' When M Vinet came into the children's room the next time, M LaPlante handed him the pages in Matey's unformed handwriting. 'The little American has done a very interesting *devoir,*' he said.

M Vinet bent his scholarly face and long brown beard over the composition and read it through. 'Yes,' he said to the teacher, laying it down, 'that picture of a good-humoured person, trying vainly to hide by pleasantness the discord between others in the group – I recognise it.'

He added kindly, putting his thin hand on her head, 'Plenty of brains in that little skull. But, my dear child, do put your mind on the rule for the agreement of your past participles!'

It was nice to be approved of, but Matey had found that French approbation seemed to take a good deal of living up to. Like Mme Vinet's liking her flexible piano hand. What long hours of piano practice that had let her in for! And after her success with one composition, old M LaPlante gave them for their next subject, 'Discuss John Stuart Mill's idea that happiness is best attained not by a direct search for it, but as one result of a life directed to other ends.' Matey felt outraged, as if she had just staggered up a steep long slope, and instead of being invited to sit down and rest were being jauntily summoned to climb yet a steeper. But when Henri, looking over Mimi's shoulder at the subject, remarked, 'Oh, I *liked* that one when I had it last year,' Matey shut her lips over her protest.

She was far behind Henri (who was her own age) and had her lessons with Mimi, although she was two years older and nearly twice as big. Henri helped them more or less in the preparation of their work. She liked Henri; she thought he was nice-looking with his thin face and big nose. She liked, too, the mild subacid of his understatements. When little Ziza, who was very *coquette* about her clothes, paraded around to show off a new dress or a new hat, Henri's habit was to meet with brotherly coolness her burning black eyes, begging him to exclaim that she looked like a princess, and to admit judicially, '*Tu n'es pas ridicule.*'

Matey, who loved the flaming little Ziza best of them all, always rushed in with 'How lovely! How wonderful! How *chic!*' But Ziza prized her brother's judgment most, though she glowered at him hard and ran a little pointed red tongue furiously around her lips. They all prized Henri's judgment most.

Mimi was not as strong as the others, her colds lasted longer, radishes upset her digestion, and so did anything flavoured with chocolate. She was distinctly a pensive child, easily depressed, the kind of person for whom 'things always go wrong.' Instead of robustly teasing and mocking her, Henri and Ziza, when Mimi drooped, surrounded her with a pitying tenderness which often made Matey impatient, toughly perfect in physique as she was. Sometimes she privately thought them a little silly.

There were many things about these new playmates which disconcerted her. Sometimes, while Mme Vinet was giving piano lessons in the salon at the other end of the long dark hall, if the little Breton maid was too busy, they took turns watching over the baby Paul, called Polo. Matey was astonished by the adoration shown for him by his brother and sisters. She had always seen older children aggrieved when their playtime was cut short by the care of a baby brother or sister. As time went on, however, her attention being called to Polo's six-months-old antics, she too began to find in them some of the engaging qualities she had always been quite willing to admit in puppies and kittens.

Except for the cooing and incense-burning during Polo's visits to the children's room, it seemed to Matey there was no let-up whatever in the dynamo hum of their work. There were practically no moments of the relaxed delicious 'fooling around', doing nothing, which had filled so much of her largely served-out leisure. They passed from their ink-stained pine work table to the piano and back again. There was hardly more than time enough to prepare and recite the long lessons, to practise the long exercises set them. Whenever they did have a minute to themselves, Henri, who had just begun four-hand music and took it with the ardour of a stamp collector with his first album, would rummage out some arrangement of something or other from the piles of dusty music in the dark little *cabinet de débarras* which was the Vinets' poor city substitute for an attic, and expect Mimi or Matey to sit down at the piano with him and read off the bass or treble. Astounded and stung by the reading facility of her new playmates, Matey flung herself desperately at the pages. Into the attempt to get through somehow, anyhow, a rapid difficult presto, to land at least on the last note of the passage at the same time Henri reached it, she transposed the fierceness of determination she had learned in hide-and-seek, racing to reach the goal before her pursuer. But try as she might, Henri never seemed impressed. He was always kind, but from chance remarks, Matey knew that he saw her not as she pictured herself, repressed, silenced, accomplishing wonders of faithful work; but as a natural unrestrained young animal, untidy, noisy, unfinished – yet not without a certain aboriginal charm.

It was another story outdoors. Mme Vinet had the firm Parisian belief in the hygienic importance of a daily dip into outdoor air. Every day at three, the baby, Polo, was put in his carriage and the conscientious mother took her children out. Perhaps once a month on fine Sundays they took their lunches in paper packages and spent the whole day in the country out of doors.

Before Matey's arrival the daily outing had been a walk, enlivened by gently rolling hoops or skipping rope beside their mother as she slowly pushed the baby-carriage along. They knew accurately how far they could go in the allotted hour along the *allées* and gravel walks of the Luxembourg gardens. The beauty of the exquisitely tended flower beds in the different seasons was an important part of their pleasure and very often a subject of their talk. They often stopped, too, to gaze dreamily at the interminable games of croquet being played under the trees by old gentlemen *en retraite*, which neither began nor ended, but were.

Without any intention of being revolutionary, indeed without thinking at all about it, Matey at once turned this routine upside down. It was the first time she had ever lived in an apartment – they were known only by hearsay in the America of her childhood – and the ordinary restrictions as to quiet, necessary because of neighbours above and below, were suffocating to her. The moment she had found herself out of doors, with real earth under her feet and over her head a sky recognisable as such though so grey, she had burst into play as a fountain flings itself up into the air. Her bacchante delight in romping was as infectious to the sensitively organised Vinet children as a peal of laughter. Ziza, quicksilver Ziza, was after her in a moment, and even Henri, the dignified and precocious, soon followed her away from his mother's side, and with his sisters began to run and shout, to play tag, hide-and-seek, and puss-in-the-corner, to use his great hoop in breathless races with one of the little girls, instead of as an exercise in dexterity to see how slowly he could keep it moving without falling over.

On their Sundays in the country Matey even organised a truncated version of one-old-cat baseball. Mimi, always a little inclined to what Matey learned to call *nonchalance*, often did not feel energetic enough to join in this play, but Ziza was soon not a bad catcher, and a real expert at running bases, although she never could learn to save her breath by refraining from wild shrieks as she ran. As for Henri, the ups and downs of this mild contest provided a quite extravagant excitement to the musicianly little boy brought up with his sisters who had never before played any outdoor boy's game more competitive than spinning tops.

Mme Vinet was somewhat taken aback by the turbulence into which the little American led her brood, but she and her husband, like most of the members of the Instruction Publique of that period, considered themselves open to new ideas, even startling ones. In addition, Mme Vinet, like most Frenchwomen, intensely wished to have the best for her children, and even the density of bourgeois traditions did not hide from her the fact that her children's faces were rosier as well as dirtier after an hour of this immoderate Americanised play, and that they were getting through the dark dripping Paris winter with fewer colds and better appetites than usual. She was obliged, of course, to draw the line somewhere. She checked the loudness of their voices, she forbade them to run or skip once they were on the street on the way home; and she firmly enforced the rule about the impropriety of appearing in public with ungloved hands; after all one could not let them act like little guttersnipes.

It was hardly one of Matey's most comfortable years,

perpetually tuned up as she was to an incredible standard of serious behaviour, good manners, and hard work, perpetually nettled and humiliated to find herself so ignorant of what her playfellows took for granted. But it was a memorable one, bringing into her life permanent new elements – new interests, new ideals – her first encounter with a living religion. Not that the Vinets were devout in the usual sense. On the contrary, they joined heartily (as became members of the still new secular system of public education) in the anti-clerical Third Republic reaction from formal faith. They lived and brought their children up conscientiously in a vivid unbelief in all the dogmas and creeds which their own parents had taught them. They spoke (with self-conscious radicalism) of Jesus as one of the great sages of the world, and taught the children to venerate Socrates and Buddha also. But this attitude, while it had more warmth of religious feeling than the quite indifferent, occasional church-going American tolerance to which Matey was accustomed, was not the glowing core of their faith, the basis of their radiant denial of the vanity of all things, which cast its reflected light into Matey's empty little soul.

Sometimes, late in the afternoon, after they had come in from their play, when it was not Mme Vinet's carefully observed 'third Tuesday at home' and when she had no lesson to give, they had a quiet visit all together in the salon. Mme Vinet was often too tired to struggle for long with the stiff difficult medium of words. It was nearly always from the piano that she talked with her music-loving children.

It is dark by five o'clock of a Paris winter. When they entered the heavily curtained living room, Mme Vinet always went to light the two candles on each side of the piano. Their pointed yellow flames were the only brightness in the room, except the red glow from the stove. When she sat down at the piano, neat in her often-mended black dress, the candles shed little light on anything but her pale plain face, as running her fingers over the keys she looked thoughtfully at the children, sitting very still and remembering to keep both feet on the floor.

What she played was a natural part of their day's life, of her daily routine, a musical comment on what some one of them had been doing. Sometimes she ran over what one of the children was practising, making out of a Bach Invention, which had been mere difficulties for Matey, a thing of clear and intelligible beauty. Sometimes she played what one of her older pupils was struggling with, a Chopin Prelude, a movement from a Beethoven Sonata, and told the children about what the student's difficulty was – here in this phrase – and how it would be ultimately overcome and forgotten by doing this with the fingers – and that with the wrist – but above all by coming to understand the phrase. 'Music is having something to say and not saying it in words,' as she often told them. Sometimes she played music that helped explain their lessons, as on the day when they first laughed over the *Bourgeois Gentilhomme,* when she played some of the crisp humorous seventeenth century music that had been written to go with the play when the ink from Molière's pen was scarcely dry on the manuscript.

Another day little Ziza encountered the death of Jeanne d'Arc and cried over it so bitterly that Mimi, not usually very imaginative, cried too. Even Matey, in spite of her astonishment that anything in a history lesson should be taken so to heart, had been moved to consider for the first time that Jeanne d'Arc had been a real girl just about Priscilla's age, and that it must hurt like anything to be burned alive. Nobody had tried to stop Ziza's tears, nobody had tried to 'cheer her up', but that afternoon, Mme Vinet had hunted out among her music a little thin album. It held, she told them, music written by Bach just for himself, his thinking aloud. 'Come here, Ziza darling. This is for you. You know, composers when they feel sad don't cry as little girls do. They have another way to say what they feel. Here is what Bach felt when he thought about the death of an innocent person who had done nothing but good. He called it "At Calvary."' As her mother played, Ziza cried a little more on her shoulder. The other children sat motionless, their eyes wide, their quieted bodies forgotten and left behind.

Because of her great ignorance, Matey was slow in beginning to understand what was being played – even to hear it distinctly and articulately. All she knew was that during these quiet hours, the dimly-lighted room became filled with something which softened her little-girl heart till she could hardly bear it.

There was occasionally talk about the music, mostly between Henri and his mother. He often left his chair and leaned over the piano to watch the notes as she played. He was never far from his mother. They had a special way of looking at each other unlike anything Matey had ever seen. At first she paid little attention to what they said because she had literally no idea what they were talking about. But as the winter went on, the music in which she was steeped from morning to night began to crystallise in her mind. By and by she did know what they were talking about and could not remember exactly when her understanding began.

It was interesting talk, for Henri had no idea of being a professional pianist but studied music as one of the elements in a liberal education. Just at that time he was working through Beethoven's Fifth Symphony so slowly that from hearing it over and over, Matey and the Vinet girls came to know parts of it by ear as well as their play songs. As they went about the apartment, they amused themselves by knocking on the doors and walls in the rhythm of the opening measures. One day Professor Vinet called them 'the young Eumenides', a joke which was Greek indeed to them till his wife explained first who the Eumenides were and further that someone, perhaps Beethoven himself, had described those opening raps as the knocks of Fate challenging Man to come out to do battle with his destiny. 'I tell you this because it is a commonplace with all the commentators,' she went on, 'but do not fall into the error of thinking that Beethoven wrote programme music. He had ideas, but he was a real musician for all that!'

Naturally this did not make the matter clearer for Matey. She had only the vaguest idea of what Fate might be, and no idea at all why Man should go out to fight with it. But, insensibly, as the winter wore on, the innumerable repetitions of the music and the ideas that came with it worked upon stuff in her mind till out of it something quite her own began to emerge. She saw clearly now a poor little Man, cowering in a little shelter, on a sloping twilight heath darkening to night, while a gigantic Fate, a dark mantle falling about him like loosened bat's wings, stood before the door.

Matey saw a hairy black arm thrust from the cloak and rap on the door those threatening notes. Would Man come out and fight? Matey wouldn't have blamed him for just bolting the door and staying quietly in his nice little life.

But it would no longer be a nice little life if it were filled with fear – Matey had met fear once and hated it. *Anything* would be better than to go on being afraid of something. Man thought as she did, apparently, for he always did answer. Matey heard pityingly the quaver in his frightened voice.

Henri was still struggling with the second movement and had gone no further than a few fumbling readings of the scherzo when one late afternoon Mme Vinet set both parts of the music before her on the piano. 'You will certainly do better work on the first parts, Henri,' she said, 'if you have some notion of what the whole thing is. Perhaps I can pick out enough notes with my ten fingers to give you an idea. Listen.'

Matey listened, too, with a real curiosity. As though it were something in a story book, she was soon hanging on the fight that was raging and shouting in the shabby little salon. Raging and shouting – but singing too. That melody which at the beginning so feebly answered the threat of Fate was no longer weak and frightened but bold and strong. Why, she could hear

✲✲✲

it plain, it snatched Fate's club away and made those knocks part of its own song – hurrah! Goody! Bang, bang, bang! At the last, 'Oh, Man *won!*' she cried, bringing her hands together hard in relief.

Later on in the year, when Henri and his mother had finally worked their way through all four movements and every note had knocked and sung its way into the heads of the little girls, his parents began to talk about giving him and themselves a great treat by going to hear the symphony played by an orchestra. 'Would you like to go too, Matey?' Mme Vinet asked. 'Do you suppose you are old enough to enjoy it?'

The phrasing of the question made Matey answer positively, 'Yes, I *would* like to,' although she had little idea what a symphony orchestra was. There were but three or four in all the United States at that time.

The cost of the tickets being a considerable item in the Vinet budget, it was decided that Ziza was really too young (she ran that pointed red tongue furiously around her lips at this decision) and that only Mimi would go with M and Mme Vinet, Henri, and Matey. When the day came and they set out together it felt like running outdoors to play in Logan Bluffs. They had gone but two or three blocks from the house when, striking his hand on his forehead in despair, M Vinet remembered he had not brought the tickets. A moment of consternation while they stood around him, suggesting yet another pocket into which he might plunge an agitated hand – and then it was remembered that Mme Vinet was the one who had the tickets *'Saperlotte!'* said M Vinet with a shaky breath. 'That gave me a scare.'

Arrived at the dingy concert hall they climbed endless stairs to the cheap seats. Matey did not know the first numbers of the concert and made nothing out of them beyond surprise at the astonishing volume and beauty of the sound which welled up from the stage far below and billowed cloudlike around them in the top gallery.

'Now they're going to begin the Fifth,' said Mme Vinet. She took Henri's hand in hers. They gave each other their special look. Matey had no premonition of what was to happen. She thought she knew the Fifth by this time, as well as she knew the look of her hat and coat, or the feel of her bed at night.

rapped out the deep-voiced menacing strings. Matey's heart turned over with a knock of its own. Why, she hadn't known *this* music at all! It was something else, something else entirely.

What was this faintingly lovely theme now barely audible after the thunder of the beginning? Was it possible, could it be the air she and the other children had hummed and whistled and sung as they had put off and on their wraps, or washed their hands? It *was!* She recognised every note. But every note was new! It floated up past her, transfigured in the voices of the violins.

Turning halfway on the bench, Matey laid her arm along the back and put her face down on it. A fold of M Vinet's well-worn professor's black coat had fallen over her knees. She took hold of this and held it hard, as though it had been a living hand – such as the one Henri was holding.

She did not move at all till after the end, when people were applauding. Then she turned around and began to clap her hands as the others were doing. Her face was very grave, and had none of its usual rosy glow. She looked pale and quiet, almost like a French child.

'Did you like it?' M Vinet asked her, wiping the happy tears from his eyes and blowing his nose with a huge handkerchief.

'*Oui, Monsieur,*' said Matey, in a low voice.

Henri and his mother sat silent, hand in hand.

They walked home to save the omnibus fare. Professor Vinet left them to give a private lesson. Henri and his mother walked together, Matey and Mimi behind them. The little girls were very quiet. Mimi stepped wide and irregularly to avoid the cracks between the flagstones as she always did on walks abroad, but absent-mindedly.

Matey was struggling fitfully with a question that fluttered like a cobweb, to and fro in her mind. How could something in her everyday life turn, as the music had, into something from another world – and yet be just what she had known it all along? How could it change to something else no more like what she had known than dry sticks are like fire – and yet be nothing new?

It was a question much too hard for her scattering wits even to keep in mind. Whenever she tried with her unskilled child's fingers to take hold of it firmly, away it blew, off into nothingness, and there was nothing in her thoughts but what was before her eyes. The walk home led them along the *quai* where pet animals are sold. They passed sad little monkeys squatting on straw in show-windows; bright clouds of goldfish in great glass tanks; restless imprisoned lovebirds in pairs, fluttering on their perches. Matey's eyes looked at them intently, but from time to time there fluttered in the cage of her brain the question that was too hard for her even to think about for more than an instant.

It had been alone at first, but presently it encountered another perplexity of much longer standing, another question that had always puzzled her, which she had never felt like asking aloud – as church language described Heaven, why in the world would anybody want to go there?

United for an instant the two questions flickered across her mind. At the glimpse of the two together she cried out, 'Oh, maybe that's the way Heaven is – just the same but all different!'

'*Qu-o-o-i, qu'est-ce que tu dis?*' asked Mimi, raising her voice above the din of the street.

'Nothing,' said Matey hastily. The Vinets spoke reverently of Jesus, but Matey knew they considered talk of God or Heaven fit only for superstitious *concierges*. Also she would not have known in the least how to answer Mimi. The flash had gone, and she was not sure what she had seen in its light. The idea, whatever it had been, faded as quickly as it came. She could not now even remember how the music sounded. She felt tired and rather cross. '*Rien! Rien du tout,*' she said impatiently to silence Mimi.

The children had forgotten themselves and used the

forbidden thick-throated Paris cockney twang. Rousing herself
from her mystic's heaven, Mme Vinet turned back to everyday
life. 'You mustn't say *"ri-e-en"* and *"qu'est-ce que tu di-i-is?"* like
that,' she corrected them conscientiously over her shoulder.

'*Non, Maman,*' said Mimi.

'*Non, Madame,*' said Matey.

CHAPTER SIX

✡✡✡

Matey never went back to Logan Bluffs; never again saw the house that had been for her childhood the centre of the universe. Another university offered Professor Gilbert a larger salary. In everybody's eyes this seemed to make their moving as inevitable as the opening of another leaf on a growing tree. So when they returned to America after their fifteen months in France they went to a city called Hamilton several states farther east than Logan Bluffs. As casually (so far as she could see) as shutting down a window, a large number of the ties she had made with the world were cut asunder.

Logan Bluffs was gone, with its houses as much a part of Matey's world till then as the sky or the earth; with its barns and yards different from all other barns and yards as one person is from another; with its school unlike all other schools because it was her school. Not a shimmer from its sunlight, different from all other light because it shone on a world that was partly Matey. Not a murmur from all the turbulent play that had been life. Like a painted scroll the place that had been home to Matey was rolled up out of her life.

With it went something that the Vinet children had, that

Matey had taken for granted she had. Henri and Mimi and Ziza and Polo were being brought up in the same rooms in which their father had spent his childhood. They walked before the same buildings and under the same trees which had looked down on their mother as a little girl. On their mother's 'third Tuesdays' the same families came to call who had called on her mother and on her husband's mother. The cross *concierge* with his wooden leg who grumblingly handed out the letters and spitefully watched to see who came to call on them had done the same things when their father had been their age. Behind them, dense and stationary as stone, stood the wall of the family, always there for better and worse, unto the third and fourth cousinship. Confident in its reality and permanence, they leaned as heavily as they liked on the world around them.

Matey too had leaned on the world around her. All during the fifteen months abroad, while she was being another person, it had never occurred to her that she would not presently go back to her old home and turn into her old self. Her thoughts had been adjusted to that return home as the muscles of a man leaning against a wall are adjusted to its solidity. Now, without warning, it was snatched away from her and she felt herself pitching headlong. She made a wild effort to recover her balance; she succeeded in getting her feet under her with enough steadiness for ordinary purposes. But she was in no hurry to lean against another world.

With flat childish letters sent to her old playmates she tried feebly not wholly to lose Logan Bluffs. Of course such attempts soon faded into silence. The fact was that she *had* lost it. Logan

Bluffs was no longer her home. But she could not at once consider Hamilton exactly her home either, any more than she could have accepted as a sister a girl she had met for the first time.

This meant that she considered nowhere exactly as home. The brick house in 'Faculty Row' on the campus in Hamilton, with well-planned shrubbery around it, was much finer than the wooden prairie rattle-trap on the corner of the block in Logan Bluffs. Yet she felt it safer not to settle down in it but to perch warily on the bough. She found perching there beside her a majority of the children and grown-ups around her. Almost without exception everybody had come from somewhere else, and expected to move again. They kept their tendrils to themselves and their roots packed ready for transportation.

'When we lived in Dayton . . . ' they would say; or 'The year we were in Minneapolis . . . ' Often they were like globe-trotters whose wanderings have outlasted their memories. 'There was a big church on the corner of the street where we lived in Detroit . . . ' someone would start a story and then, hesitating, 'or was that in Minneapolis? Helen, where was that big church that the boys used the wall of to play handball against?' To which Helen, 'Oh, that was in Grand Rapids, don't you remember?' Once Matey had heard an absent-minded professor ask his wife, 'Where was it that we knew those people . . . he was a professor of geology, I think – whose son fell out of the third storey window of his fraternity house and was killed. Don't you remember, he'd had a pet dog that his parents took, after . . . ' He was interrupted by amused laughter among his auditors and by his wife's annoyed, 'Why, *Rossiter*, that's right here in Hamilton – the Craigs!'

Matey was a good-looking, well-grown girl now, with pleasant grey eyes and long bright brown hair, and had learned enough of the necessary formulae of social existence so that she found no more difficulty than anybody else in gravitating into the group where she naturally belonged. She joined in the life of the high school where she was sent, learned her lessons, went to dances, played the piano occasionally at assembly, did whatever the others did, and in this process took part in a good deal of young fun. From her fourteenth to her seventeenth year, her external life was active and what is called normal for that age. But the currents of her life were turned in upon themselves at this by much more than the disappearance of the violently playing children of Logan Bluffs – among whom introspection had about as much chance to develop as among cowboys or pirates or lumberjacks. She had known a year of life which had softened her heart as well as her hands. She had begun inexorably to grow up. She did not welcome the new phase. It was even hard for her to admit that it was there. She refused to lengthen her skirts at the age when other girls did, or to put up her hair. At fifteen she was racing about the playground playing hide-and-seek, as wistfully as a man of forty dresses up in a red fez or white apron. But it was her turn now. Like Priscilla's, her eyes were opening for the first conscious look at life. They saw what was nearest them, and, as Priscilla had, took that for life itself.

In a panic she looked about her. Even in a provisional world you must be able to find something to lean against. Of course Priscilla was still there.

But was she? Matey waited and waited for the sister she had known to come back into the lively popular young lady, who after graduating at the University in Hamilton went on living at home and taking a year or so of postgraduate work, 'majoring in English' as was the custom of faculty daughters when they did not know exactly what to do with themselves. She was still in the same house with Matey, was always flashing in or out of the front hall with one of her cavaliers, in a hurry to go somewhere or do something. She and Matey shared the same bedroom just as they always had. But somewhere in the years when Matey had not known enough to notice or had been too absorbed in her own life to see, Priscilla had disappeared. Matey still had the nicest kind of big sister, envied by the other girls, kind and serviceable, always ready to help with Latin lessons or hair-ribbons, very clever in the trimming of hats, very good-natured in the matter of hiding minor transgressions of family rules from the family rulers. As long as the moral atmosphere around them was the brisk one suitable for catching a trolley-car, or deciding which colour to go with which, Priscilla seemed like herself. But she had thoroughly learned, long before Matey came blundering into a new self, how to surround herself perpetually with matter-of-factness.

For a time, as Matey nursed a bruise or cut from an encounter with an angle of life new to her, or felt her new young heart kindled to flame by a glimpse of beauty, she tried to share it with Priscilla.

'Say, Priscilla, today at church, you know what the rector said about Christ's paying God to stop hating us, by getting himself crucified . . . honest, Priscilla, doesn't that make you *sick!* How can people think such a horrible thing about God!'

Priscilla had disappeared. In her place was a preoccupied young lady who answered vaguely. 'Oh, I don't know. I never thought much about that,' and who added quickly, 'Matey, you know that blue hat of mine? Don't you suppose that would look well with your white swiss?'

'Priscilla, quick, come out and look at the sunset! Look at the way that fierce-looking orange down by the horizon goes up and up and somehow gets itself turned into clear, clear green . . . I should think an angel's eyes would be that colour, wouldn't you? How *can* that sort of angry orange get itself changed into such a *quiet* colour as that green?'

To nobody else in the world would Matey have said such things. She did not long go on saying them to Priscilla, who told her good-naturedly now, 'Well, Matey! Anybody'd think that was the first sunset you'd ever seen!'

To which Matey, if she had known the truth, would have answered that it was.

'Priscilla, did you ever turn off Main Street, toward the river? I did today. Hannah Warner said there was a carpenter over there that we could get cheap to make the scenery for the high school play. It turned out he lives on the other side of Main, the right side. But I thought it was the left and turned that way and got into the awfullest streets you ever saw. So dirty and smelly . . . I never knew there were such streets in Hamilton! And such horrible old wooden houses jammed up together. And the children, babies too, sitting about on the steps. Honest, Priscilla, you never *saw* such dirty kids. Not just dirty either – sickly-looking, and dumb! Their mouths sort of hanging open. Priscilla, listen, stop reading just a minute. Priscilla, why should there be such poor people? *Babies* can't help themselves! We had ice-cream for dinner tonight. Doesn't it make you feel *bad,* to have nice things to wear and eat and everything . . . Priscilla, don't you think something ought to be *done* about it? *Priscilla!'*

No, call the name as often, as loud as she might, Priscilla never answered. What she said was, *'Matey!* If Father and Mother knew you'd been poking around in such a place they would just go through the roof! I won't say anything about it, this time. But don't you ever do it again, not *ever.* It's not safe. Did you find the carpenter you were looking for? I know one of the University boys, working his way through, who's always looking for odd jobs. He'd do it lots better. I'll talk to him about it and see what he says. I'd be glad to help you kids out.'

Priscilla was always glad to help out. Matey's classmates often said she had the most *won*derful big sister in the world. Matey replied in a familiar formula, 'How nice of you to say so.' Out of these attempts to talk things over with Priscilla emerged a phrase which became a new formula, pronounced by Matey with a bewildered accent, 'What was it we were talking about?'

Priscilla always answered, vaguely, 'I don't seem to remember *what* it was.'

Matey could not for a long time realise that this was final. As she grew less and less sure she was on the right path, she tried harder and harder to throw her arms around Priscilla to see if it was all right, to make sure that Priscilla under her nonchalant airs was really not afraid. Some of the things Matey ran into really did scare her like everything.

'Priscilla, one of the girls in my class . . . you know her, that Pelham girl with the red hair . . . well, she got to talking today. I don't know how we got started on that . . . Well, anyhow, she got to talking about . . . boys . . . and things. She said . . . she said one of the boys kissed her last night, after the show. She said he tried to . . . to . . . Priscilla, she says when a person gets married . . . Priscilla, *is* it all right to . . . What is . . .'

Matey might have struggled through as far toward Priscilla as that, groping her way painfully around the heaped-up shyness, shame, and ignorance that cut her off from plainer speech. But she never advanced further.

'Matey! She must be a *horrid* girl! Don't you have anything more to do with her Why, I *never* think about such things, never. And you mustn't either. Put it right out of your mind.'

This was worse than usual. It almost seemed to Matey that for an instant she had touched the real Priscilla. And found out that she *was* afraid.

Having told Matey to put it right out of her mind, Priscilla chose to consider this done. She neither spoke of 'such things' to Matey again, nor ever enquired what might be in Matey's mind as she sat sometimes of an evening, apparently studying her algebra, but quite obviously thinking of something else.

Strangest of all was the way Priscilla acted about Matey's music. Matey had been intensely proud to find that the austere discipline of the Vinet life had made her a pianist far in advance of most of her new associates, even those who had been 'taking piano' all their lives. She had thrilled with satisfaction when Father or Mother, smiling confidently, had called on her to take her part in their 'evening at home.' But – after she had got over the first intoxication of the generous applause – somehow the savour seemed to go out of it. She still played in public when she was asked, banging her way through brilliant selections, the sort of thing people liked to hear, with plenty of easy runs and obvious chord sequences, but she was devoutly thankful Mme Vinet was not there to hear her.

Real music came when she was alone late in the afternoon with the busy day behind her. Sometimes she played music she had learned with Mme Vinet, sometimes new things she had read alone, or something she had studied with her Hamilton teacher, a conscientious musicianly German lady, to whom Matey with her capacity for hard work came as a sending from Heaven. This was the one time when she recaptured something of the feeling of permanence. It was not the music alone but all its associations which brought sometimes the softened fullness of heart which precedes happy tears.

Fullness of heart always seeks an outlet. With whom could Matey share hers? 'Priscilla, I've got the nicest Bach Invention you ever heard for my lesson this week. Come on, let me show you how it goes.'

'Priscilla, Mrs Mulhauser has given me the Minuet in Sonata No. 12. It's just *sweet*. Listen for a minute.'

At first Priscilla had come in good-naturedly, as she did everything, had stood or sat quietly listening while her little sister played. But very soon she withdrew herself. This time

Matey saw her doing it, could not doubt the intention with which Priscilla always remembered something else to be done. Why? *Why?* When Matey fairly cornered her, and asked more plainly than she ever could about anything personal to herself, 'What's the matter with you, Priscilla?' the older girl said, almost with a tremor of wildness in her usually smooth cheerful voice, 'Oh, Matey, let me alone! I – I don't believe I like music very well. It makes me feel . . . queer . . . some of the things you play.' She pulled away. She was gone, pushing shut the door Matey was trying to open.

Francis lived mostly in the fraternity house of the 'swell frat' which he had joined in his freshman year at Hamilton. Not that it mattered where he lived. What could she share with Francis? And if Father or Mother came into the twilight room where Matey was playing they always turned the gas up and lighted another jet. Father often said, 'Well, Matey, I see you've got to the Romantic School age.' Mother generally said, 'Matey dear, can't you find anything more cheerful than that to play?'

So, since Priscilla had slipped out of reach, Matey and her music were left alone together.

Some of the pages she played in those years came to seem to her like living things, like persons – only much more sure and unchanging than persons. The home-feeling of permanence was gone, the old joy in games was gone, she was becoming a new person and not a person she altogether liked, and something she had always feared to look at grew plainer and plainer before her eyes. But Beethoven and Schubert, and Bach – Bach most of all – were still there, unchanged, unchangeable.

There was one Bach Prelude in particular, the Sixth, which sounded to her exactly like an answer. An answer that knew how difficult the question was. As she wound her way through it, in and out those unexpected various phrases, as different each from every other as every leaf and branch on a tree is different from all the rest, her mind sometimes lost its way. Her fingers went on as nimbly as ever, but she felt that they were lost in meaningless twirlings which had nothing to do with each other. But when the end drew near she was reminded that all the leaves and all the branches only make one tree.

With the last chord, which summed it all up, Matey sometimes felt as though she had put her arms around a forest tree and shared its steadfast strength.

Compared to Priscilla, Bach was very far away. But he was not afraid.

CHAPTER SEVEN

Soon after they settled in Hamilton, Mrs Gilbert's family noticed that her energy was focusing itself about a new centre. She tossed the civilising influence of dramatics into the limbo of oblivion where the history of art had passed before it. In its place she began to care greatly about details of their entertaining, about the way the table was set. As for the house, everything in it was wrong! With her usual decisiveness she threw herself into re-arranging the two parlours till the rest of the family scarcely knew them, justifying the changes by quoting aesthetic principles which they heard for the first time, but of which they now heard a great deal: principles of the balance of spaces, of the value of shadows, of Japanese austerity of line, of the hideousness of Victorian over-ornamentation.

As this new wave of motive energy began to penetrate the deep absorption in their own affairs of her husband and children, their first feeling was of surprise. Then with the instinctive knowledge of long experience, surprise changed to questioning. They cast their eyes enquiringly here and there among the various personages of their world. Who was it this time? When finally over Mrs Gilbert's shoulder they saw Mrs Whitlock, they ceased to look enquiring and began to look resigned – but not for long. . . .

Mrs Whitlock was the wife of the professor of – what was he professor of? Nobody could remember. The important thing about her was not her husband nor the subject he taught, but the fact that some time after her marriage she had, quite unexpectedly, inherited money, a good deal of money. This set her apart from most people around her. In addition to her independent income she carried a lorgnette, had the aristocratic Southern-sounding odd first name of Meade, drove about in a closed carriage with a coachman in livery (the only one in Hamilton), and had the prestige, extremely rare in those early Whistlerian days, of having travelled in Japan – 'of course' (as anyone who mentioned the fact hastened to explain) '*not* as a missionary.'

Altogether she was too vivid a personality to be ignored, and too forceful to be diminished by taking toward her a pose of resigned amusement. Back in Millerton and Logan Bluffs Professor Gilbert had never seemed to mind in the least Professors Mathewson and Marlin, but his bristles soon began to rise visibly over every contact with Mrs Whitlock with her thin swarthy smoothed-up middle-aged face, her daring chatter, her quizzical look of indulgent toleration for the crude life about her. And the deeper his detestation grew, the more his wife seemed to delight in her new friend, clinging to her, passing her arm around her as they walked out of the room, calling her up on the telephone for long talks, even when they had been together hours of that very day.

✿✿✿

Mrs Whitlock, with plenty of money, no children, and a negligible husband, was free to drop in at the Gilberts' whenever the whim prompted. As time went on she often stayed to luncheon. Those inflexible noon-hours at the table, barren of a single plausible excuse for escape before the end of dessert, intensified the family attitude to the point of drama. Daily Matey watched Father come in, saw him look black at finding Mrs Whitlock there again, reluctantly rise to the family tradition, and drag out his company manners. Daily she heard Mrs Whitlock sticking little pins of ironic comment into everything he said, into all his pet admirations, into the phrases which he had always counted as sure-fire. And all the time she was loudly protesting that she found him '*perfectly fas*cinating!*'

This bitter little comedy, Matey soon discovered, was another round in the never-ending struggle as to who should come out on top which had always been in the background of their family life. No matter what the setting, this was always the only question that mattered. And now Mother had a new ally.

Up to that time Father had come out on top much more often than Mother because he was – Matey knew this very well – much stronger and cleverer than Mother. And ever so much quicker. He could see her, long in advance, getting ready to make one of her trys to get her share of importance, and when the moment came, he had all ready exactly the practised blighting word and accent to reduce her kind of importance to nothing at all. Mother had been very successful in the Dramatic Club at Logan Bluffs, had been Professor Marlin's star actress for several years. Even so early in her childhood,

Matey had winced with pity to see her mother vainly trying to use this hard-won success to force Father's recognition. Father had managed that by staying out. Professor Marlin could never drag *him* into taking a part! This was how Father always managed. At first Matey had naïvely imagined that Father was so clever he could use any situation to show his superiority. But as she grew older she saw that his method was simply to avoid situations where he couldn't.

Even after one of the big successes, like the outdoor production of *A Midsummer Night's Dream,* it had been enough for him to give that little curl to the ends of his moustache which he could make as he needed, jaunty or thoughtful or scornful, and begin to talk eloquently about the Shakespearian actresses he had seen, Mary Anderson, or Modjeska, or Ellen Terry. Without a word of direct comparison he created a twilight which dimmed the brightness of Mother's success. To the result of those weeks and weeks of rehearsals and costume making he seemed to ask, 'Is this all?' Mother might read as much as she pleased the friendly enthusiastic reviews in the local newspapers. That twilight of Father's creating was on her face as she read.

It was no twilight that Mrs Whitlock created on Father's face. It was a thunder-cloud. She had no moustache to curl as she made blighting remarks, but she managed very well without. And practised as he was in reducing to insignificance whatever he did not choose to recognise, he could not lessen her prestige by an atom, based as it was upon the unshakeable solidity of money. He went through all his usual skilful slighting manoeuvres. Often he seemed to be succeeding. But it did not last. Her discreetly gleaming carriage with its liveried driver had but to roll up to the door, and she was back on the pedestal. She *was* important. And Mother was her intimate friend.

Francis took it as he took most things, as a huge joke. 'Gosh, how they scrap!' he remarked carelessly after one of his infrequent lunches at home. 'Just the same, Dad's losing his sense of proportion. You don't see me getting peevish because a lady draped in Government Bonds tells me I'm fascinating. She did, you know! Gave me a lift in her gold-plated chariot up to the Main Building yesterday. You bet I didn't hide in the corner and sulk. I let myself be seen. Next time I'm going to kiss her hand. I'll bet she'd think that was too adorably "foreign"!' He rehearsed the gesture, bending low over an imaginary hand with the graceful half-mocking ease which he had brought back from France in place of any information about the spelling of subjunctives. 'I bet she falls for it. I bet those highbrow frills are only trimmings. What saith the Bard: "The corporal's lady and Judy O'Grady . . . "'

Priscilla went on looking fixedly the other way. 'I can't make Mother out,' Matey told her. 'She doesn't seem to *like* Mrs Whitlock. What makes her act so? She *can't* like her!'

Priscilla answered negligently, 'Oh, Mrs Whitlock's not so bad, I guess.' But she cut short Matey's attempt to go on. 'Well, don't think about her, kid, if you don't like her.' Matey noticed that whenever her sister was cornered by Mrs Whitlock, she raised to an even higher degree of hovering uncertainty her habitual air of expecting the telephone to ring at any moment.

⚜⚜⚜

This time Mother was on top. For once a situation where Mother showed to advantage had dropped right around Father so that he couldn't keep out of it, as he had kept out of dramatics. When he used the wrong fork in the suddenly appearing array of silver beside his plate, no turning of his moustache ends, no sneers about absurd formality, could in the present atmosphere of the house turn that mistake into a superiority. One blow to his prestige followed another. He sat morosely silent when the talk was turned to Japanese prints – or if they dragged him in, said brusquely that he had no time for such kickshaws. But he couldn't pass it off that way. They all remembered (and he knew they remembered) the fun he always poked at one-sided half-civilised pedants. His wife's manner silently reminded him of those biologists and chemists whom he had so enjoyed enticing into showing their ignorance of Molière.

When he stayed obstinately silent, they talked across him, about how petty and cluttered French civilisation was, compared to the conscious artistry-in-life of the East. Once, helping herself to an olive, Mrs Whitlock referred casually to Flaubert's *Salammbô* (the darling subject of Father's best senior lecture) as 'that side-whiskered, middle-class, lambrequined idea of antiquity.' Matey saw an expression of greedy exultation on her mother's face, and on her father's a dangerous look of anger. A foreboding of disaster turned the food in her mouth to wormwood. Priscilla pretended to see the postman at the door, and slipped away. Dessert was brought in, the conversation shifted, Francis laughed his careless laugh, ostensibly at some later remark, and Matey's untried new heart, just emerging into adult life, drew back quivering, and looked wistfully at the cocoon of childishness which had been its refuge.

Father was losing his old craftiness at staying out when he wasn't sure he was right. He knew, of course, that 'the American admiration for Bouguereau was one more proof' (he collected such proofs with enthusiasm) 'of this country's aesthetic impotence.' Matey had heard him say that lots of times. But apparently he had missed hearing that Meissonier had stopped being a great artist, and one noon at lunch, the painter's name being mentioned, he brought out a well-turned phrase of admiration, which Matey had often heard him use before. Mrs Whitlock smiled and began to quote the deliciously witty spiteful remarks of a French art critic who despised him.

She had gone too far. Matey saw Father lay down his fork with a formidable deliberation, and waiting before launching his counter-attack till she should have finished her sentence, face her menacingly. Matey sprang up, terrified, murmured something about needing to be back early at the high school, and leaving her food untouched, ran out of the house, hatless.

It was a pleasant day in spring. In the soft moist air, the grass was greening, the tulips and crocuses blithely unrolling their many-coloured petals. Matey saw nothing but the hate and triumph and resentment and anger in the three faces she had left, glaring through the urbane glaze of 'conversation.' She twisted her shoulders nervously and moved her head from side to side, trying to bring something to mind.

Someone hailed her by name. A high school comrade, Dick Ransome, the registrar's son, came running out of a house on Faculty Row. 'Hold on, Matey. I'm going your way.'

He had walked with her several times lately. Matey rather liked him and very much liked the attention he paid her. But today as he fell into step beside her and began talking about baseball prospects, he was struck by her unresponsive silence. He looked at her and saw that her teeth were set on her lower lip as if to keep it from trembling. 'What's eating you, Matey?' he asked with real concern. 'You look as if you'd lost your last friend.'

After one sidelong look into his honest face Matey's lip trembled more than ever. She was sick with longing to accept his sympathy, with longing to escape from the loneliness of her dread and misery. But what could she say? 'My father and Mrs Whitlock are having a discussion about whether Meissonier is a great painter.' Her wretchedness was not even tragic. The only part of it that could be put into words was ludicrous. To make him understand she would need to tell him things she had never acknowledged to herself, things which, as she watched her parents, lay at the bottom of her mind like a geologic stratum dropped down, grain by grain, through all her memories of family life. No, she never could make him understand – or anybody else.

When the friendly boy beside her said again, 'What *is* the matter, Matey?' she cut him short with a brusque 'Oh, nothing.'

What else could she say?

He understood very well that he was being told it was none of his business, and with an offended look fell silent. Matey tried now with an unpractised young clumsiness to make talk, herself. But the boy had his own sensitiveness. He answered her questions about baseball glumly, taking the manner of a boy to whom a girl is making advances. Matey added a nettled resentment to the rest of her distress, and fell silent herself.

Footsteps pattered behind them, and a well-built fox-terrier appeared trotting by Matey's side. They both knew that he was the dog who had belonged to Professor Craig's only son. Since his young master's tragic death, everybody had seen him sitting sadly on the empty porch of the Craig house, turning his pointed face listlessly here and there, or trotting soberly about the campus, his nose to the ground. Matey had seen him a thousand times. He trotted close to her side now, occasionally brushing against her. It occured to her that he must have rather a forlorn time of it, all alone with a couple of elderly people.

'What's his name? she asked.

'Sumner,' said the boy.

'What a funny name for a dog,' said Matey, looking down on the top of his bony triangular head and powerfully muscled shoulders.

'Seems as though I'd heard there was some kind of joke about it – the reason why he got named that, I mean,' said the boy. 'You know he used to belong to the Craig boy, who fell – '

'Yes, yes, I know,' said Matey, hastily.

She looked down at the little dog again and wondered if he had been in the fraternity house that night when his young master's skylarking had ended so. . . .

'Well, so long,' said the boy beside her, breaking into a lope to join a group of tall lads tossing a baseball around the playground.

They were now before the high school building. Matey stopped. The dog stood before her. Matey stooped down to him and put her hand on his head. He lifted his eyes to hers, brown eyes, very clear, very deep. The two exchanged a long look.

'Well, goodbye, Sumner,' she said softly, stroking his head before she left him to enter the school.

But it was not goodbye. He was waiting for her in front of the high school building when she came out quite late at five o'clock, and he trotted seriously beside her all the way home.

When they reached the pleasant, dignified, shrubbery-framed house on Faculty Row where Matey lived, she hesitated. She was in no hurry to go back into that house. Indeed she wished that she need never enter it again. She sat down on the bottom step and drew a long breath. The dog came up at once and sat down close to her. She put her arm around his small lean warm body.

There was a beautiful sunset that night. This one she saw with her arm around Sumner, his head pressed against her shoulder. She sat there a long time, sunk deep in colour, her eyes reflecting the unearthly magnificence in the sky. When she finally stood up to go into the house, she felt tired and let down, her feet hard to lift. But the close-fibred misery which had been like an evil growth inside her was dissolved. 'Well, goodbye, Sumner,' she said again, stroking his head. He looked up again into her eyes, a long searching gaze. 'Well, goodbye,' she said, and opening the front door, let herself into her home.

But it was not goodbye. The dog was waiting for her the next morning on the bottom step of the porch. 'Oh, Sumner!' she cried. At this he faintly wagged the short stump of his tail. It was as if he had spoken to her. And had said the right thing. She bent to stroke him and this time he arched up his head under her caress with a friendly welcoming gesture. 'Well, Sumner!' she said. She did not know how to talk to a dog. The Gilbert children had never had pet animals.

But he seemed to be satisfied with what she said and trotted beside her all the way to school. 'How green the grass is getting all of a sudden, since yesterday!' Matey thought to herself. 'And the crocuses out! I don't believe they were above the ground yesterday.' For an instant she stood again beside the newly arrived tulips in the old garden at Rustdorf. She understood Aunt Connie's cry more and more. Yes, it was incredible in such a mess as life, that a person could still feel so relatively cheerful as she did this morning.

'Want to have a run, Sumner?' she asked, running a few steps herself. He bounded forward with a bark. It was the first time she had heard his voice.

By the end of the fortnight he was hers.

When she asked Mother if she could keep him, Mother had first made her usual effort to take her attention from what was in her mind and put it on what Matey was talking about. Then she said readily, kindly, 'Why, of course, dear!' She added, 'You could have had a dog any time, Matey, if you had said you'd wanted one.'

Matey's playmates often commented enviously on the fact that her parents gave her everything she wanted.

When she timidly approached the Craigs she found they knew all about it. 'Yes, I noticed Sumner had taken to you,' said Mrs Craig. She patted his head and looked down at him. 'It's better so,' she said. 'He's been lonesome with us.' She called toward her husband's study, 'It'll be all right to let Professor Gilbert's daughter keep Sumner, won't it, Father?' He came to the door to look at Matey. The dog was standing close beside her.

'You'll be good to him,' said Professor Craig.

He stated it as a fact, but Matey answered as if it had been a question.

'Yes, I'll be good to him,' she said in a low voice.

CHAPTER EIGHT

✾✾✾

The fourth year of their stay in Hamilton, when she was a senior in the high school, Matey was almost like an only child in the house. Francis, with graduation day looming ahead, was making the most of what was left of college life; and Priscilla, now twenty-three, having taken her MA in English and flightily refusing to marry another eligible young professor, went off to teach in a high school in Detroit. She secured this position for herself; preferring it to the place in the Hamilton high school which her father was sure he could obtain for her. He was always an influential figure in any community where they lived.

One night, shortly before Priscilla went away, she was in the bedroom packing and deciding what to take with her for the new venture. Matey sat at the study table, doing her geometry lesson for the next day. Priscilla came and went energetically between open bureau drawers and open trunk. The house was quite still. Through the open door the girls heard the telephone bell ringing downstairs. As though the drawling self-conscious voice had sounded in the room, they both knew that Mrs Whitlock was calling. Their father evidently stepped quickly from his study on the ground floor to the telephone. They could not hear what he said, but they caught perfectly the personal, intimate man-to-woman murmur in which he now spoke for a moment or two. Then, changing to a matter-of-fact tone, he called upstairs to his wife. 'Mrs Whitlock on the phone, Jessica.' His steps, brisk and rhythmic as though set to a lively inner tune, went back into his study.

In her room, next to theirs, the girls heard their mother stir, come out on the landing, and without answering her husband, go laggingly down the stairs. There was a pause as though she stood for a time motionless before the instrument. Then her voice, bright, hard, animated, 'Oh, *Meade* dearest, how *are* you?'

Priscilla got up from her knees beside the trunk, and went quickly to shut the door. The hard high voice was dimmed to a murmur. Priscilla looked at her little sister's shadowed face. It was bent over the geometrical figures on the pages of her textbook. But the eyes were tightly shut. Priscilla said, 'Say, kid, I wish I could take you with me.'

She was frightened – and so was Matey – by the wildness of Matey's answering cry as she sprang up and ran to her sister. 'Oh, Priscilla, if you only *could!*'

Even as she threw her arms around her sister, Matey knew again that she could not escape. Priscilla knew it too. Matey knew by the nervous way Priscilla was patting her on the back that Priscilla had startled herself as much as her sister by those impulsive words, was now desperately anxious to set up again her usual protecting screen of not recognising what was before her.

❦❦❦

'Hush, hush, Matey! don't! don't!' she said. 'You've been studying too late. I've kept you up with my packing. I'll stop. You must go to bed right off.'

But she could not at once relax the loving pitying pressure of her arms, nor take her cheek away from her sister's tear-wet face. Nor could she instantly check the impetus of the feeling which had spoken those revealing words. It drove her now, frightened though she was, to go farther, to half-admit that there was something behind the screen, 'Listen, Matey, listen,' she said brokenly in her sister's ear, 'the only thing that helps is to keep busy . . . keep going. You remember that, Matey, when I'm gone . . . *keep busy!*' It was all she had salvaged for herself out of her defeat. She offered it tremblingly as the only help she could give – and retreated in a panic. Her broken spirit feared emotion of any kind. She would not allow Matey to go on crying till she had washed her heart clean but told her again that she was tired, was sleepy, that she needed to go to bed. She began to undo the buttons and hooks of her dress and said with a flat attempt at humorous bluffness, 'Gracious, Matey, take a brace! What's the matter with you, kid? Take a brace. Take two braces!' She dipped a towel in cold water and made Matey rub it hard on her flushed face glazed with tears. She made her drink a glass of cold water, and going to the open window, take several deep breaths. She brought out with energy a practised technique of how to drive emotion under cover, and continued to apply her recipes till she had Matey in her nightgown tucked up in bed, rather pale but composed and quiet. 'There, that's better, kiddo,' she said in a bright chattering tone, 'you look more like a man and a fellow citizen.'

Matey turned her head away and closed her eyes. She had nothing in her mind now but a weary wish that Priscilla would stop talking and turn out the light.

That year was something that Matey tried in vain to push down into the black hole in her mind where she kept the unbearable things out of sight. But there was too much of it. It rose up and up around her and over her head till there was no difference between her daily life and the black hole.

It was dreadful when she and Father and Mother had to sit through dinner by themselves, the air in the room stifling with what they ignored – the preposterous nightmare of Mother's position, where to preserve even the appearance of dignity she must pretend brightly to be perfectly satisfied. It was not easy to do one's share in the talk during such meals, to report with an appearance of animation what has been happening in the high school classes, to listen to Mother's brittle accounts of callers, to hear Father telling which students were chosen for Phi Beta Kappa this year or what had been on the table in Faculty meeting that afternoon, or say, 'Your friend Mrs Whitlock came into the office today for a consultation about that paper on Flaubert she is writing in my seminar. You were right about her, Jessica, and I was wrong. She really is a very intelligent and charming woman.'

When he said this, did Mother answer? Did she keep silent? It made no difference. Her defeat had once more been marked. Matey saw waves of falseness shimmering in the air like heat, renewed by every word or every silence.

✤✤✤

It was worse when Mrs Whitlock was there, and Francis. Francis found nothing but comedy in Mrs Whitlock's swallowing Father's hook, in her dropping her hard knowingness for yielding femininity, in her incense-perfumed questions to her new mentor about debatable points of French literature, in their intimate exclusive atmosphere of apostle and disciple of culture which turned the tables on Mother with a delicate absurd poisoned irony. Francis had always thought Mrs Whitlock a fool (he thought most people fools) and no worse a one now that she so naïvely surrendered to his father's transparent tactics.

He followed those tactics himself, flattering her grossly and hilariously till Matey was ashamed to meet his sparkling eyes. Whose eyes could she meet? The seventeen-year-old girl often looked from her father, his aquiline face more striking as the hair and moustache whitened, to her dark vivid mother with her air of gallant energy (poor Mother, what good had it ever done her – those foolish Japanese prints on the wall behind her!) and thought to herself, 'If they would only let me eat my meals with Sumner!'

It was worst of all when there was an evening party, when they must all conspire to fill the house to the brim with a flowing certainty that everything was perfectly all right. How they worked at that! How they played up to Father's unvarying tactics about travel-talk! They leaned forward as though it were the first time they had ever heard him do it, listening intently, while, early in the meal, he skipped lightly about over European travel routes, dismissing with a neutral word everything with which any guest claimed familiarity, until by elimination he found some town or *château* or gallery that was his alone. They helped make the necessary silence for his ensuing monologue of praise of Segovia or Loches or Albi. Even when once again he spoke of Siena as the 'heart of mediaeval Italy' none of them raised an eyebrow. When he described his passionate enjoyment of Holland and the Hals, Mother said not a word about the passionate discomfort of being with him in a foreign country where he did not speak the language. They collaborated with each other in a secret pact to keep the surface smooth, all that lay between them drawing them for the moment into as united a front as devoted affection could have created.

'We always have such *gay* times at your dinner parties, Mrs Gilbert,' her guests often remarked.

'Yes, isn't she an inspired hostess!' Mrs Whitlock would reply, as she passed her arm fondly around her friend's waist.

Faculty people wondered to see the two women still almost inseparable. Mrs Whitlock's affinities had always worn out so quickly. She now seemed to outsiders like an old friend of the Gilbert family.

Yes, after a heart-sick evening of watching those faces and presenting the right one herself, Matey had forgotten that there could exist anywhere in the world such honest eyes as those of Sumner when he jumped down from the foot of her bed and came trotting to meet her. He was a quiet little dog, rather offish with everybody but his mistress. Even with her, although he was often playful, he was not exuberant, never exploded into barks and tail-wagging and contortions of joy. Matey always respected him greatly as well as loving him more than she could begin to say – it was really almost terribly that she loved him that year.

'Oh, Sumner *darling!*' she often whispered foolishly, astonished, really astonished, that he could go on being himself so simply, so invincibly. The hard warm solidity of his living body seemed the first real thing she had touched for hours. She had an adult's limiting knowledge that he could not understand words, and did not talk to him as perhaps she would if she had owned him from his puppyhood. But it did not matter. She sat soberly, holding him on her lap, looking deep into his eyes. 'A dog's eyes are so *true,*' she told herself as earnestly as though she were the first person to use the phrase.

Sumner lay warm at her feet as she studied. He was part of the loosening of her inner tension as her mind began to reflect the calm certainties of mathematics, or the cunningly devised interlacings of Latin sentences. He helped when she remembered Mother's artificial voice, answering Father's veiled taunt with 'Yes, isn't Meade *delightful!*' When thick around her rose the recollection of Father's acrid admiration of his own easy masculine rout of the two women's offensive, Matey did not, as Priscilla had, vainly try to go on fixing her attention on Latin or geometry fading from the page, nor did she end by laying a defeated head down on her arms. She pushed her chair away from the study table and called 'Sumner! Here, boy!' Sumner was alive. His flesh and blood and bone and love did not fade away before unwanted thoughts.

He did something else for her. Always before she went to bed she took him for a little turn out of doors. Priscilla had never thought of leaving the house at night, but had gone to bed straight from the living room, all its tones and accents echoing in her ears. But for the owner of a dog, it was a natural part of the routine of his care. Matey and her dog never went far; around the yard perhaps, down to the corner of the street and back. Never out of sight of the house. It was far enough. It was off into another dimension Matey stepped when, preceded by Sumner's scurrying little feet, his toenails clicking briskly on the porch floor, she walked out of her home into keen starry winter nights, or into black velvet summer softness. Sometimes she stood motionless, with upraised face, drawing long deep breaths, filling her lungs with new air. Sometimes she stretched her arms wide in the gesture of one suddenly freed from bonds. Her home and all that was in it sank down to nothingness under the steady eyes of the stars.

It vanished quickly, this sense of escape. It was all gone by next morning when she took breakfast with Father and Mother, when to her ear all they said echoed with the overtones of what they did not say; when at a word from one of them in a natural comfortable voice, her spirits rose flutteringly, in the hope that this was going to be a 'good day', or at an ironic or resentful tone her heart sickened in the fear of a bad one to be lived through. It did not last long, what she found under the open sky at night, but enough of it clung to her garments, along with the fresh night air unscented with house-life, so that she was still breathing it when she fell asleep. She sometimes remembered Priscilla's reading till all hours, and admitted to herself that she was better off than Priscilla had been.

✲✲✲

She did not always think so. In Priscilla's time there had
been respites. Matey remembered them well. Long respites
day after day, when a warmth of the heart seemed to shine
transformingly into their much-admired home; times when
she and Priscilla had thought (but never said), 'Why, Father
and Mother are *all right!*' Those had been sweet days. At such
times they could not walk, they must jump and run. What
passionate gratitude the little girls had felt for their splendid
brilliant father, their wonderful vital mother.

The respites never lasted. The little girls always knew they
would not. Priscilla began to look anxious again. The house
gradually became filled with the old corrosion of competition;
everything lost its own value, and became nothing but a tool
more or less useful in the old struggle.

Now there seemed to be no respites at all that could be
counted on. Perhaps it was worse because that year Matey was
like an only child. Francis came and went between his fraternity
house and his home, according to a purposeful rhythm of his
own, based on what he could get out of home, with a finished
technique of avoiding bother. Matey remembered from the
old days his amused questions to Priscilla, 'Well, how's the old
soul this evening? Still finding life-is-real life-is-earnest, or can
it unbend to a game of backgammon?' Her time clock rang its
alarm all that year, but never more clearly than when she saw
her handsome brother come bounding up the steps of the
porch. His pleasant 'Hello, Matey, old girl, how's everything?'
turned the key of his sister's heart. But she knew better than
to open the door. She knew that nothing would come in save
a derisive 'Gee whiz, kid, what is it to *you*? Why shed tears over

a comic strip?' Francis needed no instruction in seeing the humorous side of life.

The warning bell of Matey's time clock kept her fiercely determined to act all through that year exactly like any other seventeen-year-old high school senior. Her father and mother, always meaning to do their duty, saw to it that she had pretty clothes and occasional parties at home. Matey knew very accurately that although they were disappointed because she had so little of Francis's dash and brilliance, they were relieved that she was not, in her father's phrase, 'throwing any adolescent fits'; and occasionally they were mildly proud of her, when she was wearing a specially becoming dress or had some marked success in her music or studies.

To this approval of her surface life, she was obliged, of course, by the conventions in which she had grown up, to make a suitable surface response. By this time she had grown fairly skilful in the invention and use of formulae and had a set ready for most occasions, even a set to cope with Mrs Whitlock's old-friend-of-the-family compliments. But what she said was so different from what she was feeling that sometimes as the formulae reeled smoothly from her tongue, she lost her sense of reality. The words they were all pronouncing were drowned out by the silent clash of their personalities. Sometimes she turned cold, thinking that she had actually cried aloud the words so often in her mind, 'Father! Don't! *Don't!*' But since he never turned on her with his invincible ironic look to ask the question she would not have dared to answer, 'Don't what? What in the world do you think you are talking about?' she knew that that cry was never audible.

That winter a débutante in the city's pretentious 'society set' shot herself dead. The circumstances of her life were well known, and there was no possibility of any of the usual motives. Her friends repeated that she had been in the best of spirits all that season. Her bright animation had been specially commented on. 'She always had everything she asked for,' her stricken parents moaned, as they often do in such cases. It was one of those baffling, causeless suicides among perfectly well-cared-for young people in perfectly lovely homes which recur with more or less regularity in all circles.

This tragedy and the interpretation which she put on it brought a new poison to Matey, also in the business of being brightly animated. For the first time she began to find a mawkish picturesqueness in her secret trouble. A martyr-Matey began to evolve. She looked into Sumner's honest eyes and saw reflected back only her own face, theatrically wistful. At the piano her fingers turned to plaintive adagios. She began regularly to go to church, finding in the blended choir and organ, in the sonorous King James English of the prayers, only what she was looking for, an aesthetic stimulus to self-pity. Alien to her character as it was, sentimentality came to her with the relief of a habit-forming drug. She liked it! The year seemed to be marking a turning point in the formation of her character when chance, which had brought the poison, brought the antidote.

One evening she went to a minstrel show in the auditorium of her high school. She had turned down Dick Ransome's bid to escort her, so that she might have the glory of going with the dressy president of her class. Soon, with stifled yawns she was regretting her snobbishness. The young dude was both dull and pretentious. He insisted on explaining everything. When the half-circle of black faces and grotesquely reddened lips formed itself on the stage, he whispered to her, 'The fat guy in the middle, he runs the show, sort of. He asks them all some question that they make a funny answer to, or dance, or something comic.'

But the cadaverous lantern-jawed end man first called on seemed to have no intention of being funny. When asked, 'Well, Brudder Johnson, what has you been doin' today?' he launched out earnestly into a complicated story of buying his railroad ticket from the conductor on the train who could not make change and who asked nearby passengers to help him. They had responded, it seemed, with nickels and dimes and quarters, exchanged and interchanged between themselves and the conductor and the narrator of the story, till Matey's head whirled. Presently he stopped talking. Apparently he had come to the end of his tale. The middle-man looked as bewildered as the audience felt, and enquired gropingly, 'But, Brudder Johnson, maybe I dun los' my mind . . . I didn't seem to get no point to dat story.'

'Point!' boomed Brother Johnson's solemn bass in outraged protest. 'Point! Cyan't you add? Cyan't you substrac'? Cyan't yo' see dey done me out o' fo'ty cents with dey foolishness? *Dat's* de point! My Gawd, man! What mo'point does yo' want?'

The high school audience, come there to laugh, tittered politely. Matey laughed too, but she did not think minstrel shows were so funny after all.

The interlocutor turned to another brother. This one responded with a story about two Irishmen quarrelling, the quite expected end of which sent the audience into the expected peal of laughter.

As this died down a little, there came tolling through it in a sepulchral bass voice, 'Dat may be all right, Brudder Jones, dat may be all right. But dat don't gimme back my fo'ty cents, do it?' His sorrowful eyes fixed the storyteller reproachfully as if to recall him from trivialities to eternal verity.

Brother Carter broke out into song, a banjo-accompanied piece of jollity, with a rattle of nonsense syllables at the end. Matey, as she applauded, glanced along the wide-opened hilarious red mouths of his fellows to the end man who had first spoken. He sat in profound dejection, the whites of his eyes gleaming under his wrinkled brows, like a disillusioned old dog. At the end of the encore his magnificently mournful lament broke again through the applause and laughter. 'What *eveh* does Brudder Carter tink dat's got to do wid my fo'ty cents?' he enquired of the world with the sincerest hurt bewilderment.

After an instant's surprise, the laughter broke out again as the simple-hearted young audience began dimly to take in the point.

After that he became the success of the evening. The very look on his black face as, first expectantly and then with fading hope, he listened to one funny story after another, doubled the fun. The intolerable continuation of his one comment on life, his one measure for all that happened, grew more comic to them with every repetition. He did not even need to say it aloud. If he but gazed in silent grief at a quick-footed rattling hoedown, the boys and girls burst into wild laughter.

Matey, without in the least understanding why, was almost helpless with mirth. She said over and over, wiping her eyes, 'He's the funniest thing I *ever* SAW! If he says that again I shall just go up in smoke!' And her shouts were not louder than those of the other adolescents around her, screaming hysterically as every stroke of the satire went home.

For days afterward, for all the rest of the school year, the lost forty cents echoed their warning gaily up and down the school corridors. For much longer than that, their light accurate admonition echoed in Matey's memory.

At the end of that year, one hot June morning, Matey was deep in a letter to Ziza. Alone among her cast-off homes, the Vinet *ménage* remained more than a shadowy memory. Matey and Ziza kept up a continual though intermittent correspondence. They wrote each other confidences they hid from their own families. Matey had just finished describing her graduation day at the high school and was trying to think of some blightingly witty phrase to express Francis's complacent progress through the social events of Commencement Week toward the AB degree which (by the skin of his teeth) he was now sure of getting next Tuesday, when the front door opened and Father came in. He walked past her into his study where Mother was doing the May accounts, but he called back to Matey, 'This is something you ought to hear too, daughter. A letter from the President of the University of Corinth, in

New York. Professor Brieux, their Romance language head, is obliged suddenly to return to France, on account of family affairs. The position is offered to me.'

Matey's trembling fingers screwed the top of her fountain pen.

Father went on, 'I'm rather inclined to accept, Jessica, if you're agreed. The salary is no higher, it's true. But there will certainly be more graduate students than here – my seminar has been a farce for the last year or so. Not a soul with a grain of wit in it!' The scornful reference to Mrs Whitlock rolled in the air like thunder.

Why, this was one of life's crucial moments. Matey tried to realise that she was not dreaming.

'What do you think, Jessica? Matey, how does that strike you?' He asked the question of his daughter's back, bent over her scattered papers.

If Matey had told him how it struck her, she would have shouted aloud. She knew her father's question had been a rhetorical one and attempted no answer.

After a pause her mother, speaking a little stiffly but steadily, answered, 'Why yes, I'd like it, Morris. Francis will be at the Law School next September. And Matey will just be starting her college life. It seems a suitable time to make a change. Priscilla would be no farther away.'

'Very well, that's settled,' said Father cheerfully, with relief in his voice. Matey had known all along that he would be as glad as anybody to get rid of Mrs Whitlock. But she had never been able to imagine any way to manage this. Professor Gilbert got up from his chair, stood for a moment, seemed to consider that everything had been said, and went out, with a light conquering tread, facing new worlds.

What, oh, what would Mother say now? With what words would she greet this opening of prison doors? Would she burst into joyful tears as Matey felt like doing?

What her mother said was, 'Did you remember, Matey dear, to get those long shoelaces for my high shoes when you were down town?'

Matey understood that she was to make no comment on the news. 'Yes, Mother,' she said. 'I'll get them now. They are in my bag.'

When she came back with them her mother was still sitting in the same chair. She did not look in the least as Matey felt, madly, wildly excited. She looked extraordinarily tired as though she had not the energy to step through those opened doors. She raised her hand with an effort, to take the little package offered by her daughter.

'Thank you, dear,' she said in a low tone, letting her hand with the package fall heavily to the desk.

'Oh, that's all right, glad to do it,' said Matey, filled with forebodings. What could this mean? She knew one thing at least, it meant that her mother could not endure an instant more of anyone's presence.

'I think I'll go out for a breath of fresh air,' she said, turning away. On the porch she stood, her hands pressed tightly together, all her body tense. She felt hideously alone and bewildered. What could make Mother look so tired after such wonderful good news? If Priscilla were only there! No, Priscilla was never there any more. If there were only *some*body she could lean on, who would explain everything to her and tell her what to feel and do. If she only knew how to pray, as people in religious books do, putting on Jesus, or God, or a saint, this dreadful responsibility for things beyond your strength. If – Sumner came trotting around the corner of the house, looking very preoccupied with his own affairs. When he saw his young mistress standing on the porch, his own affairs vanished from his eyes. He bounded up hastily to her, leaping against her skirts, inviting her with laughing eyes to come and play.

It came over Matey that they were really going away from Hamilton, that they would never again need to see Mrs Whitlock, that they were going to begin over again. She was seventeen years old, and it seemed to her that their removal settled everything. Everything would be different. Everybody would become somebody else. She forgot Mother's strange tired look. She forgot everything except that the locked door stood open. 'Oh, Sumner, Sumner, *Sumner!*' she cried, running down the steps of the porch and racing wildly around and around on the grass, the delighted little dog leaping beside her. 'What a kid that youngest Gilbert girl is,' thought a member of the faculty, enviously, passing on the other side of the street, his head full of anxiety about a class that had flunked in appalling numbers.

So they moved again. The furniture was packed up, and a train bore them away from all that had made their lives for four years. Just as from the first Matey had thought it might, Hamilton disappeared behind the curtain of change. It was a good thing she had never tried to steady herself against it.

Yet she did not leave Hamilton with empty hands. She went forward into the next phase of her life, if not with her father's conquering tread, at least with three considerable additions to the armour which was to defend her in the years to come – an album or two of music, a fox-terrier, and a minstrel joke.

CHAPTER NINE

✡✡✡

In a way Corinth was an improvement on Hamilton. Replacing a foreigner who had never been quite at ease in English, and who had long been half an invalid, Father scored the success of his life. He became very popular with his classes, and was so elated with the chance to use his old effects on a new audience that for more than a year he radiated good humour. Mother started nothing new at first, her hands being full with getting the new establishment running, and learning the ins and outs of the faculty circle. She seemed older, too, not quite so valiantly tireless, though she did not show again that queer lassitude – discouragement – fatigue – what had it been? – which startled Matey for an instant in Hamilton. That memory soon became as unreal as the older dream memory of Priscilla weeping as she prayed. *Priscilla* either weeping or praying! Priscilla was teaching French in a very exclusive girl's school in Chicago now, every year better paid, better dressed, more vivacious.

Time went on, another vacation came. They made a flying visit to France and saw the Vinets, still entirely themselves. Ziza and Matey made again an intimate contact. Sophomore year arrived. Matey wrote short story themes, took notes on comparative Lit, messed around in the chemical lab, badgered the freshmen girls in mild imitation of her male classmates – and conditions at home began to drop back to normal again.

Mother was having a great deal to say about the duty of citizens. Equal suffrage was on its way, she told people. Women must prove their right to it by showing an interest. Her interest was in school improvement. As it grew stronger and more expressive, city officials became deferential to her; the house was soon full of committee meetings. The Principal of the largest high school, an energetic disciple of Lucy Stone, became *the intimate* friend. Presently was the intimate friend.

That summer the family did not go away from Corinth. Father was working on a collection of French prose specimens. Mother helped Miss Wood lay siege to the Board of Aldermen. Priscilla took a party of girls to England. Francis was visiting a classmate in Pittsburgh. Matey swam and boated on the lake, stayed outdoors as much as possible, for, busy as father was, he found time to – to – how could you describe what he did? He conveyed an atmosphere. He gave the impression that Mother's work was all very well in its naïve way, but was after all a little absurd, 'worthy', 'well-intentioned', 'American', YMCA-ish. His manner to the city school officials who admired Mother led them to think him a very affable person, and emphasised to Mother (and Matey) his amused tolerance of such second-raters. The glint in his eye as he called Mother to the telephone when one of them asked for her made delicate tarnishing fun of their civic seriousness. He never allowed himself to get grim, never laid himself open to counter-attack as he had at Hamilton. It was all carried on under the surface. But nowadays Mother's nerves seemed less under control. She did not so often lie passive in baffled bewilderment. Sometimes she struck out in a blundering passion, like a maddened castaway in a jungle trying to fend off a swarm of mosquitoes with a club. Her suppressed resentment over the injustice of an intonation sharpened her own intonations to asperity for a long time afterward, just as it always had. But now sometimes it broke out an hour later, in quite unjustifiable anger over a harmless remark. Father always passed this over in a silence, to which he gave the effect of good-natured submission to injustice, by an uplifted eyebrow, a mild philosophic twisting of his moustache, and a certain down-dropped innocence of eyelid. Sometimes Mother was driven to an instant of open undignified fury, new to Matey. And at other times when Matey thought everything was quiet, she was startled by seeing angry tears in Mother's eyes. Her confused sympathies continually started out toward her mother, were continually chilled by the memory of the greedy hardness of her mother's triumph in the early days of Mrs Whitlock. She did not know what to feel any more than what to think. So she felt as little as possible. She learned how, in a bad moment, to clench her hands as at the dentist's when he hurt, and keep very quiet lest the pain find her out in a more agonising spot. She learned how to drug to somnolence the core of her being so that it lost some of its natural sensitiveness to hurts – and to everything else.

No, not to everything. She still had moments of penetrating joy in her music. She still had passing instants of strange transfiguration under the wideness of night skies. But more than music and night magic, immaterial stuff of the imagination as they were, Sumner it was who brought comfort to her daily life, solidly, prosaically, unmistakably real as he was, with his ingenious ability to pick up fleas where no other dog could find one. He was beginning to age somewhat, had fewer dog-interests of his own. Matey was everything to him. And he was more than dog to her.

She loved Priscilla and Ziza, too, the one as remote as the other. In spite of everything she really loved her parents. Sometimes it was even possible to live comfortably with them. But she had lost her old ability to relax during the comfortable periods. She knew now that they were brittle, that at any moment a chance reference or phrase or tone was enough to splinter them like a hammer on glass. Yet those impermanent intervals were sweet. To her, her parents were always kind. They sympathised when she suffered from the terrible incapacitating headaches which had grown on her ever since her little girlhood, and which resisted all attempts to find and cure a physical cause. And they sent her to the doctor when one eyelid developed a spasmodic twitch, that came and went for no apparent reason. They were anxious too when she fell into periods of lassitude, and she felt them relieved when, instead of falling like Priscilla into a half-decline, her health and spirits came back after a long romping walk with Sumner; although such relief was tinged with impatience they neither voiced nor concealed at the slightly silly, really almost distasteful absorption in a pet animal of so tall and physically so well-developed a young woman. They were on the whole satisfied with her for being a normal young person – perhaps not very interesting, a little lacking in zest and colour, perhaps rather commonplace – she detected these added shades of judgment in her father's manner, when she had fallen into one of her listless moods of not caring.

But he was always kind, and sometimes playful with her. She discovered that he was amused by her undergraduate goings-on. It was a good safe subject, capable of expansion at need. Never – not once – did they drop their father-and-daughter 'company manner' to speak of anything they really felt. By the time that Matey was nineteen that would have been as impossible as moving out of length, breadth, and thickness into another dimension. Mother was never playful, but she was kind too, earnestly kind. Her general attitude was expressed by a phrase she often used when she offered to do some shopping for Matey, 'If you'll just tell me what you want, Matey dear, I'll try to get it for you.' The difficulty of course was that Matey could not very well tell her what she wanted, for she did not, in her inexperience, know what was possible. Perhaps she had all there was to expect, all that anybody had.

It was in her junior year that Matey first registered in one of her father's classes. Always she had heard him praised as an almost inspired lecturer. 'Remarkable how Gilbert manages to wake up his students! With all the handicap of dealing with a foreign literature he quickens their sodden Saxon minds to some sort of glimmering conception of writing as an art form – far beyond anything they ever get from the English department.' So spoke his contemporaries, and Matey's contemporaries echoed according to their sex, 'Your father was perfectly *won*derful today,' or 'Gosh! That man certainly has got a line!'

She always answered, with the appearance of smiling pleasure, 'You're very kind to say so.' Why did it make her feel furtive, to smile and look pleased!

She hated feeling furtive and sat down for the first time in her father's classroom, fluttering in a nervous hope that her escape from that kind of furtiveness was at hand. 'Perhaps,' murmured this hope in her heart, 'perhaps when he teaches, he is different. Perhaps *that* is where he really – '

Father came in, leaned gracefully against the corner of his desk and began to speak. Matey stopped fluttering. Her heart sank. For an instant she stared bleakly at something from which it was her life-work to avert her eyes. Who was the brilliant vital lecturer holding his class enthralled? It was Father with his company manners on, showing off. That was all. She glanced around the intently listening class, surprised that they didn't feel at once, from the ring of his voice, that he didn't care a rap about Balzac or Flaubert, except as they gave him a chance to prove how clever he was. She looked down at her notebook, sourly recognising the put-on intonation that Father never used when he was off the stage, when he was talking about something he really meant. But after all she was there to take notes. She began to write.

And at once, she realised that what he was saying was good, very good. More important, it was alive, as professors' lectures seldom were. And yet he had been saying those things for years (she recognised many of them). Lots of them were not even his own, but from other people's books. He must care about something, sincerely and intensely, to have it last him so long. Whatever it might be, his vivid interest did not come from Balzac's merits as a novelist. Matey knew that he'd have talked in that same flashing, eager, convinced way about chemistry (if he'd been professor in that department), or about life insurance, or a two-headed calf. Perhaps this eloquence came from Father's much-talked-of magnetism. What *was* magnetism? It occurred to Matey now, keeping her eyes fixed on Father, that perhaps when you happened to be placed so you could look behind it, you saw that it is no more than willingness to pay any price of apparent interest in any one or anything in order to hold the centre of the stage.

Her pencil was as trained to automatic writing as that of any other college student. In all her classes, as she took notes, her young mind roamed about in fumbling speculations, very remote from the things she was scribbling down. 'Balzac was the first author to base his stories solidly on the fact that cash and nothing else is the key to modern relationships.' The twenty-year-old Matey jotted this statement down as the eight-year-old schoolchild had set down the rules for subtraction. Teacher said so. It was no new idea to her. Her history and economics notebooks were full of the same idea. She had never thought much about it, putting it down in her notebooks rather than in her mind. Like other girls of her generation, like most human beings, she had accepted docilely whatever was told her in a positive voice by those who claimed to know more than she. She did wonder sometimes how you could fit this theory of money as the basis of human life with the other theory you found in books, that sex was the key to everything (her mastery of French had opened to her some very adult books indeed). Not the sweet little love you found in English lyric poems – Matey privately thought those pretty enough but affected and silly – but a hideous malady that might strike you down at any moment and maim you for life. *Amour* – people who wrote novels apparently thought of it as of a homicidal maniac let loose with an axe.

Matey wouldn't have taken this seriously on the say-so of books alone. But this conception of love was not new to her when she found it in nineteenth-century novels. It only gave the clue to things she hadn't understood before – Mother's sick anger when a jolly young German cook had taken up to her room the jolly young man she said was her cousin – Priscilla's startled face of fear as she cried, 'Never think of such things. I don't, ever!' – phrases she had heard whispered between girls in her high school – faculty ladies hinting more than they whispered over a tea table – a Negro woman back in Hamilton calling pleasantries over an alley fence – Dominiqua and the kitchen terrace at Biriatou. So that was the choice that lay before you when you began to live. Either cold-blooded grabbing for money, or the long torture of passion. How could anybody not want to put off living as long as possible?

She thought about her classmates, her pencil racing along the page. They seemed in a positive hurry to begin. Or was that pretended? They talked as if they cared terribly about a lot of things which did not stir her – fraternities, college politics, attention from boys, religion, art, crushes, sports. But did they?

Matey's ear, trained to detect real from put-on accents, recalled the lively untroubled voices in which they dissected their souls. In her heart she thought that probably all lives were encased like hers in company manners very different from the feelings underneath, and suspected that poetry and religion and romance and all the rest of it were also only different kinds of company manners.

The vivid little girl whose small person had been shaken by rapture and panic in the ups and downs of games, the adolescent who had trembled at the sunset and at the injustice of poverty, was growing into a dry young woman, every day adding another thickness to the soundproof walls about her.

There were times, of course, in all classes, when she thought about what she was writing down in her notebook. One day she jotted down, 'Balzac and Victor Hugo represent the difference between the two most opposite human temperaments. To have understood the difference between them is to have understood that things do not exist in themselves but as they appear to different minds. If you are naturally romantic-school in temperament, Balzac makes Victor Hugo seem like a demi-god, no less. If you are a realist, he makes Hugo seem like a posturing second-rate actor. Victor Hugo on the other hand makes Balzac seem (according to your temperament) either like the first eye that ever looked honestly on human life, or like an old-clothes dealer who thinks his account-book is the world.'

Matey thought, 'Now that's good! Even a football player could understand that! A general idea hitched to it, too. Father *is* good!'

She looked up and saw that he was heartily agreeing with her. On his lips was the almost invisible smile of self-congratulation so familiar to her. His eye roved plunderingly from one ingenuous face to another, revelling in the golden honey-dust of their admiration.

'Oh, I *wish* I could bring Sumner to class!' thought his daughter, fretfully.

Another day, her inattention was pierced by the statement, 'The moral – though Stendhal is too fine a master to obtrude a moral – is that there are two ways to meet life; you may refuse to care until indifference becomes a habit, a defensive armour, and you are safe – but bored. Or you can care greatly, and live greatly – till life breaks you on its wheel.'

'Why, that's just what I've been thinking!' thought Matey, startled, sitting up in her chair, 'only better expressed. It's *true!*'

But was it safe to believe anything Father said when he was being eloquent?

CHAPTER TEN

✟✟✟

One morning when Matey and her father were leaving the house, he slipped, fell over the old-fashioned foot-scraper on the doorstep, and gave his ankle a long, jagged, though rather shallow cut. He got up – Matey running to help him – shaken, but relieved that he had not broken a bone, told Matey not to wait for him, went back into the house, washed off the blood, dirt, and bits of black thread from his sock which had been ground into the flesh, bandaged the torn place, and went to his classes as usual. Matey remembered very well his lecture that day.

His opening phrase, 'This morning we take up *Salammbô,*' jerked her back four years as if his words had been a lasso thrown around her neck. *Salammbô!* The Mrs Whitlock battle in the long war for prestige – Father's anger – Mother's ugly exultation – her own soreness of heart. And, most disheartening of all to remember, her childish delusion that because they were going to live in another place, everything was going to be different! She reached desperately for familiar defences. 'Quick! push it down out of sight! Think of something else. Repeat the exorcising, "Don't let your forty cents fill your mind."' In feverish haste she began to fill the page of her notebook with scribblings.

Professor Gilbert did not take his small accident seriously, nor did anyone. The ankle was swollen and painful by night, and worse the next morning. Still he hobbled to his classes as usual. The second night after his fall he could not sleep for the pain, and on the morning of the third day, Matey's mother, looking rather tired, told her that she had been up since four, putting hot compresses on it, and although Father pooh-poohed the idea, she intended to call a doctor.

That was Thursday. Tuesdays and Thursdays were full days for Matey, her laboratory work coming on those afternoons. She had only half an hour at noon, and always lunched at the University. She chanced, that day, to sit down at a table with a group of girls from her own sorority. They were the kind who discuss the meaning of life. 'We've got to get this sex-question straightened out,' one of them was saying earnestly. 'It's up to our generation. Our parents just muffed it. And it certainly is at the bottom of everything. Don't you feel that, Matey?'

'Oh, I don't know,' said Matey neutrally, as she said most things.

'And yet,' said another girl, 'I am sure that the abolition of marriage would be a *great* mistake.'

Matey swallowed a large bite from her sandwich. 'Yes, I guess it would,' she answered.

The others thought she was being prudish. 'I believe you're sexually cold, Matey,' one of them diagnosed.

'Well, maybe,' said Matey, trying to think whether she were or not. 'I like boys pretty well,' she offered, 'some of them.'

‘That's a sure sign of coldness,’ cried one of the girls tensely. ‘If you weren't sexually cold, you'd *hate* them! Sex-hostility, you know. Don't you ever read anything modern? Wells? Shaw?’

Matey examined her own mind and found nothing in it either for or against this theory, or any other; found the habit of drifting from day to day without any theories whatever. ‘Well, maybe,’ she agreed.

But when she came back from the counter with her dessert she sat down at another table to eat it. At the far end of this some boys on the tennis team were also earnestly discussing life. ‘The trouble with Bill,’ said one, thrusting out his jaw, ‘is his overhead! He can drive, and he can volley, but once you get on to his game, you can lob him to a fare-thee-well. That backstop practice of his is – ’

As if through the wrong end of a telescope Matey saw a tiny mental snapshot of Priscilla, furiously beating the ball up against the board fence. She wondered how Priscilla was getting along – *really*, that is.

When she went home late that afternoon she had almost forgotten about her father's ankle. As she stepped in through the front door, her mother was coming downstairs with two men, one of them the family doctor. They were looking very serious, and there seemed, from some words she caught, a question of taking Father to the hospital.

‘Oh, as serious as that!’ she commented, very much surprised.

Her mother and the doctors shifted their eyes to her face for an instant, looked at her as though they did not see her, and looking back at one another, made some arrangement about the coming of the ambulance.

'For heaven's sake, Mother!' she cried when the doctors had gone out. 'Is it just that trouble with his ankle?'

'It may be nothing,' said her mother in a steady voice; 'they say not to worry. But they are rather afraid of blood poisoning.'

She went upstairs quickly.

Among the many things which Matey did not know was how serious blood-poisoning might be, but she was startled by something in the air of the house. She went upstairs on tiptoe and looked in through the open door at her father, lying in bed. His eyes were closed. She could see no more because the room was darkened. Her mother, sitting near the bed, put her finger on her lips and shook her head. Matey went on into the bathroom and began to wash her hands. Presently she came to herself and perceived that she had stood there washing her hands for a long time. What had been in her mind? Had she been thinking that something serious might come of this injury to Father? No, of course not. Impossible. A little cut on his ankle! She had skinned both knees ten times as much as that last winter playing basketball, and never thought of it again. She looked in once more, saw her father and mother in exactly the same position in the darkened room, and tiptoed away. Something about her mother's expression struck her. They were as a family seldom ill – Father had never been sick since Matey could remember. She had never before seen her mother taking care of him.

The ambulance came, Father was carried downstairs, a mere long bundle of bedding. Mother put on her hat to go with him. Matey felt as though she herself had become invisible or had dropped off the earth. But just before Mother left the house she remembered, turned, kissed her, and said, 'I'll telephone from the hospital, dear, don't worry.' She spoke the words clearly, but something about her tone made Matey wonder if she knew what she said.

As the ambulance drove away, Sumner appeared and thrust his cold little nose into Matey's hand. 'Oh, Sumner!' she whispered. She sat down on the floor and took him into her arms. 'I couldn't get along without you,' she murmured in his ear. She knew this was a silly thing for a twenty-year-old girl who had read Kant and Plato to say to a dog. But it was true.

It was the maid's afternoon and evening out. Matey got herself and Sumner some dinner and ate hers, stopping between mouthfuls to make sure she had not missed the telephone bell. By eight o'clock she had had no message. She called up the hospital and asked for news. After a short wait a business-like woman's voice said, 'Your mother was just sending a nurse to telephone you that you had better come to the hospital, Miss Gilbert.'

Sumner jumped up against her as she put on her hat, thinking he was to be taken out for a walk. She did not know he was there, not even when she had pushed him back into the empty house as she shut the door behind her. Three-quarters of an hour later she walked rapidly into the hospital office and said in a low tone that she was Professor Gilbert's daughter and could she see her father and mother.

The nurse in charge nodded, rang a bell, answered a telephone call, said firmly into the mouthpiece, 'But you *said* it was the inch-and-a-half width you wanted!' and turning from this gave Matey a searching glance, and exclaimed impatiently, 'See here, you're not going to faint, are you? You are pretty white. If you're too frightened, you stay right here in a chair. Do you *feel* sick?'

Matey had not known she was pale. With an effort she tried to discover how she felt. 'I'll be all right, I think,' she said, surprised to find her lips hard to move.

An attendant appeared, led her down a corridor, and opened a door into a brightly lighted room. A doctor standing inside lifted a chair and placed it noiselessly for her. Another doctor, their own, was standing by the bed, holding Father's right wrist. Matey's mother sat holding his other hand in both hers. His eyes were still closed. Under the white glare of light his sunken face was grey. Matey could not believe that face was her father's. All that she had thought of as Father was gone from it. As she looked, it drew together with a spasmodic contraction into sharp contorted lines, as if in a nightmare effort to get those sealed eyes open. When finally the heavy lids lifted it was to show his eyes fixed in a horrified unseeing stare on the ceiling. The grey pinched mouth opened too, and a sharp frightened voice cried out, 'Jessica!'

'Here, Morris,' said his wife, bending over him instantly.

He turned his face toward her, running a shaking hand up her arm, gazing at her as though through a mist, as though he must penetrate it to see for himself that she was there. Then slowly the anguished look of fear faded from his face; his eyes grew quieter, and the lids fell shut.

At the sound of his voice Matey had recoiled violently, her hand clutching at the back of her chair. When her father's face once more lay motionless on the pillow, aloof, remote, she began to cry silently, not thinking to raise her hands to her face.

After a time she heard her father's voice, his own old voice, in a quiet reasonable tone asking collectedly, 'Doctor, am I dying?' and then instantly, without waiting for an answer the loud terrible voice of panic burst out, *Jessica, you haven't gone?*'

'Right beside you, Morris dear,' said Mother's voice – oh, was that *Mother's* voice? Could it be Mother's voice? Matey dashed the tears away enough to see, and watched again that unbearable look of terror fade away into quiet as he looked into Mother's eyes . . . could those be Mother's eyes?

The door opened noiselessly and a nurse appeared. She looked from the group around the bed to the girl weeping silently on her chair. One of the doctors half turned to her; a question and answer passed wordlessly. She stooped over Matey. 'Perhaps you'd better wait outside,' she whispered with a kind intonation.

Jessica! Don't go away!' in that piercing wail of mortal fear.

'No, Morris dear, I won't leave you,' said Matey's mother, lifting his hand to her bosom. The tears were running down her cheeks, but her voice was quite steady.

'Ah, Jessica . . . ' said her father, in a deep murmur of exhaustive relief.

'Yes, yes, I'll go,' whispered Matey to the nurse. She followed her stumblingly to a room down the corridor. There was a bed in it, across which Matey fell. She could scarcely breathe for her sobbing.

'You musn't give way so,' said the nurse gently. 'While there's life there's hope always. The doctors haven't given him up at all yet, you know.'

Matey heard these words, but little of their meaning reached her mind. It was not filled, it was not even touched by alarm for her father's life – it was bursting, cracking, all but crushed under the immensity of this new knowledge of more between Father and Mother than she had ever guessed – Why, in some way of their own . . . they *belonged* to each other, and knew it.

Oh, Mother's look of tenderness and sorrow! Father's murmur of relief when he knew she was still there . . .!

So Matey had understood nothing – had it all wrong – so all those years of her childhood had been shadowed and chilled by . . .

It came over her so bitterly that she cried aloud as though defending herself from an intolerable reproach. 'But I never knew . . . '

Across the years the child she had been looked reproachfully at her, the little girl standing in the cold shadow – if she could only make her hear! 'No! no!' cried the Matey who lay across the hospital bed and sobbed. 'No! It doesn't mean what you think! There is more! That is not all! *Don't* grow up thinking that is all!'

But she flung herself against the barrier of time. The little girl had grown up thinking that was all.

That child of the past – there were before her long crooked

years that never could be lived straight. 'But I never knew . . . ' sobbed Matey, over and over.

The door opened behind her. She sat up, blinded by her tears. A group of strangers stood there, well-dressed, indifferent strangers who looked at her in surprise. She slid off the bed, staring back at them stupidly. How long had she been there? What was she doing in this strange place?

'Oh, I beg pardon, I thought you said this was the room, nurse,' said a man's voice, speaking crisply, as people do who have nothing particular to care about.

A nurse appeared behind them. She came gently up to Matey, put her arm about her shoulders, and drew her through the little group of newcomers.

'Poor girl,' she said to them in a low voice. 'You must excuse her. Her father has just died.'

PART TWO

CHAPTER ONE

✾✾✾

The first tulip was out in the front yard of the Rustdorf Savings Bank, and when Adrian Fort came stepping along, whistling *'Auprès de ma blonde,'* he stopped to look at it. Then he glanced up at a small white cloud contributing an ingenuous pearliness to its corner of the universe, and marched briskly up the gravel walk to the building, whistling 'Turkey in the Straw.'

There was, he reflected, no reason for cheerfulness on his part in this what-next period of his life; but little ground for anxiety either, he that is down having no fall to fear. The spring air was spirited, the yellow tulip like a small sun. On the front porch of the Bank, Adrian turned to look at the flower again, waiting till the vibrations of its pure colour reached his inner eye. 'Monet was the fellow who took off our blinkers for that sort of thing,' he thought to himself, unlocking the door and stepping into the shuttered twilight of the small building.

He pulled up the blinds, opened the window, and leaned out to push back the shutters. Oblique rays of spring clarity poured in on the black grillwork above the counter. Beyond the slanting gold of these lines lay a sizeable high-ceilinged plain old room, with quiet grey and brown surfaces of wall and floor. A side window, the commonplace squares of its cross-bars foreshortened to a sprightly pattern of diagonals, made an amusing break in the soberness of the planes about it. Adrian stood for a moment considering the play of light in this composition.

As he moved toward the safe he began to whistle 'There'll be a *hot* time ...' 'Decidedly,' he thought, noting the lively tune that had come into his head, 'decidedly, it does not take much of a Monet feather or a Vermeer straw to tickle this infant.' He swung open the heavy door and extracted the cash-drawer, ledger, and other paraphernalia of the day's work.

'Good morning, Mrs Terbosh.' The first depositor was pushing her bank book and a ten-dollar bill through the cashier's window. 'Oh, no, Father's all right. Aunt Tryntje insisted that the storm door couldn't be taken down without his personal attention, that's all. He'll be here a little later. But I can enter this deposit for you, all right.' . . . 'Well, yes, a good many people have asked me that since my return. But how would you expect Rustdorf to seem to a Rustdorf boy? If you'd been living in Yokohama would Rustdorf look different when you came back? Did it ever? Here's your bank book. I entered the interest too, while I was about it. I noticed you hadn't brought it in since the first of the year. . . . Oh, that was why you wanted to see Father. Well, I never heard of this particular oil company, but I know Father would advise against it. Except of course for folks who have money they don't mind risking. Father sticks to it that anything that promises to pay too much can't help being risky. He always says he doesn't advise people against taking risks. . . . "What is life but one long risk?" . . . you know how Father talks. But he does against taking a risk without knowing you're doing it. Leave the circular here and I'll ask him when he comes in. Remember me to Madeleine and John. I hear their baby is a wonder. What are they going to name him?' . . . 'Myndert? *Myndert?* Oh, yes, for John's Father. And Terbosh for your family.' The young man laughed. 'Say, listen! Myndert Terbosh LeRoy. . . . And you can stand there and ask me whether Rustdorf is changed!'

Still smiling over this small joke when his father came in, he passed it on.

'The child's lucky they didn't name him Van den Bogert for his grandmother's family,' remarked the older Adrian. He took his hat from his thickly thatched grey head, hung it on a peg near the window, and went into the small inner office, remarking drily, 'They will, the next one.'

Adrian, tearing the paper from a roll of nickels, began to whistle abstractedly, looking out of the side window at the tennis courts on the Square. They had an early-in-the-season, rain-channelled aspect of desolation, but Adrian, who knew every inch of them, estimated that it would not take him long to put them in shape, the frost being out of the ground.

A young girl came in, nodded soberly to Adrian, pushed her bank book through the window, and told him that she wanted to take out fifteen dollars. 'I'm glad you're here, Adrian, and not your Father. I was afraid your Father would look hard at me. I'm taking it out to go to New York to buy a hat.'

'Now, Janey Whiteley!' came from the inner office. 'I wish you kids would ever get things straight. How many times will I have to tell you that I *like* to have you spend your savings for something you want? I'm just worn out, trying to get through your heads that that's the whole point of saving anyhow, whether it's money or time or health – so that when you really want something you'll have the wherewithal to get it.'

'All right for *you*, Mr Fort!' the girl answered. 'On the strength of that I'll just buy my hat on Fifth Avenue instead of Fourteenth Street.'

Laughing and looking lightened, she fluttered out into the street. Adrian's mind went back to tennis. 'Dirck Davis and I could get those courts ready to play on in two half-Saturdays,' he thought.

A tall girl in grey pushed open the door of the bank with a free graceful thrust of a long arm, hesitated, and looking back over her shoulder at a fox-terrier behind her, asked, 'Are dogs allowed in here?' She put the question vaguely to Adrian, having glanced at him without seeing him, as at a ticket-seller behind his window. Adrian thought he detected in her low-toned speech a faint trace of an accent. Perhaps only that the syllables were more neatly articulated from the teeth out than is usual with English words.

'Yes, indeed,' said Adrian gravely through the cashier's wicket. 'Dogs and babies and cats come into the Bank quite as often as depositors.'

The young lady flashed a quick look at him between surprise and uncertainty. Adrian saw that she had grey eyes, which even in that unpremeditated glance gave him an impression of guardedness and reserve.

'You're very kind,' she said formally, with a slight cool smile, evidently no more than part of the formula for acknowledging a small courtesy. 'We have a responsive live wire before us,' thought Adrian, slightly nettled. He wondered who she could be. Perhaps come in to ask her way. Certainly no depositor. Ever since he could remember, Adrian had known them all by sight.

The fox-terrier had walked in past her and now stood looking up at Adrian behind the grill. Adrian looked back cordially. He liked dogs. No young-ladyish guardedness about those eyes!

'I would like to speak to Mr Adrian Fort,' stated the young lady.

'I am Adrian Fort,' said Adrian, passably astonished and looking it.

The young lady was even more so. 'Why . . . ' she murmured, looking dubiously through the cashier's window. Adrian was rather nondescript as to hair, eyes, and skin, and nothing particular as to figure, bearing, and small sandy-red moustache. But nobody could mistake the fact he was not much older than the newcomer. She went on, 'I had thought Mr Fort would be . . . would be a much . . . '

'Oh, now I have it,' said Adrian. 'Of course. It's my father you want to see, and you must be Miss Penelope Gilbert, come in answer to Father's letter.'

His father came out hastily from the inner office, his snatched-off spectacles in one hand, the other outstretched. 'Come in, come in, Miss Gilbert. I hardly expected to see you so soon.' He was outside the counter now, her hand in his as he went on. 'So this is Cousin Constance's great-great-niece. You're very welcome indeed. My son, Adrian, Miss Gilbert. Won't you come into my office?'

('What under the sun is there in that desperately banal greeting to make her look surprised?' Adrian wondered.)

He held the half-door of the counter open to let her pass, and as she hesitated, guessed that she would like to have her dog with her. 'Come on, sir,' he whistled cordially in dog-language, snapping his fingers at the fox-terrier and motioning him in. But he was not rewarded this time even by a formal smile of thanks.

The three went into the inner office, where, the door remaining open, Adrian could hear and see as if they were still in the same room. Miss Gilbert sat down in the battered leather armchair in which all Rustdorf had sat at one time or another, laying secrets of their pocketbooks down on the table under the eyes of Adrian's father and grandfather. This visitor looked to Adrian as though she had the habit of not laying her secrets down on any table whatever. The momentary expression of surprise had disappeared. She seemed, Adrian thought, as self-possessed, not to say cautious, a young person as he had ever seen, with a face as impulsive and open as a padlocked door. But she certainly was graceful. There was something classic about the way her long arms and legs fell into quiet restful lines.

Her small dog sat soberly by her knee. He was an old fellow, Adrian could see that now; his face had the wizened sadness of elderly fox-terriers. As Miss Gilbert prepared herself to listen, she put out a gloved hand to stroke him. He turned his head up toward her, an expression of adoration in his sunken brown eyes.

'Oh, well, a dog will love anybody!' Adrian told himself. And then turning the blade inward with an accurate practised thrust, he thought, 'Vanity, vanity! Certainly all is vanity. Because a good-looking young woman refuses to observe that I exist, I turn cynic.'

He listened but absently to the explanation his father was giving of Cousin Constance's curious little bequest. It was an old story to him. For years it had been one of the few small picturesque oddities in the commonplace routine of the bank. His father was now, by the aid of a condensed table of compound interest rates, showing their visitor how the original five thousand had grown since the old lady's death to the slightly more than eleven thousand which was now at the disposal of her great-great-niece. 'It was not a very business-like arrangement, Miss Gilbert,' he said, 'but one had to get on with old Cousin Constance as best one could. She called me in one day when I was walking past, told me what was in her mind, and then and there signed over to me the securities she wanted me to sell for her. It was no way to do things and I tried to have something in writing, or someone else in as witness. But she specially did not wish this, as part of her plan was that no one should know about it – especially not your father. She did not get on very well with your father, to tell the truth, as you probably have heard. Cousin Constance was . . . well, perhaps not the most amiable of characters; although she had reasons for that. I tried to explain to her the danger there would be if

I should die before she did and before I could regularise the transaction. But she cut me short . . . '

('Yelled and threw a paperweight at his head, was the version I always heard,' thought Adrian, amused by his father's decorum of wording.)

' . . . and assured me that she would die before I did. As a matter of fact she was even then very ill, though we had no idea of it. No doctor was ever allowed to set foot in her house, you know. She was in her grave before the money came in from the sale of those securities, but she had told me just what her wishes were, so I started the account in your name, as she had specified. The gift is entirely without conditions. She didn't even leave a message for you. But from her talk it was clear enough what was in her mind. Your family had been here on a brief visit not long before and some little incident or other had convinced her that you showed unusual intelligence . . . well, I'm not sure that she didn't mean unusual character. . . . '

(Adrian smiled again at his father's expurgated version of Cousin Constance's – 'The child has real brains. But that's nothing. Morris's children would have brains, of course. The miracle is that she's honest in spite of his false egotistical blood running through her!')

' . . . I thought she was perhaps rather imagining than observing,' his father was saying. 'You were really a very small girl then, only seven, I think . . . it was while your father was still professor at Logan Bluffs; you were just beginning school. I ventured to point out that it was rather early to have any proofs either of your brains or of your manner of using them, but she wouldn't listen to me. She had made up her mind. Well, she wouldn't need much proof. You were always her favourite. It was a pleasure to me to see the satisfaction she took in leaving this small bequest, the only personal one she made. The rest of her money went, you probably heard, to endow beds in the hospital at Poughkeepsie.'

Adrian wondered what would be the first comment of the legatee. From the startled expression which had again come into her face, he gathered that the news of her inheritance had made the strongest possible impression on her. Well, cash always did.

She said, her rather low voice slightly raised by emphasis, 'But, Mr Fort . . . how did you ever know we lived in Logan Bluffs? How did you know my father was Professor there? How *could* you know when I began to go to school!' These questions came out in a crescendo of surprise.

'Why, my dear young lady, you are a relative of mine,' said Mr Fort. 'Why shouldn't I know something about you?'

'A relative!' said Miss Gilbert. 'I didn't know we *had* . . . ' she stopped as if fearing to sound ungracious.

Mr Fort laughed. Adrian liked to hear his father laugh. 'Well, perhaps people outside Dutchess County wouldn't call it much of a kinship. One of your great-grandmothers was a sister of one of my grandfathers.'

'And our Aunt Connie, too, was a . . . '

'She was one of those forty-second cousins of everybody's with which Rustdorf is filled to this day. Why, you have a townful of relations here. We've been looking forward to seeing you, to hear the news from your branch of the family. After Cousin Constance's death there was of course nothing to bring your parents back here. We heard very little, and nothing direct . . . the newspaper notices of your father's death, and then last year, your mother's. I thought often of Jessica with so much sympathy after your father's death had left her alone. I lost my own wife, many years ago, and I know what that solitude is. How *was* your mother, during those later years?'

Miss Gilbert did not answer at once. She looked down first at her gloved hands and then at the dog by her side. He turned his old head toward her again, and as she leaned toward him, jumped up stiffly upon her lap. She put a hand lightly on his head. Adrian noticed for the first time that she had beautiful hands, large, shapely, long-fingered.

'I hope I haven't said anything to . . . ' began Mr Fort with compunction.

'No, oh, no!' she told him quickly, raising her head and showing a face in which there was neither caution nor neutrality. 'No, it's not that. But I can't tell you how strange it seems to me to come here . . . I thought of course it would be just business . . . and find that you know about us. That you did, all this time, when I never dreamed that we had anybody who . . . We've moved about a good deal, you know; never very long in one place. Always with people we hadn't known for very long, and who didn't know much about us. It's . . . it's very . . . ' she hesitated for a word, did not find it, and went on, her voice shaking a little, 'I don't think that I've heard anybody call my mother Jessica since the day my father died.'

('I'm all off about this girl!' thought Adrian hastily. 'What made me think she was conventional and shallow?')

His father was saying, 'But I used to play with your mother when she was a little girl and came here from Newburgh in the summers to visit her Van Benthuysen cousins. And I used to know your father, too, when he came once in a while to see Cousin Constance. I went over to their wedding in the Newburgh church. In fact one of my old shoes had the honour of landing on top of their carriage as they drove away, and disappeared with them.'

Miss Gilbert said again wonderingly, 'You can't think how strange it seems to me! Mother as a little girl! . . . and their wedding day . . . ! I think I never thought of my parents as just like anybody else . . . who had been just a little girl and boy sometime.'

Adrian heard his father's voice say seriously, 'My dear child, how unfair! I am a parent myself; let me speak up for them. It is cruelty to anyone not to remember that he was once nothing more than a little boy, and never can become very different from anyone else.'

'Is it?' murmured the girl. She kept her eyes fixed on him as though (thought Adrian) she were getting from his aspect some unspoken comment on his words. Then she said, 'But, Mr Fort, all that was so long ago!'

'Why, it's not more than thirty-three or -four years ago,' objected Mr Fort laughingly; 'that's certainly not too long for ordinary human feelings to survive. . . . '

'Isn't it?' Her eyes rested deeply on his.

Over his ledger Adrian thought, 'What is that oddity in her accent? Funny how it makes her sound sort of appealing.'

His father was standing up now. 'See here, Miss Gilbert,

I must have some old photographs with your mother in them . . . yes, I'm sure of one, a group of us playing croquet on the Van Benschotens' front lawn . . . side-whiskers and crinoline. It would amuse you. But of course your mother must have had a copy too. Perhaps you know it.'

'No, I never saw any old photographs. There were some, I think, but they were in a box that was burned up in a freight wreck the time we moved from Logan Bluffs . . . no, it was moving from Lincoln to Millerton it was lost, I think. When you move a good many times, things do get lost.'

('It's a sort of *French* accent!' said Adrian to himself.)

His father came out to where he was leaning over the ledger. 'Adrian, take Miss Gilbert over to the house, won't you, and ask Aunt Tryntje to get out some of the old photograph albums. I'd go myself, but I'm expecting John Davis in about his mortgage. Won't you leave your dog here, Miss Gilbert? He'd be no trouble.'

'Oh, no, thanks, he always goes with me.'

'I'll be enchanted to go,' said Adrian, laying down an inkless pen. 'Tell Mr Davis, will you, Father, to pass the word along to Dirck that the tennis courts are about ready to work on.'

He used this as a gambit to start talk as they walked down the front steps. 'Do you play tennis, Miss Gilbert?'

'Yes, I play. Not so well as my sister. She's quite an expert – won the Middle Western ladies' championship last year.' She spoke in a correct, colourless manner.

'Yes,' thought Adrian, 'her conversation *is* like what I expected! And she still hasn't observed that I exist.'

But at that moment Mr Fort put his head through the side window of the Bank and called, 'Oh, Adrian, hold on a minute. I wonder if Miss Gilbert couldn't stay to have lunch with us. We'd be so glad to have you, Miss Gilbert. And I'll get my aunt to set out the spoons with the Van Benthuysen initials on them. Your mother always ate with those when she had meals with us.'

The girl glanced at Adrian almost as if consulting him about what to answer. No, it couldn't be her accent, he decided, that made her seem appealing, for she seemed so now and she hadn't said a word. Perhaps it was a trick of turning her head. At any rate he was moved to say hastily and heartily, 'Yes, do stay.'

'Thank you,' she called back to the older Adrian, hanging out of the window; 'I'll be glad to.'

As they walked on, 'Your father seems such a kind man,' she said.

Adrian saw in the turn of her phrase an opportunity to exhibit a small verbal neatness. 'Father doesn't seem anything he's not,' he said lightly. 'He *is* a kind man.'

At this she looked for an instant straight at him, said, 'Doesn't he?' in an enigmatic accent and looked away again.

Adrian was so taken aback that he was on the point of asking stupidly, 'Doesn't who?' when in a polite tone, 'Where *is* your house?' she asked him.

'I can't make connections with her at any point,' thought Adrian. 'What in the world was all that about?' Aloud he answered, 'That low grey stone one across the Square, with the locust trees about it.'

Like a swallow swerving suddenly upward, her voice broke into fresh personal vividness. 'Oh . . . locusts! Why, I believe I can remember them in Rustdorf. I'd forgotten those trees were *locusts!* '

'There are plenty of them all around,' said Adrian. 'Probably the ones you remember are those in Cousin Constance's back yard.'

'Why! Are they *still* there?' asked the girl.

Adrian laughed. 'You make me feel like my father. It's not so long since you were a little girl. Not long enough for a tree even to notice.'

'I suppose . . . I never thought of it before . . . ' her voice dropped to a solemn lower note . . . *'Does Aunt Connie's house still stand?'*

'Sure it does,' said the young man, finding this naïveté unexpected and pleasing. 'There it is, down the street, the fourth house on the right. What would you think could happen to it?'

'I can't make you understand,' said the girl, 'how strange it seems to me that it has been here, really, all this time. And you and your father knowing about us. It's like – as if you saw there had been all along another dimension to things. Why, the first thing I can remember is Aunt Connie's tulip bed.'

'We can go over and see if any tulips are out in it now,' said the young man. 'Or no, we'd better go first and tell Aunt Tryntje about lunch.'

'Is that a real name?' asked the girl.

'Well, sort of real. Katherine's a great family name around here. The Dutch like it. And Katrintje is short for Katherine, and Tryntje's short for that. Aunt Tryntje's great on old-time ways and it suits her to have the same nickname her something-or-other great-grandmother had. Her real name is Miss Katherine Brinckerhoff Van den Bogert.'

'Goodness gracious!' murmured the girl, smiling. It was the first time her seriousness had been broken. She looked very nice and young when she let herself smile, Adrian thought.

'But you'd better call her Aunt Tryntje,' he told her. 'You are certainly a relative of hers. Anyhow everybody's called her Aunt Tryntje for so long she's probably forgotten she has any other name.'

'I know,' said the young lady; 'when you said just now at the Bank that I must be Penelope Gilbert it sounded like somebody else. I'm always called Matey.'

'Matey!' said Adrian. 'What a nice nickname. I never knew a Matey.'

'Why do you find it nice?' she asked in what was evidently a sincere wonder. 'A good many people find it rather silly-sounding, I think.'

'Oh, what it seems to mean. Comradely. Somebody who shares things with you. Shipmate on the voyage of life . . . that sort of thing.'

She considered. 'Well, I never thought before of any meaning to it. I always took it just like any name . . . such as Gladys or Bernice.'

'It's a real privilege,' he told her with feeling, 'to rescue you from Gladys or Bernice. I would hate to think of anybody being stranded for life on one of those swampy malarious islets.'

This time she laughed out loud. 'How ridiculous!' she said, appreciatively.

Adrian thought to himself, 'I sort of like this girl.'

He decided that he went on liking her, as she sat opposite Aunt Tryntje in their living room, a photograph album on her knee, listening to Aunt Tryntje's exposition of her ancestry and its ramifications. Several times he thought he had detected her eyelids flickering down over her quiet eyes to hide amusement. And so, when the old lady turned her back on them to look for yet another daguerreotype, he caught the girl's eye, expecting her as a matter of course to exchange with him a smile over Aunt Tryntje's genealogical mania. But she did not allow herself to understand this invitation to laugh at her old hostess, and returned nothing but a pleasant nod and smile of reassurance.

'Why, she's a *nice* girl!' thought Adrian.

He looked at her with respect which he soon forgot in his pleasure over a faint light striking up on the shadowed side of her face which brought out the details of the low-relief modelling in her cheek. The light was reflected, he noticed, from his father's old Montaigne, glossy with long handling, which lay on the table beside her.

'And now,' said Aunt Tryntje, 'I hope I've got you all straightened out about the way the Smiths are related to the Howlands. Just remember about those English names in the family, Whiteley and Russell and Smith – they were Quakers driven out of New England, every one of them. *But not the Browns.* They'd gone to Holland first – well, well, I mustn't go into that now. It's your turn. Do tell me about your family.'

She turned to Adrian. 'Doesn't she look a little like Cousin Mary Howland? Something about the way the eyes are set in, far apart and rather deep. Cousin Mary's mother was a LeRoy, you know, and the LeRoy eyes are all. . . . '

'Well,' said Adrian judiciously, 'as I only remember Cousin Mary when she weighed two hundred and twenty and wore a wig. . . . '

The visitor broke into laughter. Adrian guessed that she had been for some time longing for a decent excuse to laugh.

'Oh, to be sure,' said Aunt Tryntje, 'I forgot you weren't your father.' She turned back to the visitor, 'I do really want to know all your news.'

'I don't know where to begin,' said the girl. 'I never met anybody who was in the least interested in my family as such. Most people I know haven't any idea whether I have any family, beyond the members they see once in a while.'

'For mercy's sake, child, where have you lived?' cried Aunt Tryntje.

'Pretty much everywhere,' said the visitor without enthusiasm.

'You were in Corinth, weren't you, when your father died?'

'Why, did you *all* know about us?' exclaimed the girl, startled.

'I should hope I wouldn't lose all track of Martha Whiteley's grandchildren. Your grandmother Whiteley was my first cousin, and my favourite relative. Well, go on, did you stay on long in Corinth?'

'We stayed another year there, till I graduated. Then I went to France for a year's study. I have some old friends in Paris, a

French family. I have stayed with them more or less ever since I was a little girl. I like them all very much and one of the daughters is my best friend. I lived with them that year and studied at the Sorbonne. When I came back I got a position in the French department at Western Reserve University. Teaching French seems the easiest thing, of course, for my sister and me.'

'And did your mother make a home for you?'

'No.' The girl paused as if thinking what words to use. 'No, I have usually lived in boarding houses. Mother . . . after Father's death . . . Mother became very much absorbed by her Church. The Church we went to in Corinth was very ritualistic and . . . ' She stooped down to where her little dog sat, and stroked his shoulder thoughtfully as she went on, 'I find I hardly know how to speak of these things. Nobody among my acquaintances in the places where I've lived lately ever knew enough about us to ask. And my brother and sister knew, anyhow, so we didn't need to talk about them among ourselves.'

She made this statement soberly in a matter-of-fact tone, but Adrian said to himself with conviction, 'It's her *eyes* that make her seem appealing.' And then remembered with surprise that he had found them guarded and cold.

'Perhaps I oughtn't to have asked you about . . . ' began Aunt Tryntje.

'No, oh, no, I think it's *sweet,* you caring to know,' said the girl, 'and there is nothing troubling about it, or hard to speak of. Mother just became more and more absorbed by the church services. There are a good many of them in a High Church. *You* know.'

'No, I don't; we are all Friends,' said Aunt Tryntje firmly.

Then, seeing that the girl did not understand, she explained, 'Yes, I know, it does seem odd, Forts and Van den Bogerts being Quakers, but my mother was a Willetts, you know.'

'Oh,' said the girl, lowering her eyelids for a moment. She went on, 'Well, there are a great many services, for the different church seasons and hours of the day. Enough to take up about all one's time. They seemed a great comfort to Mother, though she'd never cared much about going to church before. And then she became a religious.'

'A what?' asked Aunt Tryntje.

'A sister, you know, in a Church Order. An Order that runs an orphanage near Corinth. That was where she went to live. She smiled always, very busy and satisfied, and we children were so glad for her.'

'But . . . ' said Aunt Tryntje, 'but . . . ' She looked up at the ceiling as if making an inner calculation, murmured, 'Hmmm, the Van Benthuysens *are* all mystics. But Jessica never . . . ' Looking back at the girl, she asked with the privileged bluntness of old age, 'Was there some person in the Order she . . . thought a good deal of?'

With a look of surprise, the girl answered, 'Yes, she had come to be great friends with the Mother Superior.'

'Oh,' said Aunt Tryntje.

'Of course, friendships aren't allowed in religious orders very much, and once she was in, they didn't see much of each other. What interested Mother most was running the business part of their orphanage. She was wonderful at that.'

'Well . . . ' said Aunt Tryntje, and then, 'How about your brother and sister?'

The visitor began, 'Priscilla is in . . . ' and was interrupted by an exclamation from Aunt Tryntje. 'Oh, they *did* name her Priscilla, did they?'

'Yes,' said the visitor, again surprised. She waited for an explanation, but Aunt Tryntje merely said, 'Nothing. It's not one of the family names like yours, that's all. Go on.'

'Priscilla has taught French in a girls' school near Chicago for quite a time. It's a private school, sort of finishing seminary, not very serious teaching, but she gets a much larger salary than I, than any college teacher.'

'What is she like?'

'Well, she's tall and blonde and very nice-looking. Plays awfully good tennis, and often takes parties of girls abroad in the summer. That pays very well. We've all been abroad a good deal. In France, that is, because of Father's work, and now ours.'

'Is *she* High Church and religious?' enquired Aunt Tryntje.

'Oh, no, not a *bit!*' said the girl hastily. And paused an instant as if startled by some unexpected thought. But she added no qualification to her statement.

'And your brother?'

'He graduated from the Harvard Law School the year Father died. And he's in a law firm in Pittsburgh.'

'Pittsburgh!' cried Aunt Tryntje. 'Why Pittsburgh?'

'Well, one of his classmates was a Pittsburgh fellow whose father is a successful lawyer there. Francis used to go to visit them in the vacations a good deal. They all liked him in the family. People do generally. And the father gave Francis a chance in his firm. He's doing very well. Francis always does.'

✿✿✿

'Well, I must say you sound like an independent, successful set of modern young people, well prepared to take care of yourselves in the world,' said Aunt Tryntje admiringly, 'as though you were getting whatever you wanted out of life.'

('No, she's not!' cried Adrian to himself with instant certainty.)

'Is your brother married?' asked Aunt Tryntje.

'Not yet,' said the girl. For the first time there was a little dryness in her accent. Adrian took this for a sign that she had stood about all of Aunt Tryntje that could be expected. He rose to his feet. 'I promised Miss Gilbert to take her over to Cousin Constance's to see if the tulips are out there. She thinks she remembers them.'

'That must have been when you were sent on to her by yourself to stay with her in '87,' said Aunt Tryntje accurately. 'I remember you very well – one of the nicest little four-year-old girls I ever saw. Constance used to say you had as good a time living as a kitten or a puppy. Once she told me, "Matey's little face is like a nasturtium blossom." And now isn't it like something in a book – an English book, I mean – the way she left this money to you? I hope my nephew told you what she said, "I want that child to have some money all her own to do just what she wants with, without anybody's approval or consent. By the time she's twenty-four, she'll know what that is." That was *her* age, you know, when she wanted so much to go away to study medicine. I suppose that's why she didn't want you to know about it till that age.'

('Can you beat it!' thought Adrian. 'First mention of that cash . . . not made by the heiress, at that!')

Aunt Tryntje was running on, 'We've wondered, every once in a while, whether as you grew up there *was* some special thing you'd set your heart on, as she had.'

She waited for an answer to this. Their visitor turned her face away and seemed to look fixedly at a steel engraving of Washington on the wall. She murmured in a very low voice, 'I should say that the matter with me is that there is *nothing* I want very much to do.'

It sounded as though she has not intended to say this aloud. Adrian felt a hasty impulse to help her pass over what was perhaps an inadvertent confession. But was that really what she had said? Perhaps he had imagined it as the sum total of his impression of her. At any rate, on the chance that she would like to have the subject changed, he said prosaically, 'It's not enough money to do *any*thing with! Not half so much as it seemed, probably, to a person of Cousin Constance's generation. What, in this *anno Domini* of 1907 could anybody do with five hundred dollars a year?'

'There are people living in comfort on that in Rustdorf, this minute,' said Aunt Tryntje with dignity.

'Then I'll put it, what could unfortunate people forced to live out of Rustdorf do with it?' amended Adrian. Had the girl really said that, or had he imagined it?

'Well, take her along to Constance's house anyhow,' said Aunt Tryntje, looking at the clock and letting Adrian have his point. 'Peter Russell has taken the children off to Fonteynkill today and the house is shut up.' She explained to the girl, 'Constance's nephew Peter Russell inherited the house. His wife died a year or so ago, leaving him with a great batch of little girls to bring up. The forlornest old widower you ever saw. He was too old to get married in the first place, and now to be left alone with a family – ! Two of the children are delicate in health, too.' She turned back to Adrian. 'But thee can go around into the back yard. Penelope, would thee like to leave thy little dog here . . . for I'm not going to go on calling Cousin Martha's granddaughter "Miss", nor saying "you" as if thee were a stranger.'

('How *can* Aunt Tryntje not have noticed what that dog is to her?' Adrian asked himself impatiently.)

'Oh, I'd like very much to have you call me by my first name,' the girl was saying. 'But no, thanks, Sumner always goes with me.'

'*Sumner!*' thought Adrian.

As they went down the steps and along the walk, Aunt Tryntje from the front door was calling instructions to Adrian. 'Don't forget to show her the Washington house, and the house where Aunt Dina died, and tell her what Rustdorf means, and that it should be Rustdorp, and point out Barnegat . . . ' Her voice died away as they advanced across the Square.

'Aunt Tryntje's a pippin' isn't she!' said Adrian.

'I never saw anybody in the least like her,' said the girl.

'I'll bet you never did!' said Adrian.

The girl answered steadfastly, 'No, I didn't mean it that way,' and turned the conversation, asking, 'What was that she said about saying "you" as though I were a stranger?'

'Oh, she's one of the older Friends who still "adhere to plain speech."' At the look of bewilderment in his listener's face he laughed and explained, 'In Quaker language "plain speech" doesn't mean saying disagreeable things and admiring yourself for being honest, but the use of "thee" for "you."'

'Oh, yes, I remember, I've heard about that,' said Miss Gilbert. 'Like the French use of *tu*.'

'I know an elder or two who wouldn't enjoy hearing you compare it to French usage,' remarked Adrian.

'Do you say "thee" too?' she asked.

'Well, most younger Friends don't much, any more, except maybe for little children. I try to remember to do it for Aunt Tryntje, because she doesn't like it if I don't.'

'It sounds picturesque,' said the visitor.

'That's no better than comparing it to the French!' Adrian warned her.

She looked amused and asked another question, 'What is the "Washington house"? Where he slept overnight?'

'No. Rustdorf antiquity hasn't any such violent episodes as that. This is a house in front of which he stopped his horse and asked a little girl in the front yard if she would give him a drink of water from the well. But she happened to be one of our great-grandmothers . . . yours too, of course . . . so we are all brought up on what he said and what she said, and what was the colour of his horse's tail, and so on.'

'A great-grandmother of mine? I'd like to hear about it.'

'There's nothing to hear, although as she grew older it took her longer and longer to tell it. My father, as a little boy, often heard her. She had worked out a peroration which never varied – "And then President Washington bowed over his saddle – *thank God! I remembered to curtsey!* – and riding magnificently, as he did everything, disappeared from my sight. But not from my mind. To have looked into the living eyes of a man greater in character than Julius Caesar or Napoleon . . . it gave me an undying faith in the human race." '

'That's a nice peroration,' said the girl.

'Here, this is the house. Aunt Tryntje will be sure to ask you about it. That's why this is called Washington Street.' He looked at the muddy ruts and added, 'Some day we're going to pave it, too, in his honour.'

They stopped before a storey-and-a-half white house, a little sagging as to roof and askew as to perpendicular, but freshly painted, with ruffled curtains at the little windows, and a huge lilac bush guarding the low door.

'Well, so he *was*, greater in character than Julius Caesar or Napoleon!' said the girl, looking at the house. 'Which way was he going?'

'Back toward New York from a visit to Poughkeepsie,' said Adrian – 'that way.'

The girl followed the direction of his finger and looked down the elm-bordered street, arched over with early-Gothic twig-tracery. 'It's absurd,' she said to her companion with a grimace of the lips which looked French to Adrian. 'Absurd, how I hear the beat of a horse's hoofs, unhurried and regular, down at the end of the road, and see a man's back, very broad, very straight . . . It's the first time I believed that George Washington ever really existed. From now on I too shall have more faith in our race.'

'It needs all the faith it can get,' commented Adrian. He added, 'It's odd, your finding any interest in such a flat little historical incident, when you've been in France so much.'

'My great-grandmother didn't live in France,' said the girl. 'Wasn't it nice that she didn't forget to make her curtsey?'

'Ah, you're real Rustdorf!' cried Adrian, laughing. He asked curiously, 'Didn't your father or mother ever tell you any of these stories? How did you escape?'

'Oh, they weren't at all the kind of people who think of old-time stories. They were both very active, absorbed in the present. We were all of us very busy. Mother did tell us a few . . . I remember one about a grandmother of hers who used to tell that in 1817 as a child of five she walked alone to town to see the travelling waxworks. Mother said that she wore a new pair of green morocco shoes and a new . . . '

Adrian snatched the words from her mouth, 'A new plaid linen dress, home-grown, homespun, woven, dyed, and made. And at the waxworks she saw Captain Cook devoured by the cannibals, Pocahontas, saving the life of John Smith, the Sleeping Beauty, and the Witch of Endor, raising – ' He was rewarded by hearing her laugh out, loud and free, as she had in the house.

'You'll believe now perhaps that we are twigs on the same tree. I can cap any story you begin. Do you know the one about the children – our great-uncles, I daresay – who were picking up apples to eat and because it was a Sunday afternoon thought they were as wicked as the "go up, baldhead" children, and set a little brother to watch for bears? Which ones did your father tell you?'

She shot a look at him from under her lashes and said, 'The only thing he ever said about Rustdorf was that he wouldn't be caught dead in it for half an hour.'

✲✲✲

'How ever did it happen, I wonder,' Adrian queried
as he laughed, 'that you suppressed that particular family
reminiscence when you were answering Aunt Tryntje's
questions? For a newcomer, you – '

She cut him short. 'That's the queer thing. I don't feel
like a newcomer. Less than ever in my life. It sounds foolish,
literary, made up – but almost from the first I've felt as though
I'd come back to a' – after a hesitation her voice changed so
that Adrian felt as though she had moved closer to him as they
walked – 'to a place I'd always known, to people near to me.
And that's strange. For I've never known any place very well.
Nor people either. The only other people who seem to reach
back into my past and sort of connect together the different
parts of my life are a family of friends in Paris – but I remember,
I told you about them in the house.'

'I'm just back from Paris.' Adrian brought this out abruptly,
without having in the least intended to.

'You are?' said the girl, surprised. 'Do you teach French, too?'

'No! heavens, no! You ought to hear me speak it. I was
studying painting there.' He had not meant to say this, either.

'Oh, you are an artist,' said the girl.

'No, I'm not,' he answered, 'I found that out. That's why I
came back.'

What under the sun possessed him to do this? He had not
said so much to any soul in Rustdorf! Good heavens! He had
told it all, all there was to tell! He shrank with a raw soreness
from any rejoinder she could possibly make, and began hastily
to tell himself not to blame her for saying the wrong thing
since he had put her in a position where there was no right

thing to say. Walking thoughtfully by his side, the girl let his words sink into a long, healing silence. When Adrian finally glanced at her, he found she was looking at him – seeing him this time. Their eyes met.

He thought wildly, as he bent to open the gate in the hedge, 'Why, she has magnificent eyes.'

They had arrived. He pushed open the gate and led the way around to the back of the old house.

'I remember more than I thought!' said the visitor behind him. 'I remember perfectly that side door in two parts. I was too little to unlatch the lower part, and when I got on a chair it seemed more fun to wriggle over and drop down outside. It's exactly like going back to the beginning of life and starting all over again!'

They turned the corner of the house and saw before them a slope of lawn, a few tall, leafless trees, the wide bare river in the distance. Several tulips stood like little painted flames beside the path.

'Oh!' cried the girl. *'Oh!'* She gave a little run, stopped, one hand at her temple in a startled attitude, and then moved slowly on.

Adrian thought it discreet to leave her to whatever memories of things past were set before her by the scene. He moved to one side and sat down on a bench. The little fox-terrier, who with his usual self-effacement had been trotting noiselessly at their heels, instead of following his mistress down the lawn, turned aside and jumped up beside him.

Adrian felt a shock of pleasure. He put his arm around the old fellow. It was extraordinary, he thought, what a liking he had taken at sight to that dog. The little lean warm body felt positively dear to him. And what an original, suitable name Sumner was! He looked down deep into the dog's eyes. They were all right, for a dog. But how limited and animal-like any dog's eyes are, compared to the awe-inspiring revelation of personality which human eyes can give!

The girl came back slowly along the path. She had taken off her gloves and now dropped them on the bench beside him. Adrian resisted with difficulty an impulse to pick up one of them and draw it through his fingers.

He looked down fixedly at the little huddle of grey suede, wondering if they were still warm from her hands. He tightened his clasp on the dog. The girl was standing close beside him, but he did not look up at her, having an obscure fear of what might happen if he did. He felt her stir. He heard her voice, crying out the thought that was knocking at his own heart, 'Why, this is incredible! All of it!'

CHAPTER TWO

✡✡✡

'Well, I don't know when I've seen a nicer girl,' said Aunt Tryntje, as she poured the second cups of tea that evening. 'They needn't tell me that all modern young people are mannerless and uncivilised. Those with Dutchess County blood, bring them up where you will and how you will, show their ancestry. I enjoyed every minute of this afternoon, after you two had gone back to the bank, when I had her to myself.'

'Yes, I found her attractive,' said the older Adrian.

'With a real family look, too,' said Aunt Tryntje.

'Oh, yes, very much so. That breadth of low forehead, and the distance between her grey eyes. It gives them the honest look I always like.'

'I *told* thee, Adrian, she had LeRoy eyes,' triumphed Aunt Tryntje. 'She mentioned having bad headaches. Now all the LeRoys have that trouble with headaches.'

But Adrian knew by his father's voice that he had not been thinking of the LeRoys but of his daughter who had died, Adrian's little sister whom he could not remember, who would have been grown up now and might have helped to fill the place left by their mother.

'No, all is not vanity,' thought Adrian, looking at his father.

'Adrian, when thee walked down to the station with her, did thee remember to tell her the story about Speck Zyn Kill?'

'No, Aunt Tryntje, I didn't. The conversation didn't seem to run naturally toward Speck.'

'Did thee show her where the old landing-slip had been?'

'We went to look at the river while we waited for her train. I'm not sure I remembered to point out the old slip.'

'Well, did thee at least tell her that Dutchess County was *always* freehold land – never any patron foolishness?'

'No, it slipped my mind. Something else must have come up.'

Adrian thought he was pronouncing these commonplace words in the most casual of tones. But he had a notion that his father pricked an ear. Now was the time, he thought, to slide into some other topic, to ask his father if he had remembered to speak to Dirck's father about the tennis.

So he asked, putting the question to them both, 'What is that slight accent of hers? Did it sound French to you?'

'Accent?' said Aunt Tryntje in surprise. 'What is thee talking about? She had no more accent than I. She spoke very nicely, I thought, not chewing and swallowing her words as young people do nowadays. I could hear every syllable.'

'No, I don't think I noticed any accent,' said his father judicially, after thinking a moment.

To himself Adrian said, 'Now this is enough!' Aloud he asked, 'Nice little dog of hers, wasn't he?'

Aunt Tryntje dissented again. 'Now that was the only thing I didn't quite like about her. That dog. I thought she acted a little foolish about him. I don't like people who are foolish about their animals. It means a soft streak. In every other way she seemed such a sensible girl.'

'I shouldn't say she had much of a soft streak,' remarked the older Adrian in a non-committal tone.

The meal was over. The two men pushed back their chairs and went into the living room. Adrian's father sat down at once with the *Poughkeepsie Evening Enterprise.*

'I'm safe,' thought Adrian, getting out his pipe, 'and just about time!' He planned to ask his father a question about the campaign for the mayoralty of Poughkeepsie, just then beginning. 'Did you notice a sort of appealing quality about that Miss Gilbert?' he blurted out helplessly. His father lowered the newspaper and looked over it at Adrian. 'Well, at least I'm too old to blush,' thought Adrian in exasperation, keeping his eyes on his pipe.

'No, I didn't think she was at all appealing,' said his father, after considering the matter. 'I should have said that appealingness belonged to another generation of girls. She struck me as a singularly self-possessed young woman. Not unattractively so. I liked her. I liked the way she took the news of that bequest. Rather unusual in my experience. Yet that might have come from lack of vitality enough to care about it very much. She seemed rather a dry personality for anybody so young.'

He waited a moment. Adrian made no audible comment, although in his heart he was crying out wrathfully, '*Dry!*' He was lost in consternation over the insensitive dullness of the older generation. The older Adrian lifted his newspaper and went on reading.

Adrian struck a match, lighted his pipe, and reached for the book nearest him. It was the old brown Montaigne which had cast a reflected light upon the suave low relief of that young cheek. He glanced from it – a natural sequence of memory – at the steel engraving on the wall before him, to which their visitor had raised her beautiful grey eyes. As he looked, George Washington's broad inexpressive face of putty became sensitive, young, looked back at him kindly. Had she really spoken those disheartened words? Or had he dreamed them? It seemed important to him that he should know, as if it would make a vital difference in his life. Well, Aunt Tryntje had been there. He could ask her.

He went through into the old kitchen where she was putting the dishes together in readiness for Rebecca, the coloured woman who 'came in mornings.' But now, he who had been able to speak of nothing else could not bring out a single word.

Aunt Tryntje began to tell him eagerly, the fourth time he had heard it, about the recent discovery of five letters, mostly legible, received from Loyalists who had emigrated to Nova Scotia at the end of the Revolution. Aunt Tryntje thought such Loyalists unjustly neglected by Americans. These letters, she told Adrian, settled once for all the question of who had been second in command on that expedition.

'Good God, who cares?' thought Adrian indignantly. Aloud he said, 'Thee must find such papers very interesting.' He was anxious to keep Aunt Tryntje in a good temper.

He stood awkwardly, bored by the necessity of paying enough attention to those papers to answer Aunt Tryntje, irritably watching every motion of her hands, trying to think of some way to bring the talk where he would have it.

Aunt Tryntje said repeatedly, 'There now, that'll do for tonight,' in the pleasantly satisfied voice of housekeeping women when surveying something that comes up to their standards. And repeatedly darted at some last thing, 'Just let me hang up this dishcloth!' or 'Oh, I haven't put out the milk bottles.'

They both finally went back into the living room. Adrian had let his pipe go out. And he had not asked his question. Abruptly he said, 'Aunt Tryntje, when thee asked Miss Gilbert if there was something she'd specially set her heart on, to do with Cousin Constance's money – '

'Yes – ' prompted Aunt Tryntje.

'What did she answer?' The words were out, thundering as they came.

Aunt Tryntje considered, 'Yes, I remember asking her that. What *did* she answer? Did she really answer at all?' She shook her head. 'I don't believe I noticed. My eye lit on the clock just then, and I remembered I hadn't said anything to Rebecca about an extra person to lunch.'

'Ah,' said Adrian.

He took up the Montaigne again. Aunt Tryntje knitted peaceably. Presently she began to murmur in a low hum, as if thinking aloud, 'Mmmm – funny – Jessica a nun – mmmmm – Van Benthuysen – Abby – Marietta – ' her thoughts dropped below the level of audibility. They rose again with some emphasis to clearer speech as she answered herself with decision, 'No, *ma'am!* Don't tell me! Jessica was no mystic. That Mother Superior – '

Adrian laid down his book to laugh. 'Why not admit the possibility that she was converted to a more spiritual life?'

The old knitter looked up, startled. 'Have I been talking to myself again! Mercy! How like Aunt Anna that is! I was just thinking over what Jessica's daughter told – ' she stopped with a look of alarm and asked quickly, *'What did I say?'*

'Oh, various charitable speculations as to some sordid motive for Mrs Gilbert's going into a sisterhood,' replied Adrian.

She looked relieved. 'Oh, that's all. I was trying to think if I'd ever known Jessica to show her Van Benthuysen blood. It was her grandmother, thee knows, who's recorded on the Reformed Church books as "a member of this church but somewhat given to enthusiasms."'

Adrian had heard this story so often that he ignored it now. 'Doesn't it seem rather queer,' he asked, 'that her parents hadn't told her anything about Rustdorf, apparently hardly mentioned the name of the place? Come to think of it, I wonder why they didn't ever stop off, between trains, sometime. They must have passed through dozens of times.'

'Oh, I don't know,' said Aunt Tryntje casually, neutrally.

As she never spoke either casually or neutrally, Adrian wondered what she was keeping from him.

She added, 'What does thee suppose Morris Gilbert would stop for, once Constance was dead and her money bequeathed?'

Adrian's father looked over the top of his newspaper.

'She was a person I used to find touching,' he said.

'Adrian, how can thee say that? Thee never could abide Jessica,' said his aunt.

'I didn't say I liked her. I found her touching. Didn't thee ever feel a sort of uneasiness about her? As if she were . . . yes, I know that piledriver way she had of going after what she wanted, but in spite of that . . . really uncertain of the value of everything she did? Dependent on what other people thought of it, maybe? Yes, probably needed to feel backed up, approved of. The kind of woman who needs to be treated with great magnanimity if she's to develop any inner life of her own.' He sighed, held up his paper, and remarked behind it, 'But as far as that goes, who ever gets treated with magnanimity?'

After a few minutes he put down his paper again, asking himself with resigned self-contempt, 'What *makes* me waste my time over newspapers?' 'Aunt Tryntje,' he went on, 'what would thee think of inviting Jessica's daughter to make us a visit this summer? She seems pleasant, and it might do us good to have another young person around. Would it make much trouble?'

'Well, it might be nice. I could think about it. I suppose the room over the wing would do for summer.'

'How about you, Adrian?' asked his father.

'Oh, I guess it would be all right,' said Adrian, taking his pipe out of his mouth. 'She said she plays tennis. I suppose we could get up some doubles.' He put his pipe back into his mouth and went on looking at the page before him.

'Let me have a little time to approach Rebecca about it,' said Aunt Tryntje.

'No hurry,' said the older Adrian; 'we're only in April now.' He wandered toward the piano and turned over the music on it. 'Will it bother thee if I try something here?' he asked.

'Not a bit, I love to hear thee pounding away,' said Aunt Tryntje kindly.

He played stiffly, with middle-aged, not very expert fingers, but with (so Adrian often thought) a certain sense of what it was all about that made his occasional false notes and halting tempo not very important. Just now he was feeling his way through a Bach Invention that looked simpler on the page than it was. After that he played, making a much more presentable job of it, a graceful MacDowell 'Woodland Sketch.' At the end he shook his head, sighed, murmured, 'Oh, what's the use!' and reached for his too difficult Bach again.

In the midst of this he said over his shoulder, 'That Gilbert girl said she plays the piano, didn't she? I wonder how much it amounts to?'

'I didn't see any indications one way or the other,' answered Adrian readily, with a competently executed casual accent. He was doing better, he thought, forgetting that he had not turned over a page since he had been holding the book.

His father swung around on the piano stool and sat there, his hands hanging between his knees. After a time Adrian glanced up at him and met his thoughtful eyes.

No, he was not too old to blush, he thought, feeling the slow heat burn its way to his temples. He looked back at the Montaigne, resolutely turned over a page, and suddenly thought, 'Oh, perhaps Father is only thinking about whether I'm going to stay or not.' The heat died out of his face.

'Well, I believe I'll go to bed,' said Aunt Tryntje cheerfully, taking off her glasses and putting her knitting inside the little walnut sewing cabinet which stood by her knee. 'If you boys want anything to eat, there's gingerbread in the cake-box, and some apple sauce in the blue bowl on the pantry shelf.'

The tall clock ticked loudly in the silent room after she had gone. Adrian laid aside the Montaigne and looked expectantly and a little nervously at his father.

'What'd I do with my pipe, I wonder?' said the older man, getting up from the piano stool. After he had found it and lighted it the two men sat smoking meditatively. Adrian got himself more in hand. When his father spoke he was ready to answer him as quietly as the question was put.

'Well, Adrian, how about it . . . have you had time to think what comes next? I'm ready for anything you decide.'

'I believe I'll stay right here,' said Adrian. 'I've had my try – a fair chance at what I wanted. It's no go.' With the words something that till then had gone on hoping for life gave up its wistful ghost and lay dead at Adrian's feet. He was somewhat shaken, having thought it dead before, but he averted his eyes and went on in a matter-of-fact tone, 'Better be a good savings-bank cashier than a mediocre artist.'

Within his father's heart rose a cry of desperate sympathy, of passionate unresignation, of reckless uncounting devotion – he ached with longing to spend his all, his life that was no longer of any use to him, so that his boy should have what he wanted. He drew a long, deep, painful breath and came back from this madness to a wonder that at his age he should still think there was any way one human being could give another what he wanted. What had the boy said with that manly finality, that had clicked like the locking of a door, and yet with a quiver in his voice, which his father recognised from his little-boy days . . . 'better a good bank cashier than a mediocre artist.'

'There's more in that, Adrian, than you probably believe now,' said his father gently.

'Oh, I believe it, all right,' rejoined Adrian steadily, tamping down the tobacco in his pipe with his forefinger. He could not have told what his father had said, or what he had answered, except that the very sound of his father's voice had been irritating to him. He struggled hard to keep out of sight this aftermath of an emotional crisis.

His father waited humbly to see if Adrian felt like adding anything to his statement, like letting his father share in what had brought him to his decision. Adrian very decidedly did not feel like letting anyone share in the consciousness of failure which had preceded that decision. His bald statement of it had been just all that he could manage, and he now sat in a moody silence, listening to its reverberations down his future.

His father heard them too, apparently, for after a long pause he remarked moderately, 'Well, there are worse things than living in Rustdorf. At least for men of our temperament. I don't want to talk like Aunt Tryntje, but there is a good deal of quiet blood in us. It's the fashion nowadays to maintain that a man can't be sure whether he's alive unless there are guns going off around him, and some weaker person to knock down once in a while, and a new woman every week or so.'

He had hoped he might win Adrian to a smile, but there was no lightening in the other's sombre face, so he went prosaically on, 'But as a matter of unobserved fact, there are several other varieties of men, and we Friends usually belong to one of the variants. At least I do.'

Adrian said impatiently, 'Oh, Lord, yes,' as though this were not the matter in question.

His father went on thoughtfully, feeling his way forward among his words as he had among the Bach notes. 'After all, I suppose you get harmony and equilibrium in life as in everything else by keeping what you have in proportion, more than by having such a lot. And harmony and equilibrium are maybe what last you best, in the long run.'

He was aware from the suppressed exasperation on Adrian's tightened lips that he was sounding like Polonius. What made parents always go through this futile business of trying to pass on to the young the incommunicable fruits of experience?

'I know what you mean,' Adrian said, evidently thinking of something else.

With an unheard sigh his father turned the subject around to another angle. 'The fact is, I dare say,' he remarked, 'that at the very moment I am talking about the reasonableness of our family stock I am probably expressing an unbridled primitive passion. Well, if you ever have one son and lose his mother and live without her for many years, and without him all the time of his education . . . perhaps you'll not be able to stifle any better than I can a whoop of selfish relief when he decides to stay near you.'

Adrian both heard and understood this. His face softened. He looked over warmly at his father and said from his heart, 'You certainly know how to give the prodigal a rousing welcome home.'

He was ashamed of his morose impatience and very glad that he had not let his father guess at it.

'What do you say we try some gingerbread?' suggested his father, rising.

In the low-ceilinged, brown-beamed, whitewashed kitchen, over the spoils' of pantry and icebox, they talked business. In the intervals of his own college work and in a period before going abroad, Adrian had been junior clerk and assistant book-keeper, so that he was quite familiar with the routine of its management.

'The trustees have always taken for granted you'd come back,' said the older Adrian, sipping his milk; 'so it'll be perfectly all right with them. Of course it's no "opening" at all in the modern sense, and never will be. The beginning salary is microscopic, but you know the ropes so well it won't be long before you'll have it all in hand. I'll soon be glad enough to step back to second place. I'm almost at the age now when my father did. Not that there's much money to be made, at best, in a savings bank. But it's always been rather a satisfaction to me, and perhaps it will be in the long run to you, that nobody makes any profit out of our kind of a bank, only salaries. To be in a business that doesn't make profits for anybody, only just decent wages for work done, I've found it tranquillising. It keeps out of your life – your own personal life, that is – the uneasiness about the real source of profits. You can be dead sure that you have not, without meaning to, put your hand into somebody else's pocket.'

Adrian was as used to this notion of his father's as to Aunt Tryntje's ancestor-worship and made no comment on it.

'I don't mind the small pay,' he said. 'What would I do with money in Rustdorf? Enough to buy tennis balls and give Aunt Tryntje my board money, that's about all I could use.'

'You might marry,' said the older man, tipping back his kitchen chair; 'people do, sometimes.'

Adrian laughed, 'Well, yes, I suppose there really isn't anything impossible about it.' He leaned across the table and broke off a piece of gingerbread.

His father said nothing for a moment, balancing on his chair, one sinewy, delicate, elderly hand holding to the edge of the table. Then, 'I hope you will, Adrian, if you find the right mate.'

He brought all four legs of his chair accurately and noiselessly to the floor and went on speaking very naturally and looking directly at Adrian so that all of his personality spoke as well as his words. 'There's a great deal said about love,' he remarked, 'some realistic brutal things, some sentimental and sugary . . . some acrid and corrosive. And I suppose that every word that's been said, each way, is true enough. As far as it goes. But nothing to the purpose. Young people ought to be told that nobody has ever been able – not even Dante – to find a way to say what it really is, true love. All that's said about it . . . well, it's like Plato's cave shadows, compared to life in the sunshine. If you are fortunate in your love.'

Adrian said nothing, feeling rather awed and, used as he was to his father's natural way of speaking out whatever was in his mind, extremely embarrassed.

'"As in old time . . . "' quoted his father –

'As in old time, a head with gentle grace,
All tenderly laid by thine
Taught thee the nearness of the love divine . . . '

With an exquisite piercing stab to the heart Adrian thought
of Matey's head laid tenderly by his. . . .

'Well, it does. Just that,' said Adrian the older, getting up to
put the milk away in the icebox. 'I hope you'll have your share,
Adrian,' he said, over his shoulder.

He shut the icebox door quietly and sat down, leaning an
elbow on the table, resting his grey head on one hand and
looking at the floor. Adrian tipped back in his chair and stared
up thoughtfully at the rough brown of the uncovered beams.
His father's words filled the room to the brim.

Presently it seemed to Adrian that what filled the plain old
room overflowed into the world beyond.

'Nobody'd need a label on us to know us for Friends,' said
his father finally, raising his head. 'We've sat here holding
meeting all by ourselves as if we were a couple of old elders. It's
past bedtime. Adrian, wind the clock, will thee? Thee's taller
than I.'

CHAPTER THREE

✿✿✿

Priscilla was in Italy, chaperoning a party of American girls, when she received Matey's letter saying she was engaged to marry Adrian Fort. The party was just about to start home (it was toward the end of August) so that there was no time for more than the noncommittal 'love and best wishes' which Priscilla sent off from Naples. But when she landed in New York, as soon as her spoiled and petulant charges had been restored to the not-too-enthusiastic arms of their well-to-do families, she telegraphed and took the first train north.

Matey had an idea that Priscilla's feelings were not very fully or accurately represented by the 'love and best wishes' cablegram. But she felt none of her old apprehensions about making her sister understand. The new joy in her life had brought with it a clear sense of freedom from old bonds. 'No, dear, you'd better not come with me to meet Priscilla's train,' she told Adrian. 'She'll want to see me first alone. The walk up from the station will give us a chance for a good talk.' It would not take her any longer than that, she was sure, to make Priscilla understand.

She was overjoyed that her sister was coming. With Adrian, Matey faced the future. She liked this. It was not merely her old sense of decent family loyalty that kept her from trying to paint her past for him, nor her certainty that it could never be made visible to any one who had not lived through it on the inside. Adrian's ignorance of her past was part of her escape from it. But Priscilla *had* lived through it on the inside. She could understand, as Adrian never could, what the present meant. Matey could hardly wait for the arrival of her train.

The small station was dozing in the sun when she reached it, rather ahead of time. Not a soul was to be seen. She sat down on an empty baggage truck. Before her, the Hudson silently spread its late-afternoon sheet of gold. Sumner jumped up beside her. From a string of barges drifting down the river came the distant creaking of a pump.

Matey's lips began to move. She was talking to Priscilla. She was at last pouring out her heart intimately and naturally to her much-loved sister. Adrian had allowed no wall to grow up between him and his sweetheart. This meant, Matey felt it instinctively, that the wall between her and Priscilla – their helpless inability never to speak seriously of what they deeply felt – was down too.

First of all the fruits of this long-awaited freedom to talk to Priscilla, she meant to share with her that last hour of their father's life, of which she had never yet been able to speak. And after she had told her, simply, what it had been, she would go on, 'Priscilla, you'll think perhaps that it might have been only a meaningless reflex – like those of drowning people. But if you'd heard, if you'd seen them, you'd never think that for an instant. I don't pretend to know all that it meant – for them. But for me, from that minute on, it has meant that there was ever so much more between Father and Mother than you and I saw – than little girls *can* see. They belonged to each other, and knew it, in some way we never guessed. It changed everything for me. I used to think, you know, that there wasn't any use trying to find the right path because there wasn't any that led anywhere. Ever since that night I've thought maybe you and I had just made a wrong turning and got lost. Yes, that's just how I felt – lost, and waiting for someone who knew the way to find me and take me home. And Adrian's the one who's come. Is that what women mean when they say they've "fallen in love with a man"? I don't know.

'When I saw he was falling in love with me, I meant to slip away out of reach as you and I have always done. But I *liked* him! And I didn't slip away soon enough. And now I'm so glad! One evening I was sitting on a rock overlooking the Hudson. He was lying on the grass close to my knee. We'd stopped talking, and I knew what he was thinking. I made up my mind that before he could say a word I'd tell him I was going away to make another visit the next day. But he didn't say a word. He just looked up at me – Priscilla! I can't wish you ever any greater happiness than to have someone look at you so! *Tenderly*, Priscilla, as if he loved me, not just as if he wanted me. And I suppose I must have shown in my face – oh, more than I knew. . . . '

She imagined her sister there more and more vividly, and felt how she would throw her arms around her as she went on, 'Priscilla, it's the first happiness we've either of us ever had.'

In the acquiescent silence about her, she went on to imagine what Priscilla would ask, and answered her in the invincibly fluent language of thought, 'No, I don't always feel as sure as that time. It often doesn't seem real. And I have scared times about it too, as I did when I was a little girl, do you remember? One night I had a nightmare that scared me terribly. I dreamed I was back in it all – you know, Priscilla, that foreboding, that helplessness. It was at breakfast – after a party, *you* remember! – the smooth-sounding talk with that will-to-hurt fumbling its way along under it. I was trying to eat my oatmeal – Priscilla, you remember how breakfast used to taste? I was so terrified I could hardly breathe, for this time the stab inside the talk was trying to find *me*. Half of me was saying, my teeth chattering, "But I'm not tied there yet. I can get up this minute and dress and take a night train away, and never –" But I couldn't stir a finger.

'And then I woke up and heard the night boat hooting, as they often do, and a train whistling back . . . night cries that filled all the darkness for a moment. And, Priscilla – I suppose I wasn't really awake yet – as plainly as I ever heard anything, the night boat shouted out

and the train called back strongly.

187

'And I remember that the day before Adrian and I had measured our height, and he hadn't minded a bit – not at all, not in the *least*, Priscilla! – that I am a little taller than he. The nightmare faded out to nothing. I lay down in bed and went right to sleep as I used to when I'd been out playing hide-and-seek.'

Her imaginary talk ran on faster and faster. 'Yet I'm not always sure that I am in love with Adrian or want to be married to him. How can I be sure when in spite of all I've read, I honestly don't know just what that means, and I've always been ashamed to ask or try to find out? To get married is stepping off into something unknown, I see that. But if I go with Adrian! . . . I *like* him so much. I like to have him near me. You know how you and I have always hated to be touched. Well, the first thing I noticed that was different was how I loved to have his hand brush against mine as we walked side by side. I like his hands. I like the back of his neck . . . isn't it silly . . . and the first time he put his arms around me I felt as though we were just one person. Do you suppose that is "being in love with a man," Priscilla?'

In the distance, down the river, the train whistled. The sound startled Matey. She had forgotten that these confidences were not being really made, that Priscilla was not there yet. Tears were standing in her eyes, so sweet had been this foretaste of intimacy.

She wiped them away to catch the first sight of the train which was bringing to her Priscilla, the real Priscilla, not the imaginary one with whom she had been happily talking.

✥✥✥

She saw the train, distant, dark, hugging the curving tracks with a worm-like twisting, darting fast toward her, a spiteful jet of steam standing at its forehead. Priscilla was on that train, coming to find out how in the world her little sister could have lost her head.

It loomed closer. Roaring and grinding its brakes, it drew up at the station. Matey looked around for Sumner and snatched him up. Holding him in her arms. she ran along the platform. A friend of Aunt Tryntje's climbed slowly down, looking very Rustdorf in her old-ladyish ignoring of prevailing styles in hats and hair; a shabby tired mother with a couple of sticky-faced children; some gum-chewing girls. . . .

And then Priscilla – tall, blonde, tailored, her face masked in the set impassivity of the well-bred Nordic traveller. At the familiar sight, Matey's past surged up from the remoteness to which Adrian had pushed it. The very odour of the sachet Priscilla always used, the very feel of her firm smooth cheek as they embraced, brought back to Matey all their other meetings. Their past loomed darkly between them.

Of course there was naturally the matter of the baggage. The leisurely elderly expressman who had now emerged from the station was, after the usual Rustdorf habit, Adrian's second cousin. He had to be approached therefore with even an increase of the humane Dutchess County tradition that business is a part of the never-ending flow of life and not part of a mechanism to be snapped briskly open or shut: 'So this is your sister?' said he to Matey. To Priscilla, kindly, 'Glad to see you back in the old town. I used to know your mother well.

She certainly was a whipstitch! You girls will have to step fast to keep up to her.' Remembering that there was a question of baggage, he guessed maybe he could deliver that trunk today. Or tomorrow morning . . . .

But there was Priscilla's suitcase. Looking into each other's eyes, and reading there life-and-death decisions to be taken, they tried nervously to decide how to get Priscilla's suitcase to the house. Should they try to carry it – or send it?

'It's not very heavy.'

'Let me take it.'

'Oh, no, Matey dear, I couldn't let you *carry* it. No porters?' (asked the girl fresh from Naples).

'Gracious! No!' (In spite of her nervous tension the girl who had been spending the summer in Rustdorf was overtaken by a sudden laugh.) 'Perhaps we could send it up with the trunk?'

'But, Matey, it has my night things in it. I'd need it tonight.'

More talk with the expressman. One by one the sparkling bubbles of reunion's new wine broke and fell flat. Yes, he guessed he could bring them things up this afternoon if there was so much hurry for them. Matey knew very well he had nothing else to do.

'Oh, thank you so very much, Mr Van Bommel.'

All this in their company voices.

At last they started, the two sisters, up the elm-shaded street. And Matey was not the one who roused herself to act on a resolution made beforehand. It was Priscilla who, as they turned away from the station, burst out, 'See here, Matey, *I* don't think you ought to . . . You know . . . you know . . . I'd always taken for granted you and I would never marry. It's not . . . It frightened me *terribly* to . . . ' She threw her arm about her sister and pressed it hard against her shoulders.

Her words were too faltering to be intelligible. But Matey knew what she meant and would not say. It was moving to have Priscilla thus helplessly shaking the door she had locked long ago. Matey was startled into a reflected agitation by the strange sight of Priscilla agitated and not trying to hide it. 'Now I musn't let Priscilla stampede me,' she thought, trying to call back the confidence she had felt while waiting for the train. But in her imaginary conversation she had made no preparation for a Priscilla trying hard to say something of her own. She tried to bring Adrian's face before her eyes, and found that in this absurd momentary confusion she could not at once seem to remember exactly how he looked. 'What is the matter with me!' she thought fiercely. 'I will not let this go on another instant. I will answer Priscilla *some*thing before I draw another breath.' She heard her own voice saying with incredible flatness, 'It's all right, Priscilla. Adrian's really awfully nice. And so is his father.' What had made her mention fathers to Priscilla!

Anything but reassured, Priscilla gave her sister a panic-struck look. 'But, Matey . . . suppose it's *not* all right,' she said in a trembling voice. 'You *can't* know. . . . Remember how everybody used to think . . . '

Matey knew now that if she tried to answer her voice would be worse than flat, that it would tremble like Priscilla's, for she was startled into a bodily tremor she could not control. Priscilla had not said out her thought, but she had pushed it into Matey's mind nonetheless. Priscilla meant that they had both been at least safe, that they had learned how to cower down so low that the roaring wind of evil passed over their heads. She was trying to find words to cry out on the madness that had induced Matey to risk all, to stand up, to take a step forward in that trackless dark.

If the younger sister turned pale and shook under this onslaught, it was partly with dismay at herself. She was silent, struggling impatiently as with a nervous seizure.

Priscilla saw nothing but her pallor and said urgently, 'Matey, you could easily get a position in the school where I am. Or I could go to teach in Cleveland near you, if you are lonely. I ought to have done this before. We could keep house together. . . . ' A dreadfulness of raw feeling throbbed in her voice. It overshot the mark. It put, quite unexpectedly, the right weapon for resistance into Matey's hands. For the first time in her life Priscilla did not seem an older, more complete person. With astonishment Matey perceived that her older sister sounded like a child, as though she did not understand at all. Really it was not very intelligent of Priscilla not to have learned more than one thing out of life. 'After all,' thought the younger sister, half impatiently, half pityingly, 'after all there may be something in the world besides our lost forty cents.' She almost said it aloud. But Priscilla had never heard what that story meant to Matey. And she never laughed herself out of overwrought ideas. How odd it seemed that it should be Matey who was trying to think of some way to quiet and reassure Priscilla!

She laid her hand on Priscilla's arm, she made her stand still on the sidewalk, she tried to penetrate into Priscilla's real self as she said firmly, 'Now, Priscilla, listen to me. *It's all right!'*

But no, her thrust went through into vacancy. Priscilla's eyes shifted, looked self-conscious, looked away. Priscilla gave the little meaningless, nervous laugh which was her parry against any stroke that threatened to come too close. Priscilla could not – would not understand.

Adrian came running down the street toward them now, Adrian dressed for the important occasion in white flannels. In spite of them he did not look very stylish, only fresh and clean. Adrian never would look very stylish. Matey knew that by this time. He looked a little nervous too at passing the inspection of the first of Matey's family and at seeing Priscilla so formidably elegant and worldly-looking. But more than anything else he looked, compared to Priscilla, grown up and complete, with his nice hazel eyes and his smile – Adrian's smile – lifting his sandy-red moustache as he halted before them, shook Priscilla's hand, and said he was glad to see her. 'I was supposed to wait for you at the house,' he explained cheerfully, 'but when I saw you both actually coming along . . . well, here I am, somehow.'

At the sound of his voice, with its inimitable naturalness, at the perfectly Adrian-like unarranged and unpicturesque words with which he first addressed his sister-to-be, Matey shook off the last reflection from Priscilla's hysteria and stepped out from the past. 'He just *hasn't* any company voice,' she thought fondly. 'He simply couldn't plan for an effect or keep his mind on what impression he is making.' It seemed to her enough of a reason, even though scarcely the traditional one, for marrying him. It was one Priscilla might understand, if she could only tell her. Or perhaps Priscilla might see it for herself.

By the end of Priscilla's stay Matey did not know whether she had seen this or anything else. And yet Priscilla had beaten Adrian at tennis once or twice and had seen for herself that he did not hate her then or sulk afterward. Priscilla *must* have noticed that. But Matey could only guess. She knew no more than ever what was going on in Priscilla's mind, if indeed Priscilla allowed much of anything to go on in it.

She regretted more bitterly than ever that she had not been able, long ago, to speak to Priscilla of the ending of their father's life. She still did not at all understand that never-forgotten hour. The recollection of it always tossed her helplessly back and forth between two impressions of it – if that had been love, and if love could do no more than that for human lives! And yet – a belonging together that outlived all else, and stood up boldly in the face of death – !

Whatever it had been, it was Priscilla's as well as hers. Why hadn't she ever been able to say the few words that would have told it? –'Priscilla, as Father lay dying, he was frightened, horribly frightened, and it was Mother he called to in his fright. And it was Mother who answered – Mother! – in a voice of such steadfast love; Mother who helped him through the dreadfulness of dying!' Why hadn't she said it like that? Time after time she had determined that she would. But always as she drew her breath for the first words, her heart began to beat thickly with the fear that if she spoke now her voice would sound self-conscious, unnatural, false. What *was* this paralysis of throat and eye which overtook them at the thought of saying simply and naturally what was in their hearts?

One evening after Priscilla had gone, when she and Adrian were taking a twilight walk together, she put this question to him. She did not explain what it was she wished to say to Priscilla, but put it as part of her general wonder at the ways of human beings. Adrian answered that his guess was that the language of saying simply and naturally what was in your heart was probably at least as difficult to learn as French or German and took as much practice.

'Father's a proficient in that language,' he told her. 'Perhaps it's his Quakerism . . . lifelong habit of not saying anything unless he means it. Perhaps because he always manages so there is little he needs to conceal. He can actually, if it happens to come into his head in a quiet hour, talk to you about his feeling the imminence of God as naturally as he asks you whether the front door is locked. Once, I remember, last spring – I think now he had seen I'd already fallen in love with you – he said something to me about love and its greatness. . . . Did you suppose there was a father living who could bring himself to mention such a subject to his son?'

Matey was astonished. 'I'm twenty-four years old and I've known lots and lots of people and I never, never heard a single living human being intimate openly that love could be great.' She added, 'What did he say?'

'Ah, I wouldn't dare try to repeat it to you. My voice would sound like a preacher's, and that's the last awfulness for a Friend, you know. I can show you – ' he snatched her to him – 'but I can't tell you. Not yet. But I'm going to lose no time in practising that language. You too, Matey darling!'

'I don't know a word of it,' said Matey.

'Well, practise a little, now,' he urged. 'What comes into your mind first of all when you remember we are going to be married?'

Matey looked at him piteously, but said bravely, 'I'll tell the truth . . . a sense of complete unreality.'

Adrian had not expected this, but after a pause for taking breath he asked, 'How do you mean, unreality? That I don't exist? Or that we aren't engaged? Or what?'

He put his arm about her as he spoke; they were strolling along the lane which led to the river, a favourite evening walk of theirs. Matey leaned against him. Physical nearness to him helped her feel and think more clearly. She listened to what was in her mind for a moment and answered. 'Everything seems unreal – myself too. Only not you, when I'm close enough to feel you. The old Matey's gone . . . or is she just waiting there in Cleveland for the autumn teaching to begin? And I don't know the new one. Is there a new one? It seems like something in a dream. Perhaps it hasn't had time to reach me yet.' She turned her face to his, in the twilight. 'You know, Adrian, I didn't mean at all to kiss you back that time. From the moment we sat down on the grass I was all ready – I even had the words picked out – to tell you that I wasn't the marrying kind, and that I was going to go away from Rustdorf the next morning anyhow. I was saying that over and over to myself to keep it clear . . . and then you just looked up at me, and I forgot it all.'

'Were you glad you were planning to say that?' asked Adrian.

Matey turned her head from one side to the other a little wildly. 'Oh, Adrian, I can't tell you whether I was or not. I don't know. I can't tell you how strange it seems. Priscilla may be right. Perhaps I oughtn't to marry.' (But she did not tell him why. She never told him why.) 'I don't understand anything about it. Whatever *made* me, when you only looked up at me so, begin to cry and kiss you back with all my heart? I didn't mean to!'

'Perhaps you love me, Matey?' suggested Adrian gently, drawing her closer to him.

'Do you suppose I do?' said Matey, half-sobbing, half-laughing, clinging to him, rubbing her cheek back and forth on his. 'When I'm *with* you, I seem to, don't I? Especially when you put your arms around me. But I thought . . . I thought I couldn't love anybody . . . except Sumner!' she ended absurdly. 'You're like Sumner anyhow,' she told him, laughing uncertainly, 'you want me to tell you the truth. Well, I thought from the very first you were like Sumner. Your eyes are like his. You don't need to tell me I'm being silly. I know it.'

'Oh, I don't mind having Sumner as a predecessor,' said Adrian; 'you probably learned a lot on him. As a matter of fact we are alike. We're both alike. We both love you. And we let you know it.'

'Do you suppose,' Matey asked him, 'that I love you enough to marry you when I can't even really believe we are engaged?'

'Well, let's try it anyhow,' suggested Adrian.

They had come out now on the rocks high above the Hudson, and saw what they had come to look at. A miracle bloomed there with every lamp-lighting time. The wide stream was as dim in the twilight as the River of Death. On the opposite bank stood a settlement which in the daytime was only a cluster of mean wooden houses. Punctually, night by night, as darkness fell, there shone out in its place the golden sisterhood of stars at which the lovers now gazed silently.

Francis made a visit to Rustdorf too, stopping off between trains on his way to New York. He was handsomer than ever, and better dressed, and more masculinely magnetic. The aroma of power scented any room where he sat, as definitely as the perfume of his very upper-class cigars.

He told Matey that he had come to see her fiancé, and to tell her that she was not the only pebble on the beach, that he was engaged to be married himself. Her name, he said, was Emily McAdams, her father was a senior partner of the law firm where he was employed; he showed her photograph, so much retouched that Matey had little impression of more than the requisite number of features; he said she was rather darker than blonde, was a graduate of Miss Spence's School, a débutante of that year, liked to wear blue a good deal, was not the athletic sporty type, but rather old-fashioned and domestic – told, in short, every imaginable detail but the one of which Matey had been instantly sure from the announcing of his news.

Francis had been engaged before (this was one of the things she had not told Aunt Tryntje) to a girl with prospects. But when the grandmother had died, it was found that her fortune had been left to the Presbyterian Church instead of to the younger generation. And not long after that, the health of Francis's fiancée had declined so that her doctor, in spite of Francis's pleadings, had absolutely forbidden her to think of marrying. In announcing his present engagement he spoke about this earlier disappointment not only to Matey but to the Forts, with dignity, in the touching manner of one who finds that after all, life has unsuspected reserves. Not that anything could be like one's first love, but perhaps something might be better, deeper and quieter.

Matey made no comment. She leaned back in her chair absent-mindedly stroking Sumner while Francis talked about his future. She had no more to say when he talked about their common past, for, finding that both their father and mother were known in Rustdorf, he fell naturally into reminiscences, painting a vivid picture, true to the last detail, of the various homes they had had, the stirring social life in which their family had always been a leader. 'Do you remember, Matey, those dinner parties in Hamilton? By George, Mr Fort, I go out a good deal in Pittsburgh, but I never heard better talk anywhere than that I heard at my parents' table. Living in a university circle, you know, one has the pick of people who know their stuff. And Father and Mother knew how to bring them out. Yes, they made an ideal home atmosphere for us. When I hear other fellows talking about family life – lots of the Pittsburgh boys have parents who were divorced – I realise more than ever how fortunate we children were in seeing such an example of teamwork before us. Father and Mother were literally never separated for more than a day or so. They were crazy about each other.'

The Forts heard more, they said, about Matey's family in the one day that Francis was there than in all the week Priscilla stayed with them. For that matter, more than Matey had ever told them. 'Oh, Matey's a regular clam,' said Francis, with a friendly laugh. 'She was a chatterbox as a kid. I remember she used to talk your head off. But as she grew up – Mother used to say it seemed as though Matey's music took the place of words. Her music and her darned little dog. You may have noticed that Matey's only confidant is Sumner. "Too much dog in her cosmos," Father always said.' He ruffled the old dog's ears playfully as he spoke.

He seemed to make his usual brilliantly favourable impression on the Rustdorf people. Adrian's father greeted him kindly, listened to him attentively, and Aunt Tryntje was quite carried away by his interest in Dutchess County history and his desire to learn the details of his ancestry. 'I never saw a more delightful young man,' she told Matey a good many times after Francis had gone away – 'so *appreciative!* When I told him what Mr Winthrop said about the Friends in Rustdorf, "a community of transparent souls where no man hides his motive," he said he had never heard a finer phrase.'

It seemed very familiar to Matey not to have any idea what to answer back. She could not very well report Francis's talk with her at the station as he went away: 'Matey, for heaven's sake, pull out of this hole! You'll suffocate, used as you are to the intelligent university crowd. You probably take that sort of thing for granted. But you just try living in an American small town, cutting yourself off from civilisation, and you'll . . . I tell you I know, just after this one day here, what Father meant when he used to say he wouldn't be caught dead in . . .'

'I remember what Father used to say,' Matey cut him short.

'Well, bear it in mind! The old aunt is enough to addle your brains. And that prosy pious old banker . . . ! God! The whole place fairly reeks with stagnation. Honestly, Matey, you're crazy!'

Struck with a new possibility, he interrupted himself to say hastily, 'See here, you're not making a mistake about this banking business, are you? Do you even know the difference between a real bank and a mutual savings bank? It's not a *bank* at all in the business sense – there's no more chance for profits in it than in one of these mutual burying associations. It's about the same thing . . . sort of charity. Honestly it is, like something a university settlement might run. Yes, *you might about as well be planning to marry a settlement worker.*'

This was the only direct reference he made to his sister's fiancé. She needed nothing more explicit. She had read in his first glance at Adrian the conviction that he was a dead loss who never would get anywhere.

'Why, Matey, the expressman here at the station is the old man's first cousin. And another of your relatives-to-be, so I gather, that ancient crone who runs a bakeshop in one corner of her house. Honestly! Matey . . . !'

Matey felt her cheeks hot with resentment, and to her shame, with discomfort. She spoke angrily to hide her flinching. 'Francis, don't be ridiculous, everybody in America has relatives like that! Those very ones are ours too, you know.'

'Why pick out the one spot where such ones live?' enquired Francis.

'Another of Mr Fort's cousins is Chief Justice of the Iowa Supreme Court,' advanced Matey, hating every word she was saying.

'But you're not going to live in Des Moines,' said Francis, with a devastating effect of finality.

His words almost gave Matey the clue to something clear and final to be said on the other side, something she had dimly felt from her first hour in Rustdorf. But with Francis's scornful eye on her, she could not get her wits together enough to grasp it. She had, after all, no defence but her old one of being ashamed of being ashamed.

Francis was too much for her, as usual. As long as he stood there she could not save herself from the abjectness of seeing Adrian, his father, Rustdorf, as Francis did. She was horrified to feel under her brother's blighting survey that she was ashamed of Adrian's lack of an air, of his future, of the very things in him and in his father which she loved. But her experience of Francis rose up admonishingly. She could at least look stubborn and close her lips with an offended air, as if she were a sulky child. Francis readily identified her expression as a familiar one. Hadn't she . . . his memory groped among old trifles . . . hadn't she as a little girl looked like this one day when she had spoiled a game for a whole crowd by being unreasonable?

He said in a brotherly tone, 'I'm just giving you the best advice I can, Matey. Get mad about it if you like, but don't forget it.' And then, on an impulse, laying a comradely hand on her shoulder, 'See here, Matey old girl, why don't you come to Pittsburgh to teach? In the university there. I could get you a job, I know. And I'm getting on, *fast*. More than I've let on to you and Priscilla, because I don't like to brag. I've got a mighty fine circle of friends around me and I'd be *glad* to introduce you to them, and let you have the entrée wherever I have. It's to whatever's worthwhile in the city, if I do say so.' His imagination caught fire. 'Why, yes, Matey, why haven't I thought of this before? You'd meet scads of the nicest sort of young fellows . . . sons of the steel magnates . . . every one of them,' he said with an emphasis that pointed a contemptuous finger at Adrian, 'with a big future before him, going somewhere and going *fast!* Emily would be awfully good to anybody I backed up, you can bank on that. So would all her family. I don't mind telling you, just to give you an idea – that I pulled her father out of a hole the old man won't forget in one while. And kept still about it afterward. *He'd* see to it that you got every . . . '

From the beginning of this proposal Matey had felt a mounting wave of vivid feeling on which she could not put a label. Did she wish to stamp her foot and slap Francis? Or to burst into bitter tears? Neither, apparently, for she now began helplessly to laugh. Francis was simply too Francis-like for anything!

'What are you laughing at?' asked Francis in amazement.

'Never mind what,' said Matey.

'It's no laughing matter,' said Francis, nettled. 'You've got to stop these childish ways of yours, Matey, and face *facts*. What you decide now decides all your future life. If Father were alive, you know how he . . . '

Matey stopped laughing and looked again, so Francis thought, stubborn and dumb. He liked this better than her laughter, divining in it a resistance less formidable. If he only had time . . . but his train was coming in. He had done his best to take his father's place and put a stop to Matey's madness; he had pulled all the strings there were to head off this foolishness, both with Matey and with her young man. He had given them each something to think over. His appointment in New York was an important one. After all, Matey was not planning to be married until next June. There was plenty of time.

He stooped to kiss his sister goodbye, and said, urgently, affectionately, 'Now, Matey, don't make a fool of yourself! Come on to Pittsburgh and join me. I'd stand by. We'd go far! Honest we would!'

'Now here is a test,' thought Matey to herself as, rather shaken in nerves, she walked slowly home under the elms. 'Shall I have the courage to tell Adrian that for a long wretched moment I was ashamed of him?'

She felt a sincere misery over what, after a summer of Aunt Tryntje's idiom, she called to herself 'the Gilbert blood coming out.' But she found she could not bring it to the light, even to Adrian – not even to be worthy of the effort it cost him that evening to tell her something which he evidently would have preferred to conceal.

She had felt him stirred and preoccupied at the supper table, usually so peaceful, and when they went out on the porch, noticed that he did not sit down on the swinging hammock beside her. 'What makes you sit off there on that straight uncomfortable chair?' she asked him as honestly as a child.

He was silent, and then, 'Matey, I'm the one who's always talking about never hiding anything from each other – I suppose you might as well know now as later, that I doubt . . . I doubt . . . if your brother and I will ever be exactly what anybody could call intimate friends.'

Matey was genuinely astonished that there should be anybody who, meeting Francis for the first time, did not like him. 'What ever happened?' she asked.

Adrian said quickly, 'That's what I don't want to tell you – yes, I know, that's not consistent. Well, I will tell you. He – he tried to – ' No, decidedly he would not say it.

Matey thought she knew. 'He tried to make you think that I'd find Rustdorf too – ' But Adrian's look at her through the dusk showed her it had not been that. 'What *did* he say?' she asked.

Adrian hesitated. 'He said he thought as the only man of your family, he ought to warn me – to tell me that you – ' he stopped, really at a loss. Finally he murmured '– that you haven't very much of what the French call *tempérament.*'

For all that Matey understood he might as well not have made any effort to speak out. She had often heard this word, but among the many things which at twenty-four she did not know was what exactly it meant. Her impression, which had seemed to suit any context in which she had as yet met it, was that a person with *tempérament* fell in love easily and often. Mme Vinet had once said impatiently of a cook with many suitors that she had so much *tempérament* it was useless to expect her to get three meals a day. Well, if Francis had told Adrian that she did not fall in love easily or often, he was right. Why should Adrian object to that?

'Well – ?' she asked.

Adrian said furiously, 'I lost my temper. I told him perhaps his taste and mine in that matter might not – I told him it was none of his business. I told him to go to hell.'

Matey had never seen Adrian angry. She was too startled to speak.

From the open door the elder Adrian's voice asked, 'Matey, how about Number Seven? Could you give an old bore one more. . . . '

'If you only knew!' said Matey, rising quickly, 'how many lonesome hours I've spent playing Bach to myself because nobody would listen!'

'I'll sit out here and hold Sumner's hand,' said Adrian. 'We understand each other, Sumner and I.'

In the middle of the Bach, Matey stopped playing. She swung around on the piano stool, flashed a quick bright glance at Adrian's father, and said, 'Excuse me a minute, will you? I've just thought of something I want to say to Adrian.'

Adrian was not on the porch. But she saw him dimly in the starlight, standing with Sumner beside him, looking up at the sky. She ran across to him and seized his arm. 'Adrian, see here . . . ' she said in a tone of quick breathless high spirits. 'Why do we wait till next June to be married? Why don't we do it right now, in September? It just came to me – while I was playing that Bach. I felt something rising and rising in me, and all of a sudden it brimmed over. . . . '

Adrian had brought his gaze down from the stars to her face, his eyes for an instant retaining a remote contemplative expression. They met hers with a shock, as if a spark had leaped out between the two. All her face was sparkling clear, as he had never seen it, as he had not dreamed it could be. Her woman's face was bright like that of a happy loving child.

He was silent an instant, dazzled.

But when she saw his eyes on her, she flung herself headlong into his arms, clasping him in hers in a little girl's tight, single-hearted embrace. 'I *want* to marry you, Adrian!' she told him wilfully. 'If ever I wasn't sure, I am now, after Francis's and Priscilla's visits. I can feel myself boiling over with *tempérament* to marry you.'

'You don't know what you're talking about,' he murmured fondly into her hair.

'Adrian! What a *Quaker* thing to say to the girl who insists on marrying you!' she cried out to him, drawing back to laugh.

He looked at her in wonder. Her face with its starry eyes seemed to give off a radiance of its own. She looked as she felt, as if with a clap of wings she could have soared into the air.

'I never saw anything in the world as beautiful as you are this minute,' he told her, in the old lover's phrase.

'*Make* it September,' she murmured, with a coaxing pretence of imploring, bringing her face close to his till he could see nothing but her shining eyes.

She was startled, a little frightened, by the roughness of his arms about her. And still more startled when she saw tears in his eyes. He said in an uncertain hoarse voice, 'Oh, Matey, if I can only make you happy!'

CHAPTER FOUR

✿✿✿

Through the open window admonishing chimes dropped down from the tower of Antwerp cathedral to tell them how lazy they were. 'Lazy but unashamed,' Adrian answered the solemn tolling of ten o'clock. 'Being now married to Miss Penelope Gilbert, I'm far too happy to care whether it's noon or midnight.'

They were still luxuriously in bed, idly debating plans for the day, although a good part of the morning had already passed and they had eaten every crumb of the frugal breakfast brought them by the red-faced brawny Flemish girl who was general help in their bare clean small hotel.

Matey agreed with her husband that being married made other things seem unimportant. She knew now what it meant to be married. And, as she had planned to predict to Priscilla, she had found out that in marriage as in everything else, the fact that Adrian was Adrian was all that mattered to her. Anything Adrian wanted, and wanted with those caressing hands, those eager lips from which hers took such living warmth – why, she wanted anything Adrian wanted. She wondered that there could be women so perverse as sometimes not to want what a husband who loved them wanted. But perhaps they had not all such darling *sweet* husbands as Adrian. She put her arms around his neck now and told him he was darling and sweet.

'Well, I never claimed to be a caveman,' said Adrian. 'You can't say I deceived you on *that* point.' He spoke whimsically but a shadow fell, ever so lightly, on his face.

'What's the matter, Adrian?' she challenged him.

He lay gazing up at the ceiling for a moment, and then turned on her his good and clear look of affection. 'I want you to love me, Matey.'

'I *do!*' she cried.

'So you do, darling,' he said gently.

The intrusive clock struck another quarter-hour. They decided they really must get up and go to look at the Plantin-Moretus.

As they were sauntering back after a late luncheon, 'Look here, Matey,' Adrian suggested, 'we've done about all these Flemish galleries we can take in for a while. Why don't we skip up to Holland and have a look at Vermeer and Rembrandt for a couple of days before we go on to Paris? It's no trip at all.'

But with an energy which startled her, Matey found suddenly that there could be cases when she did not want what Adrian wanted. 'No, let's take the Paris *rapide* this afternoon. I hate Holland,' she said peevishly.

'Why, what have you got against the Dutch?' asked Adrian, surprised.

'Oh, I don't know,' said Matey. But she did know. She had remembered. On a street corner outside the museum in The Hague a well-dressed mother and three attractive young people stood waiting for her to join them and suffer, while coming toward them, red and furious, obviously wishing they had been dead rather than there to see his . . . 'I can't bear Holland!' she said.

'We will have it eliminated from the map,' Adrian assured her. 'On to Paris! I never did think much of the Dutch.'

When they reached the tall old hotel on the rue de Seine in Paris they found a letter from Adrian's father which informed them among other Rustdorf news that if they were thinking of buying any furnishings they must bear in mind that the colour scheme of their new living room was settled by the three coats of Quaker grey with which he had just painted the floor. He also told them that he and Sumner got on well together, Sumner being company for him after Aunt Tryntje had gone to bed, 'although I can't say that he appreciates my piano practice as yet. To tell the truth his real affection has gone out to Rebecca. No, not merely at mealtimes. He often goes out in the kitchen of an evening when there is nothing whatever on his plate and sits there, breathing in the memory of Rebecca's presence. It is not an unrequited attachment, I am happy to say. Rebecca loves him. I am sure she cuts out the tenderloin of our Thursday steak to give him. Where else can it go?'

'Isn't Father the world's champion quietist?' said Adrian. 'That line about the colour of the floor paint is to break the news to us that he's gone ahead and bought that Washington Street house for us as a wedding present, just as he threatened to. He can't afford it, you know. It'll take a good deal more than half his savings.'

Matey folded the letter and put it away in her handbag.

'I *love* your father,' she said. 'I loved him from the first moment I saw him.'

'Well, don't forget to love me too,' said Adrian, taking off her hat to kiss her hair; 'I'm the one you married. You keep getting off that subject.'

Matey laughed. 'I'm not allowed to get very far off it.'

'It's hard work to keep you on it,' he assured her; 'I never saw such a wandering mind. Suppose you try putting your arms around me this minute. It might remind you of me again.'

And as Matey a little shyly lifted her arms, he cried out roughly, catching her to him with passion. 'Oh, Matey! Matey! If I can only make you happy!'

'I am happy,' said Matey, wondering at him a little, as she often did.

'Not happy enough!'

'Happier than ever before.'

'That's *nothing!*'

'As happy as I know how to be,' said Matey.

'Maybe, but that's a subject you must study and learn more about,' Adrian told her seriously.

'This afternoon,' announced Matey, 'we must call on Mme Vinet.'

'In that case,' replied Adrian, 'I'll have to buy a shirt and some collars. This homeless tourist business is hard on laundry. I've nothing left but the négligé-est of négligés. Suppose we walk over to the Bon Marché. You can stock up on ribbons or hairpins or handkerchiefs or whatever girls buy in department stores while I clean out the haberdashery counter.'

As they walked, Matey went over again the information she had given him about the Vinet family so that he would make no mistakes in conversation. 'Mme Vinet is a widow now, you remember,' she said, beginning at the top, 'and lives with her two sons, Henri, who's about my age and a professor in a *lycée*, and little Paul – the one we used to call Polo – who must be thirteen now. He was a baby that first year we knew them. Henri's a mother's boy, regular French eldest son, never leaves her side, never has. I suppose he's what you'd call a sissy, but if you do call him that I'll never forgive you. He's always seemed like a brother to me – though not a bit like Francis. To play four-hand arrangements on the piano together, that's their idea of heaven, Mme Vinet and Henri. The children were all educated at home so that they could have more music than at the *lycée*. At least that's the reason they gave. Since I've been grown up I've suspected it was because Mme Vinet never could bear to have Henri away from her. Polo has always been a nice little boy, not spoiled as much as you'd think by being adored by his older brother and sisters. Mimi married six years ago, when she was only nineteen, not very romantically – a manufacturer much older than she – but very comfortably. Everybody was relieved. She's rather delicate, sort of nervous, not much vitality. She has three children and seems about the same as ever. A new baby since I was here last. She's the only one who has any money. They have two houses, a nice comfortable one in La Ferté-en-Valois, out beyond Meaux, and a smaller little country place right on the Marne. Ziza is the best-looking of the family, quite striking in a vivid way. She's three years younger than Mimi and I . . . must be twenty-one now. She and I have always been closest to each other. She's the one I told you was always so excitable. She's married, too – to a Belgian – just recently. But she and her husband are making an after-the-honeymoon visit to her folks, so we'll be sure to meet them sometime if not today. They'll probably arrange a family reunion, and that includes us, for when I'm with them I seem just like one of the girls. They all say thee and thou to me, as if I were blood kin, and Mme Vinet still brings me up in the way I should go.'

Adrian started to say his lesson over, checking the Vinets off on his fingers, but Matey interrupted him shyly. 'Adrian, I know you don't like secrets; still . . . let's not tell Mme Vinet where we got the money for this trip? She's a dear, but they're all so everlastingly thrifty. . . . '

Adrian stopped her with a laugh. 'I get you! Not a word – not a syllable. Any French person would be sure to agree with Aunt Tryntje that a solemn thing like a year's interest on your *dot* ought to have gone into hardwood floors and a furnace.'

'There's one thing more,' said Matey, constraint in her voice. 'They none of them understand a word of English.' She had kept out of her mind any picture of this part of the meeting as resolutely as she had pushed Holland out of sight.

'Oh, I'll get along,' said Adrian comfortably. 'None of my studio friends understand any English either. I've plenty of French of a sort.'

Yes, he had, but what a sort! She had gauged its quality in Antwerp on the few occasions – buying tickets, or ordering meals – when she had not managed to slip unobtrusively ahead of him. She felt herself wishing that he did not know a word – could stay in safe uncompetitive aloofness.

They were at the door of the Bon Marché and she found that The Hague was not the only place peopled for her with unlaid ghosts of memories. 'It's going to be hot inside, Adrian,' she said. 'Do you mind if I wait for you on a bench in the square?'

She sat down on the bench, her back to the big shop. She was afraid to go in. She was afraid of the silk counter, afraid that she would find her mother there, unable to make herself understood by a slow-witted, slightly deaf salesman, while her father leaned on the counter, apparently absorbed in admiring the quality of the silks, intervening finally with a start, as though just now noticing the difficulty and delivering the necessary explanation in a French especially diamond-faceted in contrast to the self-distrustful woolliness of his wife's. Matey was afraid she would forget that she was grown up and married to Adrian and would become again the drooping little girl who stood between the two, the child who had entered the shop bouncing with joy at the prospect of a new dress, but who now, wincing and looking down at her shoes, thought of nothing but how soon she could get back to the Vinets. She heard herself asked once more which colour she wanted, and said once more, 'Oh, *I* don't care,' in a tone so dull that her father was justified in exclaiming, 'If you don't, who's going to? Do you think we're buying this dress to amuse ourselves? I never saw such a dead-and-alive child!'

✲✲✲

It wouldn't stay down in the black hole where she had pushed it. It streamed up like the genie coming out of the bottle and settled down around the married Matey on her bench. She might as well have gone into the shop with Adrian.

When finally she saw him coming toward her, a paper parcel under his arm, she ran to him, crying, 'What in the world took you so long?'

'I struck a poor uneducated salesman from out Limoges way who couldn't understand my pure Théâtre Français vowels!' he told her, laughing. 'See here, Matey, how about having a bust-up to celebrate our arrival at the old stand? How about – laying a wreath on Aunt Connie's grave as we go – how about a duck at Foyot's?'

'I'm awfully sorry, Adrian, but one of my sick headaches seems to be starting up. Calling on Mme Vinet will be about all I can stand.'

Adrian looked at her keenly. 'You do look terribly tired, all of a sudden. Funny! You were all right a minute ago. Well, we'll be sensible and have dinner at the hotel,' he said patiently.

The call on Mme Vinet didn't turn out to be difficult. Adrian managed a few conventional phrases of greeting well enough, and for the rest of the visit there was nothing for him to do but be a correctly in-the-background new husband, while his wife and her old friend occupied the centre of the stage with family news.

'What luck that you come at this time!' exclaimed Mme Vinet. 'Just when Ziza and her husband are down from Belgium spending a few days with Mimi. Why don't we all go out on Sunday to spend the day together? There's an early train to La Ferté, the one we used to take – remember, Mété? – for Sundays together in the country. It would be charming to have all you children together, you girls with your husbands. Wasn't it curious, little Ziza marrying an Adrien, too?'

'I never heard,' said Matey, 'how they happened to choose Louvain to live in.'

'Choose? How did thy husband happen to choose R-r-rusdorf?' asked Mme Vinet, her tongue tripping a little over the name. 'Ziza's husband would ask you, "Where else would a Conacq live but in Louvain?" One of those old plain provincial families, you know, who live for centuries in the same town. His father is professor of German literature there.'

When Ziza and her new family had been thoroughly explored and commented on, the talk turned to Mimi. 'Think of Mimi with three children!' marvelled Matey.

'Why not? She has been married six years.' Mme Vinet considered Mimi's case for an instant, and then, 'The queer thing for me is to think of any Vinet with money! One would think, brought up as she was, she'd feel shy in the presence of real cash. But she seems to find it perfectly natural.'

'It's the absence of it that bothers people,' contributed Adrian, his American r's harsh and heavy.

Matey did not look at him, feeling it more decent not to. What a terrible accent he had! He must be wincing over those r's. They were like her mother's, and brought before her the tense expression of her mother's face when she was speaking French. What time was it? she wondered. The large ornamental clock on the Vinet's mantelpiece had never run since she could remember, and she dare not look at her watch. She was more tired than she thought, and her headache was evidently going to be one of the bad ones. Depression fell on her gloomily. She laid it to the prospect of a day with the complete Vinet family – so many of them, and a new baby to exclaim over. It would be noisy! People tired her, *en masse* like that. And French families were always *en masse*. The familiar ache at the base of her brain began to hang its black veil between her and life. Mme Vinet looked to her very plain and commonplace. With a malicious desire to give pain, which after the words were out quite shocked her, she asked, 'I thought surely by this time I'd find Henri engaged to be married?'

Mme Vinet's face changed. 'Henri never seems to think of marrying,' she said carefully. 'His profession absorbs him wholly. And his music.'

'She is as frightened as ever at the idea of living a minute without him,' thought Matey crossly. She remembered the intimate special look the mother and son had had, and how it made the rest of them feel left out.

In the third-class railway compartment on the early omnibus train on Sunday morning, she saw the same look pass between the grey-haired widow and the slight, pale, seriously bearded young man into whom the slight, pale, serious Henri had developed.

He did not remain serious very long in Adrian's society. It was the first time Matey had seen Adrian in French company. There was simply not room in her mind for the astonishment she felt as the train slowly rumbled along. He spoke French, as he had told her long ago and as she had heard for herself, very badly, with (it is true) a sort of wild student fluency and slangy abundance, but with inconceivable oddities of grammatical incorrectness, and an American accent as full-flavoured (Adrian said to himself that morning) as molasses and buckwheat cakes. This was evidently not the first time he had been off for a Sunday in the country with vacationing French people. He seemed to know very well what they expect of such an outing. And being himself in his usual good spirits, he lent himself heartily to this expectation, using his unique French as a comedian would use a natural gift for farce. It flavoured richly with its drollness the mildest of his humorous remarks, and rose at times through some particularly happy combination of current slang and unexpected mispronunciation to heights of absurdity which made even grave Mme Vinet laugh to tears, as Matey had never seen her laugh before. His fantastic explanation, always in this extraordinary fluent comedy language, of what molasses and buckwheat cakes are to American life, reduced little Paul to such shrieks of laughter that he had to go out into the corridor to get himself a drink of water. Mme Vinet and Henri looked at each other with an enchanted expression of satisfaction. One of their worries was lest little Paul, alone with them, should have too serious a life. The Vinets had always been a cheerful enough family in their subdued civilised way, but Matey had never suspected them capable of such outbursts of *le fou rire*, so much beloved by sober French people, as Adrian knew how to produce by his linguistic tomfoolery.

They poured out of the train at La Ferté in a state of hilarity which made Mimi – looking very matronly and settled, and rather too stout – enquire what the pleasantry was. 'Me – I am the pleasantry, Madame Mimi,' said Adrian, bowing, his hand on his heart.

Mimi shook hands with him, introduced him to her grave, substantially-built husband, M Bouvard; there was a fusillade of two-cheeked kisses among the Vinets, and they moved out of the station to dispose themselves in an elderly, well-kept carriage, dating from an earlier generation of the Bouvard family. Matey took her place between Mimi and Mme Vinet on the back seat. The three men, Henri and Adrian already like old friends, and Mimi's husband, stout, dignified, and inexpressive, crowded together opposite. Thirteen-year-old Paul, his cheeks still glowing from the resounding greetings of his provincial kin, had been put up beside the driver, from which elevation he continually turned his head not to lose a word of what Adrian might say.

Ziza and her husband were waiting for them at the house, it seemed.

'How do you like her husband?' asked Matey.

'I like him,' said Mimi, 'but . . . I could wish Ziza did not like him quite so much.'

'What is this talk,' enquired Adrian, 'of limits set to liking husbands? M Bouvard, it is time for us to stand *en garde.*'

'Ah, Ziza is only just married,' remarked Mme Vinet. 'Give her time.'

'*Fix* bayonets!' said Adrian to M Bouvard, imitating exactly the raucous speech-tune of an army sergeant. '*E-e-e-n avant! 'arche!*' His accent added a colour of burlesque to this which brought an explosive astonished laugh from the massive

M Bouvard. From the driver's seat came a delighted cackle. Adrian turned, his hazel eyes shining with fun, looked up at the little boy, and gave him a grave nod and look of understanding as from husband to husband which sent Polo off into rockets of laughter again.

Mme Vinet made an effort to think of the right conversation for people who do not live in Paris. 'Did you have a good wheat harvest?' she asked. M Bouvard, whose business was the manufacturing of plumbing fixtures, stared out of the carriage as if looking for evidence, and gravely assured his mother-in-law that he believed it had been good.

The wheat had been cut long ago, but as Matey followed his eyes over the bare brown fields, there came back vividly – more vividly in memory than ever to her seeing eyes – the magnificence of the wheat in this part of France. The stubble in the broad sloping fields was brown now, but the hoarded seed was only waiting for the fall ploughing for next year's glory. New ideas sprang nimbly up in her brain. What a history it had, wheat! Why had she never thought of it before? Handed down from the Aryan forefathers, their chiefest treasure, alive more than ever when they were crumbled dust in their graves . . . living as ideals live on, long past the death of those who cherished them. It was wonderful to be out in such a countryside. And what air! To come here from Paris was like going out from a stuffy room into a west wind. And yet she had not noticed in Paris that the air seemed stuffy. Oh, it was because her head had stopped aching! What a relief. It was going to be a lovely day.

They had arrived. She sprang from the carriage and ran

✣✣✣

to kiss darling Ziza, hung like a poppy on the arm of a blond young man as stout as he was tall, which was saying a good deal. *'Un vrai homme du Nord!'* thought Matey as she shook hands with him.

In the house, as the women were taking off their wraps in Mimi's pretty, over-furnished bedroom, 'Thy husband seems like a French boy,' remarked Mme Vinet; 'he seems like one of us. I feel already intimate. And Americans are usually so remote. Why, I would hardly know him for an American at all!' she said, struck with the idea. She added casually, 'Except for his speech.'

What was this singular lightening of the heart which Matey felt as she ran down the stairs? She felt like capering. It was absurd. She felt exactly, she thought, with no reason at all, as though she had had very good news – when she had been expecting bad. She laughed at almost everything – at the fatness of Mimi's new baby, at the way they avoided the stuffy French ceremoniousness of Mimi's over-draped bourgeois salon, and all piled into the kitchen, sunlit and copper-saucepan decorated, where the picnic baskets were being filled – at the frantic objections of that absurd, lovable Ziza to any plan of a walk to the river which would separate her from her husband.

She noticed that Mimi looked at her curiously, as, snatching her four-year-old boy by the hands, she began to dance *'Savez-vous planter les choux'* with him. And later on she caught the same look of enquiry from Mme Vinet as, picnic baskets in hand, the comfortable family party strolled along the country lane that led from Mimi's house to the banks of the Marne. 'It is such a lovely, lovely autumn day,' thought Matey. This friendly autumn sun was enough to make anyone leap and run. And how deep-hearted these civilised French people were, how warm the family feeling which kept them all together! How nice it was to be with them again! She began to sing at the top of her voice *'M le Curé n'a pas deux souta-a-nes,'* a light-hearted marching song Henri had brought back from his military service. Leading the others, she kept it going through all of its interminable variations.

As they finished the song, Mimi called out to Adrian, 'You have brought back our old Mété to us!'

'How so?' enquired Adrian.

'She was such a gay little barbarian as a child . . . how she did upset all our rules the year she stayed with us!'

'Never!' cried Matey, astonished. 'I was crushed! Submissive as a little mouse . . . I obeyed more rules than I had thought I could. . . . '

They interrupted her with derisive laughter, even Henri. 'We always called that year "our trip to America," ' he told her.

Adrian shook his head over a disillusionment. 'All those stories of Matey's about how suppressed she was!'

They drifted apart in a narrow place in the lane, Henri and Adrian walking together. 'Well she *has* been suppressed since then,' said Henri. 'I have not seen her like this, not since she was grown up.' He added pleasantly the obvious 'It speaks well for her husband.'

For an instant Adrian did not hear him. He had been as mystified by Matey's high spirits as the Vinets, as Matey herself. He was thinking sadly that Matey seemed happier now than she ever had with him. This was the light-heartedness into which he had so longed to open the door for her. He had seen one glimpse of it, the night of Francis's visit, the evening when they had decided not to put their wedding off till June. He had tried, tried with all his love, his tenderness, his passion, to free her for it again. But he had been in the dark. He had not known where to throw his effort. What was it that kept her hesitating, sent her in the midst of cheerfulness into those inexplicable numb fits, made her unable to step off freely into gaiety as she was doing today? Henri's remark finally penetrated to his attention. 'I'm afraid it can't be laid to her husband,' he answered, trying to speak lightly. 'It's rather improbable that the best of husbands should affect her all at once, today, like this.' He returned with the equally obvious, 'It's probably being with old friends of whom she's very fond.' But to himself he thought eagerly, wistfully, 'Could it be she's just waking up to our being together . . . for always . . . and liking it? I'll ask her. Why not?'

'How is it, Mété,' Mme Vinet was saying as she walked beside Matey, 'that thy husband knows our marching songs and the commands of our army?'

'He spent a year and a half in Paris, studying painting,' explained Matey.

'I thought you said he is in a bank.'

'So he is.' She hesitated, decided that the plainest possible statement was the best, and explained, 'He thought he had not enough talent to give himself to painting.'

Mme Vinet needed no embellishments on this statement. 'Ah?' she murmured. 'Not an ordinary young man.' She looked ahead to where Adrian was carrying Mimi's delighted four-year-old. The sound of his laughter and the delicious mirth of the child came back to them. She said seriously to Matey, as she would to a daughter, 'Mété, I think thou hast a good husband. Thou must be a good wife to him.'

Matey was a little surprised by this. It was very different from any of the comments, spoken or unspoken, she had received on her marriage from her American circle. No one had ever put it to her from that side. 'Thou must learn how to make up to him for what he has put away,' said Mme Vinet earnestly, as though Matey were still a little girl under her care.

But it was Ziza, little mad inflammatory Ziza, who challenged Matey most directly. After the lunch, stuffed and somnolent, they lay about the river bank, smoking and 'making their digestions.' The two Adrians with leisurely gestures were bailing out a waterlogged boat, preparatory to taking their brides for a row on the river. Matey and Ziza sat together, their backs against a great sycamore, looking down on their men. '*Are* you happy in marriage, Mété *chérie?*' Ziza asked pouncingly. 'Are you making your husband happy?'

'Well, I hope so!' said Matey, heartily, she thought.

Ziza replied, 'No, you're not! Not what I call happy, or you couldn't answer in that voice. You are not happy as I! I am crazy, crazy, crazy about my husband!' Each impassioned *folle! folle!* burst up from her like a ball from a Roman candle. 'You're not going to be happy like Mimi, are you?' she enquired. 'Like a hen or a cat?' Her great dark eyes glowered at the idea.

'How can anybody tell what he's going to be?' asked Matey.

'Well, I can,' said Ziza; 'I know exactly how I'm going to

be. I'm going to worship Adrien every hour of my life. Do you worship your Adrian?' she asked. 'Do you think him the most beautiful man in all the world?'

Matey looked down at Adrian and saw him distinctly as an ordinary-looking young man with a sandy red moustache, rather lean and small compared to his heavy red-faced companion. The two young men were resting now, sprawled in the sun, smoking and talking quietly together. They were probably comparing notes, thought Matey, about conservative investment yields. Adrian's rather leather-coloured face wore an expression made up of mild interest and of perfect quiet and composure. The murmur of their voices came up to Matey's ears. Even at that distance she could hear his strong un-French intonations. She looked at him more keenly, watching him as he smoked and talked and listened peaceably. After a moment, feeling her eyes on him, he glanced up, gave her a tender smile, lifted his hand in greeting, and turned back to his companion. He looked as natural and at ease, as little concerned with the impression he might be making, as – 'as Sumner ever does,' thought Matey, in a superlative of her own private language.

She said in a belated answer to Ziza's question – not that Ziza had noticed, having caught her own Adrien's eye and sent him an impassioned kiss – 'Well, he makes me feel . . . ' she stopped because the words that came to her mind seemed rather odd and inappropriate . . . 'he makes me feel – different,' she said finally. This was certainly a non-committal statement, she thought, to set by Ziza's fireworks. But Ziza never did the expected. She flung her arms about Matey's neck and cried out, almost sobbing, 'Yes, darling, darling, isn't it like being in a different world' – this was not nearly strong enough – 'like being in another universe.'

'Ziza is the same crazy little thing she always was,' thought Matey. 'I know why her mother and sister feel uneasy about her.'

She glanced down at the stalwart young Fleming there with Adrian, and wished he looked less opaque.

Mimi came sauntering over and asked, 'What are you children talking about so excitedly?'

'Our husbands!' cried Ziza, as if it were self-evident.

Mimi lowered herself a little heavily to the grass beside them, prosperity and maternity having made picnics slightly difficult for her. 'Wait till you have children,' she said.

'Do you *want* children, Mété?' asked Ziza, but she evidently had no interest in whether Matey did or did not, for she went on hastily, 'I suppose I do. Adrien would like it, I imagine. But I would hate them if they got between Adrien and me – for a minute – for an instant!'

'You don't know what you're talking about,' said Mimi. 'Wait till you have your first baby.'

'I'm no setting hen,' said Ziza, running her pointed red tongue around over her red lips as she spoke, in her old expression for exasperation.

'You don't know what you are,' said Mimi with older-sister complacency.

'I am Adrien's wife!' cried Ziza. 'And that's enough for me!' She got up impatiently and ran down the bank to join the men.

✴✴✴

Mimi gave Matey a look which said, 'You see what we mean.' She said aloud, self-righteously, 'Now that's not the way *I* feel about my husband at all.'

Matey made no answer. Out of this familiar tossing about of the idea of being married, a singular idea had occurred to her with great force. Why, she was married too – really married – permanently. This was not one of the things that would disappear behind the curtain of change. Adrian was always to be there, would never disappear or fade into the background with a move to another town. How strange that she should feel this only now? She had known it before. Why was it only now that she believed it? It took time, didn't it, for anything to happen?

Mme Vinet, followed by Henri, now joined them. 'Mété, tell us something about thy husband's family and home. It may be years before we see thee again.'

Matey was very sure it would be years before they saw each other again. So, sitting on the bank of the Marne, the rich humanised French countryside about her, she tried to paint for them the small old Hudson valley town, and the rich humanised Dutchess County countryside. There was little in her picture that was new to them. The slow old town full of blood-kin and set traditions, the great-aunt with her passion for ancestors, the humorous, unambitious, musical father-in-law – they had seen all those in French provincial towns. It was not unlike what lay before Ziza. And Adrian's salary of $1200 a year which Francis had found so pitiable sounded normal to them. About what Henri had.

It was only when she chanced to speak of going to Meeting

with Adrian and his father that they looked surprised. A darkening came over the face of the conscientiously anti-clerical Mme Vinet. 'Is thy husband a *pratiquant* of a church?' she asked, looking down at Adrian, her old dislike and fear of the inhumanities of religion shadowing her eyes.

'Well, not like any church you ever heard of,' said Matey hastily. 'I'll tell you about it.'

They listened in astonishment. 'No professional priests? Why, *I* might like a religion that nobody made his living out of,' cried Henri.

'No music!' murmured Mme Vinet, horrified.

'No toleration of war, really and truly?' said Mimi, already a European mother with sons.

No one made any comment during her attempt to give them some idea of a Quaker meeting. 'It's not a bit like a church service with something active going on every minute,' she told them. 'It's an exercise in contemplation, really. Most of the time is spent in silence. Silences longer than you'd think possible. At first I fidgeted and coughed and noticed my finger-nails. But I was quite astonished to feel myself becoming, little by little, very quiet! At first just an empty quiet, like a waking sleep. But do you know, even that's awfully restful. And then, once in a while, up through the space cleared from the clutter of surface things, you feel a deep lifting of something more . . . like a slow tide rising. . . . '

She was silent. They looked at her in surprise. She was a little surprised herself.

'Do you – do you pray at those times?' asked Mimi, timidly, wistfully. 'Now that I have children I . . . '

‘No,’ said Matey, trying to tell the truth. ‘You know I’ve never been at all religious. I don’t think I have ever prayed.’

‘I call *that* praying . . . ’ said Henri decisively.

All this talk about praying made Mme Vinet a little uneasy. ‘Won’t they ever get the boat ready?’ she asked, looking down at the group by the water’s edge.

‘All ready for the boat ride. Brides first!’ sang out Ziza, turning toward them.

They left Mimi sitting under the tree, musing, her head bent down. In spite of her good husband and prosperous home and nice children, Mimi’s old pensive look seemed close to the surface.

In the rumbling, jolting, badly lighted interior of the third-class compartment going back to the city, conversation was difficult. And they were all pleasantly drugged with their dose of fresh air and exercise. The Vinets slept frankly, peaceably, little Paul with his head on his older brother’s lap. Matey’s eyes slowly flickered open and shut. For a moment it seemed to her that she was a little girl again, returning with the Vinets from a Sunday expedition into the country. Adrian leaned to her ear. ‘This morning,’ he asked her softly, ‘when you were all at once so gay, singing and dancing . . . *what was it?*’ She opened her eyes and tried sleepily to remember. ‘I don’t know,’ she answered. ‘Do you ever know the reason for a change of mood? I just seemed all of a sudden to enjoy things more.’

She saw that her answer had disappointed Adrian and added, ‘I’d tell you, Adrian, if I knew, truly I . . . ’ And then it came to her. ‘Oh, yes, I remember perfectly now. It was the country looking so lovely – and something or other about the wheat that came into my head. And the fresh air had stopped my headache.'

'Ah,' said Adrian.

He added, 'I hope it doesn't ache now.'

'Not a bit,' she told him; 'I never felt better. It's been a lovely day, hasn't it? Aren't the Vinets nice? Isn't Ziza a wild little darling?'

She laid her head down on his shoulder and fell again into a waking doze, all sorts of disconnected pictures wavering through her mind, like things slowly falling down through water – Sumner sitting sentimentally in Rebecca's kitchen of an evening ; the enigmatic expression in Priscilla's eyes, during the long silences of their Quaker wedding; a chemise she had left lying across a chair in the hotel bedroom, in which she must remember to run a ribbon, the long flexible themes in the Arietta of the Sonata Mme Vinet had played while they were waiting for supper at Mimi's; and then, as clearly as if she had seen them out of the train window, a preposterous pair of big Dutch country boys, pedalling madly along on a tandem bicycle, their huge, their voluminous, their incredible trousers bellying in the wind like homespun sails. She remembered perfectly where she had seen them, though she had not thought of them from that day to this. It had been in Amsterdam, in the midst of the city traffic. How ridiculous they had looked, and how heartily and good-humouredly they had returned the laughing shouts and greetings of the city crowd. They had looked up at the little girl she was then, leaning from the hotel window, laughing and waving her hand at them, and had lifted their flat Dutch caps with a gay gesture of comedy. Funny that should come into her mind now!

'Adrian,' she said impulsively, 'I don't know what made me so contrary about Holland. Now I think of it again, I think it would be fun to sail for home from a Dutch port, and stop over in Louvain to see Ziza on the way north.'

'Rising from the vasty deeps of non-existence, I salute thee, Holland,' said Adrian. 'I always did sort of like the Dutch.'

CHAPTER FIVE

✝✝✝

Of the honeymoon fortnight in Paris Matey remembered best, after that day with the Vinets, the visit to Minarossi's, and the first time she went to the Louvre with Adrian. The Vinets being musical rather than artistic, she was very much more familiar with the Salle Gaveau than with the Louvre and had never so much as heard of Minarossi's. There was little to see when they reached there, for in the dull midsummer season the mouldy old rookery was almost deserted. The calico-clad *concierge* billowed out from her *loge* with a wide smile, a copious greeting, a handclasp for Adrian, and a searching look of scrutiny for his new wife. 'I hope you will make M Adrien happy, Madame,' said the whiskered, triple-chinned, coarse old woman, 'for he has a beautiful nature!' She and Mme Vinet! thought Matey. Everybody in America had concentrated, as far as she could remember, on hoping Adrian would make *her* happy!

Adrian was laughing over his beautiful nature and accusing Mme Dol of saying the same thing to every returned student, when some chance remark brought out the news that among the few painters still clinging to the old place in summer for the sake of reduced rent for studios was *le petit* Marceau.

'Oh, we must see him,' said Adrian to Matey. 'He's one of the old gang.'

They went down the dilapidated stone steps into the unkempt small courtyard and clambered up steep narrow wooden stairs, glancing in through open doors to big dusty bare deserted rooms. Through the half-open door of one she caught a glimpse of an elderly Italian model posing in a banal attitude, leaning on a long staff. A few young men with easels sat in a semi-circle around him, looking up intently at the nude brown withered body which Matey found as unlovely as the rest of this dingy palace of Art.

Le petit Marceau being found (a study in still life on his canvas, a cheese, a pear, a brass candlestick and an orange posing for him) proved to be a small young man with an immense brown beard, who at the sight of Adrian raised arms to heaven, and then springing forward with loud cries, kissed him soundly on both cheeks.

There was a flurry of introduction, greeting, the brown beard bent solemnly over Matey's hand while a pair of sharp brown eyes looked hard at her. ('He's wondering,' thought Matey to herself, 'whether I will make Adrian happy. They all are.') There were rapid-fire questions and answers about a dozen names strange to Matey, in the midst of which *le petit* Marceau interrupted Adrian by another ardent embrace. *'Bon Dieu, mon vieux!* If I could only tell thee how sweetly that monumental accent of thine rings in my ears! If only the rest were here to listen to it!' To Matey he explained what had already been very apparent to her. 'Your husband, Madame, is a great favourite among us all.'

'He's rather a favourite of mine,' said Matey.

The little Marceau drew back with a Mounet-Sully gesture of dramatic surprise and admiration. 'But you have no accent! you are French! *Mon* Adrien has married a French ...' He was about to rush on her with an embrace.

'No, he hasn't,' said Adrian hastily, laughing. 'She's as American as I am. In fact she is a cousin of mine. Don't you see the strong family resemblance?'

'You must persuade him,' said Marceau to Matey, 'to return here, to give up this melancholy plan of his for making a bourgeois of himself. . . . '

'God did that, not I,' said Adrian, beginning to look restless. Passing quickly into farewells, he steered Matey back into the street.

'How did it look to you, dear?' he asked Matey.

She made the little sign with finger and thumb which had been whimsically agreed upon between them as an announcement of truth told with difficulty, and answered, 'About as alluring as an empty barn. How did it look to you?'

'I don't believe I'll tell you,' said Adrian. He so seldom spoke gravely to her, except of his love, that Matey was startled.

'Are you – do you *regret* – ?' she asked him, expecting the usual instant reassurance that nothing was of any consequence to him so long as she was beside him.

'Well, why wouldn't I?' he asked. He seemed to feel no need to say anything more, walking along in a silence that was rather sombre.

She felt a chill. She had supposed it an understood matter that she completely filled his life, his capacity for joy. Was that not the basis for marriage? She thought to herself that this was the traditional first step away from the honeymoon glamour.

At the Louvre Adrian was increasingly silent, a quite different companion from the one with whom she had 'done' the Belgian galleries, as new to him as to her. The Louvre was evidently anything but new to Adrian. His feet carried him here and there, from one favourite canvas to another, with no thought on his part. In the room of the Italian primitives, one of the bored elderly guardians, shifting his weight from one aching foot to the other, looked hard at Adrian, broke into a smile, and came shuffling forward to shake hands with him. 'Where have you been this long time, M Fort?' he asked, and on being presented to Matey. 'Ah, getting married? Well, half a year is not too long for that.'

Would he, too? wondered Matey. Yes, it was obvious that he was asking himself, European fashion, as he looked at her, whether she would make a good wife for Adrian, rather than the other way around. 'I used to copy here a good deal,' explained Adrian briefly to her as they moved away.

He had never talked much to Matey about his painting, and had apparently not taken home from Paris a single canvas.

They walked around the room now, passing from the candour of the pink and blue and gold Angelicos to a canvas which gave Matey a quiet unaesthetic emotion. It was an Italian painting of a grotesquely ugly bald old man with a bulbous red nose, leaning down to welcome a small fair-haired boy who came running happily into his arms.

Matey cried out, 'Oh, Aunt Connie! The expression in the old man's eyes reminds me of Aunt Connie!'

And when they went away, as they did very soon, she stopped in the ante-room and bought a photograph of that picture.

'We'll hang it in the living room over the mantel,' said Adrian, 'in memory of Aunt Connie. I always liked that too . . . but it was the red in the cloak that struck me. I like Ghirlandaio anyhow. He wasn't one of the great ones. None of his canvases ever gives you the authentic thrill. He knew that too. He just offered what he had, so simply, so . . . It seems as though . . . '

He was silent again.

In the silence they came down the steps of the Louvre into the little shrubbery jungle of the small park around the Lafayette statue.

'Let's go and sit on that bench behind the lilac bushes,' said Matey, and when they were there, as unabashedly as any *midinette* she gave her husband a long kiss. 'I believe I love you, Adrian,' she said, drawing away to look at him.

'Well, it's high time you . . . ' Adrian made an attempt to strike the whimsical note, but his voice failing him, gave it up. His hazel eyes searched her grey ones deeply. 'Oh, *Matey* . . . ' he said with a long sigh.

It was the first time he had asked anything of her, the first time – was it not? – that anybody had asked anything of Matey. Up from unknown depths in her heart came a flood of tenderness such as she had never felt. She flung open her arms to her husband. 'Ah, *Adrian,* if I can only make you happy!' she murmured, her lips on his cheek.

CHAPTER SIX

✡✡✡

The first summer after Matey's wedding, Priscilla was personally conducting a party to the North Cape and the sisters saw each other only for a day or two. The second summer Priscilla decided not to take her usual trip with a group of girls. She was rather tired of Europe, she wrote, and very tired indeed of girls 'from the nicest families.' She thought it might be a good idea to get acquainted with her small namesake. If Matey was really sure she wouldn't be too much trouble, with the baby and all . . .

Adrian agreed with Matey that Priscilla wouldn't be too much trouble. 'But whatever can she find to do in Rustdorf for a whole summer?' he asked, answering himself, 'Oh, of course, tennis. We must get the courts in extra good shape.'

Except for a few mild outings and an occasional Saturday afternoon match of the Rustdorf Tennis Club with players from Newburgh or Poughkeepsie, there was nothing at all to amuse Priscilla, and for years she had been used to a great deal of amusing. In the winter Rustdorf people were not without diversions. They went occasionally up to Poughkeepsie to a concert, or to a lecture at Vassar open to the public, or after

much planning and arranging of time and finances, went
down to New York on the 5.20 train, coming back from concert
or opera or theatre on the 1.30, almost too sleepy to trudge
home from the station. There was a Rustdorf chorus too, in
which Matey and Adrian and Adrian's father sang, which every
spring gave a public performance of one of the less difficult
oratories or cantatas. As long as the ice held and the snow was
good there was plenty of winter fun. Of course a Bridge Club,
and a Village Improvement Society, and a District Nursing
Association, if you could call their meetings diversions. And
people invited each other around for the evening meal which
was still called supper. But the summer Rustdorf was of an
abysmal quiet. It is hot in the Hudson valley. All nature settles
down to a slower-paced life. Adrian's father said, 'Our Dutch
blood comes to the top in summer.'

Of course young mothers with first babies are never anything but hurried. Summer brought no slackening of speed to
Matey that year. Except at Meeting, she seldom had an instant
of leisure in which to think connectedly of Priscilla or anything but the next task to be done. But when Adrian called
her attention to it, she agreed with him that it was a wonder
that Priscilla, who at this time of year was usually making the
rounds of the leather shops on the Ponte Vecchio or taking
for the tenth time the drive to Amalfi, could endure such an
existence as theirs.

Even the daily tennis outing was Rustdorfian. They usually
walked down Washington Street, Adrian pushing the baby-
carriage, the three rackets lying across the foot. From the other
direction came Dirck Davis and his young wife, also pushing

a baby-carriage. Adrian sometimes asked Matey, 'How *does* Priscilla stand us?' Sometimes they had to wait before a court was free, for tennis was one of the fixed Rustdorf traditions and both courts were often occupied. They sat about on the old green-painted benches then, chatting with neighbours they found there. Everybody was related to everybody else by blood, or marriage, or old neighbourhood habits; everybody knew the resources, financial and intellectual, of all the rest; it would have been impossible for anyone to pretend to be other then he was, so nobody bothered to try. Matey had never heard such natural talk as there was in Rustdorf or felt so natural herself as she did, sitting under the old elms, exchanging impressions of the day's news, watching with one eye the players flashing about the courts, and with the other keeping track of the baby sleeping in her baby-carriage. But she realised that what seemed restful to her might easily seem a frightful bore to Priscilla, used to people for whom social contacts meant assuming an attitude, a manner, an expression, quite different from their natural ones.

If Priscilla had been at all musical she might have been interested in the odd relationship growing up between Matey and Adrian's father. But music was one of the many things which Priscilla had long ago locked out. On Sunday afternoons, the usual time for one of the joint weekly séances before the piano, Priscilla wrote letters. So the only break in the monotony of the tennis-less Sundays was going to Meeting, in the old stone Friends' Meeting House.

For Priscilla went to Meeting as naturally as she fell into other Rustdorf ways. Nobody had dreamed of asking her to go. Everybody was surprised that she did, everybody, that is, except Aunt Tryntje, who diagnosed it as 'the Van Benthuysen coming out in her.' Matey spent considerable time in Meeting wondering why in the world Priscilla had ever thought of coming. Sometimes she sat looking at her sister's serious, absent profile, marvelling at the invisible thickness of the wall that could stand between human beings so close to each other. For she had been able to share her marriage and motherhood with Priscilla as little as her courtship. Even over the exciting new daughter and niece, she had never been able to say anything better than 'I can hardly believe she's real. Wherever *do* they come from – a new person like that, all at once?' or 'Aren't little babies too funny when they sneeze!' and once when together they were bathing the baby, 'Who do you think she looks like, Adrian or me?'

That last question, trivial as it seemed, had received a silent answer from Priscilla louder than her words, which were merely, in a casual tone, 'Why, a little like Francis, don't you think?' Ominous as a mutter of distant thunder, something unspoken passed between the two women. Matey answered, looking at the mysterious unknown new member of humanity on her knee, 'Oh, do you think so? I never noticed.' But she had. And though it startled her to hear in what Priscilla did not say an echo of what was in her own mind, she felt comforted to know that Priscilla shared it with her as Adrian could not. 'Hand me the talcum powder, will you, Priscilla?' she asked.

During an especially silent Meeting one Sunday it occurred to Matey that if she could put out of her head the idea that words were the only expression of what people felt, Priscilla and she might enjoy more peaceably their affection for each other than if she continued always trying vainly to drag into the net of syllables something which – for them – lived in another, deeper medium. To accept, once for all, this mute speech as their true one might free her from her troubling sense of the disharmony between their trivial talk and the strength and beauty of the tie between them.

As they walked home together through the Sunday stillness of the old town, she took Priscilla's hand in hers. For a time they walked hand in hand as they had when they were little girls. She felt Priscilla's fingers gently return the pressure of hers. Matey thought, 'How lonely women must be who have no sister!'

Presently Priscilla said in a low peaceful voice, 'Elms are nice for street trees, aren't they, when they get old?' As she spoke she looked up at the roof of the leafy arcade over the sidewalk.

'Yes, I think they're more graceful than maples,' Matey answered, following the upward look.

A quiet happiness seemed to fill the old street from side to side. Matey was not sure, but it seemed to her that Priscilla felt it too.

As the summer days slid by, Adrian began to guess that Priscilla was not too frightfully bored by Rustdorf. He said to Matey once, 'Who'd have thought that Priscilla could draw her breath in our equatorial domesticity?' and added, 'Maybe she is too suffocated by it to get out.'

She never said whether she liked it or not, but she stayed on and on, making herself more or less useful, refusing various

vacation invitations to Maine and the Adirondacks from one
or another of her wide circle of acquaintances. Hearing Matey
say once that in her letters to the Vinets she never felt she
gave them any idea of what her life now was, Priscilla bought
a camera and took some snapshots of Matey and Adrian and
the baby, and their old storey-and-a-half stone house, green-
shuttered, with the tall locust trees towering slimly over it, and
of the distant view of the Hudson from the windows of her
bedroom. Prints of these were sent to the Vinets and to *le petit*
Marceau and others of Adrian's studio comrades with whom
he kept up, at long intervals, a desultory correspondence. In
due time the Vinet girls sent back letters with snapshots of
their children, homes, and husbands. For Ziza now had a baby,
a little boy. 'I'm ahead of you, Mété,' she wrote exultantly;
'I have two Adriens to your one.' Priscilla had never known
the Vinets as well as Matey did, but she read these letters all
through and looked attentively at the photographs. She made
no comment on them beyond 'Isn't it queer, Mme Vinet has
four grandchildren now, and all boys.'

Adrian said, '*Le petit* Marceau – do you remember him,
Matey? – has a boy too, he writes me.'

Aunt Tryntje interrupted her count of knitting stitches to
remark, 'People used to say that was a sign of war.'

Priscilla's tolerance of her namesake was perhaps more
marked than any other sentiments she might be having in
Rustdorf, and this although the cocoon-like little Priscilla
was in the two-months-old somnolent, sometimes damp,
occasionally sour-smelling and vociferous stage of development

usually disliked by sophisticated unmarried aunts. Matey herself, excited and fatigued by the complications of caring for a baby, was occasionally out of all patience with her small daughter. But Priscilla, though she was a little shy of taking responsibility, seemed never to tire of being with the tiny scrap of flesh, so amusingly human. She often volunteered to be nursemaid while the baby slept in her carriage out of doors or lay there waiting for her next meal, regarding the world with very round blue eyes. Aunt Priscilla always had a book with her, or a writing tablet. But she wrote few letters and did not read much. Glancing out of the window as she flew about the housework in the precious interval of the baby's nap, Matey often saw her sister sitting idly, her head tipped back against a tree, doing nothing at all in the warm shadow woven out of tree-green and sun-gold.

'Never,' she told Adrian, 'never since I can remember did I see Priscilla doing nothing. She was always busy about something every minute.'

'Maybe making up for lost time,' suggested Adrian. 'If I'd been busy every minute of my life I'd want to rest by the time I was thirty-three.'

Matey herself was rather often nervously and physically tired, *'wild'* she sometimes told Adrian, because there were more things to do every minute than she had thought possible. She grabbed at one, half did it, and was summoned imperiously to something else, until she was sometimes crosser than ever before in her life. She snapped at Adrian occasionally, and he rather snapped back, for his nights were broken, too. But it oddly did not matter much. Sometimes Matey, remembering the tragic importance which the very intonation of a word had had for her, how a mere impatient look from her father to her mother had filled her heart with foreboding, could not understand why a hearty exchange of impatient exclamations with Adrian seemed to leave no more impression on the colour of her day than did the chance small discomfort of setting a hairpin crookedly in her hair and taking it out to set it straight.

The point seemed to be that Adrian was entirely different – to her – from anyone else living. It was not, as Ziza seemed to feel, a passionate adoration of everything her husband did which made her married life unrecognisably different from anything she had known before. Little habits of his, his unpunctuality, his whistling, his waiting too long before going to the barber's to have his hair cut, annoyed her to the point of exasperation. It seemed to be rather his permanent nearness to her, and hers to him, a nearness immeasurably beyond anything she had dreamed possible. One Sunday morning as they lay talking together in the peaceable quiet of a rare vacation dawn when the baby slept late, she gave him an impression that had come into her mind as she had waked and found herself with her head on his shoulder. 'Honestly I hardly knew for an instant which was my flesh and which yours,' she said. 'Do you know, Adrian, lots of times I feel closer to you than to me.'

'I know what you mean all right,' said Adrian. 'I've thought of it too – I believe I'd tell you things I've always kept dark from myself.'

'Well, that would mean,' began Matey, in the trail of a new idea, 'that sex helps bring people – instead of the way everybody – '

But then the baby did wake up with her usual vital, hungry, attention-demanding yell, and whatever abstract idea had been crudely before its time trying to come to life in Matey's mind, slid back safely into the fertile formlessness where during this period most of her ideas lay, darkly striking roots into rich soil. The unending urgent tasks of their always disorganised day had begun. They had separated to go to their different watches, Adrian now on one deck and she on another. In a moment she had the baby in bed with her, and Adrian, gone sleepily downstairs in slippers and dressing gown to start Sunday breakfast, was shouting up to her that the milkman had forgotten to leave the milk and was there any left from yesterday. Over the greedily nursing baby she shouted back uncompromisingly, 'No, not a drop!' so loudly that it sounded almost like an oath, and grimly left him to wrestle unaided with this problem.

They had begun another day of their cruise, during which they would both rush about from side to side of their small undermanned craft, pulling at this rope and frantically letting out or furling this sail, like excited inexperienced sailors in windy weather. For whatever else they were, they were not becalmed. The lifting plunge forward of the deck under their feet as the following wind pushed hard on their sails made them stumble sometimes, and catch at each other, and for a moment stand unsteady, locked together close, the keen forward-rushing wind of life loud in their ears.

It was not at all either what the sentimental or the brutal reports of marriage had led Matey to expect, although she had really 'expected' nothing, drifting forward in that carefully

acquired scepticism of all theories of life which she had learned
in college. She had 'expected' nothing very exactly and she did
not know very exactly what she was getting because she had no
time to consider the matter. The raw material of life poured
in on her with such speed and in such bulk that she could not
even begin to get it in order, could only toss it here and there
in heaps, to make room for what would be borne in by the next
day's high tide.

She could not have reported accurately on any part of all
this newness. Sometimes she loved her small daughter almost
to agony; again, on the very same day, when she was tired, it was
not love she felt but indignation over the egotism with which
the baby insisted that the universe revolve around her small
person. Sometimes this indignation toppled over from a too
swelling crest into outrageous laughter. She and Adrian were
often overtaken by helpless mirth at the Nero-like tyranny of
the newcomer. 'The nerve of her,' cried Adrian, 'pushing us
off the centre of the stage like this!'

Matey had not laughed so much – or scolded so much – or
cared so intensely about anything – or been so tired – or felt
herself so flooded with vitality – not since she had been a little
girl, playing. If Priscilla had ever asked her, 'Well – ?' Matey's
report on marriage would have been only a wild half-laughing,
'Why, now, blow wind, swell billow, swim bark! The storm is up
and all is on the hazard.'

Washington Street – the one which was always going to be
paved – had been filled up in modern times to make the grade
more even. The large front lawn of the young Fort ménage

was several feet below the street, from which a short flight of stone steps led down to their front path. The sidewalk thus lay about on a level with the eyes of the people in the house or on the lawn, and Adrian pointed out to Matey how the passers-by on foot or in carriages (there were as yet but few automobiles), coming and going in each direction, made a long moving many-coloured band or frieze, sharply defined below by the empty green plane of the lawn and above by the dense foliage of the elms. The figures on this decorated band were for the most part far enough away to be soundless, which Adrian insisted brought out their colours more brilliantly. Matey would never have seen this for herself, but once her attention had been called to it, was quite taken by the idea and now saw it with Adrian's painter-eyes.

Whenever they glanced up there was a new design, a new composition to look at. Sometimes a group of children loitered along the sidewalk, talking loudly, tagging each other and leaping suddenly to one side with deer-like bounds; sometimes a farmer's wagon went slowly by with a red-and-white calf in the back; or a nicely painted ancient phaeton with one of Aunt Tryntje's old-lady friends driving a jogging horse; or a half-grown boy flashed along swallow-like on a glistening bicycle; sometimes, going to or from the factory, a line of powerfully built workmen in rough old clothes sculptured to significance by the strong bodies under them; or a well-dressed suit of clothes went satirically by, folding and opening the creases of its trouser legs in the motion of walking, the face of one of the merchants of town topping the coat and white collar; or rattling and shiny, a smart red-wheeled dog-cart from one of the 'estates' out in the country. If it were no more than the grocer's wagon, or elderly Peter Russell with his brood of unkempt motherless little girls, something was always being painted by the airy brushes of sun and shadow on the frieze which hung there, halfway up that eastern wall of their world.

One day it had rained hard in the morning so that the courts were too wet for tennis. Adrian spent the tennis hour pushing the lawnmower over the (always!) too long grass of the front lawn. Priscilla went out on the front porch with a book which soon fell shut on her knee as she sat idly brooding. The baby was 'being good' although awake. She lay on a blanket on the grass, making futile grabs at the unattainable feet dangling in the air at the end of her short legs, occasionally murmuring a good-natured remark to herself about the game she was playing.

Matey stood for a moment at the house door to look at all this. She was tired, as she often was, too tired even to remember what there was urgently needing to be done. She went slowly to where the small Priscilla lay and sat down beside her on the blanket. At once her released body drifted into a sort of physical somnolence. She leaned against the tree and thought of nothing at all, the only thing in her mind a vague wonder that she could possibly feel, as she often did in these days, too tired to draw her breath, and yet have this new savage magnificent underswell of conviction that there was nothing – *nothing!* – that she could not do if necessary. The whir of Adrian's lawnmower was rhythmic. On the outdoor frieze sunlight and shadow painted three small children, tumbling forward with a furry black puppy. Behind them towered a golden hay-wagon, pulled by two bright bay horses, stepping slowly with a firm air of being adequate to what there was to do, like an echo to what was in the background of Matey's fatigue.

Her eyelids dropped shut, as though the sunny quiet and the singsong of the lawnmower had put her to sleep.

Did she go to sleep? It seemed to be from a wide realm of other-consciousness that she emerged with the slow beat of her eyelids opening. The baby still lay beside her, placidly untroubled by never reaching her feet, the puppy's laughing yelps came clearly though faintly from down the street, the hay-wagon was just ponderously moving off at the end of the frieze. It could not have been long. And yet, for a heartbeat Matey opened her eyes upon another world.

It was just what it had been, of course. And yet wholly something else. Oh, lovely! lovely! heartbreaking with beauty! This was her world, her corner of life, just what she had known she had . . . but transfigured as if it and she had been carried up to another new, unthinkable dimension . . . and yet it was not new at all. Once before she had felt this melting into strange heavenliness of something quite familiar and old. She remembered now. The two moments fused together . . . she was still Matey Fort, sitting under one of her own trees, a grown woman, a mother . . . and she was also a little ignorant surprised child leaning over a red-plush railing while up from the depths, borne past her on the angel wings of the violins, came the voice of revelation.

She was on her feet. She turned to Adrian now as naturally as she moved from one thought to another in her mind. She ran across the lawn to him. 'Adrian, Adrian!' she said in an eager low voice, shaking his arm a little. 'Now I know what heaven will be . . . the same, the same as life, and yet transfigured . . . all glory . . . like something you've heard on the piano played by the whole orchestra, *you* know!'

No, he did not know. Had no idea what was in her mind, looked bewildered. He could not, of course, Matey remembered now, share in a long-past moment of hers, which had been too impalpable for her to tell herself in words. But she could tell him more in words than she had ever been able to tell herself. She knew she could! Was he not closer and clearer to her than her own unknown self? She could say it out, if she could hold his hand as she now did in both hers, if she could feel that physical nearness which had first taught her the road out of solitude. Quick, before the glow faded – 'Why, Adrian, here is just what I have always had . . . what everybody has . . . sunlight, the earth, trees, a shelter, food . . . they meant nothing to me . . . I don't believe I ever in my life really looked at them till just now. But for an instant, over there, in the quiet, I saw what it all makes for me . . . with you, with the baby. Why, *now* it's . . . '

After all it was not with words she told him.

They stood hand in hand, smiling into each other's quiet eyes.

On the porch behind them, Priscilla – they had forgotten her – stirred in her chair.

That night before she dropped off to sleep Matey's memory presented her with an old picture – a little girl, not so very many years older than her own little girl, trotting along a narrow path, unquestioningly, turning her head from one side to the other to watch the tall green bushes of the broom. Down the path, out of sight of the child, waited terror. But Priscilla had been there, who knew there was nothing to be afraid of. Matey thought drowsily, 'It's the other way around now.'

CHAPTER SEVEN

✝✝✝

Matey had always wanted a listener for her music. At least, years before, she had thought it would be lovely if Priscilla would share what she was doing at the piano. And now she had a listener, Adrian's father. In a way Adrian was a listener, too. He liked to hear her play, especially if it was something he already knew and liked. But he soon became accustomed to the sound of the piano in the house and was capable of getting up in the middle of a favourite piece of music to open the furnace draught or to make sure the baby-carriage had not been left out in the rain. This was the way most people listened to music, Matey knew. That is, they thought about other things a good deal. The difference between most people and Adrian was that he did not pretend to anything more than he was.

Adrian's father, on the contrary, took root in his armchair with her first note and never stirred till after the last one. Yet for a long time his way of listening rubbed Matey's susceptibilities the wrong way as much as Adrian's 'naturalness'. He listened with intensity to every note, but there was no more recognition of Matey in this concentration than in Adrian's way of remembering a house errand that needed to be done.

There were moments in that first period of her Rustdorf life when she was out of all patience with her father-in-law for his way of reducing her to no more than a sheet of glass through which he gazed at the composer's intention. His silences were monumental. And when he broke them it was never to refer to Matey's playing, no matter how good it might have been. What he said was, 'Funny, isn't it, how that change of key, just a mechanical mathematical device, should get down through your brain into your feelings.' Or, 'Well! who ever would have thought that to set a triplet in the middle of a run would give it wings like that.' Often he said nothing at all. Sometimes did not even remember, when she finished, to thank his daughter-in-law.

In many encounters of that first year with Adrian and his family Matey was piqued by what Dirck Davis's young Maryland wife, Flora, called plaintively 'their Quaker ways.' She and Flora as newcomers occasionally sympathised with each other about Rustdorf customs and had a catchword in common – 'There, Isaac, that is a good hat' – which they often quoted to each other with a smile. It was drawn from a story of Aunt Tryntje's about a Friendly hatmaker of the town in early days who had been asked by an elderly Quaker neighbour to make him a beaver hat. When he presented it to the purchaser he said, 'There, Isaac, that is a good hat that will last thee all the rest of thy life, if thee dies in any sort of season.'

Matey sometimes repeated this phrase spitefully to herself at the piano, her father-in-law at her elbow. She could not but be affected by the intense interest Adrian's father took in the music open to him through her playing; she was, as a matter of fact, insensibly coming to be half of a musical personality of which her father-in-law was the other half. But she was nonetheless often vexed and exasperated by him and agreed heartily with Flora Davis when she said in confidence, 'Seems as if Quakers just make a *point* of not having nice manners, doesn't it.'

That is, she had thought she agreed with her, until the evening when she played at a benefit musicale given at one of the handsome 'estates' near Rustdorf. It was the country home of a wealthy New York family of Dutch origin who from time to time took a notion to 'join in the life of the community.' Young Mrs Fort had been asked to play and prepared her music and her gown with more care than she would have been willing to admit to anyone but her brother. She and her father-in-law were working their way through the earlier Beethoven Sonatas that winter, but she knew better than to offer such undramatic fare as that. She began to practise some showy Liszt, but Adrian's father so took the lustre from it by his silent bewilderment at her choice that she threw it down pettishly and decided on the Chopin Étude in C Minor – the 'Revolutionary'. She found it outrageously difficult to get up to tempo, quite beyond her usual capacity, and she was obliged to give hours of work to it for several weeks before the musicale, revenging herself on her father-in-law by never letting him hear a note of it.

The musicale was held in a handsome drawing room and was carried out according to the recipe for what is known as a 'brilliant affair'. 'Like a faculty party,' thought Matey, looking out over the restless glitter as she sat before the piano. She was stirred and pleased to be the centre of these moneyed men and women, but before striking her first note she waited with a sternness taught her by Mme Vinet, till perfect quiet filled the room. 'If faculty wives had as much money to spend on their clothes as these,' she added to herself.

Perfect silence finally did fill the room. Matey played. Chopin's tocsin clanged out its bronze notes savagely in the midst of a decorous silence.

When the vibration of the *fortissimo ed appassionato* ending had died away, the audience applauded. They applauded generously, having been surprised by the unexpectedly vigorous performance of the young provincial matron, invited only to gratify local pride. And what they applauded was the player's skill and not the music. There was no doubt about that. After the concert was over, they crowded about her, filling the air with the correct catchwords which they had learned from their parents and which they were teaching their children, 'Perfectly *fas*cinating!' 'Such a lovely touch!' 'How can you ever keep up such a *won*derful technique!' Here were the nice manners Matey and Dirck Davis's wife had missed. These people were well bred enough to admire her and not Chopin. But living with the two Adrians had trained her ear to too fine a pitch of accuracy; it heard a crackled flatness in this good breeding. She did not feel exhilarated, she felt grim, as she put off her excited sharing of Chopin's violence and put on the correct smile to match the nice manners of these nice people. And when she heard her own voice saying brightly, '*So* good of you to say so!' and 'Oh, you're so *very* kind!' she felt belittled and trivial and depressed. She looked from one smiling pleasant face to another, trying to find in one of them the awakened expression of someone who has really heard music. But they were all alike, masked to uniformity by their formulas. Formulas were what Adrian – what all Quakers – lacked. Matey, smiling and grimacing by the corner of the piano, felt she did not miss them as much as she thought she had.

One man said, 'It's absurd to think of such a pianist being buried in a place like Rustdorf.' His intention was evidently no more than to say in a slightly new manner the 'how perfectly *fas*cinating!' of the others. But Matey heard in his words a complacent implied assumption of superior musical intelligence in the audience before her. She found this so unexpected and naïve that all at once her grimness vanished in a laugh.

The Sunday after, without warning him, she played that Étude for Adrian's father. He sat motionless from the opening cry to the peremptory violence of the last four chords, and then rising all in one piece, went blindly out, not noticing that she existed. That was one time when she had not minded in the least his Quaker ways.

In fact from that time on she slipped with less friction into the dual personality which she and her father-in-law were creating, became little by little, as far as he was concerned, more of a Quaker herself. She leaned more consciously on his capacity for musical attention, far riper and firmer than hers. It never wavered or slipped for a bar or two, as hers did. She felt him sometimes, half inside her own head, warning her to take care lest she lose the significance of a single phrase. Never before had Matey felt so physically the difference between music that has meaning in every phrase – and the other kind. Under their scrutiny 'the other kind' withered up and blew away.

Sometimes her listener made inventive suggestions: 'How about pausing just a breath before the end of that run? Wouldn't it add a freshness to the climax not to have that last note come as a matter of course?' Or 'Hold on, hold on! Isn't the bass the important part of this?' Together they worked out small delicacies of interpretation, the sum total of which transformed their music into something richer than Matey had ever dreamed it could be. As she looked back on the playing she had done, it sounded childish and obvious.

The Minuetto of one of the Beethoven Sonatas was one of the things she had learned to play in Hamilton. The difference between what she made of it then and now was like a diagram, she thought, of what growing up amounted to. 'You simply learn to see what's there instead of missing the important things by taking them for granted as a child does.' She sometimes thought, 'Isn't it strange how you go on accepting childishness for all there is, never guessing the depths of understanding that lie beyond, waiting for you to grow up to them?'

CHAPTER EIGHT

✻✻✻

It was, however, not at all with any depth of understanding but with stupefaction that Matey greeted Priscilla's announcement during her second summer vacation in Rustdorf of her intention to marry the faded elderly widower who lived in Aunt Connie's house and whom Matey had come to accept in the character of harmless neighbour under the title of Cousin Peter Russell. No, she acted toward the news just as Francis would have if he had known of it. She recognised in her consternation at Priscilla's having thus 'thrown herself away' the very quality of Francis, and it kept her mute. The exclamations of alarm, of anxiety, of disappointment, might rise to her lips fast enough, but how could she bring them out save in Francis's voice? Never before had she seen so clearly how Francis had stood between her and that part of their common inheritance which Aunt Tryntje would call their Gilbert blood. How Francis's example had coloured her estimate of values! The pictures he painted of his success in Pittsburgh, how profoundly they had affected her judgment of Rustdorf life!

'*Some*body ought to talk sense to Priscilla,' she told Adrian, excitedly, 'but *I* can't!' She could not, because the sort of sense she thought Priscilla ought to hear was the Francis sort.

She did not spare Adrian at least; she poured out her self-reproach to him, she cried out on herself for having been so blind. For she saw now that nobody had dreamed of hiding anything, that it had all been happening before her eyes. She had been so absorbed in her own interests she had not seen what was there. She could now trace it step by step back to the beginning which she had seen but had not recognised.

For that second of her summer visits, Priscilla had chanced to arrive in time for the Fourth of July celebration. The old town had its own way of celebrating the Fourth. As long as daylight lasted, it seemed like any American town on Independence Day. The children went about firing off crackers and flinging torpedoes down on the flagstones. Each child for himself, they created noise as copiously as each father and mother allowed. But from time immemorial the fireworks in the evening had been a communal affair. No true Rustdorfian ever bought any fireworks of his own. The money that he would have spent on them he gave to a common fund, administered (origin of this tradition lost in the mists of time) by the postmaster. It was one of the duties of the office of postmaster in Rustdorf.

On the evening of every Fourth as soon as darkness began to fall, people sauntered in pairs and groups out toward the rocks over the Hudson at the end of Barnegat Lane. The postmaster with the fireworks and a group of the more reliable adolescent boys were at the base of the rocks, on a half-circle of sandy beach in a cove, visible from above. To help with the Fourth of July fireworks was one of the Rustdorf rites of initiation into adulthood. All the little boys in town looked forward eagerly to the time when they would be down on the beach instead of leaning tamely against their mothers and fathers among the family groups scattered about in the dark on top of the cliff.

The Fourth when Priscilla was there for the first time was clear and starry. She had come in from Chicago on the late afternoon train and had received but the sketchiest account of what to expect when they all set off along the twilight lane, Adrian walking with Aunt Tryntje and carrying his fourteen-month-old daughter, Matey, Mr Fort, and Priscilla coming after with cushions. By the time they came out on the rocks, darkness had fallen deeply. They could see nothing, but a sixth sense made them aware that all about them were groups of waiting people.

Across the river shone a garden of fire-flowers, each steady blossom of flame supported by the long wavering stem of its reflection in the water.

'How lovely those lights are!' said Priscilla. 'Are they part of the celebration?'

'They are kerosene lamps,' said Adrian's father in his quiet voice, 'some of them smoky, set on kitchen tables in poor men's houses.'

'Here is a rock with nobody on it,' announced Adrian from one side.

They settled themselves to wait, hearing and feeling about them the rustlings and stirrings of the unseen crowd. A faint breeze came in from the river, flitted about, stepping capriciously on its light feet from one group to another, lifting locks of hair with invisible fingers.

From the cove below came spurts of boys' laughter.

With a majestic rush, up soared a rocket, tracing toward the stars a curve of fiery speed.

'Ah-ah-ah!' breathed the unseen, earthbound crowd.

The rocket put all its soul into that upward flight toward infinity. But it was not enough. The poor finite thing could not reach even the fringes of the stars. It hung an instant in the blackness, and then with a soft explosion that was like a long-drawn breath, made its failure beautiful in a bouquet of many-coloured falling sparks.

'Ah-ah-ah!' breathed the invisible crowd. A child's startled voice shouted out, 'Oh, p'itty! p'itty!'

'That's a child seeing it for the first time,' said Mr Fort. He added in a musing tone, 'I can remember very well when I saw it for the first time, sixty years ago. Can you remember your first time, Adrian?'

'Never'll forget it,' answered Adrian.

'They're lovely here,' came Priscilla's voice through the darkness with a surprised accent. 'I never liked fireworks much before. You're always too near. You hear people scolding about the fuses being wet, and how somebody's not holding the Roman candles right.'

'Sh-sh-sh-sh!' Up sped another rocket, its tense flight cleanly drawn, up and up – all those human faces lifted toward the stars to follow its aspiration. The bright curve halted in mid-air, recognised its defeat, bent its head in resignation, and sighed out its life in a golden rain.

'The baby's watching it,' announced Aunt Tryntje, who had claimed the privilege of holding little Priscilla. 'She really does take it in, I'm sure. She lifted her face to follow it and put out her little arms.'

'I wonder,' thought Matey to herself with a start, a pang, at the idea that her baby might be beginning a life of her own, 'I wonder if perhaps this will be one of the "really" remembered things for her.' And with the thought she saw it all differently, with a new richness and depth. She saw it as it might look to little Priscilla years from now, she saw the golden curve of beauty which had just died before her eyes, shedding an immortal brightness along the unknown future toward which the baby's feet were tending. Tears came to Matey's eyes. She felt herself humbled and exalted. It was the first step she had taken forward from physical maternity.

A flare of red flame blazed up luridly around the edge of the beach, showing the rocky walls of the cove and a line of black figures, arms melodramatically upraised toward the sky. 'Roman candles now,' explained Adrian's father to Priscilla. To Adrian he called, 'Adrian, when was the first time you began to feel grown up?'

Adrian laughed. 'Sure thing!' he said. 'Same time you did, I bet – first time I was allowed to hold one of the Roman candles.'

From each arm sprang up a ball of coloured fire, leaping nimbly into the air, vanishing to leave the darkness free for those that followed. They rose in flocks like little sprightly birds, they died down, they rose again. 'The allegretto after the largo,' murmured Adrian's father in the ear of his son's wife.

The red fire faded down to darkness, the Roman candles were still. People stirred and rustled as though for a moment they had forgotten to breathe.

A child began to cry. It was quite near the rock where the Forts sat, but they could not see it. There was no quick maternal murmur of reassurance. No other sound at all but the low wordless complaint. They looked into the darkness, on this side and that, saying, 'Why doesn't somebody quiet the little thing?'

Adrian said, 'Perhaps it's lost. I'll see if I can't find it.'

He left the rock and moved off, saying, 'Somebody strike a match so we can see.'

'It is here,' said Priscilla, 'near where I am. I felt its hands just now.'

Adrian's father struck a match. In its yellow light they saw, painted on the darkness, a tiny flaxen-haired child, her face glistening with tears, her thin small hands groping out toward Priscilla. They saw Priscilla quickly lean and draw the little thing into her lap. The match went out.

'Yes, she must be lost,' said Priscilla through the darkness. 'I'll just hold her till the fireworks are over and we can find her mother.'

'It's Peter Russell's youngest,' Aunt Tryntje told her; 'she hasn't any mother.' She went on, in a lower tone, 'The idea of Peter bringing that great brood of young ones here, with only himself to look out for them! He might have known he'd lose some of them.'

'I suppose he wanted them not to miss what other children have,' said Adrian's father.

'*Sh-sh-sh-sh!*' Another rocket burst from its pasteboard chrysalis and fled upward into its golden moment. In the faint

light cast by its soaring, Matey could see that the little girl had
settled down into Priscilla's lap, one arm around her neck, her
flaxen head laid on Priscilla's bosom.

'Right then and there,' cried Matey to Adrian at the end
of the summer, in one of her most Francis-like moods,
'anybody with a grain of sense would have risen up and taken
that child away from her. One look at her there ought to
have been enough. But I never dreamed . . . how *could* I have
dreamed!'

If she had not had sense enough to think of it then, the next
day ought to have put her on her guard, she told Adrian in
one of those later fits of remorse. But on that second occasion
too she was absorbed with her own life. The fifth of July fell
on a Sunday that year; Adrian's father and Aunt Tryntje had
come to dinner, and after the meal was over the family divided
into two parties, porch and piano, Adrian's father, with the
smile he gave to no one but Matey, having said, 'How about a
little music?' The others had gone out to the porch chairs and
hammocks, to collapse into after-dinner coma and to watch
little Priscilla staggeringly practise what Adrian called her
'walking steps'.

A strange voice sounded from the porch. Glancing out of
the window Matey saw mild Cousin Peter Russell, stooped and
grey, his rather unattractive, unkempt, sober-faced children
clustered about his thin legs. But she did not leave the piano
to greet him. Adrian and Aunt Tryntje and Priscilla were
surely enough of the family to do the honours, especially for a

neighbour whom one saw every day. He had probably stopped in to thank them ceremoniously all over again for taking care of little Mary Ellen last night. The Russells were not Friends, any of them, and Matey had so far acquired Quaker tastes that she was sometimes impatient of Cousin Peter's wearyingly polite insistence on treating each small event decently and in order with conventional formality.

There! The interruption had made her lose the thread of the music. Debussy was hard enough to follow without interruption. She was playing the notes now as though they were words in a language she could pronounce but didn't understand. And Adrian's father hated that. She started over again, forgetting the existence of so negligible a person as Cousin Peter.

Later, delightfully worn out by her struggle with a new musical personality, she joined the outdoor group, rejoicing that she had before her so restful a job as putting the baby to sleep. Looking around she asked, 'Where's Priscilla? Writing letters again?'

'No,' said Adrian, from where he lay on the grass beside his small daughter, both of them absorbed in watching the manoeuvres of a beetle. 'No, she went along with the Russells. Little Mary Ellen seems to have taken a shine to her and teased her to go to see – something or other her father has made – a doll's house, wasn't it, Aunt Tryntje?'

'Peter would do well to pay more attention to their buttons and to see that their faces were washed more often and spend less time on doll's houses,' said Aunt Tryntje over her knitting. 'Those children look like I don't know what. Rebecca says that woman Peter has to take care of them is no better than a dirty slut, but Peter will keep her because she's good-natured.'

Matey had been a little surprised that Priscilla did not come back that afternoon till supper time, and a little more surprised to see her after this so often strolling over to the Russell house or appearing with one of the children beside her. But little Priscilla's reactions were so much more important to her mother than anything else that she paid small attention to the older Priscilla's interest in the Russell children. Up to this time little Priscilla had lived, like all first babies, hermit-like, marooned on the desert island of babyhood in the ocean of grown-up life. Little Mary Ellen Russell, only two years older than she, was the first who ever burst into her silent sea. Matey was so touched by her baby's excited interest in a near contemporary that she welcomed in the three-year-old neighbour without wondering how she happened to be there so often.

In her mind, as in that of any woman just emerging from the physical excitement of bearing and nursing a child, there was a deep-rooted conviction that *her* baby was absolutely different from any other. Mary Ellen was all right, a nice little thing, though her eyes were too close together, and she was sometimes rather noisy and spoiled. But it was obvious that she was made of wholly other stuff than Matey's own child, whose life Matey shared with a literal nearness not unlike that before her birth. When little Priscilla cried – or laughed – or ate – or slept, her mother felt a mystical reflection in the cells of her own body. When Mary Ellen Russell cried, Matey suggested to Priscilla that perhaps it was time for her nap and hadn't she better be taken home?

That Priscilla might not feel the same difference between the two children never occurred to her sister. What did occur to her, with a naïve shock of newness, was the thought that since the baby was so delighted with a playmate, she ought to have a little brother or sister. 'Well, Adrian,' she said to him one night, when their murmured before-going-to-sleep talk had been of this, 'it's simply *laughable* how different I am from what I thought I was! I'm not only simply crazy about you and the baby, but the minute I think of our having another one, I just love him to death, already!'

Before she dropped asleep she said with a drowsy laugh, 'Do you remember my saying I thought I couldn't love anything but Sumner?'

'Yes, I remember very well,' said Adrian, more distinctly, more awake than she had expected to hear him.

'Doesn't that seem a million years ago – somebody else!' she murmured.

Adrian made no answer. She supposed he had gone to sleep.

Yes, looking back over that summer, Matey could see how it had been nothing but her absorption in her own affairs that had blinded her to what had been openly going on.

'But you didn't see it, either, did you, Adrian?'she challenged him.

'I can't see it now,' said Adrian. 'Talk about going through the woods to pick up a crooked stick! Not that there's anything crooked about Peter. He's straight, all right, what there is of him. But what on earth does Priscilla want of a gentlemanly old nonentity after the chances she's had!'

Such phrases had been all that came into Matey's mind after Priscilla had exploded her small bombshell. She had been on the point of bursting out, 'Oh, *Priscilla!* After all the chances you've had!' But as the words shaped themselves in her mind she saw that they had fallen into a Francis pattern, and was silent. When she was able to speak, she had said guardedly, with a horrid care in choosing her words not to say what she meant, 'Well, Priscilla dear, of course I'm surprised. You must have known I would be. I'll have to wait a while before I can really take it in.'

Priscilla did not seem to notice her sister's guardedness. She said in a low trembling voice, unlike her own, 'I had thought I would never have any children – '

Matey restrained herself with an effort from shouting, 'But *these* aren't *your* children!' As she heard these unspoken words Matey did not like the sound of them. And yet how perfectly justified they were!

For the first time since they had begun to talk, Priscilla looked up. With a startled shock Matey thought, 'Why, Priscilla never before let me look into her eyes.'

'Four little daughters – ' murmured Priscilla.

Her face, which Matey had thought set forever in its mechanical brightness, softened into the wavering misty look of young helplessness before emotion. Priscilla looked like a little girl! This was too much. Matey had been as helpless as her sister before the gust of emotion which flung her into Priscilla's arms, crying out 'Oh, darling, darling, sister!', her cheeks wet with tears half of sympathy, half of pity, wholly of love.

All through the interval between the announcement of Priscilla's engagement and her marriage, the absent Francis kept Matey from speaking out. But he did far more than that for his younger sister. Her repeated wordless struggles with his standards forced her over and over to take accurate stock of what was in her own mind. Even in thought she could scarcely finish wholeheartedly some of the outcries that came naturally to her lips. 'Think of Priscilla, with her professional ability to make good money, drudging her life away taking care of another woman's children.' Or 'How *crazy* for anybody who's learned to dress so beautifully as Priscilla to bury herself in a place where nobody'll care how she looks.' By the time she had begun to put such ideas into words she was again on the railroad platform hearing Francis's unanswerably prudent objections to her own marriage. Time and time again Francis made her draw back, thinking, 'No, *this* cannot be the real reason for my heavy-heartedness over Priscilla's marriage.'

But although Francis forced Matey to drop one after another of the conventional objections to that marriage, she did not grieve the less over it. Her heart, freed from its meaner cares, ached with all the purer sorrow to see Priscilla, so brilliant, so blonde, so accomplished, beside the listless life-weary man with whom she was to share the rest of her years. Nor was she the more reconciled when she learned that Priscilla and Cousin Peter were to share life only as house-mates, not as man and wife. When Priscilla managed to tell her sister in a shy reticent word or two that her distrust of life had abated only half, that there was to be no question of love or real marriage for her, but only the sharing of another's burden of parenthood, Matey felt a pang that was half passionate relief and half passionate unresignation. 'I don't know whether that's better or worse,' she told herself wildly.

Nor did the sight of Priscilla's fondness for her foster-children to be (touching as Matey found it) soften in the least her fury of compassion. 'She thinks that's all, poor Priscilla!' Matey often thought, watching with a lump in her throat Priscilla's beginnings of motherly ways. She felt for her older sister during those days an almost maternal yearning, as if she were an adult watching a child make an ignorant wrong choice among life's values.

Why this heat about Priscilla's marriage? Whence came the shadow which Matey saw Priscilla unsuspectingly entering? From a light, of course, as every shadow must. And the light streamed, Matey saw it now, from the centre of her life with Adrian, from their love, from their union, from their marriage. That was what gave the meaning to every breath she drew. That was what Priscilla would never know. She had hardly known it herself. She had been living in marriage as inattentively as she sometimes played music, striking the mere notes with correctness but making no sense of them. She had been loving Adrian without knowing what she was doing. Somewhere, behind her, lost in the million other insignificant moments of the two years of her marriage, had been the moment when she stopped being a cool shallow child yielding passively to caresses, and had begun to be a woman who loved. This was the moment Priscilla would never pass.

One morning as she made their bed a memory came to her of some of the books she had read in college, some of the lectures to which she had listened. Those childish notebooks of hers, filled with docile notes! Well, thought Matey, beating a pillow to lightness and setting it back, nothing, nothing at all of what she had been told to expect by all those life-experienced elders had turned out true . . . for her. Money had been neither the lock nor the key in her life, and for her, sex had not been the ignoble concession to animality that the older generation by word and gesture and ugly grimace had led her to expect. It had been the foundations of the bridge over which she and Adrian had crossed the unplumbed salt estranging sea of human isolation.

Like the refrain to a litany came her new heartache – Priscilla would live her life out on her island prison, alone.

How strange that it had been her selfless concern for Priscilla which had made her look up from her small busy thoughts and perceive the greatness into which life had led her. Was advance always haphazard, oblique like this? Suppose Priscilla had never made her anxious? Would she have gone on being childish and flat, missing love because she took it for granted?

One Sunday in Meeting, Rebecca was moved to speak. Matey heard nothing but the quotation with which she began. She heard that as if for the first time and always after heard it clad in that velvet Negro voice, 'As if a man should cast seed on the earth, and should sleep and rise, night and day, and the seed should spring up and grow, he knoweth not how; first the blade, then the ear, then the full grain in the …' Around the words, quiet circles began to widen in Matey's mind. All those older people, set there in her youth to point her to the way ahead, why had they never told her that love could come in any other way than as a flash of lightning comes – comes and blazes and burns and goes? Nothing could possibly be more unlike a stroke of lightning than love as it had come to her . . . like a field of wheat rather, first the blade, then the ear, then the full . . . 'Alas! my dear Priscilla will never feed on the harvest.'

Late on the afternoon of the next day she sat sewing on buttons and waiting for the baby to wake up. Rebecca's quotation echoed in the small sewing-room – 'As if a man should cast seed upon the earth, and it grows, he knoweth not how.'

How was it possible the harvest could come to one who so little deserved it? She had but slept and risen, night and day, giving no thought to the seed.

The door opened and Adrian, back from work, stepped in. He looked as for the first time that summer he often looked, rather tired, not very fresh, no longer in his first youth. 'Hello, Matey, what makes you look so solemn?' he said, dropping his hat in a chair with a gesture expressing weariness.

('Yes, yes, Ziza!' cried Matey silently across the ocean. 'I *am* crazy, crazy, crazy about my husband!')

'Did I look solemn?' she said, laying her work aside. 'Well, I was feeling so. I had been thinking what Priscilla is going to miss... .'

Adrian's face darkened. He said literally, drily, with none of his usual playful lightness, 'Look here, Matey, I'm tired of hearing you go on about that. What do you *think* she's missing? You're hardly in a position to think it's tragic that she won't

273

have much money. Peter Russell's income is about as much as we're likely to have. He lives in as good a house, on the same street. Why isn't hers as good a marriage as yours?'

Matey searched her husband's hard unsmiling face. She was thankful that there was in it no trace of the indulgent patient gentleness which she had seen there in the first days of their marriage. She was past needing indulgence from him now. He would never need to be patient with her any more.

'How can you ask me such a question, Adrian?' she said in a rough low tone.

Her husband paled. 'She will have plenty of children to mother,' he said. 'Isn't that enough?'

With a cry Matey sprang up from her chair. She ran to him, taking his arm in her two hands. She said violently, 'No, it's not enough! It's not enough! And you know it! And you needn't pretend I don't know it, either! Don't you ever *dare*, Adrian Fort, to say such a thing to me again!'

They were foolish childish words. No matter! If they did not say what she meant, she would find others that would.

She needed but one other. Adrian shook off her hands with a rough gesture. He held her at arm's length and looked at her. She said his name, *'Adrian!'*

There was no word at all in his answer. He caught her violently to him, no gentleness in his touch.

CHAPTER NINE

✇✇✇

Did they get everything wrong, those cocksure mentors of her youth? Matey often asked herself during the next years of her life. Were *all* their wise sayings mere traditional rules of thumb? That axiom of theirs that the emergence from adolescence is the period when human beings live most intensely – ! Why had they not once given her a hint that people might vary in this as in all other matters? Why did they not tell the young people under their charge, so touchingly, helplessly ignorant of what might be before them, something of the infinite diverseness of the paths which lead human beings toward the great moment of conversion to life and faith in it?

Matey in college had 'taken' many courses in English literature and 'passed' them all. Yet now poetry came to her like a revelation. Why, now she knew what people were talking about when they said those excited exaggerated things about poetry.

One Saturday afternoon she took advantage of Adrian's being at home to play with the baby, and with broom and duster attacked a neglected corner of the attic. On the dusty

shelves, among other books from Adrian's college days, was
an old volume of Whitman. It fell open in her hand. The bold
words on the page leaped up. It was as if this were the first
poem she had ever read.

'Oh despairer, here is my neck,
By God! you shall not go down! hang your whole weight
  upon me.'

She gave a shudder of pleasure.

She turned the pages over and came to 'Poem of Wonder
at the Resurrection of the Wheat.' After a few lines, 'Adrian,
oh, Adrian, do come up here a minute,' she called from the
top of the attic stairs. With his solid little girl on his shoulder
he came running up to where his wife stood, turbaned by a
dusting-cloth, leaning against her broom, the book in her
hand. 'It's about the earth, the earth we live on,' she told him
and went on:

'Behold this compost! behold it well!
Perhaps every mite has once form'd part of a sick person
  – yet behold!
The grass of spring covers the prairies,
The bean bursts noiselessly through the mould in the
  garden,
The delicate spear of the onion pierces upward,
The apple-buds cluster together on the apple branches,
The resurrection of the wheat appears with pale visage
  out of its graves.'

She looked up at him, chanting:

'The summer growth is innocent and disdainful
    above all those strata of sour dead.'

'Grand!' said Adrian, and 'Gosh! Matey, I never knew you could read aloud like that. You make the cold chills go up my back.'

'I couldn't for anybody but you,' said Matey.

It was not only poetry which thus sprang into life. It was all the visible world with its drama. The sun, moon, and stars, darkness and light, dawn and noonday, came into sight. There had been skies, too, had there not, wherever she had lived before? But with the slowing down of her young pulses her eyes had forgotten that it was not a wood-and-plaster ceiling over her head. No, not wholly forgotten. There had been the night skies to which she had been led by Sumner! The Matey, mother of one child and hoping for another, who stepped out of an evening with her husband for a last look at the stars, held out a hand to the wistful little Matey with her dog.

It was not only beauty which fed Matey's new hungriness for life. Roughness and hardship – yes, even suffering – were part of the banquet spread before her.

One bitter winter night as she and Adrian stepped off the late train from New York (they had been down to hear *The Valkyrie*) they found themselves facing a sudden wild snowstorm. There was nothing to do but to fight their way home on foot from the deserted station through the empty streets.

Afterward Matey could not separate the music from that boisterous battle with night and cold and the screaming wind. She leaned forward against the force of the wind; she clung to Adrian, her head bent to shield her face from the slash of the hard-driven snow; the grinding roar of the storm-tossed ice in the Hudson back of her sounded like the tumult of the orchestra. She could scarcely draw breath into her lungs, so smothering was the hand of the tempest on her face, but she shouted in Adrian's ear, 'Isn't this *great!*' as, on turning the corner of the Square, they were set upon by the full sweep of the storm.

They buffetted their way forward, stumbling in drifts, wrestling with the storm like Jacob at the ford. Under the piercing cold Matey felt the flame of her life in her burn up strong like a blast-furnace under forced draught. Was she the one who was shrieking out the Valkyr *'Ho-yo-to-ho!'* or was it the yell of the tempest? And when half-frozen they staggered up to their door, unlocked it, and found themsleves inside, in the incredible quiet of their living room, warmed and rosy-lighted by the coal fire in the grate, Matey flung her hat in one direction, her coat in the other, and cast herself violently into her husband's arms, crying out, 'Hurrah! Hurrah! Hurrah!'

Adrian kindled at her eyes. 'Great Scott, Matey, I'm sorry for the folks who aren't married to you!'

Later, as he was brushing his teeth, he remembered that his father had thought her 'dry'.

'What's the joke?' she called from the next room, and then looking in, 'Oh, it's brushing your teeth. It sounded as though you were laughing.'

Spring came and went, and drooping under the summer heat, Matey needed all her new-found strength and serenity. Long hours every day were spent in resisting and succumbing to the physical wretchedness of pregnancy, and then afterward doing hurriedly and with exasperation what she could easily have accomplished in those lost hours. But this vexation, real as it was, blew over the surface lightly. It did not reach the steady warmth within.

Even boredom, perhaps the most difficult of human ills to resist, occupied now but a corner of the spaciousness into which she had stepped out. A new careless fortitude, like a grown-up's attitude toward a child's troubles, sustained her when she went with Aunt Tryntje to the meetings of the DAR and attended those endless committee meetings whose dragging, lagging existence seemed to be a necessary part of running Rustdorf, from the Tennis Club to the District Nursing Association. 'They're simply *terrible,*' she reported to Adrian, just as she always had. But she really minded them no more than the slight bother of brushing her hair or lacing up her shoes.

With Adrian she seemed now to be reading out of life a thousand times more of its meaning than she had dreamed could lie on its familiar pages. It was exactly like the change in her reading of music.

One sunny morning, late in November, on the day after the first snowfall of the year, she went out into the back yard to burn some waste-papers. The three-year-old Petella (this was the version of her name which the little Priscilla had made as soon as she began to talk) was always tagging at her mother's heels like a little dog, and helped carry out the bushel-basket from the woodshed. Together they emptied the crumpled papers upon the cinder-covered corner dedicated to bonfires. It was transfigured now to whiteness by the new-fallen snow. As a treat, Petella was allowed to touch the match to the pile of papers. They took fire with a flash. The child drew back quickly to the shelter of her mother's skirts. The two stood for a moment to watch.

The tongues of flame flared up, their fiery red and orange chastened to transparency by the sunlight. Petella and her mother could see through their shimmering clarity the feather-light cold crystals of the new snow.

The soul of heat . . . the soul of cold . . .

The woman watching them, woven firmly into human life by a thousand blood-ties, felt her imagination soar up on a new wing. Even as she stood there in the body heavy with its double humanity, she caught through those disembodied flames a glimpse of the beautiful, fierce, unhuman life of the elements.

'I visited Saturn and Jupiter and the moon for a moment today,' she told Adrian that night at the supper table, 'when Petella and I were burning up waste-papers on the snow.'

As she spoke the vision cast a reflection of its brightness up into her rather weary face, shadowed by physical weakness. She too was beginning to show that she was no longer in her first youth.

'Don't get so far away you can't come back to us, dear,' said Adrian, his eyes deeply on hers. She thought, 'I have seen the soul of heat, and of cold – and now the soul of tenderness.'

Petella glanced up from her milk toast in time to catch the interchange of this look. She pushed her plate forward for another helping. 'Petella empty like hired man,' she said heartily, in an old-time phrase of Aunt Tryntje's.

One of the many changes which these years brought to Matey was an astonishing difference in her feeling about her home. When Adrian's father had first shown them the old house Matey had seen it flatly, literally, as she saw other things, a storey-and-a-half stone building with a white-painted clapboarded wing on one end. She had no suspicion that a house could be anything more than a house. The course of her life had moved her in and out of so many houses that she thought she knew how to see one. It had amused her a little to feel so like her mother as she competently examined kitchen, pantry, and plumbing.

After that first inspection of the house the family party of four had strolled about the yards, front and back, Matey, in the haze of golden unreality in which she had wandered through the period of her engagement, listening dreamily to Aunt Tryntje's talk, and dreamily wondering if she were really to be married and live there.

' . . . the locusts around the house came from Long Island. All the *English* families planted locusts as house trees. They were thought more elegant than forest trees. The elms in front are of course part of the regular street planting that New Englanders did wherever they settled. The big beech here was planted right after the Revolution by one of the LeRoy cousins back from the war. The LeRoys lived in this house then. He went away a private and came back a colonel, and that's more than any LeRoy of *that* branch has done since. The story was that when he came home from the war his uniform was so full of vermin he wouldn't wear it into the house. He went out into the barn . . . in those days there was a barn standing where the weeping willow in the back yard is now. No, that was the smoke-house stood there. Where *did* the barn stand? Oh, I know, farther back where the stone wall is now. Some of those stones are . . . '

How absurd, how amusing, how quaint Aunt Tryntje was, thought the young Matey – but very dimly, because she was tingling to the touch of Adrian's hand as it brushed hers.

' . . . and so they *baked* his uniform in the oven next to the fireplace – it was the kitchen-dining room then, what thee's going to use as a living room – and his wife, Henrietta Richmond, she was one of the pi'sen neat Yankee housekeepers, said she never could bear to eat anything in the oven after that, and that was how it came to be bricked up. It's still there, thee knows, under the wallpaper. . . . '

Adrian's eyes were the colour of sherry wine when the light shone through them from the side.

'The willow was planted in 1835 by Madeleine Ter Bosch – she was thy great-grandmother's cousin, Matey – because weeping willows were in fashion then. She'd been down to visit relatives in New York and they were all working weeping willows in crewel. She brought back the slip from there. But she died before it ever amounted to anything.'

* * *

At that time, all this had been for Matey but a part of Aunt Tryntje's quaintness. To be polite to an old lady she had looked at the trees, but she had certainly not seen them. Why were they now, like the house, like the sky above it, become living personalities? There had always been trees – she supposed – near all the houses she had lived in, but were never any more to her than the people who get into the train at one station and get off at the next.

By the time she was expecting her second child, she had taken root beside these trees. The certainty that she would be looking out on this very sky and these very trees to the end of her days deepened her present with overtones of her past and future, making her peaceably one with the old woman she would grow to be, as she was with the adolescent she had outgrown. She felt herself not only a part of Adrian, of the child she had, of the child who was coming, but a part of the piled-up old stones that had sheltered so many other families like hers, part of that old humanised piece of earth, full of root treasures, left there like the traits in her own personality by her predecessors in life. Like her strength, her weaknesses, they had been there before her time and would go on opening out into immortal freshness with each spring. They were all dear to her, the things that grew around the house, from the lilies of the valley to the rhubarb, down to the very blades of vigorous grass, but she came to have a particular affection, a particular intimacy, with the trees. Whenever she turned into her own yard after being away from home they looked themselves to her, unlike other trees as much as she and Adrian were unlike other people.

How differently they took life! The willow was almost a hundred years old, but it had never grown indifferent to the miracle of spring, rushed out to greet it with the same eager, pale-green young welcome, long before its more prudent comrades had stirred from their winter torpor. It was under the willow that Matey had chosen to make Sumner's tiny grave when, a little while before Petella's birth, he had faded out of life.

How differently they acted in thunderstorms! The line of Levantine elms with their dramatic, excited gesturings in the wind, the Nordic oak surly and stiff and insensitive and strong. And the tall old locusts, cut off from self-expression by their height like gentlefolk by their breeding, so that all that could be seen of their emotion in the most violent storm was the slight swaying motion of their long brown trunks.

How differently they stood up under the recurring adversity of winter! On the stormy day in December when Matey lay down on her bed, shuddering in the onset of labour-pains before the birth of her second child, she saw out of the window the old beech, stripped to the poles, magnificently glorying in the battle with wind and snow. She faced her own battle with a new heart. The present, anguish that it was, dwindled to its proper place in the great perspective.

She remembered with pity the faltering panic of her first confinement. The pains were as great now. But she was so much greater.

'No, no! Adrian!' she cried to him, seeing him turn very white at an outcry of hers, his teeth set in his underlip. She beckoned him to her. He came to kneel by the bed. When she could get her breath to speak, 'It's worth it!' she told him, with all her heart.

He turned paler than ever, his face transfigured by love and by shared suffering.

Oh, wonder and glory of life that could bring such moments, thought Matey, bracing her soul against the old beech as a new rage of pain swept over her. This too was part of the banquet spread before the living.

When she was up again, later in the month, her new son in her arms, she sometimes held him up at the window through which the beech was to be seen. And on her first outing with her two children, the baby in the baby-carriage, the little sister trudging through the snow beside it, she stopped under the tree and said fancifully, 'That's *your* tree, Adrian the fourth.' It stood quiet enough, that sunny day, holding up its branches to the winter sun, casting a faint twig-shadow down on the woman with whom it had shared its strength.

Petella gazed up at the tree seriously. The resemblance to her Uncle Francis was particularly marked when she lifted her little fair face. 'Oh, dear!' thought Matey with a qualm. 'I've made a mistake in saying that. She will not want the baby to have more than she. I must remember, now there are two, not to . . .'

The child trotted through the light snow to the tree. She laid a mittened hand on the great mottled grey bole. 'Brother's tree,' she said, smiling back at her mother.

Darling!' cried Matey, falling on her knees in the snow to catch her little daughter to her.

She longed to have had Aunt Priscilla there, to see that smile on that Francis face.

She did share another such moment with Priscilla, later that winter, one day when Aunt Tryntje was telling the children stories. Priscilla had brought her brood to spend a snowy afternoon at Matey's house with paper-dolls. Was it possible, thought Matey, that these were the same children, these rosy, noisy, vital little girls? Could these be the children who, conscious of ugly clothes and ill-cut unkempt hair, had drooped shyly in corners, trying to escape disapproving looks by being invisible?

'Those young ones just wear thee out, Priscilla,' said Aunt Tryntje that afternoon, looking at Priscilla's faded radiant face. 'It's enough to make a hired man take to his bed to have them always on top of thee like that. Now, children, let your mother alone for a while and I'll tell you a story.'

Matey, her baby in her arms, and Priscilla leaning back in peaceful weariness, listened too, although they now knew all of Aunt Tryntje's stories.

'It's about the Colonel LeRoy who was born and brought up in this house, the one whose uniform was baked in the oven downstairs, you know. But this was long before he went to the wars with General Washington. It happened when he was about sixteen, and he was sent to take home across the river an old-maid seamstress who had been working here. Indians never did any harm around here, but across the river things weren't any too settled in those days. Bartholomew was a big fellow then, and rowed the boat across the river all right in good time. They were halfway up the path toward the settlement where the seamstress lived when she remembered she'd left her work-bag in the boat. So Bartholomew LeRoy told her to wait while he ran back for it. He hadn't even got as far as where he'd tied the boat when he heard her scream . . . a scream that fairly shook the leaves on the trees, he always said. . . . '

The little girls at Aunt Tryntje's feet huddled together like startled chicks. Matey asked herself impatiently, 'What was I thinking about, to let Petella hear such a story?'

Aunt Tryntje went on, 'Bartholomew felt for his knife and started back up the path. He heard her scream again and then, round the corner of the path, men's voices talking Indian talk. He had just time to jump into the bushes and hide when they came along, four Indians and two renegade white men dressed like Indians. They had the seamstress gagged now so she couldn't scream, and they were hurrying her along as fast as she could go, stumbling and tripping on her long skirts. Well, what should the boy do? He couldn't fight six men. What good would it do anybody for him just to go and get captured himself? So he decided to stay safe in the bushes and . . . '

'No, no, *no!*' came shrilly from little Petella. 'No, he didn't stay safe! No, he didn't!' She glared at the narrator.

'Why, what does thee *mean*, Petella?' asked Aunt Tryntje in astounded rebuke. 'Yes, he did, too.'

'*No!*' cried Petella passionately. 'He ran right out of doze bushes and went right along with dat lady!'

She began to cry furiously now and rushed to her mother's knee, looking up at her with Francis's face, filled with outraged generous pain.

'Oh, *Matey!*' said Priscilla on a deep note.

287

'Listen, darling little daughter,' murmured Matey in Petella's ear, 'it all comes out *quite* nicely in Aunt Tryntje's story. Just let her go on and you'll see.' She made room for her beside little Adrian on her lap, while Aunt Tryntje, somewhat ruffled, went on, 'Well, of course, he *wasn't* to blame' (this with a glance at the still defiant Petella) – 'not a bit! And everybody told him so. But he couldn't seem to get over it. I've heard the old people tell how he used to sit right in this room by this window – just sit and sit, his face hidden in his hands. In the spring of that year he disappeared. With nothing but his gun. He was nearly eighteen years old by that time. They didn't have any news of him for about a year. Everybody thought he was dead. And then one day the next April his mother sat on the front stoep out there, churning, and looked up, and there down the road he came, all in ragged old buckskins, thin as the last run of shad, a great scar across his face, but the seamstress was with him . . . '

Priscilla's noisy little girls had been quiet as long as they could, and now began to shout and laugh and clap their hands and turn somersaults on the rug.

'Thee *sees*, Petella,' said the old lady triumphantly.

But Petella had quite forgotten the story and her remote kinsman. These were the first somersaults she had ever seen. She gazed at them fascinated, and scrambling down from her mother's lap, began clumsily to try to imitate her foster-cousins.

Priscilla's husband came in now, stamping the snow from his feet, and calling out to the children that he'd got the biggest sledge and was going to pull them all home on it.

Cousin Peter was almost as much changed as his little girls, thought Matey, noting his sleek look and the animated expression on his mild face.

'If you'll let me have that pattern for the baby's cloak,' said Priscilla, rising to go, 'I can get it cut out and basted by tomorrow. Peter is going to be at lodge meeting this evening.'

But it no longer made any difference what Priscilla *said*.

CHAPTER TEN

✿✿✿

In those very first lean years, when Adrian's salary as book-keeper was too small to mention and the house needed everything, the interest on Aunt Connie's money had melted uninterestingly, each half year, into mattresses and chairs and a new furnace and tiny expensive woollen baby shirts, and taxes and doctor's bills. But by 1913, the fifth year of their marriage, Adrian had become teller at eighteen hundred a year, and the house was moderately well furnished. 'Let's save it all up this year and buy a Ford!' said Matey daringly. There were but few automobiles owned in Rustdorf as yet, and mostly by people who had much more money than the Forts.

'Everybody'll think we're crazy,' said Adrian, 'buying a car before we either of us own a fur coat. Let's.'

So they did. And with its purchase in the spring of 1914 they went for a time ridiculously back to the joys of childhood and venturesomely forward into unexplored emotions of the future, as no generation before them did, nor after them can ever do. To be transported through the air at the speed of light by merely wishing it will not so astonish and ravish the *blasé* generations of the future as to be whirled along familiar roads at four times the speed of a trotting horse astonished and ravished the generation to which, in maturity, the automobile was new. The very process of learning to drive the contraption was an adventure. There were no driving instructors in those days. The Ford agent from whom Adrian bought the car took him out on the road once, gave him a lesson in the use of the pedals, exhorted him above all to remember where his emergency brake was, and told him to go to it. On a back road, Matey perched on the bank, Adrian went to it, perspiring from every pore. 'I haven't felt the pit of my stomach come up so, not since I was three years old and starting to slide down the banisters the first time,' he told his wife, halting the infernal machine with difficulty and wiping streams of sweat from his scarlet face.

As a rule now Matey took Adrian for granted, but the idea did come into her head that it was not Francis who would have allowed a witness to watch his fumbling unheroic struggles with a new power. 'It's awfully nice of you, Adrian,' she told him, leaning down from her refuge on the bank, 'to let me come along.'

But Adrian, naturally, did not know what she was talking about. 'I need you to pick up the *membra disjecta,*' he told her, bringing himself with a visible effort to let the clutch in again and start off. 'Let me see, turn on a little more gas, press on the left pedal, take your foot off the . . . '

When, a week or so later, Adrian first drove out his wife and children, their excitement was almost as great as his. Petella, at five, was considered old enough to sit on the front seat beside her father. Matey sat in the back, clasping the small Adrian tightly to her. 'Are you planning to use him as a cushion to fall on?' asked Adrian as he climbed over the side into the driver's seat. 'Looks like it. Petella, how'll thee and I do that? Will thee fall on me, or I on thee?' Petella laughed and relaxed her grasp on the side of the seat which had been in imitation of her mother's tensity. Matey laughed too and set the fat two-and-a-half-year-old boy down on the seat beside her, one arm around him.

'Release the emergency, press on the left pedal, raise the foot from the . . . ' murmured Adrian prayerfully. And they were off.

In the first months of their car-ownership, Matey and Adrian, along with other responsible family people of their generation, were carried away by an exquisitely childlike delight in a brand-new kind of fun. They swept Priscilla along with them. Seeing Petella and little Adrian as rapt over the Ford as their parents, she coveted it for her own little girls. Adrian told Matey, 'She'll never get Peter Russell to take money out of the savings-bank to buy a *car.* He's as Hudson valley Dutch as if his name were Van der Poel.'

But all Priscilla's dammed-up life-forces were now pouring along the channel they had found. Nothing, not even Dutch blood, could withstand her determination that her little girls should have whatever other children enjoyed for their own good. The Forts bought their Ford in April of 1914. In May Peter Russell came to the savings-bank to draw out the sum of $795, a sum as closely associated in that year with the idea of a Ford as two cents is associated with the idea of a postage stamp.

'Goody! Goody!' said Matey, when Adrian came home from the bank with this piece of news. 'Good for Priscilla!'

She never did, as a matter of fact, overcome the physical terror which her timid elderly husband felt (along with the majority of his generation) for the unholy speed of automobiles. She never succeeded in persuading him to learn to drive. So she herself learned to drive long before Matey did, one of the first women in Rustdorf to sit behind a steering wheel. Adrian said it must be the sporting blood that used to show in her tennis (which she had now entirely given up), coming out in a new form. But by this time Matey knew very well that Priscilla had never had a drop of sporting blood.

'Both you girls are perfectly crazy with the heat,' Francis told them jovially when, on one of his infrequent visits, he learned about their Fords. '*I* can't afford a car!'

'You could afford a Ford!' said Matey, using a pleasantry which was still young and unwrinkled in those days.

'Oh, *I'd* just as soon ride in a Ford as not,' he told them generously, 'but Emily has one of these fool prejudices against them. She says she wouldn't be caught dead in one.'

This energetic statement did not sound at all to Priscilla and Matey like their effaced young sister-in-law whom they had seen only twice in Francis's between-train visits in Rustdorf. They did not even need, now, to look at each other to know that this impression was common to them both.

It was extraordinary, thought Matey, how her Gilbert blood pursued her. From that day on she was, under the surface, a little deprecatory about their having a Ford and not a more expensive car. She joined with cowardly haste in the jokes made about its cheapness and was not too glad to be seen in it by the wealthy people on the estates round about, with most of whom she had now a nodding acquaintance.

Nothing, however, could mar her enjoyment of it when the wheels were really going around on one of their drives, long, *long* drives of forty or forty-five miles. Like everyone else who owned a car for the first time, it became their occupation. They drove and drove and drove. Up the river to Poughkeepsie and beyond to Rhinebeck, where none of them had ever been, though they had passed through it a thousand times on the train. South nearly to within sight of New York. Inland toward Pawling and Amenia, along the boundaries of what Aunt Tryntje still called the Great Nine Partners and The Little Nine Partners and the Rombout Patent, exploring roads known till then only by farmers.

One clear June evening when at the end of a late drive they drew up in front of their house and happened to find Adrian's father there on the sidewalk, Matey knew from the amused expression on his face that they were all four wearing naïvely happy smiles. 'Yes, we've gone back to our infancy,' she called to him.

'It never did take much of a straw to tickle me, you know,' admitted Adrian.

It was the twenty-ninth of July, and too hot for anything in the late afternoon. Too hot even for the Ford.

'She'd boil her old head off,' said Adrian.

'Mercy, yes, and we'd have to wear stockings if we went out,' murmured Matey.

❦❦❦

They sat on the porch, which Aunt Tryntje faithfully called the stoep. It faced east, so that the scorching splendour of the sun setting over the Hudson behind them wreaked its fury on the back windows of the house. But it was quite hot enough in front. Matey wondered how Adrian, after a day's work at the bank, could have the energy to pretend to be interested in Petella's struggle with her reader. It was at least her five hundredth try at the everlasting story of the Little Red Hen. Matey reached up idly to pick off a dead leaf from the vine over her head, enjoying the elasticity of her muscles. Heavens! how alive she was at thirty-three compared to what she had been as a girl! 'Did I remember to tell you, Adrian,' she asked drowsily, 'that Ziza has another baby? I had a letter from Mme Vinet yesterday.'

'A girl, I should hope, this time,' said Adrian, tightening his arm around his own little daughter.

'Another boy,' said Matey. 'They're going to name him Henri for Ziza's father.'

'But the hen said to the duck, "No, you did not help me with the corn. Now you shall not have any of the bread,"' read Petella with wonderful fluency, adding in the same breath, 'But I know that part by heart, Father, that's not really reading it.'

This seemed so natural a statement to Adrian that he evidently did not notice it. But Matey gave an inaudible hail back over the years to Aunt Connie, who had watched another little girl, and blew an invisible kiss toward the top of Petella's Francis-golden hair.

'And the turkey said,' went on Petella, adventuring stumblingly into new worlds, ' "Let me have some of that nice bread!" But the hen said, "No, you did not help me with the corn. Now you shall not have any of the nice –" ' Wasn't she the mean old thing!' said Petella indignantly.

'But she'd done all the work,' advanced her father.

'She might have let them have a taste!' said Petella, shutting up the book.

'Mme Vinet writes that Ziza doesn't seem like herself,' said Matey, although she knew that Adrian was only moderately interested in these details, 'doesn't seem to get up as well as she ought.'

'How old is her first boy?' asked Adrian.

'Oh, he's as old as Petella almost, born in 1909, just as she was. No, it can't be any effects left over from that confinement. Mme Vinet says it seems almost like a lack of nervous energy. Ziza seems sort of discouraged, doesn't want to get up.'

'That doesn't sound much like the livewire Ziza you've always described to me,' commented Adrian, 'nor like the way she seemed that day at La Ferté. I should have said motive-power was the last thing she didn't have enough of!'

'Oh, it can't be anything serious,' said Matey.

'Where's Brother?' enquired Petella, bored by her parents.

'Under his tree, in the sandpile.'

'May I take a piece of candy from Padre's box?'

'Yes.'

'And one to take to Brother?'

'Yes.' Matey's answers were no more than murmurs, but she was not too drowsy to smile at the picture Petella made, hanging over the candy-box, deliberating soulfully which two pieces to take. Her golden head drooped in the pose of a pre-Raphaelite angel, her half-open lips took on a seraphic curve. 'I believe the ones with nuts are the best,' she said thoughtfully, at last.

After she had gone her mother sank dreamily down below the surface of the ocean of well-being. The late summer afternoon was compounded of all golden elements of peace. It was after working hours, it was midsummer, it was Rustdorf, it was home. The locusts sang with all their might and the dark silent trees listened gravely. From around the corner of the house came a murmur of children's voices. 'How well they get on together,' observed Adrian, 'and isn't it heaven's own mercy there are two of them to amuse each other.' He added in an ecstasy of inertia, 'Do you suppose if I tried I could get as far as to the hammock?'

'I'm sure I couldn't,' said Matey, closing her eyes.

'Why move when you're perfectly all right as you are?' Adrian admonished himself. And to his wife, 'Honest, Matey, could anybody *be* more perfectly all right – and surer of it? There isn't anything that *could* happen to us – except one of us dying.'

'Nothing,' agreed Matey.

She relaxed still more, leaning with her weight on the fabric, firm at last, of life around her, partaking effortlessly of the sun's dynamic force, of the rooted strength of the trees, of the children's young affection, of Adrian's love.

She had enough.

Everything was all right.

In her mind the two thoughts were one.

PART THREE

CHAPTER ONE

✿✿✿

Into this beatitude came Adrian's father, an open newspaper in his hand. As he walked up the path toward the house, Matey began calling out to him in a lazy protest. 'Don't expect a note of music from me this hot evening, Padre! I've just been telling Adrian I haven't energy e – '

Adrian's father had reached the porch now and at the sight of his face Matey stopped in the middle of a word.

'What's happened now, Father?' asked Adrian sharply.

His father held out the newspaper. Two headlines of equal size stood out boldly. Matey's eye caught the wrong one first, 'No Swine to be shown at County Fair,' and after a bewildered glance at her father-in-law, looked at the other. 'French troops being concentrated along the frontier.'

'What's that?' she asked, jumping up and snatching the paper from him. She stared at the words, believing her eyes as little as if she had seen the old beech walking across the lawn. 'Not *French* troops!' she cried. She had been very busy with raspberry jam for the last few days and had not taken time to glance at the papers.

Neither Adrian nor his father replied. Over her shoulder

Adrian was silently devouring the scanty telegraphic news on the front page.

'But *France* hasn't anything to do with that quarrel between Austria and Serbia,' protested Matey indignantly.

'Russia's started or getting ready to start, you see,' said Adrian's father to his son. Something in his tone told Matey that the two men had decidedly not been missing the paper lately. Her father-in-law put his finger on a sub-head. 'Tsar's troops wreck bridge.'

'My *God!*' said Adrian, who seldom swore. The two men looked at each other.

For the first time since her marriage, Matey felt what she had heard other wives speak of, the chill of being ignored.

'Still,' said the older, 'you notice this.' He pointed out a smaller headline, 'Wall Street easier.' They seemed much closer to each other than to her.

'Yes, *that's* a darn good omen,' said Adrian. 'I can't believe it is anything but a scare.'

Matey drew a long breath of relief. 'Of course it's only a scare,' she told them impatiently. 'What are you thinking about, to imagine for a minute that modern European nations are going to war! Why, Adrian, don't you remember, when we were in Louvain with Ziza and the Conacqs, how everybody was singing "L'internationale"? Ziza's husband said it was much more like their own national anthem then the real one.'

'That day of the picnic at Namur they showed us some all-fired big frontier fortifications,' Adrian reminded her.

But Matey had recovered her poise. 'Oh, of course it won't come to anything. It can't,' she said. She looked at the paper again. 'I suppose if the French troops really are manoeuvring toward the frontier, little Paul Vinet's with them. He's in the last months of his military service, you know. Mme Vinet and Henri will be wild till the scare is over and they have him back. They hover over that boy like a couple of old hens.'

'The Belgians – Ziza's husband may be called out, too, perhaps,' said Adrian.

'Oh, that *would* be serious!' admitted Matey.

The next day's paper reported, 'Austrians in first battle, one thousand killed.' This was not to Matey's purpose. She ran her eyes hastily down the column, impatient for other news. There was no mention whatever of France or Belgium. 'You *see!*' she told Adrian triumphantly, as if it had been a perverse idea of his that there might be war.

After the children were in bed that night Adrian's father and Aunt Tryntje came over and sat on the porch with the 'young people'. They were both rather subdued. 'The news in the paper brings back the War of the Rebellion,' said Aunt Tryntje.

For the first time Matey heard that her father-in-law had run away from home at sixteen in the second year of the Civil War.

'Why, I thought Quakers didn't . . . ' began Matey, surprised.

'Not as a *soldier!*' cried Aunt Tryntje and Adrian and his father, all speaking together. Aunt Tryntje added, 'As a stretcher carrier. And there was talk of reading him out of Meeting for that!'

Matey measured from the sharpness of their correction the intensity of their Quaker horror of war and felt a little nettled.

They needn't think that Friends were the only ones who knew that war was barbarism. All moderns did.

Aunt Tryntje was launched on a reminiscence, one which Matey had not heard before. 'I'll never forget how thee looked to us, Adrian, when thee came back. The Rustdorf boys were to come, Matey, by boat, up from New York, after they were mustered out there, and were to be at the dock here at three in the afternoon. The whole town was there. Everybody. I remember we borrowed a wheelchair and took thy grandfather down, Adrian. All sorts of preparations had been made to celebrate. Our Rustdorf boys had been in the thick of everything! – at the Devil's Den at Gettysburgh and – '

'Never mind all that,' said Adrian's father in a muffled voice.

'Well everyone wanted to do them honour, you can imagine. Most of the band were away in the army, but some of the old fellows who'd stopped playing long ago got out their old uniforms and tuned up. The schoolchildren had been drilled in a patriotic song. The little girls up to the fourth grade were all in white, dressed with red-white-and-blue sashes, and every one of them had a bouquet of flowers. The Seminary boys had torches, ready for a torchlight procession as soon as it got dark. The returned soldiers were to march up the hill to the Square, hear an address of welcome, and disband. Mercy! How excited we were.

'Well, half an hour ahead of time we were all there on the landing. But the boat didn't come. Not a sign of it. The schoolchildren practised their songs. The little girls shifted their bouquets from one hand to the other. Finally the word was passed around that they would not come till next day. So we all went home.

'But some of the big boys sat up at the end of the pier to keep watch, and along about two in the morning didn't they see the boat all lighted up, swinging around the corner of the river, by the Danzkammer. They put out up the hill as fast as they could lay foot to the ground and roused the town. In about a minute, seems though, every house in town was blazing with lights. People scrambled out of bed and got into their clothes double quick. The Seminary boys grabbed their torches and lighted them as they ran down the hill. The little girls took their bouquets out of the water where they'd been put to keep them fresh. And away we all went to the landing again. I'd been grown up for a good many years, but it was the first time in all my life I'd been outdoors after midnight. I remember how queer it seemed.

'The boat was pretty close then, drifting in without any noise. We could make out people passing back and forth on the deck in front of the lighted windows. My! how black and still the Hudson looked! Our band struck up, sort of quavery. The boys with torches formed a double line and we crowded up close behind them. The boat slid up and bumped a little against the landing. A couple of deckhands jumped off with a rope and made her fast. The gangplank went down with a bang. We heard a loud voice give a command. And two by two, shoulder to shoulder, they began to march past us – what was left of the men who had been boys when – when we – last – saw – '

For some words Aunt Tryntje's voice had been trembling. It now stopped altogether. She wiped her eyes, blew her nose resolutely, and went on, 'Well, we didn't have any more of that celebration.' She turned to Adrian's father. 'Does thee remember, Adrian, how the band stopped playing . . . first one instrument and then another... ? I can see thy face now just as I saw it then.' Her voice failed. She tried again. 'I wish I could forget it!' . . . This time she did not go on at all.

After a silence, 'Well, what *did* you do,' asked Matey, 'if you didn't carry out the celebration?'

'Everybody cried,' said Aunt Tryntje, 'that was all. Everybody cried.'

'Why in the world did you cry, *then,*' asked Matey, 'when you had them safe back?'

The older people did not answer her.

From now on Matey did not omit to read the newspaper on account of raspberry jam. On August first the *Poughkeepsie Evening Enterprise* informed her that Germany and Russia had broken and that the price of Ford cars was to be cut. One piece of news was about as interesting to her as the other. What did she care about abstract ideas like Germany and Russia? Little Paul Vinet was not in the Russian army, was he? nor was Ziza's passionately loved husband in the German. The Vinets were always in her thoughts. She kept trying to imagine where they all were. Was Mme Vinet still in Louvain with Ziza? No, by this time she must be back in Paris with Henri.

The second of August was a Sunday. Newspapers were not delivered in Rustdorf on Sundays, and Matey, though the day seemed endless, would not acknowledge her anxiety enough to ask Adrian to go down to the station to buy one from a train.

On Monday, August third, she read in the headlines that 'Great Britain orders mobilisation' and that French troops had fought with Uhlans at Petit Croix. Where was Petit Croix? Where was Polo? She turned the page over and read, 'It is expected that France will declare war within a few hours.' 'Adrian! Adrian! It's not possible!'

But Adrian was not there. He had gone to work as usual. Everything went on as usual. Most people were much more interested in the cut in the price of Fords than in anything else, except a recurrence of an old hope of paving Washington Street. Matey laid down the paper and went about her own usual work. It was time to get the children in from play, washed, fed, and to bed. Brother addressed himself whole-heartedly to his food, but Petella asked, as she often did, for a story 'when you were a little girl, Mother,' and Matey told them about a jolly baby she had played with in France, 'the first baby I was ever acquainted with,' she said. 'I was like one of his big sisters, you know. He used to play peekaboo with us. And even then he always played fair and kept his eyes shut.'

She fed and undressed her children, with a kiss she tucked them up in their safe soft beds, she left them, and going out into her own bedroom, stood for a long time, one hand at her temple, staring at the floor, remembering Polo . . . how he had enjoyed Adrian's fun on that last visit.

The day went by. Matey varied between determined incredulity and moments of sudden physical sickness such as she had when she was pregnant.

Belgium refused to allow passage to the German troops.

'They're crazy!' said Adrian to his father.

'What else could they do!' he answered. 'That was one of the terms of the neutrality treaty. They signed that.'

On the day after that, Matey read, 'Belgium troops marching to frontier.'

All day she heard them marching.

That night she woke up with a cry.

'What is it?' asked Adrian. He flashed on the electric light. Matey, sitting up in bed, stared around the familiar room wildly. 'Oh, a dream,' she said.

She lay down again. Adrian turned out the light. She had thought she heard Ziza's voice screaming.

In the morning she asked, 'Adrian, how quickly you woke up! You had that light on instantly.'

'I wasn't asleep,' said Adrian. 'I was wondering where *le petit* Marceau is. He has three children now.'

And then began the advance into Belgium. How long did it last? It lasted till the end of Matey's youth. Day after day the headlines read, 'Liège battle still on,' 'Liège forts still holding,' 'Germans still held up at Liège.' Matey resolved that she would not again read a single world of the bloody description of the attack and defence, and every day read all of them. Liège fell. The headlines then read, 'Belgiums retreating on Antwerp.'

It was August 20th. A letter from Mme Vinet arrived. Matey wildly tore it open. It was a pleasant chatty letter, full of her return to Paris, how hot the train had been, and Henri

❦❦❦

had had the hall papered during her absence. She knew Matey would like the new paper, of which she enclosed a sample. Ziza's new baby was sweet, looked just as Polo had when . . .

Matey looked wildly at the date – July 21st. It had been almost a month on the way.

On August 24th the first account of German atrocities in Belgium was printed in the paper. Matey burned like a torch. Adrian's father said gravely to his son, 'War's always the same.'

Matey was furious. Partly because he would not talk to her. 'You don't mean to say, Padre,' she flared at him, 'that our American men in the Civil War . . . '

He looked at her strangely, an expression on his face she had never seen there before. 'Oh, there's no use talking about it,' he said, turning away.

That afternoon there was a regular meeting of the Rustdorf DAR chapter. It was Aunt Tryntje's turn to entertain them. (They were mostly old ladies, friends of hers.) Matey went across the Square to help out with the refreshments.

She found Aunt Tryntje turning over the pages of the immense album in which she kept old photographs. 'I got to thinking about Adrian, thy Adrian's father, in the war,' she explained over her shoulder as Matey came in. 'I thought I had a photograph of him in his stretcher-carrier's uniform, but I can't find it.'

Matey went to look over her shoulder. 'Who's that man?' she asked, pointing to the photograph of a bare-headed, bearded soldier standing in front of a tent.

'That's General Grant.'

Matey looked into the tragic eyes of the old photograph. 'It's *dreadful!*' she murmured. 'I never saw such a sad face in my life.'

'It was taken during the Battle of the Wilderness,' said Aunt Tryntje.

She turned over the page. In the moment before she turned another, Matey caught a glimpse of half a dozen faded photographs of battle scenes. Corpses in uniforms, scattered sand bags, thrown-down rifles lay scattered about the trenches. But these dead men did not shock her. They did not look real. Either they were so peacefully relaxed that they looked enviably asleep, or they were in grotesque and impossible attitudes so that they looked like nothing but badly stuffed rag dolls. They did not horrify her half as much as the steady patient misery in the eyes and on the lips of Grant.

'No, I can't find that photograph of Adrian,' said Aunt Tryntje, shutting the book.

'I've brought over some of those thin wafers,' said Matey, 'to serve with the lemonade. Rebecca made an extra lot the last time she was at the house.'

'They'll be nice,' said Aunt Tryntje.

Life slid forward in its usual grooves. Not another word had come from the Vinets, any of them. The papers reported civilian mail delayed. Where could they all be? Had Ziza escaped to Paris with her children? No, Matey did not see her in the crowds of refugees reported by the newspapers. Ziza would never leave her husband. *Je suis folle, folle, folle de mon mari!'* cried Ziza again to her old comrade. With perfect distinctness Matey now saw Ziza coming and going in the well-remembered pretty little Belgian suburban villa and felt herself sicken in the suspense which must be beating wildly in Ziza's breast.

'Come, come, this is hysterical,' thought the Matey who was sewing on the porch of her comfortable home, the locusts singing the old trees to sleep outside, her own children and Priscilla's little girls playing pussy-wants-a-corner with an astonishing degree of noisiness. 'This is melodramatic nonsense. I've lost my nerve. After all, this is the twentieth century, *voyons!*' (Her thoughts came to her often in French in those days.) 'There are trains and telephones and automobiles. And non-combatants are never involved in a modern war. Ziza's husband is older than mine, past military age. Only the young men with the colours will be expected to take part in a war. Adrien Conacq has probably long ago piled his wife and babies into their little motorcycle and side car and trundled them away from Louvain to Paris to stay with Mme Vinet till this preposterous business is over.' Ziza's American sister-friend looked up from her darning, calmed and reassured. Along the outdoor frieze flashed the spokes of the newsboy's bicycle. He reached his hand into the brown canvas bag slung on his handlebars. Riding with both hands free for an instant he folded an *Evening Enterprise* into a hard-twisted baton, and with a practised gesture slung it far into the Forts' front yard.

Matey walked out over the hot grass to pick it up.

'Mother, can we put on our bathing suits and play with the hose?' asked Petella from the side yard.

311

'Yes, if you want to,' said her mother absently, unrolling the paper. Halfway down the front page, among longer telegraphed dispatches, were two lines which read, 'Louvain wiped out. Its civilian population has almost ceased to exist.'

CHAPTER TWO

✾✾✾

Except for Adrian and his father, Matey now felt herself in the midst of perfect strangers, almost on a strange planet. Priscilla, as ever, was absorbed in her convert's fanaticism. As long as her little daughters had what they needed and were happy . . . ! And the others, these Rustdorf men and women, what could they be made of to go about as usual, cold and self-centred and hideously indifferent to suffering and death? They read the war news, it is true, they commented on it – she shuddered to hear the comments they made. They complained of the difficulty of pronouncing those queer-looking foreign names or even of remembering what they were from day to day. They said, 'I see the French government was moved to Bordeaux yesterday. Looks as though Paris was a goner, doesn't it? Isn't it terrible! My! Aren't we lucky to be out of it! I wish you'd save me some of the seed from those pansies, they're like we used to have years ago.' Matey loathed the sight of them, shallow, vegetating provincials . . . feeling herself of a superior race. She tried to cable Mme Vinet for news of Ziza – had she left Louvain in time? – and was told it was impossible to guarantee the arrival of any telegram with a French destination. No letter came.

'Germans only forty miles from the capital,' said the headlines. Matey sat up till all hours, reading. She read straight through page after page of the *Encyclopaedia*, wherever she chanced to open a volume, and never knew afterward which ones they had been. Every day now, if the newsboy who brought the Poughkeepsie paper was at all later than his usual time, she went down to the train which brought the afternoon papers from New York. On September 7th she was late. The papers were in. People stood about, reading. Matey pounced on the nearest man to her, the elderly owner of the iron factory. 'Mr DuBois!' she cried, 'What's the news?'

He lowered his paper and looked at her absently, recalling his mind from his reading with an effort. Then, 'Ah, Mrs Fort,' he said, smiling. 'How do *you* do, these days? Children all well, I hope.'

She was incapable of answering him. Her question reached his ear. 'The news?' he said vaguely, and then, 'Oh, yes, yes, Paris, of course. I hadn't looked yet.' Matey saw that he had been reading the financial page. Now he did look. 'Not taken yet,' he told her. He added gravely, with a deacon's intonation, 'How thankful we Americans should be to have no connection with all that.'

The next day the newsboy brought the afternoon paper early. Matey caught it from his hand, her heart standing still to see on the first page enormous headlines, the biggest, the blackest she had ever seen, three times as large as any *The Enterprise* had used before. They danced and wavered before her eyes. It had come. Mme Vinet too . . .

She held the paper off, trying to steady herself to read.

But the words were not 'Paris taken'. No, not at all. Matey made them out now. Like a startled yell they rang out from the paper:

POUGHKEEPSIE MAN SLAIN!

Among the lists of German soldiers killed in a battle with the Russians was, it seemed, the name of a man who had lived in Poughkeepsie for a time before going back to Germany; a man people had known; a real man, who only just now had been walking down Market Street like anybody. And he was dead. Killed. In broad daylight he had been thrust through with a bayonet by a man he had never seen before.

POUGHKEEPSIE MAN SLAIN!

shrieked the horrified printed voice, and all the Hudson valley woke to the knowledge that murder was being done.

Before even she looked to see the news from Paris, Matey was pierced as by a bayonet by her first deep intuitive understanding of something not personal to her. For an instant she saw that Rustdorf people were acting as they did according to a universal law – not because they were bad or inhuman, not even because they were indifferent, but because they did not see what was happening. As soon as ever they saw – !

But how was it possible that human beings could fail to see such events? The rebuking answer to that question lay written large in her own thick-skinned indifference to the 'thousand Austrians killed!' Could Mr DuBois himself be any more stone and ice to human agony than she? She began to understand what lies at the base of cruelty.

The instant of vision flashed and disappeared as her other first guesses at reality had come and gone. Her eyes leaped over the corpse of the slain Poughkeepsie man and ran hurriedly through the telegrams, looking for news of Paris.

On September 9th the headlines reported, 'Germans forced to change plans.'

On September 10th came the news of the battle of the Marne.

And a letter from Mme Vinet.

CHAPTER THREE

✡✡✡

The children were scuffling in the next room. Matey could hear some sort of heated discussion going on. But lively tilts between them were not uncommon. Petella was devoted to her little brother, but she often found him exasperating and contrary-minded, and he on his side was often wrought to frenzy by her big-sister attempts to bring him up. Their mother took this for one of such encounters, not serious, a mere part of the process of settling down to live together. She continued to rush about feverishly cleaning the dining room (the third time that week) and paid no attention to them till she heard Petella's voice saying urgently, 'No, *honest!* Brother, don't call her. *I'll* buckle it for you. She feels so bad – *you* know! – that baby she used to play peekaboo with . . . Let *me* do it for you!'

Matey stopped short. Where had Petella heard that? Did children know everything you tried to hide? She thought she had hidden from the children not only the news of Polo's death but all her fever of sorrow and anger and alarm. She had carefully come and gone about the house as usual, she had played with the children, she had sung to them. (But, oh! not the old French nursery songs she had sung with Polo and

Ziza!) She had kept a rigid grimace of cheerfulness on her face. She had been doing her duty, she thought, by keeping them shut out of her real life, by pushing them outside her door.

She had forgotten that she was Petella's mother and not her nurse and caretaker. But Petella had not forgotten. Matey began helplessly to cry. To think that her baby girl had been sorry for *her!* She knew that Petella had heard her and had pushed the door open. But she did not stop. She stood in the middle of the floor, her hands over her face, the first tears she had shed for the murdered Polo streaming down her face. She heard the child come in and felt about her knees the pressure of short arms, squeezing earnestly. She sat down on the floor and took her little girl into her arms, weeping more than ever – but not wholly now from sorrow.

Very dimly, calling in a faint voice from far in the past, came the question – had *her* mother, to protect her, shut her out so from her real life? And she had not known how to find her way in, like Adrian's deep-hearted little daughter. She had only run away to play – like Francis.

They cried a little while, Petella and her mother, hugging each other very hard, and ten minutes after, Petella had shed it from her five-year-old mind and was arguing with Brother about whose turn it was for a ride on the kiddie-car. Her mother was working again, but not so hysterically, capable now of noting the inimitably wheedling tone of Brother's soft little voice. He was once more getting around Petella.

During those days of suspense Matey could do nothing but work. There was not, she felt, work enough in the world to occupy her. 'No, Rebecca, leave that. I'll do it,' she said over and over. She could not bear her piano. A note struck by chance on it by the children made her wince. She could not bear to go to Meeting. She had never found in the Quaker 'silences' more than quiet and rest and occasionally a vague but comforting sense of a greater, more powerful current of life in which she was sharing. Now those long pauses were filled with sights and sounds which appalled her. Incessant activity of the most primitive kind was the only screen between her and the sight of Paul Vinet as his mother saw him in the hospital where he died, armless, blinded, mutilated beyond her recognition – little Polo! the harmless, loveable boy . . . It was almost with a recurrent cry that she sprang upon scrubbing-brush and broom to shield herself from that sight. But she only sprang into a wave of terrified surmise about Ziza and her children. It was almost worse not to know what had happened to them than to know as with Polo. At least he lay in his grave, safe from further tortures. Not a word had reached Mme Vinet from Ziza. Henri's summons had come, he had joined his regiment and perhaps now lay on a battlefield – Matey thought, 'like one of those tumbled corpses in Aunt Tryntje's photographs'– Mimi's husband, obese and middle-aged, was with the reserves, who were digging trenches all across the north of France. Mimi was to stay with her boys in the house at La Ferté-en-Valois to do what she could to keep the business together. 'La Ferté of course, so far to the interior, is perfectly safe.' So wrote Mme Vinet in mid-August. By the time Matey read the letter, La Ferté too had been engulfed and swept down to the abyss. Had Mimi left in time? Had she been caught like Ziza? Where were those little rosy boys of hers? Mimi had not Ziza's vitality. She never would survive a great shock.

'Petella, is that the mailman?' her mother called out a dozen times a day. In the midst of her restless misery it comforted her that she did not need to keep a company face for Petella.

Another letter came. Petella stood by anxiously, halving her mother's fright by sharing it. Matey raced through the first page and sent her daughter away happy with the news that the little boys who lived in La Ferté were all right. Yes, Mimi had been caught by the tide of invasion, had lived through the passage of the Germans' advance and retreat. The house had been ransacked and fouled, some of the furniture had been carried away, but no harm done to Mimi or the little boys beyond a week of deadly fear and venomous hate. Mimi was sticking it out in La Ferté to try to keep the business going. Most of the workmen were mobilised, of course, but she was using the older ones. Her oldest boy was thirteen, old enough to help her a little at the factory.

At the factory! The soft, well-served, domesticated Mimi trying to understand business accounts! Soiling her white fingers with machinery! Mimi, who had never been able to endure with steadiness even the most sheltered life. It was unthinkable to Matey. 'Mimi writes that she must save what she can out of the wreck for her children's future,' wrote Mme Vinet. ('Of course Mimi would feel so. Any mother would,' said Priscilla when Matey read this letter to her.)

❦❦❦

Mme Vinet had not in the least given Ziza up in spite of the terrible silence from Louvain. She wrote: 'I can feel that she is still alive. And if she is, as soon as she can escape she will come home. I hear her knocking as soon as I drop off to sleep. Last night I sprang out of bed and ran to open the door three or four times. I must not leave the apartment for more than an hour at a time. She may come at any moment. Providentially, the Government has declared a moratorium on rents. If I had to pay rent I should not be able to stay here. Henri's salary has stopped, of course. Mimi's husband is practically ruined. I have no music lessons – oh, what a chaos of mean and tragic miseries, my Mété!'

At the end of this letter, 'We can't be thankful enough, can we, Matey, that *our* children are safe and all right,' said Priscilla earnestly.

CHAPTER FOUR

Along with all the rest of the world, Matey passed into the next phase – the phase when nothing different happened – into a state of suspended animation in which it seemed at first she could not live another day, a condition which all wise experts, financial, political, military, economic, said could not last another day, and which lasted on, week after week, month after month.

Henri still lived. During the first period of maladjustment in the army he had been put back into the place in the regiment – in the line, as a common soldier – which had been his years before, as a young man during his military service. He had gone through three battles, receiving 'only' a slash in the face, which was superficial and treated on the field. Now, as some glimmerings of order began to appear, he had been assigned to semi-clerical work; at the front, but not actually in the trenches, not charging with a bayonet. Adrian had had word from *le petit* Marceau, his old comrade. He had long ago, as completely as Adrian, given up painting for bourgeois life, and earned a comfortable living as a travelling salesman for a large silk manufactory in Lyons. Like Henri he had been sent at first into the front-line troops, but was now, like other men past thirty, transferred to 'lighter' service. In his case it was carrying stretchers along the front lines, to pick up wounded and carry them back to the dressing stations. *'Imaginez-vous!'* he wrote to Adrian in surprise, 'that one of the sections of automobile ambulances which take the wounded from the first dressing-shelters back to the hospitals are American Fords, driven by young Americans. I call that *chic!* Lads who could be at home in comfort with their girls. *And not even their expenses paid!'* Matey could not repress an involuntary smile over the French 'realism' of that last underlined exclamation. Mimi was struggling on in La Ferté, trying to learn to manufacture plumbing fixtures with a working force of old and infirm men. She had been able, finally, late in October, to make a flying trip to Paris, to see her mother. 'There is grey in her hair,' Mme Vinet reported, 'at thirty-two. She looks like someone else. A Mimi I never saw.' They had decided, the two women who were the only members of the family who could come together for a council, that at all costs Mme Vinet should keep the apartment, in case Ziza might even then be struggling toward that refuge. 'We hear now that it is not safe to trust to a moratorium for rent, because it will be ruinous after the war is over to pay the accumulation. But I have things I can sell. My mother's Indian shawl will bring in quite a sum. And that little Greek statuette presented to my husband by his old students, I could probably find a purchaser for that.'

Her American foster-daughter saw her sitting alone in the old home fighting down grief and fear and looking about her to see what pounds of flesh would be saleable. That letter brought Matey for the first time a possibility of relief. All that day she was turning over this possible escape from the horror of her own inaction, trying to think of words that would do to begin to speak of it to Adrian.

While Matey cleared the supper table Adrian usually went upstairs with the children, told them a story or two while they undressed, and sat between their beds while they fell asleep. That night she did not hear him come down. She finished and went into the living room. It was smiling warmly with lights and books and the sea-coal fire, but Adrian was not there. Looking out, she saw in the light from the street lamp that he was pacing up and down the front walk, his hands in his overcoat pockets. She snapped off the electric lights, put on a wrap, and went out, Mme Vinet's letter in her hand, desperation in her heart.

When he saw her coming he said in a constrained tone as though he owed her an apology, 'I couldn't settle down indoors.'

Matey slipped her arm through his. They began to walk up and down together, coming as they approached the street into a circle of white light, stepping into deeper and deeper darkness on the way back toward the house. Matey was asking herself, 'How can I begin? With what words can I – ' Adrian said in an uncertain tone, so low that she could scarcely hear his voice, 'I haven't said much to you about it before, Matey – I – I had another letter from Marceau today – I don't suppose you can realise how it makes a man feel to – ' Forgetting her, he burst out loudly, 'It makes a man feel like a *dog* to be wallowing here in comfort and safety, while . . . other men, old friends, old comrades . . . '

Matey felt as if he had struck her, and instantly struck back at him in a reflex of anger. 'How do you think it makes a woman feel? You think it's perfectly all right and natural, I suppose, for a woman to be in a position that makes a man feel like a dog?'

Their vehemence had stopped them short. In the light from the street lamp Matey examined her husband's face as if he were an enemy, resentment burning darkly in her eyes.

There was no answering resentment in Adrian's face, rather an expression of apology. 'I ought to have known you'd feel it too,' he said, 'but I've been wrapped up in my own problems . . . yes, I can see now that it must be worse for a woman . . . she has to stand it without even the consolation of thinking there's anything she might do about it.'

Matey stared at him, her resentment mixed with astonishment at his grim accent and the set lines of his face. 'Why, Adrian, what could you possibly do any more than I? As much as I? You aren't thinking . . . even if you were French you wouldn't fight?'

'Matey, I don't know! I can't tell you how hellishly I go round and round between what I believe and what seems necessary. . . . I don't know what I'd do if I were French . . . it's all out of the question anyway. I didn't mean to say anything about it . . . but if I weren't married, if it weren't for leaving you and the children . . . No, I don't suppose I'd fight, though that would be the logical thing to do – the way I feel. No.' He laughed unsteadily. 'I suppose I'd compromise, try to help out somehow, short of actually taking my share . . . there's the

Belgian relief . . . and Marceau mentioned those ambulances. *I* can drive a Ford.'

Matey took his hand in hers as they walked, and said, pressing home her words as though they were swords, 'Adrian, where do you think *I* would have been by this time if I had not been married?'

It was Adrian's turn to be astonished. 'Why, what could you do?' he echoed. 'There are plenty of women – poor things – to look out for everything that can be done behind the lines.'

'Most of them are busy trying to earn a living for their babies and their old people!' All the passionate accumulation of her thoughts burst out. She told him of what was in Mme Vinet's last letter. 'Of all her children, she hasn't one with her. . . . I am like one of her daughters, I owe her much of whatever it is one owes a mother. She hasn't any money to live on, she can't keep the apartment there for Ziza perhaps to come to, without more money. And we have Aunt Connie's. She writes in every letter of being swamped in trying to help destitute refugees – with nothing but the clothes on their back – half-crazy some of them – all women and children and old men. That's woman's work. Why should I wallow here in safety and comfort any more than you?'

Adrian reminded her in a horrified voice, 'But, Matey – the children!'

'They're your children as much as mine,' she said steadily, and loosed her hand from his, walking at his side, waiting.

After a startled look into her face, Adrian turned his eyes away. They paced up and down silently. Her demand was something so new for him. She saw now with patience how new it was for any man. She could feel how long it lay on the surface of his mind before he could let it in.

In her heart she was saying over and over passionately, 'Let me in. Let me in. We are man and wife.' She thought, 'This must be the way religious people pray.' And later, 'This is perhaps prayer.'

Presently, as they turned again from the house out toward the lighted street, Adrian had come to the point of being able to say, not contentiously but more in his usual voice, with an Adrian-like wish to consider everything fairly, 'But, Matey – look here – how *could* we both? The children have *got* to be . . . I don't see . . . '

'I don't see either,' said Matey. 'That's what . . . What I want is to think about it together, instead of separately!' She took his hand again.

They marched off toward the future, looking for the path together. They walked out toward the world and turned back toward the children, over and over, up and down the old flagstones of the old path.

It was now very late. The street light went out. A thin moon showed itself palely through the elms, rose higher, and shone more brightly as they walked and talked. The mere fusing of their overwrought nerves brought – miracle of human fellowship! – more quiet, more steadiness than either had known for months. They went round and round the situation, pushing against every locked door, trying the strength of every bar. Time and again they put away the whole idea as madness, only to return immediately to considering possible ways and means. Aunt Connie's money – yes, they could use that – if they had the right to endanger their one small nest egg of capital. From the money they passed to talking of Aunt Connie, feeling as never before the meaning of her frustrated life. 'She must have walked up and down here, right up and down this very street, as raging to use herself to some purpose as we are now. But all alone! Never any mate, never any comrade! She never did find a way out.'

'It takes two,' said Adrian, 'to find a way out. A real two at that.'

They looked across to Aunt Connie's house, where Priscilla slept beside her foster-children. Matey said, 'How shallow-minded I was about Priscilla's marriage! I'd forgotten about Aunt Connie's fate. I never see the real sense of things at first.'

'There are all sorts of ways of being shut out from life,' said Adrian. 'Priscilla isn't as bad as some.'

'Adrian, I feel as though Aunt Connie were walking up and down with us right here, telling us to take her money and go. She'd *want* us to.'

'Well, that's one way of putting it,' admitted Adrian. 'What would she say about taking the children, I wonder?'

'I tell you one thing,' said Matey with conviction, 'if Aunt Connie had lived with Petella for five years as we have, she'd know the child wouldn't want to be left out of a chance to help.'

'What in the world could a child of that age . . . ?'

'When you *live* with a person, even a child, you *know*,' said Matey. She felt that Adrian thought this a womanish notion, and tried to think of specific proofs. Were those incidents of child life anything a man would call 'proofs'? Could you reason so from small to great? Yes, you could. Most of what understanding she had, had come to her from the light cast on great events by small ones. 'Well, anyhow I know!' she repeated.

Adrian put the question aside. 'Probably it's not so life-and-death as we think,' he suggested. 'The war can't last long – six months at the outside. You and they'd be safe enough in Paris.'

They went on to talk of details, of letters to be written, enquiries to be made. Matey interrupted this planning to make a confession. 'Look here, Adrian, I musn't set up to be any less self-centred than you. It hadn't occurred to me you might be feeling it as I did. If I'd spoken first I'd have left you out too, I'm afraid. I couldn't think of *anything* but – '

'I know, I know,' said Adrian, 'civilisation going to the scrapheap and – '

'No, I wasn't feeling anything thoughtful and abstract like that,' Matey interrupted. 'I don't feel that way now. I know all that. But I don't feel it. If it hadn't been for the Vinets I wouldn't have felt it any more, probably, than – old Mr DuBois.'

'Oh, as far as that goes, I too,' said Adrian humbly. 'I've a lot of old friends in the French army myself.'

They went back to their equal-to-equal talk of ways and means, talk of action which, vague though it was, drew out some of the poison from their inaction.

Once, as they halted for a moment under the old beech tree, something very tiny and light eddied down from the darkness of the branches. Matey put up her hand to see what it could be. Dandelion fluff could not be flying in November. It was a tiny downy feather. 'From an owl, perhaps,' said Adrian dreamily. Their excitement and tension had slowly poured out through their hope to act and left them in a tired tranquillity.

For a time as they walked and talked Matey held this morsel of down between her fingers. It was so fine and small she could scarcely feel it. And yet – she held it up when the moon shone out brightly – every one of its clustering hundreds of fronds was fringed with flawless symmetry. 'How can it be so infinitely perfect – so infinitely small,' she wondered, musingly.

'There's no big or little in infinity, is there?' said Adrian.

She blew it from her finger and watched it settle to the earth through the still, cold night air.

The moon sank behind the house. They still walked up and down, hand in hand. Finally it sank behind the hills across the Hudson. And yet they were not in darkness. They looked around and saw their old home world standing steadily about them.

'We've walked the night out, sweetheart,' said Adrian. 'This is the dawn.'

CHAPTER FIVE

✷✷✷

When Francis wrote, as he did in February, Matey thought wildly, 'I don't care if he is my brother. This is too much!'

What had been in his hurried note was the advice to put every penny she and Priscilla could lay their hands on into Steel. 'Fortunes are going to be made there. This war is going to last lots longer than most people think. The European factories can't begin to supply their demands. It's a wonderful new market. Every American manufacturer who's got anything to sell is going to make money. They say the people in the foodstuffs business feel the upward pull already. But steel products! That's what Europe's going to need most, of course, arms and ammunition. Emily's sister is married to one of the steel men here, so we get the inside dope. If you take that little nest egg Aunt Connie left you out of the savings-bank and put it into Steel you'll be on Easy Street, take it from me. Emily and I are selling everything – we've even put a big mortgage on the house – and buying stock. Common, you understand. Don't buy preferred. It's the common that's going to soar.'

Matey tore this letter up angrily. It was one of the things

about Francis she did not tell Adrian. She thought, 'I feel as if I never wanted to see him again!'

Yet the next time her brother came, she ran with a cry of pity to put her arms around his neck. For nine days Francis had had a little daughter. And now she was dead. So much his sisters had learned from a letter written them by an aunt of his wife's. The very next day Francis stumbled up the steps to Matey's door. She opened to his knock, she looked into her brother's face –'Why, Francis! *Francis!*' she cried.

They went down the street to Priscilla's. 'I just wanted to see you girls,' said Francis pitifully, taking Matey's hand as they walked over the glittering gaiety of the sunlit snow. 'Seemed as if it would do me good to see you. I never left my little girl, Matey. I stayed right there in the hospital. They thought a blood transfusion would save her, perhaps. They took mine.'

When they reached Priscilla's he went on talking, although his lips shook so that he could scarcely form the words. 'They took my blood for her, Priscilla. She was the nicest little kid! At first I couldn't think who she looked like. But after a while – do you remember how Matey looked when she was a baby, Priscilla? Sort of wide between the eyes? That's how my poor little girl looked. I was going to get a dog for her. Matey always took so much comfort in that old dog. You were an awfully nice kid, Matey. *She'd* have been – I sat there planning what I'd do for her. And – only nine days! I couldn't believe it when the poor little thing stopped breathing. You girls are all I've got in the world of my own, now.' He began frankly to cry, reduced to childishness by grief and sleeplessness and loss of blood.

His sisters, shocked and compassionate, got him food, got him to bed, cared for him as though he had been a sick person, and sent a telegram saying he was safe with them, to that aunt of Emily's who had written them. Since Emily was in the hospital, ill, this was the only name and address they had.

He fell asleep soon, his mouth sagging wearily, peace at last on his tear-reddened eyelids. Matey, looking in at him, shuddered. Suppose she had already quarrelled with him about that letter, had shut her door against him! How touching he looked, defenceless, appealing, human! Calamity had brought to the surface a Francis she had never known. So it had been for her father! How different they both would have been, if there had been more pain and sorrow in their lives! But they were so competent in avoiding pain. Her head ached with trying to understand. She could get no further now than understanding that deprivation like Aunt Connie's was not the only thing that frustrated what might have come to be. Success, too, could check growth. How terrible if she had already shut him out! How like her, to feel so angry at him just the first time he needed her!

Bewildered, always wrong Matey! She was discouraged by the steepness of the uphill road that led from her childish hardness towards a little understanding of the rich complexity of life. It seemed to her that she stood still, never advanced at all unless swept forward – why, like Francis! like her father! – by a blow, by calamity.

Francis slept almost twenty-four hours, and when he woke, a little refreshed though still weak and sad, 'I must get back to Emily,' he said. 'Where's a timetable?'

Matey abased herself remorsefully with the resolve never to forget that his first thought was for his wife.

At the station, pacing together soberly up and down the snow-covered platform, he and his sisters, freed from themselves for a moment, had a talk such as they had never known.

'Father and Mother lost their first child, too,' said Francis. 'Mother always thought it was a judgment on them. It was a little boy.'

'I never heard about a first child!' said Matey.

'No, Father never talked to you girls as much as he did to me. You were always hard on them, Matey, in your way. I've often thought you and Priscilla held them off – '

'Held them off!' cried Priscilla.

'Well, anyhow, after you grew up, you didn't make it easy for them to feel close to you, you know you didn't.'

Priscilla laid an unconsciously dramatic hand on her heart and stared beyond her brother at her past.

'I've always wanted to talk to you about them. But *you* know – it's not easy to begin. And you girls always took everything so hard. Maybe now you're married yourselves – *they* were all right, Father and Mother were! Fitted each other. I know they never did get it settled which one was going to be kingpin. But scrapping over that kept them up to the mark. Scrapping's what keeps people fit, anyhow. Suppose Mother'd been the soft, resigned kind of woman. Inside of three years Father wouldn't have been fit to live with. It does a man *good* to have to fight to keep his end up. Fighting's the law of life. And faithful to each other – ! There was a Mrs Whitlock in Logan Bluffs – no, Hamilton it was – you were probably too young to take it in, Matey, and it was after you left, Priscilla. Well, she fairly threw herself at Father's head. Rich, too. But did he dream of taking her seriously? Not on your life. And Mother knew that. She never had to worry a single minute about her husband's being taken with another woman.' He looked at his sisters, astonished at their lack of response, 'Great Scott, girls! what more can a woman ask!'

They found no answer.

'And Mother too . . . I bet the first girl Father was engaged to wouldn't have had the nerve to keep him up to his best as Mother. . . . You did know, didn't you, that he was engaged to another girl when he met Mother? That was one of the things that made them so – '

'No!' cried Matey.

They had not noticed that the train was there, the wind of the locomotive's passage blowing their long skirts about.

'Another time …' said Francis, kissing his sisters. But they knew this was the only time. 'All I wanted anyhow was to sort of stand up for them a little, and to tell you, Matey, don't be so *hard* on folks!'

He was gone. His astounded sisters looked into each other's eyes. But a neighbour of theirs had left the train, a DAR member. She walked home between Mrs Fort and Mrs Russell, telling them about an eighteenth-century letter, sent back from England recently to the Dutchess County Historical Society, which gave an irate account of how the soldiers of the Revolution, camped at Fonteynkill, had taken the rail fences for miles around for their camp cooking and had even stripped off the siding from the Reformed Church as high as they could reach. Matey thought, 'When we get to the house and are all by ourselves, Priscilla and I must – '

'That's why the lower clapboards of the Fonteynkill Church are of a later period!' explained Mrs Deyo.

As the three passed the bank, Adrian raised a window and called, 'Matey, come in a minute, will you?'

Priscilla went on with Mrs Deyo. Adrian came out on the walk bareheaded although the cold was intense. He held an open letter in his hand. 'I've got the answer from the New York office of that ambulance service,' he said to his wife. Matey read its few lines in one glance. Looking at each other silently, the Forts made their decision.

CHAPTER SIX

✟✟✟

Two months later, when they announced their plans, the young Forts expected to stand quite alone when the storm of horrified disapproval broke over them. But to their surprise, at least to Matey's, Adrian's father stepped quietly over to their side out of the crowd of protesting prudent people who had ordinary good sense. On the evening when they first told him he said nothing at all. He listened through to the last word of their somewhat agitated explanation of their plan. After they had said everything over twice, he sat a long time thinking, his eyes closed, his grey head propped on one hand. Sharing that silence with him, they felt something of his quietness come into their troubled hearts. Matey thought, 'It's like letting turbid water stand still till it clears itself.'

Finally he lifted his head, looked at them, smiled, shook his head, and said, 'I'll have to have more time, I'm afraid,' and putting on his hat and coat, he let himself out of the house. Two days later he came in, and finding his daughter-in-law, told her, 'I'm glad Adrian is not going alone.'

'Oh, Padre!' said Matey, thanking him with a look. She asked him timidly then, longing for his approval, not hoping for it, 'Padre, about taking the children – it's not – I know they would be safe here with you and Priscilla – but – '

Struggling with herself, she tried vainly to break her silence about the moral atmosphere of her childhood. 'I think the risk of – I feel – ' She looked away from his attentive eyes and said in low shamed voice. 'I learned when I was a little girl that *anything* is better than letting a barrier grow up between parents and children.'

He waited a moment before he answered. She ventured a hurried glance at him and saw in his face a silent fatherly compassion.

When he spoke he humanely made no reference to the words wrung from her, answering her in a judicial tone, 'Petella and little Adrian are human beings as well as children. Older people are apt to forget that. Why should we take for granted that if they knew what the choice was, they would, any more than you and Adrian, prefer safety and comfort to . . . '

'Oh, yes, yes!' cried Matey. 'That's just what I felt, but I didn't know how to put it.'

Adrian's father used rather steadily his ability to 'put' it from the time his children's plans were known until they were gone. One such talk of his helped her over the worst, Priscilla's feeling. He met Priscilla one day going out of the Fort house, crying as though there had been a death in the family. 'I can't *stand* their going!' she told him.

'I don't think they'll regret it,' he said moderately. Inside the house (it was April then, and the windows were open) Matey stood to listen.

'But the children, Mr Fort!'

'I doubt if the children will ever regret it, either.'

'Regret it! . . . Will they live through it to have any opinion!'

'There must be several million children of their age in France,' said Mr Fort. 'Matey made enquiries about supplies, milk and schools and everything. Mme Vinet reports everything near enough normal for health.'

Priscilla redoubled her protests. 'Honestly, Mr Fort, it seems to me wickedly wrong, to do anything that might in any way be a disadvantage to your children!'

'Ah, there are various kinds of disadvantages,' Mr Fort reminded her. 'Perhaps when they grow up, to know that they did not stand in the way of a generous-hearted action of their parents but shared it will be no disadvantage.'

Priscilla caught at the word 'generous'. 'You mustn't think I'm – Francis has perhaps written you that – It's *not* the money. I wouldn't care a bit if Matey gave every cent of Aunt Connie's money to them . . . just sent it to Mme Vinet by the first mail. But to . . . '

'Do you suppose Mme Vinet would accept it?' asked Mr Fort. 'Self-respecting people retain their self-respect, I imagine, even in wartimes. If you were alone, in distress, two of your children gone, the others in danger, yourself in want, how would you feel if Matey just sent money to you? Is there any decent way to give money except to give yourself with it? And anyhow, I haven't the faintest idea that the war *can* last much longer. I expect them back in the autumn. The children will get a good French accent out of it.'

Priscilla was outraged by his lack of heroics. 'Mr Fort, how *can* you! Those darling babies. You're their *grandfather!*'

'I'm Adrian's father, too,' Mr Fort reminded her. 'You must remember that I too couldn't stand it to be safe. I ran away to be a . . .'

'But you weren't *married* and a father!'

'It will be a sorry day,' said Mr Fort, energetically, for the first time losing his implacable patience, 'when getting married and becoming a parent puts an end to being a member of humanity!'

For an instant Matey feared he had gone too far and criticised too plainly Priscilla's ingrowing maternity. It was all she had salvaged, and it was natural – it was perhaps essential – that she should think it all there was to be had.

After her sister had gone, she went out on the porch to thank her father-in-law. 'It's wonderful, Padre, how you know what to answer them, every time,' she said gratefully. She wished she dared give him a hug, as she did to Adrian when her feelings overflowed. But that was one of the things you did not do to the cool old Quaker. So she went on, straining words to make them say what a hug would have said, 'We just wouldn't have the courage to do this if it weren't for you, Padre.'

'Oh, yes, you would,' he drily corrected her sentimental overstatement. And nodding, went on his way.

Matey looked after him, abashed, nettled, respectful. 'Every word of his is fresh from the mind, full value,' she reflected, 'but I know what Dirck Davis's wife objects to in them!'

She and Adrian felt better, calmer, quieter, now that it was decided. Matey went back to her piano, and never played so much for her father-in-law as in the period when the last preparations were being made, their tickets bought, the manner arranged for Adrian's father to forward to them the necessary instalments of Aunt Connie's money.

Francis's wife had had a relapse and was so ill he could not leave her. But he wrote. Matey held the letter in her hand a long time. She remembered the use he had wished her to make of Aunt Connie's money. But she remembered too how softened her heart had been on his last visit, and how startled she had been to learn that Francis had been, all during their youth, more tolerant than she. Or was it only that he had been more insensitive? Or were those two ways of saying the same thing? At any rate he was her brother. She laid the unopened letter on the fire and wrote to him, 'I didn't read your letter, Francis. I knew what would be in it, and what's the use? Be good to Priscilla while we're gone. And don't let's ever ever forget that we grew up together.'

He wrote to Adrian then. 'Francis thinks we're perfect soft-hands,' reported Adrian, knowing nothing of the first letter, 'fooled by all this "pro-Ally guffs", as he calls it, about France and Belgium being martyred nations. He says that invasion of Belgium is what any modern nation would have done, and that the war isn't anything but a commercial scheme to ruin Germany because she's efficiently industrial. *You* know! *That* line!'

His father nodded his familiarity with that line.

But Matey did not know it at all and said so. 'My goodness, why bring in political economy? Does he think we're going because . . . why, I'd like to tell him that if it was a German family that I loved as much as the Vinets, and owed as much to, I'd go to Germany just as . . . '

'Well, *I* wouldn't!' said Adrian. 'You've got another guess coming if you think that's the way I feel. I'm going to do my share to help France win the war, and don't you forget it!'

'You're a better Friend than your husband,' the older Adrian said to his daughter-in-law.

'See here, Father,' his own son challenged him, 'you weren't so impartial yourself. Would you just as soon have joined the Confederate medical corps as the Federal? You know you wouldn't.'

His father's face darkened. Matey remembered he had never said a word about those three years of his life. There was a silence. Then: 'When I went away from home I wouldn't. After the first battle . . . ' He got up, a strange expression in his eyes. 'It's one of the things there's no use talking about,' he said roughly, walking away.

Matey was not always as sure as her words. There were mornings when she woke up thunderstruck by their madness in even thinking of taking the children away from physical safety. On such a day Francis came to see her. He did not exclaim or reproach or protest. He simply talked the plainest sort of common sense.

'What do you think you can do, Matey,' he asked, 'to help the cause of the Allies? You and the children will be only more mouths to feed, more dependents to look after. Let Adrian go if he thinks he ought to. This is no job for women and children. You're not cut out for a *vivandière* anyhow.'

'But there are women and children there, Francis, who need what a woman could – '

'Now, Matey, use the old bean a little. France is a rich modern country. Don't you think she'll take care of her own without help from Rustdorf in Dutchess County? What good do you suppose a woman and two young children are going to do? You're not any wonder of strength yourself, you know, with those sick headaches of yours.'

Matey thought. 'I did use to have sick headaches! I wonder when they stopped?' To Francis she said, 'I'm perfectly well and strong now, Francis, much better than when I was a girl.'

'Use your strength to take care of your own children then,' he told her with his first severity. 'How anybody who *has* a child to look out for . . . '

Matey knew what he was thinking of and said nothing.

He went on, 'It's not surprising that you are carried away almost hysterically by this. That's the trouble with you home-keeping women, when you *do* make an exception and take some interest in public matters you haven't anything to judge by. Nothing in your sheltered lives corresponds to the realities of the great world, of course. Take it from me, there is not a pennyworth to choose between the two sides in this war. They are all in it for what they can get out of it, and they all brought it on themselves. The thing for Americans to do is to let them stew in their own juice. For heaven's sake, why get into the mess when we *are* out of it, in a safe place – '

His voice went on, for a moment Matey no longer heard the words. The rug of her living room turned into bare barn boards and on them a hapless, blindfolded, befooled little boy staggered about, reaching out desperately into vacancy for the comrades who must be there if he could only find them.

✲✲✲

That night she told Adrian, 'Francis was here today.'

'What did he say?'

'A lot of unanswerable common sense. I hadn't a word to say for myself.'

Adrian looked at her hard.

'Now I'm *really* sure we ought to go,' she said. 'I won't doubt it again.'

Adrian's father was the last of their own they saw on the dock as their steamer pulled out. He had put his by no means new hat on the end of his umbrella and was waving it absurdly at them as though they were off for a summer vacation. Matey could scarcely see him through her tears as she put away in her memory his last words to her.

Standing beside her on the deck, while Adrian at the other end of the ship showed the children how the donkey-engine worked, he said in his inimitably natural voice, 'Matey, I'm nearly seventy, you know, and the Forts are not long-lived. I fully expect to be here when you come back, but it's possible that I may not be. I don't mention that because it's of any consequence, of course. A few years more or less . . . ! But it *would* be a pity if I let you go without making sure that you know what you have been to me. It's not only that I've seen you grow from a nice girl into a deep-hearted woman who's the best wife I could imagine for my son. But for me . . . I'd thought I'd go down to my grave, always feeling the emptiness left by the death of my little girl. Yet you have filled it. I *have* had a daughter after all.'

Matey forgot her shyness of him then, put her arms around

344

him and kissed him with all her heart. She longed to tell him that she who had missed having a father, perhaps by her own fault, had found one after all. But deeply moved as she was, she could think of no words that would not sound theatrical. She was so much more fluent than he and could say so much less.

Now as the ship was slowly leaving the dock, she could only wave her handkerchief at his small lean elderly figure, and strain her ears to hear what last greeting he was shouting to Petella, who, Adrian clutching at her skirts, leaned herself half across the railing, shouting excitedly, confusedly, 'Goodbye, Padre! *Good*bye! Come again! *Good*bye!'

'What did Padre call out to you the last thing?' asked her mother.

'Oh, he just hollered, "Be a good girl, Petella!" '

He never bothered about what words to use, thought Matey. Any words would do for him.

CHAPTER SEVEN

✣✣✣

They passed at once from a world where their action had
been melodrama to a world where it was a commonplace.
But few Americans were in the second class with them. The
first class was almost deserted. People with money enough to
travel in comfort naturally stayed away from France because
of the trouble there. It was, of course, the trouble there that
was taking back the second-class passengers. The men, mostly
no longer young, were going to help out women relatives
left manless, to get in the crops, to hold small businesses
together till the head could get back from the front; to do, in
short, what there was no one to help Mimi do. Many of the
plain, self-supporting women were doing just what Matey was
doing, going back to take with service and money the place
of members of the family dead, or buried alive in the regions
occupied by the Germans. No one thought it surprising that
the Forts were going back to France, too. Matey's French made
them suppose that she was a French-woman married to an
American. 'But perhaps your husband is of French parentage,
too? Adrian Fort. There was a family of Forts living down the
street from us in Noyon. He is perhaps related to them?' The

✣✣✣

Rustdorf, accepted, taken for granted, sank unnoticed into the second-class passenger list. Adrian asked his wife, 'What in thunder made us wait so long?'

The first part of the trip was fine, sunny and quiet. People walked up and down the decks or took the May sunshine in steamer chairs, played shuffleboard, flirted and gossiped as if it were any crossing. Matey and Adrian smiled shamefacedly a good many times at the beating on the emotional drum which had preceded their departure. The children were enchanted with the new experience, and Brother was enchanted with the new language. He inhaled and exhaled it as if it were air, embellishing his baby-talk English with scraps of baby-talk French which sent his father into fits of laughter. *'Mon dieu!'* exclaimed Brother, dressing himself with difficulty on the floor of their cabin, *'Mon dieu!* I dot my left slipper on my wight *pied.'* His language had a great success. As he trotted about the deck, people stopped him to hear this bilingual babble. Petella, on the other hand, suffered Anglo-Saxon agonies of self-consciousness. At the very idea of saying a word in the strange language she felt and looked wild. But she was very proud of Brother's French, and Matey often heard her showing it off to bystanders.

Halfway across, talk of a submarine attack began. Before they left it had been considered certain that passenger ships would never be attacked. There was a rumour among the passengers of a French armed ship being sent to convoy them through dangerous waters. Anxious eyes searched the ocean. Portholes were darkened. No one was allowed to strike a match on deck at night. A notice appeared in each cabin warning passengers to have their lifebelts at hand. It no longer seemed in the least like vacation travel. No one made any pretence of enjoying danger. Matey woke up a good many times during the last nights out and lay listening to the vibration of the ship's engines till they seemed the pulse of her own being, the mysterious rhythm which was driving her forward over a dark sea to an unknown destination.

She recognised this thought as one which Adrian's father would feel an impulse to deflate. 'How he takes the dramatic quality out of things!' she told herself impatiently. Later she perceived that his dry coolness was enemy only to melodrama, and that deflating its falsity, he allowed the real drama to emerge. 'As if it were only *now* that I am driven by a mysterious rhythm to an unknown destination!' she thought.

Late one evening the ship came into the mouth of the Garonne. The passengers were told they would dock at Bordeaux early the next morning. Everyone packed before going to bed. Matey was tired and fell asleep as soon as she lay down in her berth. The children had long been tucked away in their upper bunks.

She woke to a sensation of panic. There was not a sound. Why was this stillness so death-like? Oh, the engines had stopped! No wonder she felt as though her own pulse were stilled. A thud of feet came along the corridor. Someone rapped on their door. 'Yes,' said Adrian, springing up to open. Out of the dark a voice said hurriedly in French. 'We are in a minefield. The captain has ordered the ship stopped till dawn, hoping she will lie quiet enough not to strike against one. Everyone is to dress and have his lifebelt at hand. *No lights.*' The feet went thudding down the corridor, a knock on the next door, *'Qu-est-ce-que-c'est?'* in a startled voice from behind the door.

Matey and Adrian groped for their clothes, dressed, and decided to let the children sleep. 'If we need to, you can carry Brother, and I'll take Petella. They'd better sleep if they can,' said Adrian.

They sat down on Adrian's berth. And waited. Matey thought, 'Now I shall know whether I can endure fear.'

Adrian took her hand. 'Are you afraid, dear?'

She began, 'Not so much, oh, not near so much as – ' and was silent.

It was true. This was not her first encounter with fear. She had met it years ago, and what she felt now could not be compared to that black helpless waiting for catastrophe of the child she had been, tragically unfortified, like all children, by experience. Nothing had then come into her life strong enough to stand between her and her fear – over the oatmeal, bitter as poison on bad mornings – that there was nothing real in life but the wish to hurt. That had been true despair. But this present danger – all that was not physical in her stood apart from it, unthreatened, secure.

She tried again to answer Adrian's question. 'I don't believe grown-ups can ever be as afraid as children. There's so much you're sure of that can't be hurt that a child doesn't know.'

'I don't know what you're talking about,' said Adrian blankly, 'and I tell you what, Matey, I may not be what you'd call scared, but this business of being shut up in a hole – see here, why can't we take the children and our lifebelts up on the deck where we could at least – '

'Good heavens, *yes!*' cried Matey fervently, her heart leaping at the thought of being in the open air. She *was* afraid, she saw that. But if fear wasn't any worse than this! How wonderful to be grown up! How tender one should be to helpless children, for whom the present is all!

'For goodness' sakes!' said Petella, opening her eyes and blinking in the sunlight. 'How'd we ever get up *here* in our sleeping-drawers! And what am I sitting on Father's lap for! How *cunning* Brother looks!'

Brother still lay, a blanket-swathed cocoon in his mother's arms, sound asleep, though one of the horizontal rays of the rising sun struck rosily across his round face.

'Mother and I thought it would be fun to carry you up on deck to see the sun rise,' said Adrian.

'Didn't we even wake up when you took us out of bed?'

'Just like sacks of meal!'

'What's that?' asked Petella, pointing to three masts emerging from the water. 'Looks like the top of a ship. It is the top of a ship! What made it sink? Why, there's some more masts, down the river a little. What made so *many* sink? What are we on a river for, anyhow? I thought big ships didn't go up rivers. What's that funny-looking building over there? Oh, who are those men in . . . '

'Petella, not a question out of you till I get my breakfast,' said her father irritably, setting her down on the deck with a shake. 'You run along and get *dressed.*' Adrian was as natural

350

with his children as with anyone else, and when he was tired and cross he showed it. Petella giggled at the idea of being on deck in her sleeping-drawers and scampered off down the stairs.

'Why,' wondered Matey, 'do the children mind it so little when Adrian speaks impatiently to them? My parents never did to me, and yet . . . ' She knew why, of course. 'It is because *they* knew, as I did not, there is nothing to fear, underneath.' She caught herself up with remorse. Here she was again, thinking in that old childish, unjust way as though she had not learned better. *Had* she learned better? Could you ever unlearn something that had grown into your memories?

Adrian said, yawning, 'Quite a night.' He looked at her sombrely and asked, 'Are you sorry . . . ?'

'*No!*'

His face lightened. 'You're a game old girl,' he told her, getting up stiffly from his steamer-chair. He looked more tired than Matey felt, although she was quite tired enough. But ever since their decision, under no matter what fatigue, she had felt as after Petella's birth a groundswell surge of conviction that she had enough strength for whatever she had to do.

'Wake up, *petit frère,*' she murmured to the child in her arms.

They watched the docks of lower Bordeaux slide slowly by. It was late in the afternoon, the trip up the mine-sown Garonne even in broad daylight having been conducted with extreme care. Matey was tired, sleepy and disheartened. Bordeaux looked like any modern city, invulnerably industrial. She wondered why they had thought France was in need. Maybe

Francis had been right. Certainly the business-like streets they passed, with trolley cars clanging and trucks moving up and down, did not look in the least like an organism blindfolded and befooled, staggering about in vacancy.

'There's the dock where we're going to land,' said one of the passengers. They approached it more and more slowly. A group of people stood there, leaning against the custom-house walls. 'Probably been waiting for the ship since four o'clock this morning,' surmised somebody else. 'The pilot said that about midnight a rumour got about in the city that our ship had struck a mine and gone to the bottom.'

Matey ran her eyes over the people waiting. How French they were! Why did any group of French people look so different from Americans? There was a small, thin old woman in black, with a long black mourning-veil, who was crying and waving her handkerchief at someone on the ship. Matey turned her head to see who was waving back at her. No one. She looked again. The old woman seemed to be looking at *her*.

With a shock Matey knew whose was that ravaged human countenance. Across the narrowing stretch of water, she was looking full into the eyes of Mme Vinet. It was her first glimpse of the war.

'Look, look!' she cried to Adrian. 'It's Mme Vinet! How can she have dared to leave the apartment! How *old* she looks!' She held up the children, calling out to Mme Vinet, *'C'est Petella! Voici notre petit Adrien!'* To Adrian she said, in a whisper, 'Can it be that they have heard Ziza is – ' She shrank nervously from the word which was soon to pass her lips familiarly enough.

But when, carrying Brother, she made her way down the gangplank and ran toward Mme Vinet she learned there was no news.

'Ziza . . . ?' she cried as she ran.

'Nothing yet,' said Mme Vinet, opening her arms.

'But how can you be here?'

'Henri is on leave – his first. He is at the apartment.' She began to cry, drawing Matey and her little boy into a close embrace. 'Oh, Mété, when last night I heard that thy ship had been – '

Matey drew back from her. 'But, Mme Vinet, you are missing some of Henri's precious time at home!' This might be the last time she would see Henri alive.

'Ziza and Mimi are not my only daughters now, my Mété,' said Mme Vinet.

CHAPTER EIGHT

Before she left home, Matey, guessing that her time would be limited and wishing to avoid repetition, had arranged to send the news by way of a round-robin letter, intended for all the family and neighbours. She had little to write, she told them, that was interesting. 'Paris is as quiet as Rustdorf,' she reported, 'and much darker at night. In fact Washington Street is like Forty-Second Street and Broadway compared to the Champs Elysées after six o'clock. And nothing could be less like a *vivandière's* life than mine. I just keep house as usual. Adrian's news is all there is. He is accepted as an ambulance driver and is going to be sent into service just as soon as he can get his uniform made and all the innumerable papers prepared. The mail service from the front is very good. I'll hear from him every day or so except when something special is happening. Mme Vinet gets a letter from Henri every morning. Petella watches out of the window for the mailman – she can spot him clear down in the street although we're four flights up – and runs down the stairs to bring Bonne-maman's letter to her. Mme Vinet wants the children to call her Grandmother. They get on very well together. She says some of Petella's ways remind her of Priscilla. And I believe it's true. The way she takes care of Brother, it is like the way Priscilla used to take care of me. And Brother thinks just as I used to, if only his big sister is there, everything's sure to be all right.

'Mme Vinet is in bed now for a while by doctor's orders. She was just about all in. Their little *bonne* had to go back to Quimperlé to help her father on the farm because her brothers are all at the front – those that are still alive. Most of the other servants in Paris have done something like this, too, so it's hard to get any help. The few that are left ask higher wages, and Mme Vinet had very little money of course. She'd been trying to do for herself, and she'd never so much as boiled an egg before. You know how French bourgeoises always left household work to the servants . . . especially those that have a profession, like Mme Vinet. Her fingers that I used to think were like ten clever people on the piano keys act like idiots and maniacs in the kitchen.

'Henri didn't have to go back to the front till after we'd been here a couple of days, and he and Adrian and I had a regular French *conseil de famille* about how to arrange things. You know I wasn't any too sure they'd feel all right about my paying the rent and our staying here. Adrian and I had some "talking points" all ready, what a help it would be to us if Mme Vinet could let us in, and so forth. But all that sort of thing seems here like bowing and scraping over who's going to step off into the lifeboat first! They were pretty desperate. We ought to have come sooner. Henri nearly cried with relief – extraordinary to see him leave behind so wholly that little caustic surface manner of his. He's been nearly beside himself with anxiety about his mother, I imagine. You know they have always been like two halves of one person. He feels Polo's death as much as his mother. Not to know *anything* about Ziza! Henri and his mother keep on enquiring of Belgian refugees. But they have only found two people who have ever heard of the Conacqs. One was cook in a house in Ziza's suburb and knew Ziza's little maid, Mélanie. But all she could report was that young Mme Conacq was one of the few ladies who stayed on in her home. Just what we knew Ziza would do. The other news comes from a student of the University of Louvain. He didn't know Ziza and her husband, but he had studied German under old Professor Conacq, Ziza's father-in-law. He tells us that the first day the Germans took the old professor as hostage and shot him before night as part of the reprisals against sniping at Germans.

'Henri and Mme Vinet always speak of Ziza as though they were sure she is alive. But I've given her up. It's ten months since Mme Vinet left her with the new baby . . . in Louvain! If she were alive I'm sure they would have had some word, through *some* refugee, by this time. Mme Vinet always speaks of Ziza as though she might return any minute. To quiet her I've put my bed in what we used to call the dining room, because it is close to the front door. This has given her a chance to go back to her own bedroom, and for the time being she is sleeping most of the twenty-four hours. Henri says he doesn't believe she's had two consecutive hours' sleep since the beginning of the war. She was always jumping out of bed and running to the door afraid she had not heard the knocking. That was one of the reasons why Henri was so relieved to have us here.

Mimi wrote me a lovely letter about coming, too. Henri says she has been very much worried about her mother all alone here, but of course she must stay on in La Ferté to earn the living. There just aren't enough people left at the rear to do all that has to be done.

'Our things came all right. The children were so enchanted to see some of their old Rustdorf playthings come out of the trunk. Adrian put the kiddie-car together the first thing, and now it trundles up and down the *allées* of the Luxembourg as if it thought it was still in Washington Street. Brother takes so much comfort in it. People turn to laugh at the fat little boy having such a good time on his odd vehicle. I've put Padre's photograph – it's *not* a good likeness, is it, except the eyes – up on the mantelpiece in the living room, opposite the photograph of M Vinet, beside that glass-covered monstrosity of a clock that never ran. You remember that clock, Priscilla?

'I can't tell you how queer it seems to me to have my children knocking around in the old children's room where I spent so much time. And to take them out to play in the Luxembourg, just as Mme Vinet used to take us! I don't believe a flower has changed in the flower beds there, and I'm sure the wallpaper in the children's room is the same. Half the time I don't know whether it's then or now.

'I do hope Petella will get over her shyness about speaking French. Brother's learning it ten times faster than she. His English gets quainter every day. He said yesterday, *"Je veux avoir* two oranges. I *s'all* have two oranges, because I got two hungries in me."* It's too funny to hear him make the same mistakes in English that French children do! But Petella turns all colours and swallows her tongue if she's asked to say a word. She'd get on so much better in school next fall if she could only feel at home in the language.'

Matey stopped the letter there, leaving in the position of emphasis this first intimation she had given her American family that she and Adrian would not be going home in the autumn. (Had she ever been sure the war could not last much longer?) She was worn out with the effort of keeping up that matter-of-fact reassuring tone. That would have to do for this time. She sealed the envelope and tiptoed to look in at Mme Vinet. Her face, sunk in the pillow, was like alabaster. Her tiny emaciated body barely lifted the bedclothes. Henri had said, 'You have saved my mother's life.' Matey wasn't so sure she had come in time.

The children were playing in the children's room. 'Petella, let's play soldiers. Soldiers going to smash Boche!' Where did they pick up things! Matey put her head in the door and asked severely, 'Brother, where did you hear anything about Boche?'

'I sawn 'em, *insectes noires,*' said Brother, 'crawling in the *cuisine* under ze table.'

'We're all right, Mother,' said Petella with a reassuring nod. Yes, she was a responsible child, as Priscilla used to be.

Matey went on into the living room and found there the thought from which she had been running away. It was the day after tomorrow that Adrian was going to the front. Their first separation. Forty-eight hours still. No, only forty-seven now.

It was a thousand times harder than she had realised. For an instant Matey thought wildly that it was going to be harder than she could stand. After all, she wasn't forced to stand it.

All of this was voluntary. If it was too hard . . . Someone was looking at her. She felt a human gaze on her in the empty room. Oh, Padre's photograph. She sat down and met those eyes.

Presently she stood up and went into the kitchen to start dinner.

'Well, Mother, where have you *been?*' asked Petella and Brother, storming in from the children's room. 'We didn't hear you anywhere, and we looked and you weren't with Bonne-maman, nor in your room.'

'We look *pa'tout . . . pa'tout!*' said Brother, expressing with a Gallic gesture how thoroughly they had looked everywhere.

'You didn't look in the living room,' said their mother. 'Padre and I were having Meeting together there.'

'Oh,' said Petella, looking hard at her mother to see what she meant.

'*Que-est-ce-que-c'est que* Meeting? *Qu-est-ce-que-c'est que* Meeting?' clamoured Brother, opening his hazel eyes very wide.

'*Brother,* you're forgetting all about *home!*' said Petella, shocked.

CHAPTER NINE

✿✿✿

'What do you think, Francis and Priscilla,' wrote Matey in her round-robin, that autumn, 'who do you suppose is peeling potatoes in our kitchen this minute, but Dominiqua! Yes, Dominiqua Iturbe from Biriatou. You'd recognise her in a minute. She's changed less than we have.

'It happened the simplest way in the world. Everybody keeps track of everybody in his circle, and when there's need, they help out. For instance, you remember, Priscilla, the cross *concierge* here. Their son was badly wounded in a recent engagement. Nobody likes them a bit, but everybody in the house is chipping in together to send the boy things to eat and to make it possible for his parents to see him in the hospital. And Mme Vinet's *bonne,* the one that went back to Brittany to help her father work the farm – she has three brothers still alive. Mme Vinet sends something nice to them at the front every week or so, and sometimes one of them comes here for his furlough, instead of going all the way back to Quimperlé. He sleeps in Henri's bed and eats with us. Astonishing to see such a dyed-in-the-wool old bourgeoise as Mme Vinet invite her cook's brothers to her table.

✳✳✳

'And more than this, Mme Vinet keeps track through Henri, and through these Breton boys, of soldiers from the occupied regions whose families, like Ziza, have just dropped off the earth. Such fellows have now nowhere in their country to go to on furlough. Many of them haven't seen the inside of a home since they left Valenciennes or Tourcoing or Chauny or wherever they lived when the war broke out. Most of them are working-men who don't know what to do with themselves for a week in Paris. They get awfully fleeced and done. One reason Mme Vinet was so run down and thin when I came was that she'd kept open house for such homeless fellows, doing for them as she does for Henri. She really starved herself to give them good things. They are coming and going, one or another, pretty much all the time.

'Well, that was what I came to do, if I could find it – *if I could find it!* Heavens! How could I ever have wondered if I could find it! And what I wanted to spend Aunt Connie's ever-blessed bequest on. But there weren't hours enough in the day for me to do it all without help in the kitchen. Mme Vinet is better now, out of bed, but not strong yet, and anyhow worse than nobody for housework. I was wondering how ever I'd find help. Well, one of the soldiers here on furlough happened to mention having some Basques in his regiment and I thought of Dominiqua and her boy Jeannot, the one who was a baby in arms when we were children at Biriatou. She had another boy, too, younger. They must be, I thought, about twenty-five and twenty-three years old, the age when they are most sent into the shock troops. I've always kept some sort of track of Dominiqua, sent her a New Year's card every year, and some little present, so I knew her address. I wrote offering, if she'd tell me the military address of her sons, to do what I could for them in the way of sending packages. She wrote that her husband, like Mimi's, had been sent with territorial troops to remake shell-ruined roads along the northern front, where he got pneumonia and died. The younger son, like Polo, was lost in the battle of the Marne. Jeannot is still alive, in the Chasseurs Alpins, shock troops, just as I thought. And Dominiqua was at her wit's end to know how to live. Her tiny allowance from the Government was scarcely enough to buy food. She had been working in the fields, digging potatoes, although she has a bad hernia. When I proposed to her to come here and work for us at good wages (*beata sancta* Connie, again!) two whole mail days nearer the front, where she could hear from Jeannot with no delay,· I got a telegram from the stationmaster at Hendaye reading, "Mme Iturbe arrives Paris Bordeaux Express tomorrow nine-thirty." '

'I went down to meet the train, taking Petella along for the treat of riding home in a taxi afterward. I was wondering if I'd know Dominiqua. But gracious! In that conventionally dressed crowd she stood out as if she had been labelled Basque from head to foot. There she was in her black dress, espadrilles on her feet, black coif twisted around her chignon, as Basque as a striped ox-cloth. She knew us too, at least she knew Petella. As we ran up toward her, she cried out, "Oh, *le petit François, que voilà!*" She says Petella is the perfect picture of Francis at her age.

'Well, she was terribly excited, first time she had ever been farther from home than up to Saint Jean-de-Luz. She called down on our heads the blessings of the Virgin Mary and all the saints she could lay her tongue to. And she wept all the way home in the taxi, and kept calling me *chère petite Mme Météh*, although she's a tiny little woman like Mme Vinet, and I'm as big as the two of them put together, and she undid her bundle to get out Jeannot's picture to show me, and couldn't find it, and thought she'd lost it, and then found it in her pocket! It was a wild trip! I thought I'd been crazy to think of transplanting her.

'But the sight of a kitchen restored her reason miraculously, like showing a laboratory to a distraught biologist, I imagine. She gave one look at it and said, "Oh! the casseroles shouldn't hang *there!*" in a perfectly natural human voice. I tiptoed out and left her hanging them somewhere else, to her immense satisfaction – and mine, believe *me!* I suppose I seem as futile in the kitchen as Mme Vinet does to me. If only the old Southerner doesn't freeze to death this winter (fuel's scarce of course) we're all set.'

There, thought Matey, pushing the paper away with a weary gesture, that might be a good place to stop, with that second intimation that they would be staying on right through the winter.

No – she pulled it to her again – she must send some news from Adrian, who wrote only to his father.

'I enclose part of Adrian's last letter from the front, which will tell you how things go with him, as much as he's allowed by the censor to say. I'll know more of course and tell you more, when I've seen him. We don't know yet when his first furlough will come, probably next February.'

❦❦❦

* * *

Autumn came, the gloomy autumn of 1915 – one Russian defeat after another, the murderous failure of the Champagne offensive, the savage invasion of Serbia, the Gallipoli tragedy. New disasters continually draped the French world in fresh black. French manpower never too numerous, seemed to be approaching exhaustion. Older and older men, younger and younger boys, were summoned from civilian life to military training. Women like Mimi who had boys of thirteen and fourteen began to count the days. 'But it *can't* last. We have come to the end of the rope, almost,' people said to each other in talk. Never in print.

Along with other changes in the world, school time came. Petella had insensibly slid into French and was now learning in this Paris public school about the same information she would have absorbed in Rustdorf, the multiplication table bulking large. Brother was in the kindergarten. He was a year younger than the regulation kindergarten age, but the teacher of that class was an old friend of Mme Vinet's who had known Matey when she was a little girl. Room was easily made for the little boy of the American who had come to France to run an ambulance at the front. Along with other mothers and aunts and maids and little boys and girls, Matey and her children trudged down the wet grey street in the wet grey mornings to the door of the *lycée*.

She clung to the children's untouched zest in life almost as pitifully now as the men from the front *en permission*. Playing with Brother and Petella was the part of furloughs which the

364

soldiers liked best. Now that she was separated from them most of the day, Matey understood more of what children meant. When they had held up their rosy faces to be kissed, had trotted off, hand in hand, to the mysteries within the *lycée*, and had left her standing on the muddy sidewalk, she often had a moment of panic at being left with her own thoughts and fears. But the never-ending list of things to be done built up another screen between herself and her thoughts. Mme Vinet was not strong enough to be much on her feet, so she sat at home, writing the never-ending letters to the soldiers 'on the list' or to their families with news of them, putting in order garments intended for refugees, wrapping up in the tiresomely exact manner prescribed by military authorities the innumerable packages of cigarettes, matches, chocolate, writing paper, and woollen things which streamed out from the apartment to the front.

Matey did the outside things – the long shopping expeditions to buy cigarettes, chocolate, and other things for the packages, the visits to the men in hospitals, the endless standing in line in *bureaux* of one kind or another, the trips to remote parts of Paris in answer to requests from soldiers at the front for help to their families. One of the addresses to which she was sent in this way became very familiar to her. Day after day, she went in to help take care of a bedridden peasant girl, heartbroken by her husband's deathbed two days after her baby was born. He had been in Henri's regiment, and from his deathbed had sent word to ask Henri's American foster-sister to look out for his wife. He had no one else. His wife's brother had been killed, her own parents were dead, his own family were under German rule in Valenciennes, non-existent for her. Matey could find no link with life which had survived in her. She would not look at her baby, she turned her face away from the sun, she said nothing to Matey but *'Non, Madame,' 'Non, Madame.'* The *concierge,* whom Matey paid to take care of the baby, and a nursing Sister of Charity who came in occasionally, both gave her up. 'She'll be better off in Heaven, poor thing,' said the Sister devoutedly. The *concierge* said, 'There's nothing to be done, Madame, with those peasants when they make up their minds to let go. . . . The baby will just have to go into an orphanage. He'll have plenty of company.' Matey thought of the soldier she had never seen who, dying, had confided his helpless wife to her, and went on doggedly with her fumbling efforts to be a doctor to the soul. But her attempts at cheerful talk sounded foolish and flat as they echoed in the dark void of the tenement-house room.

One day she stopped at a street flower stand and bought a bunch of country violets, last flowering of an outdoor bed, to take to the woman who would not get well. Young Mme Letellier looked at them, put up her hand to them before she turned her face away. 'There were violets in our garden at home,' she said.

An intuition came to Matey. She found out from the *concierge* that Mme Letellier's native village was Crouy, on the Ourcq. That was not far from La Ferté. Matey wrote to Mimi, explaining her plan and asking for information. Mimi's answer was prompt, accurate, detailed, sympathetic, unlike anything the old Mimi could have written.

A day came when Matey said to the listless invalid, 'I have

just heard about a piece of property that is for sale in Crouy. A small stone house, the Boutry family used to own it, near the canal, next door but one to the house where you lived as a little girl. I know of an American fund for war troubles, and if you liked, I could get from them money enough to buy this, as a place for you to bring up little Jacques. You probably remember the house. It has a big garden plot behind it. It would be nice, don't you think, to have little Jacques grow up where you and your brother lived?'

The invalid did not stir or speak. Matey dared not stop. She went on, 'A friend of mine who lives near there has gone out to Crouy to see it. She spoke specially of a fine old apple tree in the middle of the garden.' From the sick woman came faintly, 'When we played hide-and-seek with the Boutry children, that tree was our goal.'

The baby was about two months old when Matey carried him and led his white-cheeked young mother into the Gare de l'Est, and settled herself with them in the train. After they had passed Meaux, Matey said, 'You must tell me when we are near Crouy so that we can be ready to leave the train.'

Mme Letellier sat closer to the window. Presently she said, 'Oh, that fine beet field of the Auvarys' going to *weeds!*' Later, 'They haven't cut those poplars yet on the Moronier farm! They'll certainly fall in some windstorm.'

They walked down the narrow cobble-paved street, Matey the one who was led now. Mimi was waiting at the door of the tiny house. Matey scarcely knew her old playmate. This gaunt, masterful, steady-eyed woman, with grey in her carelessly arranged hair, and machine-oil ground into her hands – could this be the pensive *nonchalante* Mimi! There was no time for exclamations, for anything more than a sisterly embrace. There was but one train Matey could take back to Paris that day; it left in half an hour, and she was not sure of success.

Mimi's manner was perfect. Not a trace of the old French bourgeois superiority to peasants, 'I happened to have a little extra furniture, Mme Letellier,' she said respectfully, 'which I thought might be useful to you till you get settled.' (This was what she and Matey had decided to say about the bits of furniture bought with Aunt Connie's money.) And, 'Some of the neighbours who remembered you and your parents are coming to welcome you to Crouy. They will be here in a few minutes. Just time for you to take a turn about the house and garden if you like. Mme Fort and I will stay here and take care of the baby.'

She and Matey sat in the low, heavily-beamed kitchen, the largest of the three small rooms of the house. Before them an economical French fire burned discreetly on a huge hearth. Matey noticed that Mimi had not only provided the necessary tables and chairs, but had put white curtains at the low windows, and pots of flowering geraniums. 'That was sweet!' thought Matey. And with a motherly gesture Mimi took the fatherless baby on her knees. 'I'll stay till the last train back to La Ferté tonight,' she said. 'I'll stay overnight if she seems to need me.'

The two old comrades had less than ten minutes together, and most of it was given over hastily to the natural question-and-answer of family news. But almost from the first word and all through the talk about health and children and the difficulties of wartime housekeeping, Matey felt a growing sense of a change in Mimi, even greater than the change in her looks. It was as if the source of light in a familiar room had been quite changed, so that, although everything was in its usual place, the shadows all fell differently. Finally Matey, aware that time was flying, glanced at her watch and asked, 'Mimi, you haven't said anything yet about your boys. Your mother will be sure to ask me what you reported about them.'

The other woman did not answer for an instant. Then she said in a constrained voice, 'My boys are very well. . . . You can tell Maman that I said that.' She added immediately, the words seeming to burst out, 'Mété, I must give my children more than my parents gave me. I must! I *can't* leave them as Maman and Papa left us.'

Matey heard every shade of the mingled exaltation and bitterness in the voice, but had not the faintest clue as to the meaning of the words. Too astonished to think of any rejoinder, she remained silent, searching the other's face for an explanation.

At that moment came a knock on the door. When she opened it Matey saw there a plump elderly nun, her black draperies sweeping the ground, the white quilled ruffling of the net under her black coif casting a pearly shadow down on her finely wrinkled red cheeks and innocent round eyes.

'Oh, yes,' called Mimi from the room, 'it is Soeur Sainte Julienne. This is our old friend Mme Fort from America, *ma soeur*. Mété, this is Sister Sainte Julienne, who is coming to help out your poor war widow.' They shook hands, Matey liking on sight the open-faced old country woman. 'How *is* the poor thing?' asked the nun, coming in, 'Does she seem to take at all a liking to it, here?'

They looked out of the window. The woman in widow's weeds was standing under the bare branches of the apple tree. The dead black of her dress and veil brought out singingly the life in the autumn colours about her, the rich brown of the ploughed garden, the yellow stubble in the sleeping field beyond. She lifted her face and looked up into the tree. Inside the house they watched her anxiously. Finally, as if something had been asked and answered between them, she stepped closer to it and laid a black gloved hand on its thick strong trunk. The three in the house drew a long breath.

'How did you ever think of this, Meté?' asked Mimi, turning away from the window.

'I don't know,' said Matey.

All during the jolting night trip back to Paris, Matey was thinking about the new vitality which glowed from Mimi and wondering what those mysterious words of hers meant. Only one thing became evident. It was nothing to ask Mme Vinet about.

With Mme Letellier gone there was one errand less. But there were always plenty of new ones. The army of refugees grew larger all the time. There were many organisations now to care for refugees, some American ones, and a good deal of what Matey and Mme Vinet had to do was to steer refugee families to the right *oeuvres* and then watch over them to clear up possible bad feeling. There was a good deal of that.

✤✤✤

Refugees were always nerve-sick, either half-crazed by their sense of injury or, more often, deadened and starved into an incredible apathy, so that you needed, Matey sometimes thought, not only to provide food for them, but almost to put it into their mouths. On the other side, the devoted heads of the various charitable organisations, both French and American, were often leisure-class women for whom this was the first contact with reality and work and the first perilous experience of being in authority. The never-ending work of trying to restore to life those mutilated human organisms was, naturally enough, broken sometimes by explosions of ungrateful ill-will on one side and mean tyranny and favouritism on the other, all to the tune, perhaps, of an air raid overhead, or news of a great German offensive which might sweep them all into the ranks of refugees.

The days went laggingly by, shortening with intolerable slowness the period of waiting till Adrian's first furlough. This had been put off several times, first because of the launching of an offensive on the front where he served (to the women in the rear, offensives meant always 'no furloughs') and after that for various exasperating exhibitions of *paperasseries* and military red tape.

At the apartment other men on leave came and went, a strange mixture of personalities, castes, and abilities, but with a few never-varying traits in common, such as their intense dislike of people who called them 'defenders of civilisation,' their profound silence on the subject of exploding shells, bayonet attacks, trench life – war in general – and their deep concern over the state of their underwear. Matey knew little about their adventures with machine-guns, but she was accurately acquainted with the condition of the shirts, socks, and drawers of every *poilu* on her list. They were always either thanking her for a fresh supply just sent, hinting hesitatingly that the old articles were giving out, or exulting in the distribution to their regiment of a new lot of shirts, 'so send socks and drawers now, Mme Fort.'

Samples of all provinces and all trades passed through Henri's room, which was now their guest room. One week, Matey and Mme Vinet struggled to make conversation with a dull, silent, kind, forty-year-old coal miner from the North, a raw-boned Fleming, whose wife and little boy, if still alive, were beyond the German lines. He was happiest on leave, M Plon, if they had some small household job waiting for him, a shelf to put up, a latch to repair. The week after his visit there would be no difficulty at all about conversation with a brilliant, cynical-talking young dandy, who had been a student in Henri's classes, a boy from a wealthy family of Lille. He wanted little of Paris vacations except long mornings in bed, a chance to renew his acquaintance with his hairdresser and raw Palais-Royal farces at night. Like many young soldiers on leave, he had a horror of being alone, and once in a while when gayer company was not to be had he pressed his hostesses into service as theatre companions. Matey sometimes sat there by him, feeling, as the boy laughed half-hysterically and applauded loudly, how opium-like to his despair and loneliness was the gay, rank obscenity on the stage.

After such a week they entertained, perhaps, the dour, silent Breton farmhand, brother of the absent cook, who much preferred Dominiqua's society and conversation about livestock to anything Mme Vinet or Matey could do for him. His particular grudge against the world was the language of the newspaper reporters. 'Our chivalrous *poilus*, the fighting blood of old Gaul blazing like liquid fire in their veins, were hardly to be restrained by their officers from swarming up over the top before the hour set for the offensive.' To Dominiqua, washing dishes, he would read out such a passage in an angry tone, striking the paper contemptuously with the side of his hand, and spitting scornfully into the ashcan. 'I'd like to have one of those pen-pushers in the trenches! He'd see how hard it is to restrain us from going into an attack ahead of time. He'd see . . . '

Finally came Dominiqua's Jeannot, whom Matey had last seen as a baby on his mother's shoulder. He was by far the most dashing of all the men they saw, a hard-bitten, handsome, swaggering, front-line fighter, recklessly outspoken in his detestation of the war and its makers. 'There'll be a strike if this business goes on another year . . . a strike of soldiers. Do you know the name for a strike of soldiers, Mme Fort? It's called a mutiny. And we'll drive the Cabinet Ministers and the people who write books about war up to the front to take our places.' Very good to his mother, Jean Iturbe, and delightfully frolicsome with Petella and Brother. But then every one of their military guests loved to play with the children. Matey often thought the children were of more use to these embittered, enduring men than all the rest of them put together, with their packages of wool socks and cigarettes and chocolate.

✣✣✣

And finally, shortly before Adrian was due, Henri came for his week of respite. His mother went, pale with excitement, to meet him at the Gare de l'Est, and came back, a girl's colour in her thin elderly face, walking so close to him that her black dress was stained by the mud plastered and caked to the tops of his heavy clumping boots. Mimi came up from La Ferté for a few hours when Henri was there, the first time she had been to Paris since Matey had arrived. Matey had wondered a little at this, since the trip was really a short one. She was perhaps too busy with this tremendous effort of hers to save her husband's business. From what she told them she seemed to be making a great success of it. Indeed she talked of little but the problem of adapting her machinery to turn out shell fuses. She made several enquiries about American screw-cutting lathes and micrometer calipers, which Matey, to her shame, was quite incapable of answering.

'Why, Mimi, you remind me of Tante Caroline!' said Henri, laughing, and explained to Matey that one of his father's aunts, left a widow, had been a master hand at managing her husband's business.

'Yes, I know how Tante Caroline felt,' Mimi agreed.

Everyone avoided talk of war. It was January of 1916. They felt that France was defeated but would not admit it aloud. Mimi, it seemed, had another topic to avoid, for she sheered off quickly from any talk of her boys. She gave evasive answers to questions as to why she had not brought them and said nothing in particular when her mother spoke sadly of seeing them so little. Finally, in reply to some point-blank questions about their studies from Henri, who as a teacher in a public school was familiar with the courses of the *collège* in La Ferté, she gave a reluctant answer of which a chance turn of phrase revealed the fact that those studies were not being carried on in the secular public school but in the *collège* at Juilly.

'But that is a religious school,' said Henri blankly. 'Isn't that the one carried on by Jesuits?'

'They're not Jesuits at all!' said Mimi indignantly. 'They are priests. And you know it. It's perfectly legal.'

'But, *Mimi – !*' said her mother faintly.

Matey remembered the sweet round-eyed old nun she had met in Crouy who seemed such a friend of Mimi's.

So this was what Mimi had meant.

Mimi said hastily, 'Now, Maman, I didn't want to tell you that. I knew you'd make a fuss. And there's no use trying to explain it to you. You couldn't understand. I must do what seems best to me for my own children, musn't I? It's too long a story to tell you anyhow.' There was a silence in which Mimi finished her cup of coffee with a defiant air of not noticing anything unusual.

Matey felt herself very much in the way and rose, calling Brother and Petella for a walk. Mimi stood up to say goodbye. She kissed Matey affectionately, evidently holding her apart from what was at issue between her and her mother and brother. 'I still can hardly believe you're here, you know, Mété. It's splendid of you and your husband to come! That young war widow seems to be settling down all right at Crouy. *That* was a splendid thing to do, too.'

'Give my love to your boys,' said Matey, kissing her old comrade.

She walked soberly enough that afternoon behind her romping children under the beautiful shadowy trees of the winter park. How virulently life pursued its way! The war with its mountainous horror and madness was after all but the background for the anthills of personal dissensions. When she went back at dusk, Mme Vinet had been crying. Henri was at the piano, very delicately playing some Debussy for his mother.

Before he went back to the front that time, he went out with Matey one day into the Luxembourg, strolling with her behind the prancing children. They talked a little of old times and how she had taught them baseball and of Petella's French, which was, after all, turning out better than Brother's, and of the fact that Henri's mother was once more giving some music lessons, and how steadying this was to her nerves. Matey could see that he was trying to say something else and guessed that it was about Mimi. But because it was something very deep and close to him he did not know how to speak of it. In all his rainbow-coloured vocabulary of sophisticated words he could find none transparent enough to show what was in his heart. Nor could Matey help him. She could only admire the skill of Adrian and his father. She had not at all learned their secret. In the end she and Henri said nothing at all, walking together in wistful intimate silence up and down under the leafless winter trees.

From the front he wrote to her guardedly, not mentioning Mimi by name, about great changes which the war with its strain and anxieties brought to personalities, changes which might or might not be permanent, but which brought new pain to those who had already suffered bereavements from death. 'I am more thankful than ever before that Maman has one daughter with her,' he ended.

Matey laid down the letter, wondering, as she had so often in the past, at the harsh rigour of French differences of opinion. For it seemed no more to her. 'With all of us more or less at death's door, why should Henri and his mother make themselves miserable over this!' she thought in astonishment. 'Why not let everybody do as he thinks best without getting tragic over it!'

In answering Henri's letter she asked him this question, muting it to discretion by a careful choice of phrases. But evidently she had not been discreet enough. His answering letter, written under shellfire in an underground *abri*, with a man dying at his feet, pointedly ignored the subject, had nothing in it but the disgust at the idiocy of the war and the self-contempt at being a helpless part of it which coloured all letters from French intellectuals at the front.

On the most affectionate and intimate terms with Mme Vinet, Matey expected every day some word from her that would make it possible to say something of the sort to her. But Mme Vinet never mentioned it.

She felt that not only in her letter to Henri but in all her letter-writing she was less and less successful. Adrian from the front wrote only to her and to his father. Matey made an effort to keep all the Rustdorf circle neighbours, as well as her family, in touch with the doings in France, but the daily entries in her journal-letter grew more and more dry and concise.

'Just back from Crouy tonight, where I'd been to take that young Mme Letellier I've written about. Think of buying a whole house, ever so small a one, and a garden and a little field for $540. Young Mme Letellier seemed to like it very well.'

'Petella came home from the *lycée* the other day saying an appeal had been sent out to all the schoolchildren to ask their parents to help save from starvation the Russian prisoners in the German prison camps. We are to save every scrap of bread that is not used at table, dry it, and send it to the *lycée*, where it will be put together in big packages and sent (by means of the Swiss Red Cross) into Germany.'

'Henri has been back. His *permissions* are filled with music. He or his mother or both of them are before the piano most of the time. Henri's hands look like a day labourer's now. And he's in almost constant pain from sciatica. A good many professional men, no longer young, get sciatica from their life at the front. But he hasn't lost his delicate touch. I often wish Padre could hear him. He still makes me feel like a piledriver.'

She fell back on items about the children, always interesting to aunts and grandfathers. 'Brother is as amusing as ever. The other day he showed me Dominiqua's rosary lying on the kitchen table, and said, struggling to get it into English so Dominiqua wouldn't understand, "You see zat necklace? Zat's ze necklace what Dominiqua love God by." He can't pronounce his *th*'s any more than any other little French boy. He pronounces his own nickname now as Dominiqua does, "Brozzer," with a very much rolled *r*.'

Mostly she commented on news from home. 'We read all your letters aloud over and over, especially to Brother, who is beginning to forget home. Petella tries hard to keep it fresh in his mind. I hear her asking, "When you go down the kitchen steps, what grows in the flower bed on the right-hand side?" And "Under which tree is Sumner's grave?" It is so good of Aunt Tryntje and Rebecca to look out for the things in our house. How could moths have got into our bedding closet!

'Francis, have you ever thought that Emily's health might be helped by a stay in a good sanatorium?'

Dull stuff, her letters home. And she found it increasingly hard to write even as much as that.

To tell them what was really happening about her – to describe the effects of the war as they touched the people she saw – she could not even begin. To give them any idea of the moral atmosphere in which she lived, the brooding dread against which they daily drew the frail outline of their lives – she had not words. Adrian's father had been right. There was no use talking about it.

CHAPTER TEN

She had lived to see it dawn, the day of Adrian's return for his first furlough. But the time from dawn until his train was due was almost as hard to live through as all those weeks and months. She had too carefully finished her work ahead of time so that she should be free for his visit. It would have been better to save some of those endless tasks for today rather than to wander around the apartment, looking in at the children's room, looking in at the kitchen, looking at her watch and thinking it must have been stopped.

'Sit down, child!' said Mme Vinet finally. 'You'll wear yourself out.' She sat down and took the everlasting knitting from the older woman's hands.

'But what shall *I* do?'

'Go play something for me,' implored Matey.

She sat knitting fast and listening to Bach, once more stating honestly the complexity of all things and once more showing that in the end they are but harmonious parts of the whole. The room was filled with the intelligent beauty of that comforting voice. At the end, 'How it does one good!' breathed Mme Vinet. They were painfully sensitive to music in those days.

'It's one of the things I owe to you,' said Matey.

'You have repaid it – dear child,' murmured the woman before the piano.

'Have you still, do you suppose, that old piano arrangement for the Fifth Symphony that you and Henri used to play years ago?' asked Matey.

'Why, certainly I have it. Come and play the bass with me.'

They began bravely:

But they could get no further. Streaming up from the notes came the past – it was Henri who sat there beside his mother, Henri the other half of her soul. Behind them sat the little girls, Mimi gentle and loving, Ziza, ardent Ziza with her great gifts for joy and suffering. And the baby Paul slept in his cradle in the next room. The two women sat motionless, staring at the familiar notes on the page as if they were ghosts.

Dominiqua put her head in at the door, and asked, 'Pardon, Madam Mété, does Monsieur like garlic with his leg of lamb?'

'Non, non, non, non!' cried Matey, springing up, horrified at the idea of something wrong in Adrian's first meal at home. *'No* garlic in *anything!'*

She looked at her watch again. It was really not too early to begin to get the children's wraps on. There were so many protections to be put on against this steady February rain.

They plodded from the Métro station into the Gare de l'Est, blue with soldiers ending or beginning their furloughs, camping out on the benches, smoking, eating, waiting for their trains. Matey put down her dripping umbrella and asked an employee which was the exit for soldiers returning *en permission*. He looked appraisingly at her bourgeois hat and gloves and asked, 'Officer or common soldier?'

'Ambulance driver,' said Matey. 'An American driving an ambulance attached to the Third Army.'

The man shrugged his shoulders, quite blank as to the status of an American. 'Does he rank as an officer or a common soldier?'

'I haven't any idea,' said Matey, surprised. 'Why?'

'Officers come out this exit, common soldiers out of the side door around the corner,' he announced and went his way.

Matey and Petella were thrown into helpless agitation by this news. Which door should they choose? Suppose he took the other one. It would be too horrible to miss him after all. If only they had brought Mme Vinet! But it was too late to get her now.

Matey, undone with excitement, lost her head and was ready to cry. Petella took command. 'I'll stay here, Mother, and you and Brother go round to the side door.'

'But I can't leave you alone in such a crowd . . . in a city!' cried poor Matey. 'You're only seven years old!'

'I'll be all right,' said Petella. 'I'll stand right here and hold on to this railing. And if he comes here, I'll holler to him and we'll go round and meet you.'

Matey dared not agree and dared do nothing else. The train was almost due. She kissed Petella and told her, 'Don't you *stir* from there on any account unless Father comes,' and went away, looking back anxiously at the valiant little figure, lost in the midst of the great echoing hall and the crowds of roughly hurrying grown-ups.

Putting up her umbrella again, she ran hurriedly with Brother along the street to the side door, the slimy February mud spattering the little boy's leggings and his mother's skirts. There could be no doubt where to go. A silent crowd of women and children stood in the mud and rain, looking fixedly at a large door in the wall. Most of them were working-people who did not carry umbrellas but protected themselves from the rain sketchily with black woollen scarves over their heads, or the hoods of their dark-blue capes. Matey and her little son joined them. 'It *is* here for common soldiers returning from the front?' she asked the woman next to her, who nodded without taking her eyes from the dingy painted panels of the door.

They waited, stepping from one foot to the other, shifting babies from shoulder to shoulder. Matey began to tremble. She saw that an old woman near her was shaking so that she could scarcely stand. 'Take my arm, Madame,' she murmured, and stood more firmly herself then, steadied by Brother's pull at her hand and the weight of old age on the other arm.

'Will I know Adrian when I see him?' she thought. It seemed years since she had been his wife, had been a person at all.

She started when an employee flung the door open. The roar and clatter of a moving train poured out loudly as if the open door were a trumpet. The women fixed their eyes on it. Matey felt their silent patience rise to a passion. She too, for her life, could not have looked away.

Heavy, rapid footsteps were heard. An unshaven, un-
handsome middle-aged little Frenchman stepped through
the door, his ill-fitting uniform of coarse blue cloth smeared
with yellow mud, his hulking shapeless shoes caked with it to
their tops.

'Maurice!' cried a woman's voice hysterically, and 'Oh,
Papa! *Papa!*' a child's. A beautiful smile came over his
insignificant face. He took one long step forward and was gone
in the crowd. Another had appeared behind him, long and
lean and rustic. 'Pierre! *Ici!* Pierre!' someone called fervently
from the back of the crowd, and everyone stepped back to let
a weeping woman in a shawl fling herself into his arms.

They came all at once then, three or four crowding through
the door together. The crowd surged forward and back; there
were cries and tears and laughter; babies were transferred
from women's to men's shoulders; Matey and Brother and the
old woman were jostled from side to side by heedless reunited
couples.

And then it was over. The open door stood empty, only a
trickle of small railroad noises coming from it, the slow rumble
of a baggage-truck, the distant hoot of a train. A handful of
women still stood waiting under the rain. An employee came
to shut the door. 'All out of that train,' he said, adding not
unkindly, 'Next train in from the east front due at two o'clock
tomorrow morning.' He shut the door. The women turned
away, two of them sobbing.

'Adrian is evidently not ranked as a common soldier,'
thought Matey.

'But where is my son!' said the old woman on her arm.

'Perhaps he came through the other exit,' suggested Matey, trying not to show her impatience.

'No, he always comes through this door. I always meet him here.'

Matey's heart contracted at that 'always'. Could she live through this *again!* She struggled against her impulse to drop the old arm and run to Petella. 'Perhaps he will come on the next train?' she said.

'Perhaps,' muttered the old woman tonelessly, dropping her head and standing motionless in the rain. Matey noticed that she looked very poor. 'Won't you let me offer you a hot supper while you wait?' she asked, pointing to a restaurant across the street. 'You could eat it by the window so that you would not lose sight of the door.'

She hurried her to the table by the window, left a bill from Aunt Connie by her plate, shook hands with her, and, Brother galloping at her side, spattered around through the mud to the waiting room. It was almost empty. Petella, a little pale, stood there steadfastly, her eyes, very wide, fixed eagerly on the door to the street.

'Oh, wasn't he at your door, either?' she cried quaveringly.

Matey's heart began to pound. Her suspense recoiled upon her in a sick reaction from hope. She felt driven half-crazy by all these dependents on her, old women, little children – for whom she must show qualities she did not have. She would have given anything to be alone, free to weep aloud, to be weak and desperate as she was. It was frightful to be grown up.

'Oh, Father probably missed the train,' she said lightly in a reassuring voice to Petella. 'You know he's always late.' It was in fact one of the family jokes.

With a crackle of her nerves it occurred to her that this might be true. Adrian must have been slow in getting ready, as he often was, and have missed the train. She flared with anger. How could he do such a thing when he knew how anxious they would be! To have missed *such* a train! All the times in the past when he had been late and she had been prompt rose up from oblivion and heaped themselves to a mountainous grievance.

'Well, what do you say, dears, shall we walk part way home and look in at the windows instead of taking the Métro here?' she asked the children in a cheerful tone.

But the first window displayed beaded funeral wreaths with *'A mon mari, mort sur le champ d'honneur'* on a good many of them. As if someone had struck her a blow in the chest Matey thought gaspingly, 'Adrian may be dead this minute. May have been hit with a shell on his last trip to the front line dressing station. When I get back to the apartment I may find a telegram. . . . '

'Children, don't you think it would be fun to take a taxi, for a treat?' The cheerfulness of her voice was wearing thin. Petella looked at her anxiously. Darling little daughter! Matey, unstrung with anxiety, was afraid that in another moment she would lay her head on her little daughter's shoulder and burst into tears. She looked fixedly out of the cab window and let Petella restrain Brother from dashing himself out of the windows as he careered about, 'playing bear'.

But there was no telegram at the apartment. Only a rich unwonted odour of roast meat, and Mme Vinet and

Dominiqua running to welcome in the *permissionaire,* very much startled that he had not come. Matey read in Mme Vinet's disappointed face another explanation of Adrian's non-appearance, something Matey had not thought of, although she was as familiar with the possibility now as Mme Vinet. Another big offensive had perhaps started suddenly and again *permissions* indefinitely recalled. At this idea she sank down in a chair, all her strength gone. 'I *couldn't* wait another month!' she thought. Dominiqua went back to the kitchen to change her plans for dinner, and Matey pulled Brother up on her lap to take off his muddy leggings. Her hand trembled so she could not unbutton them. 'Sit *still,* Brother!' she said tearfully, although the weary child had not stirred.

'*I'll* unbutton them!' cried Petella, springing forward.

There was a knock on the outer door. Hearing Dominiqua step to open, they all froze into listening statutes. The door opened, a murmur of voices, a *'Oui, Monsieur'* from Dominiqua. The door to the living room opened. A slight, pale, unshaven man in a muddy uniform stood there, his great shoes caked with mud. As he looked at Matey and the children a beautiful smile came to his lips.

'*Adrian!'* cried Matey, incredulously, springing up from her seat.

'Father!' shouted Petella, running to throw her arms around his knees.

'*C'est mon papa,'* explained Brother proudly, with a Gallic sweep of his little hand, to Mme Vinet, who had snatched at him as his mother let him fall.

'But how *did* you get here without our seeing you!'

demanded Matey breathlessly, her arms still around his neck. She hardly knew what she was saying.

'Two sections to the train,' explained Adrian.

'Why didn't the man at the Gare tell us?'

'Didn't know, probably – I'll bet he didn't try to find out very hard.'

Matey's taut nerves snapped. She cried out angrily, 'Adrian, how *like* you to miss the first one! Can't you ever get anywhere on time!'

Before even the ugly echo of this greeting had time to reach her ears, she turned sick. What answer could a man make to such a woman save to turn and leave her for ever!

Well, she had forgotten him, it seemed, had in her hysterical loss of any sense of proportion forgotten that he never lost his. His answer was not in the least to turn and leave her. It was given with a grin. 'The stars in their courses, Matey, didn't seem to care as much about my *permission* as I did. It's been quite a day. First the *camionette* I started on bust a rear axle. I jumped a ride on a RVF truck and bribed the driver with cigarettes to step on the gas. Got to Bar-le-Duc. More cigarettes to the Maréchal des Logis to stamp my papers in a hurry. Got out on the platform just in time to see the train I expected to take breezing through like the Empire State passing Rustdorf. Mob of *permissionaires* – me too – acting like the mob in *Julius Caesar*. Despair. Then along comes another train. Somebody calls out "Chalons! Epernay! Paris!" and we all surge on, several hundred of us. Packed like sardines. First I stood on one foot and then on the other; there wasn't room for both. Anyway here I am.' The clasp of his arms tightened about her. He had

not even listened to her poor wrong words except to recognise
them as part of the strain of her longing for him. Adrian was
not a dream, after all.

He looked well, they began to say then, all talking at once –
rather pale from driving at night and sleeping by day. But quite
like himself. Quite like all men back from the front too, in that
his first thought was for a bath. They had the flat tin tub ready
in the little *cabinet de toilette,* the reservoir of the cookstove
full of hot water. Matey laid out clean underwear – bought
at the department store in Rustdorf! – and while he bathed
went into the kitchen. For weeks she had been planning and
re-planning what to have for that first dinner and had run all
over Paris to find the ingredients for the Boston brown bread
and the pancakes.

But after all Adrian did not eat much of it. 'I spoiled my
appetite with bread and cheese in the train. I'm afraid I can't
do justice to dinner,' he said apologetically at the last.

Matey's heart sank in alarm. She lost her head again. She
saw herself as perhaps she looked to Adrian with the elaborate
dinner to celebrate his homecoming, trivial – or callous.
He would despise her. From his letters it had been evident
that he had been profoundly affected by what he saw at the
front. Perhaps he had grown away from her, would feel that
her wildness of longing for him was grasping and personal,
indecorous in the midst of tragedy. In a flash she imagined
him grown like his father, old, remote, disembodied, beyond
passion, beyond her, lost to her . . . and because she imagined
him so, she knew he was so. Mme Vinet said, 'You two haven't

had a moment to yourselves yet. Let me put the children to bed.'

Petella and Brother said hastily *merci bien, Bonne-maman,* but they *would* like Father too, because there were certain things he always did, a certain story he always told, the same, only different. . . . 'Putting the children to bed is one of the things I'm here for,' Adrian said.

'He doesn't *want* to be alone with me,' thought Matey, wildly.

He helped the children undress with a great deal of noisy play, he tucked them up, told them an instalment of a serial saga of his invention, in which Brother figured as an elephant tamer and Petella an explorer in African jungles, and afterwards, according to the tradition which dates before the beginning of the children's memories, said, 'Now I'm going to sit here and hope you'll always be good children,' and sat between their beds in the dark, holding in each of his hands the small warm hand of a drowsy child.

After a time, 'This is a *sort* of "Meeting", Brother,' Petella's voice came sleepily through the darkness.

J'aime ça alors,' murmured the little boy.

Their father stood up finally, felt his way to the door, and stepped out into the hallway. The apartment was quiet. No light in the living room; Mme Vinet had humanely gone to bed. He drew a long breath.

He turned out the gas in the hall and opened the door to his wife's room. At the sound she turned, tall in her white nightgown, her beautiful wide grey eyes, dark with emotion, fixed on his.

He gave a cry, 'Why, it's true! I'm here!' And went toward her, trembling like a bridegroom.

She came into his arms like a bride.

'Well, M Fort,' said Mme Vinet the next morning, surprised to find Adrian up and dressed at the hour of the children's early breakfast. 'Think of seeing a man from the front, *en permission,* awake before noon.' She herself never could eat a mouthful before the arrival of the mail and Henri's daily letter and was now walking around and around the apartment in her usual morning restlessness, looking at the clock, trying to think of small tasks, picking up loose ends. Returning from the hallway with the children's wraps and overshoes in her arms, she asked him, 'What are you going to do to amuse yourself in these precious few days? It's always interesting to us to see the different ways the soldiers take to get the good of their *permissions.'*

'What am I going to do to amuse myself? I'm not going to let my wife out of sight, of course,' said Adrian, tying Brother's napkin around his neck.

'Oh, goody!' said Petella. 'Will you take us to school when she does?'

'Sure thing,' said her father. 'Wherever Mother goes you're going to see a new shadow beside her.'

Brother, who still understood English, made a little joke. 'A *lady's* shadow in trousers!' he said in French, shaking his head over his orange.

Adrian burst into a laugh, the first since he had come back. 'The little scallywag!' he cried, turning to Matey.

Brother was enchanted with the new word. *'Scadavague!
Scadavague!'* he cried proudly, laying a plump hand on his
breast. *'Je suis un petit scadavague!'*

The hours spent in the children's world were gay hours
for Adrian as for all the men on leave. But they were the
only gay ones. There was no gaiety in the painful excited
happiness of their hours together, a happiness which ran the
scale from the hungry passion which flung them wildly into
each other's arms as if to make up by present ardour for all
those arid past and future months of separation, down to the
mere home-like sharing of such uninteresting jobs as carrying
packages of mail for the front to the branch post office near
them. There were, too, certain hours of comforting tiresome
homely reality when they talked over accounts. They seemed
almost home again in Rustdorf in those matter-of-fact porings
over bills and budgets. Matey was sole treasurer of their fund,
and got out her records to see if Adrian could not help her
to plan with more foresight. But of course the one element
necessary for foresight was lacking – any sort of notion of how
long they would be required to hold out. The war was then in
its nineteenth month. 'It can't last much longer,' Matey often
affirmed, making a statement out of a wish.

'How much are you spending, altogether?' asked Adrian.

'At the rate of $250 a month,' said Matey anxiously. 'We
keep down our own expenses as closely as we can. But food,
both here and what we send in packages to the front, is more
expensive all the time. And we have so many men coming and
going whose only chance it is for decent meals. And of course,

though it was a great bargain, a lump sum out like the price of the Letellier house brings up the average. I can't make it less. It'll be more, even; the children must have some new clothes. They are growing so fast.'

She thought she saw his eyelids drooping in the perpetual drowsiness that was the most visible effect of his night driving, and left him to take a nap in his chair as he did at intervals during the day, no matter what was happening. But when she stepped back half an hour later, he said as though he had been turning the matter over in his mind, 'Well, I'm damned if I can screw expenses down any more closely either.' (One of the things he brought back from the front was a new habit of copious profanity, apparently quite unconscious.) 'In fact I'd like to spend more. There are often chances to help – families still living in the war zone, with children. And I'd like to send something every month to Marceau's family in Lyons.'

'Oh, do take more, if you have ways to use it,' cried Matey. 'The war must be over soon. Everybody says so. By next autumn at the latest!'

Adrian began to make figures on a piece of paper. 'At this rate, with the interest, diminishing though that is, we'd last for four years,' he said.

'You mean the *money*'d last,' said Matey desperately. '*We* couldn't! Oh, Adrian! Four years! It's not thinkable!'

'No, damned if I believe it,' said Adrian considering the calculations on his paper. 'I don't believe anybody'd last that long. I think it would be safe to spend more.'

Matey thought of what Aunt Connie's money had done and

exclaimed, 'Adrian, wouldn't it have been too awful if we had stayed at home!'

A bleak expression came into his eyes.

She said, shocked, 'Adrian, you don't ever wish we had!'

He laid the paper carefully down on the table. 'I often wish I could give up and lie down in my grave,' he said in a low voice.

Matey brought up hastily a familiar defence of her own against that thought. 'But, Adrian, don't you feel it a great consolation that we are doing what we can to help?'

'God! *no!*' said Adrian with a bitterness that made her tone sound smug. 'What the hell does it matter about us, compared to what's going on?'

She clung to something she felt was real. 'But it *is* better – at least a little better – at least for us – because we are doing what – '

'It might have been better for us if we had never been born,' said the man from the front, 'and hadn't brought two more human beings into the world.'

Matey was shocked into silence. But she was not shaken. Something had risen up, some sustaining certainty that had been – she saw it now – at the far back of her every thought about the war. Yes, even in the worst moments. That day last month when she sat in the hospital beside a dying man, taking his messages for his children, and on leaving him had passed between two ghastly rows of wounded men, fixing their death-shadowed eyes on her – when she had come out into the street, she had leaned against the hospital wall unable to stand, weeping all the tears of her heart. But they had been tears of sorrow, not of despair.

✲✲✲

Adrian broke the silence to say in his father's dry, self-controlled voice, 'I don't feel that way all the time, of course. In fact almost never on my top layer. I didn't mean to say it. It gives much too melodramatic an impression. I get along all right. Mostly my thoughts are quite taken up with wondering whether I remembered to put grease in the differential, or whether the engine is hitting on four. I forget all about what I'm carrying – you wouldn't think it possible, but I do – then we hit a bump and someone behind groans and calls out *"Doucement,"* and I drive very carefully for a while until I forget again. It's the forgetting that keeps me from going insane – until all of a sudden something makes you wake up and realise what's going on. I'll tell you – we've got a big map in the mess-shanty with pins to show the lines. The other day the *communiqué* reported a British gain, and I was moving pins forward and feeling good about it . . . then it came to me what the eighth of an inch of map must have been like, with the barrage and the machine-gun fire and the wounded screaming themselves to death . . . I was so ashamed of myself that I wanted to cut my throat.'

He laid his hand gently on her knee and went on more calmly. 'Don't pay too much attention to what I'm saying, Matey; I'm tired, I guess. You musn't think I'm suffering or a hero. The danger doesn't amount to much, and as for hardship, we live like princes compared to the infantry. More often than not we're positively gay at the section – get up parties, play cards and sing, and up at the *poste de secours* we swap yarns with the *brancardiers*. There are lots of times, too, when I'm carried away by the men at the front. They are amazing – what they can stand and go ahead. It gives you a new conception of what's possible. And just as a spectacle it's beyond anything. The other day – our section was driving in the daytime last week, from the field hospital back to the base hospital – I had two Germans wounded in the ambulance. As I started up a hill I saw pouring over the skyline down toward me a French regiment going up to the front. They went by me – it was magnificent, Matey! There's no hurrah, you know, along the front, no brass bands, no cheap banging on nerve centres, just a thousand silent resolute men, slogging steadily along too – ' He was silent, his lips twisting into a sick, ugly grimace that looked like disgust.

Matey said quickly, 'Adrian, after all, they *are*, aren't they, marching forward to die for what they think is right?'

He corrected the formula with a dry fierce grimness, 'Or murder for it. They don't all of them die. A good many of them kill.' His voice rose. 'People always forget that, Matey. I'm not going to have my wife forget it! Those that don't die have generally seen to it that some other fellow has.'

He drew his hand down over his face as if he were trying to wipe away the violence which in spite of himself had come into his expression and went on in a lower tone, 'When we got to the hospitals one of the Germans was dead. He looked like a nice little kid gone to sleep. But I suppose he had killed other nice little kids too, before one of them killed him.'

He looked away from his wife, down at the floor, 'Some days I can't make anything out of it at all. But there are plenty of others when I understand it all right, when we all seem to be demons in one big hell, and the truth is that there is nothing strong in life but the wish to hurt.'

Matey knew then what had been the old base of the sustaining certainty she had and Adrian had not. She confounded
in one hot impulse of compassion her husband sickened in
a blood-smeared world and the little girl sickening over the
intonation of a voice. She burst out to Adrian, her voice
breaking in her intensity, 'No, Adrian, no! That's not all. You
musn't think that's all. We couldn't live a minute if it were
all. That wish to hurt – it doesn't mean there's nothing but
hate! Compared to what's underneath, what keeps us alive – a
belonging-together of us all that's so much greater – that'll
last – outlast anything – outlast the worst in us – and stand up
in the face of death!' No, she couldn't get it into words. She
never could.

Adrian found some words for her. As he looked into her
passionately moved face his own softened. He quoted under
his breath, 'Despairer, here is my neck. By God, you shall not
go down.' He put out his hand to take hers.

There was a hurried knocking at the door. Before Matey
could open it Mme Vinet flung it open and burst in, her face,
usually pale and steady, distorted by joy. *'Mété, Mété!'* she cried,
waving a letter. Adrian and Matey had the same thought: 'Ziza
has been found.'

'Henri is wounded!' cried Henri's mother exultantly. 'In
the arm! In the arm – a beautiful arm wound. He's to be sent
to a hospital here in Paris. Tomorrow! It will take at least six
weeks before it will be healed. Six weeks! Six weeks!' She began
to cry and flung her arms around Matey, sobbing out, 'Six
weeks! He will be safe for six weeks!'

Over her shoulder, Matey saw Adrian's face take on again

the bleak stony expression that made him look like another man.

Adrian went back to the front on February 21st. The newspaper of the next morning announced the terrific bombardment which began the siege of Verdun.

CHAPTER ELEVEN

✲✲✲

Matey did not know – never did know till he returned for a leave – along which front Adrian's ambulance section was working, but during the endless spring of 1916 his brief and irregular bulletins of incessant activity sounded as though he were near Verdun. Dominiqua did not hear from Jean for a fortnight at a time that spring and went about like a woman in a trance. Henri's beautifully broken arm had lasted until May. Then he too had disappeared into the furnace, his letters no longer arriving every morning, sometimes not arriving till after many days of silence.

No men had returned on furlough for many weeks.

Death after death struck into their circle. The boy from Lille who put perfume on his hair and loved good clothes and Palais-Royal farces was part of the human chaff blown into eternity at Douaumont. Louis Plon, the illiterate home-loving exiled coal miner from the North who loved to put up shelves and mend broken locks, was sent from Mort Homme to one hospital after another, dying in Paris with Mme Vinet beside him. The stubbornly land-loving Breton farmhand lay down in the earth for ever at Avocourt. The last remaining son of

Petella's widowed teacher in the *lycée*, the two younger brothers of Mimi's husband, the only son of the family in the apartment below them, were killed and buried. Matey had walked beside Mme Vinet in one funeral procession after another. She shed no tears. And neither did Mme Vinet, leaning heavily on her arm, limping and faltering as she walked, like an old woman. They were below – or above – beyond, perhaps – the realms where tears could fall.

During the evenings as long as the children were awake they kept some aspect of quiet and cheerfulness. Mme Vinet often substituted music for words, as she had for her own children and Matey. On some evenings Matey sat with Brother on her lap, Petella, leaning against her knees, Dominiqua knitting across the room, Mme Vinet at the piano, until it was bedtime for the children. Sometimes she said to Mme Vinet, 'Play something a little louder, won't you, please?' Although it was materially impossible many women in Paris that spring heard in quiet moments a ghostly roar from the guns at Verdun.

After the children had gone to bed this sounded louder, sometimes rose till they thought an air raid was beginning. The hours after the children had gone to sleep were hard ones. The three women sat up till all hours, knitting or sewing or reading, or frankly pacing up and down in uncontrollable anxiety. The nights of air raids were almost the best, putting, as they did, something else to think about into the dark hours of waiting. But after these periods of wakefulness there always came a blessed time when the body claimed its rights, and they slept deeply, as if this nightmare, as if life itself, were over at last.

It was from such a death-like sleep on a hot night in early

June that Matey started up and sat for an instant in her bed. 'Aunt Tryntje? Is that you?' she called.

The present struck her out of bed and into the hall. She had begun to fumble for the gas-jet beside the door when she woke to the possibility that it might be the *concierge,* come with a telegram from the front. With nothing but Verdun in her mind she flung the door open.

It was not the *concierge.* In the dim light on the landing stood a small stooped woman in shabby clothes, a battered hat casting a deep shadow over her face. She held a young baby over one shoulder and seemed to hold the hand of an older child, half-hidden behind her skirts.

Matey's tall figure with long brown hair streaming over the shoulders was not apparently what she had expected. She said falteringly, half turning to go, 'Mme Vinet, then, is no longer here?' Matey knew her then. *'Ziza!'* she screamed.

Her cry, echoing down the corridor, brought Mme Vinet. She called out as she ran down the hall, and Matey answered, she did not know what, and stood back. She hurried to make a light and drew gently inside the door the two women locked in each other's arms. The sleeping baby did not stir, but the little boy slipped away like a shadow into a corner of the room and sat down on the floor behind a chair.

Now she could see the yellow-grey face of the woman who had Ziza's voice. She was startled. It did not look at all like Ziza. Nothing in eyes, mouth, or expression was like Ziza. And it was evident that the newcomer did not know Matey. Over Mme Vinet's shoulder she was looking strangely at her from sunken eyes.

'It is Météé, little Météé Gilbert, come from America to – ' began Mme Vinet.

The strange woman seemed to hear this and nodded. But after a long look into Matey's face she said, as though she had made the discovery for herself, 'Why, it is Météé. What are you doing in France, Météé?' The voice, though toneless and without personality, was recognisably Ziza's.

The baby woke up and began to cry. The woman in Mme Vinet's arms was wavering to and fro. It was no time for explanations.

'I don't suppose you have any milk?' said Ziza, wearily giving up the baby to Matey's outstretched hands.

'Yes, yes, we have plenty!' cried Matey, blessing Aunt Connie. She laid the baby on her bed and ran into the kitchen, where she was setting some milk to warm when she was aware of a small white figure near her. Petella stood there in her nightgown. Her eyes were open, but her face had a fixed blankness. 'Mother,' she said earnestly, 'didn't I hear the front door open?'

'Yes, dear,' said her mother, wondering if the child were really awake. The little girl put her hands together imploringly. 'Oh, Mother, *was* it somebody come to say the war is over?' she said, her chin trembling.

Matey drew a long breath and said gently to Petella, turning her around so that she faced the door, 'No, dear, it wasn't that. Not this time. Run back to bed, darling.'

The child pattered soberly away, and when Matey, a moment later, the bottle of warm milk in her hand, looked into the children's room, Petella was in her bed as sound asleep as her little brother.

✣✣✣

Mme Vinet had led Ziza into the bedroom which had been waiting so long for her and was helping her undress, uttering no words but broken murmurs of compassion.

Where was the little boy? Matey went back into the living room. There he sat still on the floor, in the corner behind the chair. Holding the fretting baby on one shoulder, she stooped down and said gently, 'Don't you want to come with me, dear, and go to bed?'

He did not seem to understand her, looking into her face with no change of expression, as if he did not see her. But when she put out her hand to help him up, he rose quickly with a dreadful docility and followed where she led. 'Would you like a drink of milk, dear?' she asked him as they passed the kitchen. He hung down his head and made no answer.

In the door of Ziza's room she asked, 'Will it be all right, Ziza dear, to put your little boy to sleep in the children's room near my children?' She spoke guardedly and softly, having the impression that even words were wounding to the exhaustion of the newcomers. Ziza answered in a muffled tone, 'I'll have to have the baby here, to take care of her.'

'No, oh, *no!*' said Matey with a soft earnestness. 'Let me take her! I'd love to.'

Ziza made no answer to this for a time. Her mother had put her into bed now and sat, one arm around her, holding a cup of milk to her lips, making her drink it in little sips. When she had finished this she said, in an expressionless voice, 'She's not my baby, you know,' and lying down, turned her back to them and to the room.

Matey and Mme Vinet tiptoed into Matey's bedroom, where they managed to feed the baby and to undress the little boy, passive in their hands as a rag doll. They put him into a nightgown of Petella's, vastly too large for him, and tucked him up on an improvised bed on the sofa in the children's room. They said not a word to each other till this was done and they were back in Matey's bedroom, where the sleeping baby was lost in the wide bed.

Matey saw that Mme Vinet was trembling from head to foot. She put her arms about the small thin figure. 'Let me put *you* to bed next, Bonne-maman,' she said tenderly.

Mme Vinet said in a frightened whisper, 'Can it really be Ziza?' They went together down the lighted corridor to the door of Ziza's room. It stood ajar. They pushed it gently open. The light fell on the bed, on the face half-buried in the pillow. It was relaxed in a profound sleep, and now it was Ziza's face! All that had made it strange and alien and frightening was wiped away. It was little Ziza come back.

Matey slept but little that night. She lay awake, or half-awake, on guard against the powers of evil which had eddied blackly in through the door she had opened to the fugitives. Lying in her bed, the frail unknown scrap of humanity beside her, Matey felt the despair and terror brought in by the victims filling the darkness as if with swooping silent batwings. She had no fear of them now, nothing but the steadfast certainty that she had grown to be stronger than they.

Once, as she lay planning how to reorganise the daily life, she heard a stir and ran quickly to see what it was. Mme Vinet was standing in Ziza's doorway, looking in at her, weeping silently. Matey led her back to bed. The older woman leaned to say in Matey's ear, 'Do you suppose she has lost her mind *entirely!* Will she ever . . . ' They both thought of other refugees from Belgium whom they had known.

Matey answered stout-heartedly, 'Inside a month – you'll see – we'll have her just like herself again.'

Later, standing guard from her wakeful bed, she thought she heard a faint sound again, and springing up, made the rounds of her little fortress. The sofa-bed in the children's room was empty. The child she had left to sleep in it was gone.

After one wild look at the open window she began to search for him, going very softly in her bare feet not to waken Mme Vinet. After looking at top speed everywhere, more and more alarmed, it occurred to her to look under Ziza's bed. There he was, far back against the wall, his eyes wide open. When she beckoned to him to come, he crept slowly out on his hands and knees and without a sound followed her back to his bed. After she had tucked him in, Matey stooped and passionately kissed his pale vacant little face. No change of expression came into it.

The black wings swooped boldly low then, beating loudly at her ear. They but fanned her courage till it glowed.

At dawn she roused Dominiqua and sent her out to the nearest telegraph station. The telegrams to Mimi and to Henri were identical, 'Ziza returned last night. Very tired and worn but will be all right after rest and good care. Letter with details follows. Mété.'

By afternoon of the first day she was putting what few details she had learned into carefully worded letters which went off to La Ferté and the front. After describing the arrival at the door: 'Ziza is still exhausted, as was to be expected of course. We are keeping her in bed and don't want to tire her with questions till she has more strength; so I haven't much information to add to my telegram. We don't know yet how she managed to escape and make her way here – she doesn't seem to have a penny with her – nor what has happened to her husband. She has not mentioned him, and we are afraid to till she does. She did tell us that her poor baby, Henri's namesake, died more than a year ago. The tiny baby girl with her (I took her for not more than four months old, but Ziza says she is nearly eight months) is the child of her young Belgian maid and the German soldier who was quartered in her house. No, not at all what you think. He was, Ziza says, a quiet dull peasant boy, very homesick, who fell in love with Ziza's maid and she with him. He was killed in battle, and the young mother died in Ziza's arms the day after the baby was born.

'Ziza's own little boy shows of course the effects of what he has been through. But there is no cause for alarm. He is so young that he will soon react to good food and good care and the knowledge that he is now in safety. I will write you both frequent bulletins of the invalids. Don't expect too many letters from your mother. She is of course absorbed. . . . '

She looked up from the letter to answer Petella, who came in to say anxiously, 'Mother, the new little boy still won't speak to us or look at us. He just crawls off in the corner and hides behind the bookcase.'

'Never mind, dear,' said Matey; 'it'll take time. Just go on playing naturally you and Brother. He'll get all right, little by little.'

But he did not. In Dominiqua's competent hands the baby girl changed from scrawniness to plumpness almost overnight. Under her mother's passion of solicitude Ziza's hollow eyes, sunken cheeks, and strengthless voice changed from one day to the next. But the little Adrien remained the same. They kept Ziza in bed still, and under cover of giving her a complete rest, shut out all four children from her room. She slept most of the time and was still too weak to protest or to doubt them when they said her little son was 'doing well'.

But he was not doing well. He would eat nothing if anyone was in the room with him. He had not said a word nor showed that he understood one. And if left to himself for a moment he still crept into the darkest corner he could find and crouched there, facing the wall, making himself small. The other children with their impetuous movements and clear confident voices seemed to frighten him rather more than the grown-ups. There was but one thing to encourage Matey. Under their brooding care his physical condition improved visibly. The only sound he had made was on the day they tried to put on outdoor wraps to take him for a walk. He had wept then, in a low hushed terrified way that froze Matey's blood, and with weak desperate gestures had plucked off his coat and hat as fast as they tried to put them on. Matey abandoned that plan at once, though she had had great hopes of the fresh air and outdoor exercise.

Dominiqua gave him up. Some weeks after Ziza's return, 'You can't do anything for him, M'ame Mété,' she said. 'I've seen children before who'd had too great a fright. They are always imbecile. There was a little girl in Biriatou who got lost on the mountain overnight. She never so much as knew her own name afterward.' This brought Izcohébie Hill back to Matey and her own first encounter with fear, and that other later meeting with war fright, the night on the Garonne, when she had found out that fear felt by grown-ups is not destroying like the terrors of children. She thought that, better than Dominiqua or his grandmother, she understood the sick little boy crouching in his corner. There had been long periods in her youth when she too had crept into a corner and turned her face away from what life seemed to be. And Priscilla, of course . . . She pulled herself up from these thoughts. She was being unjust again.

There was a Zeppelin raid that night, through the noise of which, as usual, the children slept unswervingly, even the new little boy. Also, as usual during air raids, Matey and Mme Vinet and Dominiqua wandered about the darkened apartment in wrappers and slippers, saying to each other that perhaps this time they had better take the children down to the basement, and remembering again the current opinion that if an apartment house were struck it would all go, crushing the people in the basement as well. They gave the baby her ten o'clock bottle, thinking it might be her last meal. They looked through cracks in the shutters out into the blackness of the threatened city; they listened to the explosions, trying to decide whether they were farther away or coming closer; they went back to look at the children; they stepped again and again into Ziza's room to tell her that it was just about finished.

Finally, after a long, dead silence, came the first ringing notes from the patrolling *pompiers,* sounding the *berloque* which always signalled the end of an attack. The three tired women stepped in their night-clothes out on the balcony, looking down into the impenetrable blackness below them, from which, like invisible rockets, soared up the voices of the bugles.

Matey went then to take a long drink of water. During the air raids she was not conscious of being exactly afraid, but afterward she always suffered from an intolerable dryness of the mouth and throat. Dominiqua always said that no Basque was ever afraid of anything mortal, but Matey noticed that her hands were icy-cold and too stiff to use. Mme Vinet's affliction was more humiliating. While the raid was going on she looked and spoke as usual, but she always had a long attack of nausea when it was over.

By the time, about three in the morning, when the three women finally went to bed, Matey would have said that any memories of her childhood brought up by Dominiqua's remark had been swept away to oblivion. Yet when she fell asleep she instantly began dreaming of Hamilton and the high school there and a play the juniors gave in which she had taken part. She was running down the school corridor calling to a classmate about the hour for a rehearsal when her alarm clock sounded its rattlesnake whir-r-r.

She opened her eyes slowly. A faint grey came in at the window. Summer rain pattered on the floor of the balcony outside. She threw off the bedclothes and slid her feet out of bed, thinking with perfect conviction, 'Now I know what to do for little Adrien.'

She could hardly wait through the morning routine, and after she had left the children at school, hurried off down the street toward the Seine. She knew where to go – the Quai along which she and Mimi had followed Henri and his mother after the concert years ago, where she had had her first guess at what a heaven might be.

By the middle of the morning, she was back in the children's room at the apartment, the doors closed. The little boy was sitting cross-legged in the corner, facing the wall. 'See here, Adrien,' she said, kneeling down beside him, 'here is a little dog for you. He is going to be yours.'

The puppy, wriggling to be free, barked excitedly in his shrill voice. At the new sound the little boy turned his vacant face toward them.

'He's only a baby dog who doesn't know how to take care of himself, so you'll have to look out for him, feed him, and all.'

The fussy little thing, down on the floor now, explosive with youth, leaped up toward the child's face. Adrien drew back nervously. A flicker of expression passed faintly over his face.

'See, he knows already he belongs to you. He's trying to tell you he's glad he has come to live with you.'

The puppy began sniffingly to investigate Adrien's shoe. The child looked down at him.

✣✣✣

'Now I've put some milk in a saucer on the table over there. Whenever you think he'd like it, just set it down on the floor where he can get at it.'

Partly because she did not dare to examine the child's face and partly out of a sense of decency she turned away from them now and stood up on a chair to dust and rearrange the books on the upper shelves of the bookcase. She had dusted them several times over and put them all back in new places before she heard a faint sound which made her turn her head. Over her shoulder she saw that the saucer of milk had been set on the floor and the puppy, his legs sprawlingly braced at wide angles, was untidily lapping it up.

She stepped quickly down from the chair and out of the door, closing it behind her. In the corridor outside, 'Well, *Sumner . . .* !' she said unsteadily.

In her general letter later that month she reported, 'Our refugees seem to be getting along better now. Ziza is still very silent and so quiet you wouldn't guess it was Ziza, but she is up and dressed every day and has been out with her mother once for a walk. The new baby is a great plaything for us all, especially for Petella, who's devoted to her. It gives the family quite a rest from Petella's questions. Ziza's little boy, who was pretty well used up when he came, has taken a real turn for the better too. We have a puppy in the family now – Irish terrier by his looks – to keep little Adrien company while Petella and Brother are at school; school here goes on, you know, till Bastille Day, the fourteenth of July. The puppy and the little boy have great times together, and Adrien won't go to sleep at night now unless Toutou is tucked up with him. That silly name, I hasten to say, is little Adrien's own idea. Yesterday, with Toutou equipped with magnificent red leather harness and leash, Adrien took his dog out for his first walk. Adrien's first, too. I went along, of course, but I didn't count. Adrien was showing the puppy the wonders of the great world. It was sweet to see the fatherly care the little boy gave his pet when we crossed the street to get into the Luxembourg, and when the foolish little thing, wriggling and bouncing all over the place, wrapped his leash around a tree and brought himself up short, with an injured goggle-eyed look of puppy surprise, little Adrien burst out laughing.' (She did not say that the tears had gushed from her eyes at the sound.) 'I think now that by the beginning of next school time, he will probably be well enough to go to school with Petella. They are about of an age, you know.

'I don't speak of the war to you because I imagine, being in a neutral country, you get more complete news and know more about it than I. Jean Iturbe, Dominiqua's son, was badly wounded in the last of the Verdun siege, at Thiaumont. But he is getting well fast and will probably be returned to the front before next winter.'

CHAPTER TWELVE

✿✿✿

Ziza made no comment on the change which gradually took place in little Adrien, although Matey thought she turned her head to listen when his voice rose above those of the other children playing or amicably wrangling in the children's room. She made no comment on the thriving condition of the baby, although she soon began to do her full share of caring for the little thing. She made, in fact, no comment on anything. Although by the end of summer she was nearly back to normal weight and seemed to have recovered her physical strength, she might almost not have been there, for any impression of personality she gave. 'I'll take those packages to the mail.' 'Let me finish that sock.' 'Tell me the address of the hospital and I'll look him up.' She seemed to have no other language. Matey noticed that the various soldiers on leave who came and went in the apartment scarcely seemed to know that she was there. Henri, thin and racked with sciatic pain, had come and gone again without venturing to break through the impalpable wall which still divided her from life.

Mimi too came up several times from La Ferté for between-train visits, but to Matey's exasperated compassion the relations

of the other Vinets with Mimi grew no easier. This in spite
of an obvious and difficult attempt to keep off the subject of
disagreement.

She still did not bring her boys to Paris. 'It disturbs their
school work,' she explained. There was now, since Ziza's
return, no reason for continuing the watch in the apartment,
and Mimi affectionately invited her mother and sister – 'you
too and the children, Mété'– to spend August with her in the
country. But Mme Vinet found reasons connected with their
war-relief occupations which would make this impossible.

'Well, send little Adrien down then,' said his Tante Mimi,
laying a kind hand on his brown bullet-head; 'he and my boys
would have great days together.'

Mme Vinet said in a quick, vehement tone, 'No, no, he
would better stay with us.' Mimi's face darkened in the ensuing
silence.

Matey was out of all patience with this misery, self-inflicted
as it seemed to her. But she dared say nothing, it was so far
from anything she could understand. It seemed to her as out of
character for Mme Vinet as if she had struck at her daughter.

Ziza sat looking at her hands passively, apparently hearing
nothing.

Time went on and she seemed to hear no more. She still
ran with nervous haste from one task to another and spoke
only of whether there was time to get one more letter in the
mail or how many petticoats were needed for layettes in an
oeuvre for Belgian refugees.

The autumn of 1916 came. The war seemed more firmly
rooted at the core of life than ever. The children went back to

school, Ziza's little Adrien skipping beside them now. Toutou was left to forlorn solitary naps in the children's room. The baby girl grew fast, had four teeth, an inexhaustible supply of smiles and naughtiness, and began to know her own name, Mélanie. 'I suppose she ought to be named for her mother,' said Ziza.

'What was her father's last name?' asked Mme Vinet, venturing timidly an enquiry about those blank years, with a glance at Matey for support.

'Müller,' said Ziza briefly, pronouncing it in the French manner. She stood up. 'Mété, there isn't enough chocolate for that package for Dominiqua's son. I'll go out and get it now while the shops are still open.' She took some money from the family purse on the mantelpiece, the purse into which Mme Vinet put the money that came in from music lessons and which Aunt Connie kept from ever becoming empty, and went away silently.

Mme Vinet drew a long sighing breath.

'Patience, patience,' murmured Matey.

The winter came on, the dreadful winter, the coldest of the war, the coldest known in France for a generation, fantastically cold, so that blood froze instantly on wounds, so that as the grim days dragged on, Matey sometimes felt as though even the sun had given up, defeated, and they were all left on a freezing planet to die slowly of the cold – those who were not cutting each other's throats. Adrian, Henri, and the other men coming and going from the front told strange stories about the cold there. Jean Iturbe, always gay with a touch of grotes-querie, delighted the children with a tale, accompanied by picturesque action, of how a man in his regiment, tormented by head lice, had recklessly washed his hair, cold or no cold, and how it has frozen stiff, in rattling knobs and wisps, on the tips of which, whenever he went out, he was obliged to hang his fatigue cap or his helmet. His encounter with his commanding officer, who rebuked him for his unmilitary aspect, and his invitation to the captain to feel for himself what the trouble was, narrated with much pantomime by Jean, sent the children into spasms of laughter. The success of this story made it grow into a serial folk-tale so that when Jean reappeared every four months the greeting of the children was to cry out, even long after the warm weather had come, even after that soldier lay in his grave in a military cemetery, 'What has happened *now* to the man with the frozen hair?'

Henri was sent into Normandy as a cog in the machinery for settling disputes between the country people and the English troops stationed there, in the matter of doors and farm utensils and window frames burned by the British. The Vinets were indignant over such lawlessness, but it did not surprise Matey, remembering Mrs Deyo and her talk of the burning of the clapboards, fence rails, and hen roosts by the American Revolutionary troops wintering at Fonteynkill.

The impression during that winter of being on a dying planet losing its vital heat was always associated in Matey's memory with the mingled dread and hope she and Adrian felt in hearing from afar what sounded like the echo of a change in American public opinion about the war. They gathered this almost entirely from their letters, as they saw few Americans save those in the ambulance service, for the most part as out of touch with home as they. And although the air was full of rumours of a change in the attitude of the United States, Adrian warned Matey not to pay too much attention to them, because rumours that winter were going beyond anything imaginable in wildness – for three days everyone Matey met was repeating the news that the United States had purchased Constantinople and would present it to the Allies as a gift. Adrian still doubted whether the United States as a whole was any more aware of Europe than when they left Rustdorf. But as far as Matey was concerned, she was once more sure about something in the great world because of a small event in her own life; she had authentic information from a private source of her own which left no doubt in her mind that the change in the United States had taken place. Francis was writing to her with hot enthusiasm for the cause of the Allies and great indignation against the Germans.

Aunt Connie stood by the little group on the rue de Fleurus all through the cold. By dint of paying five prices and following up every hint as to where fuel might be found Matey succeeded in keeping a fire in the cook-stove and even one in the salamander in the living room. That upper-class stove, supposed by French tradition to be incapable of burning anything but the best of anthracite, came down from its pedestal along with other aristocracy and sulkily burned coke and low-grade soft-coal sweepings. Aunt Connie also provided the expensive woollen underwear that was so necessary for life, for the four children and four women of the family as well as for the innumerable soldiers that were on their list.

One day in February, when they had not half a pailful of coal between them and zero weather, Matey vanished, following a clue given her by the father-in-law of one of their soldiers – for the ramification of their circle now led high and low into all sorts of connections. She returned hours later, followed by a grimy man bearing a huge sack of coke. 'Where did you get it?' they cried as she appeared in the door, the man and the sack behind her.

'Sh! the gas works – Issy-les-Moulineaux – it's not allowed – the side door – and a taxi from there here,' she told them under her breath.

After the carrier had gone, 'What did it cost you?' Mme Vinet exclaimed.

'Never you mind!' said Matey, kissing her.

That day for the first time Ziza said something a little personal to Matey. They were walking together to the omnibus station where they were to take buses to different destinations. Ziza said uneasily, 'Meté, I don't understand . . . about how you – I hadn't really thought before. . . . Is it *your* money we are all . . . ?'

'No, it's not mine,' said Matey quickly. 'It's some that belonged to an old relative of mine who wanted it used in this way.'

'Oh,' said Ziza. She asked no more questions, climbing into her bus without another word. But Matey thought she noticed from that day that Ziza was perhaps more at ease with her than with Mme Vinet, as though the effort to speak had a little broken down the wall.

But the winter had gone before she spoke again.

Much was happening in the great world to take their minds from their personal lives. They forgot even the cold in the excitement over the painful, joyful, tragic, splendid news of the Russian revolution. The newspapers were full of foreboding talk of the blow it gave to the cause of the Allies. But on her hospital visits, from the beds full of shattered men Matey heard very different comments. One day when she came into the ward where one of their soldiers lay wounded, a wheelchair patient was reading aloud from a little radical sheet which told of the redressing of old wrongs in Russia and spoke especially of the return of the soil into the hands of those who cultivated it. From the beds came approvingly, 'They've got something out of the war anyhow!' 'Sounds like our revolution.' The peasant she had come to see, almost an illiterate, asked in a shocked voice, 'Didn't the country people in Russia own their own *land!*'

Another result of the Russian Revolution was the appearance among other refugees of the first of the touching, exasperating, charming, conscienceless Russian aristocrats who later poured in crowds into France, penniless and helpless. These first heralds, like the later hordes, drove to distraction the thrifty French bourgeois women directing the *oeuvres* for refugees. What could be done for unreasonable cherry-orchard paupers who could not resist the desire to spend on one day of champagne and caviare money painfully provided out of many self-denying economies and intended to keep them alive for months!

Before spring came they had all also lived through the period of frenzied waiting to see whether the United States would continue diplomatic relations with Germany in spite of ever-increasing friction.

The answer came on a Sunday, when Matey and the children were on their way to their daily outing in the Luxembourg. Little Adrien and Petella (very good friends now, and allies against Brother's younger-child tyranny) had come to a standstill halfway to the park and were insisting that he take his turn at being horse and let one of them be driver. Brother was receiving this righteous ruling in the spirit of an aristocratiç Russian refugee. Matey let them fight it out.

Over their heated discussion, carried on in a clipped crackling elliptical French which reminded Matey of her old sharp play-discussions with Ziza, she looked idly up the street. It was quite empty this cold grey Sunday morning. As she looked an old news-woman in a ragged shawl, an armful of newspapers under her arm, came running around the corner. In front of her she carried the bulletin printed in large letters which, to save nerves nearly severed with long tense anxiety, was the only form of 'crying the news' allowed on the streets in those days.

RUPTURE OF DIPLOMATIC RELATIONS BETWEEN GERMANY AND USA

Matey held out a two-sou piece. The woman snatched at it as she ran by, leaving one of her single-sheet papers in Matey's hand, and pounded on down the street.

'Oh, *let* him be driver then!' said Adrien. His mother's fiery impatience was in his voice.

Petella said stubbornly, 'No, it's not *fair!*' Her intonation was like her Fort grandfather's.

Brother invented a Brother-like solution. He cocked his head on one side and said in his bird-like voice, 'I'd just as *soon* be the horse if you let me be a *white* horse, with spots.'

'Why, of course!' said Petella. 'You can be any kind of a horse you like!'

'Why didn't you say so, then?' said Brother, submitting with a smile to having the harness slipped over his head.

Devouring the news in the paper as she walked behind the children, Matey was asking herself, 'Will this mean war – real war – for my country? Men and boys from Rustdorf, old tennis partners, neighbours, cousins, lying in those dreadful hospital beds, looking their last at the world with those dreadful death-shadowed eyes?'

She read the paper all through, folded it, put it under her arm, and tried to give her attention to the children. They were running races now.

She stood looking at them blankly, not seeing them, but in their places the people for whom the shortening of the war would mean deliverance – Mimi's older boys nearer with every day to military service, Henri and the men of his age, worn and old, with grey in their thinning hair, the thousands and thousands of people in the occupied regions, listening passionately for the footsteps of liberators. And the women, all the women – behind the playing children, row upon row, the shadowy millions of heartsick women everywhere, waiting –

She turned from the children and the phantoms behind them and asked of the frozen trees, 'Do I even hope it will mean war for my own country?'

She never knew the answer to that question.

The end of March brought drying country roads and made possible a long-planned expedition with Ziza out into the Seine-et-Oise where they had heard of a school for chicken farmers. Matey wanted to investigate this as a possibility for one of their soldiers soon to be discharged from the hospital where he had left one arm and part of one leg. The doctors there had told Matey he needed light outdoor work.

She welcomed the chance for a momentary escape from brooding over what she wanted her country to do, and what, regardless of her wishes, it would finally do. When she and Ziza climbed into the third-class compartment of the train for Gambaix she had resolved at all costs to put them out of her mind. The sight of the open country came to her like a revelation. She had not been out of the city since the trip so many months before to Crouy with Mme Letellier. She had forgotten there was such a thing as country sky, and this was a spring sky, of a tender bright blue, with small very white clouds in it, each one shedding its own pearly light. Sitting close to the open window, she stared out hungrily. The larks were rising from the new-ploughed fields, a faint angelic echo of their song penetrating even the rattle of the train. The smell of the awakening earth came in through the window as if it were the fragrance of the untarnished country sunshine.

The train climbed painfully up a grade, through a cutting,

its old-fashioned engine (all the good ones were on trains at the front) badly fed by poor-grade fuel, panting and shaking its sides. At the top it emerged from the cutting and disclosed a magnificent field stretching to the horizon, the earth lovingly ploughed and harrowed and fitted till it lay like a mantle of brown velvet on the bones of rock. *'Oh! le beau champ!'* cried Matey, and turning, found Ziza's eyes on her with something of their old expression.

To Matey's astonishment, she said, 'You look more like yourself today, Mété, than I've seen you. You can't imagine what a relief it is to me. You've looked fairly frightening.'

'*I!*' said Matey, astounded, and with a wild, bone-breaking effort of the imagination, guessed that she perhaps had been seeming as strange to Ziza as Ziza to her. How long it took self-centred human denseness to learn that there are always two sides to any human relation! She moved over to Ziza impulsively and put her arm around her shoulder.

'Why, Ziza, dear, I was only trying not to be intrusive with you, to . . . '

'You're always too reasonable, Mété!' said Ziza. 'Too stable and . . . '

Matey laughed ruefully. 'Listen, Ziza, let me tell you the idiotic ups and downs I went through the day Adrian came back from the front for his first *permission!*' She had just reached the end of her account of that irrational day in which she had felt and acted like a naughty child and was describing her hopeless deadly certainty, while she was undressing that night, of being unloved and forgotten, when 'We approach Houdan, *mesdames,*' said the conductor at the door.

✝✝✝

They were to go by diligence from Houdan to Gambais and found the battered muddy vehicle waiting behind the little station. It was full of silent country women with baskets, returning from market. They made room for the two city ladies, who, separated from each other by the length of the wagon, yet looked at each other with an intimacy which brought them closer together than they had been since Ziza's return.

When they stepped down, in front of the school of aviculture, Ziza went on as if they had not been interrupted. 'Did you *really*, Mété? *Did* you lose your head and act unreasonably?'

'Never anybody more so,' said Matey. 'What in the world ever makes you think I'm calm and well balanced?'

Their ring at the door was answered, and their inspection of the school began.

When it was finished and arrangements made for the admission of LeGuily, their soldier, there were still a couple of hours to wait before the diligence returned to the train. They had brought a lunch of bread and cheese and apples and now borrowed a canteen of water from the school kitchen. Matey suggested half timidly, fearing that Ziza would at any moment slip back into her aloof impersonal manner, that they climb to the top of a small hill to eat and wait there for the hour of the diligence. Ziza nodded and the country woman who, in the absence of her husband at the front was directing the school, pointed out the beginning of the path and told them that in the clearing at the top they would find a bench.

Unused as they were to country walking, they had no breath for talk as they climbed up the path. Arrived at the top, they ate

✝✝✝

their lunch at once, soberly talking over the possibilities of the
poultry business for an ex-farmer with one arm gone.

They were silent after this, looking out over the brown
countryside. Early in the season as it was, the earth was no longer
in its winter sleep. Ploughing teams, greening willows, grazing
sheep, and the shouts of distant cocks were calling it back to
life. The sun shone ardently upon the motionless women. In
a bush of *aubépine* near them, leafless, but studded thick with
glistening swollen buds, a flock of tiny birds were carrying on
some sort of secret chittering discussion, incessantly bursting
up from the bush in a fluttering indignation of tiny wings, and
at once sinking back into it with low protesting murmurs.

Yes, Matey could for an instant forget the war. She began
dreamily, 'Ziza, do you remember one Sunday expedition in
the country when we all sat like this after lunch and talked
about – '

Ziza did not make a sound, but before she had finished
her sentence Matey became aware that it was not being heard.
She turned her head. Ziza was looking off at the horizon, very
pale, her face so drawn that she was scarcely recognisable.
When she lifted her eyes to meet Matey's, they seemed to have
sunk back into their sockets. Matey put out her hand and took
Ziza's small thin fingers into hers. They were hard and tense
like bird claws. She said in a murmur, 'Ziza – darling . . . '
Ziza drew a long breath, fought down a nervous tremor of all
her body, and said in a high shaking voice. 'Mété, I can't tell
Maman . . . she wouldn't understand. She and Papa were so
peaceable, so *raisonnable*. Or if they weren't, it's so long ago
she's forgotten. And I can't tell Mimi. She has only one answer

for everything now, her new one. Do you suppose *you* could – '
Matey put an arm around the little trembling body and drew it
close. Ziza fixed her eyes searchingly on Matey's and brought
it all out at once. 'Mété, *I* brought on the war. And it was *I* who
killed my Adrien.'

At the thought which came instantly into Matey's eyes, she
protested passionately, 'No, no, don't think that. Oh, Mété, if
you turn out to be only literal-minded and American, I won't
have *anybody!* Mété, don't just think I'm crazy, or I *will* be!
Listen to me first! Do you think there isn't any way for things
to be true except literally, materially?'

She began talking very fast, in so low a voice that Matey,
straining her ears, caught only disconnected phrases. 'Mété,
you know how crazy I was about Adrien? You know how
I . . . Well he was getting tired of . . . he was getting enough
of being loved by me. That spring before my second baby was
born – a girl – a neighbour – very young – just a little girl. Not
seventeen – daughter of a cousin – I was sick, clumsy, no good
for – she grew up that spring, all at once. You know. You've
seen girls. Dazzling. Intact. Adrien didn't know really, I think,
what he . . . *She* didn't know at all. He seemed like an uncle
to her. But – she was half woman – she felt it. She smiled at
him in a special way, lifted her eyebrows. Mété, she had such
beautiful eyebrows –

'Everything I did was wrong because it was I, not Marie-
Jeanne. I acted like a . . . Marie-Jeanne wore red. I bought a
red dress, but Adrien – I saw how he liked her being gay, so I
laughed too, till he gave me the blighting look that asks why
you are making a fool of yourself.

'If he had only shared with me – I could have – But he never thought of me – except as being in the way.

'He used to sit brooding . . . forget that it was time to go to his work. And he was furious if he was not reminded. Before I spoke, every time I prayed, "Oh, let me find the right word, the right tone, so that he will not look at me with that –" But I never did, never! never! never! He used to answer me, every word hard as a stone, "Yes. What is it you want?" like a knife-edge at my throat. But if Marie-Jeanne came running in, he was all bright softness at once, gentle, eager, kind.

'Mété, it was like being burned at the stake. And I couldn't even scream out, "Jésu! Jésu!" like Jeanne d'Arc.

'I know, I know, if I had been gentle, submissive . . . Marie-Jeanne was sweet. A good girl. She would have been married safely in a few years. But I can't be submissive. I couldn't stand it.

'I thought over and over, *"If only they could be separated for a while"* . . . a respite.

'If Marie-Jeanne's family would go away to live! Or if she would die! I would have killed her in a minute if I could, and Adrien not know. Or if *we* could go away! But what could take a Conacq away from Louvain! Mété, how I loathe that town! Nothing could ever induce me to set foot in it again.

'In May before my baby was born I thought of a way – I thought, "If there was a war, Adrien would be mobilised, for a while at least," I only thought of war like longer manoeuvres. Mété, you must understand that. I never *dreamed* of anything more than something like longer manoeuvres.

'And from that moment I willed a war to come. Night and day, I was praying for war. Every time Marie-Jeanne walked past the house – that tripping girl's step – I sent up my soul to call for war. I felt it coming. I used to lie awake at night and feel it like a huge roller slowly moving toward us in the dark. I lay there tugging at it to make it move faster.'

She drew away from Matey's arms and struggled up to her feet. She said something in a rapid whisper which Matey could not hear, and like a little hunted animal she darted off across the stony open field, doubling and turning silently as though she felt her pursuer close at her heels.

Matey made short work of reaching her and caught her firmly in long, strong arms. It was dreadful to feel how the thin body was shaking. Matey and the powers of evil were fighting hand to hand now.

She said, 'Ziza, look at me.' She trusted to the steadiness of her own eyes to hold the distraught ones which were lifted to them. 'Ziza, no, I don't think you are crazy. I see a truth in what you say. But if it is true for you – it is for everybody. You were right, I have been literal-minded. I see I brought on the war too, by my beastly satisfaction with my own share. Ziza, yes, we all brought it on together, that is the truth. *But that's done now.* We must make what amends we can, or be too base! Ziza, it would be cowardice not to stand by your own little boy. Ziza, you're no coward. . . . '

Ziza said, her eyes flickering to and fro in their sockets, 'Marie-Jeanne was one of those killed, the day – I saw her – her beautiful eyebrows all – '

'No, no, *no!*' cried Matey on a mounting note of intensity. 'No, you did not kill her any more than we all kill with our thoughts.'

The flickering black eyes steadied themselves against the steadfast grey ones, then slowly closed. The tense little body in Matey's arms went limp. Ziza's head fell to one side.

Matey laid her down on the ground. She was not frightened to have her faint, rather relieved. It gave them both a respite. And she hoped that a moment's unconsciousness might stand like a barrier between her and this hour. There was still water in the canteen. She poured a little of it on Ziza's forehead and rubbed her hands. When she saw the shut eyes flutter open she said in a quiet voice, 'Come, Ziza dear, we must not lose the train to Paris. The children – '

Ziza drew a long quivering sigh and sat up, lifting her hands to her wet disordered black hair. After she had pinned it into place she said, 'Ought I to tell Maman?'

'There is nothing to tell her,' Matey reminded her. She took this chance to set before Ziza the picture of reality as she wished her to see it. 'There is nothing to tell anybody, or to have in your mind, except a passing episode – nothing more – that might have happened to any woman in your condition. If the war hadn't come you would have forgotten it by now. Do you suppose that Adrien, once he held his second son in his ...'

Ziza sighed. 'You talk like a child, Mété. Of course he would.' She put on her hat.

Matey felt an almost droll collapse of her impression of masterfully leading Ziza where she would. But she noticed that Ziza's voice had infinitely more of its old personality.

Ziza went on now, 'It would have been the same thing over and over, probably, if he had lived. I couldn't change. And neither could he.'

Matey broke in roughly now, speaking with the incautious sure affection of an old playmate. 'Who's talking like a child now? Why shouldn't you have changed? Everybody else does! Everybody else grows up.' She suddenly understood something that had been said to her years ago, and went on, hearing the voice of Adrian's father, 'Why shouldn't you have come to realise that your husband was a human being and that it is cruel to expect anybody to be any more than that! And anyhow that's gone. Listen to me now, Ziza. I've made an effort, hard for me, to see the truth of something that is not literally so. Now it's your turn to look at what *is* literally true and see what there is to do that nobody will do if you don't.'

As if she had not heard a word, Ziza murmured, 'You have such good honest eyes, Mété!' She stood up. 'And though you often don't seem to understand at all – I don't know why it is, but when it is a question of what to do, you are often so right . . . ! You're right now. No, I didn't die, not quite. I wanted to, but Maman kept me alive. I tried not to feel her waiting for me. But she won. And now I must do my share of living.'

She went closer to Matey, and reaching up to kiss her cheek, said, 'Mété, you have the gift of healing. Not what you say. Just yourself.'

'It's only the relief you feel in saying it out,' said Matey humbly.

They clambered down the hill and found the directress of the school for aviculture in sabots, spading up a corner of the garden near the foot of the path. From the look she gave them, Matey guessed she had seen from the distance the pantomime of Ziza's flight across the field and her pursuit. Ziza went on into the kitchen to return the borrowed water canteen. The country woman, leaning on her spade, watched her out of sight, and then turning to Matey, tapped her forehead and lifted enquiring eyebrows.

Matey explained, 'A refugee. From Louvain.'

The country woman nodded her understanding. 'Oh, I see. Yes,' she said and went on with her spading.

CHAPTER THIRTEEN

✺✺✺

She wrote home, 'America's decision seems to make the world over here different. Henri knows a newspaper reporter who was at the Chambre des Députés when the announcement was made that the United States would stand by the allies and had declared war on Germany. He tells us that the oldest men there could not remember any such scene of pure emotion. Everyone of all parties was crying, and M Ribot, the Premier, very old, said brokenly that now he was ready to die, knowing that the human race would not go down to destruction . . . . Our own news is that Adrian has been made Chef de Section. He hasn't told me much about it in detail – evidently assuming that I know as much as he does about the ambulance service – but I make out that he no longer drives an ambulance but is head of one of the newly formed sections, responsible for the work and morals of some twenty young Americans, mostly fresh from the States. He grouses about the change, as all men at the front do about everything, says he is sorry to leave old comrades and his old Ford, but I think he's very much interested in his bigger job and takes a fatherly interest in all his new boys. Ziza seems better. She is often absent and preoccupied, but she enters into life more. She has been able to bring herself to tell her mother and Henri a little more about that blank year-and-a-half in which they knew nothing of her. Not many details – long gaps, but they know for instance that she never saw her husband from the time he went off. His regiment was sent to Liège and disappeared practically to a man. We know now too that Ziza supported herself and her household by doing cleaning and cooking in one of the Louvain hospitals. Her little maid, Mélanie, came from a Chauny family and had to stay on with Ziza because she wasn't allowed to leave Louvain. Ziza speaks of that time briefly, dryly, with the greatest effort. Never when her little boy is near. Just a sort of telegraphic statement of what some of the facts were. The only thing she has *described* is the tocsin that called the Belgian soldiers out from their homes. All one long night the church bells clanged together, hour after hour, clang! clang! clang! while inside the homes the women were helping the men get ready to leave. Ziza says no Belgian will ever get that sound out of his ears. In clear weather we sometimes hear the bells of Saint Sulpice come over the roofs to us. It's painful to see Ziza wince and turn pale.

'We still have no idea how she came out alive, and we feel we must not tax her with questions. I have a notion from one phrase of hers that she and little Adrien saw the massacre. She has told us a little about how she made her escape from Belgium. It was with the help of a German Frontier sentry, older brother to the boy who was lodged with them, to whom Ziza had been kind. She says – most of the refugees do – that the savages we hear about among the Germans are nearly all in the professional army caste, those who make their living in peacetime by being soldiers. The ordinary soldiers, the citizen army, are like any men. I find it touching that many of the French and Belgian refugees say that they were often *sorry* for the private soldiers in the German army. Ziza says the lad who was billeted with them, Mélanie's sweetheart, burst into humiliated tears one day when telling them of some military "discipline" inflicted on him by his lieutenant. Of course there were brutes among the common soldiers too, since everybody is in the army there as here, but Ziza says there were no more of them compared to the rest than the toughs and thugs in the slums of any town, and on the whole they were kept in rather stricter order by army regulations than by police regulations in peacetime. Of course none of this applies to the first days of the war, the invasion. That was, I gather, just one unbelievable nightmare of madness and terror on both sides, for the German soldiers seem to have been in as much of a panic as anyone over the idea of being fired at from the houses. On the whole after the first she apparently suffered no more, physically, personally, from the German occupation, than slow starvation and incessant rudeness and arrogance from lesser officials carrying out autocratic, often absurd orders with the usual brutality of underlings – mean, petty interference with personal liberty and human dignity – the way they say immigrants are sometimes treated on Ellis Island, or like the roughness often shown to poor and ignorant people everywhere by the police. But of course these French and Belgian women and old men were not at all poor or ignorant, but very proud and used to respect. They were practically maddened by such nagging tyranny, under a frightful strain as they were from anxiety and hate.'

As fast as the mails could bring it she had an answer to this letter from Francis, rebuking her sternly for sentimental sympathy with the enemy. 'We are at war with a race of beasts and barbarians who are proud of their beastliness,' he told her, 'and that's the thing to keep steadily before our minds. They must be exterminated if the world is ever to know peace and civilisation again. How do you expect to keep fighting spirit up if people at the rear undermine the morale! It's the least non-combatants can do, to support the Allies morally. Your own country is rousing itself, let me tell you.'

To prove this he enclosed a newspaper clipping telling of the scene in one of the movie-houses in a nearby city where the leader of the orchestra had been hissed out of the theatre for playing music by a composer with a German-sounding name. Matey turned the clipping over and in some local news on the back read an item about the arrest of a pedlar because it was thought the plaster he was selling had been poisoned by German chemists.

Henri, in Paris on leave, came in to announce that a friend had sent him some tickets for the annual concert of the Bach Society. 'The "Passion according to St. Matthew" this year,' he said; 'my favourite.' Seeing her with letters in her hands, he asked. 'Good news from home?' 'Well – yes,' said Matey.

The series of *permissionaire* guests was now occasionally varied by one of Adrian's section on leave. It did Matey's homesick heart good to have them arrive with their Anglo-Saxon tongue-tied shyness, their frank boy's eyes, and their sprawlingly kind American manners – each bearing a torn scrap from Adrian's notebook – 'Matey, if you can, take in Jack Rawling (or Steve O'Donnell, or Red Elliot). He doesn't know a soul in France.'

One of them proved to hail from Dutchess County, inland from Poughkeepsie. With him Matey had long hours of reminiscence. 'Yes, sure, I've been in Rustdorf. My folks went over there when I was a kid almost every fourth of July to see the celebration in the evening.'

At this Petella lifted her golden head from her book with an astonished expression. 'Oh, *I* remember *those!* Way back when I was a baby. The rockets going sh-sh-sh!' She traced an upward curve with her hand.

The boy from Dutchess County made a wry face. 'I've sort of lost my taste for fireworks since being on the front so much,' he said soberly. Matey made haste to change the subject. 'Did you ever drive over from Millbrook to Amenia?' she asked. He brightened. 'Sure thing! That view you get just before you start downhill into Amenia looks awful pretty in the fall, don't it?' His words hung before them the rich Inness-like gold and plenty of their home country, the opulence of its russet earth-colours, blue distances, and orange-coloured sunsets hiding the pale, transparent brightness of the Paris spring.

'Say, Mrs Fort,' said the American boy, 'it sounds foolish to care – but if – well, I'd sort of hate to think I *never* was going back there any more. If I should get mine, do you suppose you and Lieutenant Fort could see that I got sent back home to be buried?'

'Sure thing,' said Matey, 'if you'll do the same for us.'

They shook hands on it.

He went back to the front, and his place was taken by a Basque comrade of Dominiqua's Jean. Endless incomprehensible conversations floating out from the kitchen filled the apartment with their mysterious language.

And finally, although it always seemed as if his turn would never come, came Adrian. The double row of braid sewed on his sleeve to mark him Chef de Section (or as he put it, honorary nothing in particular) brought him no salary, not even a minute French one like Henri's. The Forts allowed themselves few treats that cost money during his leave. Mostly, taking along a picnic lunch, they spent days in the country or in the gardens of Versailles, long, beautiful, tragic, gay days memorable with their double burden of joy and fear.

The Fourth of July approached and brought the announcement that the new allies would parade in Paris on their Fête Nationale. The crowd promised to be enormous; windows along the rue de Rivoli commanded fancy prices. Military shows were rare in Paris, especially since the unacknowledged but everywhere talked-about mutiny after the failure of the great spring offensive. Troop movements had been routed around the city, not through it, for fear of anti-war demonstrations.

'I hate to disappoint the kids,' said Adrian, talking it over with Matey, 'but they wouldn't be able to see a thing in the jam that's certain to turn out. I have to take an early train on the fifth, too. I'd sort of like to spend the last day in Versailles together. Do you suppose they'd be satisfied if we compromised and took them to see the troops come in and march to their barracks? The paper says they're to arrive early on the morning of the third. Hardly anybody'll be there. We can have a good look.'

He was wrong. When they reached the freight station where the parade detachment were to leave the train they found the sidewalks along the line of march already packed by a crowd, curious and watchful rather than effervescent. Adrian's khaki uniform passed for that of a French Colonial or English soldier, the children spoke the purest Paris slang, so that their presence imposed no check on the talk of the people about them. Everywhere they heard the sort of questions which in politer form their own circle had put to them, the answers to which they knew as little as anyone. 'Had the Americans really any soldiers at all?' 'Would they send them if they had?' 'Weren't the Americans in the war as the Japanese had been . . . with a few warships in the Mediterranean?' 'They were all "beesness-men," weren't they, who as such would expect their money to do their fighting for them?' Adrian hoisted Brother to his shoulder, and Matey paid a franc for a packing box as a grandstand for Petella. Nothing was to be seen except a long high wall, broken by great iron gates, now tightly closed. They settled themselves to wait. After a pause filled with ponderings Matey said to Adrian, 'I wonder if perhaps they are right. How can we get any real soldiers to send? *Is* there an American army? I never saw any trace of it.'

Brother had forgotten all his English by this time and detested conversations he could not understand. He wriggled now and demanded to know what Maman was saying. 'Never mind,' she told him and said no more, joining her silence to that of the expectant crowd.

They were in a poor quarter of Paris and the people about them were mostly in the clean worn self-respecting clothes of French working men and women. They had evidently just stepped out from shop and lathe and bench and laundry to see the new show. They stood passively – overworked, quiet folk, curious, tired, doubtful. A good many men in faded uniforms like Adrian's held, as he did, a child perched on a shoulder.

From the distance a train whistled shrilly and came roaring in behind the wall. People stopped their desultory talking and pressed to the curb. Petella began to jump up and down on her packing box.

The invisible train stopped, a scream of brakes pouring over the top of the wall. There was a sound of doors flung open and many irregular footsteps. A silence, through which, sharply running down the scale from near to far, came a crackling of barked-out short words in harsh voices. The words were meaningless to the crowd, but its ears, trained by three years of war, recognised the tone as unmistakably that of professional military commands. A band struck up, the iron gates opened, and out they came, with a long supple swinging stride, quite different from the close-knit quickstep of the French . . . row upon row of men utterly different from the nation in uniform which that crowd knew as an army.

Here were no sober fathers of families with serious eyes, no pink-cheeked lads with sensitive scholar's faces, no mild, weedy clerks from small-town shops, no stalwart, burly, vacant-faced farmhands, no spectacled desk workers. Here were lean, lanky, stony-faced men, all of an age apparently, and certainly all of one predatory breed, with bulging jaw muscles, hard, reckless eyes, and leathery skins burned to a uniform sallow brown by the sun of the Mexican border. Their inharmoniously assembled features were not all of one pattern; some were beak-nosed and some had broad bulldog faces. But all were compact of bone and gristle and grim insensitiveness; dangerous customers every one, by their looks, of an ugly, powerful, dauntless, low-grade humanity, as unfamiliar to Matey as to the French people around her.

'Mother!' whispered Petella in the intense silence which greeted their appearance. She pulled at her mother's sleeve. 'Mother, are those *Americans?* They don't look like Father's ambulance boys a bit!'

The crowd of spectators stared, fascinated, without a murmur. The head of the column had advanced by this time to the middle of the street, where in response to a curt and unintelligible command, they swung to the right by fours, executing the manoeuvre with the inimitable careless ease of professional skill. And now they were marching by the crowd on the sidewalk – *left!* right! *left!* right! – swinging their long legs from loose hips, their hard small eyes impassive and expressionless in the leathery faces with the high cheekbones. Not a sound had yet come from the astonished crowd. The slap! slap! of their heavy shoes sounded loud on the pavement. Then an old woman in front of Petella lifted up a loud exultant cry, 'God! how *ugly* they are!' she shouted enthusiastically and began to clap her hands. It was the voice of the crowd. A roar of applause and cheering broke out like thunder, rolling its way down the street abreast of the marching men. The hard-faced soldiers continued to march, without a quiver of their eyes. The noise of the shouting seemed to rebound from their callous unresponsiveness like the echo of a yell from a cliff. It was the manner which suited their looks. The applause became a madness. People shouted, *'Vive l'Amérique!'* and *'Hourra!'* throwing up their hats, waving aprons and handkerchiefs. The long brown line of khaki-clad men continued to file out from the iron gates – *left!* right! *left!* right! – and to swing at the exact middle of the road with the same flexible perfection.

Petella and Brother caught the madness, shouting shrilly, *'Vive l'Amérique! Vive l'Amérique!'* till their voices gave out, and after that screeching inarticulately with the others. An American flag went by, bright, new, silken, gold-fringed. Adrian stiffened to a salute, and wild sudden tears of pride and love and homesickness came to Matey's eyes. Some young working girls near the Forts had turned and struggled through the crowd to a flower-stand and now were fighting their way back to the curb with posies in their hands. At first they only waved these and threw a few at random, but soon, frantic with noise and excitement, they ran out close to the marching men, calling to them, pelting them with flowers. Their clean black cotton working-dresses fluttered, their tenement-dwellers' young pale faces flushed to pink.

The first change of expression came into the faces of the marching soldiers. For a moment they looked almost boyish, almost naïve in surprise. Then as their eyes rested on the girls, the corners of their mouths began to twist into knowing grins that were neither boyish nor naïve.

Another bright American flag went by. The tears did not come to Matey's eyes. Bang! bang! bang! went the drums, inaudible above the shrieks of the crowd, perceptible only as a rapid throbbing pulse. 'Let's go back, Adrian,' said Matey; 'I've seen enough.'

'The old Adam's never far from the surface, is he?' said Adrian as they walked away. 'How does that poem go – do you know it, the one that begins

War I abhor, and yet how sweet
The sound along the marching street
Of drum and fife . . . ?

Well, that's me.'

'Is that the one,' asked Matey, 'that has the couplet,

For yonder yonder goes the fife
And what care I for human life!'

'You said it!' answered Adrian.

At the lunch table Mme Vinet enquired, 'I hear the American soldiers were given a fine welcome. How did they look to you? Was it like a glimpse of home to see them?'

'Not in the least,' said Adrian. 'Not the very least in the world.' At her look of enquiry he went on, 'For all I know they may be exemplary citizens, but if you want to know how they *looked* to me, I can only say that every face I saw looked as if it belonged to a man who'd kick in your ribs after he'd knocked you down, and who'd be ashamed of his softness if he ever

442

felt tempted to keep his word to a woman – and, to give 'em their due, who'd stick to a wounded buddy through hell and high water. Did they make me think of home? They did not. Wallenstein might have commanded that outfit, or Sir Henry Morgan, or Du Guesclin.'

Matey described their aspect in a little more detail. Adrian explained their status as professional fighters and why there were so few of them available.

Mme Vinet nodded her head, looking sick. 'I know. I know what kind of men you mean. Like our Foreign Legion.' She allowed herself a burst of thin-skinned feminine disgust. 'I can't bear such men! I can't bear to think they are to be used to take the place of such men as those who have died in the war.'

Matey had come home both excited and depressed by the morning, above all freshly awakened to a bewildering world filled with all sorts of men and women whose standards were alien to hers – oh, different beyond imagination, and yet firmly, vitally held, and a part of the whole of which she was a part. She felt as puzzled as when she had first seen that perhaps Francis's very insensitiveness had made him a kinder, more helpful friend to their father and mother than she and Priscilla. She answered Mme Vinet lamely, 'Oh, I don't know.'

'What don't you know?' asked Ziza, who had been paying no attention to the conversation.

'I don't believe I know much of anything at all,' said Matey.

'I know one thing,' said Adrian, 'no collection of worthy citizens could have given that war-tired crowd such a swig of the raw whisky of hope as was poured out by that bunch of roughnecks.'

Mme Vinet was a little shocked at the Forts' attitude. 'If that's the truth,' she said with a grimace of distaste, 'it's a horrible truth!'

'Oh, I don't know,' murmured Matey again, sure of nothing except that things were vastly more complex than Mme Vinet seemed to see.

CHAPTER FOURTEEN

❦❦❦

From that time on, many more burning drinks of raw American whisky were tossed down parched French throats. The 'American phase' of the war advanced to the centre of the stage. Both because it was all good news of the most inspiriting kind and because the *mot d'ordre* to the press was to play up American war activities for the sake of the effect on German spies, there seemed to be little in any magazine or newspaper save items about the stupendous American effort. The staggering figures of American Red Cross financial resources, the prodigious sums expended on warehouses for the vast American supplies, the speed with which the American engineering corps rushed up barracks and hospitals and built railroads and installed telephones – French talk, all in admiring superlatives, turned on nothing else. The now forgotten rumour of the purchase of Constantinople was less fantastic than some of those visible realities.

It was all as dazzling to Matey as to anyone else, and she was distressfully unable to answer the innumerable questions put to her by her French connections about 'American methods.' Nothing in the academic life of her youth, nor in the life of

Rustdorf had prepared her for such an America. She was staggered – proud, happy, excited. A little uneasy too, she did not know why.

American soldiers of the newly forming citizen armies were of course (all war-experienced French people understood this) slow in arriving on the field of combat. Everybody knew it took time to give them the training and preparation necessary to fit them for their new occupation. But almost at once Paris was filled with civilian war workers in the handsome uniforms of big charitable organisations who, apparently, needed no training or preparation. Their appearance did a great deal of good. French people, long reduced to the ultimate lowest margin of everything, took a starved childish pleasure in hearing the fairy-story accounts of American war relief work. Aladdin built his dream palace no more rapidly than, in the French legend, American war relief organisations leased huge buildings and filled them from top to bottom, in the twinkling of an eye, with typewriters, steam radiators, roll-top desks, telephones, and self-possessed ladies in khaki uniforms, ready to bind up the wounds of war on a large scale. French women, who for three years had been doggedly and economically binding them up on the smallest possible scale, lost their sense of reality. The refugees, wounded soldiers, war widows, war orphans, and war *oeuvres* in the Vinet circle naturally looked to Matey, the only American they knew, to canalise toward them their share of this river of golden beneficence. Matey was not very adroit about it. She began going timidly to the offices of the new American organisations and to the older ones, now immensely enlarged in this new shower of gold. Mingling with these prosperous strangers, she felt shabby and refugee-like in her plain worn clothes. She thought she knew how she probably looked to these vital, athletic, expensively shod war workers – as war victims had often looked to her, too unpromising and discouraged and hopeless to be worth helping.

If she did, they did not show it, receiving her in no recognisable European manner, but in one or another of the several American ways of making contracts, some of them easy, comradely, some of them woundingly brusque and business-like; breezy and familiar in one organisation, in another bound about stiffly to the eyes with red tape and card catalogues. Not one of them, however, gave the appraising European caste-glance at the quality of her gloves and shoes. They must (Matey supposed) have other standards of judging – their own – but she never learned what they were nor when she was conforming to them. She never found her way with any certainty about the labyrinth of suites of outer and inner offices nor even knew at all beforehand what response would be evoked by any particular one of her requests for help. She knew it couldn't be a mere matter of mood that they granted a hundred dozen costly woollen blankets one day and refused to give a bottle of milk the next. She guessed that this impression, not at all in keeping with their unfailing good will as individuals, came from the immense impersonal vastness of their organisations. Accustomed to depending on static, personal small French war charities, she was perpetually amazed to the point of stupefaction by the shifts and changes in these large ones. When, in order to go on with some arrangement started, she had threaded her way to an office where she was beginning to be a little familiar with the faces, it was always breathtaking to her to find there an entirely new personnel and to be told that the people with whom she had been dealing had been transferred from the child welfare department to the war hospital department and that the new incumbents in this office were starting to 'reorganise the work along new lines.' Matey sometimes wondered whether the intense desire of these non-combatant Americans, middle-aged men and women, to 'get to the front' had anything to do with this instability. Why in the world, she asked herself, did they all so wildly yearn to get to the front? None of the French non-combatants with whom she had been living all this time had ever thought of it.

The new people in any war relief organisation usually looked a good deal like the old ones: a clean-shaven middle-aged professional man in the inner office, his civilian chin and middle bulged into odd shapes by his uniform; in the outer office one or many energetic youngish women in uniform with much better figures than his. Most of them with the quality of eye of a bank cashier looking at a man trying to pass a bogus check. 'I don't blame them a bit for this,' she wrote to Adrian, describing an uncomfortable experience trying to get some supplies for a group of refugees under her charge. 'Everybody with money to spend gets that eye, I suppose. Has to. It's natural enough in business. But it makes you think there must be something inherently wrong about charity if the minute it gets big it gets this way.' Adrian wrote back, 'The minute anything human gets big, it gets wrong. I didn't invent this, William James did. He was dead right.'

But although the new office workers always looked like the ones whose places they took, of course they did not know Matey, and asked her to state her appeal all over again and to spell out once more those queer French proper and place names. Matey wrote to Adrian, 'You feel like a rat in a perfectly new kind of maze, with the bells ringing at all the times when they never rang before. And everybody reacts to every stimulus in just the Alice-in-Wonderland way you would be sure they wouldn't! There must be of course some general lines of policy that are being followed; they have such splendid people in the managing offices. But from the ones you actually do business with it seems impossible to make out even the outlines of any plans that stay put. You come to feel that there's no use trying to act consecutively or to count on anything's being carried out as it was planned. I'm reduced to thinking that the best you can do is to grab at the times when the grabbing seems to be good. And often the grabbing is simply epic. You know that *vestiaire* in the rue Pascal, where Mme Vinet and Ziza and I have worked so much – oh, yes, I remember now, you went with me there on your *permission* in April to help carry some bundles of clothing. Well, you should have seen me driving up to the door in glory yesterday afternoon on the front seat of an American truck, sitting beside one of those nice, nice Americans – you know – the exquisitely candid kind, who look pityingly at every French person as a war martyr. Well, he was part of a red-letter experience for me. Only a day or so ago I had put in an appeal at the Red Cross building for some more supplies of what we mostly give out from the rue Pascal place, clothing, shoes, medicine, and nursing supplies. No French organisation would have got around even to considering it so quickly. But yesterday when I went to the same office I was told that my supplies had been taken out of the warehouse and loaded and the driver was waiting for detailed directions about how to reach the *oeuvre*. I said, "Why can't I just go along and show him?"

'I gasped when I saw the size of the truck, but of course you never understand exactly all that may be going on, and I supposed it was going on several other such errands, and only a part of its contents were for us. When we got to the rue Pascal I found Mme Vinet and Ziza had come in to help mend some old clothing that had been sent us. When I opened the door and went in they sat there sewing away with two other of our regular helpers, the woman who keeps the stationery store across the street and that nice old refugee from Brussels, the Marquise something-or-other, who pays for the food and lodging she gets from the *oeuvre* by sewing for it. I didn't know how to find words for what I had to announce. I felt as though I ought to float in, singing at the top of my voice like a prima donna. What I did was to say, as though I were a born Quaker instead of just having married one, "Can you come and help me, please, carry in some supplies the American Red Cross has sent us?"

'They came. You should have seen their wild look up at that vast truck. And when we began to unload it, it was *all* for us! Yes, that entire moving-van of a thing was full of shoes and malted milk and flannel petticoats and quinine and baby shirts and aspirin and wool socks, underwear, caps, bandages, disinfectants – everything I had set down on my list was

there, by the dozens, by the hundreds! It was one wild orgy.
We unpacked and carried in, the nice boy from New Mexico
working like ten, till we were fairly walking on air. I'll never
forget it.

'The French women kept their dignity as long as the
representative from America was there, insisted on making
him drink some coffee and eat some little dry cakes (he must
have hated them, but he swallowed them down like a hero),
and before he climbed up on his seat in the truck they each
shook hands with him and made him a little speech of thanks,
nicely worded and heartfelt, and of course just that much
Choctaw to him.

'But when we were by ourselves with the doors shut we
ran around like crazy things from one to another of those
magnificent piles, exclaiming and handling them. Mme Vinet
stood, the tears running down her cheeks, in front of the heap
of malted milk cartons, and the old Belgian Marquise kept
saying, "Oh, the beautiful woollen drawers! Oh, the lovely
woollen shirts!" I was so disappointed when I went back this
morning to thank Major Woodhull (by the way, he's a doctor
from Hamilton who used to be a student of Father's at the
University) to find that he had been "sent to the front on a
mission".'

Ziza had become specially interested in a group of undernourished refugee children and had made one try at finding
her way to the right American war relief organisation to ask for
help. She had emerged from this so daunted by the magnitude
and the English-speakingness of everything, so shamed by

the penetrating personal questions asked her, so nettled at seeming to be put in the position of a beggar, and so sure that she had filled out the wrong blanks and given the wrong answers, that she asked Matey to go on with the undertaking. Matey did not at first have much more success, because the group of children in question did not (for various reasons of technical classification lore) come exactly under any of the subdivisions into which the field had been systematically divided by American card catalogues. No sooner had she finished explaining their status and her own than she was found to be in entirely the wrong place and was passed from one office to another ('as if,' she wrote to Adrian, 'exactly as if I were the buck in person').

Coming in from the unprofessional outside world as she did, she never grasped the intricacies of filing systems, nor which kind of information blanks should be filled in for which undertakings. She made a good many mistakes, but she kept persistently filling out application blanks and explaining her own status until she arrived one day in a new office where a friendly American girl in uniform took out a new application blank and began to ask new questions.

'It's just a matter of form,' she explained comfortably to Matey, 'not that anyone cares a whoop what year you were married. It's only that they've got a new set of blanks they're trying out and I'd get skinned alive if I didn't write on every dotted line.'

How good it sounded, thought Matey, in the intervals when this nice girl was writing down the answers to her questions, to hear this open American intonation, unaware to its last un-European syllable of the existence of reticence and caution.

'Cute handbag you've got,' remarked the girl. 'Made by the war blind in the Phare? Yes? Isn't it pretty! I'm going to get one to send home to Momma. What did you say your husband's middle name is? Mercy! How *do* you spell it?'

When Matey was asked the name of her American residence, she said, 'I'd better spell that, too. It's such a little place, nobody ever heard of it. R-U-S-T-D-O-R-F.'

The girl laid down her fountain pen with the gesture of one stopping work to give vent to emotion. 'Well, for goodness' sakes, are you from Rustdorf! Is that the way you pronounce it, by the way? We none of us knew how *to* pronounce it!'

'No,' said Matey, 'not like "rust" on iron, like "roost" in "rooster," you know. It is an old Dutch name that means "village of rest." '

'Oh, I know what it means, all right,' said the girl even more unexpectedly. She looked at Matey in mounting astonishment. 'So you come from Rustdorf. Well, can you beat that!' She hastened to explain, 'Funniest thing you ever heard of. Just before I left home (I live in Mason City, Iowa) an old-maid aunt of mine – great-aunt she was really – died, up in Alberta, Canada. She'd lived up there with one of Mamma's brothers for years and *years* – oh, she was *awfully* old, must have been past seventy. Well, when she died, didn't they find in her will that she wanted to be buried in the Quaker cemetery of Rustdorf, Dutchess County, New York. No reason given, nothing more than that Rustdorf meant "resting place". You can just see our whole family can't you, trying to figure out why in the world an old lady who was one of the first settlers in Calgary wanted to be buried near the Hudson River? She hadn't lived there ever that anybody knew about; our folks came from Ohio, though she had gone to a ladies' school somewhere back east when she was a girl. The only thing anybody could think of was a story one of Momma's old cousins used to tell about this aunt's having been crossed in love, that she'd been engaged when she was still living back east, and another girl had taken her young man away from her. But that cousin was dead by this time and nobody could remember exactly what she *had* told. Anyhow the old great-aunt hadn't ever married. But maybe she just wasn't the marrying kind. She certainly was not, the only time *I* ever saw her.' She gazed at Matey again. 'Well, to think that when you go home you'll live right near the cemetery where my Aunt Priscilla is buried.'

Distinctly as thought Aunt Tryntje stood there beside her, Matey heard her voice saying, 'Oh, they did name her *Priscilla*, did they?'

Through this voice she heard the girl before her going on. 'Why, maybe you know something about that end of it? Though it would be a pretty old story, I guess, by this time.'

'I have only lived in Rustdorf since my marriage,' said Matey.

'Well, let's get along,' said the friendly girl, looking down at her desk again. 'What American war relief outfit do you belong to, anyhow? American Fund for French Wounded? I hear they've changed the name of that, but you know which one I mean.'

'I don't belong to any,' said Matey. 'I'm just living here, you know, with my family.'

'Oh, you've *got* to belong to something!' said the girl from Iowa, laughing. 'You've *got* to! There's a blank on this card that's got to be filled up!'

CHAPTER FIFTEEN

✹✹✹

It was through the help, Matey always felt sure, of the friendly girl from Iowa that she and Ziza were able – not, as they had hoped, to get cod liver oil and better food for their eighteen undernourished, rickety, war-worn refugee children – but to send them south for the winter. 'As if they were millionaires!' cried Ziza incredulously. 'Mété, are you *sure* there's no mistake!' They had all by this time learned to scrutinise every possibility of misunderstanding with American philanthropic organisations.

'There doesn't seem to be!' said Matey, as excited as Ziza. 'Let me read their letter over again.'

She read it through once more, very slowly. 'No, there's no mistake. It's plain in black and white. Arrangements have been made to admit them to a convalescent home right on the seashore – they'll be out of doors in the sunshine all winter long! One of the nurses in that office told me they had wonderful cures of rickets there . . . undernourished children of six, like the little boys in that family from Lille, who have never stood on their feet, running around playing tag, inside five or six months.'

Ziza said, awestruck, 'It'll save every one of them. It seems incredible! Why, Mété, what a wonderful nation yours is!'

Matey still felt very uneasy when French people burst into superlatives about Americans. Perhaps, she thought, it was the Quaker atmosphere of 'plainness' striking in which made her ill at ease with any superlatives. She wondered now what Ziza would say to the passion the American women war workers had for 'getting to the front'; for that matter, to the liberal use of rouge and lipstick on the pleasant face of the nice girl from Iowa. 'Don't go idealising us,' she said, knowing that she sounded to Ziza as Adrian's father did to her.

'It's impossible to!' said Ziza with a flare of her old ardour.

Matey had an opportunity to see what Ziza would think of the girl from Iowa, for on the evening of the children's departure for the south she appeared in the railway station, trim, smiling, painted, kind, a large khaki bag marked 'USA' slung over her shoulder. 'I just thought I'd like to see 'em off,' she said in her cheerful loud voice to Matey. 'I've stacked up so many cards in the filing-box about this gang of kids, I wanted to see what they look like.' She turned her head and saw the lamentable little creatures climbing feebly up or being carried into the railway carriage. Her bright face sobered into a beautiful pity. '*Well* – they don't look like much, do they?' she said. Matey perceived that she was capable, when she chose, of speaking in a low voice. She moved toward them. 'Oh, say, Nurse!' she called to the Red Cross official in charge of the convoy. 'I've brought along some little tricks and things for them to play with to keep 'em from being homesick on the train. *No candy!* Is it all right to pass 'em around now?'

'Sure,' said the nurse over the shoulder of the white-faced child she was carrying. 'Could you find a better time! I can see by the looks of them they're getting ready to holler their heads off. And if you knew how little baby-talk French I've got on tap!'

The girl from Iowa clambered nimbly up the steps. Matey stood on the platform in charge of the group of anxious mothers who tearfully demanded fresh assurances from her that their little crippled children would be returned safely to them in the spring. Through the windows of the railway carriage she saw Ziza, pale and thin in her widow's dress, put a child down on the seat and turn to greet the smartly tailored newcomer. They stood together for a moment talking (in what language? – Matey wondered) and then passed among the children, putting into each outstretched skinny hand a bright toy from out of the bag of the girl from Iowa. A joyful babble of children's voices followed the progress of the two women. Matey noticed how eagerly they looked up into the face of the American girl, turning like little sunflowers following the sun from Ziza's pale quietness to that brilliantly lipsticked smile. The agitated women clustering about Matey took their handkerchiefs down from their eyes to watch. After the first dazzling surprise the children remembered their mothers, standing on the platform outside, and turned their thin radiant faces toward the windows, crying out, *'Maman! Maman! Regarde! Regarde!'* and holding up comic little dolls, checker-boards, celluloid babies, wooden ducks. *'En voiture!'* called the employee running along beside the train. Ziza and the American girl hurried down the steps to the platform. The train began to move. The mothers clenched back the tears under their eyelids to see the last of the happy child faces; the train moved more rapidly and was gone.

'That's the best time I ever gave myself in all my young life!' said the girl from Iowa emphatically. 'I was going to spend that money on a permanent wave – think of it! And a shingle-cut just as good-looking!'

Ziza came up to her and said very earnestly, 'I wish that you would tell your family that there are in France women and children who love America because of your kindness.' The girl from Iowa did not understand a word of this, but its meaning was apparent. 'Oh, *that's* all right,' she said, heartily shaking Ziza's hand.

Ziza went off to escort one of the more ignorant mothers to the right Métro train, making a rendezvous with Matey to meet her in the waiting room.

'I've got to get a move on,' said the girl from Iowa, 'or I'll miss a swell time. Another girl and I have got to know two dandy fellows – in the Marines, both of them lieutenants. We've got a date with them at Maxim's tonight . . . "girls from Maxim's"! This is the life!'

She pulled a little enamelled case from the pocket of her uniform and began to apply more lipstick to her mouth. 'I never used make-up like this at home,' she explained laughingly to Matey. 'The older girls and the alums. in my sorority would have slain me if I had. But in Paris you've got to do like the Parisians do!'

She snapped her little case shut and asked, 'Oh, say, Mrs Fort, where is Maxim's anyhow? I don't mind telling *you* that

I wouldn't know the place if I met it! Off the comic-opera stage.'

Matey reflected, gathering together half-memories of old walks in Paris streets, 'That's the one, isn't it, that's on the rue Royale, left hand as you go up from the place de la Concorde?'

The girl from Iowa laughed out admiringly, 'I guess you're more of a live wire than you look, Mrs Fort,' she said. 'The rue Royale, left-hand side. Well, *good*bye!'

She ran up half a dozen steps lightly, turned and skimmed down them again, bounding up to Matey, her face aglow, 'Honestly!' she said. 'Just between us, Paris has got Mason City and Rustdorf beat a mile, *n'est-ce-pas* what?'

Matey found Ziza waiting for her, still admiring the American nation. 'It goes beyond anything I could imagine, Mété,' she said. 'You don't seem to appreciate it! A girl like that, a *jeune fille*, leaving her *parents*, and her *home*, and coming to a distracted foreign land to devote herself to suffering! Do you suppose for a moment a French girl would do what she is doing?'

'Certainly not!' said Matey with conviction.

'Well, then – ' said Ziza, observing with dissatisfaction Matey's enigmatic expression. 'What *is* in your mind? Her rouge and lipstick? Mété, how narrow of you!'

'Well, perhaps it is narrowness,' admitted Matey.

They walked together to the exit. Ziza said, pulling out her notebook to look at an address, 'Why not go to Mme Allier's to see about that sewing material now? Her place is on the rue Pasquier. It's only a step if we go up the rue Royale.'

'*Not the rue Royale!*' cried the startled Matey in a panic. Before Ziza could speak she added, 'We're in no hurry. Don't you think it would be nicer to take the longer way around?'

CHAPTER SIXTEEN

✿✿✿

Splendid reports came back from the children in the Hendaye Convalescent Home.

Splendid reports came from America. Every letter, every newspaper, was full of the spectacle of a mighty nation, united to the last citizen, rousing itself for a crusade. Priscilla's letters told of the change in American cooking, the use of cornmeal for wheat, all Rustdorf subscribing to Liberty Loans. Francis's letters were on fire with patriotism. He wrote at the head of one Drive after another.

The nurse in charge at Hendaye wrote to Matey that those children from Lille with the terrible rickets were getting bones in their legs so fast that you could almost see them grow.

Adrian's father wrote that the entrance of the United States into the war had upset Aunt Tryntje's eighty-year-old mind. 'She now thinks apparently that I am my father and Adrian is I, gone to the Civil War. One war to each generation of our family!'

A thick envelope came from Hendaye containing a grateful note from every child in the home, addressed to 'Our American benefactors.'

* * *

Some American troops began to appear, new citizen soldiers these, who looked to Matey's homesick eyes like her own kin. At first she sometimes stopped an especially boyish one on the street to shake his hand, ask where his home in the States was, and to give him her address if he needed letters written or interpreting done. Not one of them looked suspiciously at her or answered with caution. She could have wept with pride and alarm at their candour.

But it became evident that candour or no candour, few of them came to Paris to waste time over mothers of families. A few did follow up her invitation and came in for a call. Once. But they showed none of the starved hunger for home life which made the French *poilus* play eagerly with the children, cling so to the illusion that this home was a little their own. When at the front, the Americans were said to be kind to the children in the army zone and helpful to the old, but once arrived in Paris, it was by no means home life they sought out. These big boyish-faced good-natured young men were brothers to the girl from Iowa and shared heartily her opinion of the relative advantages of their home towns and of Paris, agreeing warmly with her dictum that this was the life.

Adrian, formally enrolled with the American Army now, was very much surprised – he wrote his wife – 'to find a Rustdorf Fort with the rank of Lieutenant in the USA army.' But this was only to regularise his situation on paper. In reality he continued doing exactly the same work with the same French Division, still seeing few Americans and getting most of his news from Matey's letters. The change had one result, however, very important to the Forts. Adrian now had a salary which, moderate though it seemed to Americans, seemed very large compared to the French military pay. The spending of what was left of Aunt Connie's money could be appreciably slowed down, which, when Matey considered how little they knew what might be before them, was something to be thankful for.

Priscilla wrote that her little girls (like all the other children in Rustdorf) were working hard for war relief in France, denying themselves candy and toys and wearing their old clothes to send more help to the 'poor French and Belgian boys and girls.' Matey found this devotion very touching and did not mind at all the superlatives in which Mme Vinet and Ziza recounted it to the members of their circle. She sent Priscilla's children the little package of scrawled thank you letters from the children at the Hendaye Home and suggested that they show them at school.

The news of the greatness of the 'American effort' was constantly more impressive, more expansively described in the newspapers. Heatless days, lightless nights, automobiles emptied of their gasoline, wheatless bread, voluntary rationing of all kinds, wild bursts of enthusiasm, tremendous drives for the new loans: Matey was swept along with her French companions in their flight from the cold tragic realities about them into the Utopian conception of a golden America entirely inhabited by selfless philanthropic crusaders of the ideal. It sounded too wonderful! It was too wonderful.

* * *

✟✟✟

In early January, which was again very cold that year, a letter came to Dominiqua from a cousin of hers who lived in Hendaye and did washing for the American Convalescent Home for children. She mentioned that she would soon have less work, because the house was to be closed before the first of February. Dominiqua showed this to Matey, who after some difficulty in making out the meaning from the phonetic spelling, told Dominiqua sharply, 'There must be some mistake, of course. *Don't speak of this to Mme Vinet or Mme Ziza!'*

She dressed rapidly for the street, ran down the four flights of stairs, and hastened across Paris to the desk of the girl from Iowa. A new face, a sweet refined one, looked at her from behind it. A gentle Southern voice told her that in accordance with some changes in general policy the personnel in that office had been changed and that the work was being reorganised along new lines.

'Is it true,' asked Matey, trembling with excitement, 'that the Hendaye Convalescent Home for Children is to be *closed,* in mid-winter, without any warning given their mothers, and those sick children returned from a southern climate to tenement-houses here without fire? It would mean pneumonia for every one of them. It would be murder.'

The uniformed girl was startled by Matey's agitation. She said, edging her chair away from where Matey leaned belligerently over the desk, 'I'm very sorry, but of course I don't know anything about this.' Appealing to Matey's sense of fair play, she added with an apologetic little laugh, 'You see, I never heard of any of this till this minute. I don't even know what you are – '

'You must have records,' said Matey grimly. 'They were always making records.'

'Oh, we have our *own* records!' explained the girl hastily. '*Our* records deal with the medical supplies given out to French hospitals.'

Matey stood still for a moment till she could control her voice. She was absurd, visiting her indignation on a well-bred girl who had no connection with the cause of it. Finally, 'Will you tell me, please, to whom to apply for information about this?'

The girl answered with an understandable eagerness to be of help in moving Matey elsewhere, 'Why don't you try the office on the next floor?' She gave complete instructions for finding it, and as Matey turned away she called after her forgivingly, 'I *do* hope you'll get it all fixed up!'

In the next office the girl in charge of the desk was obviously not one of the *universitaires* and seemed ignorant of anything but stenography and the phrase, 'Dr Taylor is in an important conference.' Matey said she would wait. She waited a long time, during which she recovered her *sang-froid* and was quite sure she was on a wild-goose chase. How foolish of her to go off half-cocked, to think for a moment that an organisation of doctors and nurses would dream of returning sick children from a warm sunny climate to a cold damp one, in mid-winter, with practically no fuel in Paris tenement-houses. When Dr Taylor (this was a new one she had never seen before) was at last finished with his conference she stepped quietly into his office and with complete self-possession, even almost apologising for asking such a question, she stated her case.

But it was true, what Dominiqua's cousin in Hendaye had said. The work, so Dr Taylor said, was being reorganised along new lines. It had been decided it would be wiser to withdraw from the running of convalescent homes for children in order to give more money and effort to other lines of work. With growing agitation Matey described the conditions of the children for whose going to the south she was responsible, and explained the home life to which they would come back, the unheated tenement-house rooms, poverty, overcrowding, all family plans laid for the absence of the children till spring, so that in many cases there would not even be beds for them.

Dr Taylor expressed regret, looked at his watch, and said it was a general order with which he personally had nothing to do. It applied to all homes for children as well as to this one in which she was personally interested, she must understand.

Matey, trying hard and unsuccessfully to keep her voice steady, explained that it was simply impossible for those children to be brought back. 'You *promised* those mothers!'

Dr Taylor reminded her, 'No American war relief workers ever enter into contracts, Madam.'

Matey cried out wrathfully, 'Oh, I don't mean *legally!*'

Dr Taylor said he was really very sorry, but he was due at a conference. Matey found herself again in the outer office, trembling from head to foot.

She went outdoors into the street wrapped in its winter winding-sheet of grey mist. She stood still, thinking hard, till her hat and clothes were beaded with the moisture and her teeth began to chatter. Presently there before her in the stony French street stood the old beech tree at home, glorying in its battle with the storm. She closed her eyes to see it more clearly, and when she opened them she had said goodbye to it.

If she sold their home and took all that was left of Aunt Connie's money …

She went back and was told that Dr Taylor was at lunch. Oh, yes, it was time for lunch. She went home, sat at table with the family, listened to Petella's account of her part in a little play to be given at the Lycée, and returned to the office. Dr Taylor was still out at lunch. Matey said she would wait.

When he came in she told him what she proposed to do. 'What is left from an American war relief fund which I am administering will just about see them through to spring,' she said in proper business-like language. Dr Taylor said that was very generous of her, but he was afraid it could not be managed. 'You see,' he explained patiently, 'our organisation is the one responsible for those children. We must return them to their homes. We can't possibly turn children entrusted to us over to private individuals. I don't doubt it would be all right in *this* case,' he said with an accent which meant he doubted it very much, 'but you see what an impossible precedent it would establish.' He raised his voice a little, resenting Matey's blazing eyes. 'How could *we* tell into whose hands they would ultimately fall? What guarantee have we that you would see the proper care is given them?'

'What guarantee would you require?' asked Matey in a suffocated voice.

Dr Taylor rose. 'There is no use going on discussing it in this unbusiness-like manner,' he said. 'Of course there is no guarantee which could be given by any private individual.'

Matey would not be dismissed. 'But suppose,' she tried another way, 'suppose I do not take over the running of the home at all, but just pay for its expenses, through your office, all regularly.'

Dr Taylor's patience was worn thin, 'How in the world,' he asked, 'could we make an exception of one home? What would all the others think of such a discrimination? And what a childish idea that your special money could be kept separate from all the rest! There must be account-keeping, must there not? Have you any idea of the complexity of the business end of an organisation like ours?'

Matey found herself in the outer office, alone with the khaki-clad stenographer. She sat for a time, clenching and unclenching her hands. Finally, 'Will you please tell me the name of Dr Taylor's superior officer?' she asked.

The girl looked at her with sympathy. 'I will, dearie,' she said, 'but take it from me, it'll get you in awfully bad if you try to go over the old man's head. And you don't seem to be in any too good right now. There's nothing that slams the doors shut any quicker than appealing over the head of the officer you're doing business with.'

Matey considered and asked for the address of the girl from Iowa. The stenographer put this question through one of the innumerable desk-phones which were the admiration of the French observers, and told Matey with an accent of envy, 'All that bunch got to go to the front – lucky people!'

Matey went home but ate no dinner. To Ziza and Mme Vinet, anxious about her pallor and lack of appetite, she said she felt a little tired. This alarmed them almost as if she had fainted away on the floor, for until now she had moved steadily through whatever was to be done, as if made of steel.

She went the next day to consult a doctor about an imaginary child of hers, rickety, who had been sent to the south. 'Would it be safe to bring him home now?' she asked.

'Now!' exclaimed the doctor, 'In this weather? With the shortage of coal in Paris? A sickly child who has been in the south since November? It would be madness, Madame.'

She managed by long waiting to have a moment's interview with a high official of the Red Cross, to ask what their policy was about bringing delicate children north from Convalescent homes in the south. 'Not before May,' he told her with emphasis.

She went back to Dr Taylor's office the next day. And the day after that, and the next day. She tried every door, told her story to every woman in khaki behind every desk she could find. She was seldom admitted to inner offices. The few higher officials of the organisation she saw usually said they were very sorry (with a wary eye on her haggard face and wild eyes), but they had no connection at all with that branch of work. The girl in Dr Taylor's office told her, 'I'm very sorry, dearie, but Dr Taylor says there's just no use going over and over that again.'

Days were sliding by. The nurse in charge of the home at Hendaye, to whom she had written at once, said the date for the closing of the house had been set for the second of February. 'It's a shame, too,' she wrote; 'I feel just as you do about it. The kids are improving a mile a minute. You ought to see those children from Lille playing tag! And I'm terribly scared of bronchitis and pneumonia if they're taken north now. I haven't said anything to them yet or to their folks, because I keep hoping the order will be changed. Can't you do anything about it? I feel sure you aren't getting hold of the right people. Have you seen Dr Pennybacker? Try Miss Nourse.'

One afternoon Matey, very pale now, for she had scarcely eaten or slept for days, sat in an outer office waiting for someone to return from lunch. She was trying to keep out of her mind the anxious tender mother-looks of the women at the station who had watched the children out of sight, and was turning over a manifestly insane idea of taking the children bodily on farther south, into Spain, over the frontier, beyond French jurisdiction, when her eye fell on a proof-sheet of a booklet describing the organisation's work and intended to help raise funds for it in America. It was headed by a list of names of prominent people high in its councils.

Mrs Meade Whitlock's was one of them.

In half an hour Matey was explaining to the *concierge* of a very handsome apartment house beyond the Étoile that she wished to see Madame Veetloque, as she was an old friend of hers. After a suspicious look at her intense white face, and a reassured look at her respectable costume, the *concierge* let her in.

She began to run headlong up the velvet-clad stairs when she perceived that someone was coming down, a woman with a thin, swarthy, smoothed-up middle-aged face, in a beautifully furred cloak, Parma violets pinned to its lapel.

Holding herself by the railing, Matey began, hurriedly, 'Mrs Whitlock, I don't know whether you remember me – Matey Gilbert – Professor Gilbert's daughter, in Hamilton.'

'Why, my dear *child!*' said Mrs Whitlock in great astonishment.

'No, for an instant I didn't recognise you. But of course I never dreamed of . . . you don't look very *well* to me. But I see the Gilbert look now of course, and your eyes haven't changed at all.'

Matey's heart leaped. She could have fallen to her knees on the velvet carpet. She began her plea in an imploring voice, her eyes fixed on the miraculously unchanged face before her. She had advanced only a phrase or two when the other woman said, 'Now, dear girl, do pardon me for being in a hurry. But these are busy days for us all. If I weren't rushed to death I'd take you right back up to my rooms to have tea with you and hear all the news of your family. About this matter too, of course. But I'm on my way to a very important tea, with an Ambassador. It may mean a great deal for Our Work. Never mind about details. I never go into details anyhow. Just tell me what it is you want.'

'I want the children's home in Hendaye to go on till spring,' said Matey, her heart in her blunt words.

They were walking down the stairs now and out toward the street.

'Who is in charge of that? I don't mean the nurse there – the official here.'

Matey told her. She smiled. How well Matey remembered her smile!

'Well, I don't know *him* very well, but I know his superior officer. I can fix that for you in ten minutes,' she said. 'You just haven't got hold of the right people, that's all. One has to go at these things the right way. Now what's your address, so I can let you know?'

472

Matey gave it. Mrs Whitlock reached into the recesses of an automobile which stood waiting for her, took out a notebook, and noted down the street and number. 'Where is this hospital for soldiers that you don't want closed?' she asked, her pencil suspended over the paper.

'It's not a hospital,' began Matey hastily, 'and it's not for soldiers but for ...'

Mrs Whitlock interrupted her gently, 'Never mind about details, dear. Just tell me where it is?'

Matey told her. The moving pencil wrote.

'*Good*bye,' said Mrs Whitlock, kissing Matey in the French manner. '*So* nice to have had a glimpse of you. *So* glad there is something I can do for your father's daughter. You were the *quaintest* little girl!'

Matey was playing the *one*-two-*three*-four infantile bass for an infantile four-handed arrangement of a Schubert folk march Mme Vinet had made for Petella, when Dominiqua brought in a telegram. It read, 'Glad to report your hospital will not close till May. Give my love to your brother Francis when you write. Meade Whitlock.' When, the next day, Matey went to thank her, the *concierge* said that Mme Veetloque had gone on a mission to the front.

Two days later came a telegram from the nurse in Hendaye, 'All set to stay till May. You must have pushed the right button.'

CHAPTER SEVENTEEN

❦❦❦

On the morning of the twenty-first of March Matey was still near the gates of the Lycée when an air raid began. She had not known one to happen in the daytime, and this one was not preceded by the usual warning yells from steam sirens. But from the noise, a bomb had just been dropped not far from the street where she was walking.

She stood irresolute, heard nothing more, thought she had been mistaken, and stepped into a stationery shop to buy some of the ruled, glazed writing paper preferred by the soldiers for their letters home. The stock of the shop was much depleted and the purchase took some time.

'That couldn't have been from a Boche plane, could it, Madame?' asked the woman in widow's black who waited on her, as she was wrapping up the package.

Matey had no time to answer before another explosion shook the walls of the room where they stood. Both women started, the involuntary flick of war-worn nerves with which in those years every one greeted any sudden sound. They stepped to the door and looked cautiously out and up. Not the slightest sign of aircraft.

'You would better stay here till it is over, Madame,' said the proprietor of the store.

Matey sat down and waited. Presently – crash! another roar resounded, apparently much farther away this time, scarcely audible.

And now the sirens began to shriek out their frantic warnings.

'It must be an air raid,' said Matey, looking at her watch impatiently. She had many errands to do.

'Would you like to go down to the cellar?' said her involuntary hostess courteously.

'No, thanks, I never do,' said Matey fatalistically.

'Nor I,' murmured the other woman.

After listening for some time to the nerve-wracking screech of the sirens and the rattling turmoil of the anti-aircraft guns, and hearing no more signs of air bombardment, Matey said, 'It *must* be over, now.' As she spoke, the room was shaken by an explosion perceptibly nearer than any of the others.

The sirens yelled more madly. The guns roared like thunder. Matey said, 'That doesn't sound just like an air raid!' the other answered, 'No, so few bombs exploding. At such long intervals.'

'I'm going to ask the *sergent de ville,*' said the shopkeeper, finally throwing a shawl around her head. Matey went with her down the street, emptied of all pedestrians but roaring like Niagara with a steam whistle being drawn through it by a red fire-truck.

The *sergent de ville* waved the two women back excitedly. But as they ran they called out, 'What is it? What *is* it?'

He threw up his hands. 'You see. No signs of airplanes. But bombs being dropped. Perhaps the Boche have invented invisible aircraft! Get back to shelter, *quick!* Orders are to allow no civilians in the streets!' The two women scudded back up the street. Matey said breathlessly, 'I have two children in the Lycée. I'm going in to be with them till I find out what this is.'

Bang! came the explosion of a bomb, apparently a block or two away. The windows up and down the street rattled loudly.

'I have a little girl there, too,' said the shopkeeper and pulled wildly on the Lycée bell. The door opened, the two women rushed into the dark vestibule.

Crossing the other end of the long vestibule was a procession of aproned children, bright-eyed, bright-haired, marching rapidly two by two toward a great door opening into blackness.

'Madame la Directrice has given orders for everybody to go to the cellar till this is over,' explained the school *concierge.* Through the half-open door behind them a couple of white-faced women now pushed their way. 'Are the children safe?' they cried to the *concierge,* who waved her hand toward the marching child army.

BANG! The massive walls of the Lycée shook.

A signal passed rapidly from one teacher to another. The one nearest the waiting women raised her hand, and from the children burst out fervently, '*Allons, enfants de la patrie!*' They sang as they marched swiftly forward, their bright beribboned blonde and brown heads held high, as two by two they passed through the great door and disappeared into the darkness, their voices pouring up to join those of the later ranks.

'Didi! *ma chérie!*' called one of the women beside Matey.

A little girl turned her head and waved her hand to her mother, smiling but not ceasing to sing. 'Petella and Adrien must have passed already,' thought Matey.

The little ones of the lower grades came now, bringing up the rear, marching hand in hand, stretching their short legs to keep step with the music. There was Brother, his hazel eyes bright in his excited little face, singing like a lark at Heaven's gate, his brown head thrown back, taking long manly strides.

Bang! a more distant explosion jarred faintly through the shut doors. The teacher marking time with her uplifted hand did not lose a beat. '*Formez nos bataill*ons! *Mar*chons! *Mar*chons!' sang the last of the little children vanishing into the darkness.

The *concierge* said, 'Mesdames, Madame la Directrice sends word that it would be most unsafe for you to return to the streets and invites you urgently to descend to the cellars till the raid is over. But please, she says, exercise the utmost calm, and for the sake of the children whose mothers are not here, do not try to have your own with you.'

Downstairs in a candle-lighted gloom were dim shapes of furnaces, steam pipes, garden tools, packing boxes, coal shovels, and serried rank upon rank of children, cross-legged on the floor. Matey's eyes soon located Petella and little Adrien. Their eyes, like those of all the children, were on a teacher standing before them, a plain, pale-faced, middle-aged woman, a crocheted black wool fichu with scalloped edges cast about her shoulders.

'Now the song for the Belgians,' she said, and blew softly on a little pipe to give them the keynote, beating time, '*now . . .*'

they burst into the Brabançonne. *'Le roi, la loi, la liberté!'* sang the little republican French children with all their might.

The noise of the falling bombs was not so loud here, deep in the earth as they were. ('Half buried already,' though Matey.) Other women kept appearing on the stairs, other mothers came through shell-threatened streets as if their poor human presence could be of avail to their children. They reported in whispers that Paris was for once in a panic, everybody frantic with the eeriness of what was happening – exploding shells dropping from a perfectly clear sky. Had the Germans some balloon anchored above Paris far out of sight, thousands of feet high? The air was now full, they said, of French aircraft, flying wildly about in a vacancy punctuated at intervals by another mysterious murderous bomb. Ziza, very pale in her black dress and hat, came flying down the stairs, sought out Adrien with her eyes, saw Matey, and came to stand beside her.

A short, powerful-looking elderly woman, with greying black hair pulled straight back from a blunt-featured dauntless humorous face, stepped out in front of the children now. 'Madame la Directrice! Madame la Directrice,' murmured the women clustered by the door. One of them whispered passionately, 'Isn't *anybody* going to have them say their prayers!'

Madame la Directrice smiled at the children, hooked her gold-rimmed eye-glasses to the front of her black alpaca dress with a homely quiet gesture, and began to speak. *'Eh bien, mes enfants,* your chance has come at last. This is a great day for you! Everybody else, your fathers and mothers, the soldiers, the hospitals, the nurses, all the grown-ups have been

✳✳✳

able, ever so many times, to show how brave-hearted men and women can be. But who ever thought that little children would have a chance, too, to add their share to the treasure-chest? For that's what every human being does, you know, when he does anything that's fine. He adds another gold piece to the only real treasure there is, proof that human life is worth living.'

Bang! came a loud nearby explosion, followed by the crash of breaking glass upstairs.

The stout, elderly woman's head went up, 'Do you hear that, *mes enfants?* That noise calls out to every one of you, "This is *your* day of glory!" Whatever you do down here, even down to the littlest ones of the kindergarten, will add to or take away from the treasure-store of France, of every country, everywhere. If you meet danger bravely here, everybody who ever hears about it, even years from now, perhaps when you are old people, will be braver when his turn comes to meet danger, because he'll think "What children did, I can do!"

'What do you say – suppose we toss into the treasure-chest our own special French coin, that's not only gold with courage in the face of danger, but bright with gaiety too. Don't you think it would be fun to give an entertainment to each other, *à l'improviste?* Some of you can give recitations, I know. Marie-Louise and Paulette Audibert have just learned a pretty dance. I'll do my share. I know how to make a franc come out of my ear . . . you never guessed that, did you? What do you say, my children? Shall we march? *Alons, enfants de la patrie!'*

She paused. The children, who had not taken their eyes from her, began to clap their hands and shout.

✤✤✤

A woman near Matey and Ziza said disapprovingly, 'I always heard she was a terrible internationalist, but I never believed it before.'

Another murmured, 'I think it's pagan of her not to have them say their prayers!'

The kindergarten children, marshalled by their black-clad elderly teacher, now stood before the rest of the school.

'This is a song everybody knows,' said the teacher. 'All of you join in the refrains.' A bird-like chirping rose in the air, sweet with the tunelessness of small children.

'Il était une bergère . . .'

The other children, amused by the little ones, came in promptly with the refrain, *'eh ron, eh ron, petit pat-a-pon!'*

Crash! the whole building shook as if in an earthquake. Bits of dirty rubbish pattered down on the smooth bright heads. The little voices quavered off into whimpers, and the children huddled together with an animal motion of panic. Their teacher's smiling face bent over them tenderly, as beating time she gave them the cue to go on. 'Qui *gardait ses moutons . . .'*

'Ton! ton!' came automatically from the older children.

'Why *don't* they say their prayers!' came in an hysterical whisper from the mother near Matey.

They were all singing, full-throated now, the old nursery song, setting about them its thousand associations of home and safety.

Madame la Directrice approached the group of mothers and stopped to say a friendly word in a low tone. 'I'm going to my office to telephone to the Ministry of Instruction and see if anything has been found out and what the other *lycées* are doing.'

When she came down again she announced to the mothers gravely, 'Nobody has any idea still what it can be. No enemy airplanes in sight, the bombardment continuing regularly from some invisible force. No children are being sent home until this is over.'

The children were laughing now over the antics of three Fifth Formers. They were going through the first part of *Le Médecin malgré lui* and had come to the always enchanting scene of the thrashing of Sganarelle.

'Aie! Aie! Aie!' shrieked the child playing the woodchopper.

Bang! crash! resounded from the world above.

'Ha ha! ha!' shouted the laughing children.

Ziza had read, as they all had, the unspoken word which had been in the mind of the Directrice when she went to ask for more news. Looking at Matey now, she shaped it with her lips silently – 'Gas?'

That was what they were all thinking. If this was the beginning of an attack on the city by poison gas . . .

Matey made with her shoulders the shrugging gesture of 'nothing to be done.' But it came to her with a shock that if it *was* gas, they would never any of them go up those stairs alive.

She fumbled suddenly in her handbag for a bit of paper, pulled out the only thing she found, an old envelope, and began hastily to write on the back.

Hours afterward, when the shelling had stopped for the day, when the explanation of the mystery had flown from mouth to mouth all over the city, when Gallic sprightliness had already given a gamin name to the great cannon threatening the city, the tired children were tucked into their beds in the apartment on the rue de Fleurus and the four women gathered for the futile council of war. As long as the children were within earshot the talk had been kept on a steady, quiet tone. Mme Vinet gave her usual sympathetic attention to little Adrien's account of how killingly funny the first part of *Le Médecin malgré lui* was, and to Petella's announcement of the wonderful news that there were no lessons to prepare – '*Chic alors! Hot* dog!' commented the bi-lingual little American girl gleefully.

But when Matey came back from her bedtime reading-aloud to the children she found Ziza giving a full account of what had happened at the Lycée to her mother, who sat very still, shading her eyes with one hand as she listened.

At the end she asked, 'Were you frightened, you and Mété? Really frightened, I mean?'

Ziza answered with her usual outspoken frankness, 'Simply scared sick! It was not knowing what it might be, of course. Did you and Dominiqua think it might be a gas attack from the air? We did. All of us at the same minute, from something the Directrice said. The woman in front of me began to pray as fast as she could, and Matey started writing her last message to her husband.'

'Did I write something?' asked Matey, surprised. 'I don't remember that.'

'You don't!' said Ziza. 'Why, yes, you scribbled away for a minute or two, and when the next shell exploded, you slipped the paper back into your handbag.'

Matey went to look for this, feeling now a dim muscular memory of the actions Ziza had described.

Yes, there was the envelope, one with an American stamp, and Priscilla's dear handwriting on it. She turned it over. On the back was scrawled, almost illegibly. 'Priscilla, when Father was dying he was afraid, dreadfully afraid, and it was Mother he – Mother stood by him and helped him through the – Priscilla, they always had so much more against them than we knew. Even to come together, it had to be over a broken heart and a broken faith. There was always …'

She looked up at Ziza. 'Yes, I remember now. It was something I'd been intending to tell my sister.'

She looked again at the bald words lying dead on the paper. What could Priscilla make of them – the Priscilla of the present as life had shaped her? With a sigh she tore the envelope across and threw it into the fire. 'But I don't believe I'll send it after all,' she told Ziza.

Now she knew there weren't any words that could make Priscilla understand. She had waited too long.

CHAPTER EIGHTEEN

✟✟✟

The day after the German advance on the Soissons front began, Mme Letellier from Crouy arrived at the door with her little son and two unknown little girls in bedraggled first communion dresses, all incoherent with fatigue and fright. 'Everybody's being evacuated this time,' she told them, 'whether they want to stay or not. When the Boche came through at the beginning of the war, some people with a sick person, or somebody very old to look out for, stayed on. But now after what happened in Belgium they don't dare let anybody stay. The big army camions came through Crouy, picking up everybody – and some American ambulances too, Mme Fort, are being used to evacuate people – not a soul allowed to stay.' She was in the first stage of refugee hysteria, the phase which came before the half-dead passivity of those who had been refugees for a longer time. She could not stop her excited account: 'They drove right up to the church – on First Communion Day! The bishop was just beginning to go down the line before the altar when two great camions drove up to the door and took us all away, the bishop just the way he was, in his – They'd put old Mme Rillier in our camion; she's been paralysed for years, and she died of the fright before we'd been gone half an hour, but we couldn't stop, we had to bring her along dead – with all those children around her corpse. Oh, when I think of my poor house! I'd just had the walls of the kitchen – '

They expected then at any moment to see Mimi and her boys arrive from La Ferté. But instead a telegram from Mimi came: 'Ordered to evacuate can Mété come to get boys.' They could make nothing of it. When Mme Letellier heard it, she began to cry again. 'Oh, they did get through to La Ferté! Then they must have gone through Crouy. Oh, my poor garden! The strawberries just ripening.'

Ziza said, 'If the Germans are as far as La Ferté they will soon be in Paris. We will be evacuated too.'

Matey had thought of a face-saving explanation of Mimi's asking for her rather than for Ziza or her mother. 'Perhaps those American ambulances which Mme Letellier says are helping belong to Adrian's section, and Mimi thinks I might be useful.'

'Perhaps,' said Mme Vinet.

'But you can't go, Mme Fort,' cried Mme Letellier. 'Nobody is allowed.'

'Or perhaps,' said Ziza, 'it's because Matey has a *permis de séjour* for the army zone.'

'At any rate,' said Matey, 'if Mimi telegraphs in this way, it must be that she has some very good reason for not coming with the boys. Perhaps she's needed to care for some sick person who's to be evacuated. I must go.'

She soon found that her *permis de séjour* was of no avail, not even supplemented by all the *Système D* she had learned in three years of evading military regulations. At the Gare de l'Est crowded with excited refugees, there was no ticket window open for tickets to the war zone. The sentry by the entrance of the train shed, on whom she began to try some of the inventions which had been worked out for getting around sentries, looked stonily over her head, as if he had been a German. She went finally to the Paris office of Adrian's ambulance service, not knowing what she expected to do. But when, as she approached the office, she saw the boy from Dutchess County standing in front of the door in the street, she knew very well what she would try to do.

'Hello, Mrs Fort,' he greeted her, 'you still in Paris? If I were you I'd take the kids and beat it. Everything with wheels is being ordered out into the Marne valley to bring in "civils." They don't tell us why, but they don't have to. It's a cinch they don't expect to hold 'em this time. At the rate Ludendorff's travelling he'll be in Paris in a week.'

Matey said, 'Do you remember you said you'd see that I was sent home to be buried? Well, there's something I want much more than that – '

When, four hours later, in the dusk of the May evening, Matey crept out from the back of the ambulance, the boy said, 'Looky here, Mrs Fort, this would get me in *bad* if – '

'Nobody'll know,' she told him, 'ever. How could they? They're coming around to evacuate this quarter at dawn tomorrow, you say. Well – I'll just get evacuated with the others. You don't suppose they're going to ask for papers of identity at such a time! Don't forget that if there's ever any way I can make up to you for helping me – '

He blushed. 'Oh, that's all right – that's all right! Not much to do for the wife of my old Chef de Section. Worst luck I ever had was to get transferred out of his section. I always did like Lieutenant Fort; he's so damned unmilitary.' He saw the last of his convoy disappearing around a turn of the street and drove off hastily.

Matey went to ring the bell of Mimi's house. No one answered. She tried the knob of the door, and it turned. She stepped in and called. No one answered. She went hastily about the house, noting the evidence in dust and disorder of the careless housekeeping recently done there. The kitchen stove was still faintly warm. They could not be far. Perhaps they were at the factory next door. She made her way there in the gathering twilight. The factory itself was dark, but there were lights in the little building where the offices were installed. Matey went up and knocked on the door. Mimi opened it, standing belligerently on the threshold till she saw who was there. Then, with a cry of welcome –'Oh, I *knew* you'd come!'– she drew her in.

Behind her stood a young girl in an apron, evidently a maid, and the boys Mimi would not bring to see their grandmother. Their faces were pale under their close-cropped dark hair, and they looked frightened and half sick, but – French to the last breath – they advanced to shake hands ceremoniously with Maman's friend. Matey kissed the youngest one, a couple of years older than Petella, whom she had seen as a baby on her wedding trip, her heart yearning over his strained wide eyes and colourless little mouth.

'I told you, boys, that Tante Mété would come!' Mimi said

487

to them triumphantly, 'Now you're all right, my darlings; you'll have somebody to go with you right to Grand'mère's door.'

The youngest began to cry, leaning his head against his mother's skirt, and saying in a low mournful voice, 'I *wish* you'd come with us, Maman!'

'You know why I am staying, René,' Mimi reminded him with a noble accent. 'Be a man, my little son. Remember a Frenchman cannot be afraid of anything.'

'But, Mimi, why *are* you staying?' Matey asked the question at last.

Mimi looked at her in astonishment and then around her at the desks, the large locked safe, the typewriters, the filing cabinets, which furnished the dingy room. 'Do you suppose for a moment I'm going to abandon my children's patrimony?' she asked indignantly.

One of the many scenes which Matey tried in vain to forget was Mimi's struggle the next morning with the weary grey-haired French reserve sergeant who, climbing down from the American Field Service Ambulance, came in to evacuate the office. 'Pardon, Monsieur,' said Mimi, standing in an attitude of authoritative self-confidence, 'I send my children. But *I* remain to protect my husband's business.'

Matey gathered the boys around her, motioned to the little serving-maid to follow her, and started down the walk to the street. Behind her she heard Mimi's voice rising hysterically. 'I have given every drop of my heart's blood to save this business. For three years I have done nothing but labour for it. Let them kill me if they will – I will *not* let the Boche . . . ' The door of the office slammed shut.

Matey hurried her little flock toward the ambulance, nodding to the American boy on the driver's seat and explaining, 'I'm an American too,' as she helped the children climb up into the back of the vehicle.

'You don't *say!*' said the boy in a slow, beautiful Southern accent. He looked around at her curiously. They waited. The office door remained closed. 'Was theh somethin' heavy to ca'y out, I wonder?' asked the driver.

'I think not,' said Matey, trying to think of something else. Little René was shivering and crying noiselessly. She drew him into her lap and began to tell him a story. Presently she saw the door of the office open. Mimi appeared, *hatless,* like a peasant woman! Her face was very red and set. She was followed by the grey-haired sergeant, both of them loaded to the eyes with huge account books. From the driver's seat came a soft comment: 'Well, I've evacuated a lot of folks and I've seen 'em ca'y out most eve'thing from canary-birds to pigs, but I neveh saw a *lady* so set on bookkeepin'!'

Matey was impressed to the point of alarm by a bourgeoise forgetting her hat, wondered whether she would better remind her of it, looked at her face and decided not to.

The books were piled in under the bench which ran along each side of the ambulance; the reserve sergeant helped Mimi in and climbed wearily to the driver's seat, where he lighted a cigarette and relapsed into silence. 'He's a good old scout if he is a Frawg,' the boy from the South told Matey as the Ford roared into low speed. 'He manages refugees bettah then anybody I eveh worked with. And, believe me, they take some managin'.'

They drove on in silence, out of the court of the factory into the street, and stopped before a poor small house, from which instantly, in humble readiness, emerged a peasant woman and three children, all carrying large bundles tied up in bedding.

'It's a good thing this is my last stop,' said the driver. 'Looks like they wouldn't be any mo' room after those bundles get stacked up.'

The newcomers stored their bundles as best they could, climbed in silently. The ambulance rolled on.

The peasant woman had a rosary in her hand and now bent her head over it, her lips moving rapidly in a low murmur. With a strange look at Matey, half defiance, half exaltation, Mimi drew a rosary from the bosom of her dress. But she did not begin to say her prayers. She paused, her eyes on Matey's. For the first time Matey felt something of Adrian's father on her tongue. She said, with no effort, naturally, with a friendly smile, just what she felt. 'Now, Mimi dear, don't take for granted that I will criticise and not understand.'

Mimi looked at her attentively with an expression Matey found very touching – as if she found sympathy too much to hope for.

She went on, 'Dear Mimi, why do you hold us all off at arm's length so about this?'

'*I* don't!' cried Mimi, astonished and indignant at the idea. This was not at all, apparently, what she had expected Matey to say. 'It's the others who do – Maman, Ziza, Henri! They're the ones who act as though I had – Mété, I've felt all along as though you were my only friend there. Tell me, *why* do they treat me as though it were – Why won't they even let me

490

tell them about it? *Why* do they keep that stiff, cold, careful silence!'

'Well, I won't,' said Matey, reaching to give her hand a friendly clasp, 'if you'll give me half a chance.'

'Oh, Mété, you don't know what it means to me – How can Maman feel anything but thankfulness for me! She must see that it has given me the first happiness I ever knew. All my life I've missed it, and after the war began – no, Mété, really, honestly we would all go mad if the world were what people without faith think it is. How *could* Maman have let us children grow up without any defence against such a world! She must have seen that I was starving for faith. Alone in hell – that's where my mother left me! How can anybody blame me for wishing to save my children from that awful desolation of living without God? I know what it is. I lived in it without knowing it all my life, and then in those first weeks of the war – I knew it for what it was. I don't see how we didn't all go insane, reeling along in the darkness – going nowhere. If it hadn't been for religion we would have. It was the sight of Soeur Sainte Julienne which first showed me the light.' She looked full at Matey and said with energetic certainty, 'Do you suppose that a woman without faith *could* face danger as she has?'

Matey thought of Madame la Directrice and the teachers, but was silent, determined not to act as the Vinets did.

'Mété, such inner peace as I have had! Since the day I was baptised. Since the day of my first communion. Peace is something nobody *can* know outside the Church. When I think how long I lived without once leaning on the inexpressible comfort of authority!' Matey did not say a word nor change the expression of her eyes, but Mimi added quickly, defiantly, 'Mété, there *must* be authority! Since I have been in active life I have seen that we can't live for a moment in the material world without it. Why should we think we can live spiritually in anarchy? We can't. I will not leave my children in spiritual anarchy, let Maman think what she will!'

The energy of her speech mounted from word to word. Her eyes were exalted. 'Mété, why won't they let me talk to *them* this way? Tell them. Explain! You do understand, don't you? Can't you?'

'Well, I don't know that I understand exactly. But I can certainly sympathise. Not because I'm any better than they. You know in America we don't feel so strongly, in fact not strongly at all, about differences of religion. My own mother went into a sisterhood before she died, and we never dreamed of feeling badly about it. It's not hard for me to . . . ' She ventured a timid plea for Mme Vinet, dreadfully afraid of alienating Mimi. 'But, *ma chérie,* couldn't you think of how it seems to your mother – to have you keep your boys away . . . '

'I *must* protect their faith till it has grown firm,' cried Mimi desperately. 'It's for Maman to understand how a mother feels for her children!'

The ambulance stopped with a suddenness which almost sent them to the floor in a heap.

Matey, nearest the driver's seat, asked him what was the trouble. In a vexed accent he said over his shoulder, 'Bridge blown up. I thought I'd beat the engineers to it, but they beat me. I'd ought to have taken the long way around, after all.'

'Why didn't you?' asked Matey.

492

'Well, there's a piece of it I sort of hated to take ladies and children along,' said the Southern boy gently. He swung his awkward car around. 'I reckon I'll have to,' he said, starting back, and beginning to whistle 'It's a long long road.'

Inside the ambulance everyone except Matey was praying. She saw that the moment had passed in which she could have gone on with her appeal to Mimi for more gentleness to Mme Vinet. She had been shocked by the bitterness in Mimi's tone when she spoke of her mother. The ambulance was filled by the sound of sibilant murmured words, the repeated appeal for help, *'Nunc et in hora mortis nostrae.'*

Mimi's boys, each with a rosary in his hand, were murmuring devoutly in unison with the three peasant children.

Mimi interrupted herself to whisper to Matey, 'You can't think, too – though that's such a small matter compared to the greatness of having found God – how happy it makes me to be one with the rest of my country – as my boys are now, brothers to these simple people we never saw before – not to stand out, as our family did, hostile hard rebels from the faith which has always saved France. For you know, Mété, this war was a punishment for the unbelief of France.'

Matey nodded something vague. Mimi bowed her head over her rosary again. As Matey watched she saw her face become serene and remote.

Matey wondered where they might be and found that by tipping her head to one side she could catch glimpses of the country through the crevice between the driver and the elderly Frenchman. They were passing through farmlands, rolling and rich in carefully tended wheat fields, already jewel-green with young wheat, the old Aryan treasure that would so long outlive them all. From time to time they passed a heap of bricks and beams that had been a house. The car was going very slowly, with many outrageous jolts. She guessed that this was one of the roads of which Adrian so often wrote, badly shelled and hastily repaired. They were passing a cemetery now, the tombs clustered around a great cross, on which was the inscription, 'Love ye one another.'

'We'll soon be out of this, ma'am,' said the American boy, apologising for a back-breaking jolt.

'How kind that boy is!' thought Matey. 'How unblunted by the war!'

His driving now took all his attention. He stopped whistling as he steered a slow zigzag way between the worst of the holes. Leaning forward more as he did, he widened the aperture through which Matey was observing the world.

Down the road she saw a small square stucco house, slightly less ruined than most of those they were passing, although one corner of the roof was out. She recognised it as they came nearer. It was what was left of Mimi's pleasant little country home. She hoped Mimi would not look up.

Odd – the house, ruined as it was, seemed full of people. As the ambulance slowly advanced she made out dark forms leaning from the windows, others apparently asleep in the little latticed summer house in the garden. But they did not stir. And what strange stiff grotesque attitudes!

The ambulance drew near. A frightful stench filled the air. She saw them plainly now, had one full view of the ruined house and the rotting dead men.

The driver looked around uneasily and saw her horrified stare. 'You see, ma'am, they had a right smart fight takin' that house, and there hasn't been time enough yet to get eve'body buried. This sector's got American troops in it now and our rule is first bury our own folks, and then the Frawgs and then the horses and then the Boche.'

They jolted by. The driver began to whistle 'Over There.'

Matey looked quickly at Mimi again. But her head was still bent. Her face was still remote and radiant. She had seen nothing but her rosary.

CHAPTER NINETEEN

✦✦✦

The summer of 1918, the summer when the tide turned, when in a daze people began to try to open their minds to the thought that the war might not go on for ever, was the summer when Henri Vinet was killed.

There had been one of the terrifying silences with no letter from Henri for a week. Then for ten days. On the eleventh the news came in a letter from the front, from a comrade of Henri's. He had been one of their guests, knew the family, and wrote to Matey, asking her to tell Henri's mother and sister.

Matey was the one who opened the door to the *concierge* with the mail. She tore open the letter addressed to her in a strange handwriting, her hands wet with a sudden icy perspiration. The news was on the first page. She read it at a glance and remained perfectly motionless, looking down at the words.

At the other end of the hall Mme Vinet's door opened. Matey did not look up.

Henri's mother stepped forward to meet the execution of the death sentence which had hung over her so long.

'*Mon fils est mort,*' she said.

✝✝✝

Like a frightened child Matey put her crooked arm up over her face as if to ward off a blow.

But it did not fall. Of all in the apartment, Mme Vinet remained the strongest. As if they were children again Matey and Ziza clung to her. She grew old, old and withered and bent, from one day to the next. But she did not falter. She was still Maman.

Once, walking with her under the summer trees of the Luxembourg, while the four children played (for little Mélanie was old enough now to run about and was zestfully thrusting her way up into life), Matey said impulsively, 'How can you? I wish I knew from where you draw your strength!'

Mme Vinet, small, bent, old in her black dress and long veil, said, 'Dear child, it is the only way left me of being worthy of Henri and Polo and their father. I mean by that of standing by their ideals – mine too. You see, Mété, there's a higher standard of courage to which we must live up, we people who have no ready-made God to fall back on who'll take care of us if we'll only worship him. We must be strong enough not to shirk our share of creating God in man.'

Quietly as this had been spoken, Matey knew it referred to the situation at the apartment. The silences there had been heart-breaking. Mme Vinet's silence during the murmur of Latin prayers, Mimi's silence when, her head high, her face set, she signalled to her sons to cross themselves at the beginning of a meal. And since Henri's death – had there been a dreadful sort of rivalry of endurance between the representatives of the two opposing creeds? That over Henri's death – ! No, no, that must be an ignoble fancy of her own, born of the nervous tension, of the almost intolerable state of siege, at the apartment . . . five women and ten children living on top of each other, mattresses laid on the floors, the daily bombardment of the city by the great cannon, and a constant expectation of summons to leave the city, valises packed in readiness for instant departure.

Then the tide turned, and with dream-like rapidity the *dénouement* of the drama drew near.

The first result of it as far as they were concerned was the permission for civilians to return to the evacuated regions south of Soissons. The first train available took Mme Letellier and Mimi back to their homes, not irreparably injured, they wrote, for the rush to and fro of troops had been too hurried for systematic looting. At once geographic separation began to perform its usual miracle of reducing personal friction. Mimi's letters sounded more natural than any of her talk had been. Ziza and her mother spoke of her in a more natural tone.

Heartened by this, Matey made her one effort toward reconciliation. Since neither Ziza nor her mother would speak to her, she would speak out herself. She chose a time when she and Ziza were alone together outdoors, walking home from an afternoon's work at the *vestiaire* on the rue Pascal.

'See here, Ziza,' she said. 'I can't understand you and your mother – so loving, so kind – why can't you let Mimi enjoy her conversion in peace? It means so much to her. What harm does it do you?'

Ziza answered quickly, 'Maman is the one who feels it – that way. I don't, not in the least. I'm perfectly tolerant in matters of religion. But for Maman – for all of her generation and Papa's – I don't suppose you could possibly understand, Mété, not being French, what it means to Maman. You seem to think it's just a personal religious matter. In France it's not. It's everything. Maman feels that it strikes at the root of all that she and Papa believed in, gave their lives to, fought for, taught to Mimi. In France it doesn't mean just going to Mass, you know, it means – to Maman, anyhow – going back on everything free and humane, attacking the public schools, personal dignity, above all, treason to humanity. That's how it seems to her, like treason.'

Matey asked, 'But, Ziza, if you don't share your mother's feeling, why didn't you let little Adrien go out to visit Mimi last summer?'

'Ah, I'd just as soon not have my son exposed to proselytising till his judgment is a little more mature,' said Ziza coolly. 'After all, you know, those two ways of looking at life are absolutely opposed. What's the use of pretending they can be reconciled? No, I don't feel at all as Maman does. It's no business of mine what other people believe. All religions are very much the same anyhow. What I can't stand is the arrogance of any one religion that claims to provide the *only* road to Heaven. That's so absurd!'

Before her trip in the ambulance Matey would have given it up then. But now she said pleadingly, 'But, Ziza, in such a time as this . . . '

'That sounds to me like Anglo-Saxon sentimentality. Because we may all be dead tomorrow, is that a reason for saying you believe in what you don't?'

Matey persisted. 'Can't you see for yourself what a transformation it has made in her?' She thought of the serene remote face bent over the rosary. 'Mimi's like another person. Happier than ever before in all her life.'

'It's discovering she has Tante Caroline's gift for business that's changed her,' said Ziza uncompromisingly. 'She's simply crazy about running that factory. You just wait! My poor old brother-in-law won't have so much as a seat in the office when he comes back.'

Matey never spoke of it again. It was, along with nearly everything else personal, thrust into the background by the news from the front. They found they could not believe it, that they had not really dared to hope that peace might come again, any more than a man whose leg had been amputated hopes ever to have it back again. September had been full of incredible news of Allied victories and the breakdown of German militarism and despotism. Matey and all about her had learned in a hard school to give little credence to what they read or heard. But this hope came to them from everywhere at once. To Mme Vinet and her circle at the Lycée, lifelong Liberals, as stirring as the approach of victory was the news of the emergence to life and power of the Liberal element in Germany, the creation of the Czecho-Slovak Republic, the promise of the Allies to create a free Poland, above all the personality of the American President. Henri's mother took with passion the hope, the only one left, that out of the evil that had come to her, to everyone, somehow good might come. Her eager joy in victories that were not military was her way of keeping alive the spirit of her husband and sons.

One of Adrian's furloughs fell in the last part of September. Mme Vinet's welcome made him feel that she thought of him as the last son remaining to her. 'But I'm no son for a Frenchwoman, let her be as Liberal as she may,' he told Matey; 'I'm nobody's son but my father's. I'm more a Friend than ever before. No, I never was a Friend before. But I am now. I don't believe in anything that's had by force. I don't think you get it at all. You just have to go back to the beginning and start over again if you're going to have it. Not that I care.' He looked, in fact, far too tired to care for anything. But he never argued with Mme Vinet, he always gently turned the subject. On the evening of the twenty-ninth of September, when she sat reading aloud to the assembled family the telegraphed account of President Wilson's speech at New York, he listened quietly, making no comment, smoking his pipe, a patient expression on his face.

'First, the impartial justice meted out must involve no discrimination between those to whom we wish to be just and those to whom we do not wish to be just. Second, no special or separate interests of any single nation or group of nations can be made the basis of any part of the settlement which is not consistent with the *common interest of all*.

'Lastly, all international agreements must be made known in their entirety to the rest of the world!'

Ziza cried out, '*Vive l'Amérique!* It's not on the old continent of Europe that such statesmen are grown.'

Mme Vinet said to Ziza, 'I wish thy father could have lived

501

to hear the ruler of a great nation speak out like this for justice and democracy.' To Matey she said, trying to control her shaking lips, 'Your President makes me hope, for the first time, that Polo and Henri did not die in vain.'

Matey said anxiously, 'You musn't idealise President Wilson.'

'Idealise him?' said Ziza. 'You have heard his words. What praise could equal them?'

After that Matey's uneasiness ebbed low and flowed high in alternations of excitement. There were times when she was caught up with everyone else into a collective madness of hope and ardour over the American attitude as voiced by President Wilson. There were nights when she woke up suddenly to a sick memory of the American bureaucrats who had almost brought those children back to winter Paris.

For one whole day, the eleventh of November, she put her doubts aside. When the announcing cannon had boomed the news she and Ziza ran wildly down the street to the Lycée, their first thought to tell the children. At the Lycée gates they met the children, dismissed from school, their first thought to tell their mothers. Matey saw Petella and Brother emerge on the run from the crowd, eyes blazing, faces paper-pale. 'Maman!' they screamed, when they saw her there. 'Maman! *La guerre est finie!*' Matey let them be the bearers of the news.

As Ziza, kneeling on the sidewalk, took her little boy into her arms he asked her, in a low tone as though he feared to say it aloud, 'Maman, can we go back home now?' Matey knew then as though she saw them on the train for Louvain that Ziza would take her husband's son back to his father's home. But in the changes that were coming to them all what would become of Ziza's mother?

They went through the roaring, shouting, weeping crowds on the streets back to that mother and found her at the piano, the tears streaming down her face. All that day, at intervals, when her emotion was more than she could endure, she fled to her music again, leaning with all her weight on it. Matey thought, 'Nobody can get along – it's not just Mimi – without souls stronger than his to lean on!'

The next weeks! They never seemed to Matey like weeks of earthly life but of a long half-fevered, half-exalted dream, filled with intense feelings set intensely against one another.

The drawing aside of the veil which had so long hidden people in the occupied regions of the north brought to the apartment in the rue de Fleurus the families of the soldiers to whom they had been *marraines de guerre*. Nothing that they had lived through was harder than thus to see men two years dead die once more. Throughout the four years of prison these sallow withered women had looked forward to the moment of reunion, and when they were released nothing awaited them but a grave.

To see them, to talk to them, to sit by and watch them weep, to try to bring to mind the last words or some living memory of the men who had been the core of their lives – for the first time Mme Vinet and Ziza shrank from what was to be done. 'Mété, you see Mme Morelle. I can't stand any more. I've just been to the cemetery to show Mme Goureaud where her son's grave is.' They dreaded a knock on the door. Matey took more of this work than the three widows in the apartment, and with justice. It did not make her live over again such losses as theirs, now freshly present to their minds. For with the cessation of actual danger to those left alive, a throbbing came into wounds that had been numb. For the first time Matey found Dominiqua weeping over her dead son's photograph, and Mme Vinet put away all the books that had belonged to Henri and Polo.

It was this freshening of grief which lay at the bottom of the intensity of the feeling everywhere about the approaching Peace Conference. Women for whom personal affection had been all, who never before had felt the remotest connection with politics, now found the dignity of their deepest personal loves helplessly dependent on politicians. Every woman Matey knew stood beside a newly made grave. With the fierceness of women guarding their dead from desecration they cried out in horror at the implication that their sons and husbands and brothers had died to win material advantages. Of all the rulers of the world the American President seemed the only one capable of understanding that to kill the hope that those deaths had advanced the cause of all humanity was to kill the dead men over again. The American President alone seemed to share their consternation at a future which brought no spiritual rewards for the ignominy of the war.

Again and again Matey saw this drama act itself out before her. For days, when the newspaper talk of the settlement-to-be echoed with material advantages, material revenges to be had, a sort of shamed paralysis of the heart descended upon the hard-working women in Matey's group, almost worse than the honest fear and sorrow they had known. And then, bold, high, generous, infinitely comforting to their half-murdered sense of human dignity, came another Wilsonian statement. The group in the rue de Fleurus, like many such groups, read aloud every word from Washington, making a little ceremony of it, keeping the children up from bed to hear. Even Dominiqua, to whose old Basque total illiteracy the war had been as without meaning as a bad dream, asked every day if *le Président Veelson* had sent another piece for the paper. She too in the evening brought her knitting in to listen devoutly to the good words she could not understand.

'It's like the Fifth Symphony played out with all the world as orchestra,' said Mme Vinet again and again. 'Just when there seems no one great enough to meet the challenge of the war – ' She ran to the piano, summoning Beethoven to say the rest.

Matey discounted this both in her thoughts and in her letters to Adrian. 'Of course there may not be many like them,' she wrote. 'The Vinets – all the Lycée faculty – belong by lifelong association to that class, so small in any country, the dyed-in-the-wool Liberals.' But how to explain – could it really be a *universal* reponse to idealism – the sort of madness for Wilson which she felt everywhere? Why were pictures of him, cut from newspapers, pinned up on the walls wherever she came and went? Why did such pictures appear in the shops, everywhere? And when it appeared, a huge photograph, in the *loge* of the *concierge . . .* !

And yet she was not in the least prepared to have Mme Vinet, who had no taste for street gatherings, and like other Liberal bourgeois detested too close personal contact with working-people, cancel a morning's appointments in order to be present at the arrival of President Wilson. Not only Mme Vinet but all the family. 'You're not going to take a two-year-old child out to that?' asked Matey, astonished, seeing Mme Vinet struggling to encase the bouncing little Mélanie's plump legs in leggings.

'I don't want to make anybody stay at home to take care of her,' explained Mme Vinet.

'Dominiqua's not going!'

'She certainly is!'

'Couldn't we leave the baby just for that hour at the Lycée kindergarten?'

'The Lycée's closed for the day!'

So they went along together, every one of them, the first time they had all been out on the street at the same time. When they came to the appointed street, lined with crowds and police, they took turns in holding on their shoulders the lively little girl whose father had been a German, while they waited in the bright winter sunshine for the American President. The crowd about them was made up of just such people as they, women in black like Ziza and Mme Vinet, hatless working-women like Dominiqua, some with men in working-clothes or uniforms, all with children.

Matey was painfully affected by the excitement of their faces and talk. Behind them she saw weeks such as the Vinets had lived, weeks of heartsick waiting for some vision of the future which would give them self-respect enough to go on into more of human life. Contact with each other here brought their collective ardour to a fever. When the guns boomed out a distant warning of the arrival of the train at the station the crowd surged forward in a rush that made Matey tremble. A woman near her shocked her by saying hysterically, 'It's on our knees we should be!' Everyone made way so that the children could see. An escort of bicycle police flashed by. Down the street a sound of frantic cheering broke out. There was no military music, no roll of drums, only a car rolling along the street. The cheering swept down toward them, the crest of its wave almost visible above the shouting crowd. Matey saw Mme Vinet begin to cheer and wave her handkerchief. Ziza was crying.

The car was before them. Matey received two staggering shocks in the same instant: one, the wild single shout that broke out as the car passed, shaking her as if she had been at the centre of a clap of thunder; the other, a clear sight of the cause of this portent – a long bony college professor's face, with a pleased smile on the thin lips.

CHAPTER TWENTY

✝✝✝

'Yes,' said Matey to the elegant *chasseur* of the hotel, 'that's the name. M Francis Gilbert.'

Francis was there in a moment, even more elegant than the *chasseur.* 'All set, Matey dear,' he said genially. 'And I've got a mighty interesting bunch to dine with us.'

He led the way into a nearby salon, said 'Just a jiff, I've got to look up Parkinson,' and left her in a room which looked to her quite incredibly handsome and well kept up. As she looked from the huge and quite unbroken panes of the windows to the brocade on the chairs and the velvet carpet, Matey thought of the threadbare dinginess of the Vinet apartment. She remembered Francis's expression as he had looked about him at the window-glass mended refugee-fashion with adhesive tape, at the patched upholstery, and his silent surprise at the meagreness of the meal offered to him – and yet they had prepared what they thought a feast. But how nice he had been! He had only looked surprised and interested, not scornful at all. How magnificently respectful he had been to Mme Vinet! Perhaps a shade too showily so; it almost set off and made more visible her threadbare shabbiness. They had really all grown very shabby, thought Matey, looking around her with Francis's eyes. But Mme Vinet might have been in point lace for all his manner showed. And this evening he had not given a glance or a thought evidently to the fact that his sister was not in evening dress. Evening dress! She wore, remodelled, the black voile dress that had been made in Poughkeepsie, still her only dress-up costume. How suspicious it had been in her to think beforehand that perhaps Francis would object to showing a plainly dressed sister to his grand friends on the Peace Commission! How mean and vengeful women's long memories are! she thought with remorse.

Francis was coming back, having found Parkinson. He presented the newcomer to his sister with a beautiful deference. 'My sister, Mrs Fort,' he said bowing as though she had been royalty, and as Mr Parkinson (if that was the name) took her hand, Francis added proudly, 'My sister and her husband have been in France in relief work *since the spring of 1915*. She has given her entire fortune to help the cause of the Allies.'

Matey blinked and shut her lips together rather hard. What a vixen she was, she thought, taking offence at the least thing.

Other people came in, guests of Francis for the dinner, big, smooth-shaven men with light-coloured eyes and square jaws, and, oh! such beautifully fine close-woven *new* cloth in their dress suits! Matey could not take her eyes from it. She had not seen such cloth – she had forgotten there were such fabrics, all new!

But this was nothing to the purple velvet in a dress which now approached them. Oh – why, it was Mrs Whitlock in the dress! Impulsively she shook the other woman's hand, saying warmly, 'Now I can thank you, really.'

Mrs Whitlock kissed her. She seemed gratified at her warmth and looked around as if to make sure the others saw it. 'I was able to be of help to this wonderful little woman,' she explained (Matey towering above her), 'in the matter of a military hospital she was interested in. For the whole period of the war she has given her entire life to the cause of the Allies.'

Matey perceived in what light Francis and Mrs Whitlock were presenting her. She also perceived that they were on very good terms with each other. As soon as the conversation came down from the rather soulful tone given to it by the mention of Matey's services to the cause of the Allies there was a lively interchange of pleasantries between them which took her back many years.

'Isn't it wonderful,' said Mrs Whitlock, addressing herself to Mr Parkinson, but aware of being listened to by all the group, 'my finding here in my old age these children of the dearest old friends of my youth.'

'You are exactly the same, haven't changed an atom,' said Francis with perfect accuracy.

She shook her sleek dark head at him. 'You Gilbert men! You always know how to turn women's heads!' Looking at another man in the group, she said to Francis, 'I never could make up my mind, Dr Burchard, in the old days whether I was more in love with the father or the son.'

Mr Parkinson turned to Matey, obviously with the thought that it was time something was said to the titular guest of honour. 'We're not to have the pleasure of meeting your husband this evening?'

'Oh, no,' said Matey, 'he's not in Paris.'

'He's not one of the Peace Commission gang, then? Oh, I had an impression from something your brother said – '

Matey guessed how that impression had been obtained. In a flurry of accumulating resentment she said, with a confused notion of bringing Francis for once to book, 'My husband is a lieutenant, running an ambulance section.'

Mrs Whitlock lifted her eyebrows with a startled look of one who thinks she cannot have heard aright, opened her mouth, and closed it again.

'Ah, indeed,' said Mr Parkinson, obviously trying not to sound too much like a man who knew no one under the rank of colonel.

For an instant, incredibly, Matey heard the title as they heard it and her mind made a quick futile gesture to snatch back her words. Why did she need to tell them that! Alas! Francis was not the one who had been brought to book. She was feeling apologetic – before these people! – for Adrian. She was exactly like Francis.

Mr Parkinson stepped warily around this topic and took out another conversational gambit, 'Have you been at the front lately, Mrs Fort?' he asked politely.

'I haven't been at all,' cried Matey.

'Not at *all!*' cried Mrs Whitlock. 'Why, you poor child! Francis! Your sister says she hasn't been able to get to the front at *all!* We must get a permit for you at once – it'll be easy to manage some mission or other for you. Though of course now' – she added with the accent of disappointmrnt, 'I forgot about the armistice – there's really nothing to see.'

'A great mistake!' burst suddenly from a thin elderly dignitary who till then had not spoken at all. 'We ought not to have stopped till we had marched all through Germany, doing what they did to Belgium, clear through to Berlin. Given them a taste of their own medicine. Our boys would have seen to it that Fritz had what was coming to him. We could have trusted them to.' He turned to the man nearest him and went on with his oration while Mrs Whitlock told Matey, 'I was at the front two days after Chateau-Thierry was evacuated by the Boche. The first American woman allowed there. Before any cleaning up had been done, you know – the real thing, I can tell you! I got right down into the trenches where there'd been hand-to-hand – '

'*Ah, M Martin, quel plaisir de vous voir!*' said Francis, stepping forward to greet a newcomer, bald, stout, with quick smiling lips and quiet attentive eyes.

Francis presented him to Matey, putting an extra polish on his French, delicately drawing out the *e* mutes like an actor reciting poetry. 'My sister, Mme Fort,' said Francis. 'My sister and her husband have been in France doing war relief work since the spring of 1915. She has expended the whole of her fortune to help the cause of the Allies.'

M Martin bowed over Matey's hand and replied in unaffected French, not in the delicate or Parisian, but heartily, broadly southern, with amusing nasals and rolled *r*'s. Francis led him on a hand-shaking circuit of the circle.

'What wonderful French your brother speaks,' murmured

one of the Americans in Matey's ear. 'The rest of us are as helpless as immigrants on Ellis Island. He'd be influential enough, anyhow, a man of his standing. But it's really beyond anything – the added advantage his French is to him. He'll be one of the few whose say-so will count.'

Matey thought, 'I wonder if he has learned to spell the endings of his past tenses,' and reflected that now he would not need to, surrounded as he was by expert stenographers to do the dreary work of being correct.

'Well, we might as well go in and peck at our humble meal,' said Francis, when the introductions were over. 'We're all here.' He bent with a fine bow and offered his arm to his sister as guest of honour. On the way into the dining room he murmured in her ear, 'Mrs Whitlock's money was *in* Steel, to begin with. How's that for luck? It's ten times what it used to be when we knew her!'

No, decidedly, Matey could not hold her own with the food. She had refused the last two dishes offered. She was sorry, she told the man on her right, solicitous for her lack of appetite, but she didn't seem to feel very hungry. Her soup, she explained, she had eaten her soup very well. 'That's all we have, often, for our evening meal,' she told him, refusing to put a spoon in a wonderful edifice, apparently of many-coloured glass, presumably of aspic jelly. Francis heard her. 'My sister,' he said proudly, 'has been absolutely living the wartime life of France for nearly four years. You can see by looking at her that she has not had more than her share!' With a gesture he presented Matey to them as a war exhibit, her thinness, her old remodelled dress, her plainly dressed hair, her lack of jewellery. Matey realised that far from wishing her to appear in an elegant toilette, it would have spoiled his effect. It was, she thought, the first time that Francis had ever been proud of her.

'*I* thought she looked *dreadfully* thin when I first saw her,' said Mrs Whitlock fondly, reaching for a bonbon. 'But I must say her thinness is very becoming to her. It makes your eyes look simply *enormous,* Matey dear, and I certainly wish I had your figure.'

Matey looked at her silently out of enormous eyes.

The Frenchman was eating his way methodically through the elaborate meal. He seemed to be doing his share of talking, in fact cast out a great many sparkling words. But Matey thought he gave as intent an attention as she to the talk which now rose just beyond Francis.

'Who is this M Martin?' she asked of Mr Parkinson, sitting next to her.

'Well, I don't know exactly. I've heard, too. Somebody or other close to Clemenceau, if I remember rightly. A kind of *officier de liaison* between the American members of the Peace Commission crowd and the French.'

'I said to him, *"Don't you worry about that!"*' announced the man beyond Francis. ' "That don't amount to a row of pins," I told him. "Do you suppose we pay any attention to all that? Our policy," I told him, "is to let the Old Man talk. He loves to. And what harm does it do? Makes a nice occupation for him. When it comes right down to what is going to be *done* he won't have a look-in. He can't! The big world's no college campus!"'

Francis nodded energetically.

Something slid gently over Matey's left shoulder. She turned to see. *More food!* She shook her head and pressed her napkin to her lips.

'Madame,' said M Martin addressing her coolly in French across two diners between them, 'to whom do they make reference, in this amusing fashion, as the "Old Man"?'

She shook her head. 'Some little pleasantry of their circle, I suppose,' she said.

She saw in his eyes that he understood her to be trying to evade his question and from his smile that he had extracted from what she said the information he was seeking. He complimented her effusively on her French. 'And your brother too! You've no idea what a bright spot his French is among the tongue-tied Americans of the Peace Commission. So many things will pass through his hands because of that. He will be a power, anyone can see that.' He looked around the table, which was in an uproar of laughter over some remark of Mrs Whitlock's Matey had missed. *'Cette dame?'* he enquired of Matey.

'Very influential in American war relief work,' she told him.

'Ah,' he answered, his eyes on Mrs Whitlock. He looked at Matey again, and said smiling, 'How like one big family they all are, already, are they not, Madame? A wonderful gift for collective action, the Americans! I envy them. Nothing of the French quarrelsome individualism and lack of loyalty to a common purpose. Your people always stand solidly together behind their leaders. It is wonderful.'

'It's very kind of you to say so,' murmured Matey faintly.

Francis of course insisted on putting her into a cab at the door of the hotel. But as soon as she was out of sight, halfway across the Place de la Concorde, she stopped the driver and dismissed him. She could not return to the apartment, she could not face the eyes that would look at her there. She would walk. She could perhaps walk it off.

She had not reached the sidewalk at the edge of the Place before she began to cry. She felt her way to a bench and sat down on it, burying her face in her hands, and sobbing as she had not – not since the night of her father's death had she wept like this, as though she were being torn to pieces.

She felt a hand on her shoulder, and remembering for the first time where she was, looked up prepared to check a manifestation of the experimental, easily repelled Parisian gallantry. But it was no seeker after adventures who stood looking down on her. A gaunt old man, shabbily dressed, a refugee. Perhaps a beggar? No. He said to her, 'Pardon . . . I see that Madame is in trouble. Madame is a refugee?'

'No,' said Matey, and then, '*Yes!*'

'Madame, in 1914 my wife died on a bench in the street. We lived in Valenciennes. Homeless, like a dog, she died. Since then – I have work now – I make it my business to . . . ' He took out of his pocket a purse and fumbled to open it.

'No, no, no, thank you,' said Matey, standing up, quiet now. 'No, you are very kind. But I – I don't deserve your help. I am not without shelter. I still have a home.'

PART FOUR

CHAPTER ONE

✻✻✻

This was all, she felt, that was left to her. She wrote to Adrian almost in the words of Ziza's little boy: 'Can't we go home?'

She knew before a single session of the Peace Conference had been held what the result would be. Around her the women in black still trustingly waited for President Wilson to perform a miracle. She could not go on living with them, knowing what lay in the future. She had seen it being constructed around Francis's dinner table. If she could only get home and be far away from them, as slowly, slowly these women with their vain hope came to learn what she knew now – that they had been fooled, that nothing at all would come from their sorrow except a firmer grip by the Francises of every nation on what they wanted!

'Can't we go home now, Adrian?' she wrote in every letter.

She was not the only refugee who now thought of nothing but going home. They all did. Matey knew no one, not one of all the human beings in her circle from high to low, who felt joy in the fact of 'victory'. Their wildness of rejoicing over the Armistice had been not of triumph but of frantic relief that the firing had stopped. The war had lasted too long. Like everything that lasts too long, it had worn out the attention of its audience. No one even talked about it any longer. They thrust it behind them and talked of nothing but how to go home.

For many of the refugees there was no home to go to. But their nostalgia did not depend on material facts. In every *oeuvre* where Matey served, ungrateful refugees were refusing dumbly, stubbornly, unintelligently offers of good pay and good work in strange localities, and were doggedly moving heaven and earth to return to what was often no more than a spot on the surface of the globe. Logical-minded heads of war relief organisations were out of patience with their unreason and as far as they could were refusing to humour it. Matey helped those she knew, using up most of what was left of Aunt Connie's money. Sometimes her refugees got off for home with no more belongings than they could load on a pushcart, prepared to walk all the way, leading children by the hand, carrying the baby, camping by the roadside. If there had been no other way for Matey to go home she too would gladly have gone that way. She felt herself one with these storm-driven exiles, beating their bedraggled wings against the kind, restraining hands of those who had fed them through the tempest. Their yearning was an echo of what she felt, even in the case of those who had lost all their families, whose longing to be at home was based on no hope of reunion with the other human beings who had made their home, but only of reunion with their own corner of the sky, their own particular clod of earth.

Her longing to be at home was like theirs, not personal, as the homesickness of the earlier years of the war had been, a desire to see after long absence her sister, her dearly-loved father-in-law, the comfortable, kind neighbours and comrades. As a matter of fact she scarcely thought of them when she thought of home. Her nostalgia was like that of a lost and bewildered dog or horse sick for a familiar smell or sound – like that of a refugee for the one spot where her pulse would again beat in unison with that of the earth and sky. It was for the feel under her hand of the familiar door-latches, for the irregularity under her feet of the well-known, broad, warped floorboards, for the faint smell of creosote in the attic which she had always struggled to prevent, for the broad gleam of the Hudson from the windows of the children's room, for the sound of the night boat's hoarse whistle, for the myriad-leaved vitality of the beech tree, different from any other beech tree; for the blades of grass growing in her own yard, different from any other grass.

It was not surprising that refugees going home when there was no home to go to found in Madame Fort an impassioned helper. They often said apologetically, 'I know it's foolish, I hear there isn't a roof left standing in our village. But – the hill is there, the hill where we – ' Or the river. Or the marsh. Yes, yes, yes, Madame Fort understood. That hill was her hill; that river, that marsh, she knew them. She went down again into the corners of Aunt Connie's purse to scrape up what was left. And she wrote again to her husband, 'Adrian, can't we go home now?'

Adrian wrote back sensible reassuring letters. Yes, they were going home – and together. His application for discharge in France, favourably endorsed by his Chief of Service, had been fed into the proper official cogwheels. An order might come any day. But Matey must remember that enlisting was like declaring war – an affair of an excited five minutes. Getting out of the army was slow and deliberate like making peace. And until he was a civilian again it would be folly to think of engaging a steamer passage. Matey must try to be patient.

She did try, patience being impossible, to keep occupied. As each task was finished she turned to a new one. She used up many hours helping an elderly cousin of Mme Vinet's, whose unit of the French Red Cross had been for some weeks stationed at the Gare du Nord, to take care of the French soldiers who had been prisoners in Germany during the war and were now filtering back into France. They came slowly and irregularly, because the Germans, at the limit of exhaustion and of supplies, had for the most part merely opened the gates of their prison camps and let the inmates make their way as best they could to the French frontiers. Thence they were being brought by French trains to Paris, where at the Gare du Nord doctors, nurses, and Red Cross workers met them with hot food, clothing, medical care, bandages, and helped them find their way either to their friends or to hospitals or sanatoria. 'We hear,' said Mme Vinet's old cousin, coming one afternoon, 'that a trainload of men on stretchers who had been in prison hospitals are coming in tonight, and I thought if any one of you here were free you might help us out. Your part would be nothing more than making and serving coffee and washing dishes.'

By this time the phrase 'men on stretchers', which four years ago would have been neutral to Matey, was steeped in lurid colours. 'We don't want to call in any of our younger helpers,' said the old cousin, 'only women we can depend on.'

Matey said, 'I'm the only one here who can get off tonight. Ziza's worried over a bronchial cold of little Adrien's, and Mme Vinet's bad knee is so lame she can scarcely stand on it a moment.' Little Adrien, though cheerful and playful as the other children, seemed to have no physical resistance in him. A cold which with Petella and Brother would have meant hot lemonade at bedtime and plenty of handkerchiefs for a few days, meant for the little boy from Louvain a high temperature, a beginning of lung congestion, and long days of slow convalescence. As for Mme Vinet's knee, it was a euphemism to call it lame. The war had grimly hastened the process of ageing. People went into it middle-aged and came out decrepit.

But Matey was perfectly strong. Except for one devastating struggle with nervous indigestion, when the fate of the children in the Convalescent Home at Hendaye had hung in the balance, she had never faltered physically since her landing in France. The body toughened and strengthened in play so long ago had served her steadily without complaint. So after Petella and Brother were in bed and had had their going-to-sleep chapter of *Sans Famille* read to them, Matey rolled up one of her well-worn, long-sleeved, long-skirted aprons, put on a warm wrap, for it was a cold January night, and set out. Once inside the smoky big station she soon located the Red Cross unit, behind a counter, and was at once installed in her place in front of an improvised sink, where she began to wash thick earthenware cups. She was thankful for the task. For, although the expected trainload of sick men was not yet in, the station was full of returned prisoners left from earlier convoys. On her way to the Red Cross counter Matey had seen nothing, it seemed to her, but gaunt, listless, unshaven men, dirty bird-claw hands, stooping skeleton frames draped around with rags too worn and drab to guess whether they had ever been uniforms. Her passage among them stirred up gusts of a stale, sour, mouldering odour compared to which the acrid smell of the hot dishwater was delicious. They came and went from the Red Cross counter to get coffee and bread. If she turned her head away from the steaming pan before her she could see nothing but grey faces and hollow eyes, passing like a procession of unburied corpses.

The wooden counter below them and the empty dusk of the high-ceilinged station above made them look like a frieze of misery painted palely on the night by sickness and war. Matey looked away from them, looked down at her dishwater. Had there not been, somewhere, in another life, another frieze, with trees above and blessed grass below, where little children played with dogs, and great hay wagons were drawn by strong, well-fed horses? It was like something she had read, no more.

'That must be the train coming in now,' said Mme Vinet's old cousin, tipping her head toward the train-shed. Yes, a train was arriving, not as trains usually do, with a triumphant whistle and a lusty sound of whirring wheels, but creeping in over the rails with a horrid caution. Matey welcomed a new tray of stained coffee cups to be washed, and plunged her hands deeper into the dishwater. She did not look up when heavy irregular steps began to go by, the steps which meant men carrying stretchers.

✲✲✲

'Oh, oh, *les pauvres, les pauvres!*' whispered her old companion, under her breath, starting and beginning to cry.

No, no, Matey would not look. She had had all she could stand. 'I want to go *home!*' she said childishly to herself, rinsing the cups with boiling water.

But it was never any use trying to go back and be childish when you were grown up. When the call came to serve the coffee, and someone held before Matey a tray of steaming cups, of course she took it and followed where she was led, out beyond the counter and the safety of the menial work behind it.

The stretchers had been set down in a grey windowless high-ceilinged stone room that had been used as a baggage storehouse. Over them hovered groups of army doctors, nurses in the French Red Cross uniform, and, of course, even here, officials occupied in the inevitable accompaniment of each step of the war, mean or tragic, the accumulating of reports.

'Here for coffee!' said a doctor, holding up his finger to Matey as though she were a waitress in a restaurant. The ragged, ashen man on that stretcher had no arms, so that the nurse, taking the cup from Matey's tray, held it to his lips as he drank from it, between answering questions. The doctor ran his hand and his eyes here and there under the dirty stained bandages and rags, wrote down medical details of his physical condition, and handed the slip to the *paperasserie* official, who asked the questions about his civic condition, name, residence in France, number of his regiment, where he was wounded. When those answers were noted the little group turned to the next stretcher. The doctor said to Matey, 'Just follow after us with that coffee, will you?'

The occupant of the next stretcher was catalogued while Matey stood by, holding her tray and trying not to look at the sick man's struggles to answer, with most of his jawbone gone. They moved to the next stretcher. And the one after that. The thin white voices of the crippled men could scarcely be heard over the careless footsteps of the travellers walking up and down the station platform outside. That prison odour of long-ago soured dirt and sweat and pus was stifling.

Most of the men answered the questions with a docile, unsurprised patience, but some of them as they tried to tell their names and their homes wept feebly. A few, crazed and brutalised by suffering, cursed the questioners and spattered the attending women with foul words. On three of the stretchers lay broken bodies, still alive, but with their humanity dead, the dirty, deeply lined, scrubby-bearded men's faces without even an animal expression, the eyes open on vacancy.

Holding her tray like a servant, Matey tried vainly to remember that there was anything else in human life. Had she not had a home once where on quiet winter evenings the sea-coal fire had dozed in the grate, where on August afternoons the locusts had sung the old trees to sleep? Had she not been one of a harmless friendly group of whole human beings who sat under brooding old trees, waiting for their turn at tennis, keeping an eye on safe and well-fed babies?

Moments came when she felt faint and wavered on her feet. Others when her resentment at what she saw was like fire burning her up. These men had been beaten and broken and made ignominious so that Mrs Whitlock's fortune might be trebled. And they were being welcomed back into human existence with a cup of coffee and questions, while almost within reach of their feeble voices, people sat before flower-decked tables, eating delicate food and talking of the thrill of going down into a trench before the dead were buried.

The doctor, unwrapping a filthy bandage to look at a wound, loosened a wave of gangrene-corrupted air. Mingled infernally with it for Matey was the remembered aroma of endlessly offered dishes of exquisite food, deferentially slipped over her left shoulder.

She propped her tray on her hip, holding it with one hand for a moment while she pressed the other hand on her mouth, feeling her body begin to quiver in the onset of nausea. Why, she would be incapable even of her poor share of this poor welcome if she could not for a moment bring *something* else to mind – where were her husband, her children, her home, that she could not pull them up between her and the hideousness of what men made of life?

When she could not by any effort of the will bring them before her she tried to make her mind empty and receptive, hoping they might come into it then. But what came into its emptiness was a little dog, trotting faithfully toward her across all those years. At the call of her need, little Sumner had jumped up from his grave and made his way to her through that foreign crowd in that dismal place. He stood by her now, wagging the stump of his tail a little, looking up at her deeply out of brown steady eyes.

'Coffee here,' said the doctor. She stepped forward with her tray, prompt, quiet, to a man who had but half his face.

His answers came in halting murmurs. 'Vincent Plantard.

From La Ferté. Wounded and taken prisoner in December, 1917. In the Holmholtzen prison ever since.'

'This ulcer on your leg since 1917?' asked the doctor.

'Yes, came when the leg was amputated.'

'Tuberculosis of the bone,' diagnosed the doctor to the nurse as they moved on. 'Better be sent to the sanatorium in the Landes.'

'Henri LeDéan. Louvain. Wounded in . . . '

From Louvain? Matey looked down at his face, sunken and feeble under its masculine masquerade of obstinately growing beard. His body seemed no more than a collection of bones, great, knobbed Flemish bones. She wondered if any chance had ever thrown him in the way of Ziza's husband. It was so long since they had questioned anyone from Louvain –

When the doctor's catechism was ended, 'Pardon, Monsieur le Docteur,' said the waitress with the tray. 'May I put one question?'

To the man on the stretcher she said, very gently, ashamed to ask him to think of anything but his own suffering, 'You didn't happen to serve in the same regiment with another man from Louvain, killed in 1914, in the defence of Liège . . . Adrien Conacq?'

'He wasn't killed,' said Henri LeDéan. 'He's here in this convoy somewhere.'

Matey paused an instant, irresolute and breathless, at the bottom of those long stairs up to the apartment. She was still in her apron, no hat, no wrap, just as she had run out of the Gare du Nord. She had thought of nothing but how to reach

Ziza most quickly. But now, her imagination already at the top of the stairs up which her feet were slowly plodding, now she could not think of any way to tell her. How could you tell news that was at once so awful and so blessed? How to let Ziza learn, as she had learned, in the same breath, that Adrien was not dead, and yet was only half-alive?

As she tapped on the door of the apartment she heard Ziza with her quick step come down the hall, advancing unconsciously toward the terrific news which lay on the tip of Matey's tongue. The sound sent every word out of Matey's mind. When Ziza opened the door she could only stand there on the landing, silently confronting her. 'Oh, it's you, Mété,' said Ziza in her ordinary voice. And then, after one look at Matey's face, 'Mété?' she said, on a higher note, hardly a word, like the sudden inner shock of an emotion.

With one of her fierce gestures she pulled Matey in under the light of the gas-jet in the hall and looked burningly into her eyes. *'What is it, Mété?'*

'Ziza . . . *chérie* . . . ' began Matey unsteadily. 'Among the *grands blessés* . . . ' She said no more. Ziza flung her arms up with a frantic gesture of abandon and screamed. A long, magnificent, primitive cry, beautiful and terrifying – a passionate heart finding its own language for the unutterable.

When Mme Vinet came hobbling out of her door she found Matey alone. Ziza had winged her way down the stairs on the last of that cry, still echoing grandly in the air. Matey, hatless, in her apron, leaned against the wall, her hands over her face.

‎✡✡✡

* * *

'But he is so frightfully crippled, such an utter wreck,' she
told Mme Vinet at the end of her story. 'I should have given
her some warning of that. It will be a terrible shock to her. His
arm and leg on the right side both gone, and he is paralysed
from the waist down. I should have told her first of all that –
but I never dreamed she would – she seemed to read it from
my very look. I hadn't time to think. When the man from
Louvain told me I couldn't believe it. I was sure there was a
mistake. And when I went to see I never would have guessed
that it was Ziza's husband. You know how bulky he was. He is
like a shadow of a man shrunk up to a skeleton.' She began to
laugh and sob hysterically. 'I remember – I remember I used
to wish he – weren't so opaque.'

'Didn't you tell him Ziza is alive?' asked Mme Vinet.

'I asked the doctor whether I should, and he said yes,
better let him have it by degrees like that. He had heard of
her death from a man taken prisoner later than he, who was
an eyewitness of the massacre . . . a man who had seen Ziza fall
with the others, and the children with her.'

Ziza's mother and Matey looked at each other with a sick
expression. Ziza had never told them any more about how she
had escaped. Perhaps that was where her baby died. Perhaps
little Adrien –

'He has been at death's door all the time. *Four years.* Three
amputations on the wounded leg – gangrene. *In a prison
hospital.* It's incredible that he is still alive. He is only alive in
name, so weak. . . . He couldn't turn his head on the pillow to

530

look at me. He couldn't put his one hand up to hide the tears that began to run out of his eyes when I spoke Ziza's name. And when I told him she is alive, here, close at hand . . . ' Matey put up her own hands to hide her tears.

'We must get Henri's room ready for him,' said Mme Vinet, wiping her eyes resolutely, and getting up, her lame knee wrenching a groan from her. Matey too felt the wartime guilt at allowing herself the luxury of emotion without work.

As she reached up to a shelf to take down clean sheets Mme Vinet said to Matey, 'Don't worry about not preparing Ziza for finding him crippled and half-dead with gangrene; maybe – probably she will not even notice it.'

CHAPTER TWO

✟✟✟

And now Ziza was the one who wanted to go home. At once! At once! She could not wait to have Adrien in his own bed, in his own house, which still, she had learned, stood upright, although stripped of every belonging. He would get better there, she knew. The air of Louvain was the right air for any Conacq. 'And of course little Adrien must grow up in Louvain, too,' she said heatedly to Matey, though nobody had dreamed of making any opposition to her plans. Matey noticed that at the very thought of opposition or even of delay Ziza's tongue once more ran a red tip hurriedly around over her lips, in her old gesture of exasperation.

The question of what they were to live on was a barrier to her plans which Ziza tore down with teeth and talons and cast away behind her. 'I have just got myself a position at the bank where Adrien worked,' she said, coming in one afternoon, looking heated and triumphant. 'I've been to the branch here; I had heard they were letting war widows take their husband's places. How much more somebody in my position?' Matey thought looking at her, that it was not surprising she had secured work – or anything else she had asked for.

That afternoon when the children came home from school and heard the news, 'Oh, we are going *home!*' cried little Adrien. He got down on his knees and clasped his arms around his dog's neck, murmuring something in his ear. 'Can you remember home, Brother?' asked Petella. 'When you come in the front door, which way is the dining room? Which one of the trees is your tree?'

Brother said dreamily, 'We kept the kiddie-car in the closet under the stairs.'

But Ziza's position at the bank was a tiny one, it turned out in later talk, ill-paid, with long hours. 'Never mind!' said Ziza. 'We can manage. Adrien will have some pension, I suppose. Not enough, but something. And Maman – oh, Mété, have I told you that Maman is coming with us? She can give music lessons as well in Louvain as here. She can't go on living here alone. And you can't imagine she'd be happy with Mimi now. By putting our earnings together we'll have enough. And Maman's work being always at home, you see, she can keep an eye on things while I am at the bank.'

Matey did see. So Mme Vinet was going to give up her own home to help Ziza keep hers. Matey had not thought of that solution. 'The things in the apartment here will just furnish our house, too,' said Ziza. 'What else could Maman do with them?'

That evening when Ziza was in her husband's sick room and the children were in bed and Dominiqua laboriously writing a letter to Jean on the kitchen table, Matey spoke about this to Mme Vinet. 'Won't it be hard for you to leave – to leave all that you *will* leave behind you?' She thought of her own sick longing to be home. She thought of what this older home meant, the lifetime accumulation of memories, all the old friends, the old habits, the old occupations, all that had been part of the past.

Mme Vinet began matter-of-factly, 'Oh, Ziza needs me far more than I need – ' But to her surprise she could not go on, and showed to Matey a face piteously stripped of its usual quiet. Her lips moved in a soundless apology for her weakness. But Matey understood. It did not seem strange to her that the older woman could stand up to the loss of a son, to the loss of another, could be wise with selfless wisdom, and still be moved at the prospect of being homeless. Here was one refugee who was never going home. She put her arms silently around her old friend. Mme Vinet leaned her head against Matey's shoulder and drew a few long breaths. Then she murmured, 'The good you do is like music, Mété; no words, just your being there.' And, lifting her head, 'Mété, you asked me once from where I draw my strength? Where does yours come from?'

'Have I any?' asked Matey in surprise.

An irrepressible laugh broke from Mme Vinet's lips. She kissed Matey's cheeks and said as if this were an answer, 'No one – no one in all the world has such honest eyes as my Mété.'

Ziza came walking in noiselessly, her eyes shining. 'He held his cup for a moment – himself! Without help!'

They were all packing to go home. All but Mme Vinet. Mimi came up to Paris to talk over plans, this time with her husband, for the older men in the 'territorial service' were already demobilised.

All of them looked older, of course, Matey thought, gazing at the bald, white-bearded old man beside Mimi, but really M Bouvard the most of all. 'Old and tired and absolutely through,' she described him in her letter to Adrian that night. No talk from him, as constantly from Mimi, about getting the factory ready to meet the demand for plumbing fixtures sure to come with the rebuilding of ruined cities; no questions about tariffs and raw materials. No. 'Emilie has done very well at that, let her go on with it,' he said with the cynical placidity of complete indifference. 'We'd quarrel if I tried to go back. And in any case all I want to do is to make things with my jigsaw in winter and go fishing in summer. I never yet had time enough for those two occupations.'

Of the transformation in Mimi's spiritual life, cataclysmic to her family, he remarked in exactly the same tone, to her mother, 'Hasn't Emilie got awfully pious all of a sudden? Have you noticed it? I never thought before she had any tendencies toward devoutness.' He dismissed the matter with a shrug and another sip of his liqueur. 'Oh, well, it takes some women that way.' Matey did not know whether he meant that what 'took some women' was the war or life. He went on to Mme Vinet with a comfortable smile. 'As long as she doesn't try to make *me* go to Mass! I did enough of that when I was a boy.'

Here was someone who accepted Mimi's conversion as Matey had wished Mme Vinet would, easily, tolerantly. But when she saw this attitude embodied in the flesh she detested it. She realised now that she had never understood anything of all this story of Mimi and her mother's reaction to her Catholicism. It had found nothing in her own life or experience with which to combine to create understanding. It was not true that all experience made you wiser. Here was the raw material of life which she had not been able to fashion into shape.

After the Bouvards had gone Ziza said, 'I told you, Mété, René wouldn't have a chair in the office.'

'He doesn't want one,' said Mme Vinet, defending her older daughter.

Ziza said with a short laugh, 'It's as well for him he doesn't,' and went off to her husband's sickbed.

He was imperceptibly better, though still too weak to see anyone but Ziza and the doctor. But day by day Ziza, coming out of the sick room even more glowingly vital than when she went in, reported those minute grounds for hope which mean so much to impassioned nurses. She was tireless, patient, indomitable, fulfilled. When the doctor told her, 'He will never be out of a wheeled chair,' she cried, '*Oh*, will he be well enough to be in a wheeled chair?' She saw herself dressing him, pushing his chair out under the open sky, under their own trees; she saw herself running to and fro all the rest of her life in the endless care of a cripple. She startled the doctor by kissing him violently on both cheeks.

Mme Vinet, rather shut out from both daughters just now, was very close to Matey in those hurried uncomfortable days of packing and planning which were for her the last days of home. Dominiqua stayed on in Paris with the family to the end, though she was as desperately homesick for her own country as any of them. One evening the three of them were in the kitchen, wrapping china and glass in newspaper and putting it into barrels. Dominiqua said, out of a silence, 'The *genêt* will be in bloom at Biriatou in a few weeks.' She tucked in the ends of paper about the dish she held and added, 'I don't suppose you remember, M'ame Mété – you were such a little thing – how the *genêt* looks when it is all yellow with blossoms.'

But, yes, M'ame Mété remembered very well how the *genêt* looked, dark and rough and prickly when you were down in it, with only a few blossoms here and there, and all one smooth golden carpet when you looked at it from afar.

The Basque and the American both looked at it in imagination silently as they worked, stooping their backs over the barrel.

Presently they ran out of newspaper – there was a scarcity of paper as of everything else in France. Dominiqua said she would run down and ask the *concierge* if she had any. Matey settled herself on a packing box and put her hand over her mouth to stifle a tired yawn. She was working three nights a week in the Gare du Nord Red Cross canteen and never had enough sleep. Mme Vinet, noticing a leaking tap letting fall a slow drip-drip of water in the sink, tried to turn it off. But French taps of that period, like other things, were worn out by long service without repairs, and all she could accomplish was to make a slightly longer interval between the falling drops. Turning her back on it, she leaned against the sink, looked thoughtfully at Matey, and said, evidently going on with what had been in her mind while the talk ran on blossoming broom, 'Do you know, perhaps Ziza will be happier with her husband – this way.'

Matey looked at her quickly to see whether there was in her face the note of blame or irony which was conspicuously absent from her voice. Matey too had thought of this, had remembered a certain hillside, where, near a hawthorn bush full of swollen buds and chittering small birds, Ziza had said, 'He never would change. And I couldn't.' The thought had seemed to her a savage criticism of Ziza.

But there was neither irony nor blame on Mme Vinet's thoughtful face, withered and elderly now. There was nothing but the clarity of her realistic sight of things as they are. In its very different and Gallic setting this sometimes reminded Matey of her father-in-law's honesty, which she had often found unsparing and bald.

Over Mme Vinet's shoulder gazed the long, watchful face of President Wilson from a lithograph which Dominiqua had pinned up beside Our Lady of Lourdes. Sitting there on the edge of a packing box in the small stuffy old European kitchen, with its old European smell of drains and garlic and dishwater, looking up at Mme Vinet and the lithographed face behind her, Matey thought once more with a pang how strange it was that Mme Vinet, so invincibly realistic about everything else, who never for a moment had lost her lifetime Liberalism in any nationalistic hysteria, should harbour the naïveté of this wild faith in the American President. And not only Mme Vinet, who had, after all, always shared her husband's political creed – the multitude of home-keeping women who never before had perceived the deadly closeness of the link which binds them and their personal affections to the impersonal problems of the rulers of governments.

'What do you hear from your brother, Mété?' asked Mme Vinet casually. She always asked after Francis with French punctiliousness about blood kindred.

Francis, with a group of other prominent men attached to the American Peace Conference Commission, was as guest of the French Government making a tour of the front, which had been prolonged into Italy. His letters, intended for the Pittsburgh papers after they had gone the rounds of the family, were full of appreciation of the attentions paid to the visiting Americans by their French and Italian hosts and of indignation over the activities of certain defeatists who wanted food sent into Germany for the women and children. 'Let such snivellers see what I have seen,' wrote Francis, 'and they'd say as I do, "Let Germany rot!" How much did the Boche think of French and Belgian women and children? It is their turn now. The fewer of that brood the better.'

'Francis is having a very interesting experience,' Matey answered Mme Vinet, and asked, thinking of the phrase 'The fewer of that brood the better,' 'Will Ziza and her husband keep the little Mélanie now?'

'What else would they do?' asked Mme Vinet in surprise, and then, 'Oh, you mean that the child's mother's family would want her? But they were Chauny people. Not a trace of them left after 1917. And Ziza never knew anything more about the child's father than his name. Friedrich Müller. Like Jean Duval in France. It would be impossible to trace his people.'

'I see,' said Matey.

'Mélanie takes the place of the poor little baby boy who – who died,' said Mme Vinet. 'Ziza can never have another child of her own. Little Mélanie really seems like her own now.'

'I see,' said Matey again. She had no intention of saying anything more. But without her will her secret foreboding spurted out in rough words that sounded like blame. She said brusquely, 'Mme Vinet, it's not *fair,* truly it's not, to expect so much of President Wilson. It doesn't seem like you. What could he do if he were a demigod, and he's not in the least! I used to hear faculty talk about him years ago when he was a college president . . . he's *full* of flaws. I can't endure it to have you expecting . . . '

For an instant Mme Vinet was startled. Then she broke in, 'I know what you mean, Mété. I've seen too that the older diplomats hate him. Already the tone of our newspapers is changing, is hostile, belittling to him. But you Americans are invincibly strong now. When you speak as a united nation, the world must listen.'

'Perhaps we won't speak as a united nation,' Matey suggested faintly, hanging her head.

Mme Vinet said sharply, 'Ah!' on an indrawn breath and was silent. Matey sat looking down at her shoes and listening to the water dripping slowly into the sink. But when at last Mme Vinet spoke her voice was not even sad. 'Ah, well, Mété dear – even so . . . even so . . . You're young and an American. You forget that time, much time, is as necessary as air for any growth. I'm an old woman from a patient old race that has lived too long to expect very much – to expect *anything* good to happen quickly.'

She was silent. The drip-drip-drip made audible the passage

of the minutes. Then she said, nodding her head, 'Yes, yes, I see. It is natural that the materialists should be in power in America too. They generally are in power everywhere. And they always hate anybody who pretends that people could be better off than they are. Your President may go down to complete failure at the Peace Conference. All those in power want him to fail and will find a way to make him fail. But what of it? Did you ever hear of a man with a noble idea who succeeded in his own lifetime?'

'But . . . ' said Matey, 'but . . . ' She felt quite bewildered. Her mind went back to the wild scenes of Wilson's arrival, Mme Vinet weeping and cheering and waving her handkerchief. Mme Vinet too, evidently remembered, for her face took on again the expression of exaltation which so distressed Matey. She said earnestly, 'What he is doing – this faulty human being – is sowing a seed that no European in power would dream of sowing. Or is it America through him that is sowing it? Perhaps he himself hardly knows what he is doing. Perhaps all our misery and shame finds him the only outlet through which it can drive a way out to the light. Don't be discouraged. It was childish to dream of success at once. He has only stated the theme. To develop it will take your grandchildren and mine – '

But Matey was no longer listening. She was repeating to herself with a long breath of liberation, 'It is not a blow he is striking. It is a seed he is planting. A seed is something that has life in it.'

CHAPTER THREE

✿✿✿

They were embarked. Incredibly, they seemed to be going home. All about them people lay in steamer chairs on the second-class deck or walked up and down, played shuffle-board, or flirted. Petella and Brother ran around investigating shipboard possibilities for fun and practising their English. Brother's lingo was an uproarious success. He still could understand not a word of English when spoken to him, but he was beginning to mix odds and ends of it with his French. 'Zis *matin* I 'av too many water *dans mon bassin,* and she run down *sur le parquet,*' he explained, waving his hands to dramatise the contents of washbasin slopping over.

Knowing that Petella would always take care of Brother wherever they were, Matey lay on her steamer chair beside Adrian's in an abandon of bodily fatigue. Her mental fatigue had not yet reached the point of abandon. As soon as she shut her eyes and tried to relax, images and memories and cares swarmed about her. At first she lived over again inconsecutively those last hurried days in Paris. They had been, as a matter of actual fact, the first ones after Adrian's discharge from the army and so should have been momentous. But they had been crammed with the incredibly trivial, incredibly important details of helping the Vinets get off, and then of settling the equally complicated mechanism of their own departure. They had felt the emotional colour of those last days in France as little as a man running to catch a train notices a sunset flaming about him.

For days Matey's brain refused to take in the fact that they were on the ship going home. Sometimes her body gave a great twitching surge. Oh, some lunch must be put up for Dominiqua to eat on the train! Or, there! she had not given Mme Vinet the key to that square trunk! The lunch eaten days before on the train to Biriatou, the key of the trunk now unlocked and unpacked in Louvain. In his deckchair beside her, Adrian did not stir. Limp and still he lay in his faded trench coat. His cap pulled low over his eyes, his collar turned up high, he smoked or dozed for hours, nothing showing of himself but a non-committal sandy moustache, which had now some white hairs in it. When she asked him a question he answered it and at once dropped back to complete silent immobility – the very picture of a tired man resting.

Packed together with the children in a tiny inside four-berth cabin, with no place more private for talk than the crowded salons or decks, they had as yet, Matey thought, not really begun again their life in common. She felt no disappointment that there was so little drama about their being together again. For one thing she was too tired. For another she and Adrian seemed to be now indissolubly two halves of one whole. It was only natural – not dramatic – their being together. As soon as they emerged from this paralysis of fatigue they would once more merge their inner lives – she took this for granted.

As the grey days of a sunless passage slid hour after hour between Matey and those trivial immediate cares, other cares and memories, not so recent, not so trivial, began to toss to and fro in her head. She tried hard to stay there in her steamer chair, her eyes on the grey sky over the grey sea, but all at once she would not be at this dubious end of the war, but still in the midst of it, coming down the walk from Mimi's house, a frightened little boy clutching at each of her hands, hearing behind her Mimi's high-pitched vehement voice. Now President Wilson's leathery cheeks, creased in a pleased smile, hung before her, replaced by Ziza's face as she asked, deathly pale, 'What is it, Mété?' Now for the last time Mme Vinet walked down those familiar stairs, talking cheerfully to little Mélanie . . . while all the time Matey was aware as it were of an eagle's wing beating there beside her. She dreaded most what came most often, the night at the Gare du Nord.

People about them started the customary steamer small talk, compared notes on impressions of France, asked the children's ages. Matey brought out the right answers and sometimes held conversations of considerable length with these casual companions, whom she liked for their simplicity and lack of pretence and for the devotion with which they had been doing anonymous hard work. But afterward she could scarcely remember what had been said. One conversation, however, she did not forget. A small wren-like, honest-faced woman, a stenographer by profession, who had been private secretary to a high official of the American Red Cross, stopped one day to lean on the rail nearby. Matey heard her saying to the woman with her, 'Well, I was sorry for him lots of times. It didn't seem to make any difference *what* they did, nobody was satisfied. Knock! knock! knock! That's all the American Red Cross ever got from anybody. Nobody made any allowances. Everybody seemed to think the people running the show made mistakes on purpose. Nobody ever stopped to think what *they* were up against. They got the boss's nerve just *busted*. He'd hate to make a decision one way or the other about anything, because he knew the Red Cross would get it in the neck no matter what! I've seen him, many's the time . . . ' The couple moved off, and Matey heard no more.

After they were gone she turned to Adrian. 'That makes me ashamed of the way I felt over the Hendaye home. I suppose it was the same in all the war relief organisations. I never thought of their side.'

Adrian looked at her absently. 'Oh, well,' he said, 'we've all got so much to be ashamed of it's no use trying to balance the books. Better call the whole thing profit and loss and forget about it.'

Matey was nettled. He evidently hadn't the faintest idea how much that miserable incident had meant to her. Should she try to explain . . . but just then Petella bounded up, exclaiming, '*Mother!* I was coming up to tell you it's time for *déjeuner* and I almost *dégringoléd* off the *escalier.*' They went to lunch, and the moment for finding out what had been in Adrian's mind passed.

He was not his usual self. She was sure of that. But neither was she. Not only did she waken every morning, sunk a little more deeply in all-enveloping depression; not a single night could she get herself safely into sleep without jerking up at least once out of her first doze, heart pounding, nerves twitching, feet and hands icy cold with consternation over some past catastrophe or over one merely dreaded, that had never happened at all. Some nights, as with a great bound she sat up suddenly in the dark, it was to look again into Ziza's face as her lips formed the word, 'Gas?' Sometimes the cabin reeked with the smell of gangrenous flesh, and she was again standing beside the stretcher of a man who wept over the effort of trying to remember who he had been. Was she awake or was it in sleep that she struggled to turn her eyes away from a long fascinated stare at the rotting Germans in the ruined house? There they stood in the dark, saying to her something they had called out silently when she had first looked into their dead eyes. It was something Adrian had told her on his first furlough home, when he had said he would not have his wife forget that war meant killing as well as being killed. But she had not listened. She had kept herself too busy to hear. Their voices had been like puffs of white from a distant cannon. The sound had had long to travel before, in mid-ocean silence, it roared sullenly in her ears, telling her from those long dead men, 'We were killed by those tired, kind, homeless men to whom you devoted yourself. You helped our murderers take our lives.'

Unprotected now by the clatter of material business, Matey began after four years of living in the midst of it – to look at war. She had drugged herself to unconsciousness of what they were all doing by the traditional woman's narcotic of small personal

✝✝✝

services. She had assumed to the fighting men she knew the domestic relation of sister and mother and so had seen them, as sisters always see their brothers and mothers their sons, as victims, never as the butchers they punctually took their turn at being. On some nights as she lay in these waking trances, she could feel the fumes of her narcotic clearing away from her brain and suffered the frightening pain which comes to drug addicts with the return to reality.

Daylight always brought relief. Morning after morning, as she looked haggardly over the edge of her berth at the children's rosy faces, she thought, 'What nightmares I am having on this trip!'

One of the most troubling of those nightmares – if they were nightmares – was the fear that she had lost their food cards. Like all women with dependents she had been overwhelmed with the responsibility for those priceless, irreplaceable bits of perforated cardboard, far more important than mere money, only to be secured once, and then by slow freezing in a waiting line. Without them neither bread not sugar nor flour nor – above all – any kind of fuel could be obtained. They never left her. Twenty times a day she felt in her bag for them, and at night she put the large envelope containing them under her pillow. Every time she waked she slipped a hand under her head to make sure it was there. Making this instinctive gesture on shipboard in her berth and finding nothing always flung her into a panic before she could get her wits together.

Once this nightmare was so vivid that Matey, still half-asleep, got out of her berth and began to feel about in the darkness. Groping hurriedly everywhere, she reached up into

Adrian's berth to make sure she had not laid the big envelope there. The tips of her fingers trailed across his bare arm lying on the blanket.

'Yes?' he said in the collected tone of one who has been long awake. 'What's the matter?'

The quality of his voice awoke her with a shock. 'Nothing,' she murmured. 'I must have been having a bad dream – I thought I'd lost the food cards . . . .'

He pulled her near so that her ear was close to his lips. 'Put that all behind you, Matey,' he whispered. 'Forget it. That's the only way to stay sane. Forget it!'

He dropped her hand. There was no sound but the throb-throb-throb of the engine's pulse and an occasional creak of boards as the ship lifted and sank to the waves.

His voice had been no more than awake and intent. But the echo it left in this silence was of mortal sadness.

She got back into her berth, narrow as a coffin. The words were nothing. The Adrian she thought she knew might have said them – but not with that undertone of desperation. Somewhere – years ago – whose was that other hopeless voice which now again after years of silence echoed back his counsel of despair? 'Keep busy! That's the only thing to do – keep busy!'

It was not of food cards that Matey was thinking as she lay awake in the dark, feeling the throb of the ship's engines thrusting her forward to an unknown destination.

The children evidently noticed nothing unusual about their father. But they had seen very little of him in the last four years – a few short furloughs – and here on shipboard he still provided all they had learned to ask of him – knees to climb on, stories at bedtime, an umpire in disputes, an answer to questions. And there were plenty of times when Matey told herself that there *was* nothing unusual about him. Outwardly he was normal enough. He gave coherent to-be-expected replies to everything she said, his nightly kiss before they lay down in their narrow beds was tender enough. It must be that he was only tired and war-worn as she was – but it would not do. Even as her mind framed these comforting explanations, all her heart was trembling in the fear that the old Adrian-like sharing openness was gone. Wasn't it only on the surface he was meeting her? Wasn't he, in everything that mattered, holding aloof? And now she began to be afraid not of the past but of the future. For the first time . . . why, since the sunset hour on the cliffs overlooking the Hudson, when Adrian had looked at her with love . . . she guessed what it would mean to face the world alone. She perceived as never before the condition on which she had accepted life. 'Not without Adrian!' she cried defiantly.

The last day of the passage had been a slow fumble through a fog which had grown steadily thicker and whiter. Arriving in the lower bay they were brought to a standstill by it, and all hope of landing that night was given up.

The power of the great engines, the trained intelligence of the officers, availed nothing against the bland impalpable wall of mist. It nullified power and intelligence not by more power and more intelligence, not by violence or opposition, but passively, by making it impossible to know which way to go. The baffled ship, which had fought its way through storms and found a path across the featureless mystery of mid-ocean, admitted defeat, dropped anchor within hearing of its goal, and waited for the only thing that was left to hope for, the dawning of another day.

Late that evening Matey and her husband leaned over the rail. 'Not without Adrian!' she said to the future, and began to speak. But though she used the plainest and quickest words she had not quite strength enough to finish. 'Adrian dear, I wish you'd let me – not keep so to yourself what is – ' She could find no more words. She threw all her frightened loneliness into one beseeching look.

His eyes met hers, then turned to stare again at the treacherous, yielding, impenetrable fog. But it was enough for the familiar miracle, the old transparent revelation of a personality in one look. Matey knew that after all these years she had once more forgotten what Adrian was. She had seen in that one dip into the honesty of his eyes that he had never dreamed he was not sharing with her all along. What he said next was palpably addressed to one who needed no explanation, only a reminder of something held in common. 'Oh, the same old thing, Matey. I'd have talked about it fast enough if I thought I'd get anywhere. That's the trouble, I don't get anywhere – except round and round. Probably there isn't any answer. At least none we're willing to accept. I keep wondering if we're ever going to find any basis for going ahead. What have we got left to base anything on? I don't know. Do you?'

'I don't even understand exactly what you're talking about,' said Matey, 'except that it's about the war. I can't keep my thoughts away from that, either. But, Adrian dear – what you told me the other night – that it's all over now. Why not forget it till we have a little rest? We're both so tired now.'

'I'm not tired, physically. You women worked harder and harder right up to the last minute. But the Armistice stopped men's work. Beyond signing a few routine papers and hauling a few sick and peasants and keeping my boys out of trouble with the MP's I haven't had a thing to do for months but think. First chance for that I've had since – ' He paused, leaning heavily on the railing, facing the fog.

As if realising that his thoughts had sunk below audibility, he shook his shoulders a little and went on, 'Well, when you come down to thinking, is there anything left to think about except that not one of our standards of decency could hold out a minute after the tom-toms got to beating? I might stand our shucking off our civilisation and grabbing our stone axes – everybody gets forced into doing things he hates. What gets me is that we all liked it.'

'No, Adrian, *no!*' Matey broke in. 'It's bad enough without making it worse than it was. Not a man of all those I saw from the French army but loathed war. You ought to have heard them talk!'

He broke in impatiently, 'Oh I heard them talk, all right. I talked, too. We all said we hated it. So we did, with our brains. But how much did our brains amount to in the sum total of what we all turned out to be? You say those men loathed war – don't you remember the expression of their eyes when they bragged about their regiments? They were proud of what the war gave them. That Basque fellow, Dominiqua's son, he's a born soldier. Didn't you hear his voice the day he told us about their getting the *fourragère* after they'd stopped the drive on Compiègne? No, they all of them enjoyed it – for different reasons. It appeals to a lot of things – not only the wild beast in us, but the sporting instinct – it was a real betting interest we took, to see how far an offensive would get before it was stopped. And the natural-born serfs, couldn't you *feel* how relieved they were to give up trying to run their own lives and have an officer tell them what to do? When I say "they" I don't mean I was different. Not since I was a kid have I enjoyed baseball so much as some games I played in just behind the lines. And what was I thinking about here just before you began to talk? You probably thought I was lost in remorse about the war. Well, I was remembering how happy and proud I felt one night – it must have been December or late November, for it was freezing – when the wounded began to be brought in and told us that the French held Douaumont again. All of a glow I was, the "pleasure of recollection" collecting, like amber round a bug, around the satisfaction I'd felt that night in thinking that maybe enough Germans had been killed to stop them for a while.'

Matey had been stricken into silence long ago. She listened painfully, trying to get her bearings. Adrian seemed to turn a number of memories over in his mind before he went on. 'I'm not blaming anybody, Matey, not anybody at all, because everybody was the same way. If that's the way we are – that's the way we are. But I don't see any stuff in us that can ever build up a civilisation. We might as well give up if we can't do better than that, mightn't we? Why, we couldn't think at all when our blood was up – all that talk about Huns, and our gallant airmen dropping tons of bombs on the non-combatants of Cologne – you know what we thought about *their* air raids. And now all this sanctimonious bother about pinning the war guilt on Germany. I understand that Germans deny it. They're right, too. Nobody wanted the war – not the sort of war they got. I thought for a while after I got to the front that we are all devils. And then I saw we are only fools. One thing is sure – we are all responsible, even compromisers like me who wouldn't fire a gun but went around helping patch up the wounded so that they could go back and kill some more.'

Matey did not need now to ask what he meant. This was the nightmare stuff which had filled her nights on the ship, which she had dismissed in the morning as dreams. But this was no dream from which she could escape by waking up. Adrian was awake, and so was she. The dead men in the ruined house looked at her from the fog, moving their blackened lips to say, 'You too helped to kill us.' She tried to answer, 'But you in your turn – ' and shrank back from the endless vista of murder unrolling from this phrase. She said in a shaking voice, 'I see; yes, Adrian, I understand. I – but we can't *stand* it to go on thinking that. There's nothing we can do now to change what's past – '

'There never was anything we could do. Sometimes, though, I wish I hadn't contented myself with creeping around, making myself feel better by picking up the pieces, without resisting, without crying out on the idiocy that did the breaking . . . '

He spoke in a low tone, but his phrase needed no hurling. It crashed like a stone through four years of Matey's life and his.

✲✲✲

Matey stared out into the fog hemming them in mildly, implacably. She tried to think and could not. Not far from them a bell clinked faintly, striking on an invisible ship brought to a standstill as they were. Behind them their own ship's bell told the hour in answer.

'What else could we have done, Adrian?' she asked him finally.

He shrugged his shoulders and shook his head, his eyes on the enigmatic airy barrier of the fog.

'Do you mean – do you mean going to prison and all that? Adrian, you don't think you would have been more useful in prison than – '

It was evidently no new idea to Adrian. He answered at once with his invincible Fort honesty. 'No, I might have had a higher opinion of myself now. But that's all.' After a pause he added, as if he had been once more considering the possibility, 'I'm glad somebody did. It had to be done. But I couldn't. I never thought of it at first – an American in Europe hadn't any responsibility, I supposed. Then, when our own country was part of it and our army took over the ambulance service, I had the choice either to enlist or go home. At my age the draft wouldn't have touched me. I could have begged the question. But that's not the whole truth. I didn't want to go home.' He laughed harshly. 'I knew it was the biggest show I'd ever see, and I wasn't willing to miss the last round. That's the way I "hated war". Later on I suppose a real pacifist might have refused to obey orders. But my orders were to pick up broken and bleeding men. I couldn't buy my self-respect at that price. My self-respect wasn't worth that much!'

Matey did not say aloud the sorrowful 'Well, then – ' which was in her mind at this admission. But Adrian heard it and answered, 'I know, I know!' impatiently aware of his inconsistency. He added, 'I *said* there was no use talking about it!'

They bent their heads to look down at the water lapping against the immovable sides of the anchored ship. It was no longer deep-sea water but humanised by its nearness to man. The ship lights showed bits of garbage floating in it, rotting orange skins and half-decomposed shreds of cabbage.

Presently Adrian said, more quietly, 'Don't take all this too seriously, Matey. I'll manage all right. I've got a living to earn and an honest way to earn it, and that's something to be everlastingly thankful for. I'm going to forget the last four years because I don't know what else to do about them. And I'm going to be cheerful. You'll see. It won't be hard, either. You and the children make my own corner of life plenty enough to live for – all anybody could dream of wanting – personally. I've still got my code. Apparently it isn't based on anything solid as I used to think, but it's part of me now and it'll last out my lifetime. I'm going right ahead with what I've been doing – trying in my small futile way to pick up a few pieces in this mess of a world. That'll keep me busy.'

His last word struck another echo from Priscilla's old counsel that sounded like a warning in Matey's ear.

The bell on the invisible ship clanked out another half hour and was answered by their own.

Adrian roused himself then and stood straighter, turning away from the rail. Behind him the fog watched them both impassively out of its blind white eyes. 'I don't think much of people who complain of what's the common lot,' he told his wife, 'but to live without any belief in a plan – or in some fixed values – '

Matey turned with him, and they began to walk toward their stateroom. She was too much shaken to speak. And yet her silence seemed hard and uncomprehending. . . . She broke it finally with some faltering Priscilla phrases, intended to do no more than to show her love and helpless sharing sympathy. 'Don't you think, dear, perhaps things will look brighter once we get back to our own life – once we get home?' she asked timidly.

Adrian pressed her hand gently. 'Yes, darling, perhaps they will.' He spoke in a loving comforting tone, answering the intention in her voice and not the shallow childish words, and Matey knew he did not believe a word he said. In his eyes, where she had always before read unshakable affection and faith, there was now nothing but defeat.

CHAPTER FOUR

✵✵✵

'What do the *musique* play for, so early in the morning?' asked Petella, as she looked down at the dock sliding slowly beside the ship. The blaring trombone notes soared from one of the openings in the wharf wall.

'It's to welcome us back from the war,' said a fellow passenger. Seeing the little girl's literal acceptance of this, he added, 'No, it's probably because there are some officers in the first class and a bunch of privates in steerage.'

'What tune are they playing?' asked Petella, accustomed only to French military music.

'I suppose "See the Conquering Hero Comes,"' suggested the facetious passenger.

'*Qu-o-oi? Qu'est-ce qu'il dit,* Petella?' Brother nervously demanded a translation in a phrase which was soon to become almost his sole speech.

'*Voici le héro conquérant,*' translated Petella.

'But where? Where?' asked Brother, turning his eyes here and there about the deck.

'Where indeed?' said Adrian. He walked to the other side of the deck and looked out through the remnants of yesterday's fog at the Hudson, city-soiled and dingy. He found his wife leaning over the rail there.

'Well, Matey?' he said.

'Well, Adrian.' She found nothing else to answer. Their hands, touching, interwined in a clasp.

A gust of wind stirred the thinning fog and poured around them the brazen breathing of the band.

'Gay, isn't it?' asked Adrian.

She asked, 'Do you remember Aunt Tryntje's Civil War story of how the Rustdorf men came home?'

Yes, Adrian remembered.

'I asked her,' said Matey, her voice trembling, 'what made them cry.'

A raucous yell rang out. *'American citizens this way!'* One more examination of papers.

'That's us,' admitted Adrian, going off to collect the children.

The vast reaches of the pier were greyly dusky in the early dawn, and empty save for a few men in uniform. War regulations still held. The general public was not allowed to pass a high barrier at the far end. In spite of the early hour a good many people were massed behind its closely-set pickets.

Although they had little idea that, after the failure of the ship to land last night, any one of the Rustdorf family would be there to meet them, Matey and Adrian and the children walked toward this barrier, trying to distinguish faces in the dimly seen crowd.

A voice called, 'Adrian!'

Adrian dropped Petella's hand and pressed his face against the pickets. Matey heard him say, 'Father?'

A hand came through the pickets, a sinewy elderly hand. Adrian clasped it in both his. 'Why, *Father!*' he said in a deep broken voice. It was as if he had forgotten he had a father. He clung to the hand as if he had been a little boy lost.

'Adrian's father can understand!' thought Matey. 'And we, who never before understood him – oh, *he* is the one who perhaps can help Adrian!'

She saw him now. At the first sight of his white hair and sunken eyes she thought with a shock, 'How old he has grown! He is a feeble old man.' But when he turned his eyes on her, when he tried to smile and to shape 'dear daughter' with his trembling lips, she too forgot everything save the miracle of having a father.

Brother, outraged at being forgotten, pulled at her skirts and clamoured, *'Je veux voir mon grandpapa!'*

Petella put both arms through the paling, shouting, 'Padre! Padre! Do you remember me?'

Matey stooped and picked up the little boy, presenting him to his grandfather. 'He doesn't speak a word of English.' Half laughing, half apologetic, she said the first trivial words that came into her mind.

'Mais si! Mais si! Je sais parler anglais,' Brother told his shadowy grandfather behind the bars. 'One! two! free! *four!'* he proclaimed triumphantly.

The customs took even more than its usual interminable time, the Forts' trunk being one of the last unloaded from the hold. There were endless war formalities about papers. The children were allowed to go out through the gate in the barrier to their grandfather, while Adrian and Matey for the last time grimly went through the ordeal of standing in a slow line inching its way toward a desk, only to be told when they reached it that they should have been in some other line.

It was three o'clock before they were free, and they were extravagantly weary when they went to look up the others. Brother was taking a nap, his head on Padre's folded-up overcoat, while Petella and her grandfather had a talk. The little girl and the old man were sitting hand in hand, the child talking earnestly, her head tipped back to look up into the old face gazing down tenderly at her. Matey knew that the sight was touching, but she felt only a nervous irritability over being so delayed.

Adrian's father saw them approaching and smiled to them. 'Petella's been telling me about Toutou's tricks,' he said, getting up. 'A very remarkable dog, I take it.' They might never have gone away, for anything in his manner now.

This time Matey found no fault with the transparent truthfulness with which his manner always reflected the reality of things. The sober everyday quality of his greeting was the right one. The friction of petty difficulties of landing had worn away their emotion. 'Wake up, *petit frère,*' she murmured to the little boy.

He bounded up. 'Are we home?' he cried eagerly. The un-home-like height and official varnished woodwork of the waiting room struck his eye. 'Oh, *pas encore!*' he said, drooping in disappointment against his mother's shoulder.

‘Priscilla and her eldest girl were down all yesterday afternoon, waiting for your ship,’ Adrian’s father told her. ‘They stayed till after dark. But Lucy has been outgrowing her strength lately . . . she’s shot up very tall all of a sudden. And Priscilla thought she was getting tired out, so she took her home. They would have been down again today if anybody’d dreamed it would take so long.’

‘How’s Aunt Tryntje?’ asked Adrian, shouldering his overcoat and taking Brother on one arm.

‘Thee’ll see for thyself,’ answered his father. ‘All right, very cheerful, quite herself . . . except that the war has thrown her into the past altogether. She still thinks I am my father, and all the rest of it. But that’s not uncommon with very old people.’ He stooped to pick up his share of the bags to be carried. ‘Well, perhaps they’re not so far off,’ he remarked. ‘Who are we, after all, but our forefathers?’

CHAPTER FIVE

✦✦✦

The four o'clock train up the river is not a fast one. There was time for much give and take of family news, for Brother to get very fidgety, for Matey to forget about the irritating delay on the dock, for Adrian's father to look older and older as his fatigue settled like grey dust on his deeply-lined face. After a while he and Adrian moved to a vacant seat and began to discuss business.

Matey was holding Brother on her lap in a vain effort to keep him quiet enough for another nap. From time to time he asked plaintively *when* they would be home. During a stop at a tiny wayside station, 'See all those birds!' said Petella, trying to amuse the weary little boy. 'What are they, Maman?'

Used as she was to it, there were still some moments when Matey was startled at being required by life to be Maman, to know everything, to be all-enduring, all-consoling, all-wise. 'Wild ducks,' she said, looking at the neatly made birds riding composedly at anchor in a small inlet, 'on their way north. Every spring they fly clear north, 'way to Canada somewhere. Perhaps they're waiting as we did last night for the fog to clear.'

'How ever do they know the way?' asked Petella.

'It's called instinct,' said Matey.

'What's instinct?' asked Brother. He did not ask so many questions as Petella, but he had an inspired gift for putting hard ones.

'Well, I suppose it's something that tells you which way to go when you don't *know* which way to go,' his mother hazarded.

'How ever does anybody get it?' enquired Petella with surprise.

The train moved on now, was speeding beside the slate-grey river, which had broadened out till through the mist the opposite bank looked dim and unsubstantial.

'I wish I knew, Petella,' said Matey wearily. 'Perhaps by trying a great many times?'

Petella was silent. Her mother's tone had again sounded as if she had asked too many questions. Somehow she never knew she was asking questions till some grown-up looked impatient. She stared out of the window, saw churches and houses and factories jumbled together on the opposite bank, ghostly grey in the mist, and turned her head quickly to ask her mother what town that was. But she did not. Her mother was looking at the town too, queerly. For once Petella remembered in time and did not put her question. She sighed, turned away, and forgot about the town, watching a line of deeply freighted barges towed down the river by a puffing tug.

Her mother said to her, 'Petella dear, do you see that town across there? It is Newburgh. And in one of the churches there – can you make out those steeples? – my father and mother were married.'

✿✿✿

It was the first time she had ever spoken to her children of her parents.

'Were they?' commented Petella, watching a little dog run barking along the top of the last of the barges. 'Brother, see that dog. He looks a little bit like Toutou, don't you think?'

Brother gave the dog but an absent look. '*When* will we be home, Maman?' he asked, wriggling on her lap.

'Let's play tit-tat-toe,' suggested Priscilla resourcefully.

Over their heads and over the grey brooding formlessness of the river, Matey watched the distant town slowly slipping back into the past as she rushed forward into the future. She had not thought of her parents for a long time, and she was astonished at what she felt at the sight of that church steeple. Not the old shrinking away, the old throb of pain for those darkened days of her youth. No, it was pity she felt as she imagined her father and mother standing there together before the altar, young people beginning life. With them she looked forward at the life they had meant to lead together, and she remembered what their life had been. Had they felt even at the beginning the cloud which hung over their coming together, their consciousness of the sorrow they had caused? Probably they held up before themselves the thought, 'But what else could we have done!' And yet . . . 'So they did name her Priscilla!' Was that name a propitiatory frightened gesture of young parents who had lost one child, who began to see that something was wrong, to guess that perhaps they had missed the path and were lost, and the passion strong enough to break through all the material obstacles which kept them apart was not strong enough to cope with their own weakness?

No, for an instant of divination Matey felt that until the very
end they had never guessed this, that her father's death had
found them still living provisionally, knowing half-consciously
that their irritability came from the temporary colour of their
lives, always feeling themselves perfectly able to turn aside
from their crooked bypath back to the real road which in the
church at Newburgh they had not doubted lay before them.
Without this faith they could not have lived. They had never
dreamed of making their whole lives out of that mean lesser
stuff which was all they had showed to their children. Not
death alone had embittered and ennobled their last moments
together, but the panic-struck realisation that their chance had
gone. They had had time but for one tragic step along the road
they had meant all along to follow.

The river was dimming now to the blue of twilight. From
the dark unlovely bodies of the small houses on the opposite
bank living souls bloomed out like stars. 'But you don't see
them till night comes . . . ' thought Matey, remorsefully.

The brakeman put his head through the door and
announced in the old local speech-tune, first questioning and
then proclaiming, 'RUST*dorf*? *Rust*DORF!'

Petella bounced from her seat and ran to the platform of the
car. She was first down, first to fall shouting into Aunt Priscilla's
arms, first to try to embrace all at the same time the four foster-
cousins. A wild babble of voices, exclamations, questions,
explanations, arose as the others followed her. Adrian's father
carried Brother. Matey and Adrian followed with the bags. From
the platform Matey caught sight of Priscilla's face as, smiling
and weeping, she bent lovingly over her small namesake.

✝✝✝

The first sight of a well-known face after long absence is like the first look at a newborn baby, sharpened by a prophetic insight which later familiarity dims into the blindness of everyday life. Matey saw that the surface of Priscilla's face was older, the flesh of the cheeks that had been apple-firm a little flaccid. New lines showed at the corners of the lips, paler than they had been. But it was still a face of girlish immaturity.

Priscilla was no older, and Matey guessed that she never would be. Her heart rose in an indignant bound of protecting affection, as if she had seen for the first time that Priscilla had been lamed by life. 'Priscilla, *darling!*' she called, running to her. But Brother's voice called for help. Frantically above the clamour he shouted from his grandfather's shoulder, '*Qu-est-ce qu'ils disent, Maman? Qu-est-ce qu'ils disent?*'

'I'd better take him, Padre,' she said, holding out her arms to the wild-eyed little boy. He flung himself into them and clung about her neck. It was sweet to be Maman, all-consoling.

Priscilla had her Ford there, a later Ford, and by dint of every grown person's holding a child or two on his knees they managed to squeeze in, to the accompaniment of much cheerful fun from Priscilla. 'Here, Petella, take Lucy on your knees, will you?' she said, disposing of them in inverse order. As she stepped on the starter she called back over her shoulder, to Petella's joy, 'All people with false teeth are hereby warned to hold them in. This road hasn't been mended since the frost went out.'

As the car in low speed ground slowly up the hill Adrian murmured in his wife's ear, 'Are you here yet?'

'No, oh, *no,*' she told him. 'In a minute I'll open my eyes on the Gare du Nord.'

'Aunt May-ee-ty!' shrilled Mary Ellen from the floor somewhere. 'Is Petella going to be in my class at school? I'm in the fourth class. Can't Petella come in tomorrow?'

'*Qu-est-ce-qu'elle dit?* Petella? *Qu-est-ce-qu'elle dit?*' came Brother's voice anxiously.

Petella told him.

'Gracious! What makes you talk French so *fast!*' complained Mary Ellen.

They turned the corner at the top of the road. The Square was on one side. To the last leafless, early-Gothic twig arch, it looked as it had to Matey on the spring day when she walked across it with Sumner, on her way to find Adrian.

They passed the Friends' burying ground, the humble low headstones glimmering faintly white. There lay the unknown woman whose name Petella carried.

The plain brick sides and barn-like roof of the Friends' Meeting House loomed up under its guardian oaks. Matey and Adrian looked from its four-square honesty into each other's eyes.

'Petella, have you forgotten all your American?' asked Priscilla. 'Do you remember any of the riddles we used to have such fun with? Do you know how much wood a woodchuck would chuck if a woodchuck would chuck wood?'

'Oh, say it again, Aunt Priscilla!' called Petella, enchanted.

Brother nestled on his mother's lap. 'When are we going to get *home?*' he murmured plaintively.

The car passed the bank. Adrian turned his head to look

at it. 'The old oak has gone,' he remarked to his father, who answered, 'Yes, the whole top blew out in a storm last year. Not enough of it left to live. I had to have it cut down.' He added, 'Thee'll have to plant a new one, Adrian.'

His son did not answer.

With every moment the twilight was becoming a deeper blue, the lighted windows in the familiar houses they were passing a deeper yellow. A few stars shone through the leafless tree branches. Matey's heart began to beat suffocatingly. They were almost home.

'We thought you'd rather have your house to yourselves just at first,' said Adrian's father with his plain dry manner. 'We're going to drop you now and come in later, after supper. If Aunt Tryntje feels up to it I'll bring her around.'

'Nobody else would have thought of that!' Matey felt, gratefully.

The car stopped. They were before their own house. Lights gleamed from its windows.

'Rebecca and all the neighbours,' explained Adrian's father, 'have been getting it ready for you. You'll find the door open. They got some food into the house, too.' Brother was set down on the sidewalk. Instantly, looking like a little goblin in the dusk, he ran down the steps, along the path, and up on the porch. After an instant's pause, *'Je ne peux pas ouvrir la po-o-rte!'* he wailed tragically.

'I'll open it for you,' cried Petella, scampering after him.

The returned refugees picked up their bags, walked down the steps and along the path. Up and down this path they had walked that night, in that other existence . . . troubled and uncertain, yes, but so young, so unaware of what it meant to be a human being. They alone had changed. Everything else, from the street to the trees, showed not the slightest alteration. The owl's feather might still be lying there, tiny in its infinity.

'Here on this porch,' thought Matey, as they stepped across it, 'I sat, thinking, "I have enough and so everything is all right."' Adrian lifted the latch and opened the door. In the lighted hall Petella knelt, helping Brother take off his rubbers. Over her head the little boy looked at them soberly. Behind the children, in the living room, a sea-coal fire glowed placidly in the grate. Adrian and Matey came in and closed the door behind them. They did not look at each other but at the children.

'Well, how do you like it, Petella?' asked Adrian, setting down the suitcases and taking off his hat.

Petella's face shone happily. As if she had never noticed it before, Matey thought with astonished thankfulness, 'But she *has* a happy face, Petella has. I wonder why!'

'I remember *ev*-ery *sin*-gle THING!' Petella told her father, 'Right through *there* is the *salle-à-manger.*'

They went through the dining room door and found the table laid for supper. 'Oh, I remember the dishes!' shouted Petella, clasping her hands in ecstasy. Brother said nothing and Petella remembered that they were to speak French for him. *'Tu vois, les petites roses sur les tasses . . .* ' She pointed them out to him like old friends.

A folded bit of paper lay on the plate at Matey's place. She opened it and read in Rebecca's unformed handwriting, a little tremulous with age now, 'Creamed potatoes, baked beans, and

Boston brown bread in the oven. Cocoa for the children on the stove. Gingerbread in the cake tin. Apple sauce in the icebox.'

That had been a favourite supper menu of the old days. That was what they had eaten so often, gathered together around the table like four children, unaware of what it means to be a human being. No part of the homecoming affected Matey more. She had to dash cold water on her eyes at the kitchen sink, and when she reached blindly for a roller towel and found a clean one waiting faithfully for her in the old place she buried her face in it, drawing long breaths.

They dropped their wraps where they took them off, and while Adrian carried the bags upstairs and Petella took Brother for a tour of the house Matey made tea, put the food on the table, and called the family.

Brother so far had not said a word, and he ate absent-mindedly with little of the gourmet's gusto for food which was part of his charm. They took pains not to say a word of the English which was so distressing to him, but he did not seem to notice. Mostly it was Petella who chattered about how big little Mary Ellen had grown, and did Maman know that Aunt Priscilla's Lucy was in the *High* School. And oh, *wasn't* Aunt Priscilla lovely! 'She's so *cheerful!*' said her niece enthusiastically. '*Elle est si gaie!* I never saw anybody so cheerful. Aren't cheerful people nice!'

Halfway through the meal Brother pushed back his chair, murmured something to his mother, and went out through the door into the hall. Petella said responsibly to her mother, 'I showed him where the bathroom is.' But he did not come back. Presently Petella was sent to fetch him. She too did not return and now from the hall came a low babble of voices, broken by sobs. Adrian and Matey hurried out and found Brother, weeping broken-heartedly, face down on the floor, near the closet under the stairs. Petella, crouching by him, looked up from her efforts to comfort him, and said, half crying herself, 'He expected to find the kiddie-car under the stairs! He ran there to look the first thing when he and I came in. It makes him feel so *bad!'*

Matey sat down on the floor and pulled the little weeping boy up on her lap, holding him close, murmuring lovingly in his ear reasonable, logical reminders of reality. 'Why, Brother *chéri*, don't you remember, we took the kiddie-car *with* us, and you had it in France, all the time . . . riding up and down in the Luxembourg. Just think a minute. We used to leave it with the *concierge* generally, you know, not to carry it up and down all those stairs every day. And when we came away you gave it to little Mélanie. You wanted to, dear. You were the one who thought of it. You had grown too big for it, anyhow, don't you remember? How could it be here when we had it there?'

Petella said, '*I* told him all that when he first looked in. And just now, too. But he just said over and over, he *thought* all the time it would be there when we got home and he could get right on it and ride off. He kept thinking about it on the ship, he said, and on the train. That's why he was in such a hurry to get home. And when he opened the door and saw the closet all empty it made him feel so . . . '

'Look here, Brother, I'll get you a new one tomorrow,' said Adrian, 'or a velocipede. With red wheels!'

Brother said bitterly between his sobs, *'Ce n'est pas ça.'*

His father and mother looked at each other. Adrian had an inspiration. 'Or I'll get you one just like the old one,' he told Brother's heaving shoulders.

The little boy repeated unreasonably, tragically, on a higher note, '*Mais ce n'est pas ça!*'

Matey ventured, 'Suppose we send a new one to Mélanie and get Tante Ziza to send the old one back here to you?'

But nothing they could say reached the solitary heart of the little boy, sobbing alone in a mysterious astonished distress, far beyond the power of Maman to console. Still a little boy small enough to be held in his mother's arms, he had come face to face with the implacable rule of life which forbids even the slightest, even the sweetest return to the past. He must go on, go on, and become someone else.

Adrian stood looking down at his son with a sombre sympathy. 'The best thing's to put him to bed,' he said, accepting their helplessness. 'He's had a long day of it.'

CHAPTER SIX

When she came downstairs from putting Brother to bed Matey found Priscilla, her stout, comfortable husband, and Lucy in the living room. Remembering what a forlorn old widower he had been, she said as she shook hands with her brother-in-law, 'Peter, you positively get younger as the years go by.'

'Who wouldn't,' he answered, 'with Priscilla to make a home for him?'

Priscilla looked pleased and patted her husband's arm. Lucy got up abruptly and went over to stand near the fire in the grate, looking down at it moodily.

'How that child has grown! She is as tall as Priscilla and I,' thought Matey.

Petella was on her aunt's knees, fingering Aunt Priscilla's brooch, one arm around Aunt Priscilla's neck. She had evidently been telling the newcomers about Brother's metaphysical sorrow, for at the first pause she went on, 'And no matter what Papa and Maman said, he kept telling them back, "But *that's* not the trouble! *That's* not it!" Whatever do you suppose it was!'

Aunt Priscilla answered, 'Why, dear child, it was nothing at all but just that poor little Brother is too tired. If it had really had anything to do with the kiddie-car he could have told you what the matter was. You just see, tomorrow morning after a good night's sleep he won't remember a thing about it. It was just tired nerves and a notion.'

During this reasonable, sensible explanation, which quite satisfied and reassured Petella, Matey noticed Lucy's eyes were fixed with an ironical expression on her foster-mother. Those eyes were shadowed, and the girlish cheek was very thin. Matey remembered now that Adrian's father had said that Lucy wasn't very well. How could the child have grown so tall? But after all, she was past fifteen. What an entirely other person a girl of fifteen was from a noisy bouncing little girl of eleven! Matey wondered if that delicate pretty face was weak or only sensitive?

'Aunt Priscilla,' asked Petella, fondly tightening her arm around her aunt's neck, 'have you still got that lovely doll's house over at your house that Uncle Peter made for Mary Ellen?'

Priscilla smiled down at the little girl. 'Yes, indeed, dear. We saved it for you and Brother. And Mary Ellen has repapered every room in it. It's *lovely!*'

On her face was the not-to-be-imitated expression of some-one who really did think it lovely. Petella looked up adoringly at her aunt. Matey thought gratefully, 'It'll be a good thing for the children to be back near Priscilla.'

She understood very well what Petella was feeling, because in a way she felt it too – felt restfully that Priscilla could be counted on always to produce cheerfulness, to reject all elements from which cheerfulness could not be extracted. At that moment it seemed right that there should be in the world childish undeveloped people like Priscilla who fixed their attention on what was pleasant and shut their eyes to what was dark and true.

'There are some little kittens in our woodshed too,' Aunt Priscilla told her namesake.

'Oh, *are* there?' breathed Petella.

'We're going to let you and Brother make your choice first.'

'Oh, are *we* going to have one for *us?*' cried Petella.

'Why not two? One for each of you.'

'Oh, Aunt Priscilla!' cried the little girl, scarcely able to endure her ecstasy.

Slow steps sounded on the porch. Adrian sprang up to open to his father and Aunt Tryntje, the white-haired older Adrian looking almost youthful beside the aged feebleness of his aunt. Matey was shocked by Aunt Tryntje's decrepitude. Seeing her, who had kept till late in life a free strong step, shuffle in, fumbling, tottering, wavering like an old baby learning to walk, Matey felt as outraged as though an indignity had been offered before her eyes to a defenceless victim.

She felt this apparently more than Aunt Tryntje did, for the thousand wrinkles of her face were wreathed into a bright expression of welcome, and the usual confusion of greeting ended by her saying loudly, looking all around, 'Where's Adrian? Little Adrian, I mean. I wanted to see him. I want to see who he looks like!'

Matey offered to take her upstairs for a look at the sleeping child. As Matey steered the bulky old body around the turn of the landing she heard Lucy's voice, 'Aunt Matey, may I come too?'

Matey looked back, saw the girl's thin face turned up toward her with an eager look on it.

'Why, of course, Lucy,' she said, a little surprised.

The three generations of women stepped as noiselessly as they could down the hall. Matey opened the door to the children's room. The light struck in and fell across the little bed where Brother lay.

Aunt Tryntje shaded her old eyes and looked at him intently. So did his mother. She gazed down at her son, lost in wonder at the immortal strength and never-dying weakness come from beyond the centuries, beyond human thought, to do battle in his breast as he struggled to find his way forward into his share of happiness and misery.

'He's all Fort. He looks exactly like his sister,' whispered Aunt Trytnje, 'exactly as Madeleine did at his age.'

Matey looked up startled till she remembered Aunt Tryntje's confusion of the generations, and startled again to find Lucy's eyes as deeply on her face as hers had been on Brother's.

Matey pulled the clothes up over Brother, tucked them in, went out into the hall, and closed the door behind her. Halfway to the stairs walked Aunt Tryntje and Lucy, side by side, Aunt Tryntje's broad sagging back, old, finished, and done for, Lucy's piteously immature, with narrow shoulders and thin hips. As Matey looked, Aunt Tryntje took the girl's arm. Lucy braced herself, but as the old woman continued, with the ruthless self-absorption of the old – and the young – to lean on her, the unhardened bones and untoughened sinews of the girl's body bent sideways. Matey thought, 'They'll never get downstairs that way.' Putting Lucy gently aside she said, 'Better let me take her down, dear.' Fearing that the girl's young vanity might be wounded, she smiled at her to ask her not to mind being thought the weaker. But she saw in Lucy's eyes only relief and gratitude.

'He's all thy side of the family, Adrian,' said Aunt Tryntje again on coming back into the living room, 'His mouth is the very double of Madeleine's.'

'I believe thee's right, Aunt Tryntje,' said Adrian's father, the only other person in the room who had ever seen the long-dead Madeleine.

'Of course I am,' she said contentedly, reaching into her bag for her knitting.

There was a silence, which Peter Russell broke with conscious geniality. 'It certainly is good to have you all back safe and sound, but I must say I shall miss your letters. You made everything so vivid. I never thought I could get so interested in foreigners. Many's the time I've said to Priscilla, "Why, those Vinets are just like Rustdorf folks." Wasn't it extraordinary that' – he fumbled a moment over a forgotten name – 'that your friend's husband should have been alive after all?'

'Yes, indeed,' said Priscilla cheerfully, '*wasn't* that the greatest piece of luck! I think the Vinets came out pretty well, Mme Vinet with both her daughters in good health, all nicely established in their own homes again, their husbands with them, and their children all around them.'

These words, with the expression that went with them of bright comfortable satisfaction, penetrated slowly to Matey's brain. She was stricken silent by them. Here was a one-dimensional truth that was staggering. What comment was possible?

None was necessary. Priscilla had turned to Adrian with a question about the weather they had had on the trip home.

'Just excuse me a second,' Matey murmured. 'I want to put the food away in the icebox.'

In the dining room she was aware of a shadow beside her. Lucy was there. 'Let me stay out here with you, Aunt Matey,' she said in a low tone. 'I'd love to help you.'

Matey looked across the table into the girl's eyes. They were fixed on her with a savage imploring intensity. What they cried out was unmistakable. 'Let me lean on you! Let me hang my whole weight on your neck. I can see that you are strong. What is your strength for if not to help me?'

Matey's weary flesh quailed at this summons. Had she not enough to carry as it was? But who was she to turn away from egotistic youth? There rose before her memory a room in a hospital years ago and a girl – older than Lucy was now – flung across the bed, a girl who had been rock-like in her obliviousness of what death meant to a dying man, absorbed only by what it meant to her.

She had looked down at the teapot in her hands. She looked up now, smiled, and said, 'Why, glad to have you, Lucy. Just bring the beans and the cream pitcher along, will you, into the pantry.'

After they had put away the food, the voices from the living room continuing voluble and animated, they began to clear away the dishes, piling them up in the sink. Lucy apparently had nothing to say, and Matey was absorbed in a thought that had come to her when Priscilla spoke about how comfortably off the war had left the Vinets. She knew what Priscilla would think about their parents – if she ever allowed herself to think about them at all. With the thin hardness of judgment based on a one-dimensional view of life she would say that they had been a vain self-seeking man and woman who between them reduced marriage to an ignoble struggle to show off better than the other one and who were of such coarse spiritual fibre that this struggle did not make them suffer much. 'That is the truth, too,' thought Matey. An echo of what she had felt on looking at the Newburgh church steeple came to her mind, but now it seemed fanciful and rather sentimental. She perceived that a good deal of vitality is necessary to hold two dimensions in a human mind. She felt Lucy's eyes on her again, knew that she must be looking sad, and tried to force her face into a more cheerful expression.

They took the tablecloth off, and Matey stepped out of the back door to shake the crumbs from it. It was a mild night, full of the moist odour of newly thawed earth and wet leaves. Matey stood for a moment on the back porch, looking at the lights on the other side of the river, very large and hazy in the damp air. 'All the same,' she thought, 'whatever else Father and Mother can have meant to do, it was not to live as they did,' and a tender pity for them stole upon her like the breath of the spring night. Lucy had followed her out and now stood beside her, looking where she looked. 'It seems good to see those lights again,' Matey told her. 'I've thought of them so often while we were away.'

The girl drew a long breath but said nothing.

They went back into the kitchen. 'Lucy, you go and get Petella, will you, dear, and let's put her to bed.'

The little girl had almost fallen asleep in her aunt's arms. While Matey undressed her Lucy watched, so silent that once or twice Matey forgot she was there. Laid in her bed, Petella came to herself enough to nestle down in it with conscious pleasure, and turning her head, to send up one smile to her mother before she closed her eyes with a long, blissful sigh.

'May I sit on the sofa with you?' asked Lucy in a whisper as they went down the stairs.

Matey made room for her, and presently felt her hand taken and held tightly by thin hot flexible young fingers. Adrian had advanced as far as the fog in his account of the weather during their trip home and was describing how thick it had been. Matey turned her head to whisper, 'Do you play the piano, Lucy? Your fingers feel like a pianist's.'

'I've been taking lessons from Mrs Steenson,' Lucy whispered back, 'but she's going away.'

'Would you like to study with me for a while?' asked Aunt Matey, and felt her hand frantically squeezed.

The clock struck.

'Goodness gracious, Lucy dear!' said Priscilla, 'What am I thinking about to let you sit up so late? Put on your things this minute, darling, and run along home. What would Dr Van der Water say if he could see you up at ten!'

As Lucy went obediently out into the hall for her wraps, Priscilla explained to Matey and Adrian, 'Lucy's been out-growing herself lately, as Aunt Tryntje says, and Dr Van der Water is giving her a tonic that has some iron in it. He says she must have lots of sleep, too.'

Matey went with Lucy to the outside door in the hall. The girl leaped fiercely at her, gave her an intense embrace, and ran out across the porch. Looking after her, Matey saw her skipping down the path like a little girl.

When Matey turned around she found Priscilla had followed her into the hall. 'I wanted to talk to you about Lucy, Matey,' she said, and then stopped, her old prison walls around her. She forced herself to go on, falteringly, her eyes a little wild like those of a person doing violence to himself. 'I'm so glad you're back, Matey, for Lucy's sake. I – I love Lucy so! And when she was still a little girl . . . ' She stopped, closed her eyes as if to think what she wished to say, and opening them again went on simply, honestly, 'You know, Matey, I never was emotional myself, and I don't understand emotional people.' She ended humbly, 'I feel that Lucy needs more than I can give her – now.'

Matey took her sister's hand in hers and pressed it. They stood for a moment in silence. Priscilla murmured, looking deeply into her sister's eyes, 'Oh, Matey, I feel so much *safer* with you near at hand.'

Together they went back to the living room. Matey looked around from one to another. Padre, looking very old, his eyes closed, leaned back in the easy chair; Aunt Tryntje's lips moved silently in time with her clicking needles; Peter Russell seemed to be dutifully making conversation, Adrian answering him with weary courtesy.

‘Matey’s letter never told us much about the details of *your* work,’ Peter was saying. ‘I’d like to know more about it.’

‘All right,’ Adrian answered; ‘there isn’t much to say about it, but I’ll tell you anything you want to know.’

‘I’ll tell thee what *I* want to know,’ said Aunt Tryntje unexpectedly. ‘I want to know if thee saw any Rebels close to – to talk to, I mean. I’d just like to know what in the world they’ve got to say for themselves.’

For an instant no one knew what to answer. Then Adrian told her seriously, ‘They’ve got just the same things to say for themselves that we have.’

‘Oh, come now,’ said Peter Russell, at a loss between the two wars. ‘The wanton destruction, you know, the devastation! What was done to Belgium. Our boys never did anything like that!’

‘They never got the chance,’ replied Adrian.

Adrian’s father opened his eyes and nodded. ‘My regiment was with Sherman,’ he said.

His words echoed in a long silence. Matey heard them tramping back and back and back through the centuries from one war to the one before it. No one found a word to say.

But Priscilla knew other tools than words with which to shatter dangerous silences. She coughed nervously, rose to her feet, tucked her handkerchief up her sleeve, and said, ‘Come along, Peter, it’s time we were going. Matey, you look tired. You look worse than tired; you look blue. Go to bed, dear. I always tell my girls when they get the blues that a good night’s sleep is what they need.’

‘It’s time for us to go too, Adrian,’ said Aunt Tryntje, struggling to her feet. Mr Fort turned to Priscilla. ‘Would you and

Peter take Aunt Tryntje home for me? I want to talk to Matey and Adrian a minute about a matter of business.'

But when Matey returned from seeing the Russells and Aunt Tryntje out of the front door she did not find business being talked. Adrian was pacing up and down the living room. His father sat looking at him out of sunken old eyes. As she came in Adrian sat down abruptly, leaning forward, his clasped hands hanging between his knees, and broke out almost as if against his will, 'Father, you lived through it! How *could* you?'

His father did not give his old rejoinder now, did not say with a darkening face and his old rough accent of impatience with ignorance, 'Oh, there's no use talking about it!' He received his son's question into one of his capacious silences.

Matey's heart fluttered in a painful hope as she waited for his answer. She had thought on the pier, when she saw Adrian's father, that he could read Adrian's riddle for him as she could not, that he could show them in a few wise words how it was all right after all.

But when he spoke Matey saw that what she had wanted of him was what those aching women's hearts in Europe had with so wild and childish a folly wanted of President Wilson, a ready-made solution. He gave her instead one of those invitations to reflect on life, deeply, bitterly if need be, which, like Mme Vinet, he brought out when asked for short-cut affirmations. He asked of Adrian, 'Has it ever occurred to thee that the imminence of death may be one of the things – as well as our bestial pleasure in violence – which gives wartime experience such intensity of meaning? I've thought of that lately. People of imagination, of course, always feel death at hand, but war makes it obvious even to the thick-witted. And there's no doubt about it, to feel the closeness of death gives dignity to life – keeps you from being too helpless before trifles.'

This was not at all what Matey had expected. Adrian was looking at his father in silence, frowning a little, attentively, as if he did not see yet what the other was meaning.

The old man left this idea with him and went on to another. 'I've thought sometimes – looking back – that perhaps the new vitality that comes to men in war may be partly like the unity that comes to a quarrelsome country when it's attacked from outside. We're all full of warring impulses stabbing each other in the back. Perhaps the outside pressure of fear in war life makes them all stand together for a time in self-defence and gives a temporary inner peace.'

He shook his head. 'No, these are non-essentials, of course. The core of the matter is that nobody can get along without a purpose. And war supplies a purpose – a poor, false, imitation purpose, but it's hard to question it as long as the noise of fighting is going on. And we are so starving for it we'll take even the poorest imitation rather than nothing.'

He ended by a question apparently addressed to Matey. 'But why do we talk melodramatically, as if war were in an outside compartment different from life? All that can be found in war – appeal to the beast in us – to the man – isn't it in every day of life, if lived with imagination?'

'If you're putting that question to me, Padre,' said Matey sadly, 'I feel as if you were standing a long way off from me, pointing out something that I can't see at all. I haven't any head for abstractions, you know. You sound to me as if you were defending war.'

'No, Matey, only men.' He looked up at the clock and went on, 'And that wasn't in the least what I stayed here to say, anyhow. Adrian's exclamation set me off on something else. I have a proposition that concerns you both.'

He explained it briefly and drily, with his usual impersonality. He was neither young nor well, he said. In fact it had been hard to hold out till his son's return. He could not go on at the bank, the doctor told him. Adrian would need someone who could learn to be bookkeeper and teller. Why not Matey? The hours were not long. The work was nothing more than any intelligent grown person could learn. The children would be in school most of the day from now on, and since he had been obliged to have a nurse-housekeeper since Aunt Tryntje's failing in strength, Rebecca was free to give all her time to the younger Forts. There was nothing picturesque about the job at the Bank, just plain useful work: but really useful, he insisted, with a depth to it that didn't show in the flat surface statement that it amounted to no more than helping people hold on to their money. The point was that in the modern world of capital, money – whether you liked to have it so or not – stood for independence – freedom – personal dignity. What did Matey think?

Matey's mind, only beginning to stagger out of the past into the present, balked stupidly at the notion of stepping toward the future. She could scarcely think what he was talking about. At her bewildered look her father-in-law said, 'No hurry. No hurry about deciding. I've thought of it a good deal of late. But it's perfectly new to thee.'

Adrian added, looking at Matey anxiously. 'Yes, it's much too soon for her even to think of it. I would like it fine, of course. When Father first spoke of it, I jumped at it – but I'd hate it if you didn't feel free to decide as you like. Wait till you get your breath.'

Mr Fort said goodnight, turned to go, remembered that he had not yet left the duplicate keys to the bank with Adrian, and handed them over. Adrian put them in his pocket and went with his father to the door. It closed behind him. The returned refugees were alone in their home.

They stepped about soberly in the usual closing-up tasks. After a discussion about whether it was warm enough to let the fire go out Adrian went downstairs to put more coal on the furnace. Matey locked the front door and drew up a fire screen in front of the still glowing fire in the grate. As she did this her eye caught the wavy irregularity of the wallpaper which had been pasted over the old wall-oven more than a century ago, after the return of another war refugee, in a vain attempt to seal away from sight a reminder of the filthiness of war.

She was overcome with a hideous, unbearable disappointment, like Brother's, at the lack of something she had confidently expected to find. She could have put her head down on the mantelpiece and wept as inconsolably as he, in as mysterious a grief. Why had she been so frantically eager to reach this house? What had she thought would be waiting for her there? Her old outgrown self? The old safe world in which she had been that old self?

She was still standing staring at the sealed-up oven when Adrian came up from the cellar. 'Ready, dear?' he asked, a hand on the button of the electric light in the hall. When Matey turned around to nod her assent he was standing under its hard, unsparing light, looking very tired.

They went upstairs without a word.

CHAPTER SEVEN

🌳🌳🌳

They lay down for that first night in their own bed as weary animals lie down on the straw of their stables, feeling in each other's presence only the blunted satisfaction which makes horses stand together under the same tree rather than at opposite sides of the pasture. Adrian put his hand out to take Matey's, and holding it, fell asleep in the position in which he had lain down, without once stirring. Really asleep. His hand relaxed to utter limpness. Matey wondered at him. It would be hours, she thought, before her troubled nerves would be still.

And yet she must have fallen asleep, for now, much later, she felt herself waking. Slowly she floated up to consciousness, did not know who she was, nor where, lay looking out at the black sky, as if she had been a disembodied spirit wandering forlornly through the vastness of space.

The night boat going up the river hooted hoarsely, and a train on the west side answered with two long calls.

Like a falling star her spirit dropped from space to its earthly home, to Matey's body, lying by her husband's. She turned toward him, laying her head on his shoulder. Still asleep, he put an arm around her.

* * *

The fog was gone. This was the first thought in Matey's mind as she woke to a morning of sunshine pouring matter-of-factly into their bedroom windows. Those windows, which during the night had opened out upon eternity, now looked only into the upper branches of a soft-maple tree. It was in bloom, its smooth young branches studded thick with a rosy fire of blossoms. A robin flew with the clumsy energy of his race to a branch and perched on it, tipping back and forth to get his balance. When he was poised, he made with loud cheerfulness the unimaginative, one-dimensional statement about warm weather and plenty of worms with which robins always greet the spring. As she lay listening to the bird's stout-hearted prose Matey was astonished to find that physical vitality had come back to her good useful faithful body and that with the disappearance of the deadly physical fatigue the world really looked another place.

She turned her head to see what the new day had brought to Adrian's face, and with the movement his eyes opened. He looked rested. He smiled at her. 'Welcome home, Matey,' he said. He raised his head to look around the familiar room. 'I believe I've almost landed,' he told her. 'Last night I was still hurtling through space.' His eyes fell on the blossoming tree in the sunshine. 'Hello, the fog's gone,' he said.

As if startled, the robin flew blunderingly out of the tree. Steps crunched on the side path, went around to the back yard, and returned again to the street.

'The milkman,' Adrian interpreted the familiar sequences.

'Priscilla or somebody must have told him to come. Sounds as though he hadn't missed a day, doesn't it? Must be twenty-five minutes to seven. Now I'm dead sure we've got home.'

They lay silent for a time, their eyes turning toward their future – upon them now, almost the present.

Adrian asked dreamily, 'Matey, did you ever think in France that perhaps we never would get home?'

'Oh, ever so many times.'

'It would have been lots more dramatic if we hadn't, wouldn't it? All four of us to go up in smoke, bombed in an air raid or something. Less of an anticlimax than just to come back and go on stodgily helping people save their money in Rustdorf.'

He spoke whimsically, but something experienced and seasoned in Matey made her protest against taking this lightly. 'Oh, Adrian, if there's anything in the world that's cheap and shoddy, it's "dramatic living." '

He turned his head to look at her, surprised at her heat. She told him, 'I know, I know you didn't mean it seriously. But it brought home to me what an awful thing life turns into when you always plan for how it's going to look from the outside. You don't know how miserable it makes you on the inside!'

'What do *you* know about it?' said Adrian challengingly. 'You're no show-off!'

Matey was silent.

The earth, tumbling headlong in its daily revolution, shifted Rustdorf and their window so that the sunlight laid a friendly ray on their faces.

✸✸✸

'I hope the sun is shining like this all along the border in northern France, on all the other returned refugees,' said Matey, sending them one by one a comradely thought.

'Why limit it to northern France?' suggested Adrian half absently.

The door of their room opened softly. Petella's eye appeared around it. 'Oh, goody, Maman, you're awake. I'm just *éreintée* trying to keep Brother in. Can we go out?'

Her parents looked in astonishment at the city-bred child. 'Why, haven't you got the sense you were born with?' Adrian asked her. 'Don't you know you're *home,* outdoors as well as in!'

Petella withdrew herself with a shout and clattered down the stairs, calling to Brother.

'They *musn't* forget their *rubbers!'* A reflex instinct in Matey uttered this cry. She sprang out of bed, clutched a wrapper about her, shuffled her feet into slippers, and ran downstairs just in time to recall the reluctant children from the damp front walk.

After rubbers were found and put on – rather a painful process, because Brother shied off violently from going near the hall closet where Petella had put his rubbers the night before – Matey thought, 'I might as well put the water on for coffee, so it can be heating while I dress.' Busy in the kitchen, she heard Adrian in the cellar shaking down the furnace. A new day had begun.

When breakfast was over Petella dragged them all out, informing them that they hadn't any idea what a lovely day it was.

591

She was right. It was a morning fine beyond words to express, as fine mornings always are. It went to the children's heads. They ran around and around in a frenzy, trying to be everywhere and see everything and feel everything at once. Brother was as effervescent as Petella, his eyes brilliant, no slightest shadow on his face.

As Matey and Adrian came around from the back yard to the front, there before them, painted by sun and shadow and April air, the many-coloured strip of their outdoor frieze hung between trees and lawn. A couple of long-legged boys glided by on bicycles, the spokes of the wheels glittering as they turned, making a staccato run of small bright reflections. Behind them an oil truck lumbered slowly forward, its crude scarlet like a trumpet note. Against its steady bulky advance a flock of little children on their way to school scurried along the sidewalk, hopping and skipping in an irregular rhythm like grace-notes. In the Deyo side yard a line of drying clothes, pink, blue, green, red, children's garments, fluttered in the wind. Older children strung themselves out along the frieze – Lucy with books under her arm. She smiled with lips and eyes and waved her hand at Aunt Matey – and gave a skip afterward like the littler ones.

A couple of neighbours passed, older men on their way to business, fathers and uncles of Adrian's contemporaries, distant relatives. Members of the Meeting, both of them.

Seeing the Forts standing together in the side yard, they smiled a greeting to Matey and called heartily, 'Hey there, Adrian! Glad to see thee home again!'

Adrian called back, 'How are you, Cousin Al?' and 'You're

looking fine, Mr Winthrop.' In his voice was a sort of surprise as if he had forgotten that transparent men existed.

Clamours and shrieks from the children made them turn their heads. Petella was showing her Gallicised small brother what to do with a slanting cellar door. 'Brother seems all right this morning,' said Adrian, looking at the little boy's glowing face. 'What was that Cousin Connie said about you as a little girl – that your face was as bright as a nasturtium? I hope he's forgotten all about that misery of last night, whatever it was.'

Matey told him then about Brother's refusal to go near the hall closet and tried to describe the painful darkening of his eyes as he looked across the hall at its door.

Adrian's own eyes darkened as he said, 'Still got it with him, then, hidden away somewhere . . . probably always will have. Something he's got to get used to living with from now on... . Oh, well, it's the common lot. We've got the war.'

Petella called frantically from the other side of the yard, 'Maman! Papa! Come quick!'

She was kneeling by a flower bed, Brother sitting on his heels beside her, looking down to where she was surrounding something lovingly with her two hands. As her parents came up, 'See that!' she said. And taking her hands away she showed the shining green of a tulip leaf's spear-head pushing its way with an almost visible vitality through the dark moist earth. 'It's alive!' she told them. 'It's been here in the ground all the time we were away, waiting for us to come back.'

Petella will always find something waiting for her, thought her mother.

Brother still squatted beside her, a hand on each knee, looking down gravely at the up-pointed finger of the leaf and keeping his counsel about what it said to him. He never was so transparent as his sister.

'Innocent and disdainful above all those strata of sour dead!' murmured Adrian.

He pulled out his watch.

'Oh, are you going to the Bank right away? Now. This very morning?'

He nodded.

He stooped to kiss his children, kissed his wife like any husband going to any day's work, and walked resolutely off down the street. The children ran away to see something in the back yard. Matey stood looking after her husband, going to the obscure, anonymous work which was his future.

After he had disappeared she dropped her eyes absently to the ground. Crowding thick about her feet was new grass, every blade glistening with vitality. How eagerly it renewed itself! Before even the old willow. No. Lifting her head, she saw that the battered aged tree under which Sumner lay buried was already showing green. The elms, too – last night in the twilight she had thought them leafless. So they were. But now the morning clearness showed, entangled in their twigs, a veil of transparent colour – *couleur de vie*, she thought, looking at them and at the maples, envying the silent tide of life which, even as she looked, must be flooding up from their roots. Everything in sight seemed to be beginning all over again.

No, not everything. The old beech which was Brother's foster-father stood stark in mid-winter bleakness. For all that the eye could see it was dead, dead to its last fibre. Motionless as a dead thing too, Matey thought, walking over to it and remembering the wild energy of its battle with the storm and how it had helped her in her own battle with the anguish which had given her a son. She put out a hand to touch the great mottled grey trunk. It felt hard and dense as a column of stone and said to her, 'Stand fast!' It stood fast, clutching its great roots into the ground, patiently enduring its apparent death, while around it all its comrades with pale visages stood up out of their graves.

How did the intimation of new life come? she wondered. Was there a thrill of all its cells at once as the buds swelled and opened? Or a rush of sap from the roots like blood returning to a drained-out heart? Or perhaps, as the rising tide of life flowed here and there along its inscrutable channels, it touched for an instant the tip of some deeply buried root, stirring its fibres to a vibration so fine that no more than a dreamy echo of it reached the tree's great crown.

The children called her to share their delight in finding the weather-beaten remnants of their sand-pile and forgot her at once as they began eagerly to put in order its circling border of bricks fallen away into ruins. She watched them for a moment, hoping that Ziza's returned little refugees were as happy. Then, thinking of Ziza, she walked away and sat down on the edge of the porch, leaning her head against one of the pillars.

The sun was warm. She was sheltered from the wind. She sat so still that presently mingled with the children's voices came an occasional brief purposeful remark passed between a pair of martins that were building a nest under one corner of the porch roof.

At first she thought of things to be done – their trunk perhaps now at the station to be brought to the house and unpacked – and was old Cousin Charlie Van Blommer still the expressman – and some food needed to be bought for lunch. But presently her bodily quiet emptied her mind of trivialities and left it still and vacant. After a time of vague staring up into red blossoms of the soft-maple tree and listening to the faint hum of early insects murmuring their way from flower to flower, she thought, 'I haven't been as quiet as this – waking – not since the last time I went to Meeting.'

Into the stillness of her emptied mind a thought, very clear, complete in words as few of her thoughts were, dropped as concretely as a stone dropping into a pool. 'I know exactly how Adrian feels,' she told herself. 'The war has made him feel about all the world as I did about Mother and Father before I knew – knew that there was so much more – that they hadn't intended that, that it was only a mistake they'd made.'

This time she did not ask herself shyly and humbly whether it was perhaps childish and silly to reason this from small to great, to interpret the world's catastrophe from her own small experience. She looked down at the spot where the tiny owl's feather had lain, thought, 'No, there is no small or great in what's true,' and sat staring at the circles widening from that thought.

When Adrian's father came down the path toward her he scarcely stirred the surface of her quiet, telling her gently, 'Don't move. Don't move. It does me good to see thee sitting still. I only came to see if Adrian is ready to – '

'He's gone already,' she answered. 'He's very – he's not yet – I think he couldn't wait to get back to work.'

'Ah,' said Adrian's father thoughtfully. He had taken off his hat and now lifted his white head and age-ravaged face toward the sky. Matey followed his gaze and saw what he was looking at, a dark V of wild ducks headed north and flying fast.

He watched the birds out of sight and then, looking down at her said, 'Adrian thinks the war is an indictment of the universe. Instead of a mistake men make.'

'Oh, Padre, if you could only make him feel that!'

He shook his head. 'Thee's the only one to do that.'

At her startled *'I!'* he sat down beside her, saying, 'Thee's done it once for Adrian.'

She said again, *'I! –* for *Adrian!'* It was a reversal of all her thoughts of Adrian.

The old man told her, 'Years ago, when there was a bitter passage of his life before him, and nothing I could do to help – while I was dreading it, thee came walking into his life – that very day.'

Matey's mind went back with incredulous astonishment to that well-remembered day and to the strengthless girl, walking about like an automaton, whom Adrian had brought back to life. 'What thee did for him then – and ever since – ' went on her father-in-law meditatively, looking down and stirring absently with his foot a tuft of grass. 'I wonder does thee know the lines,

> As in old time, a head with gentle grace,
> All tenderly laid by thine
> Taught thee the nearness of the love divine . . . '

Matey's shamed protest rose into words. 'No, *no*, Padre,' she said, nervous and abashed, 'don't think I'm like that. I'm – I'm not, at all. I don't even understand such ideas. "The nearness of the love divine" – honestly, I haven't any idea what those words mean.'

'They don't mean anything theological,' said Adrian's father mildly. 'I never mean anything theological.' He stood up to go. 'As for understanding – ' He looked around him, saw the naked beech standing fast, and said, 'I don't suppose that old fellow understands very much about where its roots find food.' Seeing her face still full of startled denial, he said like a grown person affectionately mocking a child's ignorance, 'What did thee think such a life as thine and Adrian's was rooted in?' He put on his hat, asked, 'Or did thee perhaps think it has no roots at all?' and went away as quietly as he had come.

'But I *don't* understand!' Matey murmured obstinately to herself, watching his retreating back. 'He can talk that way all he likes. I never have understood religious ideas.'

She tried to consider this. But sitting so long blankly and passively in the sun had put the upper layer of her brain to sleep. "The nearness of the love divine," she said vaguely, wondering what it could mean, but she could not arouse herself to drive away by thoughts the meaning which lay still and golden about her, warm as the silent sunshine.

'No,' she told herself finally, giving it up, 'I have no head for abstract ideas. I'm good for nothing but to plod along, one step after another, following the windings of the path wherever it leads.'

As if in sequence from this chance phrase came an idea so inconsequent that she was astonished to find it in her mind. 'I wonder if the ants are out yet this spring?' she asked herself abruptly and absurdly and looking down saw, sure enough, a busy tiny creature fetching and carrying to a hole near her feet. Why in the world had she thought of – oh, yes, the notion of following a path had made her think of Biriatou and then of the ant she had watched so many years ago on another ideal April morning, leaning on the back terrace wall, eating a *tartine* with such gusto. This memory was so real that in this floating musing haze she scarcely knew which she was now, the little girl leaning over the wall, or the woman whose own children murmured happily in the sun as they reconstructed something that had been spoiled. She was both, of course. The little girl sat here listening with a contented sympathy to the other children's voices; the woman leaned over the wall in her past – and now lifted her head from the labouring ant, looked out again over the miles and miles of blossoming broom, and thought again how different it looked when you were up above it from the way it was when you were down in it, sunk below the tops of the unlovely, rough bushes, valueless millions of them, anonymous and obscure as human lives, like them earth-rooted, thorny, dark, a few sparse blossoms scattered along their years. And it was the woman who was on the lookout rock again, a fresh wind blowing in her face the great wind of the high places, from which as far as the eye can see there stretches out illimitable living gold.

The martins flew in and out, more and more boldly over the head of the motionless woman. Her eyes were wide open, but she sat as still as though she had fallen asleep.

She had instead fallen awake, knew again the startled waking to complete vision out of the half-sleep of ordinary life, as she had known it once as a little girl at a concert, once as a young wife. With a startled flutter the birds darted back from the porch as the woman rose suddenly to her feet. After she had walked down the path to the street they returned cautiously to their nest-building.

It was only for a moment that Matey was surprised to find herself not on the porch but on the sidewalk under the elms. She knew in an instant why she was there, what impulse had sent her hurrying, to share with Adrian – to tell him –

She walked more slowly. To tell him? She could no more tell him than one tree can make another share the renewed life which thrills along a deeply buried root.

She walked more slowly still. She could not only not tell him. She could not keep it herself. It was going from her. She was not big enough to hold it fast. She felt it going back whence it had come, back into the myriad sources from which for an instant it had drawn the stuff of understanding – back into the owl's tiny feather – and into those words of Adrian's father which she did not understand – and into Biriatou with its paths that led home and its by-paths that led to terror

✣✣✣

– and into Mme Vinet's long resolute look into a remediable future – and into her children's play with bricks – and into the memory of the anguish of childbirth – and into her father's dying voice. It was leaving her, the emotion and the certainty of this last awakening; it was streaming up into the leafless trees like a mist, sinking into the ground like rain. But as it went it transformed everything. That radiant meaning – it was no longer within her, but all about her. The trees looked down upon her, as the tulips had looked up so long ago, with a kind conscious wisdom as if to promise they would not let her forget.

And now it was all quite gone. She had only the memory of it. She was no more than Matey Gilbert, on the sidewalk of Washington Street, in her small home town, walking toward the savings bank where her husband worked. For she continued to walk steadily forward to find Adrian. She would keep nothing for herself, not even a memory; she would have nothing she could not share with Adrian. But when she tried to put even her memory into speech she found among the millions of human words only one and another battered copper symbol of the gold she had seen. Put into words, what was it she wanted to tell her husband? Fragments of it could perhaps be forced into speech – that it takes anguish to bring new life to birth; that the war had not shaken the bases of human life but only made them visible; that human beings die tragically, having no more time left to repair their mistakes, but that their deep-rooted race goes on, goes on into new springtimes; that to have missed for a time the right path and to be lost in a bypath is no ground for terror; that the only despair lies in thinking that one's life is all, in not seeing the vastness of which it is a part – the preacher-like sound of that last phrase gave her a warning. No, no, this would not do. She was maligning by her awkwardness with words the might and majesty of the life-current which had passed through her.

She tried again. She had quite missed the very core of what had happened to her, the knowledge that there is no small and great, that what Adrian had planned to do with his life, the obscure anonymous helpful work to which he had resigned himself, was all there was, the best there was, and gloriously enough. If she could make him see it – all those anonymous millions of human lives, each with a poor flower or two – what if you could not see the golden whole! There it was, miles and miles, of beauty, ever renewed.

She stopped short, shuddering away from the misshapen clumsy metaphors which were all she could find. It was unfaithful to that memorable certainty of wholeness to try to put it into speech. She had no skill with words. Had she ever yet in all her married life found a single one that would tell Adrian anything of what she deeply felt?

Her years with Adrian answered that question, stood before her, beckoning her on. She walked forward again. Had Adrian ever needed words to share with her all she had learned from him? The medium for the communion of the spirit is not words, but life.

At this, literal reality closed in around her with its opaque walls. All that was left of her memory was a manageable purpose not in the least mystic or hard to put in speech. She thought,

'My job in life just now is to keep Adrian from making of work and cheerfulness a dreary substitute for joy. It's the other way around with us from the way it used to be – I seem to have more capacity now for joy than he. It's something that can't be talked about, but if we share life wholly, if we work together, why, whatever's in my life will be in his.'

She went up the steps and pushed open the door. Adrian was with his father in the inner office. Hearing the door shut behind her, he came to see who was there and looked at her through the cashier's window. At the idea that she would soon be in there beside him, an exclamation of pleasure, clad in innocent childishness like one of Petella's, sprang into her mind. 'It's going to be *nice* to work together!'

Aloud she said, 'Oh, Adrian, I thought I'd run in to tell you that after you left I got to thinking about your father's idea, and of course I want to take that job. It'll be the best thing in the world for me. As soon as ever I get the children settled in school I'm coming to start work.'

At the deepening of his eyes, at his long breath – she had not dreamed he wanted her so! – 'It takes so long for me to get anything through my head,' thought Matey humbly.

PAUL DAVIES

Quantum 2.0
The Past, Present and Future of Quantum Physics

A PELICAN BOOK

PELICAN
an imprint of
PENGUIN BOOKS

PELICAN BOOKS

UK | USA | Canada | Ireland | Australia
India | New Zealand | South Africa

Pelican Books is part of the Penguin Random House group of companies
whose addresses can be found at global.penguinrandomhouse.com

Penguin Random House UK
One Embassy Gardens, 8 Viaduct Gardens, London SW11 7BW

penguin.co.uk

Penguin
Random House
UK

First published in Great Britain by Pelican Books 2025
001

p. 6: 'Quantisierung als Eigenwertproblem' by E. Schrédinger. *Annalen der Physik und Chemie*, 1926: Volume 79 Issue 6; p. 47 (bottom): Dr Tonomura and Belsazar of Wikimedia Commons; p. 53: adapted from: upload.wikimedia.org/wikipedia/commons/9/91/Schrodingers_cat.svg

Book design by Matthew Young
Set in 11/16.13pt FreightText Pro
Typeset by Six Red Marbles UK, Thetford, Norfolk
Printed and bound in Great Britain by Clays Ltd, Elcograf S.p.A.

The authorized representative in the EEA is Penguin Random House Ireland,
Morrison Chambers, 32 Nassau Street, Dublin DO2 YH68

A CIP catalogue record for this book is available from the British Library

ISBN: 978-0-241-65580-1

Penguin Random House is committed to a sustainable future
for our business, our readers and our planet. This book is made from
Forest Stewardship Council® certified paper.